THE TREATMENT OF PRISONERS
UNDER INTERNATIONAL LAW

The Treatment of Prisoners Under International Law

NIGEL S. RODLEY

Second Edition

OXFORD
UNIVERSITY PRESS

OXFORD

UNIVERSITY PRESS

Great Clarendon Street, Oxford OX2 6DP

Oxford University Press is a department of the University of Oxford.
It furthers the University's objective of excellence in research, scholarship,
and education by publishing worldwide in

Oxford New York

Athens Auckland Bangkok Bogotá Buenos Aires Calcutta
Cape Town Chennai Dar es Salaam Delhi Florence Hong Kong Istanbul
Karachi Kuala Lumpur Madrid Melbourne Mexico City Mumbai
Nairobi Paris São Paulo Singapore Taipei Tokyo Toronto Warsaw

with associated companies in Berlin Ibadan

Oxford is a registered trade mark of Oxford University Press
in the UK and in certain other countries

Published in the United States
by Oxford University Press Inc., New York

British Library Cataloguing in Publication Data
Data available

Library of Congress Cataloging in Publication Data
Rodley, Nigel S.
The treatment of prisoners under international law/Nigel S.
Rodley.—2nd ed.
p. cm.
Includes bibliographical references and index.
1. Political prisoners—legal status, laws, etc. 2. Torture.
I. Title.
K5519. R63 1998 341.6'5—ddc21 98-45050
ISBN 0-19-826564-6

3 5 7 9 10 8 6 4 2

Printed in Great Britain
on acid-free paper by
Antony Rowe Ltd, Chippenham

Preface to the Second Edition

The number of developments that have taken place since the first edition of this book have required substantial rewriting and extensive additions to the text. They are also too numerous to list here. Of a particularly far-reaching nature is the adoption by the United Nations of a Second Optional Protocol to the International Covenant on Civil and Political Rights, providing for abolition of death penalty, the Body of Principles for the Protection of All Persons Under Any Form of Detention or Imprisonment and the Declaration against Forced Disappearance.

In the Inter-American Court of Human Rights, the *Velásquez Rodríguez* case has been influential beyond the region in clarifying the normative status and legal consequences of torture, extra-legal execution, and enforced disappearance. The same impact may be expected of a series of European Court of Human Rights decisions, involving Turkey, in respect of the same practices, particularly *Askoy, Aydın, Kaya* and *Kurt*. Its decision in *Soering* v. *United Kingdom* concerning extradition on capital charges to the Commonwealth of Virginia has proven to be of landmark significance.

International inspection of places of detention has been pioneered at the regional level with the adoption of the European Convention for the Prevention of Torture, Inhuman or Degrading Treatment or Punishment. Its system has inspired an initiative at the universal level, with the process now under way of drafting a protocol to the UN Convention against Torture and other Cruel, Inhuman and Degrading Treatment or Punishment.

The creation by the United Nations Security Council of *ad hoc* criminal tribunals in respect of the former Yugoslavia and Rwanda has spurred efforts culminating in a diplomatic conference aimed at establishing a permanent international criminal court. I expressly excluded this proposal from the first edition's general conclusion, considering it not feasible in the short or medium term.

In 1993, I was appointed by the Chairman of the United Nations Commission on Human Rights to succeed Professor (now Judge) Peter Kooijmans as its Special Rapporteur on the question of torture. Where it has been necessary to refer to this mandate, I have sought to depersonalize my own role by using the third person—I hope readers will not take this as a kind of inverse royal plural.

Many people have helped me by providing ideas and information. The following have been among the more frequent victims of my importunings: Christina Cerna, Federico Andreu, Professor Kevin Boyle, Carla Edelenbos, Camille Giffard, Professor Geoff Gilbert, Christopher Keith Hall, Professor

Françoise Hampson, Ahmed Mothali, Eric Prokosch, Aisling Reidy, Ian Seiderman, Trevor Stevens, Wilder Taylor, and Dr James Welsh.

Again the editorial assistance of my wife, Dr Lyn Rodley, has been of immeasurable help, and her moral support has been decisive in getting me through the ordeal.

While it has been possible to take account of some more recent developments, including the status of ratification of international treaties, the book aims to be accurate as of 31 March 1998.

N.S.R.

Colchester
June 1998

Stop Press

On 17 July 1998, the United Nations Diplomatic Conference of Plenipotentiaries adopted the Rome Statute of the International Criminal Court (UN document A/CONF.183/9). Designed to make it possible, when national jurisdictions fail, for an international tribunal to bring to justice the perpetrators of genocide, crimes against humanity and war crimes, it is a millenarian achievement.

The Statute confirms numerous notions heralded in various chapters of this book, especially chapters 4, 6 and 8. In particular, by Statute article 7, the systematic or widespread practice of torture, murder and enforced disappearance are confirmed as crimes against humanity, when committed as part of an attack directed against any civilian population. So are practices involving '[o]ther inhumane acts of a similar character intentionally causing great suffering, or serious injury to body or to mental or physical health'. Indeed, the list of crimes against humanity includes '[i]mprisonment or other severe deprivation of liberty in violation of fundamental rules of international law'. This latter may be relevant to chapter 11. The vexed question of the definition of enforced disappearence is resolved as follows (approximating the approach proposed in chapter 8):

> 'Enforced disappearance of persons' means the arrest, detention or abduction of persons, by or with the authorization, support or acquiescence of a State or a political organization, followed by a refusal to acknowledge that deprivation of freedom, or to give information on the fate or whereabouts of those persons, with the intention of removing them from the protection of the law for a prolonged period of time.'

A crime against humanity may be committed without having to be linked to an armed conflict.

As well as covering war crimes committed in international armed conflict, article 8 of the Statute includes those committed in non-international armed conflict. Although the Court's jurisdiction over war crimes applies 'in particular when committed as a part of a plan or policy or as part of a large-scale commission of such crimes', it is not restricted to such a context. In other words, individual acts qualify for the description of 'war crime'. They include, as had been expected, 'serious violations of article 3 common to the four Geneva Conventions of 12 August 1949'.

Also, in a clear rebuff to some retentionist states, the Court will not be empowered to impose the death penalty (chapter 7).

Colchester
August 1998

Contents

Contents

Selected Abbreviations

AJIL	*American Journal of International Law*
BYIL	*British Yearbook of Interntional Law*
CIOMS	Council for International Organizations of Medical Sciences
Ecosoc	Economic and Social Council of the United Nations
EHRR	European Human Rights Reports
ESCOR	*Official Records of the Economic and Social Council*
ETS	European Treaty Series
GAOR	*Official Records of the General Assembly*
HRLJ	*Human Rights Law Journal*
HRQ	*Human Rights Quarterly*
IAPL	International Association of Penal Law
ICJ	International Commission of Jurists
ICJ Rep	Reports, Advisory Opinions and Orders of the International Court of Justice
ICLQ	*International and Comparative Law Quarterly*
ICRC	International Committee of the Red Cross
ILO	International Labour Organization
ILR	International Law Reports
NQHR	*Netherlands Quarterly of Human Rights*
OAS	Organization of American States
PCIJ	Permanent Court of International Justice
SIM Newsletter	*Newsletter of the Netherlands Institute of Human Rights* (Studie- en Informatiecentrum Mensenrechten)
UN	United Nations
Unesco	United Nations Educational, Cultural and Scientific Organization
UNTS	United Nations, Treaty Series
WHO	World Health Organization
World Court	Permanent Court of International Justice and International Court of Justice
Yearbook	Yearbook of the European Conventions on Human Rights

Table of Treaties and Other International Instruments

Table of Cases

General Introduction

THE DEVELOPMENT OF AN INTERNATIONAL LAW OF HUMAN RIGHTS APPLICABLE TO PRISONERS

WE THE PEOPLES OF THE UNITED NATIONS DETERMINED

To save succeeding generations from the scourge of war, which twice in our lifetime has brought untold sorrow to mankind, and to reaffirm faith in fundamental human rights, in the dignity and worth of the human person . . .

Thus begins the preamble to the Charter of the United Nations, adopted on 26 June 1945. It was more than a solemn statement of revulsion at the massive destruction of World War II, or at the 'disregard and contempt for human rights' that had 'resulted in barbarous acts which have outraged the conscience of mankind'.[1] It was more than a reaffirmation of commitment to prevent the recurrence of those barbarous acts. Beyond all this, it was an implicit statement of an argument made explicit three years later in the preamble to the Universal Declaration of Human Rights, which says that 'recognition of the inherent dignity and of the equal and inalienable rights of all members of the human family is the foundation of freedom, justice and peace in the world'. Thus it asserted that assaults on the inherent dignity of human beings were recognized as being relevant to the stability of the international order. It follows that a profound transformation of international relations was being heralded and with it a profound transformation of international law; for international law, like any law, is largely a description, in terms of rules of behaviour, of the society it aims to regulate.

That transformation, engendered by growing concern for human rights, has certainly taken place. Before World War II there was virtually no general international law of human rights: in a major work on human rights published in 1982 the bibliography of analytical legal writing contains no entry for a book or article on international human rights law for the period before 1945.[2] As with all revolutions, there were of course antecedents: before World War I, international law had already begun to set its face against slavery, and by 1926 the Slavery Convention had been adopted. Also in the first quarter of this century, under the League of Nations, treaties guaranteeing the rights of some minorities were concluded, and populations living in territories subject

---

[1] The quoted words are from the second preambular paragraph to the Universal Declaration of Human Rights; see *infra* n. 7.

[2] Vasak (general ed.), *The International Dimensions of Human Rights* (revised English edn. by Alston, 1982), ii, Annex III, 701.

to the League mandate system were to have their human rights respected. The establishment of the International Labour Organization by the Treaty of Versailles in 1919 brought the real prospect of effective international legislation and action to protect trade union rights (a species of the right to freedom of association). International law had also already developed rules for the conduct of international warfare to protect non-combatants, especially prisoners of war. There were, therefore, diverse moves in the recognition of human rights on an international scale, but still, in principle, human rights were seen as a matter to be left to the *domaine réservé*, or domestic jurisdiction, of states. In other words, for most purposes governments could do what they wished with those under their jurisdiction and international law had no opinion on the matter, much less any means to act.[3]

Events leading up to, and most particularly the events of, World War II changed all that. There was widespread denial of civil rights and liberties on the basis of racial, religious, and political discrimination; forced labour; public and clandestine deportations of groups of people, or of individual 'undesirables' or 'subversives'; confiscation of property; routine and systematic detention and torture of prisoners; wanton murder; the ultimate atrocity of genocide; these things took place and require no documentation here. Of crucial importance to those left among the ruins was the recognition that the carnage had been perpetrated by a government that had unleashed a war of aggression, involving more bloodshed than the world had ever known, within living memory of a war that had already cost a generation of lives and whose wounds were still felt, and that much of the population taking part in this aggression was itself coerced and intimidated. It became clear to the Allied Powers who founded the United Nations that no peace could be secure where governments were free to break and obliterate their own people. Where there is no restraint at home, no limit to the exercise of official power, there need be none such abroad either. And law could not just rest at addressing the behaviour of a state beyond its frontiers. International law could no longer just be the law regulating behaviour between states, it had also to concern itself with what went on within them.

[3] Although in the nineteenth and early twentieth centuries some states claimed a right of armed 'humanitarian intervention' when certain population groups were threatened with massacre (a claim that has surfaced again in the post-World War II era), this is a doctrine that has not won widespread acceptance: see Ronzitti, *Rescuing Nationals Abroad and Intervention on Grounds of Humanity* (1985); Franck and Rodley, 'After Bangladesh: the Law of Humanitarian Intervention by Military Force', 67 *AJIL* 275 (1973); cf. Tesón, *Humanitarian Intervention: An Inquiry into Law and Morality* (1988). It is particularly noteworthy that there was no question of any such intervention to protect the Jews or other minorities in Hitler's Germany: id., at 292–3. Since the end of the Cold War, it may be possible to detect the emergence of a doctrine whereby collective armed intervention, notably when authorized by the United Nations Security Council, may be considered a legitimate response to widespread or systematic gross violations of human rights: see Rodley (ed.), *To Loose the Bands of Wickedness—International Intervention in Defence of Human Rights* (1992); Murphy, *Humanitarian Intervention: The United Nations in an Evolving World Order* (1996).

Much of the thinking of those responsible for framing the new post-war human rights instruments was generated, naturally enough, by the events of the recent, grim past. Development of the law on the conduct of international armed conflict (*jus in bello*) preceded that of international human rights law and indeed had its forerunners in religious principles and practices of antiquity. It has been the subject of much learned writing and it is unnecessary to add to it here. Suffice it to say that in the immediate post-war period its inadequacies were bleakly obvious, and existing humanitarian law relevant to the conduct of international armed conflict and the protection of those caught up in it was considerably developed by the Geneva Conventions of 1949. The refinement of rules of humanitarian law on the treatment of prisoners of war, for example, even now in many respects goes far beyond that of rules of human rights law relating to the treatment of prisoners in peacetime.[4]

The concern here is primarily with the development of the new field of international human rights law, but the humanitarian law rules will be considered to the extent that they help elucidate the scope of the human rights rules generally, and also to the extent that they impose significant obligations in the case of violation of rules that are common to international human rights law and international humanitarian law (sometimes called, indeed, 'the law of human rights in armed conflict'). One branch of international humanitarian law will, in fact, be given special attention, namely the law applicable in non-international armed conflict. The development of this branch postdated World War II and can be ascribed to the same causes that led to the development of international human rights law. Its particular significance lies in the fact that it overlaps in many crucial respects with international human rights law and each will be seen to help clarify the other.[5]

The result of post-war efforts to protect people from serious abuse by their own governments has been the evolution of a general international law of human rights. Both the evolution and the general features of this law have been amply described by others and it is not intended to reiterate them

---

[4] The relevant law relating to the treatment of persons in the hands of a party to an armed conflict was codified in the Geneva Conventions of 12 August 1949: Geneva Convention for the Amelioration of the Condition of the Wounded and Sick in Armed Forces in the Field (Geneva Convention I); Geneva Convention for the Amelioration of the Condition of Wounded, Sick and Shipwrecked Members of Armed Forces at Sea (Geneva Convention II); Geneva Convention Relative to the Treatment of Prisoners of War (Geneva Convention III); Geneva Convention Relative to the Protection of Civilian Persons in Time of War (Geneva Convention IV). These instruments were supplemented in 1977 by the Protocol Additional to the Geneva Conventions of 12 August 1949, and relating to the Protection of Victims of International Armed Conflicts (Protocol I) and by the Protocol Additional to the Geneva Conventions of 12 August 1949, and relating to the Protection of Victims of Non-International Armed Conflicts (Protocol II). See, generally, Best, *Humanity in Warfare* (1980); Cassese (ed.), *The New Humanitarian Law of Armed Conflict* (1979); International Committee of the Red Cross and Henry Dunant Institute, *Bibliography of International Humanitarian Law* (2nd edn., 1997).

[5] See Green, 'Human Rights and the Law of Armed Conflict', 10 *Israel Yearbook of Human Rights* 9 (1980); Meron, *Human Rights and Humanitarian Norms as Customary Law* (1989).

here.[6] But two broad aspects of the field need to be mentioned. The first is the area of standard-setting, often called the promotion of human rights; the second is that of giving effect to the standards, commonly called the protection or implementation of human rights. Effort during the immediate post-World War II period, especially at the United Nations level, focused principally on standard-setting, the first achievement of which was the Universal Declaration of Human Rights, adopted on 10 December 1948.[7] This instrument was to be the first of four, the other three being the International Covenant on Economic, Social and Cultural Rights, the International Covenant on Civil and Political Rights (the Covenant), and the Optional Protocol to the latter.[8] The Covenants encompassed elements aimed both at standard-setting and at initiating measures of implementation, the latter including the creation of the Human Rights Committee. These instruments are known collectively as the International Bill of Human Rights. Similar developments at the regional level produced the European Convention on Human Rights,[9] the American Declaration of the Rights and Duties of Man (an analogue to the Universal Declaration) and later the American Convention on Human Rights,[10] and more recently the African Charter on Human and Peoples' Rights.[11]

Just as it was hardly possible to write a book on the international law of human rights before the advent of the United Nations over fifty years ago, this study of human rights with particular relevance to the treatment of prisoners could not have been written even twenty years ago. It was not until 1975, for example, that the United Nations General Assembly adopted its landmark Declaration on the Protection of All Persons from Being Subjected

[6] See especially, *The International Dimensions of Human Rights*, *supra* n. 2, and Meron (ed.), *Human Rights in International Law: Legal and Policy Issues* (1984). Excellent introductions to the field are to be found in Robertson and Merrills, *Human Rights in the World* (4th edn., 1996) and Buergenthal, *International Human Rights in a Nutshell* (1988). Sieghart, *The International Law of Human Rights* (1983), is an important reference work on the scope and meaning of various rights. To the extent that the rights are articulated in the International Covenant on Civil and Political Rights (see *infra.* n. 8), valuable commentaries on them are to be found in Henkin (ed.), *The International Bill of Rights—The Covenant on Civil and Political Rights* (1981).

[7] GA res. 172 A (III), 10 Dec. 1948.

[8] GA res. 2200 A (XXI), 16 Dec. 1966. A second Optional Protocol, aiming at the abolition of the death penalty, was adopted in 1989: GA res. 44/128, 15 Dec. 1989.

[9] Council of Europe, Convention for the Protection of Human Rights and Fundamental Freedoms, done at Rome, 4 Nov. 1950, and its eleven protocols.

[10] Organization of American States: American Declaration of the Rights and Duties of Man, adopted by the Ninth Conference of American States, Bogotá, Colombia, 1948; American Convention on Human Rights, signed at the Inter-American Specialized Conference on Human Rights, San José, Costa Rica, 22 Nov. 1969. The Convention has since been supplemented by an Additional Protocol in the Area of Economic, Social and Cultural Rights ('Protocol of San Salvador'), signed at San Salvador, El Salvador, 17 Nov. 1988 at the 18th regular session of the OAS General Assembly, and Protocol to Abolish the Death Penalty, approved at Asunción, Paraguay, 8 Jun. 1990 at the 20th regular session of the OAS General Assembly.

[11] Organization of African Unity, African Charter on Human and Peoples' Rights, adopted by the 18th Assembly of Heads of State and Government, Nairobi, Kenya, June 1981.

to Torture or Other Cruel, Inhuman or Degrading Treatment or Punishment (the Declaration against Torture).[12] The Covenant did not enter into force until 23 March 1976, and the authoritative 'general comments' of its Human Rights Committee on the scope of the provisions in question emerged only in 1982. The United Nations Commission on Human Rights had traditionally considered itself powerless publicly to investigate specific human rights violations. A major departure from this reluctance came when, in 1975, it established a working group to investigate human rights in Chile.[13] Since then it has examined the human rights situation in a number of countries, but, because the Commission is a body composed of governments, not all countries meriting attention have received it. The first mechanism created by the Commission to deal with a specific category of serious human rights violations wherever they occur was the Working Group on Enforced or Involuntary Disappearances, established in 1980. It was followed by the appointment of a Special Rapporteur on Summary or Arbitrary Executions in 1982. Only at the end of 1984 was it possible for a far-reaching UN Convention against Torture and Other Cruel, Inhuman or Degrading Treatment or Punishment to be adopted by the General Assembly.[14] Like the Covenant, this Convention contains elements of standard-setting and implementation. Hard on its heels, in March 1985, the Commission on Human Rights, following the models of its existing 'thematic mechanisms' on 'disappearances' and on summary and arbitrary executions, decided to appoint a Special Rapporteur on Torture. Later, in December 1985, the General Assembly of the Organization of American States adopted its own Inter-American Convention to Prevent and Punish Torture;[15] and, in 1987, the Council of Europe adopted the European Convention for the Prevention of Torture and Inhuman or Degrading Treatment or Punishment[16] which provides for a system of international inspection of places of detention. These are just some of the recent developments that have contributed to the growth of a complex branch of international human rights law which relates to the treatment, or rather the limits on ill-treatment, of prisoners.

Before proceeding further, it will be as well to define the central term of this book. Unless the text shows clearly a different intention, the terms 'prisoner' and 'detainee' (used separately or together) should be taken as referring to any persons who are so positioned as to be unable to remove themselves from

---

[12] GA res. 3452 (XXX), 9 Dec. 1975.

[13] The Commission had in 1967 set up an *ad hoc* working group of experts on southern Africa, but apartheid was not seen as a matter of domestic jurisdiction. There had also been investigations into the human rights of people in the occupied territories of the Middle East after the 1967 war; but here, by definition, there was no question of the territories falling within the domestic jurisdiction of Israel: see Rodley, 'The United Nations and Human Rights in the Middle East', 38 *Social Research* 217 (1971).

[14] GA res. 39/46, 10 Dec. 1984.   [15] OAS, *Treaty Series*, No. 67.

[16] Done at Strasbourg, 26 Nov. 1987, *European Treaty Series*, No. 126.

the ambit of official action and abuse. The term 'prisoner' is not therefore limited to its most familiar usage, implying a person confined, after due legal process, to a formal institution of detention, as a result of conviction for a criminal offence, or on remand pending trial. Although such prisoners are as entitled as any others to have their basic human rights respected, much of what follows will be more relevant to the prisoner or detainee denoted by the broader definition just given.

A word of explanation about the scope of the book is also in order: just as international humanitarian law is concerned only with the rules pertaining to the conduct of armed conflict (*jus in bello*) and does not address itself to the legitimacy of resort to armed force in the first place (*jus ad bellum*), so this book is concerned with international law as it relates to the treatment of prisoners, not to the propriety of their detention. It may be that many of the people whose cases will be discussed ought never to have been deprived of their freedom—for example, they may be detained in violation of the right to freedom of conscience, or of expression, or of association or assembly. In such cases the primary international legal response would be that such persons should be released. Nevertheless the rights that are the subject here apply regardless of the legitimacy of the detention. They are the rights of all prisoners, whether entirely innocent of any offence or guilty of the most heinous. They are, precisely, rights inherent in the dignity (in the sense of value or worth) of every human being.[17]

Not all the rules referred to in this book apply only to prisoners. Someone not detained may suffer violation of, for example, the right to life or the right not be subjected to degrading treatment: people may be shot for disobeying a curfew of which they were fully aware and which they were free to observe—their killing may well violate the right to life, though in a manner totally unconnected with detention. Similarly, refusal on racial grounds to admit persons to a country whose nationality they bear has been held to be degrading treatment,[18] but is again unconnected with detention. To this extent the book does not explore the full scope of the rules it deals with, but is concerned only with their application to the treatment of prisoners or detainees.

Much of this text is, therefore, concerned with the scope, in relation to the treatment of prisoners and detainees as defined above, of a small number of provisions that appear in most of the instruments mentioned earlier and are quoted here from the Universal Declaration of Human Rights:

Everyone has the right to life, liberty and security of person. (Article 3.)
No one shall be subjected to torture or to cruel, inhuman or degrading treatment or punishment. (Article 5.)
No one shall be subjected to arbitrary arrest [or] detention . . . (Article 9.)

[17] For an acute analysis of the term 'human dignity', see Schachter, 'Human Dignity as a Normative Concept', 77 *AJIL* 848 (1983).
[18] *East African Asians* v. *United Kingdom*, 3 EHRR 76 (1973).

These provisions have, as will be seen, been the object of sustained international legislation as well as application in specific cases by the bodies empowered to implement the instruments noted above. Moreover, new mechanisms have been, or are in the process of being, established to deal with certain kinds of violations of the provisions. It is not intended here to examine the general human rights bodies established under the several conventions, but to look at their specific findings on the relevant provisions and to pay close attention to the emerging implementation mechanisms which are particularly aimed at combating violations of the provisions.[19]

THE NATURE AND SCOPE OF THE PROBLEM

TORTURE AND OTHER ILL-TREATMENT

For working purposes, torture may be understood to be the officially sanctioned infliction of intense suffering, aimed at forcing someone to do or say something against his or her will. While the concept of torture has sometimes embraced severe punishment of persons convicted of crimes—and this may indeed be the case today (see Chapter 3)—torture has traditionally been a method of arriving at the 'truth', of determining responsibility for offences by means of eliciting confessions or other information. Less obviously, it has also become a method of inspiring fear among the population at large, or specific segments of it.

The history of torture has been written elsewhere, in depth, and is not the aim of the present volume; a brief summary, however, may be of use in understanding the nature of the practice.[20]

Until the end of the eighteenth century, torture had been prevalent, and legal, in western Europe for about seven centuries. It had an earlier history still in ancient Greece and in the Roman Empire, where it was used to elicit the truth in cases of serious crime. Its use was, at least in theory, limited to slaves, foreigners, and other persons without full legal personality, but in the

---

[19] There are also non-treaty-based mechanisms aimed at curbing violations of human rights generally, of which the best-known is the (confidential) procedure approved by UN Economic and Social Council resolution 1503 (XLVIII) of 27 May 1970, whereby the UN Commission on Human Rights is empowered to investigate or make a thorough study of an alleged 'consistent pattern of gross and reliably attested violations of human rights and fundamental freedoms'. On this and other general mechanisms see, for example, Robertson and Merrills, *supra* n.6, and Hannum (ed.), *Guide to International Human Rights Practice* (2nd edn., 1992), especially chapters 4 (Rodley, United Nations), 5 (Marks, Unesco), 6 (Swepstone, ILO), 7 (Shelton, inter-American system), 8 (Boyle, Europe).

[20] See, generally, Langbein, *Torture and the Law of Proof* (1977): Ruthven, *Torture—The Grand Conspiracy* (1978); and Peters, *Torture* (1985). Extensive research on the existence or otherwise of torture in non-European civilizations still remains to be done. Nevertheless, it seems to be the case that torture was alien to Jewish and Islamic law (albeit the political leadership of the Ottoman Empire had recourse to it, despite its incompatibility with religious injunction).

later Roman Empire it was gradually extended to other categories of the population, and was particularly used on those suspected of treason. Away from the influence of the classical world, early medieval Europe did not, strictly speaking, use torture. It did, however, employ physical suffering as a method of arriving at justice, in the trial by ordeal, wherein the extent to which an accused person could withstand pain was taken as an indication of guilt or innocence. This was, therefore, a method of resolving disputes between accuser and accused, based on the belief that the deity would indicate justice by determining the outcome of the ordeal.

In twelfth-century Europe, perhaps stimulated by a revival of classical learning, perhaps linked to the rise of state authority (and the consequent erosion of individual power), trial by ordeal was gradually replaced by the inquisitorial process. This change was based on the belief that perception of truth need not be left to the deity, but might be determined by rational analysis of the facts of a case. Once this sort of inquiry was deemed to be necessary, rules of evidence or proof had to be developed. In cases of crimes for which the penalty would be death or mutilation, circumstantial evidence was considered insufficient proof for conviction. Two other types of proof became recognized as conclusive: the testimony of two eyewitnesses, or a confession. Given the scarcity, in serious crime, of two eyewitnesses, the confession came to be regarded as the most secure proof, 'the queen of proofs' in the language of the day. This need for confession seems to have led to the introduction of torture into legal process. In theory, there would be no resort to torture ('the question') until there were sufficient indicia (circumstantial evidence) to make a very strong case; further, torture would be used only on those known to be of bad character, and even then only as a last resort. Complex safeguards were intended to ensure that torture was not prematurely used, and that, when it was used, it would not kill or maim. In fact, however, there was widespread abuse of torture by judges and, in a context where religious heresy was regarded as the equivalent of treason in the secular world, the zeal (or corruption) of ecclesiastical inquisitors led to considerable relaxation of the 'rules' of torture.

Those who defended torture, by no means all corrupt or sadistic, argued that it was essential to arrive at the truth in cases of crime which incurred mutilation or death as punishment. They argued that torture was the only possible method of obtaining truth when all others had failed, and they saw the shortcomings of the method as the result of corrupt or inept application of a basically sound principle. Such defences met objections that had been offered probably since torture was first used: it was unacceptable on moral grounds, and unacceptable on the logical ground that it was unlikely to achieve its stated aim, since it tested the resistance to pain of the victim, rather than his or her capacity for telling the truth. Torture persisted, nevertheless, as an aspect of the inquisitorial process in both secular and ecclesiastical law, until the mid-eighteenth century. Then came the Enlightenment, an intellectual environment unsympathetic to the religion-dominated past, to superstition, to conventional assumptions, wherein the moral and logical arguments carried more force than before. Just as important, perhaps, for the demise of torture, was the increased sophistication of the legal process: the confession became less in demand as rules of evidence were refined. In addition, imprisonment and other punishments came increasingly to replace the death penalty and other corporal punishments, reducing to some extent the concern for absolute certainty in judgments. In the space of about half a century, torture was abolished as part of legal process and was virtually gone from Europe by the end of the eighteenth century. From this point, it was considered to be a thing of the past, until the rise of the Nazi party in Germany in the 1930s, which went so far as to legislate the permissibility of 'third degree' interrogation. It need hardly be restated that, during World War II, torture was used, notoriously, in occupied territories, particularly on persons suspected of resistance activities. When peace brought the chance to review the atrocities of war, torture was perceived to be an aberration that must not be allowed to recur. It was natural, therefore, that the Universal Declaration of Human Rights in 1948 should prohibit torture. Nevertheless, the practice persists.

It is not possible to give precise statistics for the current prevalence of torture and ill-treatment of prisoners. It is in the nature of such practices that they take place without independent witnesses. Physical scars, if any, may not be long-lasting; the tortured and those close to them may be too afraid to complain; doctors and lawyers, where available, may be silenced by fear that even the little alleviation they can offer will be curtailed if they do not keep silent. Geographical isolation also often plays a part: detailed information may not reach the cities, or transcend the frontiers of the state, where aid might be solicited. The only certainty is that the authorities can be expected to deny the existence of anything resembling torture.

Despite these obstacles to information, a rough picture emerges. In its first report on torture[21] Amnesty International discussed allegations that torture or other ill-treatment had taken place in over sixty countries. A decade later its report *Torture in the Eighties*[22] discussed a similar number of countries and presented clear evidence that torture had taken place in a majority of them. In 1997, the UN Special Rapporteur on Torture decided that the information he had received about the practice of torture was such as to justify his approaching the governments of sixty-nine countries or territories.[23] In view

---

[21] Amnesty International, *Report on Torture* (1973).

[22] Amnesty International, *Torture in the Eighties* (1984); see also Lipmann, 'The Protection of Universal Human Rights: The Problem of Torture', *Universal Human Rights*, vol i, no. 4 (1979), 25.

[23] UN doc. E/CN.4/1998/38 and Add. 1. Some approaches concerned isolated cases of urgent appeals aimed at avoiding torture and some others were directed to countries from which

of the hindrances to the flow of reliable information, the number of countries practising or tolerating torture must be reckoned to be higher than has been reliably documented. Most of the available information concerns political prisoners, many of whom will be articulate, well educated, less prone than others to conceal the whole matter afterwards, more likely to be aware of, or in contact with, organizations able to take the matter to the public or even international level. How many more there may be, with less facility for communication and less knowledge of channels of complaint, may only be conjectured.

There seem to be no geographical or ideological frontiers to the incidence of torture. In the 1970s and 1980s the typical victim was a political opponent of the government—violent or non-violent, a real force for change or a minor irritant to the regime—seized by the security forces. The latter would have been military or police (or both, acting together) but more commonly the military. They may or may not have been in uniform; their vehicles may or may not have had number plates; frequently, though not inevitably, the government of the state concerned would have been ousted unconstitutionally by the armed forces which would then be able to operate free of restraint. In the 1990s, there are still all-too-many such victims, but the ordinary criminal suspect has also been revealed as a frequent victim.

Once seized, the prisoner will be transported to a place of detention. This may be a police station, or an army barracks, or a place belonging to neither category, but commandeered for the purpose. It may be a secret place. The torture and ill-treatment will take place there, unless it has already started during the transportation. The methods are as infinite as the inventiveness of the dark side of the human imagination, but among the more common are prolonged beatings, especially on the soles of the feet or genitals, immersion in excrement, near-asphyxiation, rape and other violent sexual assault, burning, and the administering of electric shocks. More sophisticated, in that they leave little physical trace, are the psychological techniques: deprivation of light (or of darkness), deprivation of sound, of sleep, general disorientation, threats of mutilation or death, mock execution, and most powerful of all in many cases, the threat that physical abuses will be extended to persons close to the prisoner.

The purposes of torture and ill-treatment are generally limited. The torture is usually aimed at securing information about the activities of the victim, or of persons connected with the victim. The activities in question may be thought to relate to the commission of criminal offences (with or without political connections) or the planned commission of such offences, or simply to political dissent that the authorities are not prepared to tolerate. The tor-

persons were threatened with removal to a country where they risked being tortured or ill-treated. But 'observations' on some 38 countries suggested an extensive practice in *at least* that number.

ture is also often aimed at securing 'confessions' to criminal acts. Another purpose is the intimidation of the victim and others, possibly even society as a whole, so as to deter people from undertaking an activity that could risk their falling into the hands of the authorities.

Torture is usually carried out while the victim is excluded from any contact with the outside world (family, doctor, lawyer, and so on—a condition known as detention incommunicado). This period is often prolonged, measured in weeks and months rather than in days (though, of course, a lot of suffering may be inflicted in a period of days or even hours). The incommunicado detention may, like the torture itself, be frankly illegal under the law of the country in question. Often the authorities will facilitate the perpetration of torture by declaring a state of siege or emergency in order to permit the suspension of legal guarantees that could have acted as checks—such as the right to contact with the outside world, the right to be brought before a judge promptly after arrest, or the right to challenge the legality of detention before a court.

EXECUTIONS

Some governments are willing not only to inflict acute physical and mental suffering on those they consider a nuisance or threat, or the repositories of useful information, they are also willing to kill them.[24] Sometimes death may be the predictable result of torture. Sometimes victims will be seized in circumstances similar to those described for torture victims, and their bodies will subsequently appear on a roadside, or washed up on the seashore, or, eventually, in an unmarked mass grave. Again the authorities will deny responsibility, claiming perhaps that the deaths were the results of shoot-outs with armed subversives, or that the victims tried to escape from detention, or were killed by fellow subversives. Sometimes they will say that the killings were carried out by groups beyond official control, despite evidence that such groups are often composed of members of the military or police, who seem to be able to operate with impunity and who never seem to be pursued with the diligence that is brought to bear on the government's opponents. In some countries such groups are called 'death squads', often targeting persons named on a 'death list'. All is denied: few governments will go to the lengths of openly calling for the 'physical liquidation of enemies of the revolution', and making them targets for 'elimination' anywhere in the world.[25]

---

[24] See Amnesty International, *Political Killings by Governments* (1983); also Kaufman and Weiss-Fagan, 'Extrajudicial Executions: an Insight into the Global Dimensions of a Human Rights Violation', *Human Rights Quarterly*, vol. iii, no. 4 (1981), 81.
[25] Amnesty International, *supra* n. 24, 69–77 (Libya).

The victims will often be perceived political opponents, violent or non-violent. Sometimes they will be suspected common criminals who seem to the law enforcement officials to be 'getting away with' crime: so the processes of law are simply bypassed. On occasion the victim will be a member of a detested minority: national, racial, religious, or linguistic, whose offence is to claim more rights than the majority wishes to accord. Not all such victims will have been physically detained before being killed, but most will have been put in a position akin to detention, in that there is nothing they can do to escape the bullet destined for them.

Not all killings by governments belong in the category of official murder just described (extra-legal executions, as they will be called). In certain circumstances international law does not condemn some kinds of killings committed by governments. It is recognized, for example, that under certain conditions law enforcement officials may, as a last resort, have to have recourse to the use of lethal force. Similarly, while waging a war of aggression may be illegal, waging one in self-defence is not, and even the most pacific state may thus find itself at war and involved in killing. There are, therefore, rules for the conduct of armed conflict: killings committed within these rules may well not fall foul of international law. Nor *per se*, does capital punishment (unless in violation of a specific treaty obligation), which persists, even though international law recognizes the goal of abolition. On the other hand, lack of procedural safeguards and other limitations when applying the death penalty may render the event virtually indistinguishable from the extra-legal executions that have just been described. In some countries, for example, the death penalty may be applicable for joining a banned political party; or it may be made applicable retroactively, that is, only after a particular accused person has committed the offence in question. The trial may have taken the form of denunciation at a mass meeting, or may have been before an *ad hoc* tribunal composed of 'judges' without legal training (often soldiers, appointed by the executive authority). The 'trial' may well have taken place in secret, with no access for the accused to a defence lawyer. The possibility of appeal is likely to have been dispensed with, and if a provision for petition for clemency exists at all, it may well be to the head of the government that has established the apparatus. International law does not acquiesce in such sham uses of the law to effect the same end as would be achieved by extra-legal execution.

There can be no precise statistics for the incidence of internationally unlawful killings, even in peacetime; the problems which beset the documentation of torture inevitably operate here also. The Special Rapporteur on Summary or Arbitrary Executions appointed by the UN Commission on Human Rights stated in his first report in January 1983 that, in the previous fifteen years or so, killings within his mandate (that is extra-legal executions and death penalties not meeting international criteria for safeguards) had been practised 'in many countries and in a number of them in a consistent pattern.

Conservative estimates would put the known victims of summary or arbitrary executions to be at least two million persons.'[26] In his latest report, he said that, for the year 1997, he transmitted to governments 'more than 960 cases of violations of the right to life as well as 122 urgent appeals on behalf of 3,720 persons, in addition to allegations concerning groups of persons for which no number of individuals was known'.[27]

DISAPPEARANCES

Of all the enormities that are considered in this book, perhaps none is more sinister than what has become known as the 'disappearance'.[28] In the typical case the victim, normally a perceived political opponent, will be seized in circumstances like those already described for torture victims and victims of extra-legal execution. The detention is not acknowledged by the authorities: the person merely goes missing and may not reappear for a long time, if ever. After a while there may well be serious grounds for fearing the person's death, but family and friends will remain in a state of anxious uncertainty. In many cases the only possibility of 'reappearance' will be the discovery of the body, often bearing marks of torture, in an unmarked grave. Early reports of the Working Group on Enforced or Involuntary Disappearances established by the UN Commission on Human Rights[29] numbered the 'disappearances' they had heard of in the thousands, alleged to involve some thirty-eight countries. Most of the many thousands of cases the Group has dealt with occurred in the 1970s. By the late 1980s, in tandem with the demise of military governments, there was a marked reduction in their incidence in several countries of Latin America, the region where their practice first attracted international attention to the problem. In 1997 the Working Group was still transmitting 1,111 'new' cases to twenty-three governments. However, the majority related to four countries (two from Latin America), with only 180 allegedly occurring in that year.[30]

PRISON CONDITIONS

It is impossible to know at any given moment how many people around the world are incarcerated. At the fifth session of the United Nations Commission on Crime Prevention and Criminal Justice, the Secretariat

---

[26] UN doc. E/CN.4/1983/16, para. 217.   [27] UN doc. E/CN.4/1998/68, para. 110.
[28] See, generally, *'Disappearances'—A Workbook* (Amnesty International USA, 1981); Berman and Clark, 'State Terrorism: Disappearances', 13 *Rutgers Law Journal* 531 (1982). Other general works are cited in Chapter 8, at n. 6.
[29] UN docs. E/CN.4/1435 and Add. 1 (1981); E/CN.4/1492 (1981) and Add. 1 (1982); E/CN.4/1983/14: E/CN.4/1985/15 and Adds. 1 and 2: E/CN.4/1986/18 and Add. 1.
[30] UN doc. E/CN.4/1998/43, para. 13 and Annex I (Colombia, 16; Indonesia, 30; Mexico, 24; Sri Lanka, 77). 686 of the pre-1997 cases came from Iraq.

prepared a table of prison populations in sixty-four countries 'as of 31 December 1993 (or nearest possible date)'. A rough calculation suggests that in those countries, at that time, some 2.4 million people were formally deprived of their liberty, of whom nearly 30 per cent were remanded in prison pending trial. This figure falls well short of the whole, for the calculation included no figures from some of the world's most populous countries, such as Brazil, China, Egypt, India, Indonesia, or Nigeria. Nearly half the countries had a prison population of over 100 per 100,000, with the Russian Federation having the highest ratio, of 618 per 100,000.[31]

There is even less information about conditions of detention. Sometimes a prison regime will be relatively humane, its main purpose and effect being to inflict no more hardship than necessarily attends upon deprivation of liberty and consequent exclusion from participation in society. Sometimes there are schemes which permit a measure of socialization with, and work among, the non-prison community. All too frequently, however, the prison will be a place of harsh deprivation: it may be overcrowded, even to the point of suffocation, and may offer little chance of exercise, or of adequate diet; its conditions may be generally poor and sometimes an arbitrary or even brutal prison administration will prevail, with the authorities willing to massacre inmates who rise against their conditions. Sometimes the worst conditions and treatment, including prolonged solitary confinement, deprivation of light during the day, or of darkness at night, wanton beating by guards, will be reserved for political prisoners.

Regulation of prison conditions is quite properly the province of domestic legislation, not least because familiarity with local custom, cultural traditions, and standards of life will be an important factor in determining what conditions are acceptable to humane society and what are not. There are some issues not susceptible to relative interpretation, however, and it is against these excesses that the international community has set its face; in particular in the drawing up of the UN Standard Minimum Rules for the Treatment of Prisoners.

THE INHERENT DIGNITY OF THE ENEMY

It is a truism that man's inhumanity to man can thrive only if the torturer or the executioner can deny the humanity of his victim. For one person to treat another in the ways that have been described above may, in the isolated case, be psychopathic behaviour. But when such behaviour is part of an institutional practice then something else is at work: the victim is—must be— dehumanized, seen as an object. This is the traditional and inevitable means

---

[31] UN doc. E/CN.15/1996/Add. 1, para. 5 and table 1.

of considering 'the enemy', be it a class enemy, a race enemy, a religious enemy, or a foreign enemy. Whatever the group, its members must be stripped of their inherent dignity as human beings in order to mobilize the rest against them.[32]

It is this dehumanization of the perceived enemy that the international law of human rights, following the international humanitarian law of armed conflict, must confront. It will do this by proscribing the destruction of the inherent dignity of the human person, and, if possible, by ordaining certain consequences should the proscription fail. Its province is universal, but the particular concern here must be that part of the law dealing with prisoners and detainees, who are, however unjustly, the archetypal outcasts of society.

What follows is to a large extent a consideration of how international law has already risen to the challenge, but it will conclude with suggestions on what more can be done to meet it. However, it must be clear from the outset that law is only one social tool for improving the lot of humanity. It can regulate only the society that has absorbed its values. This is as true for international law as for national law. International law will be seen to have been decidedly ambitious in the limits it sets on the behaviour of government authorities towards those in their hands, by comparison with the grim picture that obtains in many parts of the world. It is a noble ambition and the thrust will now have to be in the direction of action to give force to the law.

THE APPROACH

This text has been prepared with a number of audiences in mind.

First, it is hoped that its style will make it accessible to the concerned governmental official who may not be a lawyer but who may be involved in the administration of justice or law enforcement or in advising others as to positions to be taken at relevant international meetings.

Second, it is hoped that it will be a useful reference work, both on the law as it is at present and on the approaches available for strengthening it, for use by lawyers and non-governmental organizations working for the promotion and protection of human rights at the international level.

Third, it is offered as a first reference work for lawyers pleading cases before national courts where cognizance may be taken of international law.

---

[32] See Ruthven, *supra* n. 20. The point crops up frequently in a series of readings on 'The Psychological and Ethical Context' in Falk, Kolko and Lifton (eds.), *Crimes of War* (1972), 419–575 and in Crelinsten and Schmid (eds.), *The Politics of Pain—Torturers and Their Masters* (1993).

This applies in particular to lawyers in countries whose national legal systems incorporate international law or whose constitutions contain statements of rights using the language of the international instruments.

Fourth, it is hoped that academic colleagues will find it a useful contribution to the literature on the topic. While there have been a number of sometimes excellent books and articles on various specific aspects of the subject, it remains the first attempt at a global consideration of the international law approach to the problem of the treatment of prisoners.

The organization of the text is as follows.

The first five chapters deal with various aspects of torture and other ill-treatment, especially that which typically occurs at the post-arrest/interrogation period. The prohibition of torture and other ill-treatment has undergone significant evolution since 1973 and is probably the most developed aspect of rules relating to the treatment of prisoners. Chapter 1 describes the beginnings of a series of standard-setting initiatives launched by the General Assembly in the mid-1970s; Chapter 2 then contains an exposition of the current legal status of the prohibition of torture and other ill-treatment. This is the main doctrinal exposition on the issue of the legal status of particular standards and frequent reference will be made to it in later chapters. Chapter 3 seeks to identify the factors involved in determining whether particular acts amount to torture or other ill-treatment. The legal consequences of committing the prohibited acts, both for the state and for the individual torturer, are the subject of Chapter 4. This chapter contains the main doctrinal consideration on the issue of the legal consequences of violations of relevant international law rules, so, like Chapter 2, it also will be the object of frequent references in later chapters. Chapter 5 explores remedies that have been or are being established with a view to securing international action to protect people from being tortured or ill-treated.

Chapters 6 and 7 deal with executions. The former considers extra-legal executions, virtually a euphemism for murder committed or tolerated by governments, and a species of what have become known as summary or arbitrary executions. Chapter 7 deals with this broader category of summary or arbitrary executions which are formally pronounced death sentences carried out without regard to the numerous safeguards that international law (which does not as yet universally forbid the death penalty *per se*) requires to be observed in capital cases.

Chapter 8 analyses the phenomenon of the 'disappearance' and explores the main legal provisions that it flouts, including the right not be tortured and the right to life.

Chapters 9 and 10 deal with formal punishment: prison conditions and corporal punishment respectively. The nature and scope of the corporal punishment problem was not discussed above, because it is necessarily treated in Chapter 10.

Chapters 11 and 12 explore internationally prescribed rules, the application of which at the national level might prevent the treatment that previous chapters will have found to be prohibited. Chapter 11 deals with legal safeguards against arbitrary arrest and detention, while Chapter 12 considers internationally approved standards of conduct for law enforcement officials, prosecutors, lawyers, and medical personnel; it also notes suggestions for an additional code for military personnel.

A general conclusion draws attention to desirable future developments in the field.

When a chapter introduces a new legal rule or instrument into the discussion it will usually follow the model of Chapters 2 to 5. That is, it will assess the legal status of the rule, describe its scope, examine the legal consequences of breach of the rule, and point to specific remedies that have been established for the purpose of implementing the rule. The chapters generally conclude with a summary, except where summaries have already been integrated at the end of particular sections.

I

The Response of the United Nations General Assembly to the Challenge of Torture

INTRODUCTION

Since the end of World War II, the need to prohibit the torture and ill-treatment of prisoners has been the focus of much activity among intergovernmental organizations. After the right to self-determination (decolonization), the right not to be subjected to racial discrimination (including apartheid), and the right to freedom of association (trade union rights), the right not to be subjected to torture has received more attention than any other from intergovernmental organizations.

It is not intended here to explore in detail the background to the establishment of the norm condemning torture. The prohibition of torture appeared naturally and uncontroversially in the Universal Declaration of Human Rights, the landmark catalogue of human rights and fundamental freedoms adopted by the General Assembly of the United Nations in 1948.[1] Its inclusion signalled the desire 'to eliminate the medieval methods of torture and cruel punishment which were practiced in the recent past by the Nazis and fascists'.[2] Specifically, article 5 of the Declaration states: 'No one shall be subjected to torture or to cruel, inhuman or degrading treatment or punishment.' The same language is to be found in article 7 of the International Covenant on Civil and Political Rights (the Covenant),[3] wherein the motivation for including the prohibition is similarly obvious.[4] The atrocities of World War II also led to the inclusion of a prohibition against torture and other ill-treatment in the Geneva Conventions of 12 August 1949 on the protection of victims of war.[5] The same motivation lies behind the prohibition against torture in the European Convention on Human Rights.[6] Subsequent instruments, such as the American Convention on Human Rights[7] and the African

---

[1] GA res. 217 A (III), 10 Dec. 1948.

[2] Robinson, *The Universal Declaration of Human Rights—its Origin, Significance, Application and Interpretation* (1958), 108.

[3] GA res. 2200A (XXI), 16 Dec. 1966. The following language is added to that of the Universal Declaration (article 5): 'In particular no one shall be subjected without his free consent to medical or scientific experimentation.'

[4] Dinstein, 'The Right to Life, Physical Integrity and Liberty', in Henkin (ed.), *The International Bill of Rights—The Covenant on Civil and Political Rights* (1981), 125.

[5] The relevant articles are mentioned in the next chapter.

[6] Article 3.   [7] Article 5.

Charter on Human and Peoples' Rights,[8] could not thereafter fail to include the prohibition.[9]

The United Nations is the body which has devoted most attention to the problem of torture and other ill-treatment.[10] While, as will be seen, many organs of the UN have dealt with particular aspects of the issue, the political initiative was taken primarily by the General Assembly. A programme of standard-setting that the Assembly started in 1974 was completed in 1988 with the adoption of the Body of Principles for the Protection of All Persons under Any Form of Detention or Imprisonment (see below). Several aspects of this standard-setting work are dealt with in detail in later chapters; the aim here is to concentrate on the period from 1973 to 1977 when the Assembly played its most creative and innovative role, since a description and review of this role provides the necessary background to matters dealt with at length in later chapters.

First to be examined are the developments leading up to the adoption by the General Assembly in 1975 of the Declaration on the Protection of All Persons from Being Subjected to Torture or Other Cruel, Inhuman or Degrading Treatment or Punishment (Declaration against Torture; see Annex 1). (The formula 'other cruel, inhuman or degrading treatment or punishment' will in this text be abbreviated to 'other ill-treatment' except where the separate parts are relevant to the discussion.) There will follow a description of the General Assembly's initiatives in developing several documents: the above-mentioned Body of Principles; the Code of Conduct for Law Enforcement Officials; and the Principles of Medical Ethics relevant to the role of health personnel, particularly physicians, in the protection of prisoners and detainees against torture and other cruel, inhuman or degrading treatment or punishment. Following this there is a brief outline of three major General Assembly initiatives: the decision to mandate the drafting of a convention against torture or other ill-treatment; the devising of a questionnaire by means of which compliance by governments with the Declaration against Torture might be ascertained; and the promotion of unilateral declarations against torture and other ill-treatment.

---

[8] Article 5.

[9] In addition, a number of treaties on specific areas of human rights include a prohibition of torture in relation to the subject matter of those conventions; see Chapter 2.

[10] Developments at the regional level, particularly within the Council of Europe and the Organization of American States, will be referred to in subsequent chapters dealing with substantive topics.

DISCUSSION OF TORTURE AT THE UN GENERAL ASSEMBLY
1973–1975

RESOLUTION 3059 (XXVIII) OF 2 NOVEMBER 1973

In 1975, the General Assembly of the United Nations adopted its landmark Declaration against Torture. This was a pivotal event in a process which had started in 1973 and was to continue for some fifteen years. Statements by the Foreign Ministers of Denmark, Sweden, and The Netherlands at the General Assembly's General Debate at its twenty-eighth session (1973) led the way for discussion of the issue of torture. The Danish Foreign Minister spoke of being 'alarmed by the many reports of torture' and referred approvingly to 'the many endeavours aimed at condemnation and the elimination of the use of torture'.[11] His Netherlands counterpart referred to 'reports from various parts of the world [which] provide evidence that this appalling practice has become rife and is often used against people suspected of having committed a political offence'.[12] Meanwhile, according to the Foreign Minister of Sweden: '[i]n recent years world opinion has become increasingly aware of the use of torture in connection with armed conflicts and internal political conflicts in different countries'.[13] There is evidence that these initiatives were prompted by the activities of non-governmental organizations (NGOs). For example, when, subsequent to the General Debate, Sweden introduced a draft resolution on the subject of torture at the General Assembly's Third Committee,[14] a suggestion of the context that provoked the initiative was apparent in the statement that to 'work actively for the complete eradication of every form of torture was a common humanitarian duty, since torture knew no frontiers, as pointed out by the Chairman of Amnesty International, the former Irish Foreign Minister, Mr. Sean MacBride'.[15] Similarly, during the same debate Denmark referred to 'the campaign launched by the Danish section of Amnesty International for the collection of signatures as a protest against the use of torture prevalent in many parts of the world'.[16] The one-year Campaign for the Abolition of Torture, launched by Amnesty International in December 1972 with the support of a broad range of NGOs,[17] may therefore be considered as having contributed the political

[11] *GAOR*, 28th Session, 2128th Plenary Meeting, para. 106.   [12] Id., para. 171.
[13] Id., 2149th Plenary Meeting, para. 33.
[14] Report of the Third Committee, *GAOR*, 28th Session, Annexes, Agenda item 56, A/9249, para. 6. (The text of the draft resolution was also contained in UN doc. A/C.3/L.2010 and was sponsored by Austria, Costa Rica, Ireland, The Netherlands, Sweden, and Trinidad and Tobago, subsequently joined by Lesotho and Nepal.) The Third Committee is a committee of the whole specializing in social, humanitarian, and cultural affairs, including human rights. Most of the General Assembly's work is carried out in such specialized committees; their recommendations can usually be expected to be confirmed in plenary session.
[15] *GAOR*, 28th Session, Third Committee, Summary Records, A/C.3/SR.1998, para. 1.
[16] Id., A/C.3/SR.1999, para. 18.   [17] Amnesty International, *Annual Report 1972–1973*, 15.

context for an initiative at the UN. The campaign included the quest for petition signatures referred to by Denmark, the publication of a report on torture
(the main part of which comprised a 'World Survey of Torture'), and an international conference that was to take place in December 1973.[18] There was
therefore intense press and governmental interest generated by the NGO
activities at both the national and international levels.

While the NGO campaign may have created the context of awareness and
interest necessary for an initiative, there still had to be the political will to act.
A principal factor here was the overthrow of the constitutional government
of Chile by the Chilean armed forces on 11 September 1973 and the death of
its president, Salvador Allende. A number of delegations to the General
Assembly made reference to harrowing press reports of repression and brutality by the Chilean armed forces. The representative of Chile, speaking in
reply to comments made by Norway, Yugoslavia, and Belorussia,[19] stated
that representatives of the International Red Cross, the UN High
Commissioner for Refugees, and the Inter-American Commission on Human
Rights had visited Chile, and he announced that a delegation from Amnesty
International would shortly do so.[20] Thus, the issue of torture became closely
associated with the expression of worldwide disgust at the brutality of the
overthrow of the Allende government, a connection that would also affect
developments in subsequent years. This, then, was the context for discussion
of torture in 1973: growing NGO action combined with the sharp focus provided by events in Chile.

It should be noted that no delegation felt able to defend the use of torture,
even though many of the governments represented had been cited publicly as
having perpetrated it.[21] Nor, as pointed out by Sweden, had anyone questioned the existence of torture.[22] It is unsurprising that no stance of outright
opposition to the initiative was taken, given that such a stance might have
been seen as an admission of guilt, or as approval of the practice of torture.

The draft resolution introduced by Sweden had two operative paragraphs:
the first provided that the General Assembly would 'examine the question of
torture' as a separate agenda item at its next (twenty-ninth) session; the second requested the Secretary-General 'to prepare a report on the question' for
presentation at that session.[23] This draft underwent changes that were to be
symptomatic of subsequent developments. First, new material was introduced: the first two operative paragraphs of resolution 3059 (XXVIII) as it
emerged from the debate had no analogues in the original draft. By them the
Assembly:

---

[18] Id., 23–4; see also Amnesty International, *Conference for the Abolition of Torture—Final
Report, Paris 10–11 December 1973.*
[19] Loc. cit. *supra* n. 15, A/C.3/SR.2000, paras. 23 (Norway), 24–7 (Yugoslavia), and 50–5
(Belorussia).
[20] Id., para. 57.   [21] See, for example, Amnesty International, *Report on Torture* (1973).
[22] Loc. cit. *supra* n. 15, A/C.3/SR.2002, para. 5.   [23] UN doc. A/C.3/L.2010, *supra* n. 14.

1. Rejects any form of torture and other cruel, inhuman or degrading treatment or punishment;
2. Urges all governments to become parties to existing international instruments which contain provisions relating to the prohibition of torture and other cruel, inhuman or degrading treatment or punishment.[24]

To this extent, the draft was strengthened by an effective reaffirmation of existing norms.

Second, although the summary records of the discussion disclose no open criticism of the two operative paragraphs of the original draft, these were significantly weakened: Sweden introduced a revised draft whereby the proposed 'report' from the Secretary-General would become an 'introductory note' that would 'tak[e] into account' consideration that other UN bodies might give to the question.[25] This was even though, during the earlier General Debate, The Netherlands had pressed 'for the adoption of an expedient such as an impartial enquiry, in order to bring the facts to light'.[26] The change was explained by Sweden as being 'to emphasize that the note should be impartial and concise, so as to constitute a starting point for the discussion of the question of torture'.[27] Clearly, Sweden's consultations had revealed opposition to giving the Secretary-General a fact-finding mandate to report in detail on the incidence of torture. Even the retreat from 'report' to 'introductory note' apparently did not satisfy those opposed to any form of fact finding. On the proposal of Egypt[28] it was decided that the Secretary-General should be requested merely 'to inform the General Assembly . . . of the consideration which may have been given to this question by the Sub-Commission on Prevention of Discrimination and Protection of Minorities . . . or by the Commission on Human Rights'.[29] This effectively became the third operative paragraph of General Assembly resolution 3059 (XXVIII).

The first operative paragraph of the original draft, by which, it will be recalled, the General Assembly was to examine the question of torture at its twenty-ninth session under a separate agenda item, was finally amended so as to provide that the General Assembly would 'examine the question of torture *and other cruel, inhuman or degrading treatment or punishment in relation to detention and imprisonment* as an item of a future session' (emphasis added).[30] The addition of the words emphasized here affords a considerable clarification of the scope of the issue, which in the original draft was referred to simply as 'the question of torture'. On the other hand, it was no longer stipulated

---

[24] GA res. 3059 (XXVIII), 2 Nov. 1973.
[25] Loc. cit. *supra* n. 14, para. 7. (The text of the revised draft resolution was also contained in UN doc. A/C.3/L.2010/Rev. 1.)
[26] Loc. cit. *supra* n. 12.   [27] Loc. cit. *supra* n. 16, para. 25.
[28] Loc. cit. *supra* n. 15, A/C.3/SR.2001, para. 86.
[29] Loc. cit. *supra* n. 14, para 8(a). (The text of the Egyptian proposal was contained in A/C.3/L.2015.)
[30] Id., para. 17.

that the consideration would occur at the next General Assembly session but only at some unspecified future session. (And even this limited commitment to future consideration would have been omitted had an Egyptian proposal on the subject succeeded.[31]) It was also made clear that any such future discussion would not be under a separate agenda item, as had been envisaged in the original draft. This was effected by the device of obliging the Secretary-General to submit his information 'under the report of the Economic and Social Council'—this wording is contained in operative paragraph 3 of the final text.[32] The advantage of a separate agenda item is that it would have given the issue greater visibility and possibly greater momentum.

The final text, then, appears to reflect a compromise between those who wanted the speediest consideration of the problem by the General Assembly and those who would have preferred no commitment to any such consideration. By adopting (unanimously) resolution 3059 (XXVIII),[33] the General Assembly may be seen to have come out of its first skirmish with the problem of torture and other ill-treatment ready to reaffirm its clear objection to the practices and its support for the existing human rights treaties prohibiting them. But at the same time it appeared decidedly unwilling to envisage any measure of monitoring the practice and reluctant to be drawn into protracted consideration of the problem. Nevertheless a number of countries had wanted to ensure consideration of the question the following year and it was apparent that they could be expected to take advantage of the information to be provided by the Secretary-General in order to press for further discussion.

RESOLUTION 3218 (XXIX) OF 6 NOVEMBER 1974

At the next (twenty-ninth) General Assembly, a number of countries took advantage of the General Debate to announce their concern with the issue of torture: the Foreign Ministers of Norway and Belgium and the Prime Minister of Luxembourg all referred to continuing reports of torture around the world;[34] the United States Secretary of State and the Netherlands Foreign Minister indicated that they would be bringing specific proposals before the Assembly;[35] the Danish, Irish, and Austrian Foreign Ministers also denounced torture, with the latter referring specifically to the torture of political prisoners.[36] Norway's Foreign Minister took the opportunity 'to pay tribute to the work carried out by Amnesty International and the campaign against torture which that organization has launched'.[37] Similar themes were

---

[31] *Supra* n. 29.   [32] *Supra* n. 14.
[33] *GAOR*, 28th Session, 2163rd Plenary Meeting, para. 37.
[34] UN docs. A/PV.2241, 83 (Norway); A/PV.2244, 12 (Belgium); A/PV.2253, 8 (Luxembourg).
[35] UN docs. A/PV.2238, 42 (United States); A/PV.2252, 29–30 (Netherlands).
[36] UN docs. A/PV.2242, 12 (Denmark); A/PV.2243, 31 (Ireland); A/PV.2244, 42 (Austria).
[37] UN doc. A/PV.2241, 83.

taken up in the Third Committee, when several delegations referred to reports of the increasing use of torture and of the negative reaction to it of public opinion, as well as to the need to end the practice.[38] For example, the Federal Republic of Germany, referring to various sources, including 'non-governmental organizations and the mass media', maintained that torture was 'one of the most serious and widespread forms of ill-treatment of human beings at the present day . . . in particular with regard to political prisoners and political opponents'.[39] Sweden pointed out that 'interest in the question seemed to have grown considerably as indicated by the conference on torture organized by Amnesty International and held in Paris in December 1973'.[40] Once again, therefore, it seems that NGO activities had contributed to the formation of a political context conducive to an initiative on torture, just as they had in 1973.

But this year, too, Chile was a formidable factor. The draft resolution on torture which formed the basis of resolution 3218 (XXIX) was discussed in tandem with draft resolutions on human rights in Chile and many delegations spoke in favour of action on both topics.[41] The effect of this may have been implicitly, at least, to invoke concern over the one in aid of support for the other. NGOs had a penumbral role in this aspect of the debate also: Belgium and Bulgaria both referred to the report issued by Amnesty International after the visit of its delegation to Chile (this was the visit that the Chilean representative had announced the previous year). Similarly, the USSR pointed to testimony placed before the UN Sub-Commission on Prevention of Discrimination and Protection of Minorities by such NGOs as the Women's International League for Peace and Freedom, the International Commission of Jurists, and Amnesty International.

This year the potentially divisive issue of fact-finding was not to be found in the draft resolution.[42] There were, however, expressions of opinion in favour both of investigation and implementation: during the General Debate, the Irish Foreign Minister had denied the right of any country 'to infringe basic human rights, let alone use torture within its territory, or to be free from inquiry, from inspection, or from condemnatory action by the international community in respect of such breaches of the rights of man'.[43] Greece, newly emerged from military government, spoke in the Third Committee of the need for 'the system of protection by the United Nations [to be] strengthened',[44]

---

[38] *GAOR*, 29th Session, Third Committee, Summary Records, A/C.3/SR.2064–71, *passim*.
[39] Id., A/C.3/SR.2064, para. 15.   [40] Id., para. 24.
[41] Report of the Third Committee, *GAOR*, 29th Session, Annexes, Agenda item 12, A/9829, paras. 15–21. (For the discussion, see loc. sit. *supra* n. 38.)
[42] Id., para. 12. For The Netherlands, which introduced the draft resolution, the aim was 'the strengthening of the rules governing the conduct of those exercising authority over the detainee . . . [as] a first step towards providing effective remedies and protection for the victims of torture'. (Loc. cit. *supra* n. 39, para. 5.)
[43] UN doc. A/PV.2243, 31.   [44] Loc. cit. *supra* n. 38, A/C.3/SR.2068, para. 39.

while Australia implied that it would, at the Fifth UN Crime Congress (see below), be working for 'the strengthening of machinery to achieve wider compliance with international laws prohibiting torture'.[45] The sponsors of the draft resolution, which was introduced by The Netherlands, probably had several factors in mind when deciding to refrain from pursuing general measures of implementation of the prohibition against torture and other ill-treatment. First, it may have seemed that no further progress was politically possible at that stage. In this connection, it must be noted that it was not until 1980, when especially propitious circumstances obtained, that the UN established its first 'thematic' mechanism (that is, a mechanism whereby a UN body would be empowered to receive and act upon information of a particular kind of human rights violation; the first instance of this was the establishment of the Working Group of the Commission on Human Rights on Enforced or Involuntary Disappearance (see Chapter 8)). Second, it must have seemed that the moment was right to secure an advance in *ad hoc* implementation through the adoption of a resolution dealing specifically with the human rights situation in Chile.[46] The initiatives taken in respect of Chile were important innovations: with the exceptions of the special cases of the countries of southern Africa[47] and the occupied territories of the Middle East,[48] there had been no systematic investigation of human rights violations within the borders of a member state of the UN. The investigation of Chile in this respect was to change that and would provide an important precedent.[49] Third, as the Secretary-General's information paper pointed out,[50] the Sub-Commission on Prevention of Discrimination and Protection of Minorities had just embarked on an 'annual review' of the 'question of the human rights of persons subjected to any form of detention or imprisonment', and it might have been hoped that this review would afford a measure of implementation (see Chapter 5). These three factors, then, may account for the absence in the draft resolution of reference to implementation.

The draft that was, with amendment, to become resolution 3218 (XXIX) was introduced by The Netherlands,[51] with the specification that the thrust was not one of fact-finding and denunciation, but one of aiming 'to provide

---

[45] Id., para. 10.   [46] GA res. 3219 (XXIX), 6 Nov. 1974.

[47] Carey, *UN Protection of Civil and Political Rights* (1970), 95–126; Zuijdwijk, *Petitioning the United Nations—A Study in Human Rights* (1982), 244–80.

[48] Rodley, 'The United Nations and Human Rights in the Middle East', 38 *Social Research* 217 (1971); id., 'Monitoring Human Rights by the U.N. System and Nongovernmental Organizations', in Kommers and Loescher (eds.), *Human Rights and American Foreign Policy* (1979), 157, 162–3; Zuijdwijk, *supra* n. 47, 281–303.

[49] Marie, 'La Situation des droits de l'homme au Chili: enquête de 1a Commission des droits de l'homme des Nations Unies', 22 *Annuaire français de droit international* 305 (1976); Zuijdwijk, *supra* n. 47, 304–19.

[50] UN doc. A/9767 (1974).

[51] Loc. cit. *supra.* n. 41, para. 12. (The text of the draft resolution was found in UN doc. A/C.3/L.2106.)

remedies for, and strengthen the defences of, those unfortunate individuals who found themselves to be the victims of torture'.[52] The remedies and defences would be normative, with the object of strengthening national legal protections. The paragraph of the draft resolution that laid the basis for formulating the Declaration against Torture requested the Fifth UN Congress on the Prevention of Crime and the Treatment of Offenders (hereinafter the Fifth UN Crime Congress) to consider 'rules for the protection of all persons subjected to any form of detention or imprisonment against torture and other cruel, inhuman or degrading treatment or punishment'.[53] It was reasonable to infer that these rules would be discussed in the light of an analytical summary that the Secretary-General was to prepare on the basis of comments requested from governments, concerning various aspects of legal safeguards against arbitrary arrest and detention.[54]

Taking up a theme that had been dormant at the Commission on Human Rights[55] for ten years and upon which the UN Economic and Social Council (Ecosoc) had recently sought to elicit action,[56] the Assembly also requested the Fifth UN Crime Congress 'to give urgent attention to the question of the development of an international code of ethics for police and related law enforcement agencies'.[57] The Assembly went on to invite the World Health Organization (WHO) to draft 'an outline of the principles of medical ethics which may be relevant to the protection of persons subjected to any form of detention or imprisonment against torture and other cruel, inhuman or

---

[52] Loc. cit. *supra.* n. 39, para. 4.

[53] GA res. 3218 (XXIX), 6 Nov. 1974, operative paragraph 4.

[54] Id., operative paragraphs 1 and 2, which read as follows:

'1. *Requests* Member States to furnish the Secretary-General in time for submission to the Fifth United Nations Congress on the Prevention of Crime and the Treatment of Offenders and to the General Assembly at its thirtieth session;

(a) Information relating to the legislative, administrative and judicial measures, including remedies and sanctions. aimed at safeguarding persons within their jurisdictions from being subjected to torture and other cruel, inhuman or degrading treatment or punishment;

(b) Their observations and comments on articles 24, 25, 26 and 27 of the draft principles on freedom from arbitrary arrest and detention prepared for the Commission on Human Rights;

2. *Requests* the Secretary-General to prepare an analytical summary of the information received under paragraph 1(a) and (b) above, and submit it to the Fifth United Nations Congress on the Prevention of Crime and the Treatment of Offenders, the General Assembly at its thirtieth session, the Commission on Human Rights and the Sub-Commission on Prevention of Discrimination and Protection of Minorities.'

[55] The Commission of Human Rights is a functional (i.e. specialized) commission of (at present) 53 representatives of UN member states. It is established by the Economic and Social Council (Ecosoc) which elects its members. Ecosoc is composed (at present) of representatives of 56 UN member states. It is a 'principal organ' of the UN and concentrates on the economic and social aspects of the UN's concerns, but not the political and security aspects. It reports to the General Assembly (composed of all UN member states), which in practice has ultimate responsibility for UN policy in the economic and social field.

[56] Ecosoc res. 1794 (LIV), 18 May 1973.

[57] GA res. 3218 (XXIX), 6 Nov. 1974, para. 3.

degrading treatment or punishment';[58] this draft was to be brought to the attention of the Fifth UN Crime Congress.

Thus, the General Assembly was following four potentially normative lines:

1. rules against torture and ill-treatment;
2. safeguards against arbitrary arrest and detention;
3. professional ethics for police and analogous officials;
4. professional ethics for medical personnel.

As will be seen, the Congress was able to deal conclusively with only the first strand of this mandate, the latter three strands constituting an agenda for post-Congress activity.

The number of issues that were to be set before the Fifth UN Crime Congress, which would report to the following (thirtieth) session of the General Assembly in 1975, now clearly justified the inclusion of a specific item on the General Assembly's agenda. The last paragraph of resolution 3218 (XXIX) expressly committed the Assembly to consider 'the question of torture and other cruel, inhuman or degrading treatment or punishment in relation to detention and imprisonment'.[59]

The decision to place the problem of torture and other ill-treatment before the Fifth UN Crime Congress deserves brief comment at this point, since torture had previously been seen largely as a human rights issue and it may be wondered why the matter was not left with the human rights bodies. The following reasons may be speculatively advanced:

(a) the Congress was already to have before it two agenda items directly relevant to the concerns of General Assembly resolution 3218 (XXIX). One concerned 'the treatment of offenders in custody . . . with special reference to the implementation of the Standard Minimum Rules for the Treatment of Prisoners'.[60] In so far as rules relevant to torture might figure as part of revised Standard Minimum Rules, this agenda item seemed to complement the substance of resolution 3218 (XXIX). The other relevant item was 'the emerging roles of the police and other law enforcement agencies, with special reference to changing expectations and minimum standards of performance'.[61] Clearly this would be pertinent for a discussion of police ethics, which matter Ecosoc had already referred to the Committee on Crime Prevention and Control, the body responsible for much of the preparatory work for the Congress.

(b) the problem of torture is indeed one of criminality, albeit criminality sometimes committed by those charged with crime prevention. Indeed, the

[58] Id., para. 5.   [59] Id., para. 6.
[60] *Fifth United Nations Congress on the Prevention of Crime and the Treatment of Offenders—Report*, A/CONF.56/10 (1976) (hereinafter *Fifth UN Crime Congress Report*), para. 260.
[61] Id., para. 193.

Committee on Crime Prevention and Control had just categorized torture as a 'major [crime] of transnational concern'.[62]

(c) the participants in the Congress are drawn largely from the ranks of national administrations of justice (judges, prosecutors, senior police officers, and so on) rather than from foreign offices, as is the case with most UN meetings. It might be expected that representatives with this background might want to confirm that torture was the antithesis of their calling.

(d) since the Congress meets only once in every five years deferral of the issue, the traditional tactic of those wishing to obstruct an initiative, was less likely to be successful.[63]

(e) the First UN Crime Congress had, in 1955, successfully completed and adopted the Standard Minimum Rules for the Treatment of Prisoners and, twenty years on, the possibility of developing another landmark document might create a certain momentum in favour of the torture issue.

(f) the Congress had implementation of the Standard Minimum Rules on its agenda, so it might have been hoped that the issue of torture would give that discussion some focus, and in turn benefit from any developments within it.

THE FIFTH UN CONGRESS ON THE PREVENTION OF CRIME AND THE
TREATMENT OF OFFENDERS (1975)

At the beginning of the Congress an informal intersessional working group was established by the Congress Steering Committee with a mandate to deal with the work of the Congress relating to implementation of General Assembly resolution 3218 (XXIX).[64] The Swedish and Netherlands delegations had, on the first day of the Congress, submitted a draft recommendation which set out the text of a draft declaration on the protection of all persons from being subjected to torture and other cruel, inhuman, or degrading treatment or punishment, to be adopted by the General Assembly.[65] Most of the

---

[62] Report of the Committee on Crime Prevention and Control, Third Session (E/CN.5/516; E/AC.57/21/Rev. 1), paras. 27 and 39 (1974). The Committee was at that time composed of 15 individual experts appointed by the UN Secretary-General, reporting to the Commission for Social Development which, like the Commission on Human Rights (*supra* n. 55), is an intergovernmental functional commission of Ecosoc. It was later composed of 27 individual experts elected by Ecosoc on the basis of nominations from governments, reporting directly to Ecosoc. In 1992, the Committee was replaced by a new Commission on Crime Prevention and Criminal Justice, another functional Commission of Ecosoc, composed of representatives of 40 member states; see generally Clark, *The United Nations Crime Prevention and Criminal Justice Program* (1994), 1–57.

[63] Professor Clark, citing most of these suggested reasons with approval, doubts this particular one, a five-year delay being 'not unheard of at the U.N.': id., 102.

[64] *Fifth UN Crime Congress Report*, para. 290.

[65] UN doc. A/CONF.56(V)/Misc. 2, 1 Sept. 1975 (not reproduced in the *Fifth UN Crime Congress Report* but copy on file with the author, who attended the Congress as an observer for Amnesty International).

working group's efforts were concentrated on discussing this draft declaration and it was unable to discuss to any conclusion the creation of a code of police ethics or amendments to the Standard Minimum Rules.[66] The group's recommendations were, therefore, limited, covering only the text of a revised version of the Swedish/Dutch draft.[67]

It is hardly possible to reconstruct the full development of this text as it progressed from the original Swedish/Dutch draft to the final approved text. The Congress Report[68] does not reproduce the original draft; which is therefore not easily accessible.[69] In addition the Report condenses two discussions into one: the draft declaration as it was adopted by the working group was discussed and amended first in a Congress committee (or Section IV as it was called)[70] and then in plenary session.[71] The Congress report, however, gives the impression that the text was finalized in one stage.[72] Furthermore, its account of the discussions is so sketchy that the reasoning behind changes remains obscure. The first articles of both texts aim to define torture; the next two articles condemn torture and other cruel, inhuman, or degrading treatment or punishment under all circumstances; the rest of the articles deal with the obligation on states to take 'effective measures' to prevent torture and other ill-treatment and with the possibility of defining the practices as criminal.

Changes in definition

As will be seen in Chapter 3, the view was expressed at the 1974 General Assembly discussion leading to the adoption of resolution 3218 (XXIX) (which gave the Congress its mandate to deal with torture) that there was a need to define the concept of torture. This task was attempted in the first article of the Swedish/Dutch draft.

Like the final text (see Annex 1, article 1) the Swedish/Dutch draft began the definition by describing torture as 'any act by which severe pain or suffering, whether physical or mental, is deliberately inflicted on a person . . .'. The only change made by the working group at this stage was the substitution of 'intentionally' for 'deliberately'. But the element of deliberation was retained; whereas the Swedish/Dutch text went on to describe torture as 'an aggravated form of cruel, inhuman or degrading treatment or punishment', the final text uses the term 'aggravated and *deliberate* form . . .' (emphasis added). A subsequent attempt to delete 'intentionally' failed.[73] So far then, changes were more of form than of substance.

---

[66] *Fifth UN Crime Congress Report*, paras. 254–8 and 283–9.
[67] Id., paras. 291–2.
[68] Id., para. 260 A.
[69] See *supra* n. 65.
[70] *Fifth UN Crime Congress Report*, para. 458.
[71] Chapman, 'Torture motion passed to UN', the *Guardian* (London), 13 Sept. 1975.
[72] *Fifth UN Crime Congress Report*, paras. 290–300.
[73] Id., para. 301. It is unclear what, if anything, the notion of deliberation adds to the notion of intentionality.

A major change came in the part of the definition which describes the purposes for which severe pain or suffering are inflicted. The Swedish/Dutch draft envisaged only two purposes, namely, that of obtaining from the person subjected to the pain or suffering, or from a third person, 'information or confessions' and that of 'punishing him for an act he has committed or is suspected of having committed'. Such a definition would, however, have been too narrow to take account of the range of purposes for which torture was known to be practised. This was doubtless made clear in the working group's discussion, for in the final text the purposes now included the broader one of 'intimidating him or other persons'. Furthermore, it referred not only to these particular purposes, but 'such purposes as' these purposes. Such a definition was far more suitable than the rather limited one of the draft to encompass the modern practice of torture as state terror. It should be noted that the purposive element was perceived as significant; this is indicated by the failure of a proposal during the formal Congress sessions to add the words 'or for any other purpose'.[74]

Another change inserted by the working group was the specification that the act must be committed 'by or at the instigation of a public official'.[75] The motivation for introducing the status of the perpetrators of torture or other ill-treatment as an issue presumably reflects the working group's wish to restrict international concern with torture to those acts which were not purely private acts of cruelty. Opposition to this limitation was expressed during the Congress, but no change resulted.[76] The limitation has obvious validity, to the extent that acts of torture or other ill-treatment committed by private citizens would in most circumstances incur criminal proceedings in domestic law. A difficulty arises, however, in the case of political entities that may not necessarily be governments but do exercise effective control over substantial populations. This problem was dealt with in the paragraph of the draft resolution by which the General Assembly would adopt the declaration 'as a guideline for all states and other entities exercising effective power'.[77]

The final change in the definition of torture took place during the formal deliberations of the Congress, first in Section IV and then in plenary session. To ensure that the definition did not catch suffering necessarily incidental to ordinary incarceration, Section IV inserted the additional sentence: 'It [torture] does not include pain or suffering arising only from, inherent in or inci-

---

[74] *Fifth UN Crime Congress Report.* The point seems confirmed by the words of the Netherlands representative, introducing the eventual draft to the General Assembly's Third Committee: for him 'it would be possible to give a precise definition of torture if the question was approached through the purpose for which it was used'. *GAOR*, 30th Session, Third Committee, Summary Records, A/C.3/ SR.2160, para. 3 (1975). See also Chapter 3.

[75] *Fifth UN Crime Congress Report*, para. 292.   [76] Id., para. 301.

[77] See generally Rodley, 'Can Armed Opposition Groups Violate Human Rights?', in Mahoney and Mahoney (eds.), *Human Rights in the Twenty-first Century—A Global Challenge* (1993), 297.

dental to lawful deprivation of liberty to the extent consistent with the Standard Minimum Rules for the Treatment of Prisoners.'[78] By the time it emerged from plenary, the only further change was to substitute the word 'sanctions' for the term 'deprivation of liberty'.[79] The broader concept of 'lawful sanctions' (covering all penalties, not just deprivation of liberty) was apparently inserted in response to concern expressed by countries that retain corporal punishment.[80] In practice it is difficult to read the sentence in a way that would meet their concerns. The Standard Minimum Rules deal with the conditions of detention and disciplinary treatment of prisoners; they are not relevant to judicial sentences which do not involve incarceration. Corporal punishment cannot, therefore, be 'consistent with' the Standard Minimum Rules in such circumstances. The Standard Minimum Rules are relevant, of course, to disciplinary corporal punishment, but would hardly serve the interests of those who sought to exclude corporal punishment from the definition of torture, since rule 31 of the Rules expressly prohibits such punishment (see Chapter 10).

International prohibition of torture

There was no change to draft article 2, by which torture and other ill-treatment, described collectively as an 'offence to human dignity', are 'condemned as a denial of the principles of the Charter of the United Nations and as a violation of human rights and fundamental freedoms proclaimed in the Universal Declaration of Human Rights'. In the version that emerged from the working group, the word 'denial' had been replaced by 'breach', and yet the final text in the Congress Report contains the original word 'denial'. Curiously, the report of the Congress discussions contains no mention of any challenge to the use of the word 'breach'.

There was no substantive change to article 3 of the Swedish/Dutch text, which prohibits states from tolerating torture or other ill-treatment, regardless of any exceptional circumstances 'such as a state of war . . . or any other public emergency' (see Annex 1, article 3). According to the Congress Report, some participants recommended deletion of the second sentence of the draft article, part of which has just been quoted and which in effect demands that the prohibition operate in all circumstances. It is fortunate that there was no consensus on this proposal, for it could have had the effect of undermining the position taken by the International Covenant on Civil and Political Rights and the other human rights and humanitarian law conventions: the human rights conventions prohibit suspension of the prohibition of torture in

---

[78] UN doc. A/CONF.56/L.6/Add. 1, para. 16. This document is the draft report of the rapporteur of Section IV, reproduced in a two-volume compilation by UNIFO Publishers: *UN Crime Conference Keynote Documents Edition—Fifth United Nations Crime Congress 1–12 September 1975* (1976), ii, 542 ff.
[79] *Fifth UN Crime Congress Report*, para. 300.　　　　　　　　[80] *Supra*. n. 71.

circumstances where derogation from several other rights is permitted and the humanitarian law conventions treat torture as a 'grave breach' or war crime.

Effective measures by states

Article 4 of the final text is the same as article 4 of the Swedish/Dutch draft and contains a general obligation on states to 'take effective measures to prevent torture and other cruel, inhuman or degrading treatment or punishment'. The remaining articles refer to specific measures to be taken by states. Thus, article 5 of the final text reproduces, with editorial amendments, the Swedish/Dutch draft article 5, which requires states to ensure that the training of, and general rules for, persons charged with custody of prisoners must reflect the prohibition on torture and other ill-treatment. Similarly, article 6 of both texts envisages the need to keep interrogation methods and detention practices under review.

A significant change concerning the formula 'torture *or other* cruel, inhuman or degrading treatment or punishment' (emphasis added) occurred in the next cluster of draft articles (articles 7, 8, and 9 of the Swedish/Dutch draft) which became articles 7, 8, 9, and 10 of the final draft. The obligations in these articles relate to criminal responsibility for, and methods of investigation into, torture and cruel, inhuman, or degrading treatment or punishment. The Swedish/Dutch draft made no distinction between the two branches of the formula. Both would have been required to be treated as criminal offences under domestic law (draft article 7); there would have been an obligation on the competent authorities to investigate both, either on the initiative of the alleged victim (draft article 9) or on their own initiative where they had reasonable grounds to believe that the prohibited acts had been committed (draft article 8); finally, there would have been an obligation to institute criminal proceedings against offenders (draft articles 8 and 9).

Articles 7, 8, 9, and 10 of the final text reflect the action of the working group, which modulated the obligations according to whether torture or other ill-treatment were at issue. Thus, the obligation contained in the final text is to make acts of torture alone necessarily criminal offences (article 7), which acts the competent authorities are expected of their own initiative to investigate, whether or not there is a formal complaint (article 9), and to institute criminal proceedings where torture appears to have been committed (article 10). As far as 'other cruel, inhuman or degrading treatment or punishment' is concerned, the obligation is to investigate only on complaint of the alleged victim (article 8) and to subject alleged offenders to 'criminal, *disciplinary or other appropriate proceedings*' (emphasis added, article 10). This distinction between the two parts of the definition was presumably made in view of the absence of a definition of the formula 'cruel, inhuman or degrading treatment or punishment' and the consequent difficulty of according it criminal status.[81] Nevertheless, it is regrettable that it was felt that acts of cruel, inhuman, or degrading treatment or punishment not amounting to torture should be subjected to investigation only upon complaint of the alleged victim.

Except for the addition of the words 'by or at the instigation of a public official', article 11 of the final text reproduces article 10 of the Swedish/Dutch draft, which provides for redress and compensation for victims of torture and other ill-treatment. Finally, article 11 of the Swedish/Dutch draft, stipulating the inadmissibility in legal proceedings of statements made as a result of torture or ill-treatment, is maintained in the final draft as article 12, but in strengthened form. Whereas in the Swedish/Dutch draft (and the draft as it emerged from the working group) the inadmissibility related only to proceedings against the person from whom the statement was coerced, in the final text it relates also to proceedings against 'any other person'. An attempt to extend the inadmissibility to include not only statements but also 'physical evidence' failed.[82]

Implementation

Article 12 of the Swedish/Dutch draft was a modest attempt to incorporate some element of implementation of the normative provisions of the preceding articles. This article underwent significant change during the course of the Congress and was eventually excised. The draft article read:

Article 12

All States shall cooperate in implementing this Declaration. Where appropriate; regional bodies may be set up for the purpose of assisting States in elaborating rules or standards or in investigating cases of alleged violations of the principles of this declaration.

Thus, international 'implementation' would be confined to an obligation of government-to-government co-operation, with an implicit expression of approval for regional multilateral co-operation. By the time this draft article emerged from the working group (as article 13), it had been transformed:

Article 13

All States shall endeavour to implement this Declaration as soon as feasible. All appropriate international governmental organizations are requested to co-operate in the implementation of these standards in accordance with international law and practice.

The first sentence of this revised text had the effect of radically weakening the nature of the obligations contained in the draft declaration. By its original terms the declaration was to be 'a guideline for all States and other entities

---

[81] This is how the Netherlands representative was to present the issue at the subsequent General Assembly discussion: loc. cit. *supra* n. 74.

[82] *Fifth UN Crime Congress Report*, para. 301.

exercising effective power'. Under the revised draft article 13, however, the obligation would be only to attempt to implement the declaration and even that was to be done only 'as soon as feasible'. The second sentence of the revised draft article may have been intended to envisage a more active implementing role for universal intergovernmental organizations such as the UN itself, but its actual wording sought only 'co-operation' between 'appropriate' intergovernmental organizations, a formulation so flexible as to have little force. The removal of the provision for the setting up of regional bodies to assist with the elaboration of standards further weakens the obligations contained in the article.

In the end, the whole article was abandoned by Section IV and, despite considerable efforts, of the Greek delegation in particular,[83] the declaration was to have no implementation procedures. Nevertheless, as the Congress recognized, 'there clearly remained the need to move towards more effective international procedures to implement that declaration'.[84] Indeed, in words reflecting the view propounded by the Australian delegation,[85] the Congress continued: 'The ultimate objective would of course be the development of an international convention ratified by all nations.'[86] Perhaps the Congress was not a suitable body to develop specific measures of implementation and its strength lay in its ability to suggest normative advances and recognize the need for future implementation.

By the end of the Congress the draft declaration was being acclaimed as 'the major achievement of the Congress, comparable in significance to the Standard Minimum Rules [for the Treatment of Prisoners] elaborated by the first Congress in 1955'.[87] According to the Congress's General Rapporteur, 'passionate concern over the use of torture . . . had been the most significant and pressing aspect of its work'.[88] Further, there had been broad participation in the Congress discussions. The first draft of the text of the declaration had been introduced by Sweden and The Netherlands, states which had taken the lead in raising the matter in the 1973 and 1974 General Assembly sessions, but the working group had been chaired by a member of the Yugoslav delegation[89] and its rapporteur was a member of the Zambian delegation.[90]

---

[83] Amnesty International, 'Report on the Geneva Congress' (Index no. NS206, 14 Oct. 1975), 4, which describes the Greek delegation as having 'let no opportunity pass during the entire congress to stress their own recent experience that once a regime is willing or determined to torture its citizens, neither natural laws nor international declarations can stop it'.

[84] *Fifth UN Crime Congress Report*, para. 298.

[85] 'Report on the Geneva Congress', *supra* n. 83, 4.

[86] *Fifth UN Crime Congress Report*, para. 298.

[87] 'Report on the Geneva Congress', *supra* n. 83, 4.

[88] *Fifth UN Crime Congress Report*, para. 379.

[89] Professor Bogdan Zlataric, Faculty of Law, University of Zagreb (author's recollection).

[90] E. L. Sekala, Director of Public Prosecutions, Ministry of Legal Affairs, Lusaka (author's recollection).

During the debate on the draft in Section IV of the Congress, representatives of twenty-five governments from all geographical and political regions are reported as having spoken, and they did so uniformly in support of the draft declaration.[91] The Congress was attended by 101 government delegations, many of the members of which were senior officials in their national systems of administration of justice. Congress support for the declaration was therefore not only a positive expression of foreign policy from all geographic and political areas of the world, it can also be interpreted as an authentic expression of their official law enforcement policies.

Other relevant aspects of the Congress's work, including extension and implementation of the Standard Minimum Rules for the Treatment of Prisoners and the development of a code of ethics for police and other law enforcement officials and of ethical principles for medical personnel, none of which came to any conclusive result, are dealt with below and in Chapters 9 and 12. Similarly, the Congress did not discuss the report of the WHO, since this did not contain the draft principles of medical ethics which had been requested by the General Assembly.[92] Meanwhile, the draft declaration left the Congress for the General Assembly with broad support. The main question was what, if any, further action the General Assembly would authorize once it had adopted the declaration.

RESOLUTION 3452 (XXX) OF 9 DECEMBER 1975—THE DECLARATION AGAINST TORTURE

As already noted, the question of torture and other ill-treatment had acquired its own agenda item by the thirtieth session of the General Assembly (1975), having first been raised in 1973 under an agenda item dealing with the twenty-fifth anniversary of the adoption of the Universal Declaration of Human Rights, then in 1974 under the report of Ecosoc. Before discussion of the agenda item in the Third Committee, the General Debate heard the United States Secretary of State and the Belgian, Dutch, and Norwegian Foreign Ministers[93] mention with approval the Fifth UN Crime Congress's recommendations on torture. Further, the Swedish, Danish, and Austrian Foreign Ministers,[94] as well as the spokesperson from Ecuador, all raised the issue of

---

[91] 'Report on the Geneva Congress', *supra* n. 83, 4; even though, as noted above, some participants also suggested amendments. The 25 countries were Australia, Austria, Belgium, Bolivia, Cameroon, Canada, Cuba, Czechoslovakia, Egypt, France, German Democratic Republic, Greece, India, Iraq, Ireland, Mexico, Netherlands, Pakistan, Qatar, Sri Lanka, Sudan, Sweden, United Kingdom, United States of America, Zaïre.

[92] UN doc. A/CONF.56/9 (1975).

[93] UN docs. A/PV.2355, 52–3 (United States); A/PV.2361, 61 (Belgium); A/PV.2362, 32 (Netherlands); A/PV.2364, 36 (Norway).

[94] UN docs. A/PV.2358, 51 (Sweden); A/PV.2360, 8–10 (Denmark); A/PV.2371, 53–5 (Austria); A/PV.2376, 94 (Ecuador).

torture, as did the Permanent Representative of Libya.[95] It would appear that by this time the issue had a momentum of its own and was less a matter of reaction to outside influence. None of those parts of the interventions dealing specifically with torture referred to NGOs, though one of the interventions in the Third Committee preceding adoption of the Declaration against Torture did so.[96]

The Netherlands introduced the draft declaration prepared by the Fifth UN Crime Congress as the first matter of business of the Third Committee under the agenda item on torture.[97] Having described the background at the Congress,[98] it went on to observe that 'without purporting to impose a legal obligation, the declaration imposed a moral obligation on States to ensure that their national legislation conformed to the standards laid down therein'.[99] Sweden also mentioned that 'the text would not be a legally binding instrument', though it would be 'a suitable basis' for 'an international convention' that it was 'clearly necessary to envisage'.[100] This statement presaged a specific initiative two years later (see below).

The substance of the draft declaration seemed to be widely approved, since it provoked very little discussion. Norway, Greece, the Federal Republic of Germany, and Australia did, however, address the theme of implementation and the need for international supervision that had been omitted from the final text.[101] Greece was particularly insistent on this theme, again invoking its own experience that, under a military dictatorship, 'domestic legislation did not suffice' and that exposure of such a dictatorship's crimes to, and their condemnation by, the international community was necessary to prevent torture. Greece also proposed a new preambular paragraph that would envisage 'appropriate systems of supervision and international measures', but this was not accepted.

The draft declaration underwent only one amendment. Where, under article 2, torture and other ill-treatment were to be 'condemned as a denial of the principles of the Charter of the United Nations', it was proposed by the German Democratic Republic that the word 'purposes' be substituted for the word 'principles'.[102] This was because 'the latter word [that is "principles"] was freely used in international law to mean specific rights and duties among

---

[95] UN doc. A/PV.2375, 57.

[96] *GAOR*, 30th Session, Third Committee, Summary Records, A/C.3/SR.2165, para. 53: Australia referred to its support for 'the activities of Amnesty International and the International Commission of Jurists aimed at exposing the practice of torture'.

[97] Report of the Third Committee, *GAOR*, 30th Session, Annexes, Agenda item 74, A/10408, para. 5.

[98] Loc. cit. *supra* n. 96, A/C.3/SR.2160, para. 3.   [99] Id., para. 5.

[100] Loc. cit. *supra* n. 96, A/C.3/SR.2165, para. 56. Australia had earlier spoken in a similar vein (id., para. 54).

[101] Loc. cit. *supra* n. 96, A/C.3/SR.2160, paras. 7 (Norway), 14 (Greece), and 20 (Federal Republic of Germany); and A/C.3/SR.2165, para. 54 (Australia).

[102] Loc. cit. *supra.* n. 96, A/C.3/SR.2166, para. 37.

states'.[103] It is not clear whether it was meant that the prohibition against torture was not a specific right or duty or that it was not a right or duty pertaining to interstate relations. In any event, the proposal was logical in so far as human rights and fundamental freedoms are referred to in article 1 of the UN Charter, dealing with the purposes of the organization, not in article 2, which deals with the principles of interstate behaviour in furtherance of the purposes. The amendment was agreed without discussion.[104] Immediately afterwards, the Third Committee adopted the draft declaration, as amended, 'by acclamation'.[105] On 9 December 1975, at a plenary meeting of the General Assembly, the Declaration against Torture was formally adopted.[106]

DEVELOPMENTS FOLLOWING THE ADOPTION OF THE DECLARATION AGAINST TORTURE

The thirtieth General Assembly, in addition to adopting the Declaration against Torture, also agreed to embark on a programme of specific standard-setting.

RESOLUTION 3453 (XXX) OF 9 DECEMBER 1975

At the start of the third meeting of the Third Committee's consideration of the torture issue, before the adoption of the draft declaration, Greece had introduced a draft resolution[107] that, after discussion and amendment, was to become General Assembly resolution 3453 (XXX). The part of the draft that survived substantially unchanged was essentially the unfinished business of the previous year's resolution 3218 (XXIX). It related to standard-setting and dealt with several specific aims.

Body of Principles for the Protection of All Persons under Any Form of Detention or Imprisonment

In the terms of the Greek draft resolution, the Commission on Human Rights would elaborate 'a code on the protection of all persons under any form of detention or imprisonment'. This would be based on the *Study of the right of everyone to be free from arbitrary arrest, detention and exile* (a document prepared for the Commission over a decade earlier), and the draft principles annexed to it.[108] While the Declaration against Torture had reflected some of

---

[103] Ibid.   [104] Id., para. 39.   [105] Ibid.   [106] GA res. 3452 (XXX).
[107] Loc. cit. *supra* n. 97, para. 8. (The text of the resolution was contained in UN doc. A/C.3/L.2187.)
[108] UN Department of Economic and Social Affairs, *Study of the right of everyone to be free from arbitrary arrest, detention and exile* (E/CN.4/826/Rev. 1) (1964). The Draft Principles on Freedom from Arbitrary Arrest and Detention form part VI of the study. The study and the

these principles (for example, the inadmissibility of coerced statements,[109] and the right to compensation in case of violation[110]), it had omitted reference to many others that could be relevant (for example, the right not to be held in detention incommunicado and the right to have the legality of detention independently determined[111]). There was still need, therefore, for a compilation of pertinent standards.

The USSR expressed reservations on this issue, on the grounds that 'the international standards of conduct in that respect were already contained, for example, in articles 7 and 10 of the International Covenant on Civil and Political Rights and there was no need to establish new standards'.[112] India would have deleted the whole paragraph referring to a code of protection (and which also referred to implementation—see below) as being 'too broad and general'.[113] Since there was no further substantive criticism of the idea, the final text required the Commission on Human Rights to elaborate 'a body of principles [not a code[114]] on the protection of all persons under any form of detention or imprisonment'.[115] The history of the subsequent development of the Body of Principles is to be found in Chapter 11.

Code of Conduct for Law Enforcement Officials

Since the Fifth UN Crime Congress had not been able to produce a text on police ethics, although it approved the aim, the proposal in the Greek draft, that the Committee on Crime Prevention and Control should be requested to assume the task, was uncontroversial. Several speakers, both before[116] and after[117] the introduction of the Greek draft, spoke in favour of developing such a code of ethics, and no substantive change to the draft was necessary. The history of the subsequent drafting process, and of the adoption by the General Assembly, of the UN Code of Conduct for Law Enforcement Officials is to be found in Chapter 12.

Principles of Medical Ethics

The proposal that the WHO be invited 'to give urgent attention' to the study and elaboration of relevant principles of medical ethics[118] was more problematic. In its report to the Fifth UN Crime Congress, the WHO had concluded that practices of extreme maltreatment of prisoners 'are in such

---

principles were drawn up in 1962 by a committee established by the Commission on Human Rights; the Commission did not act on them.

[109] Id., Draft Principles, art. 24.   [110] Id., art. 10.
[111] Id., arts, 10, 19, and 36.   [112] Loc. cit. *supra* n. 96, A/C.3/SR.2167, para. 36.
[113] Id., para. 50.
[114] The dropping of the word 'code' that would imply a more solemn document than 'body of principles' was a concession to the USSR, India, 'and others': loc. cit. *supra* n. 96, A/C.4/SR.2172, para. 14.
[115] GA res. 3453 (XXX), 9 Dec. 1975, para. 2(b).   [116] e.g. loc. cit. *supra* n. 101.
[117] e.g. loc. cit. *supra* n. 112.   [118] Loc. cit. *supra* n. 97, para. 8.

flagrant contradiction to the principles of health ethics implicit in the WHO Constitution that it would be idle to pursue the matter further'.[119] Thus, the Greek draft seemed to be urging action on a reluctant specialized agency that saw no need for a new text. Following this, the United Kingdom voiced the concern that 'Governments should reflect on the content of the WHO's report before any action was taken',[120] and for India, the WHO report meant that the relevant paragraph of the draft was 'superfluous'.[121] This led Greece to substitute the term 'further attention' for the term 'urgent attention', otherwise leaving the meaning intact.[122] Despite India's reiterated opposition,[123] the text underwent no further change. The history of the subsequent development and adoption by the General Assembly of the UN Principles of Medical Ethics relevant to the role of health personnel, particularly physicians, in the protection of prisoners and detainees against torture and other cruel, inhuman, or degrading treatment or punishment is to be found in Chapter 12.

Implementation

In one respect, the Greek draft underwent a substantial change. It had envisaged that the Commission on Human Rights would 'give urgent consideration to further steps for ensuring the implementation of international norms prohibiting torture or other cruel, inhuman or degrading treatment or punishment'.[124] However, the USSR expressed unspecified 'serious doubts' about this, and since the paragraph concerned was also that which provided for the elaboration of a code for protecting detainees or prisoners from torture or other ill-treatment, India's opposition (see above, under Body of Principles) was applicable to this as well. Greece was therefore led to propose a reformulation whereby the Commission on Human Rights would 'study the question of torture and all necessary steps for: (a) Ensuring the effective observance of' the Declaration against Torture.[125] With the substitution of the word 'any' for 'all', this was the wording of the final text. It was, of course, weaker than the draft, in that 'implementation' had been replaced by 'effective observance' and 'urgent consideration' had become 'study'. Nevertheless, there was here an embryonic mandate for the Commission on Human Rights to embark on implementation. That it failed to do so—until ten years later—is described and discussed in Chapter 5.

[119] UN doc. A/CONF.56/9, para. 26(1975).   [120] Loc. cit. *supra* n. 112, para. 3.
[121] Id., para. 50.   [122] GA res. 3453 (XXX), 9 Dec. 1975.
[123] Loc. cit. *supra* n. 96, A/C.3/SR.2172, para. 17. See also UN doc. A/PV.2433, 78, where India's continuing misgivings were voiced after the adoption of resolution 3453 (XXX).
[124] Loc. cit. *supra* n. 107.
[125] Id., para. 10 (the text of the revised draft resolution was contained in UN doc. A/C.3/L.2187/Rev. 1).

RESOLUTIONS 32/62, 32/63, AND 32/64 OF 8 DECEMBER 1977

By adopting resolution 3453 (XXX) the General Assembly was again agreeing to have a specific torture item on its agenda the following year,[126] as happened annually for several years and now happens biennially. Most of the Assembly's work under the item during the period being reviewed was to supervise the development of the standard-setting programme it had initiated in 1975. This, for example, was the thrust of the 'essentially procedural'[127] resolution 31/85 of 13 December 1976. The only matter of substance in this resolution was a call on governments and on intergovernmental and thirty-one non-governmental organizations 'to give maximum publicity' to the Declaration against Torture. Valuable as good-faith compliance with this call might have been, mere publicity for the Declaration against Torture could be expected to have limited practical value in regard to its enforcement.

In 1977, however, the thirty-second session of the General Assembly was to exhibit increased initiatives on the torture issue. It set in motion the drafting of a treaty against torture (resolution 32/62), authorized the development of a questionnaire to governments on their compliance with the Declaration against Torture (resolution 32/63), and developed the technique of encouraging unilateral declarations by governments which would commit them to obey the terms of the Declaration against Torture (resolution 32/64).

The context in which the debate on the issue of torture took place was suggested by one of the resolutions (32/63), which described the General Assembly as 'gravely concerned over continued reports from which it appears that in some countries State authorities are systematically resorting to torture and other cruel, inhuman or degrading treatment or punishment'.[128] These reports were in the main coming from non-governmental sources which were continuing to demand effective international action to deal with the problem. Denmark, Austria, Spain, the United Kingdom, and Libya all cited the work of Amnesty International in this area.[129] The United States also referred to 'the careful work of independent organizations such as Amnesty International, the International Commission of Jurists and the International

---

[126] GA res. 3453 (XXX), 9 Dec. 1975, para. 5.

[127] These are the words of the Portuguese representative when introducing the draft of what became General Assembly resolution 31/85, 13 Dec. 1976: *GAOR*. 31st Session, Third Committee, Summary Records, A/C.3/31/SR.63, paras. 23–6. The resolution was mainly aimed at encouraging progress in the development of the instruments set in train by resolution 3453 (XXX). It also encouraged Ecosoc to consider an amendment to the Standard Minimum Rules for the Treatment of Prisoners that sought to assure the applicability of the Rules not only to persons charged or convicted, but also to persons arrested or imprisoned without charge or conviction (para. 3).

[128] GA res. 32/63, 8 Dec. 1977, sixth preambular para.

[129] *GAOR*, 32nd Session, Third Committee, Summary Records, A/C.3/32/SR.35, para. 14 (Denmark) and para. 17 (Austria); A/C.3/32/SR.36, para. 40 (Spain); A/C.3/32/SR.37, paras. 10 and 13 (United Kingdom); and A/C.3/32/SR.38, para. 20 (Libya).

League for Human Rights', which had 'indicated that the current list of practitioners of torture was a long one'.[130]

Another important influence on the debate was the recent death in detention of the South African Black Consciousness movement leader Steve Biko.
The discussion is replete with references to his death,[131] and a special resolution was tabled, discussed, and adopted under the torture item, by which the
General Assembly was to express its strong condemnation of 'the arbitrary
arrest, detention and torture which led to the murder of Stephen Biko by
[South African] agents'.[132]

A convention against torture

Introducing the draft of what was to become resolution 32/62,[133] by which the
Commission on Human Rights would be requested 'to draw up a draft convention against torture and other cruel, inhuman or degrading treatment or
punishment', Sweden argued that the Declaration against Torture 'should
not be the ultimate goal of United Nations efforts to protect all persons from
torture, and that the work should lead up to a legally binding international
instrument'.[134] This echoed similar statements made by Sweden and
Australia at the time the Declaration against Torture was adopted (see
above). Political support for this resolution was notable. It was the first resolution on the topic to have the sponsorship of countries from all the geographical regions (and thus all political tendencies) within the membership of
the United Nations.[135] No doubts about the substance of the idea were
expressed in the debate. At this stage, the proposed convention was proffered
with the aim of giving conventional legal form to the principles contained in
the Declaration against Torture. Neither the text of the resolution nor statements made during the debate explicitly envisaged the establishment in the
convention of implementation mechanisms. Sweden's own intentions were
made clear when, a few months later, it presented to the Commission on
Human Rights a draft convention that contained a proposed implementation
mechanism with pioneering elements (see Chapter 5), in addition to providing for universal jurisdiction over suspected torturers (see Chapter 4). In 1980
the General Assembly, following a suggestion of the Sixth UN Crime
Congress, confirmed that the convention should include 'provisions for the

---

[130] Id., A/C.3/32/SR.36, para. 35.   [131] e.g., loc. cit. *supra*. n. 129.
[132] GA res. 32/65, 8 Dec. 1977.
[133] Report of the Third Committee, *GAOR*, 32nd Session, Annexes, Agenda item 80,
A/32/355, para. 8 (1977).
[134] *GAOR*, 32nd Session, Third Committee, Summary Records, A/C.3/32/SR.35, para. 22.
[135] The sponsors were Austria, Cuba, Denmark, Ecuador, Egypt, Ghana, Greece, India, Iran,
Jamaica, Kenya, Mexico, Morocco, Netherlands, New Zealand, Portugal, Spain, Sweden, and
Yugoslavia, subsequently joined by Angola, Australia, Cameroon, Colombia, Costa Rica,
Cyprus, German Democratic Republic, Hungary, Iraq, Ireland, Italy, Lesotho, Mali,
Mozambique, Nigeria, Norway, Panama, Poland, Tanzania, Upper Volta, and Zambia.

effective implementation of the future convention'.[136] The subsequent developments in drafting the convention and its adoption in 1984 are examined in Chapters 2 to 5.

Questionnaire on the Declaration against Torture

A more positive step towards implementation was contained in resolution 32/63 whereby the Secretary-General was requested 'to draw up and circulate among Member States a questionnaire soliciting information concerning steps they have taken, including legislative and administrative measures, to put into practice the principles' of the Declaration against Torture. The Netherlands introduced the draft that became resolution 32/63 in highly nuanced language that suggested a temporary stocktaking exercise.[137] Further, it noted that the information received as a result of the questionnaire 'might provide the Commission [on Human Rights] with useful guidance in drafting the convention'.[138] Although the resolution was adopted without a vote, the fears of some delegations of a potential implementation measure were reflected in 'explanations of vote' in the Third Committee discussion.[139] Five delegations expressed doubt about a preambular paragraph that portrayed the General Assembly as 'gravely concerned over continued reports from which it appears that in some countries State authorities are systematically resorting to torture . . .'.[140] For Argentina, the paragraph was 'dangerously ambiguous',[141] while for Laos it was 'unacceptable, as it left the door open to outside interference'.[142] Of the dissenting faction, only Laos went as far as to say that on these grounds, and also because the procedure itself 'was too complicated for implementation by developing countries',[143] it would have abstained had there been a vote. That the fears of these countries were misplaced can be seen in Chapter 5 where further developments relating to the questionnaire are discussed.

Unilateral declarations against torture

Resolution 32/64, which was also adopted without a vote, was initiated by India.[144] In it the General Assembly called upon all member states 'to rein-

---

[136] GA res. 35/178, 15 Dec. 1980, para. 2.

[137] Loc. cit. *supra* n. 134, para. 27: 'It was now propitious to assess, even if only provisionally, the progress made towards abolishing all forms of torture. Information on the action taken by Member States to put the Declaration into practice would be useful in evaluating what had been accomplished as well as in determining what action was still to be taken by the United Nations in that field.'

[138] Id., para. 31.

[139] The system of adopting texts 'without a vote' is a device to permit a measure to pass even though particular states may have reservations about it. These reservations are often expressed by way of statements made 'in explanation of vote' even though no proper vote has taken place.

[140] *GAOR*, 32nd Session, Third Committee, Summary Records, A/C.3/32/SR.42, paras. 22 (Argentina), 29 (Uganda), 33 (Laos), 34 (Iran), 35 (Guinea) (1977).

[141] Id., para. 2.   [142] Id., para. 33.   [143] Ibid.   [144] Loc. cit. *supra* n. 133, para. 15.

force their support' for the Declaration against Torture 'by making unilateral declarations . . . along the lines' of a model annexed to the resolution and 'by depositing them with the Secretary-General'. According to the model unilateral declaration, a government would declare its intention to 'comply with' the Declaration against Torture and to 'implement, through legislation and other effective measures, the provisions of the said Declaration'. The resolution was the first to be initiated by a 'Third World' country.[145] In its introduction to the draft that was to become resolution 32/64, India said that the unilateral declarations called for by the resolution 'would be an expression of the good faith of governments and their moral commitment to the provisions of the Declaration on Torture'.[146] There was no questioning of the value of the resolution during the Third Committee debate, but eight delegations later indicated that they would have abstained had there been a vote.[147] The only reason given was that of Madagascar (supported by four of the others), whose representative reserved his government's position in the absence of instructions on the point.[148] The moral, political, or legal effect of such declarations is discussed in Chapter 2.

SUMMARY

In the wake of vociferous non-governmental activities aimed at exposing and denouncing widespread practices of torture, the General Assembly in 1973 embarked on its first, tentative consideration of the issue. Governments playing a leading role in the process linked their concern to the NGO activities and, as the Assembly gathered, the brutality of the sudden overthrow of the Allende government in Chile served to highlight the problem of torture and harness it to the general revulsion at events in that country. The Assembly's action in 1973 was modest, confined essentially to a rejection of torture and ill-treatment and a vague prediction of further consideration of the problem at an unspecified future session.

Nevertheless, the problem was again before the Assembly in the following year. Once again, NGO reports were invoked by the initiating governments, and the unimproved human rights situation in Chile continued to provide an illustrative focus as well as to provoke parallel action. In contemplation of the

---

[145] In a subsequent plenary meeting of the General Assembly the same year (1977), Belgium observed that 'it is to the Government of India, principally supported by the Governments of Bangladesh and Egypt, that we owe the draft resolution'. (*GAOR*, 32 Session, Plenary Meetings, vol. 111, 98th Meeting, para. 54). Belgium then announced that it would be the first to deposit a declaration (id., para. 55).

[146] Loc. cit. *supra*. n. 140, A/C.3/32/SR.37, para. 27.

[147] Loc. cit. *supra* n. 140, paras. 21 (France), 23 (Togo), 27 (Madagascar, Mali, Cameroon, Benin, and Venezuela), and 35 (Guinea).

[148] Id., para. 27.

Fifth UN Congress on the Prevention of Crime and the Treatment of Offenders, to be held the following year (1975), the Assembly selected a number of aspects of the problem of torture that it deemed suitable for consideration by the Congress. These were all normative in character: the possibility of developing rules against torture and ill-treatment; safeguards against arbitrary arrest and detention; rules of professional ethics for law enforcement agents and medical personnel who may encounter abuses of detainees or prisoners. Torture and ill-treatment would be a specific agenda item for the General Assembly's 1975 session after the Congress. Despite expressions of opinion in favour of UN action to implement the prohibition of torture and other ill-treatment contained in existing international instruments, no such action was formally proposed.

The Fifth UN Crime Congress considered that torture was the most significant issue before it and a working group was specially created to deal with a proposed draft General Assembly declaration against torture. Delegations from all parts of the world spoke in favour of the draft that emerged, which stressed the impermissibility of torture under any circumstances and raised violation of the norm against torture and other ill-treatment to the level of non-compliance with the UN Charter. It specified a number of national measures to be taken against torture, but avoided any reference to international measures of implementation.

The Declaration against Torture adopted by the General Assembly some two months later was, with a minor amendment, the text forwarded by the Congress. A growing number of states represented at the General Assembly expressed concern about the problem of torture. Recognizing that the Congress had not been able to initiate the formulation of specific rules against arbitrary arrest and detention (a terrain in which torture thrives) nor to develop relevant rules of professional ethics, the Assembly set in motion the drafting of texts on these matters. While avoiding the word 'implementation', it also this time laid the groundwork for the Commission on Human Rights to take steps to ensure the effective observance of the Declaration. The results of these initiatives are considered in subsequent chapters.

The 1976 session of the General Assembly was not one of major activity on the torture issue, but by 1977 a new spate of initiatives was undertaken. Again, some of the governments spearheading the drive invoked NGO information on the issue. The recent death under torture of Steve Biko, like the brutalities of the military rulers in Chile, served to galvanize attention to the problem. With the broadest sponsorship of any initiative yet taken, the Assembly agreed to call for the drafting of a convention against torture and other ill-treatment. It also decided that member states should respond to a questionnaire on their compliance with the Declaration. Finally, in response to the first initiative to originate from among the non-aligned countries, the Assembly decided to invite formal unilateral declarations pledging such compliance. Developments in these areas are also to be found in later chapters.

Thus, international awareness of the problem of torture, instigated by the activities of NGOs and focused by the notorious developments in post-1973 Chile and the death of Steve Biko, stimulated the General Assembly to embark on a major programme of standard-setting. Two years after it first considered the issue, it adopted the Declaration against Torture. Subsequent developments form important segments of a number of later chapters. Highlights are the adoption by the General Assembly of a convention against torture, in 1984 (see Chapter 2), and the establishment by the Commission on Human Rights, in 1985, of a Special Rapporteur on Torture (see Chapter 5).

The Legal Prohibition of Torture and Other Ill-treatment

INTRODUCTION

As noted earlier, many aspects of international public order in the modern world were formed in reaction to the events of World War II. The United Nations, at the centre of post-war international co-operation, was itself initiated by the Allied Powers that had defeated those of the Axis. In seeking a structure for post-war international co-operation, those who supported the establishment of an international body to maintain international peace and security were keenly aware from recent experience of the relationship between aggressive behaviour at the international level and tyrannical domestic regimes.[1] For this reason the first article of the Charter of the United Nations proclaimed that one of the purposes of the new organization was to 'achieve international cooperation . . . in promoting and encouraging respect for human rights and fundamental freedoms for all without distinction as to race, sex, language or religion'. When the United Nations came into existence and began to draft instruments that would identify the chief human rights norms (these had not yet been defined in the Charter), the same recent experience made it inevitable that the issue of torture would be addressed.

The Universal Declaration of Human Rights (1948)[2] prohibited torture and 'cruel, inhuman or degrading treatment or punishment' (hereinafter 'other ill-treatment') and gave rise to the ban which now pervades the extensive network of international and regional instruments dealing with human rights and humanitarian law. In addition, a number of other documents have been adopted, or are in the process of being adopted, aimed specifically at hastening the eradication of torture (see Chapters 1 and 5).

The aim of this chapter is to examine the international legal status of the prohibition against torture or other ill-treatment, beginning with a brief description of the existing treaties prohibiting it. Since treaties bind only those states that are parties to them, the next section will deal with the extent to which what is known as 'general international law' prohibits other states from committing torture or other ill-treatment.

---

[1] Humphrey, 'The Universal Declaration of Human Rights: Its History, Impact and Juridical Character', in Ramcharan (ed.), *Human Rights: Thirty Years After the Universal Declaration* (1979), 21 (hereinafter 'Humphrey').

[2] GA res. 217 A (III), 10 Dec. 1948.

TREATIES PROHIBITING TORTURE AND OTHER ILL-TREATMENT

The first action taken by an international lawyer seeking to establish what a state's international legal obligations on a particular point may be is to determine whether that state is a party to any treaty dealing with the question. The Convention against Torture and Other Cruel, Inhuman or Degrading Treatment or Punishment (Convention against Torture) has now become the benchmark reference in this field. By resolution 39/46 of 10 December 1984, the General Assembly adopted the Convention against Torture without a vote (that is, by consensus). At the time of writing, the Convention has been ratified or acceded to by 105 states, a figure equivalent to more than half of the membership of the United Nations, having entered into force on 26 June 1987. As will be seen subsequently, it is nevertheless indicative, in many respects, of the position under general international law applicable to all states.

Within the region of the Americas, an Inter-American Convention to Prevent and Punish Torture was adopted on 9 December 1985 at the Fifteenth Regular Session of the General Assembly of the Organization of American States (OAS). Incorporating much of the content of the UN Convention against Torture, only two of the thirteen states which have become party to it are not also parties to the UN Convention, perhaps suggesting that they prefer to become bound at the regional rather than the universal level, at least at the first instance. The Convention entered into force on 28 February 1987.

The Council of Europe has also adopted a European Convention on the Prevention of Torture and Inhuman or Degrading Treatment or Punishment. This is not a normative treaty. It takes as its premise the prohibition of torture and ill-treatment contained in article 3 of the European Convention on Human Rights. Rather, it focuses on the 'prevention' aspect, putting in place a system of international inspections of places of detention and will accordingly be discussed in Chapter 5.

In fact, it is the case that most states are parties to one or more non-torture-specific treaties that also prohibit torture and these treaties may be crudely divided into two broad categories: the human rights treaties and the humanitarian law treaties. The human rights treaties are, generally, formulated in terms of the rights and immunities of the individuals they seek to protect, while the humanitarian law treaties tend to be formulated in terms of obligations on governments to do, or to refrain from doing, certain things to those protected by the treaties. Apart from this formal distinction there is also a rough substantive distinction between them. The human rights treaties aim basically at regulating the behaviour of governments towards their own citizenry,[3] whereas

---

[3] Or towards others under their jurisdiction: while the exercise of some human rights, e.g. the right to vote, may be conditional on the link of citizenship, this would not generally be the

the humanitarian law treaties seek mainly to protect the nationals of one country from unacceptable behaviour by the government of another country, where the two governments are in conflict. Indeed, the issue of conflict raises a further distinction between the two categories of treaty, in that human rights treaties are designed to operate in normal times, while the humanitarian law treaties are designed to ensure humane limits to the conduct of armed conflict. In fact, as will be seen, this distinction is not entirely clear-cut, since the planes of operation of the two types of treaty overlap, particularly in the area of internal disruptions of up to civil war proportions. The two types of treaty also overlap in terms of those protected by them, a condition which will be seen to be especially pronounced in some fields, including that of the prohibition of torture and other ill-treatment. The UN and OAS Conventions against Torture will be briefly introduced in the next subsections, and then the relevant treaties of human rights law and of humanitarian law will be presented.

THE UN CONVENTION AGAINST TORTURE[4]

In 1978, pursuant to a 1977 mandate of the General Assembly (see Chapter 1), the Commission on Human Rights began the task of drawing up 'a draft convention against torture and other cruel, inhuman or degrading treatment or punishment'.[5] The bulk of the Commission's work was based on a draft text submitted to the Commission by Sweden, whose delegation at the previous General Assembly had introduced the proposal that the Commission should assume the task. Almost concurrently, the International Association of Penal Law (IAPL) had convened a meeting of experts to consider a 'draft convention for the prevention and suppression of torture',[6] which met just over a week after the General Assembly took its decision. The text that emerged from this meeting was submitted by the IAPL and the International Commission of Jurists (ICJ) to the Commission on Human Rights. In fact, this text was not the real focus of discussion, but it had many points in common with the Swedish draft and it may well be that it influenced the content of the latter.[7]

---

case. Certainly the norms described in this book are beyond peradventure applicable as against any state regardless of national status: see the Declaration on the Human Rights of Individuals who are not Nationals of the Country in which They Live, GA res. 40/144, 13 Dec. 1985, Annex, arts. 5(a) and 6.

  [4] See, generally, Burgers and Danelius, *The UN Convention against Torture—A Handbook on the Convention against Torture and Other Cruel, Inhuman or Degrading Treatment or Punishment* (1988).

  [5] GA res. 32/62, 8 Dec. 1977, para. 1.

  [6] 'La Prévention et la suppression de la torture—The Prevention and Suppression of Torture', *Revue internationale de droit pénal*, vol. xlviii, nos. 3 and 4 (1977), 13.

  [7] For example, one of the experts at the IAPL meeting was Mr H. Romander, Attorney-General of Sweden.

From 1979 to 1984 an open-ended working group of the Commission on Human Rights, meeting in the week preceding the annual session of the Commission, developed the convention in draft. The working group operated on a consensual basis. In view of the implicit veto that such a procedure gives to any state determined to prevent adoption of a text, it is understandable that the exercise took so long. On the other hand, it is a matter for satisfaction that the group was able to complete its work in 1984. Except for an aspect of the question of implementation (which the group could not resolve and left for final determination by the superior bodies, see Chapter 5), a consensus text on all other aspects was submitted to the Commission on Human Rights. The Commission then took the decision to forward the text (including the unresolved aspect of implementation) through Ecosoc to the General Assembly.[8] The text adopted by the General Assembly is reproduced as Annex 2a to this volume.

As indicated in Chapter 1, the Convention was to be based on the Declaration against Torture, and it indeed broadly follows that document. But the Convention defines 'torture', for its purposes, with some significant changes to the wording of the Declaration (article 1—see Chapter 3, below). States parties are obliged by the Convention to 'take effective legislative, administrative, judicial and other measures to prevent acts of torture' (article 2). Torture may not be justified by invoking exceptional circumstances such as 'war or a threat of war, internal political instability or any other public emergency', nor by invoking an 'order from a superior officer or a public authority' (article 2). The latter point, rejecting the defence of *respondeat superior*, borrows from the Nuremberg Principles (see Chapter 4) and adds to the obligations contained in the Declaration.

Torture is to be made punishable as a crime of a 'grave nature' (article 4) and (again going beyond the Declaration) states are to consider it among those crimes that they treat as extraditable (that is, for which alleged offenders can be sent to another country to stand trial) (article 8). Unless a state extradites an alleged torturer to another country to stand trial, it is obliged to institute criminal proceedings against any such person within its jurisdiction, regardless of the latter's nationality, or of where the crime was committed (articles 5–7). This is the principle of universality of jurisdiction; it is clearly innovative and is discussed further in Chapter 4. There is an obligation to afford transnational assistance in respect of criminal proceedings based on the offence of torture.

States are committed to educate their law enforcement personnel, and other relevant personnel, about the prohibition of torture and to include the prohibition in the rules and instructions of such personnel (article 10). As a further means of preventing torture, they are to 'keep under systematic

[8] Resolution 1984/21, 6 Mar. 1984, Commission on Human Rights, Report, 40th Session, *ESCOR*, 1984, Supplement No. 4, Chapter 11A.

review interrogation rules, instructions, methods and practices as well as arrangements for the custody and treatment' of detained or imprisoned persons (article 11). The Convention introduces another obligation not spelled out in the Declaration by providing that people are not to be deported or extradited to countries where they may face torture (article 3—this obligation will be revisited in Chapter 4). The competent authorities of a state party are required not only 'promptly and impartially' to examine allegations of torture by the alleged victim (article 13), they are also, of their own motion, similarly to investigate 'wherever there is reasonable ground to believe that an act of torture has been committed' within the state's jurisdiction (article 12—and see Chapter 4). The individual complainant and witnesses are to be protected against 'all ill-treatment or intimidation' (article 13). Victims of torture (or their dependants if death results) are to have means of redress; among these are 'an enforceable right to fair and adequate compensation, including the means for as full rehabilitation as possible' (article 14—and see Chapter 4). Statements extracted by torture cannot be used in proceedings against the victim or anyone else the victim may have incriminated (article 15).

All the above articles refer to 'torture'. They do not all automatically cover other ill-treatment. As will appear in the next chapter, not all acts of 'cruel, inhuman or degrading treatment or punishment' necessarily amount to 'torture'. Under article 16 of the Convention, states 'undertake to prevent' such other ill-treatment. But the only detailed provisions of the Convention that are made explicitly applicable to other ill-treatment as well as torture are those contained in articles 10 (education of law enforcement and other relevant personnel), 11 (review of interrogation and detention rules and practices), 12 (ex officio investigation of information), and 13 (examination of individual complaints). The omission from this list of articles 14 (the right to compensation) and 15 (inadmissibility of statements made under torture) is a regrettable retreat from the Declaration. The omission of reference to article 3 (non-explusion) is similarly regrettable. On the other hand, the application to other ill-treatment of the obligation contained in article 12 represents an advance on the requirements of the Declaration.

The implementation provisions of the Convention are discussed in detail in Chapter 5. It may simply be noted here that the Convention establishes a Committee against Torture (article 17), provides for its functioning (article 18), and empowers it both to examine periodic reports from states parties (article 19) and to make inquiries into apparent systematic practices of torture (article 20). Where the state in question expressly agrees, the Committee may also receive complaints from other states of non-compliance with the terms of the Convention (article 21) or from individuals against that state (article 22). The Committee is mandated to report annually on its work, both to states parties and to the UN General Assembly.

THE OAS CONVENTION AGAINST TORTURE

The OAS has a tradition of drafting regional analogues to major UN human rights instruments. Thus it evolved its own American Declaration of the Rights and Duties of Man at the same time as the UN was drafting the Universal Declaration of Human Rights; indeed, the regional text was adopted some months ahead of the UN text.[9] It also adopted the American Convention on Human Rights, in 1969, as a regional equivalent of the UN's 1966 International Covenant on Civil and Political Rights.[10] Some months after the UN General Assembly had authorized the drafting of a UN convention against torture, the OAS General Assembly held to tradition: it requested the Inter-American Juridical Committee to prepare 'a draft convention defining torture as an international crime'. The Committee was to do this in co-operation with the Inter-American Commission on Human Rights.[11] A text was produced in 1980[12] and a revised version in 1984.[13] The latter text underwent further change, so that by the time of the 1985 session of the OAS General Assembly only one issue was left to be resolved by the Assembly.[14] On 9 December 1985, the Assembly adopted the 'Inter-American Convention to Prevent and Punish Torture', with all reference to the terminology 'international crime' removed. The text is reproduced in Annex 2b of this volume.

Like the UN Convention, the OAS Convention contains a definition of torture (article 2). As will be seen in the next chapter, this is a broader definition, potentially encompassing more acts of coercion than may be covered by the UN Convention's definition. States parties are obliged to take effective measures to prevent and punish torture (articles 1 and 6). No special or emergency circumstances may be invoked as a justification for torture (article 5), nor is the defence of *respondeat superior* available (article 4).

Still following the UN Convention, the regional text requires acts of torture to be punishable by 'severe penalties', reflecting the 'serious nature' of such acts (article 6), and states parties are to consider it as one of the crimes that they would treat as extraditable (article 13). Universality of jurisdiction is provided for in this text also, in the sense that, unless an alleged torturer is

---

[9] The American Declaration was adopted by resolution XXX of the Ninth International Conference of American States, held in Bogotá, Colombia, 30 Mar.–2 May 1948; the Universal Declaration was adopted on 10 Dec. 1948.

[10] The American Convention on Human Rights was signed at the Inter-American Specialized Conference on Human Rights, San José, Costa Rica, 22 Nov. 1969: the Covenant had been adopted on 16 Dec. 1966.

[11] AG/RES. 368 (VIII-0/78).   [12] OEA/Ser. G CP/ doc. 1061/80.

[13] OEA Ser. G CP/doc. 1524/84.

[14] This was whether or not torture covered by the Convention would be limited to acts perpetrated or otherwise aided and abetted by a 'public servant or employee' (alternative A of article 3): OEA/Ser. G CP/doc. 1622/85. The Assembly chose to limit the scope of the Convention to the acts of such officials.

extradited to another country to stand trial, there is an obligation on any state party that may find the person within its area of jurisdiction to try the person, regardless of nationality or of where the torture was committed (articles 11–14).

The text continues to parallel the UN model by providing for the proper training of law enforcement officials in the prohibition of torture (article 7). It also requires investigation by the relevant state authorities of allegations of torture, either on the complaint of an alleged victim, or by accusation of others, or where there is 'well-grounded reason to believe that an act of torture' has occurred (article 8). National law is to guarantee 'suitable compensation' for torture victims (article 9). Statements obtained by torture are to be inadmissible as evidence against the victim or anyone else incriminated by the victim (article 10). The only provision in the OAS text comparable to that in article 3 of the UN Convention (prohibiting sending people to a country where they face torture) is to be found in paragraph 4 of article 13, the rest of which article is concerned with extradition of alleged torturers. Paragraph 4 would prohibit extradition of 'the person sought' to a place where there is a risk of torture or certain other undesirable results. It is thus not clear whether the intended beneficiaries of this safeguard are confined to alleged torturers. Certainly only extradition is referred to, not other forms of *refoulement* such as deportation or expulsion. Interestingly, among the undesirable results other than torture towards which the beneficiaries of article 13(4) may not be extradited, is other 'cruel, inhuman or degrading treatment'. In this respect the protection is broader than that offered by the UN Convention.

The only other references to such other ill-treatment in the operative parts of the OAS Convention are in the creation of a general obligation on states parties to take 'effective measures to prevent and punish other cruel, inhuman, or degrading treatment or punishment' (article 6(3)) and in the applicability of the obligation regarding training of law enforcement officials to address the prevention both of torture and of such other ill-treatment or punishment (article 7). However, as will be seen in Chapter 3, the definition of torture in the regional Convention may well be thought of as including most acts that elsewhere might be treated as prohibited ill-treatment not amounting to torture. If such acts are subsumed under the rubric of torture, in respect of which all the Convention's obligations apply, then the need for special coverage of other ill-treatment is correspondingly abated.

The OAS Convention hardly deals with implementation. It provides that, after exhaustion of domestic remedies, a 'case may be submitted to the international fora whose competence has been recognized by' the state in question (article 8(3)). This appears to be no more than an obligation not to interfere with an existing right. The Convention also requires states parties to report to the Inter-American Commission on Human Rights on 'any legislative, judicial, administrative, or other measures' taken to give effect to the Convention (article 17). No periodicity is laid down for the submission of such reports. By the same article the Commission is to 'endeavor . . . to analyze the existing situation in the member states of the Organization of American States in regard to the prevention and elimination of torture'. While this seems like a lukewarm approach to implementation, it should be borne in mind that all OAS member states are subject to the jurisdiction of the Commission. This body has an automatic right to take up individual complaints, and to inquire into alleged systematic practices of violation of any of the rights contained in the American Convention on Human Rights (*vis-à-vis* states parties) or in the American Declaration of the Rights and Duties of Man (*vis-à-vis* other OAS member states).[15] Accordingly, its powers as regards torture and ill-treatment are already, arguably, more extensive than those to be available to the Committee against Torture under the UN Convention.

THE HUMAN RIGHTS TREATIES

The human rights treaties which deal with torture and other ill-treatment may most usefully be considered under three headings: first, the International Covenant on Civil and Political Rights, which is a general human rights treaty of universal applicability; second, treaties of universal applicability which deal with specific human rights and which prohibit torture; and third, regional human rights treaties.

The International Covenant on Civil and Political Rights

One of the first tasks undertaken by the United Nations as it began its existence was the drafting of an International Bill of Human Rights.[16] After some years of debate on the format of the Bill, it finally emerged as a package consisting of the following:

1. the Universal Declaration of Human Rights (1948);
2. the International Covenant on Economic, Social and Cultural Rights (1966);
3. the International Covenant on Civil and Political Rights, including an Optional Protocol (1966).

The first of these, the Universal Declaration of Human Rights, is not a treaty and will be dealt with below.

---

[15] See generally Buergenthal and Shelton, *Protecting Human Rights in the Americas: Cases and Materials* (4th edn., 1995); Medina Quiroga, *The Battle of Human Rights—Gross, Systematic Violations and the Inter-American System* (1988); Shelton, 'The Inter-American Human Rights System', in Hannum (ed.), *Guide to International Human Rights Practice* (2nd edn., 1992), 119.

[16] See, for example, Humphrey, *supra* n. 1, 22. See also Pechota, 'The Development of the Covenant on Civil and Political Rights', in Henkin (ed.), *The International Bill of Rights—The Covenant on Civil and Political Rights* (1981), 32, 33–9 (hereinafter 'Henkin').

The International Covenant on Civil and Political Rights is the treaty that contains the prohibition against torture.[17] The Covenant was not adopted and opened for adherence until 1966[18] and took until 1976 to come into force;[19] by 4 June 1998, 140 states had agreed to become bound by it. Compliance with the Covenant is monitored by the Human Rights Committee, a body set up by the Covenant especially for this purpose.[20]

Article 7 of the Covenant reads: 'No one shall be subjected to torture or to cruel, inhuman or degrading treatment or punishment. In particular, no one shall be subjected without his free consent to medical or scientific experimentation.' The question of what acts amount to torture or other ill-treatment will be discussed at several points in this text, especially in the next chapter and in Chapter 9.

At this stage, there are two basic points to note. First, the article is formulated in absolute terms envisaging no exception to the rule.[21] Second, although article 4 of the Covenant allows that states may 'in time of public emergency which threatens the life of the nation . . . take measures derogating from their obligations' under the Covenant, it specifies that a number of articles may not be thus derogated from, and these include article 7 which prohibits torture and other ill-treatment.[22] While neither the Covenant nor the Human Rights Committee, when commenting on article 4, indicate what is meant by 'public emergency threatening the life of the nation',[23] it has been persuasively argued by Thomas Buergenthal that the formula includes war, since 'war is the most dramatic example of a public emergency which might

---

[17] See, generally, Nowak, *U.N. Covenant on Civil and Political Rights—CCPR Commentary* (1993).

[18] GA res. 2200 A (XXI), 16 Dec. 1966.

[19] That is, to become binding on states ratifying or acceding to it. It required 35 such states to bring the Covenant into force.

[20] The Human Rights Committee is composed of 18 nationals of states parties, serving in their personal capacities (art. 28), each from a different state elected by states parties (art. 30). The Committee reviews reports submitted periodically by states parties on their compliance with the Covenant (art. 40); it can hear complaints by one state party claiming that another has not complied with its obligations, under Covenant article 41, which applies only as between the (so far) 45 states that have accepted this optional procedure; and it can receive complaints from persons claiming to be victims of violations of the Covenant where the state in question has ratified or acceded to the Optional Protocol to the Covenant. There are 93 such states as of 4 June 1998. See, generally, McGoldrick, *The Human Rights Committee: Its Role in the Development of the International Covenant on Civil and Political Rights* (1991).

[21] This may be compared with articles 18 (freedom of conscience and religion), 19 (freedom of opinion and expression), 21 (right to peaceful assembly), and 22 (freedom of association), which permit restrictions on the rights on such grounds as the need to protect national security, public order, public health, or morals; see Kiss, 'Possible Limitations on Rights', in Henkin, *supra* n. 16, 290.

[22] The other articles which article 4 exempts from derogation in time of emergency are articles 6 (right to life), 8 (prohibition of slavery and servitude), 11 (no imprisonment for breach of contract), 15 (right to recognition as a person before the law), and 18 (freedom of thought, conscience, and religion).

[23] The Committee has adopted a 'general comment' (as to which see below) on article 4 of the Covenant which does not clarify the idea: general comment 5(13), in Report of the Human Rights Committee, *GAOR*, 36th Session, Supplement No. 40 (1981), Annex VII.

"threaten the life of the nation" '.[24] Thus, despite the fact that the Covenant is drafted on the assumption that normal, peacetime conditions prevail, it makes clear that a state party has 'to ensure to all individuals within its territory and subject to its jurisdiction' (article 2(1))[25] the right not to be subjected to torture or other ill-treatment, however internally or externally pressed it may be.

Two other articles of the Covenant contain norms relevant to the prohibition of torture. Part of article 9 provides that '[e]veryone has the right to liberty and *security of person*' (emphasis added). Article 10, paragraph 1, states: 'All persons deprived of their liberty shall be treated with humanity and with respect for the inherent dignity of the human person.' Both articles may be suspended, if necessary, 'in time of public emergency which threatens the life of the nation'. These articles (reproduced in full in Annex 9b) will be dealt with more fully in later chapters, since article 9 is mainly relevant to the question of arbitrary arrest and detention (Chapter 11), while article 10 focuses primarily on prison conditions (Chapter 9). They are mentioned here to underline the extent of the Covenant's aim to protect individuals in the hands of the authorities from a broad range of indignity, including torture and other ill-treatment.

Specific human rights treaties of universal applicability

Five treaties, each aimed at protecting groups or categories of persons, contain provisions that would make torture or other ill-treatment a violation of the treaty.

The Convention on the Prevention and Punishment of the Crime of Genocide (1948)[26] includes 'causing serious bodily or mental harm to members of the group' among the acts which amount to genocide when 'committed with intent to destroy, in whole or in part, a national, ethnical, racial or religious group, as such' (article II).

The Supplementary Convention on the Abolition of Slavery, the Slave Trade, and Institutions and Practices Similar to Slavery (1956)[27] provides for the criminalization of 'the act of mutilating, branding or otherwise marking a slave or a person of servile status in order to indicate his status, or as a punishment, or for any other reason'; it also provides for the punishment of convicted perpetrators (article 5).

The International Convention on the Elimination of All Forms of Racial Discrimination (1965)[28] lists a number of rights in respect of which states

---

[24] Buergenthal, 'To Respect and to Ensure: State Obligations and Permissible Derogations', in Henkin, 72, 79.

[25] Id., 73–7; also *supra* n. 3.   [26] GA res. 260 A (III), 9 Dec. 1948.

[27] Adopted by a Conference of Plenipotentiaries convened by Ecosoc res. 608 (XXI), 30 Apr. 1956, and done at Geneva on 7 Sept. 1956.

[28] GA res. 2106 A (XX), 21 Dec. 1965.

parties undertake to guarantee equality before the law to 'everyone, without distinction as to race, colour, or national or ethnic origin'. Included among these is the 'right to security of person and protection by the State against violence or bodily harm, whether inflicted by government officials or by any individual, group or institution' (article 5).

The International Convention on the Suppression and Punishment of the Crime of Apartheid (1973)[29] defines 'the crime of *apartheid*' as consisting of a number of 'inhuman acts committed for the purpose of establishing and maintaining domination by one racial group of persons over any other racial group of persons and systematically oppressing them'. Among these inhuman acts are: 'Denial to a member or members of a racial group or groups of the right to life and liberty of person . . . by the infliction upon the members of a racial group or groups of serious bodily or mental harm, by the infringement of their freedom or dignity, or by subjecting them to torture or other cruel, inhuman or degrading treatment or punishment' (article II).

The Convention on the Rights of the Child (1989)[30] requires states to ensure that '[n]o child shall be subjected to torture or other cruel, inhuman or degrading treatment or punishment' (article 37). This is the most widely ratified human rights treaty (191 ratifications or accessions).

It must be understood that, under the first four of these treaties, the infliction of torture or bodily harm on a member of the group in question is not *per se* a violation of the treaty: the harm must be perpetrated against the individual *because* he or she is a member of the group. Further in the case of the Genocide and *Apartheid* Conventions, it must be inflicted for the stated purposes. Thus the prohibitions against torture and other ill-treatment contained in these treaties apply only in very specific circumstances.

Regional human rights treaties

There are three general human rights treaties of regional applicability, as follows:[31]

1. The *European Convention on Human Rights* (1950), open to acceptance by and, since 1982, binding on, all 40 members of the Council of Europe, a regional organization originally of western European states, now expanded to become pan-European;
2. The *American Convention on Human Rights* (1969), open to acceptance by the 36 members of the Organization of American States, 25 of which are presently parties to the Convention;

[29] GA res. 3068 (XXVIII), 30 Nov. 1973.
[30] GA res. 44/25, 20 Nov. 1989. Art. 1 defines a child as 'every human being below the age of eighteen years unless under the law applicable to the child, majority is attained earlier'.
[31] For full citations, see General Introduction, nn. 9, 10, and 11.

3. The *African Charter on Human and Peoples' Rights* (1981), open to acceptance by all 53 members of the Organization of African Unity, all but two of which (Eritrea and Ethiopia) are parties.

With insignificant variations in wording, all three of these treaties prohibit torture or other ill-treatment in terms similar to those of article 7 of the International Covenant on Civil and Political Rights. In the case of the European and American Conventions (see Annexes 9c and 9d respectively), a parallel with the Covenant is also maintained with regard to the impermissibility of derogations from the prohibition, even in time of public emergency.[32] The same cannot apply to the African Charter (see Annex 9e), which has no provision regarding derogations or suspension of guarantees and therefore is not required to entrench specific rights.

THE HUMANITARIAN LAW TREATIES

The pertinent treaties dealing with international humanitarian law applicable in situations of armed conflict are the four *Geneva Conventions of 12 August 1949*, on the protection of victims of war, which are augmented by the two Additional Protocols of 1977.[33]

The Geneva Conventions were designed primarily to establish a detailed network of rules for the conduct of international armed conflict, especially for the treatment of persons from one party to the conflict who find themselves in the hands of another party to the conflict. They also set out to define a regime of protection for those entitled to benefit from the rules. The first Additional Protocol (*Protocol I*) expands upon some of these rules and on the regime of protection. Reference will first be made, however, to the one article, found identically in all four conventions (common article 3), that deals with 'armed conflict not of an international character' and to the second Additional Protocol (*Protocol II*) which, according to its article 1(1), 'develops and supplements' common article 3. The reason for this order of presentation is that common article 3 and Protocol II cover the areas that most nearly overlap with the regime of the human rights treaties. Indeed, this area of overlap is recognized by the parties to Protocol II when, in the second preambular paragraph, they recall 'that international instruments relating to human rights offer a basic protection to the human person'.

Common article 3 and Protocol II

Common article 3 applies, as just noted, to armed conflicts not of an international character. The concept of such armed conflicts is not further defined,

[32] European Convention on Human Rights, art. 15; American Convention on Human Rights, art. 27.
[33] For full citations, see General Introduction, n. 4. 188 states have adhered to the Geneva Conventions; that is, all UN member states except Eritrea and Marshall Islands.

either in terms of the threshold of violence, or in terms of the characteristics of parties to the conflict (see below). Those protected by the article are 'persons taking no active part in the hostilities, including members of armed forces who have laid down their arms and those placed *hors de combat* by sickness, wounds, detention, or any other cause'—in other words, anyone in the hands of, or under the control of, a party to the conflict. These persons must 'in all circumstances be treated humanely, without any adverse distinction founded on race, colour, religion or faith, sex, birth or wealth, or any other similar criteria'. To this end, a number of acts against these persons 'are and shall remain prohibited at any time and in any place whatsoever'. The acts include 'violence to life and person, in particular . . . mutilation, cruel treatment and torture', as well as 'outrages upon personal dignity, in particular, humiliating and degrading treatment' (see Annex 9a).

The prohibition of torture or other ill-treatment could hardly be formulated in more absolute terms. In the words of the official commentary on the text by the International Committee of the Red Cross (ICRC), 'no possible loophole is left; there can be no excuse, no attenuating circumstances'.[34] The motivation, as with the Covenant, was to reach 'acts which world public opinion finds particularly revolting—acts which were committed frequently during the Second World War'.[35] Common article 3 has no clause concerning reciprocity and clearly applies, at least to a *de jure* government, regardless of reciprocity.[36]

The language of Protocol II is very close to that of common article 3 as far as torture and other ill-treatment are concerned, except that the common article 3 phrase 'violence to life and person' is somewhat expanded in article 4 of Protocol II, which refers to 'violence to the life, health and physical or mental well-being of persons'.[37]

The importance of Protocol II is that, in addition to the prohibition of torture and other ill-treatment (and certain other prohibitions also contained in common article 3), it lays down a range of further obligations; several of these will be referred to in later chapters. This extension of a government's obligations led to the reopening of a debate that had preceded the adoption of common article 3 and concerned the nature of the armed conflict to which common article 3 should be applicable. Since the debate was unresolved at the time of adoption of the article, 'armed conflict not of an international character' remained, as noted, undefined. This lack of definition permitted a certain flexibility in the assessment of applicability of common article 3. Protocol II, however, does define the formula in question, in a manner which results in certain specific restrictions of applicability. These restrictions are couched in terms both of threshold of violence (level of hostilities) and of characteristics

[34] Pictet (ed.), *The Geneva Conventions of 12 August 1949—Commentary: III Geneva Convention Relative to the Treatment of Prisoners of War* (1960), 39 (hereinafter 'Pictet').
[35] Ibid.   [36] Id., 37.   [37] 142 states are parties to Additional Protocol II.

of the parties to the conflict. Article 1(1) of Protocol II uses a mixed threshold and characteristics test, in that the Protocol applies only to an armed conflict between the armed forces of a party and 'dissident armed forces or other organized armed groups which, under responsible command, exercise such control over a part of its territory as to enable them to carry out sustained and concerted military operations and to implement this Protocol'. A further threshold test is contained in article 1(2): 'This Protocol shall not apply to situations of internal disturbances and tensions, such as riots, isolated and sporadic acts of violence and other acts of a similar nature, as not being armed conflicts.'

The effect of article 1, then, is to restrict the field of application of Protocol II to serious conflicts, perhaps amounting to full-scale civil war.[38] Given that Protocol II was designed to develop and supplement common article 3, the question then arises as to whether the field of application of common article 3, which contains virtually the same prohibition against torture and other ill-treatment and which is more widely ratified than Protocol II, is to be read as restrictively as that of the Protocol. The authors of the ICRC commentary pointed out that those who framed common article 3 had considered including in it tests similar to those now contained in article 1(1) of Protocol II, but they abandoned the idea, arguing that 'the scope of application of [common article 3] must be as wide as possible'.[39] Further, article 1(1) of Protocol II purports to develop and supplement common article 3 'without modifying its existing conditions of application'. It may well be, therefore, that the strict demands of article 1(1) of Protocol II are not retroactive and do not require of common article 3 a similarly narrow interpretation of the field of application.

The terms of Protocol II article 1(2), however, do have significance for common article 3 and must be accepted as an authoritative interpretation, by the intergovernmental conference that adopted the Protocol, of the scope of common article 3. The point is that since the Protocol denies the classification 'armed conflict' to 'internal disorders and tensions', and so on, it removes conflicts of the latter type from the applicability of common article 3. However, there may exist also conflicts which do not reach the level of hostilities envisaged in Protocol II article 1(1) and are not fought by parties with all the characteristics specified there, and yet may be of greater magnitude than would be specified by 'disturbances and tensions'. It would appear that such conflicts would continue to be the province of common article 3. This is certainly the view expressed in the ICRC commentary on the Protocols which affirms that 'common Article 3 retains an autonomous existence, i,e., its applicability is neither limited nor affected by the material field of application of the Protocol'.[40]

---

[38] See Veuthey, *Guérilla et droit humanitaire* (1983), xxiv.　　　　　　[39] Pictet, 36.

[40] Pilloud et al. (Protocol I) and Junod (Protocol II) (eds.), *Commentary on the Additional Protocols of 8 June 1977 to the Geneva Conventions of 12 August 1949* (1987), para. 4457. See also

To sum up, common article 3, which remains applicable to parties to the Geneva Conventions, probably does not apply to internal disturbances and tensions as described by article 1(2) of Protocol II. Further, while the strict criteria of article 1(1) of Protocol II (territorial control, and so on) may not need to be met to trigger the applicability of common article 3, the latter article was and is limited, in the words of the ICRC commentary, to 'armed conflicts, with *armed forces* on either side engaged in *hostilities*—conflicts, in short, which are in many respects similar to an international war, but take place within the confines of a single country'.[41]

The Geneva Conventions and Protocol I

The Geneva Conventions are primarily concerned with the traditional subject matter of the laws of war, that is, the protection of persons in the hands of a party to an international armed conflict. All four Geneva Conventions prohibit the infliction of torture and other ill-treatment on persons protected by them;[42] nor may such persons be subjected to reprisals.[43] A small number of acts are specifically defined as 'grave breaches' of each of the Conventions, and these include 'torture or inhuman treatment, including biological experiments, [and] wilfully causing great suffering or serious injury to body or health . . .'.[44]

Certain victims of international armed conflicts and wars of self-determination were not covered by the Geneva Conventions, and Additional Protocol I was developed in recognition of this. The protection of the Fourth Geneva Convention may not extend, for example, to all refugees, such as those having the nationality of the occupying power. This gap is closed by article 73 of Protocol I, as far as parties to it are concerned.[45] Some armed conflicts may be difficult to categorize as either non-international, within the meaning of common article 3, or international, since one of the parties to a conflict may not be a state and would thus be incapable of becoming a party to the Conventions. The conflicts often called, during the Cold War, 'wars of national liberation' could fall into this category. Protocol I aims to extend Geneva Conventions protections to the victims of such conflicts.[46] To the

Veuthey, *supra* n. 38, xxv; and Bothe, Partsch, and Solf, *New Rules for Victims of Armed Conflict: Commentary on the Two 1977 Protocols Additional to the Geneva Conventions of 1949* (1982), 628.

[41] Pictet, 37.

[42] Geneva Convention I, art. 12; Geneva Convention II, art. 12; Geneva Convention III, arts. 17 and 87 (see also arts. 13 and 99); Geneva Convention IV, art. 32 (see also arts. 118 and 119).

[43] Geneva Convention I, art. 46; Geneva Convention II, art. 47; Geneva Convention III, art. 13; Geneva Convention IV, art. 33.

[44] Geneva Convention I, art. 50; Geneva Convention II, art. 51; Geneva Convention III, art. 130; Geneva Convention IV, art. 147.

[45] 150 states are parties to Additional Protocol I.

[46] According to article 1(4) of Protocol I, the armed conflicts to which it applies include 'armed conflicts in which peoples are fighting against colonial domination and alien occupation and against racist regimes in the exercise of their right of self-determination, as enshrined in the

extent that it does so, then torture and other ill-treatment are automatically prohibited in these circumstances. Some persons may be 'affected by a situation' dealt with by the Protocol, but otherwise not covered by it, in which case they enjoy the benefit of the 'fundamental guarantees' of article 75 of the Protocol, including protection from torture and other ill-treatment.

UNILATERAL DECLARATIONS AGAINST TORTURE

One way in which a state may enter into a treaty obligation *vis-à-vis* another state or states is by making a unilateral declaration of commitment to perform the obligation in question.[47] The question therefore arises as to whether the unilateral declarations made in response to General Assembly resolution 32/64 of 8 December 1977 (see Chapter 1) create such obligations.

It will be recalled that, by this resolution, the General Assembly called upon member states 'to reinforce their support of the Declaration on the Protection of All Persons from Being Subjected to Torture and Other Cruel, Inhuman or Degrading Treatment or Punishment' (Declaration against Torture). This was to be achieved by making unilateral declarations by which they would agree 'to comply' with the Declaration and 'to implement, through legislation and other effective measures, the provisions of the said Declaration'. The unilateral declarations, according to the chief sponsor of the resolution (India), 'would be an expression of the good faith of governments and their moral commitment to the provisions of the Declaration'.[48] Thirty-three states are reported to have made such unilateral declarations.[49]

'Good faith' and 'moral commitment' are not of themselves indicators of legal commitment and it is not easy to see the purpose of such unilateral declarations if they were not to provide *juridical* reinforcement to a text (the Declaration against Torture) that was not *per se* binding. By 1979, the representative of India, appealing for further declarations, was describing such a declaration as 'a commitment by a government on behalf of its citizens' and 'a guarantee for these citizens which they could claim whenever their rights were threatened'.[50] This language comes closer to suggesting a commitment of a legally binding nature.

It may be, therefore, that the states that have made unilateral declarations would not be able to argue, should they seek to do so, that they are not juridically bound by the terms of the Declaration against Torture. In fact, of the

Charter of the United Nations and the Declaration on Principles of International Law concerning Friendly Relations and Co-operation among States in accordance with the Charter of the United Nations'.

[47] *Eastern Greenland* case (*Denmark* v. *Norway*), PCIJ, Series A/B, No. 53 (1933).
[48] *GAOR*, 2nd Session, Third Committee, Summary Records, A/C.3/32/SR.37, para. 27.
[49] UN docs. A/33/197 (1978); A/34/145 and Adds. 1–3 (1979); A/35/370/Rev. 1 and Add. 1 (1980); A/36/426 and Add. 1 (1981); A/37/263 (1982).
[50] *GAOR*, 32nd Session, Third Committee, Summary Records, A/C.3/34/SR.32.

thirty-three countries only seven are not now parties to either the UN or OAS Conventions against Torture and, of these, only one, Qatar, is not a party to any general human rights treaty prohibiting torture. In any event, as will be seen below, the basic demands of the Declaration are probably already an accurate reflection of general international law and, as such, already binding on all states.

GENERAL INTERNATIONAL LAW AND TORTURE

There was international law before the modern network of multilateral treaties, just as there was national law before the still relatively modern network of statutes or codes. While in national societies the code or the statute has become the predominant 'source' of law, it has not completely displaced traditional sources of law, especially (but not only) in the common law countries. This is also true of the international legal system. International lawyers commonly refer to the Statute of the International Court of Justice[51] for the standard enumeration of the 'sources' of international law. In addition to international conventions (that is, treaties), these are: state practice (as evidence of 'customary international law') and general principles of law, as principal sources, and judicial decisions and the teachings of publicists, as subsidiary sources. The term 'general international law' refers to that law that may be derived from any one or combination of these sources.

   Resolutions of the United Nations General Assembly have also been considered a possible source of international law, and much of the writing on this point has dealt with the legal status of the Universal Declaration of Human Rights. In formal terms the status of these instruments is prescribed by the Charter of the United Nations as normally being that of recommendations (articles 10–14). It is not seriously doubted, however, that such resolutions can serve as evidence either of what is meant by potentially ambiguous terms of international treaties or of customary international law.[52] Two declarations of the General Assembly are especially pertinent for consideration of the general legal status of torture: the Universal Declaration of Human Rights and the Declaration on the Protection of All Persons from Being Subjected to Torture and Other Cruel, Inhuman or Degrading Treatment or Punishment (Declaration against Torture—see Annex 1).

[51] Article 38(1). The Statute of the International Court of Justice is an integral part of the Charter of the United Nations. The Court, frequently referred to in this text by the commonly used term 'World Court', is 'the principal judicial organ of the United Nations' (UN Charter, art. 92) and is the successor to the Permanent Court of International Justice, established under the League of Nations (also commonly known as the World Court). See, generally, Meron, *Human Rights and Humanitarian Norms as Customary Law* (1989).

[52] See Higgins, *The Development of International Law Through the Political Organs of the United Nations* (1963), 1–10.

THE CHARTER OF THE UNITED NATIONS[53]

The promotion and encouragement of respect for human rights and fundamental freedoms has already been mentioned as a purpose of the UN Charter. References to human rights and fundamental freedoms occur in several places in the Charter, but the obligation imposed by article 56 is of particular importance. By it, UN members 'pledge themselves to take joint and separate action in cooperation with the Organization for the achievement of the purposes set forth in Article 55'. Among the purposes stated in article 55 are the promotion of 'universal respect for, and observance of, human rights and fundamental freedoms for all without distinction as to race, sex, language, or religion'. Nowhere does the Charter define the term 'human rights and fundamental freedoms'. Proposals to this end, made when the Charter was drafted, did not carry,[54] but it seems to have been understood that this would be the function of the International Bill of Human Rights to be drafted by the new organization.

The first instrument of the Bill was the Universal Declaration. It has been consistently argued by many, including government representatives at the time of its adoption, that the Universal Declaration is an authoritative catalogue of the human rights and fundamental freedoms referred to in the Charter.[55] Indeed, the seventh preambular paragraph of the Universal Declaration, alluding to the pledge contained in articles 55 and 56 of the UN Charter, specifically asserts that 'a common understanding of these rights and freedoms is of the greatest importance for the full realization of this pledge'. Therefore, according to this argument, each right contained in the Universal Declaration is effectively incorporated into Charter articles 55 and 56.

Against this it may be argued that a General Assembly resolution, which is formally only a recommendation, cannot, or at any rate should not, be lightly presumed to be a document defining legal obligations. Indeed, the text of the proclamatory paragraph of the Universal Declaration seems to argue a more modest intent when it states that the Universal Declaration is 'a common standard of achievement for all peoples and all nations'. Also, one might ask what need there was to translate the rights into legally binding treaty form, by means of the two covenants that were subsequently to be drafted, if the Charter had already made them legally binding. Further, at the time of its

---

[53] The Charter of the United Nations is, of course, a treaty and a case could be made for including it in the previous section. This has not been done, because the Charter has evolved to become something different from a mere treaty. It is a virtual constitution for the overwhelming majority of the world's states and populations and the basic rules of behaviour it sets out are generally considered to be rules of general international law.

[54] See Humphrey, 21–2.

[55] Robinson, *The Universal Declaration of Human Rights—Its Origin, Significance, Application and Interpretation* (1958), 40–7.

adoption some governments explicitly denied that the terms of the Universal Declaration were *per se* binding.[56]

Nevertheless, protagonists of the juridical nature of the Universal Declaration refer to the increasingly common practice of the General Assembly and even the Security Council to invoke the Universal Declaration among the obligations with which states are expected to comply. This argument will be dealt with under the next subheading (customary international law).

For present purposes, it is submitted that the adoption of the Declaration against Torture in 1975 has effectively concluded the discussion as regards article 5 of the Universal Declaration, since the Declaration against Torture expands and refines its content. Article 5 of the Universal Declaration states: 'No one shall be subjected to torture or to cruel, inhuman or degrading treatment or punishment.' Article 2 of the Declaration against Torture reads:

Any act of torture or other cruel, inhuman or degrading treatment or punishment is an offence to human dignity and shall be condemned as a denial of the purposes of the Charter of the United Nations and as a violation of the human rights and fundamental freedoms proclaimed in the Universal Declaration of Human Rights.

The Declaration against Torture, having been adopted by acclamation in the Third Committee (see Chapter 1), was then adopted by the General Assembly without a vote and with no reservations expressed at the time of adoption. The Declaration therefore represents a most authoritative interpretation of the UN Charter.[57]

The question of the legal status of principles contained in the Declaration against Torture remains, of course. It was adopted 'as a *guideline* for all States and other entities exercising effective power' (emphasis added). Such language was probably necessary both to clarify that the articles of the Declaration did not necessarily require verbatim incorporation into national law, and, perhaps, to indicate that some of the articles might not impose strict legal obligations or that governments may need to make legal adjustments to give full effect to them.[58] It might even be asserted, however dubiously, that all the articles designed to give effect to the prohibition of torture, that is articles 4 to 12, fall within the denomination 'guideline'. Article 2, however, bears

---

[56] Robinson, *The Universal Declaration of Human Rights—Its Origin, Significance, Application and Interpretation* (1958), 40–7.

[57] Article 1(3) of the UN Charter describes among the 'purposes' of the UN; 'to achieve international cooperation in . . . promoting and encouraging respect for human rights and for fundamental freedoms for all without distinction as to race, sex, language, or religion'.

[58] For example, compliance with article 11 of the Declaration (see Annex 1), requiring compensation for victims of torture or other ill-treatment, might involve legislating a right of action against the state that did not previously exist. Similarly, article 12 on inadmissibility of statements made under such duress could well mean that a juridicial concept would have to be incorporated into the legal systems of states that at present have no such rules of inadmissible evidence.

no resemblance to a guideline for governments; it is a formal and solemn statement of principle.

The same holds for article 3, which could not define the basic obligation in more absolute terms:

No State may permit or tolerate torture or other cruel, inhuman or degrading treatment or punishment. Exceptional circumstances such as a state of war or a threat of war, internal political instability or any other public emergency may not be invoked as a justification of torture or other cruel, inhuman or degrading treatment or punishment.

As noted above, it may be argued that the 1977 General Assembly decision to initiate the drafting of a treaty based on the Declaration against Torture casts doubt on the legal significance of the Declaration itself, as perhaps did the above-mentioned call for unilateral declarations of commitment to the Declaration. While, as already indicated, this may be so for some of the articles of the Declaration, it is submitted, for the same reasons, that it is not the case for articles 2 and 3. As suggested in Chapter 1, an important motivation for the elaboration of a treaty was that the prohibition of torture be given effective tools for its enforcement. To the extent that the norms and obligations contained in the Declaration are now also to be found in the Convention against Torture (itself adopted by consensus), this too argues against the 'guideline' nature of the pertinent provisions of the Declaration. The point seems to be confirmed by the language of resolution 39/46 of 10 December 1984, the resolution by which the UN General Assembly adopted the Convention against Torture. The fifth preambular paragraph of this resolution which, it will be recalled, was adopted by consensus, describes the Assembly as desiring to achieve 'a more effective implementation of the existing prohibition under international and national law of the practice of torture and other cruel, inhuman or degrading treatment or punishment'. Moreover, four days later the Assembly, by resolution 39/118 of 14 December 1984, reaffirmed 'the existing prohibition under international law of every form of cruel, inhuman or degrading treatment or punishment'. The language could hardly be less ambiguous: the practice of torture and other ill-treatment is the object of an already 'existing prohibition under international law'.

CUSTOMARY INTERNATIONAL LAW

Most writers on the topic of human rights in international law argue that the standards laid down in the Universal Declaration, although perhaps devoid of legal obligation at the time of adoption, have become part of customary international law as a result of subsequent state practice.[59] The state practice most commonly mentioned is the adoption of a plethora of resolutions,

---

[59] e.g. Higgins, *supra* n. 52, 118–30; Humphrey, *passim*.

mainly by the General Assembly, which call upon states—either individual countries or the UN membership as a whole—to comply with the Declaration. Particularly persuasive in this argument is the invocation of the Proclamation of Tehran, whereby the International Conference on Human Rights:

solemnly proclaim[ed] that . . . the Universal Declaration of Human Rights states a common understanding of the peoples of the world concerning the inalienable and inviolable rights of all members of the human family and constitutes an obligation for the members of the international community.[60]

Statements such as this may be adduced either as subsequent evidence for interpreting the human rights clauses of the UN Charter (as discussed above) or, more traditionally, as evidence of state practice in the sense of indicating states' understanding of the rules by which they are bound.

This view has been challenged on the grounds that many states violate human rights norms with impunity and that there is a dearth of mechanisms for their effective enforcement.[61] A number of writers have refuted this challenge,[62] and it is not proposed to rehearse the polemic in these pages. Suffice it to say that since governments which practise torture not only do not seek to justify their behaviour but in fact deny it vehemently, human rights violations in the form of torture cannot be offered as evidence of state practice. It may be asked whether the many armed conflicts that have occurred since World War II prove that there is no international law rule prohibiting the use of force to settle disputes. As to the lack, or inadequacy, of enforcement machinery, this can hardly be offered as proof that the rule requiring enforcement does not exist. In fact, there has in the last two decades at the UN been a burgeoning of newly created machinery,[63] a trend that suggests slow, and

---

[60] The Conference, held in Tehran, Iran, by the United Nations, from 22 Apr. to 13 May 1968, in the year marking the twentieth anniversary of the adoption of the Universal Declaration of Human Rights, adopted the Proclamation of Tehran on 13 May 1968; its text is reproduced in United Nations, *Human Rights—Compilation of International Instruments* (1983), 18–19. The quotation is from para. 2.

[61] For example, Watson, 'Autointerpretation, Competence and the Continuing Validity of Article 2(7) of the UN Charter', 71 *AJIL* 60 (1977); id., 'Legal Theory, Efficacy and Validity in the Development of Human Rights Norms in International Law', *University of Illinois Law Forum* (1979), 609; Lane, 'Demanding Human Rights: A Change in the World Legal Order', 6 *Hofstra Law Review* 269 (1978); id., 'Mass Killing by Governments: Lawful in the World Legal Order?', 12 *New York University Journal of International Law and Politics* 239 (1970).

[62] For example, Sohn, 'The International Law of Human Rights: A Reply to Recent Criticism', 9 *Hofstra Law Review* 347 (1981); Higgins, 'Reality and Hope in International Human Rights', 9 *Hofstra Law Review* 1485 (1981). An excellent survey and rebuttal of a range of objections to the legal status of the Declaration may be found in Alston, 'The Universal Declaration of Human Rights at 35: Western and Passé or Alive and Universal', 31 *The Review* (International Commission of Jurists, Dec. 1983), 60. See also Szabo, 'Historical Foundations of Human Rights', and Vasak, 'Toward a Specific International Human Rights Law', in Vasak (ed.), *The International Dimensions of Human Rights*, i, 11 (Szabo) and ii, 671 (Vasak) (1982).

[63] See, for example, the establishment of the UN Working Group on Enforced or Involuntary Disappearances (1980, see Chapter 8), the Special Rapporteur on Summary or Arbitrary

perhaps inadequate, but definite incremental steps towards more effective implementation of human rights norms.

Briefly, then, it is submitted that the best evidence for a customary rule of international law is to be found in what states say they think the rule is (*opinio juris*), and what they say they are doing (or not doing) in terms of that rule. The fact is that a large number of the governments that proclaim their adherence to the prohibition of torture and their compliance with it, actually commit acts of torture in the dark and secret reaches of their power.[64] But this no more undermines the validity of the prohibition than the covert activities of secret services invalidate international law rules on non-intervention against state sovereignty.

GENERAL PRINCIPLES OF LAW

The concept of general principles of law has seldom been invoked to articulate a substantive rule of international law, either by the World Court or by international arbitral tribunals referring to the sources of law contained in the World Court's Statute.[65] As Professor Brownlie puts it, 'the most frequent and successful use of domestic law analogies has been in the field of evidence, procedure, and jurisdictional questions'.[66]

Most, perhaps all, countries would claim that torture is prohibited as a crime in their domestic law,[67] and many constitutions include a prohibition against torture explicitly or implicitly.[68] Indeed, the prohibition is often advanced as proof of (or at least as evidence in support of) government denials that torture is taking or has taken place.[69] While several constitutions include the prohibition of torture in the cluster of rights that may be suspended in time of emergency, there appears to have been no attempt at formal authorization of torture during such an emergency. If, therefore, the notion of general principles of law is available as an independent source to

Executions (1982, see Chapters 6 and 7), the Special Rapporteur on Torture (1985, see Chapter 5), the Working Group on Arbitrary Detention (1991) and the Special Rapporteur on the Independence of Judges and Lawyers (1994).

[64] In 1977, Lady Gaitskell, representing the United Kingdom at the General Assembly's Third Committee, had referred to a statement attributed to Amnesty International according to which 'the confrontation between the individual and the limitless power of the State, between the torturer and the victim, took place in the darkest recesses of political power'. (UN doc. A/C.3/32/SR.37, para. 13.)

[65] See Cheng, *General Principles of Law Applied by International Courts and Tribunals* (1953); Friedmann, *The Changing Structure of International Law* (1964), chapter 12.

[66] Brownlie, *Principles of Public International Law* (4th edn., 1990), 18.

[67] See, for example, the responses to the UN questionnaire on compliance with the Declaration against Torture, discussed in Chapter 5.

[68] Bassiouni and Derby, 'An Appraisal of Torture in International Law and Practice: The Need for an International Convention for the Prevention and Suppression of Torture', 48 *Revue internationale de droit pénal*, vol. xlviii, nos. 3 and 4 (1977), 17, 139–211 (hereinafter 'Bassiouni').

[69] See n. 67 *supra*.

determine the existence of an international law rule against torture, existing constitutional and criminal law rules in national legal systems would be weighty evidence of the rule. It is noteworthy that General Assembly resolution 39/46 quoted above refers to the 'existing prohibition' of the practice of torture and other ill-treatment 'under international and *national* law' (emphasis added).

JUDICIAL DECISIONS

A small number of World Court[70] pronouncements have alluded to human rights in a way that indicates a certain trend towards recognition of their juridical nature. Before considering these, the nature of decisions and opinions of the World Court must be understood. Article 38(1) of the World Court Statute says that judicial decisions are 'a subsidiary means of determining rules of law'. Furthermore, there is no doctrine of precedent whereby World Court decisions may be binding on either the Court itself or on others.[71] This said, the Court's views nevertheless have impact in the realm of international law. Even in the absence of a doctrine of precedent, the Court frequently invokes its own earlier opinions and decisions and its decisions have been highly influential in determining the shape of treaty codifications of issues with which the Court has dealt. Accordingly, international lawyers tend to treat World Court judgments with respect and to turn to them for guidance. Three cases are of particular interest in this respect.

The *Barcelona Traction* case[72] concerned a Canadian corporation, with subsidiaries operating in Spain, which was sued for bankruptcy in Spanish courts. The company was allegedly owned largely by Belgians and the issue before the World Court was whether Belgium might exercise diplomatic protection of its nationals, who claimed that their interests had been harmed by action of the Spanish courts. It was fundamental to the World Court's finding against Belgium's standing to bring a claim against Spain that there was a distinction between what it called bilateral obligations and obligations 'towards the international community as a whole'. The latter were:

By their very nature . . . the concern of all States. In view of the importance of the rights involved, all States can be held to have a legal interest in their protection; they are obligations *erga omnes*. Such obligations derive, for example, in contemporary international law, from the outlawing of acts of aggression, and of genocide, *as also*

---

[70] See n. 51 *supra*.

[71] Article 59 of the Court's Statute states: 'The decision of the Court has no binding force except between the parties and in respect of that particular case.'

[72] ICJ Rep. (1970), 3. See Rodley, 'Corporate Nationality and the Diplomatic Protection of Multinational Enterprises: The Barcelona Traction Case', 47 *Indiana Law Journal* 70 (1970); id., 'The Nationalization by Peru of the Holdings of the International Petroleum Company', in Rodley and Ronning (eds.), *International Law in the Western Hemisphere* (1974), 112, 121–3.

from the principles and rules concerning the basic rights of the human person, including protection from slavery and racial discrimination [paragraphs 33 and 34—emphasis added].

Thus the World Court articulated the proposition that obligations towards the international community as a whole derive from, *inter alia*, the principles and rules concerning the rights of the human person. The prohibitions of slavery and racial discrimination are given as examples of such principles and rules, but they are only examples. Their inclusion may be attributed to the need to give a clear retrospective reference to another case, the *South-West Africa* case (1966), wherein the World Court's decision had provoked widespread criticism.[73] Further, as with the reference to genocide, these categories are the subject of specific treaties. Indeed, an extensive list of inclusions would have risked adverse interpretation of unintentional omissions of certain principles and rules. None of the separate or dissenting opinions challenges this statement of the Court.[74]

A year later the Court handed down its Advisory Opinion on the *Legal Consequences for States of the Continued Presence of South Africa in Namibia (South-West Africa)*.[75] This Advisory Opinion was sought by the General Assembly precisely because of the unsatisfactory nature of the 1966 decision referred to above, and an expectation that the World Court would wish to pronounce on the substance of the problem, something which it had avoided in 1966. The Opinion confirmed the view of the UN Security Council that the continued presence of South Africa in Namibia was illegal. The Court stated in its Opinion:

To establish . . . and to enforce, distinctions, exclusions, restrictions and limitations exclusively based on grounds of race, colour, descent or national or ethnic origin which constitute a denial of fundamental human rights is a flagrant violation of the purposes and principles of the Charter [paragraph 131].

A distinguished commentator has already pointed out the importance of not claiming too much from this statement.[76] Not only is the World Court Opinion advisory and therefore not formally binding on anyone, but it also deals only with the sort of discrimination explicitly covered by the relevant

[73] *South West Africa. Second Phase*, ICJ Rep. (1966), 6. The Court had held in this case that Ethiopia and Liberia, having no direct interest at stake, had no standing to receive a decision of the court against South Africa, despite the fact that the subject matter of the case related to the human rights provisions of the League of Nations mandate under which South Africa administered South West Africa (now Namibia).

[74] ICJ Rep. (1970), 55–357. The Court subsequently pointed out that not all states have 'the capacity to *protect* the victims of infringements of [human] . . . rights irrespective of their nationality' (para. 91, emphasis added).

[75] ICJ Rep. (1971), 16. See Schwelb, 'The International Court of Justice and the Human Rights Clauses of the Charter', 66 *AJIL* 337 (1972).

[76] Humphrey, 36.

UN Charter articles.[77] It is authority, however, for the proposition that there is under the UN Charter a clear legal obligation on governments not to commit such discrimination. The Charter provisions are therefore not just hortatory and programmatic.[78]

The clearest statement on the juridical nature of human rights is to be found in the judgment in the *Tehran Hostages* case.[79] This judgment found that Iran had incurred responsibility towards the United States as a result of the continued detention of United States diplomatic and consular staff in Tehran, mainly in the premises of the United States embassy. At one point in the judgment it is stated:

Wrongfully to deprive human beings of their freedom and to subject them to physical constraint in conditions of hardship is in itself manifestly incompatible with the principles of the Charter of the United Nations, as well as with the fundamental principles enunciated in the Universal Declaration of Human Rights [paragraph 91].

In respect of the plight of diplomatic and consular staff held hostage, the jurisdiction of the World Court had been based on the Vienna Conventions of 1961 and 1963 on Diplomatic and Consular Relations.[80] Its jurisdiction in respect of 'two private individuals of United States nationality' was based on the Treaty of Amity, Economic Relations, and Consular Rights of 1955 between Iran and the United States.[81] The statement quoted above goes beyond both these instruments and was presumably made pursuant to the Court's finding that Iran had committed 'successive and continuing breaches of the obligations laid upon it by . . . the applicable rules of general international law' (paragraph 90).

Neither the separate opinion of Judge Lachs[82] nor the dissenting opinion of Judge Tarazi[83] contest this aspect of the Court's decision. However, Judge Morozov in his dissenting opinion complains that the statement in effect 'serves . . . to level at Iran the unfounded allegation that it has violated the Charter of the United Nations and the Universal Declaration of Human Rights'.[84] In the context in which this opinion is found the basis of Judge Morozov's objection is not clear. It may be that he doubted the jurisdiction of the Court on a matter (human rights) not covered by the Vienna

---

[77] See, for example, article 1(3) of the UN Charter quoted in n. 57 *supra*, as well as articles 55 and 56 by which member states pledge themselves 'to take joint and separate action in cooperation with the organization for the achievement' of certain purposes including the promotion 'of universal respect for, and observance of, human rights and fundamental freedoms for all without distinction as to race, sex, language, or religion'.

[78] See Schwelb, *supra* n.75, 350–1.

[79] *Case Concerning United States Diplomatic and Consular Staff in Tehran (United States of America v. Iran)*, ICJ Rep. (1980), 3.

[80] Vienna Convention on Diplomatic Relations, done at Vienna, 18 Apr. 1961, 500 UNTS 85; Vienna Convention on Consular Relations, done at Vienna, 24 Apr. 1963, 596 UNTS 261.

[81] Cited at para. 77 of the Court's judgment.   [82] ICJ Rep. (1980), 47–50.

[83] Id., 58–65.   [84] Id., 51–7, 53.

Conventions and the Treaty of Amity which permitted the unilateral application to the Court;[85] or that he felt that responsibility should not be attributed to Iran for the acts of the 'militants' who seized control of the embassy and the personnel; or he may have considered that the evidence capable of demonstrating such violations was insufficient; or, finally, that the behaviour in question did not amount to violations of the Charter or the Declaration. There appears to be no challenge, however, to the contention that, under general international law, it is possible to commit acts against human beings that are incompatible with the principles of the UN Charter and those of the Universal Declaration of Human Rights.

Thus, the apparently unanimous view of the World Court is that the Universal Declaration of Human Rights is a document of sufficient legal status to justify its invocation by the Court in the context of a state's obligations under general international law. This opinion would seem to imply much more than simply the respect which is accorded to a resolution (that is, a recommendation) of the General Assembly. Further, if 'wrongfully to deprive human beings of their freedom and to subject them to physical constraint in conditions of hardship' entails acting in a manner 'manifestly incompatible' with a state's obligations under the Charter and the Universal Declaration, and if such behaviour involves breaches of the applicable rules of general international law, then there can be little doubt that violations of the prohibition against torture and other ill-treatment are similarly incompatible.

One further World Court case is relevant specifically to the area of humanitarian law. In *Nicaragua*, among a number of counts of violations of international law, for which the Court found the United States responsible, was the distribution to irregular forces seeking to overthrow the Nicaraguan government by the Central Intelligence Agency of a manual which, among other things, encouraged the selective 'neutralization' of government officials. By this the United States had 'encouraged the commission . . . of acts contrary to general principles of humanitarian law'.[86] The principles in question were to be found in common article 3 of the Geneva Conventions discussed above. The Court did not apply article 3 as a treaty obligation since, in this case, it had no jurisdiction over matters that were covered by multilateral treaties. Accordingly, it was central to the Court's reasoning that common article 3

[85] The Court's jurisdiction was based on art. I common to the Optional Protocol to each Convention Concerning the Compulsory Settlement of Disputes (*supra* n. 80), but the jurisdiction is stipulated to concern 'disputes arising out of the interpretation or application of' the conventions. It may be that, in Judge Morozov's view, human rights issues were not addressed by the Conventions and therefore did not fall within the scope of this provision.

[86] *Military and Paramilitary Activities in and against Nicaragua (Nicaragua v. United States of America)*, Merits, ICJ Rep. (1986), 14, at para. 292(9). (In this case the Court also addressed, negatively, the controversial issue of a state's use of armed force to redress human rights violations in another state, on which see Rodley, 'Human Rights and Humanitarian Intervention', 38 *ICLQ* 321, 327–32 (1989), parts of which borrowed from the same section of the first edition of the present work.)

also stated rules of general international law; they were 'a minimum yard-stick', containing 'rules which . . . reflect . . . "elementary considerations of humanity"'.[87] The same 'general principles of humanitarian law' were reflected in the Conventions' common article 1 which obliged states to respect and to ensure respect for the Conventions 'in all circumstances'.[88] Encouraging acts violating common article 3 therefore violated the principle contained in common article 1. Accordingly, for the Court, torture and other ill-treatment contemplated in common article 3 inflicted on a protected person in any armed conflict would be a violation of general international law.[89]

The World Court's findings in the *Barcelona Traction, Tehran Hostages* and *Nicaragua* cases are binding only as between the parties, and in the Advisory Opinion on *Namibia* the Court's findings are, by definition, advisory. Further, judicial decisions are subsidiary 'sources' of international law. Bearing all this in mind, the following seems to emerge from the modern case law (jurisprudence) of the Court:

   (a) the human rights clauses of the UN Charter contain binding legal obligations (Advisory Opinion on *Namibia*);
   (b) the principles and rules of international law concerning the basic rights of the human person engender obligations *erga omnes* (*Barcelona Traction* case);
   (c) such obligations may be found in the UN Charter and the Universal Declaration of Human Rights (*Tehran Hostages* case);
   (d) wrongful deprivation of freedom involving physical constraint in conditions of hardship is an example of a breach of such obligations (*Tehran Hostages* case);
   (e) violations of common article 3, including torture and ill-treatment, are violations of the 'laws and customs of war' relevant to any armed conflict (*Nicaragua* case).

In the case of item (d), the breach in question presumably arises from the incompatibility of the treatment described with the Declaration's principles on liberty and security of person and against torture or other ill-treatment. Since the former principle is one from which derogations are permitted in time of war or public emergency (see above) while the latter is not, it may safely be inferred that, according to the World Court's line of reasoning,

---

[87] *Military and Paramilitary Activities in and against Nicaragua (Nicaragua v. United States of America)*, *Merits*, ICJ Rep. (1986), para. 218.

[88] Id., para. 220.

[89] The Appeals Chamber of the International Criminal Tribunal for the Former Yugoslavia, following the *Nicaragua* reasoning, held that common article 3 reflects the customary international law notion of 'laws and customs of war', and acts may violate it, 'regardless of whether they occurred within an internal or an international armed conflict': *The Prosecutor* v. *Duško Tadić*, Decision on the Defence Motion for an Interlocutory Appeal on Jurisdiction, Case No. IT-94-1-AR72, 2 Oct. 1995, para. 137, reprinted in 35 *ILM* 32 (1996).

torture and other ill-treatment would be a clear violation of any state's obligations under general international law, even in the absence of armed conflict.

An up-to-date comparative survey and analysis of national judicial decisions on the international legal status of the human rights provisions of the UN Charter and of the Universal Declaration of Human Rights does not yet exist, and this is not the place to fill that gap. Mention must nevertheless be made of one national court judgment that has found torture to be a violation of customary international law. This is the celebrated United States case of *Filártiga* v. *Peña-Irala* that, together with some other relevant cases, will be dealt with in Chapter 4.

TEACHINGS OF PUBLICISTS

Most recent writing by experienced and distinguished scholars and practitioners of public international law appears to support the thesis that in one way or another the principles of the Universal Declaration of Human Rights have entered the realm of general international law. The details of this literature will not be covered here, since the basic arguments have already been laid out above. There has been little writing specifically on the legal status of the prohibition against torture, but little, if any, of what has been produced appears to contradict the thesis that torture is a breach of general international law.[90] Finally, it must be noted that this topic is not one upon which the teachings of publicists can *per se* be expected to have decisive influence.

SUMMARY

To sum up, torture and other ill-treatment are prohibited by the Universal Declaration of Human Rights, an instrument whose legal value, to put it modestly, 'exceeds that of a simple recommendation'.[91] They are prohibited by the International Covenant on Civil and Political Rights and by the three regional human rights conventions. Those treaties that permit derogation from some of their provisions in time of public emergency make no such allowance for the prohibition against torture and other ill-treatment. The Declaration against Torture has described such treatment as a denial of the

---

[90] See Bassiouni, *supra* n. 68; Draper, 'The Juridical Aspects of Torture', *Acta Juridica* (Capetown, 1976), 221; Ackerman, 'Torture and Other Forms of Cruel and Unusual Punishment in International Law', 1 *Vanderbilt Journal of Transnational Law* 653 (1978); Klayman, 'The Definition of Torture in International Law', 5 *Temple Law Quarterly* 449 (1978); Lippmann, 'The Protection of Universal Human Rights: The Problem of Torture', *Universal Human Rights*, vol. i, no. 4 (1979), 25. See also Dinstein, 'The Right to Life, Physical Integrity and Liberty', in Henkin, 114, 122–6; Meron, *supra* n. 51, 95 (citing the *Restatement of the Law: Third Restatement of the Foreign Relations Law of the United States*, Vol. II (1987), sec. 702).

[91] Szabo, *supra* n. 62, 24.

purposes of the Charter of the United Nations. Not only do the Geneva Conventions of 11 August 1949 prohibit such treatment in time of non-international armed conflict, they also do so in time of international armed conflict, and violation of the prohibition is considered a 'grave breach' of the conventions. Subject to what will be said in subsequent chapters regarding certain difficulties in determining what practices and punishments may fall within the limits of the prohibition against torture and other ill-treatment (it will be seen to have 'a fixed core of settled meaning'[92]), no country is known to tolerate it as formally lawful. Several World Court decisions have suggested that human rights norms form part of general international law, one in language ('deprivation of freedom . . . in conditions of hardship') coming close to specific reference to the prohibition. It has said so unmistakably in respect of torture committed in armed conflict. Furthermore, the UN and OAS Conventions against Torture confirm the absolute prohibition of torture and other ill-treatment under all circumstances. Indeed, they require states that subscribe to them to exercise jurisdiction over suspected torturers wherever they come from and wherever they may have committed the torture. Moreover, the resolution by which the UN Convention was adopted expresses the General Assembly's consensus view that the practice of torture and other ill-treatment is already the object of an existing prohibition under international law.

This being so, it is safe to conclude that the prohibition is one of general international law, regardless of whether a particular state is party to a treaty expressly containing the prohibition. Indeed, it may well be that the same reasons, especially the fact of non-derogability of the prohibition in the human rights treaties, permit acceptance of the view that the prohibition is itself a norm of *jus cogens* or 'a peremptory norm of general international law' which is 'a norm accepted and recognized by the international community of states as a whole as a norm from which no derogation is permitted and which can be modified only by a subsequent norm of general international law having the same character'.[93]

---

[92] O'Boyle, 'Torture and Emergency Powers under the European Convention on Human Rights: Ireland v. United Kingdom', 71 *AJIL* 674, 688 (1977).

[93] Article 53 of the Vienna Convention on the Law of Treaties (A/CONF.39/27 (1969)); it provides that a treaty is void if it conflicts with a norm of *jus cogens*. The argument that torture constitutes such a norm is asserted by the first UN Special Rapporteur on Torture, in his first report (UN doc. E/CN.4/1986/15, para. 3), and by O'Boyle, *supra* n. 92, 687–8.

3

What Constitutes Torture and Other Ill-treatment?

INTRODUCTION

Having concluded in the previous chapter that there is an obligation under general international law prohibiting torture and other ill-treatment, it is now necessary to examine what is meant by these terms. As has been said, the basic formula, 'torture or cruel, inhuman or degrading treatment or punishment', is that of article 5 of the Universal Declaration of Human Rights. All the human rights treaties that contain the prohibition effectively reproduce this formula, except for the European Convention on Human Rights, whose article 3 omits the word 'cruel', a change of little significance.[1]

It might therefore be thought that the single question to be answered is 'what is torture or cruel, inhuman, or degrading treatment or punishment?', with the words of the formula being understood as contributing to an 'umbrella' description of a range of severe ill-treatment. A problem has arisen, however, in that it has become necessary to distinguish between the different limbs of the formula. This was clearly not the intention of those who framed the Universal Declaration of Human Rights, who were seeking a formula that would not be so rigid as to exclude practices such as the medical experimentation that took place on concentration camp victims in World War II. The various changes through which the text went afford no further guidance as to the drafters' intentions.[2] Perhaps it is vain even to seek them: it is in the nature of such a formula to be elastic and capable of evolving interpretation over time. The practice of the Human Rights Committee[3] reflected this global approach, in that the Committee has tended generally to speak of 'violations of article 7' of the International Covenant on Civil and Political Rights, without reference to the formula itself. As will appear below, however, it has in a few cases concluded that *torture* has been inflicted.

This approach, of dividing the formula into its component parts, was started by the European Commission of Human Rights in its report on the

---

[1] See Klayman, 'The Definition of Torture in International Law', 51 *Temple Law Quarterly* 449 (1978).

[2] Verdoodt, *Naissance et signification de la Déclaration universelle des droits de l'homme* (1964), 105–7.

[3] 'It may not be necessary to draw sharp distinctions between the various prohibited forms of treatment or punishment.' Report of the Human Rights Committee, *GAOR*, 37th Session, Supplement No. 40 (1982), Annex V, general comment 7(16), para. 2. See also general comment 20(44) in Report of the Human Rights Committee, UN doc. A/47/40 (1992), Annex VI A, para. 4.

Greek case.[4] Here the Commission made its well-known statement on the formula contained in article 3 of the European Convention on Human Rights: 'It is plain that there may be treatment to which all these descriptions apply, for all torture must be inhuman and degrading treatment, and inhuman treatment also degrading',[5] thus understanding the terms of the formula to refer to separate and different types of treatment. In fact, the distinction was of limited relevance to the findings of the Commission, since the report went on to use the phrase 'torture or ill-treatment' for the purpose of describing generally acts prohibited by article 3 of the European Convention.[6]

It was perhaps understandable that when Sweden and The Netherlands, two of the countries that had instituted the application against Greece, came to formulate a draft UN declaration against torture (see Chapter 1), they should have been influenced by the Commission's analysis of the general prohibition. Responding to the felt need of some countries for a definition of torture,[7] they offered such a definition in their first draft and it included the statement: 'It is generally an aggravated form of cruel, inhuman or degrading treatment or punishment . . .',[8] thus again separating the formula into at least two branches. Subject to some wording changes, this approach was adopted in the final text of the Declaration against Torture (see Annex 1). The fragmentation of the formula would have had little significance had there not also been a substantive modification of the original text that concerned the consequences attaching to the separate terms of the formula. In the original draft all the proposed obligations on states would have applied in respect of 'torture and other cruel, inhuman or degrading treatment or punishment'. But, as may be seen in Chapter 1 and will be examined further in Chapter 4, it was decided that some of the obligations were too strict to apply in cases involving the undefined concept of 'cruel, inhuman or degrading treatment or punishment'. Further, at the stage that the distinction was made, it began to appear that even punishments prescribed by law after conviction for an offence might have to be included in this undefined concept (see Chapters 1 and 10), and so it was doubtless felt undesirable to make those involved in the administration of such lawful punishments open to mandatory criminal proceedings. The separation of the terms of the formula was therefore much reinforced by the creation of a distinction of obligations or consequences incurred by the two branches. The UN Convention against Torture and Other Cruel,

---

[4] 12 *Yearbook of the European Convention on Human Rights* (hereinafter '*Yearbook*')—*The Greek Case* (1969). The case was brought by Denmark, Norway, Sweden, and The Netherlands against Greece in the wake of the 1967 military coup in Greece. The complaining governments alleged a wide range of human rights violations, eventually including torture.

[5] Id., 186.

[6] However, as will be seen below, the Commission did at one point use the term 'torture *and* ill-treatment' (emphasis added).

[7] For example, Iraq: *GAOR*, 29th Session, Third Committee, Summary Records, A/C.3/SR.2065, para. 45.

[8] UN doc. A.CONF.56(V)/Misc. 2; see Chapter 1.

Inhuman or Degrading Treatment or Punishment (see Annex 2a) adopts the same approach.

The *Greek* case affords the first and most extensively reasoned formal finding, by a body called upon to apply a human rights treaty, that torture has taken place. In this case the European Commission of Human Rights found 'a practice of torture *and* ill-treatment by the Athens Security Police, Bouboulinas Street, of persons arrested for political reasons, and that . . . this torture and ill-treatment has most often consisted in the application of "falanga" or severe beatings of all parts of the body'[9] (emphasis added). The Commission described '*falanga* or *bastinado*' to have been 'a method of *torture* known for centuries. It is the beating of the feet with a wooden or metal stick or bar which, if skilfully done, breaks no bones, makes no skin lesions, and leaves no permanent and recognizable marks, but causes intense pain and swelling of the feet.'[10] (Emphasis added.) To categorize such behaviour as torture is uncontroversial: it is classic, having been 'known for centuries'. There are, of course, many other specific methods of inflicting pain that would without controversy fall into the category of torture. It is obvious, however, that a juridical definition cannot depend upon a catalogue of horrific practices; for it to do so would simply provide a challenge to the ingenuity of the torturers, not a viable legal prohibition.

DEFINING TORTURE

Most elements of the definition of torture as it emerged are to be found in the European Commission of Human Rights report in the *Greek* case just mentioned. Having indicated its view that 'torture' comprises inhuman and degrading treatment and that 'inhuman treatment' comprises degrading treatment, the Commission went on to describe its notion of 'inhuman treatment'. This covered 'at least such treatment as deliberately causes severe suffering, mental or physical, which, in the particular situation, is unjustifiable'.[11] It then described treatment or punishment of an individual as 'degrading if it grossly humiliates him before others or drives him to act against his will or conscience'.[12] Further, 'torture' was 'inhuman treatment, which has a purpose, such as the obtaining of information or confessions, or the infliction of punishment, and it is generally an aggravated form of inhuman treatment'.[13] So, for torture to occur, a scale of criteria has to be

---

[9] 12 *Yearbook—The Greek Case* 504 (1969). [10] Id., 499.
[11] Id., 186. [12] Ibid.
[13] Ibid. See, generally, Duffy, 'Article 3 of the European Convention on Human Rights', 32 *ICLQ* 316 (1983); also Doswald-Beck, 'What Does the Prohibition of "Torture or Inhuman or Degrading Treatment or Punishment" Mean? The Interpretation of the European Commission and Court of Human Rights', 25 *Netherlands International Law Review* 24 (1978); Klayman, *supra* n. 1; Sudre, 'La Notion de "peines et traitements inhumains ou degradants" dans la

climbed. First, the behaviour must be degrading treatment: second, it must be inhuman treatment; and third, it must be an aggravated form of inhuman treatment, inflicted for certain purposes.

Clearly the factors comprising degrading treatment, according to the Commission's approach, represent the lower threshold for behaviour to fall within the scope of the prohibition as a whole. The difficulty of determining the threshold in practice is considered below. Here it need only be noted that the Commission's words should not be taken literally. Thus 'grossly humiliates him *before others*' (emphasis added) should not be taken as indicating that, unless there were present on the occasion in question persons other than the victim and the tormentor, there was no relevant humiliation. Similarly, 'drives him to act against his will or conscience' should not be taken as indicating that, unless the victim capitulates, the torment will not be degrading. The point presumably is that the behaviour must be aimed at one of these goals (humiliation or action against will or conscience) or reasonably calculated to achieve them.

Once having established the treatment as being degrading, it must, again according to the Commission's language in the *Greek* case, then be asked if it is also inhuman; that is, certain elements must be present: (a) it must cause mental or physical suffering; (b) the suffering must be severe; (c) it must be deliberately inflicted; and (d) it has (seemingly) to be unjustifiable in the particular situation. Elements (a) and (b) will be returned to below. As regards element (c) (deliberation), this seems aimed at specifying intentional rather than merely negligent ill-treatment and is presumably designed to shield those who might unwittingly cause suffering.[14] Nevertheless, negligent behaviour leading to severe suffering (in a very inadequate prison regime, for example) might well incur condemnation as inhuman and/or degrading treatment or punishment (see Chapter 9). The final element (d) requires greater discussion.

JUSTIFIABILITY?

The Commission's inclusion of the concept of justifiability in its definition of torture in the *Greek* case gave rise to controversy.[15] It seemed to be saying that torture or other ill-treatment might in certain circumstances be justifiable, despite the fact that the European Convention on Human Rights couched the prohibition against torture and other ill-treatment in absolute terms and permitted no derogation from it, even in time of war or other pub-

---

jurisprudence de la Commission et de la Cour européennes des droits de l'homme', 88 *Revue générale de droit international public* 825 (1984).

[14] According to the Declaration against Torture, the pain or suffering has to be inflicted 'intentionally' (article 1). The UN Convention against Torture says the same (article 1) as does the OAS Convention against Torture (article 2).

[15] e.g. Amnesty International, *Report on Torture* (revised edn., 1975), 35–6.

lic emergency threatening the life of the nation. Aware of the difficulties to which the notion of 'justifiability' had given rise, the Commission took the opportunity afforded by the *Northern Ireland* case (1976) to note that, as a result of its *Greek* case report, 'the term "unjustifiable" (in the particular situation) has given rise to some misunderstanding and [the Commission] therefore finds it necessary to state clearly that it did not have in mind the possibility that there could be a justification for any treatment in breach of Art. 3'.[16]

The Commission then asks whether the prohibition is: 'an absolute one, or whether there may be special circumstances, such as those existing in the present case, in which treatment contrary to Article 3 may be justified or excused'.[17] Pointing to the non-derogability of article 3 of the European Convention and the prohibition of torture or other ill-treatment 'at any time or in any place whatsoever' by common article 3 of the Geneva Conventions ('although not directly applicable here'), the Commission concludes that the prohibition 'is an absolute one and that there can never be under the Convention or under international law, a justification for acts in breach of' the provision prohibiting torture or other ill-treatment.[18]

This seems to be an effective retraction of the relevance of the notion of justifiability, and yet the Commission's formulation still begs the question to some extent. The Commission 'maintains its understanding of the basic elements of Art. 3, expressed in earlier cases, in particular, as regards "inhuman treatment"'.[19] Given that 'justifiability' is an integral element of that understanding of what is contained *within* the provision, then the Commission's disclaimer does not answer the criticism that 'justifiability' should not have been such an integral element. The possibility of justification in some circumstances for acts that might involve the infliction of the degree of suffering required for torture or inhuman treatment may therefore be mooted. First, one may offer the case of the person confined and treated in a mental hospital; next, the case where pain is inflicted for the benefit of the recipient (for example, the mountaineer trapped under a rock, who can be saved only by amputation of a limb);[20] third, the utilitarian case wherein pain is inflicted with the object of achieving a greater good for others (for example, in order to extract information about a concealed bomb that threatens many lives).

One line of approach to the question of justifiability here is consideration of the *purpose* of the treatment: that is, the suffering inflicted must be for no other purpose than the benefit of the recipient. Such an approach might be applicable to the first two hypothetical cases given above, which both involve

[16] *Ireland* v. *United Kingdom*, 19 *Yearbook* 512, 750 (1976).   [17] Ibid.
[18] Id., 752.   [19] Ibid.
[20] A range of similar examples is given in the dissenting opinion of Judge Fitzmaurice in the case of *Tyrer* v. *United Kingdom*, European Court of Human Rights, Series A., No. 26, 23, para. 4 and footnote 2.

the question of potential benefit to the recipient of treatment which may cause suffering. The problem with this approach is that there is apparently no end to the suffering that some will inflict on others, convinced that the pain is for the greater or long-term good of the recipient. An alternative approach would rely on the principle of *consent* or presumed consent. Where such consent can be given in the case of a conscious trapped mountaineer or the commitment to a mental hospital of a rational patient, then the action in question must not take place without consent, even if failure to take it is unambiguously detrimental to the condition of the potential recipient. Where consent is freely given, then, there is no question of torture or other inhuman treatment. Where consent cannot properly be given (in the case of an unconscious mountaineer or severely mentally ill patient) then it can be elicited from (or withheld by) someone acting in the best interests of the recipient (next of kin, lawyer, and so on).[21] In the absence of anyone able to act for the person in question, or in case of an emergency, it may be proper to assume consent. The approach based on consent has the advantage of being analogous to the principle underlying the second sentence of article 7 of the International Covenant on Civil and Political Rights, which prohibits medical or scientific experimentation without the 'free consent' of the recipient.[22]

The utilitarian argument for justifiability (that ill-treatment is justified in order to elicit information that may save others) has been advanced in a number of cases. This argument has rarely been made by governments themselves (indeed, the United Kingdom did not advance it in the *Northern Ireland* case), but, nevertheless, it has sufficient following to merit serious attention.[23]

Those who argue in the language of utilitarian reasoning, when seeking to rebut the utilitarian challenge, tend to point to the impossibility of confining the facts to the classic example of the lesser evil for the greater good: how many broken bodies equal how many lives? How many broken wills to save a government? Will torture create more terrorists? It is a version of the 'slippery slope' argument: once torture is permitted on grounds of necessity, nothing can stop it from being used on grounds of expediency.[24] Further, the

[21] It is common for legal systems to recognize such a person as being empowered to act on behalf of another person, where the latter person does not have the capacity to make legal choices for him or herself (e.g. very young children, insane persons, senile persons).

[22] As Judge Fitzmaurice put it, in his separate opinion when the *Northern Ireland* case went to the European Court of Human Rights: '[t]orture is torture whatever its object may be, or even if it has none, other than to cause pain, provided it is inflicted by force (of course the suffering experienced in the dentist's chair, however intense, is not technically torture because the patient submits to it of his own volition)'. European Court of Human Rights, Series A., No. 25, 129–30, footnote 19.

[23] 19 *Yearbook* 750 (1976). See Levin, 'The Case for Torture', *Newsweek* (New York), 7 June 1982, 4. For a response, see Leys, 'The Case for Torture: A Rebuttal', *Newsweek* (New York), 12 July 1982, 4. For extensive discussion of the issues in a specific context, see Hebrew University, *Proceedings of a Seminar . . . The Issue of Torture* (1995), *infra* n. 37.

[24] See Twining and Twining, 'Bentham on Torture', 24 *Northern Ireland Legal Quarterly* 305, 345–56 (1973).

incorporation of 'justifiability' on utilitarian grounds would cut across every formulation of the absolute prohibition against torture and other ill-treatment in legal instruments.

Moreover, it is clear that the Commission in the *Northern Ireland* case specifically intended to exclude this approach. Although the United Kingdom did not advance the argument of 'justifiability' in the proceedings of this case, the Commission, in arriving at its view that the prohibition of torture and other ill-treatment should be absolute, referred to precisely such utilitarian arguments. Such arguments were contained in the report of an official committee commissioned by the United Kingdom to examine whether authorized interrogation procedures required amendment.[25] More importantly, the Commission dealt with the kind of hypothetical situation being considered here. In a passage of its report (separate from its above-quoted remarks on justifiability) which dealt with the issue of evidence of what constitutes official tolerance of torture, it considered the possibility of taking into account the stress imposed on the security forces by the situation: 'it is not difficult, to take a hypothetical situation, to imagine the extreme strain on a police officer who questions a prisoner about the location of a bomb which has been timed to explode in a public area within a very short while'.[26] The Commission's view of the situation could not be less ambiguous:

any such strain on the members of the security forces cannot justify the application on a prisoner of treatment amounting to a breach of Art. 3. On the other hand, as a matter of fact, the domestic authorities are likely to take into account the general situation as a mitigating circumstance in determining the sentence or other punishment to be imposed on the individual in a case which is brought against him before the domestic authorities and courts for acts of ill-treatment. This does not, of course, in proceedings brought under the [European] Convention [on Human Rights], affect the responsibility of the High Contracting Party concerned under the Convention for the acts in question. However, where a penalty has been so mitigated by the domestic judicial or disciplinary authorities, having due regard to the severity of the acts involved and *the necessity of preventing their repetition*, this fact cannot in itself be regarded as tolerance on the part of these authorities . . . [emphasis added][27]

According to the Commission, then, the responsibility of a state for acts of torture and inhuman treatment remains, even in the sort of case presented above; the concept of justifiability on utilitarian grounds is clearly excluded.

As noted, the passage just quoted occurs not during the Commission's own discussion of 'justifiability', but in its discussion of what amounts to tolerance

---

[25] *Report of the Committee of Privy Counsellors Appointed to Consider Authorized Procedures for Interrogation of Persons Suspected of Terrorism*, Cmnd. 4901 (1972). See O'Boyle, 'Torture and Emergency Powers under the European Convention on Human Rights: Ireland v United Kingdom', 71 *AJIL* 674, 678 (1977). The 'five techniques', described further below, consisted of wall-standing, hooding, subjection to noise, deprivation of sleep, and deprivation of food and drink.

[26] 19 *Yearbook* 764–6 (1976).   [27] Ibid.

of an administrative practice. The late Commission member Mr Fawcett used a similar hypothetical case when directly addressing the question of 'justifiability'. He felt that 'there can be situations of urban guerrilla conflict where information is urgently needed to save lives and if this is obtained by . . . illtreatment, I think that disciplinary punishment or judicial sentence imposed on those who inflicted it, could be mitigated'.[28] By this, Mr Fawcett did not seem to be challenging the Commission's view that the acts of ill-treatment would engage the responsibility of the state, but that the normal responsibility of the state to punish such acts severely might itself be mitigated. In the European Court of Human Rights, the late Judge Sir Gerald Fitzmaurice referred approvingly to the relevant passage in Mr Fawcett's separate opinion.[29] The Court itself did not address the matter of 'justifiability', contenting itself with the observation that, despite the uncertain nature of the severity of ill-treatment required to trigger the application of article 3,[30] 'the Convention prohibits in absolute terms torture and inhuman or degrading treatment or punishment, irrespective of the victim's conduct . . . there can be no derogation therefrom even in the event of a public emergency threatening the life of the nation'.[31]

Later case law has confirmed this analysis. In *Tomasi* v. *France*, the government invited the European Court of Human Rights to take into account, when considering the ill-treatment of the applicant, the '"particular circumstances" obtaining in Corsica at the time and the fact that he had been suspected of participating in a terrorist attack which had resulted in the death of one man and grave injuries to another'.[32] The Court, unanimously finding a violation of article 3, responded robustly:

The requirements of the investigation and the undeniable difficulties inherent in the fight against crime, particularly with regard to terrorism, cannot result in limits being placed on the protection to be afforded in respect of the physical integrity of individuals.[33]

Indeed, at the European level, the issue seems to have been laid to rest by the *Chahal* case. Here the Court found that the deportation of the applicant to India would violate article 3. The United Kingdom had argued effectively that national security interests either override the risk in deportation cases or should be part of the process in assessing the risk of ill-treatment, should deportation occur.[34] (Exactly how the threat to national security is relevant to identifying the risk threshold is unclear.) The Court rejected the argument in unambiguous terms:

[T]he Convention prohibits in absolute terms torture or inhuman or degrading treatment or punishment, irrespective of the victim's conduct . . . Article 3 makes no pro-

---

[28] 19 *Yearbook* 497.   [29] *Supra* n.22.
[30] Id., para. 162. On the relative nature of degrading treatment, see below, text accompanying nn. 106–13.
[31] Id., para. 163.   [32] European Court of Human Rights, Series A, No. 241-A, para. 114.
[33] Id., para. 115.   [34] *Chahal* v. *United Kingdom*, Judgment, 15 Nov. 1996, para. 76.

vision for exceptions and no derogation from it is permissible under Article 15 even in the event of a public emergency threatening the life of the nation . . .

The prohibition provided by Article 3 against ill-treatment is equally absolute in expulsion cases . . . [T]he activities of the individual in question, however undesirable or dangerous, cannot be a material consideration.[35]

While the Court reached its conclusion by twelve votes to seven, the dissenting opinion of the seven effectively confirms the Court's basic approach. The dissent accepted that in deportation cases the risk to national security could be balanced against the risk of ill-treatment. This was because the 'situation is different' when 'the extra-territorial (or indirect) application of the Article is at stake'. As to the basic proposition, the minority 'agree with the majority that national security considerations could not be invoked to justify ill-treatment at the hands of a Contracting State within its own jurisdiction, and that in that sense the protection afforded by Article 3 is absolute in character'.[36] In other words, there is unanimity that torture or other ill-treatment can never be justified.

The position would seem to be the same at the universal level. Certainly it is logical that it be so. The status of the prohibition of torture is equally non-derogable and expressed in equally absolute terms under the International Covenant on Civil and Political Rights (Annex 9b, articles 7 and 4) and under the Convention against Torture (Annex 2a, article 2).

The problem surfaced in the case of Israel's use of 'moderate physical pressure', the nature of which is discussed below. The use of the types of pressure in question have been the subject of controversy in Israel, where there has been debate on the justifiability of torture in what has become known as the 'ticking bomb situation', that is, the sort of extreme case mentioned earlier.[37] As it happens, Israel's main line of argument is that the techniques constitute neither torture, nor cruel, inhuman, or degrading treatment. The Committee against Torture and the Special Rapporteur on Torture have both taken the view that the techniques, as used, can constitute torture and have rejected any notion of justifiability. The Committee against Torture expressed its position when examining a 'special report' that it had sought from the Government of Israel in response to information that the Israeli Supreme Court had not contested the legality of the techniques.[38] It states:

---

[35] Id., paras. 79–80.

[36] Id., Joint Partly Dissenting Opinion of Judges Gölcüklü, Matscher, Freeland, Baka, Gotchev, Bonici and Levits, para. 1.

[37] Hebrew University of Jerusalem Centre for Human Rights, *Proceedings of a Seminar on Israel and International Human Rights Law: The Issue of Torture*, 9 June 1995. The 'ticking bomb' example is the same as that referred to by the European Commission of Human Rights in the *Northern Ireland* case, *supra* n. 26 and accompanying text; see also Benvenisti, 'The Role of National Courts in Preventing Torture of Suspected Terrrorists', 8 *EJIL* 596 (1997), explaining the idea of 'self-defence' as a defence to a charge of torture (pp. 606–9).

[38] Report of the Committee against Torture, *GAOR*, 52nd Session, Supp. No. 44 (1997), paras. 24–5. On the Committee generally, see Chapter 5.

The Committee acknowledges the terrible dilemma that Israel confronts in dealing with terrorist threats to its security, but as a State Party to the Convention Israel is precluded from raising . . . exceptional circumstances as justification for acts prohibited by Article 1 of the Convention. This is plainly expressed in Article 2 of the Convention.[39]

Similarly, while appreciating the same 'challenges posed by politically motivated terrorist activities', the Special Rapporteur considered that 'as the Government itself acknowledges, these cannot justify torture or cruel, inhuman or degrading treatment'.[40]

The present position on 'justifiability' as an element in the concepts of torture and other ill-treatment may be summarized as follows: the notion is not available as a defence against the charge of violating the prohibition against torture and other ill-treatment; this prohibition is absolute. Nor can it be used to excuse acts of torture or ill-treatment on the general utilitarian grounds that they are intended to serve a greater good. It is necessary, however, to take account of the fact that in certain circumstances severe pain or suffering may be inflicted on a person without contravening the prohibition on torture and other ill-treatment, but these seem to be limited to those wherein the sole objective is the direct benefit of the recipient. The infliction of pain in these cases may be embraced by a limited concept of justifiability but other concepts are also available, namely that of *purpose* (that is, for the benefit of the recipient) or that of *consent* or presumed consent (of the recipient). It is argued above that the latter, consent, is the better concept.

Having established, following the Commission's reasoning, that degrading treatment is treatment tending to humiliate or to drive a victim to act against will or conscience, and that inhuman treatment is the deliberate infliction of severe mental or physical suffering (without the qualifying notion of justifiability), it is now proposed to examine the additional elements required to denote torture. These, it will be recalled, were the elements of purpose and aggravation.

PURPOSE

As has just been seen, in certain circumstances the notion of 'justifiability' becomes entangled with that of *purpose* which, according to the *Greek* case, would seem to be an additional element for inhuman treatment to amount to torture. This element appears to have been reaffirmed by the European Commission of Human Rights in the *Northern Ireland* case (see below). Not only did the Commission maintain 'its understanding of the basic elements' of the article 3 prohibition against torture and other ill-treatment, it also twice

[39] Report of the Committee against Torture, *GAOR*, 52nd Session, Supp. No. 44 (1997), para. 258.
[40] UN doc. E/CN.4/1997/7, para. 121, On the Special Rapporteur generally, see Chapter 5.

referred to the *purpose* of obtaining information, in the passage of its report where it finds the five in-depth interrogation techniques that were used by the United Kingdom in Northern Ireland to constitute torture. The European Court of Human Rights, to which the *Northern Ireland* case was referred after it had been dealt with by the Commission, did not address the issue directly, but offered some implicit confirmation of the 'purpose' element in the passage of its judgment that concluded that the five techniques did not amount to torture. It arrived at this conclusion '*although* their object was the extraction of confessions, the naming of others and/or information' (emphasis added).[41]

This element of 'purpose' is confirmed by developments at the international level. The examples of relevant purposes referred to by the Commission in the *Greek* case (obtaining information or confessions; punishment) are reproduced in the Declaration against Torture (see Annex 1) and augmented by 'intimidating' the victim or other persons (article 1). The UN Convention against Torture (see Annex 2a), which in turn follows the model of the Declaration, further expands the list to include 'coercing [the victim] or a third person, or any reason based on discrimination of any kind' (article 1).

Similarly the OAS Convention against Torture (Annex 2b) contains a purposive element. Specifically the pain or suffering would be inflicted 'for purposes of criminal investigation, as a means of intimidation, as personal punishment, as a preventive measure, as a penalty, or for any other purpose' (article 2(1)). No doubt the framers considered that the purposes of obtaining information or confessions were covered by the reference to criminal investigation. However, the securing of information may well be pursued by the authorities outside the framework of a formal criminal investigation, for instance, as part of a counter-insurgency strategy. Since the object of the Convention is to prevent torture under all circumstances, it may be presumed that torture committed for such a purpose would at least be covered by the term 'or for any other purpose'.

DEGREE OF PAIN OR SUFFERING/AGGRAVATION

It will be recalled that, in the view of the European Commission of Human Rights, 'torture' comprises an aggravated form of severe physical or mental suffering; the same requirement is found in the Declaration against Torture.

Examples of such *physical* suffering are to be found in authoritative findings which interpret the human rights treaties. The first such finding is that of

---

[41] Id., para. 167. Cf. the robust argument against the inclusion of an element of purpose in the extract of Judge Fitzmaurice's separate opinion quoted above at n. 22. In a recent case, one Commission member took the view that the impugned acts (see below), while capable of being 'assimilated to acts of torture', should not be treated as torture 'in a formal sense', as it had not been proven that ill-treatment had been inflicted for the relevant purposes: *Selmouni* v. *France* (Application No. 25803/94), Report, 11 Dec. 1997, Separate Concurring Opinion of Mr Herndl (the quoted words are translated from the French version).

the European Commission of Human Rights in the *Greek* case, quoted above, relating to the use of the *falanga*. Other findings come from the Human Rights Committee and concern a series of individual cases mainly from Uruguay. The *Bazzano and Massera* case was one of these: in its first ever adoption of views, under article 5(4) of the Optional Protocol to the International Covenant on Civil and Political Rights, the Committee found that mathematics professor Luis Massera, a former deputy to the Uruguayan National Assembly, 'was tortured as a result of which he suffered permanent physical damage'.[42] The damage in question was that one leg was left several centimetres shorter than the other. This came about because 'having been forced to remain standing with his head hooded for long hours, he lost his balance, fell down and broke his leg which was not immediately taken care of . . .'.[43] It is not clear from the text of the Committee's 'views' whether or not the ill-treatment in question was part of that alleged by the author of the communication (Professor Massera's stepdaughter) to have been administered to him on his arrest, which included '*plantón* (the prisoner was forced to remain standing for 14 hours) electric shocks and *bastinado* (blows)'.[44] If so, then the brutalities in question would not have fallen within the jurisdiction of the Committee, since they happened in October 1975, six months before the Covenant came into force. Even so, the offence was continued, by virtue of the denial of medical treatment, after the Covenant entered into force on 23 March 1976. At this stage, therefore, it is probably reasonable to conclude that, in the view of the Committee, the combined cruelties of *plantón*, electric shocks, and *bastinado*, together with the denial of necessary medical treatment and the resultant permanent physical damage, constituted torture.

In another case, the Committee found that Alberto Grille Motta had been subjected to 'torture and inhuman treatment',[45] basing its opinion on his 'unrefuted' evidence that he had suffered 'the application of electric shocks, the use of the "*submarino*" (putting the detainee's hooded head into foul water), insertion of bottles or barrels of automatic rifles into his anus and forcing him to remain standing, hooded and handcuffed and with a piece of wood thrust into his mouth, for several days and nights'.[46] The Committee made no attempt to refine its finding of 'torture and inhuman treatment' by indicating which of the above practices could be placed under which heading.

In the case of Sergio Rubén López Burgos, the Committee found 'treatment (including torture)' in violation of article 7.[47] Mr López Burgos had

---

[42] *Bazzano and Massera* v. *Uruguay* (5/1977), Report of the Human Rights Committee, *GAOR*, 34th Session, Supplement No. 40 (1979), Annex VII, para. 10 (ii).
[43] Id., para. 2.   [44] Ibid.
[45] *Grille Motta* v. *Uruguay* (11/1977), Report of the Human Rights Committee, *GAOR*, 35th Session, Supplement No. 40 (1980), Annex XI, para. 16.
[46] Id., para.2.
[47] *López Burgos* v. *Uruguay* (52/1979), Report of the Human Rights Committee, *GAOR*, 36th Session, Supplement No. 40 (1981), Annex XIX, para. 13.

suffered a fractured jaw on his seizure in Buenos Aires by Uruguayan personnel and his jaw was injured still further during subsequent interrogation. For the first ten days of this interrogation he was 'kept hanging for hours with his arms behind him, . . . given electric shocks, thrown on the floor, covered with chains that were connected with electric current, kept naked and wet'.[48] During subsequent interrogation he was beaten and given electric shocks. Again, no guidance is offered as regards which particular cruelties constitute torture and which other prohibited ill-treatment.

The Committee moved towards greater precision in the case of the Tupamaro leader Raúl Sendic Antonaccio. It held that Mr Sendic had for three months been 'subjected to torture (*"plantónes"*, beatings, lack of food)'.[49] This wording was an abbreviation of the allegation by Mr Sendic's wife that 'for three months, he was made to do the *"plantón"* (stand upright with his eyes blindfolded) throughout the day; he was only able to rest and sleep for a few hours at a time; he was beaten and given insufficient food . . .'.[50] In forming its opinion, the Committee must have considered the particularly protracted duration of the treatment, and may also have had in mind Mrs Sendic's fears about the precarious state of her husband's health due to an untreated hernia and heart disease, particularly since the Uruguayan government had ignored the Committee's repeated requests for information on the victim's medical condition.[51]

In a case concerning a 'disappeared' person (see Chapter 8), the Committee found that for ten months until his feared death in August 1976, Eduardo Bleier had been subjected to 'severe torture'.[52] The tortures seem to have included continued physical beatings and being buried alive.[53] Witnesses testified to his shrieks under torture,[54] but there are no further details of the physical assaults. The same is true in another case of a 'disappearance', that of Elena Quinteros.[55] There were witnesses to her cries, one of whom heard her say 'why didn't they kill me, why didn't they kill me?',[56] but no specific details were available. The Committee nevertheless found that she had been subjected to torture, though it apparently had no information as to its nature.[57] Indeed, the Committee is likely to be satisfied with very little in the way of specific information where death has occurred subsequently[58] or is found to have occurred in the context of a 'disappearance'.[59]

---

[48] Id., para. 2.3.
[49] *Sendic* v. *Uruguay* (63/1979), Report of the Human Rights Committee, *GAOR*, 37th Session, Supplement No. 40 (1982), Annex VIII, paras. 16(2) and 20.
[50] Id., para. 2.4.   [51] Id., para. 19.
[52] *Bleier* v. *Uruguay* (30/1978), Report of the Human Rights Committee, *supra* n. 49, Annex X, para. 13(4).
[53] Id., para. 2.3.   [54] Id., paras. 8.1, 10.1, and 10.2.
[55] *Quinteros* v. *Uruguay* (107/1981), Report of the Human Rights Committee, *GAOR*, 38th Session, Supplement No. 40 (1983), Annex XXII.
[56] Id., para. 1.5.   [57] Id., para. 12.3.

More detail is available in the case of the Argentinian pianist, Miguel Angel Estrella, detained in Uruguay in 1977. According to Estrella's unrefuted evidence he and three others were subjected to torture: 'The tortures consisted of electric shocks, beatings with rubber truncheons, punches and kicks, hanging us up with our hands tied behind our backs, pushing us into water until we were nearly asphyxiated, making us stand with legs apart and arms raised for up to 20 hours.'[60] The Human Rights Committee found that he had been 'subjected to severe physical . . . torture'.[61] As in the other cases, it did not specify whether each, all together, or just some of the above acts constituted torture. Nor did it need to; in all the cases the totality of the treatment meted out was of such extreme cruelty that it obviously amounted to torture.

Indeed, this agglomerative approach of the Committee could be said to represent something of a pattern where torture is an explicit part of the finding. Other cases have involved: 'beatings "electric prod", stringing up';[62] four days of incommunicado detention involving 'beatings, stringing up, asphyxiation, electric shocks and long periods of forced standing in the cold without anything to drink or eat';[63] being placed naked on a bed, subjected to electric shocks to various parts of the body, having buckets of dirty water thrown at one and suspension by the arms, over a week-long period;[64] ' "submarine", hanging and beatings', accompanied by threats that the parents would be killed unless there was a confession (there was);[65] fifteen days of 'physical beatings, electric shocks (*picana*) and immersion in water (*submarino*)';[66] and being strapped to a concrete floor, electric shocks being administered to the genitals and heavy beatings with a metal bar with barbed wire wrapped round the end.[67]

---

[58] See, e.g., *Miango* v. *Zaire* (194/1985), Report of the Human Rights Committee, *GAOR*, 43rd Session, Supp. No. 40 (1988), paras. 8.2, 10 (death caused by blows with a blunt instrument); and *Arhuacos* (*Villafañe Chaparro et al.*) v. *Colombia* (612/1995), UN doc. CCPR/C/60/D/612/1995 (1997), para. 8.4 (autopsy results had concluded, as indicated by the death certificate, that torture had occurred before death).

[59] See, e.g., *Bautista de Arellana* v. *Colombia* (563/1993), UN doc. CCPR/C/55/D/563/1993 (1995), para. 8.4 (a government administrative tribunal had already found that she had been tortured).

[60] *Estrella* v. *Uruguay* (74/1980), Report of the Human Rights Committee, *supra* n. 55, Annex XII, para. 1.6.

[61] Id., para. 8.3.

[62] *Arzuaga Gilboa* v. *Uruguay* (147/1983), Report of the Human Rights Committee, *GAOR*, 41st Session, Supp. No. 40, Annex VIII B, paras. 13.2, 14.

[63] *Berterretche Acosta* v. *Uruguay* (162/1983), Report of the Human Rights Committee, *GAOR*, 44th Session, Supp. No. 40 (1989), Annex X A, paras. 10.2(a)(b), 11.

[64] *Rodríguez* v. *Uruguay* (322/1988), Report of the Human Rights Committee, *GAOR*, 49th Session, Supp. No. 40 (1994), Annex IX B, paras. 2.1, 12.1.

[65] *Herrera Rubio* v. *Colombia* (161/1983), Report of the Human Rights Committee, *GAOR*, 43rd Session, Supp. No. 40 (1988), Annex VII B, paras. 10.2, 11.

[66] *Lafuente Peñarrieta et al.* v. *Bolivia* (176/1984), id., Annex VII C, paras. 1.3, 15.2, 16.

[67] *Kanana* v. *Zaire* (366/1989), loc. cit. *supra* n. 64, Annex IX J, paras. 2.1, 5.3.

The same is true for the European Court of Human Rights. For example, in *Aydın* v. *Turkey*, 'the accumulation of acts of physical and mental violence inflicted on the applicant and the especially cruel act of rape to which she was subjected amounted to torture'.[68] The violence other than rape consisted of her being 'blindfolded, beaten, stripped, placed inside a tyre and sprayed with high pressure water'.[69] In fact, in this case the Court did opt to separate out the rape question, affirming that '[i]ndeed the Court would have reached this conclusion on either of these grounds taken separately'.[70]

Thus, the Court, while maintaining a natural disinclination to classify every individual act of ill-treatment, took the opportunity, as requested by counsel for the applicant,[71] to confirm a view already widely shared that *rape* involves the infliction of pain and suffering at a level that puts it into the category of torture. As had been pointed out by Amnesty International in a written submission to the Court,[72] that position had already been taken by the Inter-American Commission on Human Rights,[73] the UN Special Rapporteur on Torture,[74] and the International Criminal Tribunal for the Former Yugoslavia.[75]

In one case, the Committee used language suggesting that each of the various sorts of assault described in one or other of the above cases can be a form of torture. Specifically it found that the victim had, over a nine-day interrogation upon arrest, been 'subjected to *various forms* of torture including beatings, electric shocks and mock executions'.[76] The beatings seem to have consisted of being 'stripped and subjected . . . to a hail of blows from cords, slaps and kicks' and of a technique known as 'the "typist" . . . which consists of squeezing the prisoner's fingers after pieces of wood have been placed between them'.[77]

Indeed, it is in the area of beatings and mental torture that problems of applying the texts arise. As will be seen below, beatings are often considered to fall short of torture. However, in a recent case, the European Commission of Human Rights concluded that numerous medically certified trauma on various parts of the body, consistent with the application of beatings

---

[68] *Aydın* v. *Turkey*, Judgment, 25 Sept. 1997, para. 86; for a case identifying a specific form of torture, see also *Aksoy* v. *Turkey*, European Court of Human Rights, Judgment, 18 Dec. 1996, para. 64 (' "Palestinian hanging", in other words, . . . he was stripped naked, with his arms tied together behind his back, and suspended by his arms').

[69] Id., para. 40.   [70] Id., para. 86.   [71] Id., para. 74.   [72] Id., para. 51.

[73] *Mejía* v. *Peru*, Report No. 5/96, Annual Report of the Inter-American Commission on Human Rights 1995, OAS Doc. OEA/Ser.L/V/II.9 Doc. rev. 7 (1996), 157, 186–7.

[74] UN docs. E/CN.4/1986/15, para. 119; E/CN.4/1992/SR.21, para. 35; E/CN.4/1995/34, para. 19.

[75] *Gragan Gagović and others*, 26 June 1996, Case No. IT-96-23-1.

[76] *Muteba* v. *Zaire* (124/1982), Report of the Human Rights Committee, *GAOR*, 39th Session, Supplement No. 40 (1984), Annex XIII, para. 10.2 (emphasis added); see also para. 12.

[77] Id., para. 8.2.

involving punches, kicks and blows with a truncheon and baseball bat, as denounced by the applicant, was proof of torture.[78]

The *Estrella* case also affords an example of the sort of *mental* suffering that may amount to 'torture'. Estrella complained of 'psychological torture' which:

> consisted chiefly in threats of torture or violence to relatives or friends, or of dispatch to Argentina to be executed, in threats of making us witness the torture of friends, and in inducing in us a state of hallucination in which we thought we could see and hear things which were not real. In my own case, their point of concentration was my hands. For hours upon end, they put me through a mock amputation with an electric saw, telling me, 'We are going to do the same to you as Victor Jara.'[79] Amongst the effects from which I suffered as a result were a loss of sensitivity in both arms and hands for eleven months, discomfort that still persists in the right thumb, and severe pain in the knees.[80]

In the view of the Human Rights Committee, he 'was subjected to severe . . . psychological torture, including the threat that . . . [his] hands would be cut off by an electric saw, in an effort to force him to admit subversive activities. This treatment had lasting effects, particularly to his arms and hands.'[81] The Committee does not indicate which of the other threats were of influence to its finding of psychological torture.

This finding is consistent with the view expressed by the European Commission of Human Rights in the *Greek* case that 'non-physical torture' was 'the infliction of mental suffering by creating a state of anguish and stress by means other than bodily assault'.[82] It reaffirmed this view in the *Northern Ireland* case, which is the case that offers the most vivid illustration of the difficulty of establishing the borderline between torture, on the one hand, and other prohibited ill-treatment, on the other.

The Northern Ireland case

Between 1972 and 1976 the organs of the European Convention on Human Rights were seized of a major interstate case brought by Ireland against the United Kingdom. The case was first heard by the European Commission of Human Rights and then went to the European Court of Human Rights. Ireland alleged that the United Kingdom had violated a number of provisions of the European Convention on Human Rights.[83] The most notable alleged

---

[78] *Selmouni* v. *France, supra* n. 41, paras. 19–27, 61, 67–70. Two Commission members (Mr Busuttil and M. Soyer), in separate concurring opinions, disagreed with the torture categorization, as it did not meet the *Northern Ireland* case standard of involving the 'special stigma' associated with torture, as to which, see below; see also Mr Herndl, *supra* n. 41.

[79] 'A well-known Chilean singer and guitarist who was found dead and with his hands completely smashed at the end of September 1973 in a stadium in Santiago de Chile.' From the decision of the Human Rights Committee, *supra* n. 60, footnote accompanying para. 1.6.

[80] Id., para. 1.6.   [81] Id., para. 8.3.

[82] 12 *Yearbook—The Greek Case* 461 (1967).   [83] 19 *Yearbook* 516–20 (1976).

violations related to the institution of administrative internment (detention without charge) and to torture or other ill-treatment of those suspected of politically motivated violence. The opinion of the Commission and the subsequent similar judgment of the European Court of Human Rights was that, under the circumstances, the administrative internment did not violate the Convention (see Chapter 11).

As for the allegations of torture and ill-treatment, there were two main categories of alleged violation of article 3 (prohibiting torture and inhuman or degrading treatment or punishment). One related to the use of physical violence against detainees in a number of places of detention. In respect of one such place, both the Commission and the Court held unanimously that the violence in question constituted inhuman treatment, but not torture; this will be referred to again below. The second category concerned the use of five interrogation techniques referred to by the Court as 'a form of "interrogation in depth"' sometimes involving '"disorientation" or "sensory deprivation" techniques', described as consisting of the following:

(a) wall-standing: forcing the detainees to remain for periods of some hours in a 'stress position', described by those who underwent it as being 'spreadeagled against the wall, with their fingers put high above the head against the wall, the legs spread apart and the feet back, causing them to stand on their toes with the weight of the body mainly on the fingers';
(b) hooding: putting a black or navy coloured bag over the detainees' heads and, at least initially, keeping it there all the time except during interrogation;
(c) subjection to noise: pending their interrogations, holding the detainees in a room where there was a continuous loud and hissing noise;
(d) deprivation of sleep: pending their interrogations, depriving the detainees of sleep;
(e) deprivation of food and drink: subjecting the detainees to a reduced diet during their stay at the centre and pending interrogations.[84]

The Commission had stated that the purpose of the 'five techniques' was 'to obtain information' from the persons subjected to them. The Court agreed, as previously noted, that 'their object was the extraction of confessions, the naming of others and/or information'.[85]

The combined use of the 'five techniques' was considered unanimously by the Commission to amount to torture.[86] The Commission had apparently been influenced by two factors: the first was the nature of sensory deprivation; it found that the intensity of 'the stress caused by . . . the combined application of methods which prevent the use of the senses' is such that it 'directly affects the personality physically and mentally'.[87] It regarded the practice as a 'sophisticated method to break or even eliminate the will'.[88] The second factor is that of *purpose*. The Commission considered that:

[84] *Ireland* v. *United Kingdom*, European Court of Human Rights, Series A, No. 25, 41, para. 96.
[85] Id., para. 167.   [86] *Supra* n. 83, 794.   [87] Id., 792.   [88] Ibid.

the systematic application of the techniques for the purpose of inducing a person to give information shows a clear resemblance to those methods of systematic torture which have been known over the ages . . . . [T]he Commission sees in them a modern system of torture falling into the same category as those systems which have been applied in previous times as a means of obtaining information and confessions.[89]

Thus, the crucial issues for the Commission were the use of sensory deprivation sufficient to break the will and the purpose of the five techniques, which was the obtaining of information.

The European Court of Human Rights (by a 13:4 vote) disagreed with the Commission, however, concluding that the use of the 'five techniques' did not amount to torture. But it did agree (by a 16:1 vote) that their use still constituted a practice of inhuman and degrading treatment.[90] It is not easy to understand the basis of the Court's disagreement with the Commission.

The Court did not challenge the Commission's concern with sensory deprivation or with the issue of purpose, but took another line of approach. For the Court, the distinction between torture and inhuman or degrading treatment 'derives principally from a difference in the intensity of the suffering inflicted'.[91] It continued:

The Court considers in fact that, whilst there exists on the one hand violence which is to be condemned both on moral grounds and also in most cases under the domestic law of the contracting States but which does not fall within Article 3 of the Convention, it appears on the other hand that it was the intention that the Convention, with its distinction between 'torture' and 'inhuman or degrading treatment', should by the first of these terms attach a special stigma to deliberate inhuman treatment causing very serious and cruel suffering.

Moreover, this seems to be the thinking lying behind Article 1 *in fine* of Resolution 3452 (XXX) adopted by the General Assembly of the United Nations on 9 December 1975, which declares: 'Torture constitutes an *aggravated* and deliberate form of cruel, inhuman or degrading treatment or punishment.'

Although the five techniques, as applied in combination, undoubtedly amounted to inhuman and degrading treatment, although their object was the extraction of confessions, the naming of others and/or information and although they were used systematically they did not occasion suffering of the particular intensity and cruelty implied by the word torture as so understood.[92]

This is unsatisfactory reasoning from an authoritative judicial body. The first two paragraphs in effect merely confirm that there is a distinction to be made between torture and other ill-treatment and suggest that the distinction is generated by a 'special stigma' attaching to torture, a notion that, although possibly true in general linguistic usage, has little or no legal implication. The invocation of General Assembly resolution 3452 (XXX) (the Declaration

---

[89] Id., para. 794.
[91] Id., para. 167.

[90] *Supra* n. 84, para. 168.
[92] Ibid.

against Torture) is hardly apposite, first because the distinction in the latter does not relate to 'stigma' but to particular legal consequences incurred by the separate limbs of the formula used for the prohibition and second because the Declaration was, in this respect, merely following, rather than adding to, the Commission's own doctrine in the *Greek* case. Accordingly, the Court's view seems to be reducible to the unexplained assertion that 'the five techniques . . . did not occasion suffering of the particular intensity and cruelty implied by the word torture as so understood'. The term 'as so understood' is presumably intended to convey that the Court is not merely voicing its own understanding but a general understanding of the meaning of the word torture. The Court's reasoning has led one commentator to speculate that the Court was influenced mainly by the notion that 'the common understanding of torture must be limited to mean extreme barbarity', thus excluding 'the systematically researched and applied subtle techniques of psychological manipulation which nullify the human will'.[93] If this be the case then the Court is playing into the hands of those governments of developing countries that consider the issue of torture to be a discriminatory one. That is, that accusations of torture made by developed countries which have devised more refined techniques to achieve the same purposes are hypocritically levelled at countries less technologically advanced.[94] It was no doubt such a consideration that provoked Amnesty International to react to the Court's decision with the statement: '[o]ur organization must continue to combat torture anywhere in the world and that task makes it impossible for us to follow the restrictive standard set by the Court'.[95]

In the same statement, Amnesty International referred to its March 1972 report of its own on-the-spot investigation in Belfast in December 1971, which stated that 'it is a form of torture to force a man to stand at the wall in the posture described for many hours in succession, in some cases for days on end, progressively exhausted and driven literally out of his mind by being subjected to continuing noise, and being deprived of food, sleep and even of light'.[96] This understanding of Amnesty International matched the unanimous similar finding of the Commission which, unlike the Court, had examined the facts in detail. Given this, together with the fact that the United Kingdom government did not even contest the finding before the Court, it might have been reasonable to have expected the Court, if only out of deference to the Commission, to explain the different basis of its own

---

[93] Spjut, 'Torture under the European Convention on Human Rights', 73 *AJIL* 267, 271 (1979).

[94] On 1 Oct. 1976, *Le Monde* (Paris) quoted the former Shah of Iran as saying: 'Why should we not employ the same methods as you Europeans. We have learned sophisticated methods of torture from you. You use psychological methods to extract the truth: we do the same.' As translated in *Amnesty International Briefing—Iran* (1976), 9.

[95] Amnesty International news release (AI Index NWS 02/04/78) 19 Jan. 1978.

[96] Ibid.

understanding. This is particularly the case since the Declaration against Torture invoked by the Court defines torture to include physical or mental pain or suffering. Would the Court not have agreed with the Human Rights Committee that the threats to Miguel Angel Estrella caused the requisite degree of mental suffering? It is to be hoped that the views of the four judges who dissented from the Court findings on this point will provide a sounder guide for authoritative understanding of what constitutes mental torture.[97] What is certain is that the notion of 'intensity of the suffering' is not susceptible of precise gradation and, in the case of mainly mental as opposed to physical suffering, there may be an area of uncertainty as to how the forum in question may assess the matter in any individual case. Its assessment may reflect, or purport to reflect, prevailing community notions of what suffering may be 'stigmatized' as torture.[98]

UN bodies, called upon to examine facts reminiscent of those obtaining in the *Northern Ireland* case, have had no difficulty in identifying the treatment in question as torture. The Human Rights Committee found torture to have occurred where the person was blindfolded (the eyes become inflamed and purulent), hooded, forced to sit up straight, day and night, for a week, in the presence of piercing shrieks apparently coming from others being tortured, and threatened with torture himself.[99]

An even closer analogy with the interrogation techniques considered in the *Northern Ireland* case is presented by those involved in the 'moderate degree of pressure, including physical pressure', approved by Israel's Landau Commission, 'to obtain information, such as that which would prevent imminent murder or would provide information on a terrorist organization'.[100] The techniques are secret, but have been presented as follows:

The following forms of pressure during interrogation appear so consistently (and have not been denied in judicial proceedings) that the Special Rapporteur assumes them to be sanctioned under the approved but secret interrogation practices: sitting in a very low chair or standing arced against a wall (possibly in alternation with each other); hands and/or legs tightly manacled; subjection to loud noise; sleep deprivation; hooding; being kept in cold air; violent shaking (an 'exceptional' measure, used against 8,000 persons according to the late Prime Minister Rabin in 1995). Each of these measures on its own may not provoke severe pain or suffering. Together—and they are frequently used in combination—they may be expected to induce precisely such pain or

[97] Judges Zekia, O'Donoghue, Evrigenis, and Matscher, *supra* n. 84, 97–100; 102–9; 136–8; 139–41, respectively; see Doswald-Beck, *supra* n. 13, 40–1; cf. Sudre, *supra* n. 13, 885–6.
[98] The Court has maintained its attachment to the notion of a special stigma recently, but not to rule out a finding of torture: *Aydın v. Turkey, supra* n. 68, para. 82.
[99] *Cariboni v. Uruguay* (159/1983), Report of the Human Rights Committee, *GAOR*, 43rd Session, Supplement No. 40 (1988), Annex VII A, paras. 4, 10. See also *Arhuacos v. Colombia, supra* n. 58, para. 8.5 (the Villafañe brothers were 'blindfolded and dunked in a canal').
[100] UN doc. E/CN.4/1997/7, para. 119.

suffering, especially if applied on a protracted basis of, say, several hours. In fact, they are sometimes apparently applied for days or even weeks on end.[101]

As indicated earlier, both the Committee against Torture and the Special Rapporteur on Torture have concluded that the techniques constitute torture. For the Committee, '[t]his conclusion is particularly evident where such methods of interrogation are used in combination, which appears to be the standard case'.[102] For the Special Rapporteur, under the circumstances described in the above quoted passage, 'they can only be described as torture, which is not surprising given their advanced purpose, namely, to elicit information, implicitly by breaking the will of the detainees to resist yielding up the desired information'.[103] While Israel is a state party to the International Covenant on Civil and Political Rights, the Human Rights Committee had not at the time of writing had occasion to deal with the matter, as Israel's first periodic report had been overdue since 2 January 1993.[104] The Israeli government would not be well advised to expect the Committee to take a different view.

Other cases

All the cases described above have involved findings of torture, albeit the European Court of Human Rights disagreed with the European Commission of Human Rights on this point in the *Northern Ireland* case. On a number of occasions, the European Commission of Human Rights and the Human Rights Committee have made findings that simply leave open the issue as to whether the treatment in question was either torture or other ill-treatment

While in the *Greek* case the European Commission of Human Rights found, it will be recalled, 'a practice of torture *and* ill-treatment' (emphasis added), consisting of 'the application of "falanga" or severe beatings of all parts of the body', it also found in respect of eleven individual cases that 'torture *or* ill-treatment' (emphasis added) had been inflicted.[105] Several of the prisoners concerned had been subjected to *falanga*; two to electric shock treatment; several others to mock execution. All had been subjected to severe beatings on various parts of the body. Some had been held in a confined space for days without food, water, or access to toilets. One had been permanently scarred, another lost her baby. The reasonable interpretation of its finding of torture or ill-treatment is that the Commission was required to assess a range of practices, some of which constituted torture, some other ill-treatment; but

---

[101] Id., para. 121.   [102] Loc. cit. *supra* n. 38, para. 257.
[103] *Supra* n. 100, para. 121.
[104] Report of the Human Rights Committee, Vol. I, *GAOR*, 52nd Session, Supplement No. 40 (1997), Annex III. It is understood that the report was submitted on 26 Feb. 1998 and was due for consideration at the Committee's 63rd session, July 1998.
[105] 12 *Yearbook—The Greek Case* 501 (1969).

96   *What Constitutes Torture?*

the Commission's report does not permit distinctions to be made as to which of the ill-treatments in the list was which.

The European Committee for the Prevention of Torture, which does not have a judicial or quasi-judicial role (see Chapter 5), has also tended to avoid drawing clear lines, generally distinguishing between 'torture and other forms of severe ill-treatment', on the one hand, and 'less severe forms of ill-treatment' on the other. The former category includes the sorts of practices found in the *Greek* case and in the cases in which the Human Rights Committee has also found torture.[106]

The language of the Human Rights Committee has been especially inconsistent in its many cases dealing with violations of article 7. Of the cases already discussed, where the Committee used the word 'torture' in arriving at its conclusions, two contained the word in conjunction with others. Thus, in the *Grille* case it found 'torture and inhuman treatment' while in the *López* case it found 'treatment (including torture)' in violation of article 7. In neither case did it indicate which, if any, of the cruelties to which the victims were subjected might *not* have amounted to torture.[107]

The practice of the Committee is probably best understood in the light of a statement in its 'general comment' on article 7: 'It may not be necessary to draw sharp distinctions between the various prohibited forms of treatment or punishment.'[108] In a number of cases it had merely used general terminology, finding 'violations of article 7', without at all specifying any further limb of the prohibition.[109] In the *Lanza* case, for example, it found such violations 'because of the treatment [Mr and Mrs Lanza] received'.[110] Mr Lanza had been subjected to 'electric shocks, hanging from his hands, immersion of his head in dirty water, near to asphyxia, "*submarino seco*"'; Mrs Lanza was tormented with '"*caballete*", "*submarino seco*", "*picano*" and "*plantón*"'.[111] In another instance, William Torres Ramírez was 'continuously kept blindfolded' and was subjected to 'lack of food and clothing' as well as to 'beatings, "*plantónes*"'[112]

---

[106] Spain, Council of Europe Doc. CPT/Inf.(96) 9 (1996), paras. 19–21. See also Greece, Doc. CPT/Inf.(94) 20 (1994), paras. 17–25; Bulgaria, Doc. CPT/Inf.(97) 1 (1997), paras. 17–27; Cyprus Doc. CPT/Inf.(97) 5 (1997), paras. 13–21; Romania, Doc. CPT/Inf.(98) 5 (1998), paras. 16–22. The same approach is reflected in the Committee's two public statements on Turkey: Doc. CPT/Inf.(93) 12 (1993), Appendix 4, and CPT/Inf.(96) 34 (1996).
[107] *Supra* nn. 45 and 47 respectively; see also *Cariboni* v. *Uruguay, supra* n. 99, para. 10; *Herrera Rubio* v. *Colombia, supra* n. 65, para. 11.
[108] *Supra* n. 3, para. 2.
[109] Thus, in one case the Committee said 'it could not find that there has not been any violation of article 7 . . .'. *Santullo* v. *Uruguay* (9/1977), Report of the Human Rights Committee, *GAOR*, 35th Session, Supplement No. 40 (1980), Annex V, para. 12.
[110] *Netto, Weismann and Lanza* v. *Uruguay* (8/1977), id., Annex VI. para. 16.
[111] Id., paras. 9 and 14; *caballete* means forcing prisoners to straddle iron or wooden bars; *submarino seco* means near suffocation, for example by placing a plastic bag over the head; *picano* means electric shocks from a cattle prod; *planton* means being forced to stand upright for long periods.
[112] *Torres Ramírez* v. *Uruguay* (4/1977), id., Annex VIII, para. 2.

and the Committee found an article 7 violation 'because of the treatment he received . . .'.[113] A third example is to be found in the *Conteris* case, where the Committee found a violation of article 7 because of the 'severe ill-treatment' the victim suffered.[114] The treatment, which succeeded in eliciting a 'confession' of politically motivated acts of violence, apparently included his being 'hanged by the wrists for 10 days and . . . subjected to burnings and repeated *submarino*—immersing the head of the victim in water fouled by blood, urine and vomit almost to the point of drowning'. In none of these cases does the information provided by the Committee suggest any basis on which the Committee might have wished to distinguish the treatment received by Mr and Mrs Lanza, Mr Torres Ramírez, and Mr Conteris from that in the cases where it specifically used the word 'torture'. Nor, given the nature of the treatment, could it not be described as torture.

In one case, the Committee decided that Ismael Weinberger had been the victim of a violation of article 7 'because of the severe treatment [he] received during the first 10 months of his detention'.[115] Except that the treatment was inflicted while 'he was most of the time kept blindfolded with his hands tied together',[116] the summary provided by the Committee does not specify what the nature of the ill-treatment was, although it states the results: 'serious physical injuries (one arm paralysed, leg injuries and infected eyes) and substantial loss of weight'.[117] The case seems to suggest that, even where details of the ill-treatment may not be clear, it will be deemed to be a violation of article 7 where its medical consequences are serious.

The last of this early group of what may be called 'unclassified cases' is the *Teti* case. Here the Committee found a violation of article 7 'because of the ill-treatment [to] which Mario Alberto Teti Izquierdo had been subjected'.[118] This finding was based on the following: 'After a visit of the International Red Cross to Libertad prison in February/March 1980, Mario Alberto Teti Izquierdo was subjected to physical attacks and threats of death.[[119]] In August 1980 he was moved to a punishment cell and held in solitary confinement. He was then in a very poor physiological and psychological state of health.'[120] Perhaps more information on the nature of the physical attacks would be necessary to make any reasoned assignment of the treatment to a

[113] Id., para. 18.

[114] *Conteris* v. *Uruguay* (139/1983), Report of the Human Rights Committee, *GAOR*, 40th Session, Supplement No. 40 (1985), Annex XI. para. 10.

[115] *Weinberger* v. *Uruguay* (28/1978), Report of the Human Rights Committee, *GAOR*, 36th Session, Supplement No. 40 (1981), Annex IX, at para. 16.

[116] Id., para. 12.   [117] Ibid.

[118] *Teti* v. *Uruguay* (73/1980), Report of the Human Rights Committee, *GAOR*, 37th Session, Supplement No. 40 (1982), Annex XVII, para. 9.

[119] He alleged that the treatment was inflicted because he had been held responsible for 'having instigated statements made by prisoners to the Red Cross mission': id., para. 1.4 (author's footnote).

[120] Id., para. 7.8.

particular place on the scale of article 7 prohibited treatment (though, after the *Estrella* case, serious death threats would presumably amount to torture).

More recent cases of a non-specific finding of a violation of article 7 suggest a reluctance to categorize where there is limited information available, or where the Committee may have doubts about the nature of the allegations. The former category is illustrated by an Ecuadorean case. Here, the individual was shackled and blindfolded, with 'haematomas and skin lesions . . . all over his body', but with nothing in the report indicating what acts had caused the wounds.[121] A Nicaraguan case seems to fall into the latter category. This case involved various interrogation sessions in different locations, with the ill-treatment consisting of handcuffing, being hung by a chain from the roof, beatings, kicking, being present when a group of which he was a member was executed. The Committee's apparent doubts are indicated by their request to the government to investigate 'the author's *allegations* of torture and ill-treatment'.[122]

The reports of the Special Rapporteur on Torture also take an approach that de-emphasizes the borderline between torture and other ill-treatment. The first incumbent wrote of a 'grey area' between the two categories[123] and, in practice, reports of the Special Rapporteur tend to include references to the kinds of practice that would be included in either category as they have come to be understood. For example, he has expressed concern about 'sleep deprivation and threats against detainees', as well as, 'beatings' in the Republic of Korea,[124] and about '[b]eating, kicking and punching' of 'asylum-seekers, or members of ethnic minorities' in Germany.[125]

To sum up on the issue of how severe or aggravated inhuman treatment has to be for it to amount to torture is virtually impossible. Only the organs of the European Convention on Human Rights have attempted to conceptualize the difference between the various limbs of the formula of the prohibition (torture, inhuman treatment, degrading treatment; cruel treatment does not arise as the word is not found in article 3 of the European Convention). If the distinctions that emerge from the practice of the Human Rights Committee are not merely accidental, it is hard to elicit any clear rationale from the earlier cases. This is even more so in respect of those cases where the European Commission of Human Rights (aspects of the *Greek* case) and the Human Rights Committee have used language which either leaves the question open

---

[121] *Terán Jijón* v. *Ecuador* (277/1988), Report of the Human Rights Committee, UN doc. A/47/40 (1992), Annex IX I, para. 5.2.

[122] *Zelaya Blanco* v. *Nicaragua* (328/1988), Report of the Human Rights Committee Vol. II, *GAOR*, 49th Session, Supplement No. 40 (1994), Annex IX C, paras. 6.5, 10.5, 12 (emphasis added). See also *Cañón Garcia* v. *Ecuador* (319/1988), loc. cit. *supra* n. 121, Annex IX M, paras. 2.2, 6.1 ('rubbing of salt water into his nasal passages', spending the night handcuffed to a table and chair).

[123] UN doc. E/CN.4/1986/15, paras. 23, 33.   [124] UN doc. E/CN.4/1998/38, para. 158.

[125] Id., para. 102.

or indicates a range of ill-treatment, only some of which may constitute torture. While there is 'a fixed core of settled meaning',[126] the specific content may vary with the ingenuity (or lack of it) of the particular tormentor.

Meanwhile, there could be some doubt as to the relevance of the element of aggravation, at least beyond the European regional level, since it has been dropped from the UN Convention against Torture (see Annex 2a and Chapter 2). Article 1 of the Convention speaks only of 'severe pain or suffering, whether physical or mental'. In this it follows the wording of article 1 of the Declaration against Torture. The original Swedish draft on which the present Convention is based had further emulated the Declaration against Torture, by providing that 'torture constitutes an aggravated and deliberate form of cruel, inhuman or degrading treatment or punishment'.[127] This formulation was from the beginning subjected to criticism on the grounds that it involved a reference to a concept ('cruel, inhuman or degrading treatment or punishment') that was itself undefined and might be differently interpreted in different parts of the world.[128] It was defended, however, by those who wished it to be made clear that torture was at the extreme end of a range of prohibited ill-treatment.[129] The latter group agreed to the deletion of the qualifying requirement of aggravation only when agreement was reached on a change of wording in another article (article 16) referring to 'other acts of cruel, inhuman or degrading treatment or punishment which do not constitute torture as defined in article 1'.[130] The clause 'which do not constitute torture' was amended to read 'which do not amount to torture'.[131] No doubt, states wishing to restrict the scope of application of the term 'torture' will invoke the idea of 'amounting to' in support of the view that torture is at the top end of a scale of rising disapproval. On the other hand, the group did not accept an alternative formulation which would have used the phrase 'which are not sufficient to constitute torture' instead of 'which do not amount to torture'.[132]

The working group's report is silent on the reasons for its preference, but the rejected version would certainly have more clearly achieved the object of those states wanting to preserve the element of aggravation. Presumably the agreed formulation was arrived at in an attempt to make further progress in drafting the Convention by way of compromise. As such the matter will be susceptible of further interpretation by organs charged with applying the terms of the Convention.

Finally, the approach of the Inter-American Convention against Torture (article 2(1)) should be noted, since it refrains from specifying any degree of

---

[126] O'Boyle, *supra* n. 25, 688.
[127] UN doc. E/CN.4/1285 (1978), article 1.
[128] UN doc. E/CN.4/L.1400 (1978), para. 12.
[129] UN doc. E/CN.4/L.1470 (1979), para. 22.
[130] UN docs.E/CN.4/1982/30/Add. 1; E/1982/12/Add. 1, paras. 7–8 and 43–5.
[131] Id., para. 45.
[132] Id., para. 44.

pain or suffering to be attained: it does not have to be severe, much less aggravated. Indeed certain acts are considered to fall within the definition of torture, 'even if they do not cause physical pain or mental anguish'. Specifically meant is 'the use of methods upon a person intended to obliterate the personality of the victim or to diminish his physical or mental capacities'. This is clearly aimed not only at sensory deprivation techniqꓴes (they do induce anxiety), but also at even more sophisticated techniques, especially chemical, of mind control.

WHO COMMITS TORTURE?

It remains only to consider one further element in the definition of torture that it has not fallen to any of the bodies charged with applying the prohibition to examine. As was noted in Chapter 1, the Declaration against Torture provides that torture must be 'inflicted by or at the instigation of a public official' (article 1). The UN Convention against Torture provides that it must be 'inflicted by *or at the instigation of or with the consent or acquiescence of* a public official *or person acting in an official capacity*' (article 18—emphasis added). The effect of such language is to suggest that the prohibition is not concerned with private acts of cruelty: international concern arises only where cruelty has official sanction. Meanwhile, in so far as the language of the UN Convention may now be taken to represent a settled position—and it is submitted that it does—government officials at all levels may be held responsible if they fail to act to stop torture where it occurs. Failure so to act could well be interpreted at least as acquiescence. Indeed, as if to ensure that any involvement in torture should be caught, article 4(1) of the Convention provides that both an 'attempt to commit torture' and 'an act . . . which constitutes complicity or participation in torture' are required to be considered criminal offences.[133]

There can therefore be no doubt that by this combination of language the Convention aims to establish the responsibility of those public officials who turn a blind eye to atrocities committed against opponents of the government in power by unofficial groups, as well as by the authorities. While the membership of such unofficial groups (often known by terms such as 'death squads' or 'paramilitary units') is frequently composed of agents of the security forces, this will not always be the case. Although it is to be welcomed that the Convention is alert to the subterfuge, in practice there may well be prob-

[133] Note further the observation of the Human Rights Committee, in its general comment 7(16) on Covenant article 7, that 'it is also the duty of public authorities to ensure protection by the law against such treatment even when committed by persons acting outside or without any official authority' (*supra* n. 3) and the similar language in general comment 20(44) (*supra* n. 3, para. 2); see Villán Durán, 'La Convención contra la Tortura y su contribución a la definición del derecho a la integridad física y moral en el derecho internacional', *Revista española de derecho internacional* (1985), no. 2, 377, 395–6.

lems in specific instances of demonstrating that a particular official has evinced the necessary consent or acquiescence.

Using different language, the OAS Convention against Torture takes a similar approach (article 3). The decision to restrict the offence to acts committed by, or within the scope of authority of, a public official was taken only on the final adoption of the text by the OAS General Assembly. Up to that point there had been no agreement on such a restriction.[134]

WHAT IS 'OTHER PROHIBITED ILL-TREATMENT'?

It now remains to determine what practices are covered by the second limb of the formula of prohibition. In some cases 'inhuman treatment' has been found: the five techniques of interrogation in depth used in Northern Ireland were, as has been seen, held by the European Court of Human Rights to constitute inhuman treatment, but not torture. Given that the European Commission of Human Rights had unanimously considered the techniques to constitute torture, they certainly represent the frontier beyond which categorization of torture is ineluctable. In other words, the practice of the five techniques will serve as an illustration of the upper limit of the formula.

In the same case, the European Court of Human Rights agreed with the Commission that certain other incidences of physical brutality amounted to inhuman treatment. Specifically, it held unanimously that 'there existed at Palace Barracks in the autumn of 1971 a practice of inhuman treatment . . . in breach of Article 3'.[135] The practices in question seem to have ranged from 'comparatively trivial beatings' leading in one case to a perforated eardrum and some minor bruising[136] to being 'made to stand spreadeagled against a wall' and being 'severely beaten or otherwise physically ill-treated', resulting in contusions and bruising.[137] In one case medical evidence disclosed 'substantial' injuries; in another it revealed the injuries to be 'massive'.[138] As noted above, the majority view in the Court was that the practices just described did not amount to torture, since 'the severity of the suffering that they were capable of causing did not attain the particular level inherent in the notion of torture as understood by the Court'.[139] Three members of the Court dissented from this opinion, however, and felt that the practices should have been categorized as torture. Once again, therefore, it is evident that some behaviour defined by the second limb of the prohibition formula comes very close to that covered by the first limb, torture. Further, except in terms of the duration of the brutality, it is difficult to distinguish the treatment described

---

[134] OEA/Ser. G CP/doc. 1622/85.
[136] Id., paras. 115 and 174.
[138] Id., paras. 111 and 174.

[135] *Supra* nn. 84, 94.
[137] Id., paras. 110 and 174.
[139] Id., para. 174.

above from that meted out to Professor Massera,[140] to Raul Sendic,[141] or to the Villafañe brothers in the *Arhuacos* case,[142] which was considered by the Human Rights Committee to be torture.

In other cases too, the European Court of Human Rights found inhuman and degrading treatment. In *Tomasi* v. *France*, beatings on various parts of the body leaving medically certified trauma were in that category,[143] as were blows leading to bruises on the inside and outside of the right arm in *Ribitsch* v. *Austria*.[144] In both cases, the applicant had claimed that the treatment was inhuman and degrading.[145] These cases would seem to confirm that beatings alone may not constitute torture.[146] On the other hand, in neither case did the applicant maintain that the treatment amounted to torture. Moreover, as noted above, the European Commission of Human Rights did find sustained beatings to be torture in *Selmouni* v. *France*.[147] If the Court were to concur with the Commission majority in such a finding, it could perhaps be reconciled with its earlier findings on the basis of the use of implements to inflict the beatings. Otherwise, it may have to be concluded that any serious infliction of physical pain leaving visible evidence now constitutes torture, at least at the European level. In any event, it is evident that the division between torture and the upper limits of other ill-treatment is not precise.

In the *Bouton* case, the Human Rights Committee found a violation of article 7 of the Covenant specifically 'on the basis of evidence of inhuman and degrading treatment' of the victim.[148] This evidence consisted, *inter alia*, of the statement that 'she was forced to stand for 35 hours, with minor interruptions; that her wrists were bound with a strip of coarse cloth which hurt her and that her eyes were continuously kept bandaged. During day and night she could hear the cries of other detainees being tortured. During interrogation she was allegedly threatened with "more effective ways than conventional torture to make her talk".'[149] This is the only case of this sort (that is, at the interrogation phase, before conviction and sentence) where the Committee did not either invoke torture explicitly or use only general terminology about 'treatment' or 'ill-treatment'. If this exceptional use of the terms 'inhuman and degrading treatment' is significant, then it provides further

---

[140] *Supra* n. 42 and accompanying text.   [141] *Supra* n. 49 and accompanying text.
[142] *Supra* n. 99.   [143] *Supra*, n. 32, paras. 108, 115.
[144] Judgment, 4 Dec. 1995, paras. 29, 39.   [145] *Tomasi*, para. 70; *Ribitsch*, para. 24.
[146] The European Committee for the Prevention of Torture seems to follow this approach; see, for example, Spain, Council of Europe Doc. CPT/Inf.(96) 9 (1996), para. 21: suspects allegedly 'slapped, punched, kicked or verbally abused', described as 'less severe forms of ill-treatment', as opposed to 'torture and severe ill-treatment', as to which, see *supra* n. 73 and accompanying text. Also, United Kingdom (Northern Ireland), Council of Europe Doc. CPT/Inf.(94) 17 (1994), paras. 31–3.
[147] *Supra*, n. 78 and accompanying text.
[148] *Bouton* v. *Uruguay* (37 1978), Report of the Human Rights Committee, *supra* n. 47, Annex XIV, para.13.
[149] Id., para. 2.3.

guidance as to the range of treatment covered by the second limb of the formula. In this case the ill-treatment of the victim, although deplorable, was not as severe as that in the cases referred to above, where the Committee used the complete formula and therefore permitted possible categorization of the ill-treatment concerned as torture. As with the Palace Barracks cases, the relatively limited duration of the treatment might have been relevant to the omission of 'torture' from the finding.

In one other case, apart from cases raising the general issue of conditions of detention (see Chapter 9), the Committee explicitly found 'inhuman treatment'. This was the case of Etienne Tshisekedi, then Zaïrean opposition leader, who was 'deprived of food and drink for four days after his arrest . . . and was subsequently kept interned under unacceptable sanitary conditions'.[150] While the language is not clear, it may perhaps be assumed that the use of the term is applicable to each of the situations to which it applies. It is noteworthy that Mr Tshisekedi was not questioned during the four-day period after arrest. Certainly four days deprivation of liquid could involve very severe suffering indeed. Of course, the purposive element required for torture was not evident.

Findings of treatment of prisoners falling specifically within the concept of degrading treatment are rare.[151] A recent Human Rights Committee case probably represents an appropriate use of the term. In *Polay Campos* v. *Peru*, the person was displayed to the press in a cage. For the Committee this was degrading treatment.[152] It was clearly meant to humiliate and demean, but, without the infliction of physical pain, the expected mental distress did not perhaps have the intensity of other examples that have been encountered. The purposive element required for torture was clearly not manifest.

Apart from this case, the scope of the notion is a matter for speculation. Some limited guidance may be found from less recent decisions of the European Commission and Court of Human Rights which have held certain practices not to be degrading. In the *Greek* case, the Commission had defined degrading treatment of a person as that which 'grossly humiliates him before others or drives him to act against his will or conscience'.[153] In that case there was evidence that some of the prisoners had received 'slaps and blows during, or shortly after, their arrest'.[154] The Commission noted that most detainees had 'tolerated . . . and even taken for granted' what it called 'a

---

[150] *Birindwa and Tshisekedi* v. *Zaire* (241 and 242/1987), Report of the Human Rights Committee, Vol. II, *GAOR*, 45th Session, Supplement No. 40 (1990), Annex I, para. 13(b).

[151] There have, however, been findings of degrading treatment not related to prisoners: see, for example, the *East African Asians* case, 3 EHRR 76 (1973) (refusal to permit British passport holders from East Africa to enter the United Kingdom). There have also been findings of degrading punishment: see, for example, the *Tyrer* case, *supra* n. 20 (corporal punishment).

[152] *Polay Campos* v. *Peru* (577/1994), UN doc. CCPR/C/61/D/577/1994 (1998), para. 8.5.

[153] 12 *Yearbook—The Greek Case* 180 (1969).

[154] Id., 501, para. 11 and accompanying footnote.

certain roughness of treatment . . . by both police and military authorities. . . . Such roughness may take the form of slaps and blows of the hand on the head or face.'[155] Denying that such treatment would fall within the prohibition of article 3, the Commission observed that 'this underlines the fact that the point up to which prisoners and the public may accept physical violence as being neither cruel nor excessive, varies between different societies and even between different sections of them'. This notion that a sort of cultural relativity may enter into the determination of what acts may amount to degrading treatment, and its implication of variability in the lower threshold of the prohibition of torture or other ill-treatment, is at first sight disturbing. Looked at more closely, however, it is to some extent inevitable. It has been pointed out, for example, that forcing a devout Muslim to fall to his knees and kiss the cross might well fall within the prohibition, whereas similar behaviour towards prisoners who have no profound philosophical or religious aversion to the procedure would have no comparable significance.[156] The point must be made, of course, that to be an offence against the prohibition an act must be one which the *victim* finds, or may be expected to find, degrading, and although there may be great variability in the nature of such acts, the criterion of degradation remains constant. Similarly, the criteria of humiliation and assault on will or conscience remain universal: but it will be a question of fact as to what acts may fall within the criteria. In the *Northern Ireland* case the Commission reaffirmed the line it had articulated in the *Greek* case,[157] and when the *Northern Ireland* case reached the European Court of Human Rights the Court confirmed that the assessment of the minimum level of severity for treatment to be caught by article 3 'is, in the nature of things, relative: it depends on all the circumstances of the case, such as the duration of the treatment, its physical or mental effects and, in some cases. the sex, age and state of health of the victim, etc.'.[158] It is essential, however, that the concept of relativity be used with extreme caution, since heavy reliance upon it could lead to a propensity to excuse cruelties on the grounds that they are socially acceptable in the given context. (One fears, for example, the government which argues tradition, or popular acceptance, in its defence of practices generally held to be cruel. Indeed one must also have regard to the propensity of officials to become degraded by the treatment they inflict on those in their charge.) In this respect, the universal criterion, noted above, of acceptability or otherwise to the victim, should always be a factor.[159]

---

[155] Id., 501 (1969).
[156] Amnesty International, *supra* n. 15,36.   [157] 19 *Yearbook* 748 (1976).
[158] *Supra* n. 84, para. 162. According to Sudre, *supra* n. 13, 842–8 and 885–6, the political context (stable situation/terrorism, dictatorship/democracy, and so on) is also relevant to establishing the threshold and the borderlines between the prohibited categories; fortunately neither the Commission's nor the Court's words sustain this thesis.
[159] Albeit not the only factor; it must also be objectively reasonable to assume that the treatment in question would have a serious adverse effect on the subject. See Duffy, *supra* n. 13, 319.

In other cases the early practice of the European Commission and Court of Human Rights disclosed a reluctance to challenge some serious abuses of prisoners and yet it is difficult to elicit clear reasons for their decisions. Thus, in the *Northern Ireland* case the Commission referred to an earlier case concerning police interrogation[160] in which it 'found that some psychological pressure applied to an applicant suspected of murder by reason of the remark that he would not leave the police station until the police knew everything could not in any way be described as exerting undue pressure amounting to inhuman or degrading treatment'.[161] It went on to deal with the facts of the *Northern Ireland* case itself: at Ballykinler Regional Police Holding Centre in 1971 prisoners were made to do certain exercises, involving the adoption of various strenuous postures on the floor; a United Kingdom court had considered the treatment 'harsh, deliberate and even illegal'.[162] The Commission considered that the exercises 'certainly caused considerable strain and hardship on the prisoners, particularly elderly persons and those in poor physical condition. Moreover, they were felt by the prisoners to be measures designed to oppress and degrade them.[163] However, even though the exercises accompanied interrogation throughout day and night,[164] the Commission was unable to determine 'the exact length of time during which the exercises were performed nor . . . the degree of compulsion used to enforce them'.[165] It concluded unanimously that no violation of article 3 was involved.[166] The European Court of Human Rights confirmed the Commission's view.[167] Describing the exercises as 'irksome and painful', it considered them discreditable and reprehensible but not an infringement of article 3.[168] By contrast, it may perhaps be speculated that a body applying the definition of torture contained in article 2(1) of the OAS Convention against Torture (it does not lay down any requisite level of intensity of pain or suffering) might have found such treatment to be covered by that definition.

Again, as with the borderline between torture and inhuman treatment, the borderline between 'other ill-treatment' and treatment falling outside the prohibition altogether cannot be precisely drawn. An element of relativity may arise from the subjective response of the victim to the treatment, and there will inevitably be an element of subjectivity in the willingness of the forum called upon to apply the prohibition to find a violation of it. The European Commission of Human Rights has in the past been particularly reluctant in this regard and this will also have been seen to be the case in respect of its approach to conditions of detention considered in Chapter 9. In this respect,

---

[160] Commission Application No. 4771/71, 42 Collection of Decisions, 22.
[161] 19 *Yearbook* 750 (1976).   [162] Id., 928.
[163] Ibid.   [164] Id., 876 and 882.
[165] Id., 928. This was probably because they did not have the confidence in the testimony of the one case they examined.
[166] Id., 928–30 and 946.   [167] *Supra* n. 84, 95.   [168] Id., paras. 180–1.

it may be hoped that in the future the Commission and other relevant bodies will pay heed to the statement found in the official General Assembly commentary to the UN Code of Conduct for Law Enforcement Officials (see Chapter 12) which states: 'The term "cruel, inhuman or degrading treatment or punishment" has not been defined by the General Assembly but should be interpreted so as to extend the widest possible protection against abuses, whether physical or mental.'

The foregoing has not attempted to give an exhaustive picture of the prohibition of torture or other ill-treatment. Rather it has sought to elucidate the nature of the prohibition, especially in so far as it applies to the period after initial arrest or capture. (This is traditionally the period when the arresting or detaining authorities are most prone to commit serious abuses.) Most of the practices discussed in subsequent chapters will also be found to raise questions of compatibility with the prohibition. This will be more particularly the case in respect of Chapter 9 (conditions of detention) and Chapter 10 (corporal punishment). These latter chapters will consider the limits on the punishments to which convicted offenders may be sentenced.

The Legal Consequences of Torture and Other Ill-treatment

THE LEGAL CONSEQUENCES OF TORTURE

When a violation of international law occurs, there are consequences for the government that has committed it and possibly also for individuals, usually agents of the government, who may be personally liable. The responsibility of the government attaches to the state itself and is often known as 'state responsibility'.[1] This state responsibility for acts of torture will be examined first, followed by consideration of the issue of individual responsibility. The legal consequences for other prohibited ill-treatment will then be similarly examined.

STATE RESPONSIBILITY FOR TORTURE

It is clear that when a state breaches its obligations under international law, its responsibility is engaged; it is less clear just how that responsibility operates. There have been attempts to find municipal law analogies to describe the juridical nature of the responsibility under international law: some have likened it to the English law of tort (non-contractual civil obligation); others prefer the analogy of contract law, especially in the case of non-compliance with treaties. Another approach, recognizing the essentially public law character of international law, is that which considers a violation of international law to be a 'delict', understood as a general offence under public law.[2]

---

[1] See Meron, *Human Rights and Humanitarian Norms as Customary Law* (1989), 146–245; also Kamminga, *Interstate Accountability for Violations of Human Rights* (1992). Furthermore, two studies on related topics, each yielding a set of proposed principles, have been undertaken under the auspices of the Sub-Commission on Prevention of Discrimination and Protection of Minorities: 'Study Concerning the Right to Restitution, Compensation and Rehabilitation for Victims of Gross Violations of Human Rights and Fundamental Freedoms—Final Report Submitted by Mr Theo Van Boven, Special Rapporteur' (UN doc. E/CN.4/Sub.2/1993/8; the latest version of the draft 'basic principles', currently under consideration by the Commission on Human Rights (see its resolution 1998/43, 17 Apr. 1998), is contained in UN doc. E/CN.4/1997/104, Appendix (hereinafter 'Van Boven principles'); 'Question of the Impunity of Perpetrators of Human Rights Violations (Civil and Political)—Revised Final Report Prepared by Mr Joinet' (UN doc. E/CN.4/Sub.2/1997/20/Rev.1; the 'set of principles', also currently under consideration by the Commission on Human Rights (see its resolution 1998/53, 17 Apr. 1998), is contained in Annex II to the Revised Final Report (hereinafter 'Joinet principles').

[2] See, on terminology, Brownlie, *Principles of Public International Law* (4th edn., 1990), 433–4 and 509.

Recently, the International Law Commission (ILC) has been propounding a dual approach: it categorizes breaches of an international obligation generally as 'internationally wrongful acts' which it calls 'international delicts',[3] and then considers certain particularly grave 'internationally wrongful acts' to be crimes.[4] Thus, the Commission follows the delictual approach in general, but adds a further category of international crime. The latter would include 'a serious breach on a widespread scale of an international obligation of essential importance for safeguarding the human being, such as those prohibiting slavery, genocide and apartheid'.[5] This formulation could reasonably be understood to cover systematic torture of prisoners.[6] The Commission has also adopted articles specifying the consequences of internationally wrongful acts in general, and of international crimes in particular.[7]

Traditionally, and the ILC approach generally confirms it, the international law of state responsibility envisages reparation for the wrongful act. The reparation will usually take the form of restitution and/or compensation for damage or loss. Other types of reparation are also known, sometimes under the general rubric of 'satisfaction'. They include, in appropriate cases, and where there is an adjudication, a declaration by the Court or tribunal that the violation has occurred, a formal acknowledgement and/or apology by the state committing the wrong, the punishment of the individuals concerned, and the taking of measures to prevent a recurrence of the harm.[8] But this traditional international law approach is not automatically applicable to all human rights violations. This is because, historically, the wrong in question

---

[3] *Yearbook of the International Law Commission* (1976), vol. ii, part 2 (A/CN.4/SER.A/1976/ Add. 1 (Part 2)), Chapter III B; Draft Articles on State Responsibility, article 19. The International Law Commission is a body of 34 lawyers appointed by the General Assembly to assist it in its task of 'encouraging the progressive development of international law and its codification'. (UN Charter, article 13 (I) (a).) A number of treaties have been adopted by diplomatic conferences convened by the General Assembly on the basis of texts drafted by the Commission.

[4] Ibid.   [5] Ibid.

[6] See, for example, id., Commentary to article 19, para. 34; Meron, *supra* note 1, 208–15.

[7] In addition to the legal consequences for internationally wrongful acts in general (see below), draft article 53 provides: 'an international crime committed by a State entails an obligation for every other State: (a) not to recognize as legal the situation created by such crime; (b) not to render aid or assistance to the State which has committed the crime in maintaining the situation so created; (c) to cooperate with other States in carrying out the obligations in sub-paragraphs (a) and (b); and (d) to cooperate with other States in the application of measures designed to eliminate the consequences of the crime.' Moreover, in respect of international crimes, draft article 52 provides for the inapplicability of certain restrictions on restitution for internationally wrongful acts in general (it should not be disproportionately burdensome as compared with compensation: draft article 43 (c); and should not jeopardize the political independence and economic stability of the offending state, unless the aggrieved state would otherwise be similarly jeopardized: draft article 43 (d)) and on the right to satisfaction (demands that would impair the dignity of the offending state are not justified: draft article 45 (3)): Report of the International Law Commission, *GAOR*, 51st Session, Supplement No. 10 (1996), chapter 3. In other words, there would appear to be no legal limit to the onerousness of measures of restitution and satisfaction that may be owed as a result of the commission of international crimes.

[8] Ibid., draft articles 43–6.

has generally been one committed by one state to the detriment of another. Even where the wrong involved injury to individuals (normally nationals of the claimant state) it was to the claimant state, rather than to individuals, that reparation was to be made. In the case of a violation of the newer branch of international law concerned with human rights, the obligation is multilateral, with no single state having an interest in material reparation, while, in the absence of special agreement (between states), the individual victim has no standing to bring an international claim.

International legal instruments tend to require an 'effective remedy' from the national authorities in case of a human rights violation,[9] but there is no explicit general reference as to what such a remedy may consist of. In any case, the mode of reparation deemed appropriate will vary according to both the nature of the wrongful act and its specific circumstances. Financial compensation will not always be the appropriate remedy and, where it is, its measure may be uncertain. As Professor Higgins, as she then was, has noted, 'it is therefore perhaps not surprising that these underlying questions seem to remain unclear and uncertain in the leading international instruments on the protection of human rights'.[10] Those instruments that establish courts capable of giving binding decisions envisage the award of 'just satisfaction' or 'fair compensation';[11] those that do not provide for courts are silent on the issue. Certain articles of the International Covenant on Civil and Political Rights specifically envisage a right to compensation in particular circumstances,[12] but strangely these do not include the non-derogable articles of which the prohibition against torture and other ill-treatment is one. This has not, however, prevented the Human Rights Committee from expressing the view that compensation is due in respect of violations of provisions other than those expressly envisaging compensation. Thus, having found that Miguel Angel Estrella had been subjected to torture, it expressed the view that the state party 'is under an obligation to provide the victim with effective remedies, including compensation for the violations he has suffered and to take steps to ensure that similar violations do not occur in the future'.[13] In similar cases, the Inter-American Commission on Human Rights also calls for investigation of the facts, submission of those responsible to 'appropriate judicial processes', and redress, including payment of 'adequate and fair

---

[9] See, for example, International Covenant on Civil and Political Rights, article 2(3)(a).

[10] Higgins, 'Damages for Violations of One's Human Rights', in Simms (ed.), *Explorations in Ethics and International Relations* (1981), 45, 46.

[11] European Convention on Human Rights, article 50 ('just satisfaction'): American Convention on Human Rights, article 63 ('fair compensation').

[12] Article 9 ('unlawful arrest or detention') and article 14 (punishment as a result of 'miscarriage of justice').

[13] *Estrella* v. *Uruguay* (74/1980), Report of the Human Rights Committee, *GAOR*, 38th Session, Supplement No. 40 (1983), Annex XII, para. 11. For the facts, see Chapter 3.

compensation'.[14] The European Commission of Human Rights restricts itself even further, leaving all questions on reparation to be dealt with by the European Court of Human Rights in appropriate cases.[15] Further, the Court's own policy is to leave it to the state in question to give effect to its awards, except in so far as the Court may itself be willing to award compensation as 'just satisfaction'.[16] It is difficult to draw firm conclusions from the practices just outlined, since these appear to be simply reflections of what each body considers to be within its competence, rather than substantive assessments of what reparation flows, as a matter of law, from a violation of the provisions of the instrument in question. Nevertheless, there seems to be a common denominator to the extent that compensation is deemed due for certain human rights violations, even where not specifically signalled in the text of the instrument concerned, and that violations involving torture or other ill-treatment do fall within this category.

In fact, there is compelling evidence that both conventional and general international law require that a state where torture has been, or appears to have been, committed is required to: 1. investigate the matter, 2. bring the perpetrators to justice, probably through the institution of criminal proceedings, 3. compensate the victims, and 4. take measures to prevent a recurrence of the problem. Moreover, where a person is threatened with expulsion or extradition to a country where there is a certain risk that the person will be tortured, then there is an obligation on the custodial state not to send the person to the latter country. Each of these obligations will be briefly discussed.

Investigation

In each of its general comments on article 7 of the Covenant, which it reads together with article 2 (right to an effective remedy), the Human Rights Committee has affirmed that '[c]omplaints about ill-treatment must be investigated effectively by competent authorities'.[17] Indeed, the Committee found

---

[14] For example, Resolution no. 31/96, case 10,526 (Guatemala), 16 Oct. 1996: Organization of American States, *Annual Report of the Inter-American Commission on Human Rights, 1996* (OEA/Ser.L/V/II.95, Doc. 7 rev., 1997), 332, 369.

[15] However, the Commission will be influenced, especially in considering friendly settlements under article 28(b) of the European Convention, by government actions to change potentially offending laws and practices. Also, as my University of Essex colleague, Professor Kevin Boyle, drew to my attention, in a case where the Commission finds a violation and which is not referred to the Court, the Committee of Ministers of the Council of Europe may request the Commission to advise it on the question of compensation.

[16] Thus, in the *Northern Ireland* case, where the complainant government indicated that it was not seeking compensation for any individual person, the European Court of Human Rights considered that it was not necessary to apply article 50 (on just satisfaction): *Ireland v. United Kingdom*, European Court of Human Rights, Series A, No. 25, 94–5, paras. 245–6.

[17] General comment 7(16), Report of the Human Rights Committee, *GAOR*, 37th Session, Supplement No. 40 (1982), Annex V, p. 94, para. 1; General comment 20/44, id., 47th Session, Supplement No. 40 (1992), Annex VI A, para. 14 (further stating that the investigation must be conducted 'promptly and impartially').

a violation of article 7, read together with article 2, in respect of an amnesty-barred investigation.[18] The absence of an investigation has been found to be a constituent of a violation of the corresponding articles of the European and American Conventions by their respective Courts.[19] Both the UN and OAS Conventions against Torture require investigation even in the absence of a complaint from the victim.[20]

The consistency of practices under the terms of the treaties, to one or more of which the majority of the countries of the world are parties, could of itself suggest that general international law expects the same. Certainly the UN Declaration against Torture, on which the UN Convention was based, requires investigation even in the absence of a formal complaint.[21] The UN Special Rapporteur on Torture (see chapter 5) also insists on investigation in his dialogue with governments, as well as considering it as a formal require-ment.[22] The UN Commission on Human Rights has affirmed that position.[23]

Bringing to justice

In its first general comment on Covenant article 7, the Human Rights Committee, reading the article together with article 2, stated that 'those found guilty must be held responsible'.[24] The language implies a duty to establish legal or disciplinary, albeit not necessarily criminal, liability for violations of article 7. The absence of explicit criminal liability may be explained by the fact that not every violation of article 7, for example degrading punishments inflicted according to law, should necessarily be considered as requiring penal sanction for those carrying out the punishment; indeed, no national law could contemplate such a course in respect of those who are complying with that very law. On the other hand, the general comment does envisage the relevance of the criminal law, when it states that 'it is not sufficient for the implementation of this article to prohibit such treatment or punishment or to make it a crime',[25] thus implying that prohibition and criminalization are just the starting points.

---

[18] *Rodríguez* v. *Uruguay* (487/1992), Report of the Human Rights Committee Vol. II, *GAOR*, 49th Session, Supplement No. 40 (1994), Annex X B.

[19] *Aksoy* v. *Turkey* (100/1995/606/694), Judgment, 19 Dec. 1996, finding, *inter alia*, torture in violation of European Convention article 3 and non-investigation in violation of article 13 (right to effective remedy), and citing the UN Torture Convention article 13 requiring the investigation to be 'prompt and impartial': para. 98; and to the same effect *Aydın* v. *Turkey* (57/1996/676/866), Judgment, 27 Sept. 1997, para. 103; I/A Court HR, *Velásquez Rodríguez Case, Judgment of 29 July 1988*, Ser. C No. 4 (case of 'disappearance' and ill-treatment violating rights to life (art. 4), personal liberty and security (art. 7), and humane treatment (art. 5), and, in respect of non-inves-tigation, the same rights read together with art. 1(1) (duty to respect rights)): paras. 159–88, 194.

[20] Annex 2(a), art. 13 and Annex 2(b), art. 8.   [21] Annex 1, art. 9.

[22] UN doc. E/CN.4/1995/34, para. 926(g).

[23] Res. 1997/38, 11 Apr. 1997, para. 10; see also Van Boven principles, principle 2, and Joinet principles, principles 1–18 (*supra* n. 1).

[24] General comment, *supra* n. 17, para. 1. See, also (second) General comment 20/44, id., para. 13.

[25] Id., paras. 1 and 8 respectively.

The second general comment goes further:

The Committee has noted that some States have granted amnesty in respect of acts of torture. Amnesties are generally incompatible with the duty of States to investigate such acts; to guarantee freedom from such acts within their jurisdiction; and to ensure that they do not occur in the future. States may not deprive individuals of the right to an effective remedy, including compensation and such full rehabilitation as may be possible.[26]

Since many such amnesties are aimed at exempting perpetrators of torture from criminal liability, this statement could be taken as suggesting that, at least 'generally', such amnesties are incompatible with the state's obligations under the Covenant. On the other hand, the absence of a specific reference to an obligation to prosecute as one of the duties of states undermined by such amnesties is notable, unless that obligation is subsumed under the notions of obligation 'to guarantee freedom from [acts of torture]' and 'to ensure that they do not occur in the future'. In individual cases dealt with under the (first) Optional Protocol to the Covenant, the Committee has generally been reluctant to call for the punishment of the perpetrators of torture or other human rights violations, since individuals do not, it maintains, have a right to require that a state prosecute another person.[27] However, in *Rodríguez* v. *Uruguay*, it edged away from this position. Dealing, in 1994, with the Uruguayan amnesty law (of the sort referred to in its general comment above), it held that the applicant, a torture victim, was entitled to an effective remedy. It urged the state party:

to take effective measures (a) to carry out an official investigation into the author's allegations of torture, in order to identify the persons responsible for torture and ill-treatment and to enable the author to seek civil redress; (b) to grant appropriate compensation to Mr Rodríguez; and (c) to ensure that similar violations do not occur in the future.[28]

Even here, the Committee's call falls short of an explicit demand for prosecution, although it was concerned that, in adopting the amnesty law, 'the State party has contributed to an atmosphere of impunity which may undermine the democratic order and give rise to further grave human rights violations'.[29] Clearly, an effective investigation, identification of those responsible, and enabling the seeking of civil redress, would amount to a certain bringing to justice, even in the absence of a prosecution.

In 1995, the Committee moved even further away from its reluctance to call for prosecution of particular individuals. *Bautista de Arellana* v. *Colombia* was a case involving 'disappearance', torture, and death at the hands of state

---

[26] *Supra* n. 17, para. 15.
[27] See Nowak, *U.N. Covenant on Civil and Political Rights—CCPR Commentary* (1993), 60 and cases therein cited at footnote 166 and accompanying text.
[28] *Supra* n. 18, para. 14.   [29] Id., para. 12.4.

agents, in which compensation had been paid to the family of the victim by the government which had also effected disciplinary sanctions against the suspected perpetrators. Nevertheless, the Committee urged the state party 'to expedite criminal proceedings leading to the prompt prosecution and conviction of the persons responsible for the abduction, torture and death of Nydia Bautista'. [30]

A particularly strong statement is found in the *Velásquez Rodríguez* case, where the Inter-American Court of Human Rights stated that 'subjecting a person to official, repressive bodies that practice torture and assassination with impunity is itself a breach of the duty to prevent violation of the rights to life and physical integrity of the person'.[31] It went on to state that '[i]f the State apparatus acts in such a way that the violation goes unpunished . . . the State has failed to comply with its duty to guarantee the full and free exercise of those rights to persons within its juridsiction'.[32]

The Court had earlier in its judgment referred to the states's 'legal duty . . . to carry out a serious investigation . . ., to identify those responsible, impose the appropriate punishment and ensure the victim adequate compensation'.[33] Interestingly, in cases involving the Uruguayan amnesty that was the subject of the *Rodríguez* case before the Human Rights Committee discussed above, and another such amnesty in Argentina, the Inter-American Commission on Human Rights found the amnesties to violate the Convention: it did so by relying explicitly on the quoted language of the Court in *Velásquez-Rodríguez*.[34] In both cases, the Commission recommended that the governments concerned 'adopt the measures necessary to clarify the facts and identify those responsible'.[35] The Commission's approach seems congruent with that of the Human Rights Committee. It may be slightly more rigorous in its invocation of language from the Inter-American Court to the effect that the impunity granted by the amnesties involved, of itself, a violation of the Convention. Moreover, as observed in respect of the Human Rights Committee's line, insistence on identification of those responsible, even without requiring the establishment of criminal liability, represents a demand for a certain bringing to justice and a measure aimed at preventing recurrence of the violations.[36]

[30] Communication No. 563/1993, decision of 27 Oct. 1995, reproduced in 17 *HRLJ* 19 (1996), para. 10.

[31] *Supra* n. 19, para. 175.   [32] Id., para. 176.   [33] Id., para. 174.

[34] Report no. 28/92, cases 10,147, 10,181, 10,240, 10,262, 10,309, 10,311 (Argentina), 2 Oct. 1992, Organization of American States, *Annual Report of the Inter-American Commission on Human Rights* 1992–1993 (OEA/Ser. L/V/II.83, Doc. 14, corr. 1 (1993), 41); and Report no. 29/92, cases 10,029, 10,036, 10,145, 10,305 (Uruguay), 2 Oct. 1992, id., 154; reproduced in 13 *HRLJ* 336 and 340 respectively (1992).

[35] Paras. 52 and 54 respectively.

[36] The problem of amnesties for criminal violations of human rights has generated a substantial literature of which the leading works are Roht-Arriaza (ed.), *Impunity and Human Rights in International Law and Practice* (1995); Joyner (ed.), *Reining in Impunity for International Crimes*

The European Court of Human Rights has taken a clear position. In *Aksoy v. Turkey*, having stated that the 'nature of the right safeguarded under Article 3 [prohibition of torture and ill-treatment] has implications for Article 13', it affirmed that:

as regards Article 13, where an individual has an arguable claim that he has been tortured by agents of the State, the notion of an 'effective remedy' entails, in addition to the payment of compensation where appropriate, a thorough and effective investigation capable of leading to the *identification and punishment of those responsible*.[37]

The absence of such an investigation, notably by the Prosecutor, entailed a violation of article 13. Of interest here, however, is the purpose of the investigation indicated by the emphasized words. Criminal accountability seems to be required.

Again both the UN and OAS Conventions against Torture require that acts of torture be treated as crimes 'punishable by appropriate penalties which take into account their grave nature' (UN Convention) or 'by severe penalties that take into account their serious nature' (OAS Convention).[38]

As with investigations, the consistency of treaty practice can be taken as indicative of the general international law approach. The UN Declaration against Torture also provides for acts of torture to be treated as criminal offences,[39] the practice of the UN Special Rapporteur on Torture follows the same line,[40] and the UN Commission on Human Rights has affirmed that position.[41]

Compensation

This aspect of state responsibility for torture has already been largely covered earlier in this chapter. The practice of the treaty bodies is entirely consistent with the approach under general international law, appropriately adjusted to the reality that it is the victims, not states, to whom compensation is due. The UN and OAS Conventions envisage the obligation on states to grant

---

and Serious Violations of Fundamental Human Rights: Proceedings of the Siracusa Conference (1998); Ratner and Abrams, *Accountability for Human Rights Atrocities in International Law: Beyond the Nuremberg Legacy* (1998); Orentlicher, 'Settling Accounts: The Duty to Prosecute Human Rights Violations of a Prior Regime', 100 *Yale LJ* 2537 (1991); Méndez, 'Accountability for Past Abuses', 19 *HRQ* 255 (1997). See also Aspen Institute, *State Crimes—Punishment or Pardon—Papers and Report of the Conference*, 4–6 Nov. 1988, Wye Center, Maryland (1989); Bronkhorst, *Truth and Reconciliation—Obstacles and Opportunities for Human Rights* (Amnesty International Dutch Section, 1995).

[37] *Supra* n. 19, para. 98 (emphasis added).   [38] Articles 4 and 6 respectively.
[39] Article 7.   [40] UN doc. E/CN.4/1995/34, para. 926a.
[41] Res. 1997/38, 11 Apr. 1997, para. 10. By the same resolution the Commission also calls for abrogation of 'legislation leading to impunity for those responsible for grave violations of human rights such as torture' and for the prosecution of 'such violations, thereby providing a firm basis for the rule of law' (para. 7, citing the Vienna Declaration and Programme of Action (A/CONF.157/23, Part II, Section B.5 (1993)) adopted at the World Conference on Human Rights); see also Van Boven principles, principle 2, and Joinet principles, principles 18–32 (*supra* n. 1).

victims of torture compensation that is 'fair and adequate' (UN Convention) or 'suitable' (OAS Convention).[42] It is beyond the scope of this work to attempt an analysis of what the quantum, or criteria for establishing the quantum, of damages may be. It may be noted, however, that, in addition to compensation for material damage, the European Court of Human Rights has awarded compensation for 'non-pecuniary damage',[43] which appears to coincide with the notion applied by the Inter-American Court of Human Rights of 'moral damage',[44] both of which are aimed at redressing the victim's suffering.

As with investigation and bringing to justice, the Declaration against Torture envisages compensation, albeit with the qualification 'in accordance with national law' (article 11). The UN Special Rapporteur on Torture calls for compensation for victims of torture[45] and this too has been seconded by the UN Commission on Human Rights.[46] The obligation on a state to compensate victims of torture must be considered as a basic requirement of general international law.

Measures against recurrence

The call for states, in respect of which the Human Rights Committee has found a violation of the prohibition of torture, to take effective measures to prevent the recurrence of torture[47] is standard practice for the Committee. What is meant by such measures is less clear. They presumably include, in addition to compensation, the obligation effectively to investigate the allegation and to bring to justice those responsible. Yet, even in a case where an investigation had taken place and compensation had been paid, and in which the Committee had called for criminal proceedings to be expedited, it still insisted that the state party 'is further under an obligation to ensure that similar events do not occur in the future'.[48] This is a firm statement that seems to require an 'obligation of result'.[49] It can best be understood by reference to the approach of the Inter-American Court of Human Rights. Using the language of a 'duty to prevent', it accepted that 'the existence of a particular violation does not, in itself, prove the failure to take preventive measures'.[50] Presumably what is required is that a state must deploy 'all those means of a legal, political, administrative and cultural nature that promote the

---

[42] Articles 14 and 9 respectively.   [43] e.g. *Aksoy, supra* n. 19, para. 113.
[44] e.g. I/A Court HR, *Velásquez Rodríguez Case, Compensatory Damages, Judgment of 21 July 1989 (Art. 63(1) American Convention on Human Rights)* Ser. C No. 7, para. 39.
[45] *Supra* n. 40, para. 926(g).
[46] *Supra* n. 41; see also Van Boven principles, principles 6–14, and Joinet principles, principles 33–6 (*supra* n. 1).
[47] See, e.g., *Estrella* v. *Uruguay, supra* n. 13 and accompanying text.
[48] *Bautista* v. *Colombia, supra* n. 30, para. 10.
[49] On obligations of means and obligations of result, see Meron, *supra* n. 1, 182–8.
[50] *Velásquez Rodríguez, supra* n. 19, para. 175.

protection of human rights', albeit these means will 'vary with the law and the conditions of each State Party'.[51] Perhaps what it boils down to is that particular violations should be very rare, and when they do occur they should be properly investigated and redressed, including by compensation, and that the perpetrators should not enjoy impunity.

Non-expulsion

A state may violate the UN Convention against Torture (UNCAT) if it sends a person to a country 'where there are substantial grounds for believing that he would be in danger of being subjected to torture'.[52] This provision was 'inspired by the case-law of the European Commission of Human Rights with regard to article 3' of the European Convention.[53] The practice under the European Convention will be returned to below. As it happens, most of the cases dealt with by the Committee against Torture concern the application of UNCAT article 3. Indeed, in a number of cases the Committee has concluded that the relevant grounds exist and that the state against which the 'communication' was brought was obliged not to effect the return.[54]

Similarly, the Human Rights Committee's second 'general comment' on article 7 of the International Covenant on Civil and Political Rights adopts the position that 'States parties must not expose individuals to the danger of torture or cruel, inhuman or degrading treatment or punishment upon return to another country by way of their extradition, expulsion or refoulement'.[55] Interestingly, this concept was not to be found in the Committee's first general comment on the article.[56] The evolution may be tracked in the Committee's case law. In the mid-1980s, it considered a claim from a Chilean refugee against expulsion from The Netherlands to Chile to be inadmissible.[57] The claim was rejected with 'the laconic reasoning that the author had no

---

[51] *Velásquez Rodríguez, supra* n. 19, para. 175. See also Van Boven principles, principle 15(h), and Joinet principles, principles 37–42 (*supra* n. 1).

[52] Article 3(1). Article 13, para. 4, of the OAS Convention seems to follow suit, though the odd drafting ('Extradition shall not be granted nor shall the person sought be returned . . .') could imply that, in the absence of a 'seeking', expulsion to a country where the danger exists could be permitted. Moreover, the text is generally concerned with extradition of alleged torturers only.

[53] Burgers and Danelius, *The United Nations Convention against Torture* (1988), 125.

[54] *Mutombo* v. *Switzerland* (13/1993), Report of the Committee against Torture, *GAOR*, 49th Session, Supplement No. 44 (1994), Annex VB (threatened explusion to Zaire); *Khan* v. *Canada* (15/1994), Report of the Committee against Torture, *GAOR* , 50th Session, Supplement No. 44 (1995) Annex VA, p. 46 (Pakistan); *Alan* v. *Switzerland* (21/1995), Report of the Committee against Torture, *GAOR*, 51st Session, Supplement No. 44 (1996), Annex VA, p. 68 (Turkey); *Kisoki* v. *Sweden* (41/1996), id. p. 81 (Zaïre); *Tala* v. *Sweden* (43/1996), Report of the Committee against Torture, *GAOR*, 52nd Session, Supplement No. 44 (1997), Annex VA1 (Iran); *Aemei* v. *Switzerland* (38/1995), id., Annex VB2 (Iran); *Tapia Paez* v. *Sweden* (39/1996), id., Annex VB4 (Peru); see also the Committee's general comment on the implementation of Article 3 in the context of Article 22 of the Convention against Torture: UN doc. CAT/C/xx/Misc. 1 (1997).

[55] *Supra* n. 17, para. 9.   [56] *Supra* n. 17.

[57] *M.F.* v. *Netherlands* (173/84), *Selected Decisions of the Human Rights Committee under the Optional Protocol, Volume 2* (1990), 51.

claim under' article 2 of the Covenant's Optional Protocol (right to bring a claim by individuals whose Covenant-protected rights have been violated).[58] While there has as yet been no case of threat of torture in which the Committee has had occasion to deal with an expulsion or threatened expulsion, its willingness to do so has been signalled in the case of *Ng* v. *Canada*,[59] the only one of a series of cases involving extraditions from Canada to the United States of persons wanted for trial on capitally punishable offences in which the Committee found a violation. In that case, which will be referred to again in chapter 7, the Committee found that Canada had violated the Covenant in extraditing Ng to California to face execution in the gas chamber, a form of execution that it considered would violate article 7.

The European Commission case law that led to the UN practice started with *Amekrane* in which a friendly settlement was reached between the applicant, whose husband, a Moroccan air force pilot, had fled to Gibraltar after a failed *coup d'état* and had been returned to Morocco, where he was executed after a military trial, and the defendant United Kingdom government. The substantial settlement evidently reflected a potential finding by the Commission of a violation by the UK of article 3 in returning Amekrane to Morocco.[60] Subsequently, the Commission developed a practice in such cases of intervening before removal and offering the government an expedited procedure.[61]

The Court confirmed the Commission's stance in *Soering*, also a death penalty case, which will be referred to in greater detail in chapter 7. There the Court found that, to extradite a person to Virginia to face the possible imposition of the death penalty, would in the particular circumstances of the case involve a violation of article 3.[62] The juridical basis for the approach is the obligation of states parties under article 1 to 'secure' the rights spelled out in the Convention[63] and the principle of ensuring 'the effectiveness of the safeguard' contained in article 3.[64] It is not a question of holding a third state responsible under the Convention: liability is on the state party 'by reason of its having taken action which has as a direct consequence the exposure of an individual to the proscribed ill-treatment'.[65] As such the ill-treatment in question is not the potential one that may happen in the state to which the extradition is effected, but that of the state party's *exposing* the person to such treatment.

---

[58] Nowak, *supra* n. 27, p. 137.

[59] *Ng* v. *Canada* (469/1991), Report of the Human Rights Committee, Vol. II, *GAOR*, 49th Session, Supplement No. 40 (1994), Annex IX CC.

[60] Application No. 5961/72, 16 *Yearbook of the European Convention on Human Rights* 356 (1973). The sum in question was £35,000.

[61] Harris, O'Boyle and Warbrick, *Law of the European Convention on Human Rights* (1995), 589–90; see also, id., 73–80 on the practice of the Commission and Court.

[62] European Court of Human Rights, Series A, No. 161 (1989), reproduced in 11 *HRLJ* 335 (1990).

[63] Para. 86.   [64] Para. 90.   [65] Para. 91.

The standard articulated by the Court in *Soering* and followed in later cases is whether 'substantial grounds have been shown for believing that the person concerned, if extradited, faces a real risk of being subjected to torture or to inhuman or degrading treatment or punishment in the requesting country'.[66]

Space does not permit a detailed analysis of how the Court has applied this standard in subsequent cases. In *Cruz Varas*, the Court agreed with the Commission that on the facts the expulsion to Chile of a Chilean asylum seeker in Sweden was not a violation of article 3. The Court took into account that 'the establishment and verification of the facts is primarily a matter for the Commission'[67] and 'all the material placed before it'.[68] Also, while the Court looks at the facts at the time of the decision, it is 'not precluded . . . from having regard to information which comes to light subsequent to the expulsion'.[69] In this case the facts subsequent to expulsion do not seem to have included the applicant's torture or ill-treatment.[70] Moreover, the Court *disagreed* with the Commission in respect of the latter's finding that Sweden had violated its obligations under the Convention by expelling the applicants despite 'interim measures' indicated by the Commission that the expulsion be suspended pending the proceedings in Strasbourg.

In *Vilvarajah*, involving five Sri Lankan asylum seekers deported from the UK, the Court again agreed with a divided Commission that the expulsions did not entail a real risk of proscribed ill-treatment. In fact, three of them were subjected to torture or ill-treatment in Sri Lanka, but all five had subsequently been permitted to return to the UK.[71] The Court also *disagreed* with the Commission's firm finding of a violation of Convention article 13 in respect of the limitations of the UK's judicial review procedure.

If these two cases suggested some reluctance on the part of the Court effectively to overrule national decisions taken after the exhaustion of careful procedures, the latest case indicates that the European Convention still has sufficient force to override national procedures.

Karamjit Singh Chahal, his wife, and two children were ordered to be deported to India from the United Kingdom on national security grounds. He was a Sikh activist suspected by the UK authorities of involvement in anti-Indian terrorist activities. In 1984 he had been arrested by the Punjab police and, he claimed, tortured, eventually being released without charge. Under national law, the Home Secretary could weigh the risk to the applicant against the risk to national security. The process of judicial review accepted that this had been done, and so could not block the deportation. An assurance was obtained from the Indian government that Chahal 'would have no

---

[66] Para. 91.
[67] *Cruz Varas* v. *Sweden*, European Court of Human Rights, Series A, No. 201 (1991), para. 74.
[68] Para. 75.   [69] Para. 76.   [70] Paras. 36–8.
[71] *Vilvarajah* v. *United Kingdom*, European Court of Human Rights, Series A, No. 215 (1991).

reason to expect to suffer mistreatment of any kind at the hands of the Indian authorities'.[72]

The European Commission of Human Rights held unanimously that there would be violations, *inter alia*, of articles 3 and 13 (right to an effective remedy) of the European Convention, if Chahal were deported. The Court agreed on the threatened violations of article 3 by twelve votes to seven. It also held unanimously that there had been a violation of article 13 in conjunction with article 3. As regards the article 3 finding, the central aspect for the purposes of this work, argument centred on factual and legal aspects. The government and the Court's dissenting minority were not convinced of the real risk of torture or ill-treatment of Chahal should he be returned. The majority of the Court agreed with the Commission that the evidence suggested the contrary. The legal issue was whether, as the government and Court's minority argued, the risk to the individual could be balanced against the risk to national security. Indeed, the government went as far as to argue that, as with international refugee law which had been the analogy on which the Strasbourg case law had been based, national security could trump the individual's right not to be exposed to torture or other ill-treatment. The majority decided that neither argument was valid. Pointing to the 'absolute terms' of the article 3 prohibition of torture and ill-treatment, with no exceptions or derogations being permitted 'even in the event of a public emergency threatening the life of the nation'[73] (see chapters 2 and 11), the Court simply affirmed that the article 3 prohibition 'is equally absolute in expulsion cases'.[74] Where the real risk obtains, the state's responsibility is engaged and 'the activities of the individual in question, however undesirable or dangerous, cannot be a material consideration'.[75]

In addition to the treaty practice described above it may also be confidently asserted that the *non-refoulement* principle is one of general international law. There is little doubt that the principle has that status as regards sending a person to a country where persecution within the meaning of international refugee law is threatened.[76] The threat of torture is in many ways an extention or a specification of the notion of persecution. It is, after all, hardly conceivable that it would be forbidden to send someone to face political or group persecution, that is, a form of human rights violation, while not prohibiting the same person from being exposed to a human rights violation that, as will be seen below, amounts to a crime under international law. Although the prohibition is not found in the Declaration against Torture, this may be because the idea was too unfamiliar at the time of its drafting. Certainly it is the practice of the UN Special Rapporteur on Torture to intervene in cases where torture may be a risk. His approach is to request that the expulsion not be

---

[72] *Chahal* v. *United Kingdom* (70/1995/576/662), Judgment, 15 Nov. 1996, para. 37.
[73] Para. 79.   [74] Para. 80.   [75] Ibid.
[76] Goodwin-Gill, *The Refugee in International Law* (2nd edn., 1996), 167–71.

proceeded with, or that both satisfactory assurances of personal security be obtained from the country in question and that the returning state take effective measures to ensure that the assurances will be complied with.[77] In such circumstances, the exposure to torture is avoided.

INDIVIDUAL RESPONSIBILITY FOR TORTURE

Traditionally international law has been a body of rules binding upon states which are represented by their governments. States have thus been both the legislators and subjects of international law, its framers and its addressees. Where one state claimed that another had violated an international legal obligation, it looked to the offending state for redress, rather than to the individual agents whose behaviour had engaged the state's responsibility.

This general rule has long known the occasional exception, whereby international law has concerned itself with the behaviour of individuals. The classic example is that of piracy on the high seas which, under customary international law, was a violation of international law that all states were expected to redress and over which any state could exercise jurisdiction. More recently international law has criminalized other acts, such as certain forms of hostage taking.[78] The hallmark of these exceptions is that they seem to permit, and in some cases require, states which find within their jurisdiction persons alleged to have committed the prohibited acts to bring such persons to justice, regardless of the nationality of the persons or of where they committed the crime. This is known as the principle of universality of jurisdiction and clearly represents an exceptional assertion of criminal jurisdiction. Where states are actually required to take action, the principle of universality of jurisdiction is coupled with the concept known by the Latin phrase *aut dedere, aut judicare* (either extradite or try). In other words, the state on whose territory the alleged offender is found must either try the person or extradite him or her to a country willing to exercise criminal jurisdiction. Piracy would be an example of a case where states are permitted, but not required to exercise criminal jurisdiction on a universal basis (permissive universality of jurisdiction), while hostage taking would be an example of a case where states are required either to exercise such jurisdiction or to extradite to a country willing to do so (compulsory universal jurisdiction). These examples are of acts committed by private individuals or groups, not by state officials (unless

---

[77] For example, the case of three Iranian aircraft hijackers threatened with extradition to the Russian Federation: UN doc. E/CN.4/1995/34, para. 513. The Norwegian government reported that it had extradited the men after receiving various assurances, including the right to visit them in detention, which had been exercised.

[78] International Convention Against the Taking of Hostages, GA res. 34/146, 17 Dec. 1979. See, generally, Randall, 'Universal Jurisdiction under International Law', 66 *Texas Law Review* 791 (1988).

acting as individuals). But the scope of what will now be called 'crimes under international law' is not limited to private acts.

The category of crimes under international law committed by public officials emerged with the post-World War II trials in Nuremberg of persons accused of 'crimes against peace', 'war crimes', and 'crimes against humanity'.[79] The General Assembly of the United Nations later unanimously confirmed the principles of international law recognized by the Charter and the Judgment of the Nuremberg Tribunal.[80] Crimes against peace and war crimes are, by definition, matters of interstate relations, committed by public officials. The category 'crimes against humanity' was framed to be applicable only 'in execution of or in connection with' a crime against peace or a war crime.[81] In other words, the Tribunal could deal only with crimes against humanity committed after the outbreak of international warfare (that is, after 1939); it did not go as far as to judge the behaviour of the Nazi government towards its own citizens in peacetime. Because the Nuremberg Charter set up an *ad hoc* international body to judge a specific set of war crimes, it had no need to deal with the issue of jurisdiction at the national level. The Geneva Conventions, however, which encompass a codification of war crimes, do make it clear that such crimes may be prosecuted on the basis of universality of jurisdiction. They provide that perpetrators of 'grave breaches' (a species of war crime) shall be prosecuted by parties to the Conventions 'regardless of their nationality', unless they are handed over to another party that 'has made out a prima facie case' for jurisdiction.[82] Furthermore, the Geneva Conventions by now covered an area that would bring many, if not all, crimes

---

[79] The four Allied Powers that occupied Germany established an international military tribunal in Nuremberg composed of judges from each of them (France, Union of Soviet Socialist Republics, United Kingdom, and United States of America) to judge the leading figures of Nazi Germany. The tribunal's mandate was contained in the Charter of the International Military Tribunal annexed to the Agreement for the Establishment of an International Military Tribunal, concluded at London, 8 Aug. 1945: 5 UNTS 251. The judgment of the tribunal (1946) is reproduced in 41 *AJIL* 172 (1947).

[80] GA res. 95(I), 11 Dec. 1946. Traditionally state officials are considered immune from jurisdiction abroad in respect of acts they committed in office on behalf of the state, under what is called the 'act of state' doctrine—the international law equivalent of the 'corporate veil' in domestic law. Thus, the Nuremberg principles represent a piercing of the corporate veil of the state.

[81] Under article 6 of the Charter of the Nuremberg Tribunal, crimes against humanity are defined as: 'murder, extermination, enslavement, deportation, and other inhumane acts committed against any civilian population, before or during the war, or persecutions on political, racial or religious grounds *in execution of or in connection with any crimes within the jurisdiction of the Tribunal*, whether or not in violation of the domestic law of the country where perpetrated' (emphasis added). The other crimes within the jurisdiction of the Tribunal were 'crimes against peace' and 'war crimes'. 'Crimes against peace' covers acts relating to the launching of a war of aggression (*jus ad bellum*); 'war crimes' covers violations of the rules governing the conduct of warfare (*jus in bello*).

[82] Geneva Convention I, article 49; Geneva Convention II, article 50; Geneva Convention III, article 129; Geneva Convention IV, article 146.

against humanity (when committed in the context of crimes against peace or war crimes) within their ambit.[83]

In fact, it is now safe to conclude that war crimes and crimes against humanity can be committed even in the absence of any connection with international armed conflict. Indeed, it would appear that crimes against humanity may be committed outside the context of any armed conflict.

As indicated in Chapter 2, common article 3 of the Geneva Conventions prohibits as regards persons in the hands of a party to the conflict 'at any time and in any place whatsoever . . . violence to life and person, in particular . . . mutilation, cruel treatment and torture', as well as 'outrages upon personal dignity, in particular, humiliating and degrading treatment' (see Annex 9a). However, the Conventions do not spell out any legal consequences for the violation of article 3, which applies only to situations of 'armed conflict not of an international character'.

A number of developments indicate that general international law now treats violations of common article 3 as war crimes.[84] In the *Nicaragua* case, the World Court affirmed that common article 3 reflects 'fundamental general principles of humanitarian law'.[85] The Statute of the International Criminal Tribunal for the Former Yugoslavia makes violations of 'the laws and customs of war' triable by the Tribunal.[86] In the *Tadić* case, the Tribunal's Appeals Chamber concluded, accordingly, that 'customary international law imposes criminal liability for serious violations of common article 3'.[87]

Meanwhile, the Statute of the International Tribunal for Rwanda provides directly for that Tribunal's jurisdiction over 'serious violations' of common article 3.[88] It is clear that the Security Council did not consider itself as imposing retrospective criminality, but rather as codifying existing international criminal law. Finally, the draft Statute for an International Criminal Court provides for

---

[83] For example, article 147 of Geneva Convention IV on the treatment of civilian populations provides: 'Grave breaches to which the preceding Article relates shall be those involving any of the following acts, if committed against persons or property protected by the present Convention: wilful killing, torture or inhuman treatment, including biological experiments, wilfully causing great suffering or serious injury to body or health, unlawful deportation or transfer or unlawful confinement of a protected person, compelling a protected person to serve in the force of a hostile Power, or wilfully depriving a protected person of the rights of fair and regular trial prescribed in the present Convention, taking of hostages and extensive destruction and appropriation of property, not justified by military necessity and carried out unlawfully and wantonly.'

[84] See Meron, 'International Criminalization of Internal Atrocities', 89 *AJIL* 554 (1995); Meindersma, 'Violations of Common Article 3 of the Geneva Conventions as Violations of the Laws and Customs of War under Article 3 of the Statute of the International Criminal Tribunal for the Former Yugoslavia', 42 *Netherlands International Law Review* 375 (1995).

[85] *Military and Paramilitary Activities in and against Nicaragua (Nicaragua v. United States of America)*, Merits, Judgment, ICJ Rep. (1986), 14, para. 218.

[86] UN doc. S/25704 (1993), Annex, as approved by Security Council res. 827 (1993), 25 May 1993, article 3; reproduced in 32 *ILM* 1192 (1993).

[87] *The Prosecutor* v. *Duško Tadić a/k/a 'Dule'*, Decision on the Defence Motion for Interlocutory Appeal on Jurisdiction, Case No. IT-94-I-AR72, 2 Oct. 1995, para. 134.

[88] Security Council res. 955 (1994), Annex, article 4; reproduced in 33 *ILM* 1602 (1994).

the proposed court to have jurisdiction, like the Yugoslav Tribunal, over 'serious violations of the laws and customs applicable in armed conflict'.[89]

Therefore, serious violations of the laws and customs of war committed even in non-international armed conflict, are to be considered as crimes under international law. They are cognizable by an international penal tribunal and would be expected to be amenable to universal jurisdiction. Whether the articles of the Geneva Conventions providing for *compulsory* universal jurisdiction over 'grave breaches' should now be understood as applying to serious violations of common article 3 is doubtful, since the 'grave breaches' articles apply only to acts committed against 'protected persons' who are defined in the context of international armed conflict.

If the jurisdiction of the Nuremburg Tribunal limited its consideration of crimes against humanity to those committed in connection with a crime against peace or a war crime, meaning in that context a connection with the international armed conflict, it has become clear that such a connection is not inherent in the notion of crime against humanity.[90] Indeed, it is a crime that can be committed in peacetime.

Genocide, the most notorious crime against humanity committed during World War II, was made the subject of a special convention: the Convention on the Prevention and Punishment of the Crime of Genocide (1948).[91] This Convention does not require that genocide be committed in connection with a crime against peace or a war crime: it may be committed within the frontiers of a state and in the absence of any armed conflict. The Convention specifies that the offence is a 'crime under international law' (article I) and it is reasonable to see this term as the generic one for crimes for which international law may permit an international penal jurisdiction or require individuals to be prosecuted. The Genocide Convention does not refer specifically to universality of jurisdiction. It requires trial 'by a competent tribunal of the State in the territory of which the act was committed, or by such international penal tribunal as may have jurisdiction' over the offence. While the absence of reference to other bases of jurisdiction is regrettable (not even jurisdiction on the basis of nationality of the perpetrators is mentioned), it should not be assumed that the Convention purported to exclude other bases of jurisdiction, including universality, at least on a permissive basis. Universality was certainly the most convincing claim to jurisdiction that could be made by the court in Jerusalem that tried Adolf Eichmann.[92]

[89] Draft Statute for an International Criminal Court, Report of the International Law Commission on the Work of its Forty-Sixth Session, *GAOR*, 49th Session, Supplement No. 10 (1994), p. 43, 70 (article 20); see Crawford 'The ILC Adapts a Statute for an International Criminal Court', 89 *AJIL* 404 (1995). (Professor James Crawford was the Chair of the ILC's working group on the project.)

[90] See, generally, Bassiouni, *Crimes against Humanity in International Criminal Law* (1992).

[91] GA res. 2106 A (III), 9 Dec. 1948.

[92] *Attorney-General of the Government of Israel* v. *Eichmann*, District Court of Jerusalem (1961), 36 ILR 5.

Other practices that have been described in international instruments as crimes against humanity are apartheid[93] and the systematic practice of enforced disappearance.[94] Also, the ILC has included a number of offences, 'when committed in a systematic manner or on a large scale', which are more or less coextensive with the notion of crimes against humanity as adjudicated at Nuremberg, in its Draft Code of Crimes against the Peace and Security of Mankind,[95] except that there is no requirement for a connection with any armed conflict.[96]

More far-reaching developments have also taken place. The Statute of the International Criminal Tribunal for the Former Yugoslavia included crimes against humanity within its jurisdiction. These had to be committed 'in armed conflict, whether international or internal in character'.[97] Thus, there was a disconnection from international conflict as required at Nuremberg, but the notion did not here extend to peacetime. As such, probably little that would not have been covered by the category of war crimes as discussed above and also triable under the Statute was added by the inclusion of crimes against humanity, except perhaps by protecting populations from atrocities committed by forces from their 'own' party.

However, the Statute of the International Tribunal for Rwanda has no limitation to a context of armed conflict in its specification of cognizable crimes against humanity. All that is requred is that they be committed 'as part of a widespread or systematic attack against any civilian population on national, political, ethnic, racial or religious grounds'.[98]

The draft Statute for an International Criminal Court would place crimes against humanity within the proposed court's jurisdiction. The ILC which prepared the draft refrained from defining the term, preferring to refer in a commentary to its text of the Draft Code of Offences against the Peace and Security of Mankind.[99] This, as noted above, required no connection with an armed conflict.

We can conclude this general consideration of crimes against humanity by affirming that genocide and other crimes against humanity may be committed, not only outside the context of international armed conflict, but without

[93] International Convention on the Suppression and Punishment of the Crime of *Apartheid*, GA res. 3068 (XXVIII), 30 Nov. 1973, art. I.

[94] Organization of American States, Inter-American Convention on Forced Disappearance of Persons (adopted at Belém do Pará, 9 June 1994, 24th regular session of the General Assembly), preambular para. 6; UN, Declaration on the Protection of All Persons from Enforced Disappearance, GA res. 47/133, 18 Dec. 1992, preambular para. 4.

[95] Report of the International Law Commission on the Work of its 48th Session, *GAOR*, 51st Session, Supplement No. 10 (1996), ch. II D, art. 18 (entitled 'Crimes against humanity'). It includes 'torture', 'rape, enforced prostitution and other forms of sexual abuse', and 'other inhumane acts which severely damage physical or mental integrity, health or human dignity, such as mutilation and severe bodily harm'. For more on the background to the Draft Code, see Chapter 6.

[96] Id., Commentary, para. (6).

[97] *Supra* n. 86, art. 5 (torture is included).

[98] *Supra* n. 88, art. 3 (torture is included).

[99] *Supra* n. 95.

an armed conflict context at all. They are amenable to any international penal jurisdiction and, while no treaty requires the exercise of universal jurisdiction over perpetrators, it may be assumed that such jurisdiction is permitted.

Where then does the individual torturer stand? Clearly one who tortures a person protected by the Geneva Conventions, in connection with an international armed conflict, commits a grave breach of the Conventions and may be tried anywhere or extradited for trial. As to torture committed in non-international armed conflict, apart from the possibility of any international penal jurisdiction, there may as yet be no requirement of universal jurisdiction, although there is probably no obstacle to any state's exercising such jurisdiction. The same appears to be the case in respect of torture committed as part of a systematic or widespread practice of persecution against certain population groups, as a crime against humanity.

What of torture committed outside one of these categories and left unredressed by the national authorities? Two modern cases go some way to elucidating the matter.

The first is that of Captain Astiz.[100] During the hostilities in the South Atlantic in 1982, Argentinian naval Captain Alfredo Astiz became a prisoner of war of the British. He was captured on the island of South Georgia and taken to the United Kingdom. Interest in this prisoner of war was occasioned by the fact that non-governmental organizations had declared themselves to be in possession of numerous statements by survivors of the secret detention camp in the Naval School of Mechanics in Buenos Aires.[101] These statements asserted that Astiz was involved in the arrest, kidnapping, torture, and illegal execution of political opponents of the military government of Argentina. Specifically, he was suspected of involvement in the 'disappearance' in Argentina of two French nuns and with the arrest and killing, again in Argentina, of a Swedish girl. These allegations led the French and Swedish governments to request the British authorities to have questions put to Astiz once his identity had been established. The questions were eventually put, but Astiz refused to answer them, shielded by the provision of the Third Geneva Convention that requires prisoners of war only to identify themselves. Astiz was subsequently repatriated to Argentina.

The case presents several problems of jurisdiction, since it concerns allegations of torture committed in Argentina, made against an Argentinian national on behalf of victims who included French and Swedish nationals; a potential opportunity for prosecution of the charges arose because Astiz was captured by the British, in the course of an international armed conflict which had no connection with the acts of which he was accused. The question is, which of the several nations concerned had jurisdiction?

---

[100] See Meyer, 'Liability of Prisoners of War for Offences Committed Prior to Capture: The Astiz Affair', 32 *ICLQ* 948 (1983).

[101] Id., 952 and International Commission of Jurists, *infra* n. 105.

It is beyond doubt that Astiz could have been brought to trial in Argentina, had the Argentinian authorities chosen to press charges, but they had not done so. There remained, therefore, the more complicated question as to whether any other state might exercise jurisdiction—in effect Sweden or France, whose nationals were the alleged victims, or Britain, in whose custody Astiz was being held. The answer to this question is further complicated by the fact the Astiz was being held as a prisoner of war. The distinction between compulsory jurisdiction and permissive jurisdiction arises at this point: none of the three states mentioned had a clearly defined obligation to exercise jurisdiction in this case. It remains to inquire whether any might have done so on the basis of a permissive rule of jurisdiction. Neither Sweden nor France formally requested extradition of Astiz from the United Kingdom but it might be inferred that their request to pose questions to him (and British acquiescence, which included transporting Astiz 8,000 miles to the United Kingdom for the purpose) took place in contemplation of the possibility of extradition. It is possible only to speculate on why, in the event, extradition was not sought. One explanation may be that the governments concerned felt they had no case for jurisdiction, but there are others. First, Astiz's special status as a prisoner of war may have been relevant: it may have been felt that the problem of extradition should be left open, in order not to create a precedent whose long-term implications could be far-reaching and possibly inimical to the humanitarian aims of the regime of prisoner of war protection.[102] Second, the evidence available against Astiz in the particular cases concerned may have seemed inadequate, especially since he availed himself of his right not to answer questions put to him.[103] Third, given the conflict then under way between Britain and Argentina, Sweden and France may have wished to avoid embarrassing the United Kingdom government by confronting it with a juridically controversial interpretation of the Third Geneva Convention (which is silent on the issue of the extradition of prisoners of war) that, if pursued, might have jeopardized Argentina's future compliance with the Conventions. Several explanations of the failure to pursue extradition are therefore available, none of which affects the issue of jurisdiction. In any event, since France and Sweden did not request extradition, their claim to jurisdiction is moot.

The possibility of such a claim by Britain was suggested at the time by a British scholar who advocated that 'thought should be given to prosecuting the same Captain Astiz in this country [that is, the United Kingdom] for

---

[102] Article 99 (first paragraph) of Geneva Convention III states: 'No prisoner of war may be tried or sentenced for an act which is not forbidden by the law of the Detaining Power or by International Law, in force at the time the said act was committed.' This language is not restricted to trial for acts committed in connection with the armed conflict which led to the capture of a particular prisoner of war.

[103] According to article 17 of Geneva Convention III, a prisoner of war, if questioned, is required to give only name, rank, birth date, and serial number.

breach of a crime under international law, namely torture'.[104] In response, the International Commission of Jurists pointed out that domestic legislation would have been required for the British courts to be able to take jurisdiction over an act of torture committed outside the United Kingdom.[105] Indeed, the enactment of such legislation would probably be required in many countries. Even without this obstacle the United Kingdom would doubtless have had the misgivings referred to above regarding both Astiz's prisoner of war status and a desire not to provoke Argentina into non-compliance with the Geneva Conventions. Once again, therefore, no action was taken and the issue of jurisdiction remained untested.

In so far as steps interpretable as preliminary to extradition were taken, the case provides some evidence that states whose nationals have been the victims of torture and 'disappearance' could have a claim to exercise jurisdiction. It gives no indication one way or the other, however, as to whether a state totally unconcerned with the alleged practices might do so.

Meanwhile, a second case is pertinent to the question of whether it is already the case that, under customary international law, alleged torturers may be tried on the basis of a permissive rule of universal jurisdiction. The case is that dealt with by a United States Federal Court of Appeals decision in *Filártiga* v. *Peña-Irala*.[106]

According to the plaintiffs-appellants (Dolly Filártiga and Dr Joel Filártiga), Joelito Filártiga, the 17-year-old brother of Dolly Filártiga and son of Dr Joel Filártiga, was kidnapped and tortured to death on 29 March 1976 by defendant-appellee Americo Norberto Peña-Irala (Peña), the then Inspector General of Police in Asunción, the capital of Paraguay. The Filártigas claimed that Dr Filártiga was a long-standing opponent of the government of President Alfredo Stroessner of Paraguay and that his son Joelito was tortured and killed in retaliation for his father's political activities and beliefs. In 1979 they brought a claim in tort (violation of non-contractual civil obligation) against Peña (who was at that time in the United States of America) in a United States federal district court, under an old, rarely invoked provision (section 1350 of the Alien Tort Statute) endowing the relevant courts with jurisdiction over 'any civil action by an alien for a tort only, committed in violation of the law of nations or a treaty of the United States'.[107] The District Court dismissed the complaint 'for want of federal jurisdiction'. The Court of Appeals however, reversed the District Court judgment and held that:

---

[104] Dr Malcolm N. Shaw, letter to *The Times* (London), 8 June 1982.
[105] 'The Case of Captain Astiz', 28 *The Review* (International Commission of Jurists, June 1982), 3.
[106] 630 F 2d 876 (2nd. Cir. 1980).
[107] Alien Tort Statute, 28 USC, section 1350 (originally the Judiciary Act of 1789, Chapter 20, section 9(b), 1 Stat. 67, 77 (1789)).

deliberate torture perpetrated under color of official authority violates universally accepted norms of the international law of human rights, regardless of the nationality of the parties. Thus whenever an alleged torturer is found and served with process by an alien within our borders, section 1350 provides federal jurisdiction.

Following this decision, the District Court awarded the plaintiffs damages totalling over ten million dollars.[108]

The judgment delivered for the Court of Appeals by Circuit Judge Irving R. Kaufman elicited a plethora of scholarly reaction, most of which greeted the decision with acclaim,[109] though the occasional voice of doubt was also raised.[110] The judgment is important in three respects: first, the court, relying on the human rights and humanitarian law instruments described earlier in this text, found that torture is prohibited by modern customary international law. Second, although it did not deal with the question of when a prohibition under customary international law imposes liability on the individual violator, it did find that an individual could be responsible. Third, it exercised jurisdiction, at least in a civil case, despite the fact that the torture occurred outside the United States and was inflicted on a foreign national by a foreign national. In support of its decision it cited article 7 of the Declaration against Torture, which provides that states are to ensure that acts of torture are offences under their criminal law. It also noted that it is possible for civil jurisdiction to occur outside the *lex loci delicti*,[111] especially where the act complained of would be unlawful in the place where it took place (as was the case in Paraguay). It did not deal, however, with the intractable question of when an international law prohibition, even one that requires penal action by states to repress violations, becomes one that requires or permits universality of criminal jurisdiction.[112]

It is worth quoting an extract of the concluding passage of the *Filártiga* judgment because, while its language is limited to the issue of civil liability, it uses terminology resonant of international criminal liability:

---

[108] 577 F Supp. 860 (EDNY 1984); summarized in 78 *AJIL* 677 (1984).

[109] For example, Blum and Steinhardt, 'Federal Jurisdiction over International Human Rights Claims: The Alien Tort Claims Act after *Filártiga* v. *Peña-Irala*', 22 *Harvard International Law Journal* 53 (1981); Paust, 'Book Review—Human Rights: From Jurisprudential Enquiry to Effective Litigation', 56 *New York University Law Review* 277 (1981).

[110] Hassan, 'Conflict of Philosophies: the Filártiga Jurisprudence', 32 *ICLQ* 250 (1983); D'Zurilla, 'Individual Responsibility for Torture under International Law', 56 *Tulane Law Review* 186 (1981).

[111] That is, outside the place where the acts of torture were committed.

[112] In the absence of a treaty stipulation permitting or requiring it, it would presumably involve the following elements: (a) that the act is criminal under most national laws; (b) that international law endorses or requires such criminalization; and (c) that states actually exercise jurisdiction without general challenge. In connection with the third factor, the basic approach of the World Court is that a state contesting another state's exercise of its criminal jurisdiction has the burden of proving that there is a rule of international law prohibiting such exercise. See the *Lotus* case (*France* v. *Turkey*), PCIJ Rep. Series A, no. 10 (1927).

In the modern age, humanitarian and practical considerations have combined to lead the nations of the world to recognize that respect for fundamental human rights is in their individual and collective interest. Among the rights universally proclaimed by all nations, as we have noted, is the right to be free of physical torture. Indeed, for purposes of civil liability, the torturer has become—like the pirate and slave trader before him—*hostis humani generis*, an enemy of all mankind.

Although this language tends to suggest that for the purposes of international law the torturer is no different from the pirate or slave trader (that is, liable to universal jurisdiction), it must be remembered that the *Filártiga* case was one of civil, not criminal law. There is no reason to conclude that criminal liability would not also be the case, but as yet there is no state practice to endorse the point.[113] Indeed, the chances of establishing such a practice will be rare: evidence is hard to come by in torture cases, especially in cases heard outside the country where the torture took place; other rules of international law (such as the Geneva Conventions, as in the Astiz case, or rules of diplomatic immunity) may inhibit the exercise of universal criminal jurisdiction.

The issue has been significantly clarified as a result of the adoption by the United Nations General Assembly of the Convention against Torture (Annex 2a). This is because the problem of having to look to general international law to determine whether or not universal criminal jurisdiction may be applied to torturers can, of course, be bypassed by international legislation.

Under the Convention, states parties are required, as described in Chapter 2, to establish criminal jurisdiction over cases of torture committed within their jurisdiction (territorial principle), by their nationals (nationality principle), or (if the state deems it appropriate) where their nationals are victims (passive personality principle) (article 5(1)).[114] Jurisdiction is also to be taken in the absence of any such link (article 5(2)) (the universality principle). There is also an obligation either to extradite alleged torturers or to try them on the basis of universality of jurisdiction alone (articles 5(2) and 7).[115] This had been one of the most controversial issues before the working group of the Commission on Human Rights, which drafted the bulk of the text, but was resolved at its last session in 1984.[116] The same approach on universality of

---

[113] It should be noted that in a later US case before another Circuit Court of Appeals, *Tel-Oren* v. *Libyan Arab Republic*, the court doubted whether, in the absence of specific legislation, new offences against the law of nations (in this case, terrorism) committed outside the United States were justiciable under section 1350 of the Alien Tort Statute: 726 F 2d 774 (DC Cir. 1984). However, in addition to several other cases based on section 1350, there is now a statute, the Torture Victims Protection Act of 1991, Pub. L No. 102–256 Stat. 73 (1992) which codifies the jurisdiction.

[114] The relevant implementing legislation in the UK is enacted in the Criminal Justice Act 1988, s. 134.

[115] The first case known to have been initiated in the UK is that of a Sudanese doctor charged in Scotland: Symon, '"Torture centre" doctor charged', *Sunday Times*, 21 Sept. 1997.

[116] UN doc. E/CN.4/1984/72. Apart from the (unstated) concern of some countries not to have their torturers tried abroad, the main argument against universal jurisdiction was that it

jurisdiction is, as noted in Chapter 2, taken by the OAS Convention against Torture (articles 11–14). This evolution is significant not only in terms of the specific obligations of parties to the Conventions, but also as an indication of the customary international law attitude to the individual responsibility of torturers: while states parties will, of course, be obliged to try alleged torturers on the basis of universality of jurisdiction (unless they extradite them), it is now hard to imagine a convincing objection to any state's unilateral choice to exercise jurisdiction on a universal basis.[117] Thus, permissive universality of jurisdiction is probably already achieved under general international law.

THE LEGAL CONSEQUENCES OF OTHER PROHIBITED ILL-TREATMENT

As seen in Chapter 3, the formula for the prohibition of torture and other ill-treatment has on occasion been treated as having two separate parts: torture, and 'cruel, inhuman or degrading treatment or punishment' (other ill-treatment). The legal consequences for the perpetration of acts of torture, involving both state and individual responsibility, have just been described. As far as the perpetration of other prohibited ill-treatment is concerned, the incidence of *state responsibility* will also be very similar. Thus, article 8 of the Declaration against Torture (see Annex 1) envisages the right of anyone alleged to be the victim of torture or other ill-treatment to complain to, and have the case impartially examined by, the competent national authorities. However, while article 9 of the Declaration places on governments the obligation to investigate possible cases of torture, even in the absence of a formal complaint, this obligation does not extend to cases of alleged other ill-treatment. On the other hand, as noted in Chapter 2, this restriction is not found in the UN Convention against Torture (articles 12 and 16). While persons alleged to be responsible for torture must be the object of criminal proceedings, article 10 of the Declaration envisages the institution of 'criminal, disciplinary or other appropriate proceedings' in respect of persons believed responsible for other forms of prohibited ill-treatment. The Convention against Torture is even less specific: states parties undertake to 'prevent' acts of other ill-treatment (article 16). Article 11 of the Declaration requires redress and compensation for victims either of torture or other ill-treatment.

---

would be very difficult for a court outside the jurisdiction where the torture took place to secure the necessary evidence and documentation. This was countered by the assertion that nothing in the draft convention would require a state to proceed in the absence of all the elements required by its legal system for a successful prosecution. The burden of the argument of those in favour of the principle of universality of jurisdiction was that there should be 'no safe haven for torturers'.

[117] D'Zurilla, *supra* n. 36, based much of his case against the *Filártiga* decision on the initial absence of agreement in the working group on the issue of universal jurisdiction.

The Convention against Torture does not make its compensation provision (article 14) applicable to other ill-treatment (article 16).[118]

The elements common to both torture and other ill-treatment, reflected in the general practice of the Human Rights Committee,[119] are summed up in the passage of the Committee's general comment on the overall prohibition of torture and other ill-treatment,[120] and may be summarized as consisting of at least the following obligations on governments: (a) to investigate complaints, (b) to establish the responsibility of individual perpetrators, and (c) to provide effective remedies to victims, including compensation. (Frequently also the Committee will call for the provision of adequate medical care for the victim.[121])

Turning to the position with regard to individual responsibility: as far as international armed conflict is concerned, the four Geneva Conventions of 12 August 1949 include among the acts they term 'grave breaches', 'torture or inhuman treatment, including biological experiments, wilfully causing great suffering or serious injury to body or health', if committed against persons protected by the Conventions.[122] Such grave breaches are to be the subject of 'effective penal sanctions' and each state party is to bring persons suspected of having committed or ordered the acts in question, 'regardless of their nationality, before its own courts', unless they hand them over to another state party for trial.[123] Thus, it seems that most of the practices described in Chapter 3 as constituting prohibited ill-treatment not amounting to torture would, when committed against protected persons in the context of international armed conflict, be crimes under international law, in respect of which alleged perpetrators would be subject to universal jurisdiction.

When these practices are used by a government outside the ambit of international armed conflict, generally against its own citizens, the position is less definite. Common article 3 of the Geneva Conventions, serious violations of which are war crimes in violation of the laws and customs of war, prohibits 'violence to . . . person, in particular . . . mutilation, cruel treatment and torture', as well as 'outrages upon personal dignity, in particular humiliating and degrading treatment'. There is as yet no practice under the rules of humanitarian law attributing acts to one or other of the terms used, though the practice under human rights treaties is likely to be influential. Nor is there any

---

[118] This might be explicable by the fact that article 11 of the Declaration against Torture provides that the victim of torture or other ill-treatment is to be 'afforded redress and compensation according to national law'; whereas Convention article 14 has a more stringent requirement of 'an enforceable right to fair and adequate compensation'.

[119] For example, *Cubas* v. *Uruguay* (70/1980), Report of the Human Rights Committee, *GAOR*, 37th Session, Supplement No. 40 (1982), Annex XVI, para. 13.

[120] See text accompanying n. 17 above.

[121] For example, *Teti* v. *Uruguay* (73/1980), loc. cit. *supra* n. 119, Annex XVII, para. 10.

[122] Articles 50, 51, 130, and 147 respectively.

[123] Articles 49, 50, 129, and 146 respectively.

practice as to which of the acts that might fall under each of the terms should be considered as a *serious* violation. Bearing in mind the approach applicable in international armed conflict, namely, that torture and inhuman treatment are grave breaches, probably a secure position would be that torture or cruel or inhuman treatment would be a serious violation of common article 3. Mutilation would clearly qualify, while perhaps not all 'humiliating and degrading treatment' would.

As to cruel, inhuman, and degrading treatment or punishment committed outside the sphere of armed conflict, the international human rights instruments are silent on the point and there has been no case law on it. Although the UN Convention against Torture provides for universality of jurisdiction over alleged torturers, it does not do so in respect of persons suspected of perpetrating other ill-treatment, although its article 16 provides that this is without prejudice to what the prevailing international legal position may be. It may be argued that although article 10 of the Declaration against Torture requires the instigation of criminal proceedings against torturers only, it still implies that criminal sanctions might be appropriate for perpetrators of some other forms of prohibited ill-treatment; this may be a basis for envisaging individual responsibility under international law in such cases. In the absence of guidance as to just what forms of ill-treatment may be relevant here, perhaps the safest approach would be to envisage the possibility of international criminal responsibility of the individual where the acts in question are, at least, serious crimes under the law of the country where they were committed and probably would be similarly criminal under the laws of most countries. It would also probably include medical experimentation on unconsenting prisoners (see Chapter 9), a practice which, it will be recalled, is not only a specific grave breach of the Geneva Conventions, but also one which was seen by those who framed the original prohibition of torture and other ill-treatment as having a gravity equivalent to that of torture. Such practices would, in any event, be close to the borderline with torture and fall within the concept of inhuman treatment.

SUMMARY

Breach of the prohibition against torture and other ill-treatment attracts state responsibility (a) to investigate the facts even, in the case of torture and perhaps also in the case of other ill-treatment, in the absence of a specific complaint from the alleged victim; (b) to bring to justice those responsible; and (c) to compensate the victim. The state is also required to take measures to prevent recurrence and to avoid sending a person to a state where there is a substantial risk of the person's being subjected to torture or ill-treatment. Under the UN and OAS Conventions against Torture, liability to trial for torture will be on the basis of compulsory universal jurisdiction in those states that are parties to the Conventions. This is also the case as regards torture and inhuman treatment when perpetrated on persons in the hands of a party to an international armed conflict. Permissive universal jurisdiction probably applies to torture committed by nationals of non-state parties to those Conventions. This may also be the case in respect of cruel or inhuman treatment, including mutilation and medical or scientific experimentation on unconsenting human victims. The same goes for such treatment when committed in connection with non-international armed conflict or in the context of crimes against humanity. At least when committed under either of the latter conditions or in international armed conflict, perpetrators may become amenable to international criminal jurisdiction.

5

International Remedies for Torture and Other Ill-treatment

INTRODUCTION

This chapter will focus on those intergovernmental measures which are aimed specifically at dealing with the problem of torture and other ill-treatment. In principle, there is no reason why there should be mechanisms tailored to this particular form of human rights violation only, since it is covered by wider instruments. Thus, parties to international armed conflicts are, by the Geneva Conventions of 12 August 1949, which most countries of the world have ratified, obliged to accept supervision of all their obligations towards persons in their hands protected by the Conventions. Supervision—including access to detainees—is by a named 'protecting power' or, more commonly, the International Committee of the Red Cross.[1] Similarly, as has been seen, there are bodies set up to monitor compliance with general human rights conventions. For example, the Inter-American Commission on Human Rights has been concerned with a large number of individual complaints of torture and the practice has been a central part of its reports on specific countries. It is the only treaty-based body capable of dealing, on its own initiative, with general human rights investigation in countries which belong to the Organization of American States (OAS), the regional body that gave birth to it.[2] The European Commission of Human Rights may receive individual complaints of human rights violations from all of the members of the Council of Europe, but, in the absence of an interstate complaint, is effectively unable to consider human rights violations or torture as

---

[1] See, for example, Abi-Saab, 'The Implementation of Humanitarian Law', in Cassese (ed.), *The New Humanitarian Law of Armed Conflict* (1979), 310. Under Additional Protocol I to the Geneva Conventions, the system of supervision is supplemented by provision for the establishment of an International Fact-Finding Commission (article 90(1)(a)) whose jurisdiction is optional and applicable only in respect of international armed conflicts.

[2] The Commission's mandate is now laid down by the American Convention on Human Rights. See Shelton, 'The Inter-American Human Rights System', in Hannum (ed.), *Guide to International Human Rights Practice* (2nd edn., 1992), 119; Medina Quiroga, *The Battle of Human Rights—Gross, Systematic Violations and the Inter-American System* (1988). 25 member states of the OAS are parties to the Convention, but the Commission's powers extend to non-parties who are OAS members. Furthermore, as noted in Chapter 2, the Commission's existing functions of protection against torture are taken for granted in the new Inter-American Convention to Prevent and Punish Torture and certain additional functions are envisaged for it (Annex 2b, articles 16 and 17).

a systematic practice.[3] Most people living in states outside these regions (that is, in the great majority of countries) have initially no effective channels of complaint to international treaty bodies available to them. This lack of access to channels of complaint is diminished in the case of the ninety-three countries that have ratified the first Optional Protocol to the International Covenant on Civil and Political Rights, which permits individuals to complain to the Human Rights Committee.[4] Although this route to the Human Rights Committee provides some opportunity of recourse, there is again no formal means for the Committee to deal with a systematic practice of human rights violations, including torture, except in the case of an interstate complaint.[5] The UN Commission on Human Rights has a confidential procedure for dealing with 'consistent patterns of gross and reliably attested violations of human rights'.[6] It also has a public procedure for examining allegations of human rights violations (including torture) but only when urged to do so by one or more of the governments represented at the Commission which have gathered adequate support for their proposal;[7] these procedures, with their shortcomings, have been fully and frequently described elsewhere.[8] None of the above-mentioned procedures envisages any preventive action and rarely affords any possibility of individual relief or redress (see Chapter 4).

---

[3] The Commission is established under the European Convention on Human Rights. All states parties have accepted the right of individual complaint to the Commission under article 25. When, as is expected by 1999, the 11th Protocol to the Convention comes into force, the Commission will be subsumed into a unified European Court of Human Rights to which individuals will have direct access, marking a major advance in the granting of legal standing to individuals under international law. On the problems for individuals of bringing systematic practices before the Commission and Court, see Kamminga, 'Is the European Convention on Human Rights Sufficiently Equipped to Cope with Gross and Systematic Violations?', 12 *NQHR* 153 (1994); and Reidy, Hampson and Boyle, 'Gross Violations of Human Rights: Invoking the European Convention on Human Rights in the Case of Turkey', 15 *NQHR* 161 (1997); also Rodley, 'Systematic Violations of Human Rights and the Individual Petition System', paper presented at British Institute of Human Rights, Conference on the European Convention on Human Rights—The Eleventh Protocol: Problems of Procedure, London, 15 Mar. 1996, available from the Institute or the author.

[4] 140 states are parties to the International Covenant on Civil and Political Rights.

[5] See articles 41 and 42. 47 states have made the optional declaration recognizing the jurisdiction of the Human Rights Committee over interstate complaints.

[6] Ecosoc res. 1503 (XLVIII), 27 May 1970.

[7] Ecosoc res. 1235 (XLII), 6 June 1967.

[8] See, for example, Möller, 'Petitioning the United Nations', *Universal Human Rights*, vol. i, no. 4 (1979), 57; Tardu, 'United Nations Response to Gross Violations of Human Rights: The 1503 Procedure', 20 *Santa Clara Law Review* 559 (1980); Zuijdwijk, *Petitioning the United Nations* (1982), 1–116; Bossuyt, 'The Development of Special Procedures of the United Nations Commission on Human Rights', 6 *HRLJ* 179 (1985); Dormenval, *Procédures onusiennes de mise en oeuvre des droits de l'homme: limites ou défauts?* (Presses Universitaires de France, 1991); Alston, 'The Commission on Human Rights', in Alston (ed.), *The United Nations and Human Rights—A Critical Appraisal* (1992), 126; Rodley, 'Towards a more effective and integrated system of human rights protection by the United Nations', United Nations, World Conference on Human Rights, UN doc. A/CONF.157/PC/60/Add. 6 (1993).

Despite the universal condemnation of torture (see Chapter 1), the world community hesitated to accept, in respect of torture, specific international measures of implementation that it would more understandably be unprepared to accept in respect of the broader range of human rights violations. A move in the direction of implementation of the prohibition of torture may have been the intention behind the General Assembly's request in 1975, formulated in the wake of its adoption of the Declaration against Torture (see Annex 1), that the Commission on Human Rights should study 'any necessary steps for . . . ensuring the effective observance of the Declaration'.[9] Such seems to have been the understanding of the governments that submitted a draft resolution to the next session of the Commission on Human Rights.[10] By this draft resolution the Commission would have invited the Sub-Commission on Prevention of Discrimination and Protection of Minorities 'to bring to the attention of those Governments concerned for their comments any reliably attested information submitted to it giving rise to concern in relation to the effective observance of the Declaration' (operative paragraph 3). The Commission would also have called on 'all Governments to cooperate fully in the implementation of this resolution' (operative paragraph 5), and would have decided to give priority consideration each year to an envisaged annual report of the Sub-Commission (operative paragraph 6).

The draft did not come up for discussion until the last morning of the Commission's 1976 session, nor was there any earlier consideration of its substance.[11] The non-aligned group of countries proposed that the paragraphs of the draft resolution just referred to should be deleted,[12] and this proposal secured the reluctant acquiescence of the sponsors of the original draft. Thus amended, the resolution as adopted by the Commission was limited to inviting the Sub-Commission to draw upon the Declaration against Torture 'as a guideline for its work' on the question of the human rights of persons subjected to any form of detention or imprisonment and to recommending that it examine 'the relevant information submitted' under this item 'in the light of the principles contained in the Declaration'. The Sub-Commission was to report annually to the Commission.[13]

The caution displayed by the Commission did not, however, end prospects for implementation of the norms relating to the prohibition of torture and other ill-treatment. The following sections deal with a number of further developments, in the General Assembly, the Commission, and the Sub-

---

[9] GA res. 3453 (XXX), 9 Dec. 1975; see Chapter 1.

[10] UN doc. E/CN.4/L.1329A (1976) (Austria, Canada, Costa Rica, France, Federal Republic of Germany, Italy, Turkey, USA). Amnesty International, taking a similar line in a statement circulated to the Commission, had suggested the setting up of a working group of experts—see UN doc. E/CN.4/NGO/189 (1976).

[11] Commission on Human Rights, Report, 32nd Session. *ESCOR*, 60th Session, Supplement No. 3 (1982), para. 160.

[12] UN doc. E/CN.4/SR.1378, paras. 44–6.   [13] Res. 10 (XXXII), 5 Mar. 1976.

Commission. Later developments will be seen to have involved major advances in this field, especially the naming by the Commission of a Special Rapporteur on Torture and the provision for a Committee against Torture to be created under the Convention against Torture, as well as a far-reaching preventive mechanism: the European Committee for the Prevention of Torture.

GENERAL ASSEMBLY QUESTIONNAIRE ON TORTURE

It will be recalled from Chapter 1 that in 1977 the General Assembly decided that UN member states should be asked to respond to a questionnaire concerning the effect they had given to the provisions of the Declaration against Torture. Pursuant to the General Assembly decision (resolution 32/63, 8 December 1977), the Secretary-General circulated a questionnaire soliciting the relevant information. The information sought by the questionnaire was essentially of two types.[14] Most of the questions aimed to elicit information on the legislative, administrative, and judicial factors that might be involved in giving effect to the Declaration's provisions, and many of the responses were informative in this regard.[15] Two questions, however, were designed to bring out information on what measures states take in practice. The responses to these questions might have been expected to give a basis for consideration of the extent to which torture actually occurred in the responding countries, and what efforts had been made to combat it. Thus, question 11 asked whether 'any investigations have been carried out or any proceedings instituted in connection with allegations of torture' or other forms of ill-treatment; and question 15 sought indications of 'the progress accomplished and difficulties encountered, if any, as regards the prevention and punishment of torture' and other ill-treatment. Both referred to the period since the Declaration was adopted.

The overwhelming majority of the sixty-two states which responded to the questionnaire either did not answer question 11, or stated that they did not have the relevant data, or claimed that no allegations of torture had been received, or that no investigations had been made or proceedings instituted (thus leaving unclear whether allegations had been received but not acted upon). Of the rest, two responses stated the belief that there had been no relevant cases and indicated that other complaints of excessive police use of force were dealt with in the normal way.[16] Another country that had only recently made torture and ill-treatment a specific offence could not isolate relevant cases from the statistics relating to acts contrary to legislation

---

[14] UN docs. A/33/196 (1978), Annex; A/34/144 (1979), Annex.
[15] UN docs. A/33/196 and Adds. 1–3 (1978); A/34/144 (1979); A/35/369 and Adds. 1–2 (1980).
[16] Norway and Sweden: UN doc. A/33/196, 65 and 83 respectively.

prohibiting the infliction of bodily harm.[17] One country asserted that 'the necessary action . . . was taken by the appropriate courts or bodies' under existing legislation.[18] Two countries referred to the existence of commissions of inquiry. One of them enclosed a copy of a report from such a commission which contained damaging findings of police maltreatment under an earlier administration during a state of emergency.[19] The other was still considering the report of a commission, but stated that 'in a recent case, two policemen were charged and convicted of maltreating a murder suspect'.[20] Also the State Attorney of that country had 'personally conducted an investigation' into allegations of maltreatment made by a journalist. Four other countries offered similar information. Two merely gave an affirmative response, one indicating the occurrence of torture 'at various times, with legal action following, both judicial and administrative';[21] the other responding that 'investigations have been carried out and proceedings have been instituted in connexion with police and prison officials'.[22] Another country noted the institution of '22 administrative investigations of mistreatment of prisoners in various prisons in the country, which represents a marked decrease in comparison with previous years'.[23] Only the fourth responded with any degree of detail, pointing to two court cases, one of prison warders convicted of wilful bodily harm and injury to prisoners (before the Declaration was adopted) and one of policemen convicted, *inter alia*, of involuntary homicide and wilful bodily harm. In each case the offenders were given suspended custodial sentences and fined.[24]

As to question 15, only one country acknowledged any difficulties in implementing the Declaration. It stated that 'the progress made is apparent from the reduction in the number of cases of torture, and the difficulties encountered are due to the persistence of a repressive mentality which has to be reformed'.[25]

Thus the responses to the questionnaire cannot be said to have provided a superabundance of information. But, as the experience of the Committee on the Elimination of Racial Discrimination[26] and the Human Rights Committee[27] have shown, a well-informed and independently briefed body of experts could have used the responses, even those not giving information on questions 11 and 15, to probing effect. In fact, no such thing happened. In introducing the question at the 1978 session of the Third Committee of the

---

[17] Spain: UN doc. A/34/144, 97.   [18] Turkey: id., 103–4.
[19] India: id., 37.   [20] Israel: UN doc. A/35/369, 18.
[21] Pakistan: UN doc. A/33/196, 25.   [22] Venezuela: UN doc. A/35/369/Add. 1, 47.
[23] Chile: UN doc. A/33/196, 25.   [24] Senegal: id., 75.
[25] Venezuela: UN doc. A/35/369/Add. 1, 48.
[26] Buergenthal, 'Implementing the UN Racial Convention', 12 *Texas International Law Journal* 187 (1977).
[27] 'Human Rights Committee', *The Review* (International Commission of Jurists, Dec. 1980), 35, 36. McGoldrick, *The Human Rights Committee—Its Role in the Development of the International Covenant on Civil and Political Rights* (1991).

General Assembly, the Director of the Human Rights Division of the UN Secretariat invited the Committee 'to consider in what manner' the information contained in the responses 'could be scrutinized and analysed'.[28] One concrete suggestion he made was that the information might be forwarded to the Sub-Commission on Prevention of Discrimination and Protection of Minorities to be considered 'together with other information that it received annually on the human rights of persons subjected to any form of detention or imprisonment'[29] (see below).

During the discussion only three delegations referred to the questionnaire. Two referred to their countries' moves to give effect to the Declaration[30] and two pointed to the gap between law and practice.[31] The resolution adopted by the General Assembly pursuant to this discussion confined itself to noting the replies, calling for responses from governments that had not yet given them, and requesting the Secretary-General to submit these responses to the General Assembly and to submit all the information to the Commission on Human Rights and the Sub-Commission on Prevention of Discrimination and Protection of Minorities.[32]

Although eight delegations referred to the questionnaire during the 1979 discussion in the Third Committee, there was no effective scrutiny of replies. Half merely mentioned the questionnaire or stressed the utility of replies to it.[33] Two drew attention to their own governments' replies, stressing constitutional or legislative provisions against torture.[34] One referred to the burden created for governments by the increasing requests for reports of this type.[35] One repeated its concern at the tendency of replies 'to limit themselves to a purely legalistic approach'.[36] The General Assembly adopted a resolution to the same effect as that of the previous year. It also provided for transmission of the information to the Sixth UN Congress on the Prevention of Crime and the Treatment of Offenders.[37]

By 1980, it was clear that the questionnaire exercise was not affording any possibility of formal consideration of individual responses. In the understated formulation of one delegation, it was to be 'regretted that the review of the various positions of Member States was proceeding so slowly'.[38] The only other delegation to refer to the questionnaire during the Third Committee debate drew attention to the increasing number of responses, including that of its own government.[39] Given this cursory consideration of the matter, the

---

[28] *GAOR*, 33rd Session, Third Committee, Summary Records, A/C.3/33/SR.69, para 4.
[29] Ibid. [30] Libya: id., A/C.3/33/SR.71, para. 62; Jordan: id., para. 130.
[31] Jordan: ibid.; Netherlands: id., paras. 133–6. [32] GA res. 33/178, 20 Dec. 1978.
[33] Australia: A/C.3/34/SR.31, para. 15; UK: id., para. 17; Panama: id., para. 24; Austria: A/C.3/34/SR.32, para. 32.
[34] Kenya: A/C.3/34/SR.32, para. 44; Spain: id., para. 7.
[35] Italy: A/C.3/34/SR.31, para. 5. [36] Netherlands: A/C.3/34/SR.31, para 7.
[37] GA res. 34/167, 17 Dec. 1979. [38] Italy: A/C.3/35/SR.76, para. 15.
[39] Spain: A/C.3/35/SR.75, para. 13.

General Assembly decided to dispose of it by asking the Secretary-General to forward replies to the questionnaire to the Human Rights Committee 'for the use of Committee members when dealing with questions relating to torture' and other ill-treatment.[40] No new responses were sought and there was no discussion of the questionnaire at subsequent sessions. To the extent that it had been a potential implementation technique, this result suggests that the General Assembly itself was not ready to embark on implementation.

SUB-COMMISSION ANNUAL REVIEW OF PRISONERS' RIGHTS

In 1973, the Sub-Commission on Prevention of Discrimination and Protection of Minorities decided that it wished to have an item on its agenda entitled 'Question of the human rights of persons subjected to any form of detention or imprisonment'.[41] The question arose in the context of a debate about the Sub-Commission's 'inadequate means for investigating violations of human rights',[42] a debate that had envinced some frustration, from both non-governmental organizations and expert members. The need for action was urged by Mr Capotorti, who wanted the Sub-Commission to examine 'the treatment of prisoners in general and political prisoners in particular'.[43] The wording of what became the new agenda item was that of Mr Gros Espiell, speaking in support.[44] As Mr Gros Espiell put it a year later, the proposal 'had arisen from concern expressed in the Sub-Commission the previous year during the consideration of the report of the working group on individual communications . . .[45] That report had contained a paragraph drawing attention to the problems raised by the situation of political prisoners in certain countries . . .'.[46] The decision to include the agenda item was taken without substantial debate.[47]

With the approval of the Commission on Human Rights,[48] which was granted after its chairman drew attention to General Assembly resolution 3059 (XXVIII),[49] the Sub-Commission considered the agenda item at its next (twenty-seventh) session in 1974. The discussion was introduced by Mr Gros

---

[40] GA res. 35/178, 15 Dec. 1980.
[41] UN doc. E/CN.4/Sub.2/SR.677, 123–9. See, generally, Burke, 'New United Nations Procedure to Protect Prisoners and Other Detainees', 64 *California Law Review* 205 (1976); Prémont, 'United Nations Procedures for the Protection of All Persons Subjected to Any Form of Detention or Imprisonment', 20 *Santa Clara Law Review* 603 (1980).
[42] UN doc. E/CN.4/Sub.2/SR.686, 188.   [43] Ibid.   [44] Id., 189.
[45] The concern stemmed from the apparent lack of action under the procedure for dealing with 'consistent patterns of gross violations of human rights' referred to above (text accompanying n. 6): loc. cit. *supra* n. 41.
[46] UN doc. E/CN.4/Sub.2/SR.690, 34–5.   [47] Ibid.
[48] Decision 6 (XXX), 6 Mar. 1974, Commission on Human Rights, Report, 30th Session. *ESCOR*, 55th Session, Supplement No. 5 (1974), Chapter XIX B.
[49] i.e. the resolution on torture (see Chapter 1); UN doc. E/CN.4/SR.1286, 222.

Espiell who, after giving the background described in the previous paragraph, said that 'the origin of the problem was political, in the reappearance of torture of prisoners as a normal situation'. He suggested the establishment of a working group to produce a draft resolution 'setting forth the essential principles underlying the human rights of persons subjected to any form of detention or imprisonment',[50] and justified this on the grounds of the topic's 'great relevance, especially for political prisoners, who were often tortured and subjected to cruel treatment'.[51] Most subsequent interventions,[52] as well as one written statement from a non-governmental organization (NGO),[53] confirm the centrality of the issue of torture, especially of political prisoners, in the minds of Sub-Commission members and observers. As had been the case in the General Assembly the previous year (see Chapter 1), the concrete example of Chile was conspicuous.[54] The working group was established and in due course produced a draft resolution[55] that, with minor amendment,[56] became resolution 7 (XXVII) of 20 August 1974.

The preamble to the resolution expressed the Sub-Commission's grave concern 'at numerous reports that violations of the basic human rights of persons detained or imprisoned persist in various parts of the world' (first preambular paragraph). It continued with an extensive enumeration, drawn mainly from the provisions of the International Covenant on Civil and Political Rights, of the 'basic human rights' that detained or imprisoned persons 'should enjoy at least' (first preambular paragraph). A further two paragraphs focus on torture, noting the persistence of torture and ill-treatment (fourth preambular paragraph) and the non-suspendability under the Covenant of the right not to be subjected to torture or ill-treatment (third preambular paragraph).

Thus in its preambular paragraphs the resolution dealt with the normative aspects of the question and the strong influence of the issue of torture and other ill-treatment as motivation for the Sub-Commission's concern. Its operative paragraphs contained the seeds of a possible mechanism for addressing allegations of violations of the human rights of prisoners and detainees. The Sub-Commission would 'review annually developments in the field'; this review would take into account information from governments, intergovernmental bodies, and concerned NGOs having consultative status with the UN Economic and Social Council (Ecosoc) (operative paragraph 1). The Secretary-General was to channel this information to the Sub-Commission (operative paragraph 2). At this point the stage seemed to have been set for a

[50] UN doc. E/CN.4/Sub.2/SR.690, 35.   [51] Id., 36.

[52] UN docs. E/CN.4/Sub.2/SR.690-2, 36-52.

[53] UN doc. E/CN.4/Sub.2/NGO/49 (Amnesty International).

[54] It was referred to especially by Mr Smirnov (of the USSR) and by Professor Newman (representing Amnesty International, on behalf of which organization he had recently visited Chile): UN doc. E/CN.4/Sub.2/SR.692, 49-50.

[55] UN doc. E/CN.4/Sub.2/L.609/Rev. 1.   [56] UN docs. E/CN.4/Sub.2/L.616 and L.617.

possible non-confidential consideration by the Sub-Commission of information alleging torture and other violations of the basic human rights of prisoners.

The next Sub-Commission discussion, in 1975, concentrated more on how to proceed with the item than on its substance. There were practical inhibitions on dealing with substance: in particular the contributions from NGOs that the Secretary-General had solicited under resolution 7 (XXVII) had not been issued as documents and became available for scrutiny by Sub-Commission members only just before the discussion.[57] The Sub-Commission limited itself to passing a resolution which isolated certain themes for particular attention in its next (1976) annual review and to requesting of the Secretary-General a synopsis of NGO information.[58]

When introducing the draft of this resolution, one of its sponsors, Mr Van Boven, indicated that he had in mind a synopsis 'with the emphasis placed on types of practices rather than on countries that engaged in them'.[59] When in 1976 the Secretariat's synopsis appeared, therefore, it contained a well-organized presentation of information submitted by NGOs, but, in the words of one NGO observer, 'in it anonymous non-governmental organizations made charges against anonymous Governments'.[60] Indeed, while the material permitted the Sub-Commission to single out particular areas on which to focus at future sessions, it was becoming increasingly clear that the full Sub-Commission was not a suitable forum for concrete discussion of specific examples of violations of the human rights of detainees and prisoners. Accordingly the Sub-Commission recommended that the Commission on Human Rights authorize the establishment of a pre-sessional working group of the Sub-Commission 'to analyse the material received . . . and to prepare the Sub-Commission's annual review of developments in this field'.[61] Perhaps such a working group would be able to move from the general to the specific.

The Commission did not act on the Sub-Commission's recommendation. The request was repeated annually at its sessions from 1977 to 1980, but each time no authorization was forthcoming. Meanwhile, during this period, the Sub-Commission dealt with a number of important general issues that will be taken up in later chapters, including the drafting of a body of principles on the human rights of detainees or imprisoned persons, the problem of states of emergency and their effect on such rights (see Chapter 11), and the practice of 'disappearances' (see Chapter 8).

---

[57] See comment of Mr Nettel (Austria): UN doc. E/CN.4/Sub.2/SR.735/Add. 1, 190.

[58] Resolution 4 (XXVIII), 10 Sept. 1975, Report of the Sub-Commission on Prevention of Discrimination and Protection of Minorities (hereinafter 'Sub-Commission Report'), 28th Session (E/CN.4/1180; E/CN.4/Sub.2/364), Chapter XXI A.

[59] UN doc. E/CN.4/Sub.2/SR.739, 230.

[60] UN doc. E/CN.4/Sub.2/SR.754, para. 33 (Amnesty International).

[61] Resolution 3 A (XXIX), 31 Aug. 1976, Sub-Commission Report, 29th Session (E/CN.4/1218; E/CN.4/Sub.2/378), Chapter XVII A.

In 1981, the Sub-Commission, taking advantage of the fact that it did not require authorization from any superior body to establish a sessional working group (as opposed to a pre-sessional one that would have financial implications),[62] decided to establish such a group to deal with the item.[63] The working group was convened for the current session. A significant proportion of its report dealt with procedural questions as to the role of the working group.[64] The remaining discussion, perhaps because group members and NGOs were unprepared for the sudden emergence of the group, seemed to be a rehearsal of the general questions that are normally discussed in plenary sessions of the Sub-Commission.[65]

When the group was re-established in 1982,[66] however, it showed itself to have potential for taking stock of specific violations of prisoners' rights in particular countries. The working group used as the basis of its work the headings of the table of contents in the synopsis of NGO materials prepared by the UN Secretary-General, which specified categories of human rights violations.[67] Typically, consideration of a subject-heading would be a mixture of discussion of problems raised by the practices described in the NGO synopsis and (although it does not appear clearly from the working groups report) presentation, mainly by NGO observers, of examples of relevant human rights violations.[68] One example of attention to a particular case is contained in the report, namely, a case of an alleged 'extra-territorial abduction' which was brought to the group's attention by the International Commission of Jurists.[69] The group recommended to the Sub-Commission that a telegram be sent to the government in question, and the Sub-Commission agreed to this.[70] This initiative was, however, seen as exceptional. The report of the working group did not otherwise refer to the particular countries alleged during the debate to have committed human rights violations.

The report concluded with a list of recommendations consisting primarily of safeguards against arbitrary arrest and detention. These safeguards

---

[62] UN doc. E/CN.4/Sub.2/SR. 902, para. 9.

[63] Sub-Commission Report, 34th Session (E/CN.4/1512; E/CN.4/Sub. 2/495), para. 150. The suggestion made by the chairman (E/CN.4/Sub.2/SR.897, para. 4) seems to have been implied by the director's opening address to the Sub-Commission (E/CN.4/Sub.2/SR.895, para. 13).

[64] Id., para. 176, sub-paras. 3–6.   [65] Id., para. 175, sub-paras. 7–16.

[66] UN doc. E/CN.4/Sub.2/1982/SR.6, paras. 3–4.

[67] For example, torture, 'disappearances', etc.: E/CN.4/Sub.2/1982/34.

[68] Recollection of the author, who attended the session as an observer for Amnesty International. One of the features of working groups is the latitude they allow for interventions by NGOs during their deliberations. This was the period before NGO denunciations of human rights violations in the Commission and Sub-Commission had become standard practice: see Rodley, 'United Nations Non-Treaty Procedures for Dealing with Human Rights Violations', in Hannum (ed.), *Guide to International Human Rights Practice* (2nd edn., 1992), 60, 76–81.

[69] UN doc. E/CN.4/Sub.2/1982/34, para. 14 and footnote 1. The case concerned exiled former Malawi minister Orton Chirwa and his wife, who were allegedly abducted from Zambia by agents of the Malawi government.

[70] Decision 1982/8, 31 Aug. 1982, Sub-Commission Report, 35th Session (E/CN.4/1983/4; E/CN.4/Sub.2/1983/43), Chapter XXI B.

duplicated and partly expanded upon those contained in the draft body of principles on the human rights of all persons under any form of detention or imprisonment (see Chapter 11). With regard to torture, one recommendation, which was adopted by the full Sub-Commission in resolution 1982/10, envisaged that, unless the Commission on Human Rights were to assume the task, the working group at its 1983 session would 'give special attention to hearing and receiving information . . . concerning the extent of and facts relating to torture or other cruel, inhuman or degrading treatment or punishment'.[71] Another recommendation also requested more time for the group's work.[72] The Sub-Commission seemed to be saying that, on the one hand, there was a need for action and that the Commission was the suitable body to deal with allegations of torture and other ill-treatment, just as it had started dealing with 'disappearances' and arbitrary and summary executions (see Chapters 8, 6, and 7), and, on the other hand, that, in the absence of Commission action, the Sub-Commission would undertake the responsibility.

In fact, the Commission, at its intervening session early in 1983, specifically requested the Sub-Commission to 'defer the implementation' of this decision, pending the Commission's own consideration of the matter at its 1984 session.[73]

A number of factors may have prompted the decision to request deferral: one was that little time was available to discuss the Sub-Commission's proposal for special hearings on torture;[74] another was that the Commission had just adopted a resolution (after a sharp debate) on the proper role of the Sub-Commission;[75] a third, as indicated later in this chapter, was that the Commission's working group on the draft convention against torture had been proceeding in its examination of implementation mechanisms to be incorporated into the draft convention; delegations may have been reluctant to adopt any posture that could risk unsettling this working group's progress.

It is not clear how the working group would have conducted its hearings on torture. Nevertheless, the Commission's decision did nothing to impair the group's continued efforts to deal with torture as one of its categories of violations of the human rights of prisoners. Thus, when the working group met again in 1983, it continued to provide a forum for NGOs to denounce practices of torture and other violations of the human rights of prisoners. But it was a limited opportunity, the substantive work being done in one half-day

[71] Resolution 1982/10, 7 Sept. 1982, para. 17: ibid.

[72] Id., para. 18. The working group had only four one-hour meetings, most of the last hour being taken up by the process of adopting the group's report.

[73] Decision 1983/104, 4 Mar. 1983, Commission on Human Rights, Report, 39th Session, *ESCOR*, 1983, Supplement No. 3, Chapter XXVII B.

[74] The proposal had been circulated only earlier the same day.

[75] Resolution 1983/22, 4 Mar. 1983, Commission on Human Rights, Report, *supra* n. 73, Chapter XXVII A. The debate preceding adoption of the resolution may be found in UN docs. E/CN.4/1983/SR.20–5 and 28.

session.[76] The Commission on Human Rights has, meanwhile, effectively taken up the implied invitation in Sub-Commission resolution 1982/10: in 1985 it created a Special Rapporteur on Torture.

SPECIAL RAPPORTEUR ON TORTURE

Despite its earlier coolness, the Commission on Human Rights decided to grasp the nettle and create its own mechanism on torture. At the close of its 1984 session, the Assistant Secretary-General for Human Rights, Mr Herndl, broached the topic. He did so in the context of recent evolution in the Commission's attitude to implementation, especially its establishment of a working group on 'disappearances' (see Chapter 8) and a Special Rapporteur on Summary or Arbitrary Executions (see Chapters 6 and 7). He said: 'Of the three fundamental phenomena, hitherto identified within the Commission, affecting the right to life—namely, summary executions, disappearances and torture, torture would seem to be in need of a fact-finding mechanism of its own . . .'.[77] In this, he was reflecting a recommendation of an international colloquium on how to combat torture, convened in Geneva in April 1983.[78]

At the opening of the 1985 session of the Commission, the chairman of the previous session (Mr Kooijmans, representative of The Netherlands) took the opportunity of the traditional speech of the outgoing chair to renew the call for Commission 'monitoring machinery' on torture.[79] Later, when introducing the relevant item of the agenda in advance of the debate, the Assistant Secretary-General for Human Rights drew attention to 'the need for a fact finding mechanism or special procedure' on torture.[80] The idea was then taken up by a number of speakers.[81] Eventually, the representative of the recently installed civilian government of Argentina—taking an initiative whose symbolic significance was clear to all—introduced the draft of what was to become resolution 1985/33 of 13 March 1985, aimed at appointing a Special Rapporteur on Torture.[82] During the discussion of the draft resolution, doubts were expressed both as to timing (just as the Convention against Torture was beginning to gather signatories)[83] and as to uncertainty about the role of the proposed Special Rapporteur.[84] A vote was taken and the

---

[76] UN doc. E.CN.4/Sub.2/1983/WG.1/2.   [77] UN doc. E/CN.4/1984/SR.63, para. 48.
[78] Swiss Committee Against Torture, *How to Combat Torture—Report of the International Colloquium, Geneva, 1983* (1984), 42, where the idea was suggested in a paper presented by the present writer.
[79] UN doc. E/CN.4/1985/SR.1, para. 7.   [80] UN doc. E/CN.4/1985/SR.27, para. 42.
[81] UN docs. E/CN.4/1985/SR.28–31 and 33.
[82] UN doc. E/CN.4/1985/SR.55, para. 50. As early as 1977, the General Assembly's Third Committee had heard mooted the idea that the Commission or the Sub-Commission might name a special rapporteur to prepare 'a report on the most serious problems' relating to torture: UN doc. A/C.3/32/SR.37, para. 43 (United States).
[83] Id., para. 57 (Tanzania).   [84] Id., paras. 55–6 (Cameroon).

proposal was adopted with no votes against, but with twelve abstentions.[85] Less than three months later consensus was to be restored when Ecosoc ratified the Commission's decision without a vote.[86] Meanwhile, on 22 May 1985 it was announced that the Chairman of the 1985 session had appointed his predecessor, Peter Kooijmans, to serve as the Special Rapporteur.[87] After serving for eight years, he retired in December 1992 and the chairman of the 1993 Session of the Commission appointed the present writer to replace him.

Before considering the mandate of the Special Rapporteur, it may be worth speculating on how, ten years after the adoption of the Declaration against Torture, it was at last possible to establish an implementation mechanism on torture for the whole of the UN. It is suggested that three principal factors coincided to make the development possible. First, the idea of an implementation mechanism to deal with a particularly grave type of human rights violation was no longer new to the Commission, which had already established 'thematic mechanisms' for 'disappearances' and for summary or arbitrary executions. Indeed, as the Assistant Secretary-General for Human Rights had implied, a mechanism for dealing with allegations of torture would fill a specific gap that was now apparent. Second, as emerges clearly from Chapter 1, it is the case that, when international public opinion is seen to be concerned about a problem, it is easier to make progress. In this case, Amnesty International had, since April 1984, been conducting a renewed campaign against the problem of torture, the springboard for which had been a worldwide survey of the scope of the problem.[88] Clearly a further standard-setting exercise by the UN, such as had occurred in the 1970s, would no longer be perceived as a pertinent response. In this connection it may also be relevant that governments had been approached by Amnesty International national sections in advance of the Commission session, urging support for the idea of a mechanism to deal with torture.[89] Third, the Commission was no longer preoccupied with drafting a convention against torture and, in particular, with debating the nature of the implementation mechanism the convention might create for states parties. The issue had been disposed of the previous year; the General Assembly had gone on to adopt the Convention, and its provisions were now known (see below). Work on it could not, therefore, be invoked as grounds for deferral. Nor could its existence be argued as obviating the need for action by the Commission; for it was clear that it would be a matter of years before the whole of the world community would be subject to its implementation procedures.

[85] UN doc. E/CN.4/1985/SR.55, para. 62.   [86] Ecosoc decision 1985/144, 30 May 1985.

[87] United Nations Office at Geneva, Press Release HR 1704. Professor Kooijmans was then Professor of International Law in the University of Leiden. He is now a judge on the International Court of Justice.

[88] See Amnesty International, *Torture in the Eighties* (1984).

[89] 'A positive step against torture', Amnesty International *Newsletter*, vol. xvi, no. 5 (May 1985), 1.

NATURE AND FUNCTION OF THE SPECIAL RAPPORTEUR

As with most mechanisms established by the Commission at that time, the Special Rapporteur was appointed for one year. In 1986 his mandate was renewed for another year, and it has been renewed until the present.[90]

The mandate is couched largely in language that is also to be found in the resolutions establishing the mandates of the Working Group on Enforced or Involuntary Disappearances (Chapter 8) and the Special Rapporteur on Summary or Arbitrary Executions (Chapters 6 and 7). Thus, by Commission resolution 1985/33, he is to 'examine questions relevant to torture' (paragraph 1) and to report on 'the occurrence and extent of its practice' (paragraph 7).

At the beginning of the mandate there was some question concerning the scope of the mandate. While all the preambular paragraphs referred both to 'torture' and to 'cruel, inhuman or degrading treatment or punishment' (other ill-treatment), the relevant operative paragraphs, from which quotation has just been made, referred only to torture. This appears to be no accident: an early version of the draft resolution, on which resolution 1985/33 was based, referred to 'other ill-treatment' in the operative paragraphs also.[91] Nevertheless, the broader formulation remained in the preambular paragraphs and the Special Rapporteur has indicated that he would not feel compelled to take too narrow a view of the scope of the problem he was to examine (see Chapters 3 and 10).[92]

There was also some uncertainty as to the range of sources the Special Rapporteur could use for the discharge of his mandate. Following the example of the Special Rapporteur on Summary or Arbitrary Executions, he is 'to seek and receive information from Governments, as well as specialized agencies, intergovernmental organizations, and non-governmental organizations' (paragraph 3). It was unclear whether this precluded resort to sources other than those mentioned. Arguably, he would receive information from a broader range of sources than those from which he could 'seek and receive' information. Also, the term 'non-governmental organizations' is itself broad, since these can presumably be national as well as international NGOs. The NGOs need not have consultative status with the Economic and Social Council. The first Special Rapporteur indicated in his first report a flexible approach in this respect: he 'received members of non-governmental organizations and individuals' and on one occasion he 'heard a witness, who

---

[90] Now the thematic mechanisms tend to be renewed for three-year terms, the latest renewal having been effected by Commission on Human Rights resolution 1998/38, 17 Apr. 1998.

[91] Compare UN doc. E/CN.4/1985/L.44 (the text first circulated) with UN doc. E/CN.4/1985/L.44/Rev. 1 (the draft formally introduced by Argentina and adopted unamended).

[92] See his first report: UN doc. E/CN.4/1986/15, paras. 23 and 33 referring to a 'grey zone' between torture and other ill-treatment. His successor appears to have followed the practice: UN doc. E/CN.4/1997/7, para. 3.

testified that he had been tortured while held in detention by the army'.[93] The present Special Rapporteur has followed this flexible policy, putting the accent on the quality of the information (it should be 'credible and reliable') rather than its provenance.[94]

Like the other thematic mechanisms, the Special Rapporteur is to 'respond effectively to . . . information that comes before him', but, also like them, he is to act 'with discretion' (paragraph 6). In his case alone, the information he is to seek, receive, and act upon is expressly required to be 'credible and reliable' (paragraphs 3 and 6). The latter requirement does not appear to have been interpreted as a restriction on mandate as compared with that of the other theme mechanisms.

The working methods of the Special Rapporteur have become well established and were summarized in his annual report to the Commission at its 1997 session.[95] Briefly, they consist of transmitting 'non-accusatory' urgent appeals direct to the foreign ministry of the country concerned, primarily with a view to preventing feared harm (119 to 45 countries in 1997[96]); sending letters to governments, via their permanent missions in Geneva, concerning alleged cases of ill-treatment within the mandate, sometimes accompanied by 'allegations of a more general nature regarding torture practices' (48 letters to 45 governments in 1997[97]); receiving responses from those governments wishing to reply (in 1997, 28 responded in respect of some 345 cases submitted during 1997[98]); and reporting annually to the Commission on his activities, including a country-by-country summary of allegations and responses. Since 1994, the report also contains, 'where applicable', observations on the situation as disclosed by the information dealt with.[99]

The mandate also undertakes fact finding with the agreement of the government in question, usually in response to a request by the Special Rapporteur, but sometimes by way of unsolicited invitation. The previous Special Rapporteur went on one such visit (Indonesia, including East Timor[100]); by the end of 1997 the present Special Rapporteur had visited:

---

[93] UN doc. E/CN.4/1986/15, para. 61; see also para. 95.
[94] UN doc. E/CN.4/1997/7, Annex, para. 7.
[95] UN doc E/CN.4/1997/7, Annex.   [96] UN doc. E/CN.4/1998/38, para. 7.
[97] Ibid.   [98] Ibid.
[99] Id., para. 8. In 1997, the 39 countries in question were Afghanistan, Algeria, Armenia, Bahrain, Bolivia, Bulgaria, Cameroon, Chad, Chile, China, Colombia, Cuba, Egypt, Equatorial Guinea, Ethiopia, Georgia, Germany, India, Indonesia, Iran, Iraq, Israel, Kenya, Mexico, Myanmar, Nepal, Pakistan, Peru, Romania, Russian Federation, Spain, Sudan, Switzerland, Turkey, Ukraine, United States of America, Venezuela, Yemen, Yugoslavia.
[100] UN doc. E/CN.4/1992/17/Add. 1. Also, in 1987, he engaged in a three-country mission for 'on-site consultations' (Argentina, Colombia, and Uruguay): UN doc. E/CN.4/1988/17/Add. 1. The consultations were with the authorities of the respective countries, rather than the non-governmental sector. It was not, as such, a fact-finding mission and should be understood as an attempt to introduce the mandate to country missions. Neither Special Rapporteur repeated the exercise.

Russian Federation (1994),[101] Colombia (1994),[102] Chile (1995),[103] Pakistan (1996),[104] Portugal (1996),[105] Venezuela (1996),[106] and Mexico (1997).[107] The first Special Rapporteur joined the Special Rapporteur on the situation of human rights in the former Yugoslavia (1992), pursuant to a mandate adopted at the first special session of the Commission on Human Rights,[108] and the present Special Rapporteur accompanied the Special Rapporteur on the situation in Rwanda (1994) at the request of the latter, under a mandate adopted by the third special session of the Commission.[109] These visits are usually made the subject of a special report to the Commission describing the information received, conclusions to be drawn therefrom, and recommendations, mainly to the government concerned, indicating measures that should be taken to address the problem.

Typically, the annual report will also contain recommendations aimed at governments in general. A compilation of these was included in the Special Rapporteur's report to the 1995 session of the Commission.[110] As he stated in that report, 'if states were to comply with these recommendations, the incidence of torture in the world would be dramatically reduced'.[111] They boil down, essentially, to the need for measures to avoid incommunicado detention and impunity for the perpetrators.[112]

It should be understood that the Special Rapporteur, being a sub-body of the UN Commission on Human Rights, itself a functional commission of Ecosoc, cannot emit binding decisions. His findings, nevertheless, have the political status that emanates from a mandate consistently supported by the Commission, a body composed of fifty-three member states of the United Nations, which has also endorsed his recommendations concerning incommunicado detention and impunity.[113] The mandate was also firmly supported

---

[101] UN doc. E/CN.4/1995/34/Add.1 and Corr. 1. This invitation was, unusually, issued at the initiative of the government: id., para. 62.

[102] UN doc. E/CN.4/1995/111. This was a joint mission with the Special Rapporteur on Extrajudicial, Summary or Arbitrary Executions, the first and, as of the time of writing, only joint mission of thematic mechanisms alone.

[103] UN doc. E/CN.4/1996/35/Add. 2.   [104] UN doc. E/CN.4/1997/7/Add. 2.

[105] UN doc. E/CN.4/1997/7, paras. 95–111. The purpose of the visit, undertaken at the initiative of the government of Portugal, was to examine allegations of torture made by East Timorese now living in Portugal.

[106] UN doc. E/CN.4/1997/7Add. 3.   [107] UN doc. E/CN.4/1998/38/Add. 2.

[108] UN doc. E/CN.4/1993/26, para. 30.

[109] UN doc. E/CN.4/1995/34, para. 7. It should be noted that he will not usually seek to visit a country that is the subject of a country-specific mechanism, unless it seems to both that a joint visit is indicated, nor will he do so in respect of a country that is the subject of a thorough study by the Committee against Torture under article 20 of the Convention against Torture, as to which see below: UN doc. E/CN.4/1997/7, Annex, para. 11.

[110] Id., para. 926.   [111] Id., para. 923.

[112] The point is made explicitly in UN doc. E/CN.4/1994/31, para. 666.

[113] See, for example, resolution 1997/38, 11 Apr. 1997, Commission on Human Rights, Report, 53rd Session, *ESCOR*, 1997, Supplement No. 3, Chapter II A, operative paras. 7, 10, 19, and 20; also res. 1998/38, 17 Apr. 1998, operative paras. 4, 5, 19 and 20. By the latter resolution

by the 1993 Vienna World Conference on Human Rights.[114] His work confirms that a person who is tortured or threatened with torture is no longer outside the concern of the main organization of the world's states; on the contrary, the organization now seeks to hold its members to account for the fate of that individual.

UN CONVENTION AGAINST TORTURE

When the General Assembly first requested the Commission on Human Rights to draft a convention based on the Declaration against Torture, neither the resolution containing the request[115] nor the preceding debate made any reference to the possibility that the convention might incorporate measures of implementation. In 1980, however, stimulated by a resolution of the Sixth UN Crime Congress,[116] the General Assembly requested the Commission to include in its draft 'provisions for the effective implementation of the future convention'.[117] It renewed its request in 1981[118] and in 1982.[119]

In fact, although there had been no pre-1980 call for the inclusion of implementation measures in the draft convention, five articles (articles 16–20) of the original Swedish draft convention submitted to the Commission on Human Rights[120] dealt with such measures. They envisaged that the responsible body would be the Human Rights Committee established under the International Covenant on Civil and Political Rights.[121] Article 16 provided for a compulsory reporting procedure, whereby the Committee would consider reports submitted by states parties 'on measures taken to suppress torture and other cruel, inhuman or degrading treatment or punishment'. Such a procedure would be analogous to that under article 40 of the Covenant. Articles 18 and 19, again following the Covenant (articles 41 and 42), envisaged a system of optional interstate complaints.[122] Article 20, following the

---

the Commission also enhanced its support for the mandate by requesting the Special Rapporteur to make an oral report to the following session of the General Assembly (para 30).

[114] United Nations World Conference on Human Rights, Vienna, Austria, June 1993, Vienna Declaration and Programme of Action, 14 *HRLJ* 352, para. 57.

[115] GA res. 36/62, 8 Dec. 1977.

[116] Resolution 11, *Sixth United Nations Congress on the Prevention of Crime and the Treatment of Offenders—Report*, A/CONF.87/14/Rev. 1 (1981), chapter I B.

[117] GA res. 35/178, 15 Dec. 1980. In the fourth preambular paragraph, the Assembly welcomed resolution 11 of the Sixth UN Crime Congress.

[118] GA res. 36/60, 25 Nov. 1981.   [119] GA res. 37/193, 18 Dec. 1982.

[120] UN doc. E/CN.4/1285 (1978) and see Chapter 2. See, generally, Burgers and Danelius, *The United Nations Convention against Torture* (1988).

[121] In this it follows the International Association of Penal Law (IAPL) draft article XIII: UN doc. E/CN.4/NGO/213 (1978).

[122] i.e., as will be seen below, a state party may make a declaration recognizing the competence of the committee to receive a complaint against it submitted by another state party.

Optional Protocol to the Covenant, foresaw an optional system of individual petition to the Committee. Article 17 contained an innovative feature: the Committee could, if it received information of a systematic practice of torture in a state party, initiate an urgent inquiry that could include a visit to the state concerned if the latter consented.

In addition, after the 1980 session of the Commission, Costa Rica submitted a draft optional protocol to the draft convention 'for use as a basis for consideration by the Commission on Human Rights when once the Convention has been adopted'.[123] The draft optional protocol which had been prepared by the International Commission of Jurists,[124] would establish a system of routine and *ad hoc* visits to all places of detention in states adhering to it. The thrust of the proposal, disconnected as it is from any specific allegation of torture, was preventive;[125] it will be returned to below.

It was not until 1981 that the Commission's working group, having adopted many of the substantive articles of the draft convention, turned in a concerted way to the proposed implementation provisions. Views ranged widely on the merits of including implementation procedures: some considered that implementation should be left to national legal systems while others argued that as 'self-enforcement had been shown to be a failure . . . implementation procedures were an indispensable part of the treaty'.[126] The discussion was overshadowed by the arrival of a telegram from the UN's Legal Counsel[127] who doubted whether, in the absence of an amendment to the Covenant,[128] the proposed convention could confer any of the contemplated powers upon the Human Rights Committee.[129] This left the group with the additional problem of devising another supervisory body.

The report of the working group's 1982 session disclosed a more detailed discussion of all the above issues.[130] There was the same range of doubt as to whether there should be any international measures of implementation, even optional ones.[131] Various proposals for the composition of an implementation organ were considered, including bodies composed either of government representatives or of individual experts.[132] There was also some discussion of the details of the specific powers the implementation organ should have.[133]

---

[123] UN doc. E/CN.4/1409 (1980).   [124] Ibid.
[125] See, generally, International Commission of Jurists and Swiss Committee Against Torture, *Torture: How to Make the International Convention Effective* (2nd edn., 1980).
[126] Commission on Human Rights, Report, 37th Session, *ESCOR*, 1981, Supplement No. 5, para. 185, sub-para. 52.
[127] UN doc. E/CN.4/1981/WG.2/WP.6.
[128] The process of amending the Covenant is complicated, involving the convening of a diplomatic conference, and acceptance by the General Assembly and subsequent acceptance by two-thirds of the states parties to the Covenant (article 51).
[129] Commission on Human Rights, Report, *supra* n. 126, para. 185, sub-paras. 51, 53, and 54.
[130] UN doc. E/1982/12/Add. 1; E/CN.4/1982/30/Add. 1 (1982), paras. 49–83.
[131] Id., para. 53.   [132] Id., paras. 54–69.   [133] Id., paras. 70–83.

By 1983, a text began to emerge. Most significantly, no further opposition was expressed to the principle of including measures of international implementation,[134] but, while most delegations favoured a mandatory system,[135] two delegations preferred an optional one.[136] Subject to these basic divergences of approach, which were maintained throughout the session,[137] the group made progress in determining the nature of both the implementation organ and its functions.

This progress was continued at the working group's 1984 session. Indeed, as indicated in Chapter 2, the text of a draft convention was agreed, submitted to the Commission on Human Rights, and forwarded by the Commission through Ecosoc to the General Assembly. However, as will appear below, agreement was not reached on all aspects of the articles on implementation, leaving some matters to be resolved by the General Assembly. In any event, the Assembly adopted the text of the Convention against Torture and Other Cruel, Inhuman and Degrading Treatment or Punishment by resolution 39/46 of 10 December 1984 (for the full text, see Annex 2a). Having received the twentieth ratification (by Denmark), the Convention entered into force on 26 June 1987.[138]

COMMITTEE AGAINST TORTURE

Article 17 of the Convention provides for the establishment of a Committee against Torture consisting of 'ten experts of high moral standing and recognized competence in the field of human rights, who shall serve in their personal capacity'. After it came into force, the states parties to the Convention elected the first members of the Committee. As a nod in the direction of the original notion that the Human Rights Committee should be the responsible body, the electorate was to 'bear in mind the usefulness of nominating persons who are also members of the Human Rights Committee'.

Review of periodic reports

A procedure for considering periodic reports from states parties 'on the measures they have taken to give effect to their undertakings under this Convention' is contained in Article 19.[139] The article authorizes the Committee against Torture (henceforth 'the Committee') to receive and con-

---

[134] UN doc. E/CN.4/1983/63, paras. 48–68.   [135] Id., para. 31.
[136] Id., para. 30. The USSR wanted an optional protocol. The Ukrainian SSR would have had the optional clauses in the body of the convention as a compromise.
[137] Id., para. 62.   [138] As of 4 June 1998, there were 105 states parties.
[139] Article 19 corresponds to article 16 of the original Swedish draft. As to the scope of the undertakings, it may be noted that, during the negotiations on the text of the Convention, the representative of the United States expressed the 'understanding that incidents covered by the Geneva Conventions and Protocols thereto would not fall within the scope of the convention against torture and that to consider otherwise would result in an overlap of the different treaties which would undermine the objective of eradicating torture': UN doc. E/CN.4/1984/72, para. 5. Were such a view to prevail, then the jurisdiction of the Committee against Torture would not

sider such reports on a quadrennial basis. However, the Committee also has the power to request 'other reports' to be submitted.

Officially the only information available to the Committee is that provided by the state itself. In practice, NGOs will frequently make their information available to Committee members and the Secretariat will furnish the Committee with relevant information from other parts of the UN system, notably, the reports of the Special Rapporteur on Torture. Accordingly, the Committee is able to assess the states' reports in the light of the 'unofficial' information.

The Committee is empowered to make 'general comments' on 'each report' and these have to be forwarded to the state party concerned, which in turn may respond with its own observations. The Committee has the discretion to make public in its annual report such general comments, together with any observations from the state in question.

The nature of the general comments has evolved over the years. When the Committee began reviewing the reports in 1989, it made no comments as such. Its annual report merely summarized the discussion, with a final paragraph reporting 'the members'' observations which themselves tended to refrain from commenting on the situation as such, preferring rather to indicate further information that would be helpful in the next periodic report, when not simply congratulating the country;[140] however, by the end of 1989, it was becoming more assertive, with requests for additional reports if the members appeared more concerned about the situation.[141] By the end of 1990, the Committee put the heading 'concluding observations' above the paragraphs in question, thus giving the impression that, although mainly couched in terms of the views of 'members of the Committee', the paragraphs were reflecting a corporate committee opinion; they were also becoming more pointed.[142] The corporate view was formalized at the end of 1991, the concluding observations being expressly those of the Committee as such.[143] A year later, the 'concluding observations' had transmuted into 'conclusions

apply to situations of armed conflict. However, the argument is difficult to sustain in a treaty that pointedly affirms that neither 'a state of war' nor 'a threat of war' may be 'invoked as a justification of torture' (article 2(2)). In any event, as Norway pointed out at the General Assembly, the United States understanding would only seem 'relevant in relation to international armed conflicts'; this would be because, for such conflicts, 'the Geneva Conventions and the First Additional Protocol established a system of universal jurisdiction and of implementation that must be considered equal to the system of the convention against torture': UN doc. A/39/499 (1984), 15, para. 6. Even this would only apply to states that had accepted the competence of the International Fact-Finding Commission set up under article 90 of Protocol I.

[140] See Report of the Committee against Torture, *GAOR*, 44th Session, Supplement No. 46 (1989), chapter III.

[141] Report of the Committee against Torture, *GAOR*, 45th Session, Supplement No. 44 (1990), chapter IV.

[142] Report of the Committee against Torture, *GAOR*, 46th Session, Supplement No. 46 (1991), chapter IV.

[143] Report of the Committee against Torture, *GAOR*, 47th Session, Supplement No. 44 (1992), chapter IV.

and recommendations'.[144] By now, also, the conclusions were capable of being frank and critical.[145] Finally, at the end of 1993, the format that largely obtains at the time of writing was adopted. The Committee's conclusions and recommendations have an introductory section, a statement of 'positive aspects', a section on 'subjects of concern', and a section on recommendations,[146] the only innovation occurring at the end of 1996, with the addition between 'positive aspects' and 'subjects of concern' of a section on 'factors and difficulties impeding the application of the provisions of the Convention'.[147] The 'subjects of concern' section is the one that expresses the Committee's assessment of the situation of torture and ill-treatment in the country. This improvement in the format of the Committee's reaction to states' reports has, unfortunately, been accompanied by the loss from the annual report of the résumé of the exchange between the Committee and the government representatives. This must now be elicited from the 'summary records' of the Committee's proceedings, which are only accessible at specialized libraries.

In previous chapters, reference has frequently been made to 'general comments' of the Human Rights Committee, consisting of that Committee's general interpretation of specific articles or groups of articles under the International Covenant on Civil and Political Rights. This practice developed because, until the 1990s, the Human Rights Committee interpreted the Covenant article 40 language that referred to general comments to be made on states' 'reports' (note the plural) as precluding it from making comments on specific country reports. In fact, in the 1990s it developed country-specific concluding observations on the state reports in the same way as did the Committee against Torture. For its part, the Committee against Torture has (as of March 1998) only once availed itself of the technique of making comments of a general interpretative nature[147a].

At its seventeenth session in November 1996, the Committee initiated a new procedure. Stimulated during the session by reports in 'the media' that the Israeli Supreme Court had declared lawful the use of 'physical pressure' by the Israeli security services, the Committee, invoking its power under article 19 to request 'other reports', requested the Israeli government to submit a special report on the matter.[148] The Committee examined the government's

---

[144] Report of the Committee against Torture, *GAOR*, 48th Session, Supplement No. 44 (1993), chapter IV.

[145] e.g., 'the Committee noted with deep concern that . . . an extremely large number of acts of torture of all kinds were perpetrated in Mexico': id., para. 228.

[146] Report of the Committee against Torture, *GAOR*, 49th Session, Supplement No. 44 (1994), chapter IV.

[147] Report of the Committee against Torture, *GAOR*, 52nd Session, Supplement No. 44 (1997), chapter IV.

[147a] UN doc. CAT/C/xx/Misc. 1 (1997). The general comment concerns article 3 and explains the Committee's criteria for offering the sending of persons to countries where there are 'substantial grounds' to believe a person risked being subjected to torture; see notes 154–5 *infra* and accompanying text, and chapter 4 p. 116.   [148] Id., paras. 24–5

special report at its following (eighteenth) session in May 1997, concluding that the practices in question amounted to torture (see Chapter 3).[149]

If Israel responded promptly, not all governments have submitted their periodic or additional reports on time. As of 1997, initial reports were over-due from the following twenty-nine countries (the bracketed dates indicating the year the report was due): Togo and Uganda (1988); Guyana (1989); Brazil and Guinea (1990); Somalia (1991); Estonia, Venezuela, Yemen, and Yugoslavia (1992); Benin, Bosnia and Herzegovina, Cambodia, Cape Verde, Latvia, and Seychelles (1993); Antigua and Barbuda, Burundi, Costa Rica, Slovakia, and Slovenia (1994); Albania, Ethiopia, Sri Lanka, Former Yugoslav Republic of Macedonia, and United States of America (1995); Chad, Moldova, and Uzbekistan (1996). In addition, several second periodic reports were overdue, as were most third periodic reports, the first of which were not, however, due until 1996.[150] Thus, over one quarter of the states par-ties had not submitted their periodic reports within at least a year of when they were due, despite constant reminders from the Committee. Such behav-iour undermines the credibility of the Convention's basic monitoring system.

Interstate complaints

Article 21[151] provides that one state party may make an optional declaration accepting the right of the Committee to receive a communication from another state party (having made a similar declaration) alleging that the first state party 'is not giving effect to the provisions of' the Convention. Under this reciprocal system, and subject to certain procedural requirements, the Committee is required to use its good offices, including the possible establishment of an *ad hoc* conciliation commission, to seek a solution. If it succeeds in doing so, then the proceedings, which are confidential, terminate with the adoption by the Committee of a report containing 'a brief statement of the facts and the solution recorded'. If it fails to do so, the Committee makes a report, again containing 'a brief statement of the facts' as well as 'the written submissions and record of the oral submissions made by the States Parties concerned'. As of 4 June 1998, forty-one states parties had made the requisite declaration. Modelled on the analogous procedure in articles 41 and 42 of the Covenant, the Human Rights Committee has not, at the time of writing, had to deal with an interstate com-plaint. Neither has the Committee against Torture. There is, therefore, no expe-rience from which to predict how this system will work in practice.

Individual complaints

Article 22[152] provides that any state party may recognize 'the competence of the Committee to receive and consider communications from or on behalf of

---

[149] Id., para. 257.   [150] Id., Annex III.
[151] Article 21 corresponds to articles 18 and 19 of the original Swedish draft.
[152] Article 22 corresponds to article 20 of the original Swedish draft.

individuals subject to its [that is the state party's] jurisdiction who claim to be victims of a violation by a State Party of the provisions of the Convention'. Such individual complaints are to be made only against a state party that has made such a declaration. Subject to certain procedural requirements, the Committee deals with the complaint, but in closed meetings. On the basis of its examination the Committee adopts 'views' that are to be forwarded to the state party concerned and to the individual complainant. The article is silent on whether the 'views' should also appear in the Committee's 'annual report on its activities' called for by article 24. In fact, they do so appear, presumably because its work under article 22 forms part of its 'activities'. As of 4 June 1998, thirty-nine states have made the necessary declaration. Here again, the model is the work of the Human Rights Committee under the Optional Protocol to the Covenant.[153]

In fact, in its ten years of existence the case law of the Committee has not elucidated the Convention to any great extent. Of the 67 cases it has opened, 32 remained under consideration at the time of the adoption of its 1997 annual report to the General Assembly. Of the 35 that had been processed, the majority had been discontinued or had been declared inadmissible *ratione temporis* or for non-exhaustion of domestic remedies, or because of prior submission to another procedure of international settlement, such as the European or Inter-American Commissions on Human Rights, or for failure to provide minimum substantiation of the claim. Only 13 cases had been decided on the merits. Eleven of them concerned claims that threats of expulsion would violate article 3 which prohibits expulsion to a country where there are 'substantial grounds for believing that [the person] would be in danger of being subjected to torture'. In 7, the Committee upheld the complaint,[154] while in 4 it did not.[155] Only 2 involved claims that torture had been inflicted in the state that was the object of the claim. In *Parot* v. *Spain*,[156] the

---

[153] The Human Rights Committee's early practice may be consulted in the 1985 UN publication *Human Rights Committee—Selected Decisions under the Optional Protocol (Second to Sixteenth Sessions)* (CCPR/C/OP/1); and in *Selected Decisions of the Human Rights Committee and under the Optional Protocol, vol. 2 (Seventeenth to Thirty-second Sessions)* (CCPR/C/OP/2, 1990). On the functioning of the Committee under the Optional Protocol, see Möse and Opsahl, 'The Optional Protocol to the International Covenant on Civil and Political Rights', 21 *Santa Clara Law Review* 271 (1981); McGoldrick, *supra* n. 27.

[154] *Mutombo* v. *Switzerland* (13/1993), Report of the Committee against Torture, *GAOR*, 49th Session, Supplement No. 44 (1994), Annex V B; *Khan* v. *Canada* (15/1993), Report of the Committee against Torture, *GAOR*, 50th Session, Supplement No. 44 (1995), Annex V A; *Alan* v. *Switzerland* (21/1995) and *Kisoki* v. *Sweden* (41/1995), Report of the Committee against Torture, *GAOR*, 51st Session, Supplement No. 44 (1996), Annex V; *Tala* v. *Sweden* (43/1996), Report of the Committee against Torture, *GAOR*, 52nd Session, Supplement No. 44 (1997), Annex V A; *Aemei* v. *Switzerland* (34/1995), and *Tapia Paez* v. *Sweden* (39/1996), id., Annex V B.

[155] *X* v. *Netherlands* (36/1995), Report of the Committee against Torture, *GAOR*, 51st Session, Supplement No. 44 (1996), Annex V; *X* v. *Switzerland* (34/1995), *X* v. *Switzerland* (38/1995), and *Mohamed* v. *Greece* (40/1996), Report of the Committee against Torture, *GAOR*, 52nd Session, Supplement No. 44 (1997), Annex V B.

[156] (6/1990), Report of the Committee against Torture, *GAOR*, 50th Session, Supplement No. 44 (1995), Annex V A.

Committee seems not to have been impressed by the reliability of the allegations of torture; it focused on whether there had been a proper investigation of the allegations, under article 13, and concluded that there had. So it found no violation. In *Halimi Nedzibi* v. *Austria*,[157] the Committee also concluded that the substantive allegations had not been sustained, but found a delay of fifteen months in initiating an investigation to be a violation of article 13. In sum, as of May 1997, the Committee had found 7 violations of article 3 (non-expulsion) and 1 violation of article 13 (investigation). A possible reason for this limited record may be that the overwhelming majority of countries accepting the optional article 22 individual complaints procedure are also subject to one or more analogous procedures under the Optional Protocol to the International Covenant on Civil and Political Rights or the European or American Conventions on Human Rights, which potential applicants may feel provide more authoritative remedies. Also, it is the author's experience that there is little knowledge of the Convention and its protection system even among lawyers. It may well be that the procedure will only be of substantial use in respect of countries to which no other international procedure is applicable or as regards Convention provisions which are more convention-specific. In this connection it should be noted that the Committee has set up an expedited procedure for dealing with threatened expulsion cases.[158]

Inquiry into systematic practices of torture

Potentially the most innovative implementation procedure in the Convention is that contained in article 20 which deals with ex-officio inquiries into the practice of torture.[159] Article 20 contemplates that where the Committee 'receives reliable information which appears to it to contain well-founded indications that torture is being practised systematically in the territory of a State Party, the Committee shall invite that State Party to cooperate in the examination of the information and to this end to submit observations' on the information. Some delegations wanted to make this procedure optional, like the individual and interstate complaints procedures,[160] so the article could not be adopted by the drafters who worked, it will be recalled, by consensus. The matter was resolved at the General Assembly, which retained the compulsory nature of the procedure in principle, but added a new article 28, permitting states to make a reservation by which they could opt out of the procedure. No doubt this arrangement was necessary to secure adoption of

---

[157] (8/1991), Report of the Committee against Torture, *GAOR*, 49th Session, Supplement No. 44 (1994), Annex V A.

[158] Pursuant to amended Rules 106 and 108 of the Committee's Rules of Procedure: Report of the Committee against Torture, *GAOR*, 50th Session, Supplement No. 44 (1995), para. 191; and Annex VI (for text of the amended Rules).

[159] Article 20 corresponds to article 17 of the original Swedish draft.

[160] E/CN.4/1984/72, para. 52, where the German Democratic Republic, the Ukrainian SSR, and the Soviet Union are reported as taking that view.

the whole text by consensus. It may at least be expected that many of the states that would not have opted for the article 20 procedure, had it been left to their initiative, have been loath to opt out of it by making the requisite article 28 declaration. For they may well have feared that the deposit of such a declaration would be interpreted as signifying that they have something to conceal.[161]

Article 20 is of particular interest in that the only limitation on the source and nature of the information imposed on the Committee is that of reliability, and it is left to the judgement of the Committee to determine when that standard is met. Further, the standard applies not for the purposes of making a conclusive finding, but only to establish 'well-founded indications' sufficient to justify an approach to the state party concerned. It is open to all states and to international and national governmental and non-governmental bodies, as well as private individuals, to submit information which may aid the Committee to determine whether the required indications exist. What is remarkable is that the Committee may take the initiative to approach a government of its own motion.

Such an approach is the first stage in this procedure. If the Committee is not satisfied by the response it receives from the state party in question, or if there is no response, or if 'other relevant information'[162] suggests that 'a confidential inquiry' is warranted, the Committee may designate one or more of its members to make such an inquiry and to report back to it 'urgently'. With the agreement of the state concerned, the inquiry may include an on-the-spot visit. After the inquiry, the Committee examines the findings and transmits these together with its own comments or suggestions, if any, to the state concerned.

So far all the proceedings described, not just the 'confidential inquiry', will have been confidential. But secrecy does not necessarily cloak the events permanently. The Committee retains a power, after consulting with the state in question, 'to include a summary account of the results of the proceedings in its annual report'. It was to have been expected that the Committee would use that discretion, at least where the findings were serious, where the government did not fully co-operate with the Committee, or where the state concerned responded inadequately to the Committee's suggestions. This has proven to be the case.

The Committee has so far issued two summary accounts of inquiries it has conducted under article 20, on Turkey[163] and on Egypt.[164] In both

---

[161] Twelve states have excluded the Committee's article 20 powers: Afghanistan, Belarus, Bahrein, Bulgaria, China, Cuba, Israel, Kuwait, Morocco, Poland, Saudi Arabia, Ukraine.

[162] 'Other relevant information' is not defined, but presumably may come from any source, as may that giving rise to the 'reliable indications' of torture practices.

[163] Report of the Committee against Torture, *GAOR*, 48th Session, Supplement No. 44A (1994) (hereinafter 'Turkey Report').

[164] Report of the Committee against Torture, *GAOR*, 51st Session, Supplement No. 44 (1996), chapter V B (hereinafter 'Egypt Report').

countries the Committee found that torture was being 'systematically practised'.[165]

Although article 20 is couched in language suggesting that the article 20 procedure is one that the Committee initiates ex officio, each inquiry was in fact instigated by submissions, explicitly under article 20, made by Amnesty International.[166] However, the Committee also consulted information from other sources, notably the Commission on Human Rights' Special Rapporteur on Torture and other, non-governmental sources.[167] The Turkish inquiry included a visit to the country by two Committee members.[168] Despite a request from the Committee to visit Egypt, the government did not give its consent.[169]

The Committee does not go into detail on the reasons for publishing the summary accounts. In both cases, the Committee cites the number and seriousness of the allegations of torture.[170] Predictably, in the case of Egypt, it implicitly points to the government's lack of full co-operation by referring to the government's failure to agree to a visit.[171] It then asserts that publication is 'necessary in order to encourage full respect for the Convention'.[172]

The accounts are indeed summary, that on Turkey consisting of fifty-nine paragraphs, that on Egypt having forty-three paragraphs. It is, therefore, not easy to assess the nature of the evidence before the Committee, nor its analysis of the evidence. It is, however, worth repeating its understanding of what amounts to a systematic practice:

The Committee considers that torture is practised systematically when it is apparent that the torture cases reported have not occurred fortuitously in a particular place or at a particular time, but are seen to be habitual, widespread and deliberate in at least a considerable part of the territory of the country in question. Torture may in fact be of a systematic character without resulting from the direct intention of a Government. It may be the consequence of factors which the Government has difficulty in controlling, and its existence may indicate a discrepancy between policy as determined by the central Government and its implementation by the local administration. Inadequate legislation which in practice allows room for the use of torture may also add to the systematic nature of this practice.[173]

This procedure is potentially the most important element in the Committee's powers to implement the major obligation of the Convention. While far from being of negligible utility, the state reporting system cannot normally be expected to have any short-term impact on a particular situation. The inter-state complaints system is optional and, in any event, the reluctance of states

[165] Turkey Report, para. 38; Egypt Report, paras. 219–20.
[166] Turkey Report, para. 3; Egypt Report, para. 182.
[167] Turkey Report, para. 4; Egypt Report, para. 183.
[168] Turkey Report, paras. 10–16.   [169] Egypt Report, paras. 216–18.
[170] Turkey Report, para. 21; Egypt Report, para. 200.
[171] Egypt Report, para. 200.   [172] Turkey Report, para. 21; Egypt Report, para. 200.
[173] Turkey Report, para. 39. The Committee quotes it in full in the Egypt Report, para. 214.

to bring such complaints is well known.[174] The individual complaints procedure is also optional and, apart from the limited acceptance of the optional jurisdiction, such complaints do not always provide a forum in which to come to grips with a systematic practice.[175] Abhorrent as every case of torture is, international awareness of and revulsion against torture today has been provoked by its widespread and systematic use, rather than by the occasional isolated incident.

There is no model for a procedure such as that provided by article 20 in a United Nations human rights treaty. The innovative character of the procedure is particularly suited to the special elements of the systematic practice of torture. The uniformly clandestine circumstances in which torture occurs make it necessary for information to be compiled from a range of sources, including families of victims and national and international organizations.

Preventive visits?

Even the article 20 procedure involves after-the-fact action and presents difficult problems of fact finding. At present, a working group of the UN Commission on Human Rights is trying to reach agreement on an optional protocol to the Convention against Torture, whose purpose would be to approach the problem from the perspective of prevention. The idea is that an international body, at present designated as a Sub-Committee of the Committee against Torture, albeit composed of separately elected members, would be able as of right to make periodic and *ad hoc* visits to states parties to the protocol and visit any place being used as a place of detention.[176]

Since such a scheme has now been successfully established with the Council of Europe, the history and thinking behind the proposal is mentioned in the following section dealing with the European experience. Here it need only be noted that Costa Rica introduced its original text in 1980, but it was kept in abeyance while the main (Swedish) draft was being discussed, with a view to its being considered after the Convention was adopted. In fact, although the Convention was adopted in 1984, it was not until 1991 that the Commission established its working group to take the project forward.[177]

At the time of writing, many of the key elements remain to be agreed, including the very obligation to accept visits without agreement or constraint. Uncertainty also attaches to the issue of whether the eventual body, whatever

---

[174] There have been none under article 41 of the International Covenant on Civil and Political Rights, and few under the European Convention on Human Rights.

[175] Attempts to use the individual complaints procedure under European Convention on Human Rights article 25 have been consistently ill-fated: see works cited n. 3 *supra*.

[176] For the present state of negotiation in the working group, see UN doc. E/CN.4/1998/42 (hereinafter 'Sixth Working Group Report'). The articles provisionally agreed at 'second reading' are contained in Annex I of that document. The 'first reading' text is contained in UN doc. E/CN.4/1996/28, Annex I.

[177] Commission on Human Rights dec. 1991/107, 5 Mar. 1991.

its powers, will be guaranteed the membership, expertise, and (substantial) staff and other resources required for the work to be carried out professionally. Anything less could jeopardize the goal of the exercise.[178]

EUROPEAN CONVENTION FOR THE PREVENTION OF TORTURE

In November 1987 the Council of Europe opened for signature the Convention on the Prevention of Torture and Inhuman or Degrading Treatment or Punishment (see Annex 2c). This was the first concrete result of a movement that had started over ten years earlier.

HISTORY

In May 1977, the Swiss Committee against Torture, a private organization founded by retired Swiss lawyer and banker, the late Jean-Jacques Gautier, convened a meeting of experts to develop a draft international convention to prevent torture.[179] Gautier's idea was to place work of the style undertaken by the International Committee of the Red Cross (ICRC) on a formal legal footing.

The ICRC, well known for its work as 'guardian' of the Geneva Conventions of 12 August 1949 which are applicable primarily in international armed conflicts, had over the years developed a practice according to which it would seek the agreement of governments to visit persons held in connection with 'internal tensions and troubles' (political prisoners).[180] The purpose of the visits was to ensure the humane treatment of the prisoners. It was generally agreed that the ICRC's work in this area had been useful in protecting prisoners.

There were, however, two obstacles to even greater effectiveness of the ICRC. First, the organization could only work in those countries whose governments agreed to allow them to do so. Second, a condition of their access was that their findings would remain confidential, regardless of any lack of

---

[178] According to the second reading text, the basic functioning of the body will be financed out of the UN budget (Sixth Working Group Report, Annex I, article 15), which is notoriously being kept at 'zero growth'. Article 13 provides for missions to include experts assisting Sub-Committee members, but states parties may 'oppose the inclusion of an expert' (id., article 13).

[179] See, generally, de Vargas, 'History of a Campaign', in International Commission of Jurists and Swiss Committee against Torture, *Torture: How to Make the Interntional Convention Effective* (2nd edn., 1980), 41.

[180] On ICRC practice, see Moreillon, *Le Comité international de la Croix-Rouge et la protection des détenus politiques* (1973); Veuthey, 'Implementation and Enforcement of Humanitarian Law and Human Rights Law in Non-International Armed Conflicts: The Role of the International Committee of the Red Cross', 33 *American University Law Review* 83 (1983); also Rodley, 'Monitoring Human Rights Violations in the 1980s', in Domínguez, Rodley, Wood, and Falk, *Enhancing Global Human Rights* (1979), 142 ff.

improvement in the behaviour of the authorities. It would only make its reports public if the authorities published its reports in a selective or misleading way, either to make them look better than was the case or to make a previous government look worse than was merited.[181] The ICRC's only sanction for governments that ignored its findings of even the worst atrocities was to withdraw, a step it was and is understandably reluctant to take for fear of abandoning its charges to an even worse fate.

The Gautier draft aimed to overcome these drawbacks, by making states parties to the eventual convention automatically bound to accept visits by the international body it would set up and by permitting the body to publish its findings in the event of non-co-operation or of non-improvement in a serious situation.[182] The principle of confidentiality would be maintained, as was appropriate for an essentially preventive approach, but the preventive goal was reinforced by the availability of the sanction of publication as a last resort.

In the light of the General Assembly's decision to draft a convention against torture to be based on the Declaration against Torture (see Chapters 1 and 2), the Swiss Committee against Torture, co-operating with the International Commission of Jurists, persuaded the government of Costa Rica to introduce the text in the form of an optional protocol to the convention asked for by the General Assembly.[183] Not wishing to complicate the work on that draft convention which was being discussed in a Commission on Human Rights working group, Costa Rica at the same time moved to defer consideration of the draft optional protocol until after adoption of the main convention.[184]

Meanwhile, the Swiss Committee against Torture and the International Commission of Jurists switched focus, deciding to explore whether the proposal might prosper within the framework of a regional organization. Given the relative homogeneity, at that time, of most of the countries of the Council of Europe, as well as the rarity of situations characterized by widespread allegations of torture in the region, the Council of Europe clearly commended itself as the locus for the experiment.

In 1983, the Council's Consultative (now Parliamentary) Assembly commended the ICJ/Swiss Committee against Torture text to the Committee of Ministers for adoption.[185] The matter was discussed primarily in the Steering

[181] See, as an example of the latter type of case, ICRC Communiqué de Presse No. 1384, 9 Jan. 1980 (Iran).
[182] The text is reproduced in *Torture: How to Make the International Convention Effective*, *supra* n. 179, 7–13.
[183] de Vargas, *supra* n. 179, 44.
[184] Id., 46; indeed, in 1986, the Commission on Human Rights further deferred its consideration, presumably feeling that the Council of Europe initiative should be completed and its early experience assessed (res. 1986/56, 13 Mar. 1986).
[185] Recommendation 971 (1983). For further background, see the official Explanatory Report to the Convention: Council of Europe, *European Convention for the Prevention of Torture and Inhuman or Degrading Treatment or Punishment—Text of the Convention and Explanatory Report*, doc. CPT/Inf(91)9, p. 13.

Committee on Human Rights, where the text was amended, and the Convention was adopted in 1987.[186] It came into force on 1 February 1989 and as of 5 June 1998, thirty-nine of the forty members of the Council of Europe had ratified the Convention, which was still awaiting ratification by Lithuania.

THE COMMITTEE

Article 1 of the Convention provides for the establishment of a European Committee for the Prevention of Torture and Inhuman or Degrading Treatment or Punishment, commonly known by the initials CPT.[187] Composed of one person per state party, its members, who serve in their individual capacities and are to be independent and impartial, are to be chosen 'from among persons of high moral character, known for their competence in the field of human rights or having professional experience in the areas covered by the Convention' (article 4). They serve for four-year terms, renewable only once (article 5(3)).[188]

VISITS

The CPT arranges both periodic and *ad hoc* visits to countries (article 7(1)). The visits may be to any place of detention (articles 7(1) and (2)), that is, a place where persons are held by, or by order of, a public authority.[189] While notification of the CPT's intention to carry out a visit to a country must be made to the government in question, there is no minimum period of notice required.[190] Nor is it required to give notice in respect of every place of detention it may wish to visit (article 8).[191]

---

[186] Id., 15. Discussions also took place in the Steering Committee's subordinate body, the Committee of experts for the extension of the rights embodied in the European Convention on Human Rights: id., p. 14. See, generally, Cassese, 'A New Approach to Human Rights: The European Convention for the Prevention of Torture', 83 *AJIL* 128 (1989); also Decaux, 'La Convention européenne pour la prévention de la torture et des peines ou traitements inhumains ou dégradants', 34 *Annuaire français de droit international* 618 (1988).

[187] See, generally, Evans and Morgan, 'The European Convention for the Prevention of Torture: Operational Practice', 41 *ICLQ* 590 (1992) and 'The European Convention for the Prevention of Torture: 1992–1997', 46 *ICLQ* 663 (1997); also, APT (Association for the Prevention of Torture), *The Implementation of the European Convention for the Prevention of Torture and Inhuman or Degrading Treatment or Punishment (ECPT)—Acts of the Seminar of 5 to 7 December 1994, Strasbourg* (1995); Anstett, 'La Convention européenne pour la prévention de la torture: succès et incertitudes' [1997] Revue pénitentiaire et de droit penal, no. 3, 197.

[188] When Protocol No. 2 to the Convention (ETS No. 152) enters into force, membership will be renewable twice (art. 1).

[189] Explanatory Report, *supra* n. 185, p. 19.

[190] In one case, notification of an *ad hoc* visit was given 'a mere 24 hours before it was due to begin': Reports on the Visits to Spain carried out by the CPT from 1–12 April 1991, 10–22 April 1994 and 10–14 June 1994, Council of Europe doc. CPT/Inf(96)9, p. 196.

[191] *Supra* n. 185, pp. 24–5.

Because there is no limit on the types of place of detention the CPT may visit (article 2),[192] the Convention allows governments in 'exceptional circumstances' to 'make representations to the Committee against a visit at the time, or to the particular place proposed by the Committee'. The grounds for making such representations are limited to 'national defence, public safety, serious disorder in places [of detention], the medical condition of a person or that an urgent interrogation relating to a serious crime is in progress' (article 9(1)). While the grounds are few, their susceptibility to broad interpretation is apparent. On the other hand, the representations are not conclusive, they merely lead to consultation between the government and the CPT 'in order to clarify the situation and seek agreement on arrangements to enable the Committee to exercise its functions expeditiously' (article 9(2)). Bearing in mind that the Convention 'applies not only in peacetime, but also during war or any other public emergency',[193] the CPT would be well placed to resist abusive resort to article 9(1) representations. In fact, no invocation of article 9(1) is reported to have taken place since the CPT began its work.

By the end of 1993, the Committee had completed its first round of periodic visits among the then twenty-three states parties.[194] Since then, it has embarked on the second round of periodic visits in respect of the same countries, while beginning the first round in respect of new states parties. It has also undertaken numerous *ad hoc* visits. Moreover, it has developed the practice of undertaking follow-up visits where these are deemed appropriate.

PUBLICATION

Despite the confidential nature of the system, there are two circumstances in which CPT concerns on a particular country may reach the public domain. First, states themselves may require publication of the CPT's reports, together with their own comments (article 11). It is the practice of the CPT to encourage states to follow this course and the experience seems to be that, subject to varying periods of delay (perhaps, in some cases, to permit the states to take remedial measures that they can announce), states generally do so.[195] Second, as indicated earlier, if the CPT considers that a state party has failed 'to cooperate' or refused 'to improve the situation in the light of the committee's recommendations', it may decide 'to make a public statement on the matter' (article 10 (2)). This sanction, central to the scheme of the

---

[192] Council of Europe doc. CPT/Inf(96)9, p. 19.   [193] Ibid.

[194] 4th General Report on the CPT's Activities, 1 Jan.–31 Dec. 1993, Council of Europe doc. CPT/Inf(94)10, para. 1.

[195] 'At the time of writing, 44 of the 60 visit reports so far drawn up by the CPT have been published. Many of the remaining sixteen reports have only recently been forwarded to governments and will in all likelihood be published in due course.' (7th General Report on the CPT's Activities, 1 Jan.–31 Dec. 1996, Council of Europe doc. CPT/Inf(97)10, para. 9.

Convention, may only be resorted to after a decision taken by a two-thirds majority of the CPT's members. This is a substantial hurdle, now that there are so many states parties and, therefore, members. The CPT has so far availed itself only twice of this power, in each case in respect of Turkey, the one country that has consistently refused to accept publication of the CPT's reports on both periodic and *ad hoc* visits. In the first instance, in 1992, it found:

In the light of all the information at its disposal, the CPT can only conclude that the practice of torture and other forms of severe ill-treatment of persons in police custody remains widespread in Turkey and that such methods are applied to both ordinary criminal suspects and persons held under anti-terrorism provisions. The words 'persons in police custody' should be emphasised.[196]

In the second, in 1996, it affirmed that:

resort to torture and other forms of severe ill-treatment remains a common occurrence in police establishments in Turkey. To attempt to characterize the problem as one of isolated acts of the kind that can occur in any country—as some are wont to do—is to fly in the face of the facts.[197]

The use of such strong language demonstrates that the CPT takes its only sanction seriously. However, it is also, in a sense, a confession of failure, the government no doubt calculating that such statements, which are perforce brief, are less damaging than publication of the reports based on the actual visits. The deeper failure lies in the persistence of the problem. Here, of course, the CPT shares the failure with the UN Convention's Committee against Torture which, it will be recalled, issued a similar statement in 1994 after its article 20 inquiry.[198]

On the other hand, the published reports disclose no country where torture is widespread, despite occasional examples of torture and other ill-treatment in police custody and somewhat more frequent inhuman and degrading conditions of detention. How far the work of the CPT has itself contributed to the relative rarity of torture in the Council of Europe region remains to be assessed. In 1996, it included in its seventh general report a chapter on foreign nationals detained under aliens legislation, manifesting a concern regarding

---

[196] 3rd General Report of the CPT's Activities, 1 Jan.–31 Dec. 1992, Council of Europe doc. CPT/Inf(93)12, App. 4.

[197] Public statement on Turkey, 6 Dec. 1996, Council of Europe doc. CPT/Inf(96)34.

[198] *Supra* n. 163. The limits to the effectiveness of such machinery is, of course, inherent in the limits of acceptable international action to give effect to the rules of international law, in the absence of a threat to or breach of international peace and security justifying enforcement action by the UN Security Council under UN Charter chapter 7. For a comparative assessment of the work of the CPT, the UN Committee against Torture, and the Special Rapporteur on Torture, see Bank, 'International Efforts to Combat Torture and Inhuman Treatment: Have the New Mechanisms Improved Protection?', 8 *European Journal of International Law* 613 (1997).

treatment and conditions of detention in all phases of the process from first holding through expulsion.[199]

VOLUNTARY FUND FOR VICTIMS OF TORTURE

While only halting progress was being made in the area of implementation of international standards prohibiting torture and other ill-treatment, in the sense of impartial examination and monitoring of practices of treatment of prisoners that might amount to torture and ill-treatment, a most concrete development took place in the field of humanitarian relief for torture victims. In 1981, the General Assembly established a United Nations Voluntary Fund for Victims of Torture.[200] Its creation was controversial and was possible only by departing from the general practice in the General Assembly and other UN bodies of adopting resolutions on the issue of torture by consensus.

ORIGINS OF THE FUND

Three years earlier, the Assembly had established a United Nations Trust Fund for Chile.[201] Its function was 'to receive contributions and distribute, through established channels of assistance, humanitarian, legal and financial aid to persons whose human rights have been violated by detention or imprisonment in Chile, to those forced to leave the country and to relatives of persons in the above-mentioned categories'.[202] By 1980 the Fund had set certain priorities[203] and made grants totalling $US 101,250 or just under two-thirds of the $US 156,250 that had been contributed to the Fund.[204] The Secretary-General quoted the Chairman of the Board of Trustees, whose members he had appointed and upon whose advice moneys would be disbursed, as saying: 'The Fund is a first step in this vital but virtually unexplored field of providing assistance to persons in order to aid them to overcome the effects of violations of human rights.'[205]

At its 1980 session, the General Assembly asked the Commission on Human Rights 'to study . . . the possibility of extending the mandate' of the

---

[199] Council of Europe doc. CPT/Inf(97)10, ch. III. For an enthralling initiation into the texture of the work of the CPT and especially the conduct of its country visits, see Cassese, *Inhuman States—Imprisonment, Detention and Torture in Europe Today* (1996). The author was the first President of the CPT.

[200] GA res. 36/151, 16 Dec. 1981; see generally Walkate and Roels, 'United Nations Voluntary Fund for Victims of Torture', 5 *SIM Newsletter* (Utrecht) 22 (1984); Danelius, 'The United Nations Fund for Torture Victims: The First Years of Activity', 8 *Human Rights Quarterly*, 294 (1986).

[201] GA res. 33/174, 20 Dec. 1978.

[202] United Nations Trust Fund for Chile—Report of the Secretary-General, UN doc. A/35/543 (1980), para. 1.

[203] Id., paras. 6 and 7.   [204] Id., paras. 9 and 10.   [205] Id., para. 11.

Fund to cover victims of gross and flagrant violations of human rights else-where in the world.[206] The vote (57 for, 39 against, and 46 abstentions) revealed a marked lack of enthusiasm for the proposal.[207] The 'Western European and Other' group voted solidly in favour, while the 'Eastern European' group voted solidly against; other member states distributed their votes in all three categories. The draft of the resolution was the initiative of the five Nordic countries.[208] The initiative was justified by the Finnish dele-gation on the simple grounds 'that assistance could be given not only to Chileans but[209] also to victims of violations of human rights in other coun-tries'. This implicit criticism of selective concern for victims of human rights violations in Chile was echoed by the Australian delegation.[210]

Opposition to the draft dwelt on three points. First, 'the draft resolution's vague criteria left room for potential misuse [and] would be open to . . . exploitation for propaganda purposes. It would contravene the purposes and principles of the Charter of the United Nations, which called for friendly rela-tions between States.'[211] The message seemed to be that, since controversy sometimes exists as to what acts amount to human rights violations and when such acts are considered to have occurred, grants by the Fund could be con-strued as an implicit allegation of such violations and perhaps also a mark of support for groups (the recipient channels of assistance) which accuse gov-ernments of such violations. Second, in the words of one delegation, 'the establishment of such a fund [with an extended mandate] would . . . be tanta-mount to doing away with the United Nations Trust Fund for Chile at a time when the Special Rapporteur had reported an aggravation of the situation in that country, and when the Fund's activities should therefore be intensi-fied'.[212] Another delegation argued similarly that this 'could only weaken the position of the United Nations with respect to human rights in Chile'.[213] Third, India had 'more serious reservations'. It referred to recent 'attempts to link the question of human rights with that of development'. Not only was it a matter of the sensitive issue of principle as to whether aid should be made conditional on a standard of compliance with human rights norms, but also, more concretely:

Developed countries had shown increasing reluctance to make contributions for development aims, so that it seemed that the voluntary contributions referred to [in

---

[206] GA res. 35/190, 15 Dec. 1980.

[207] UN doc. A/35/PV.96, 67. In the Third Committee the vote had been even closer: 48 for, 40 against, 46 abstentions (UN doc. A/C.3/35/SR.80, para. 25).

[208] Denmark, Finland, Iceland, Norway, Sweden.

[209] *GAOR*, 35th Session, Third Committee, Summary Records, A/C.3/35/SR.77 (1980).

[210] UN doc. A/C.3/35/SR.79, para. 86.

[211] UN doc. A/C.3/35/SR.80, para. 3 (USSR). Argentina also feared abuse: id., para. 17.

[212] UN doc. A/C.3/35/SR.79, para. 81 (Yugoslavia), referring to the Commission's Special Rapporteur on Chile.

[213] Id., para. 82 (Poland); the view was shared by the USSR: UN doc. A/C.3/35/SR.80, para. 3.

the draft resolution] might well be made at the expense of development projects in developing countries. Those countries had requested more help, which had not been forthcoming, and they would not welcome any diversion of the aid they received.[214]

One element that was brought out during the debate on the proposal to make the Chile Fund into a general fund for torture victims[215] was the question of contributions to the Chile Fund. Sixty-four per cent of it had been contributed by three Nordic countries (Denmark, $25,000; Norway, $25,000; and Sweden, $50,000), while another 32 per cent came from The Netherlands ($50,000), which had spoken in support of the proposal.[216] Yugoslavia, the largest of the remaining three contributors, had supplied 3.2 per cent[217] and spoke against the proposal. Thus, the greatest contributors to the fund wished to expand its scope. It was also pointed out by proponents that the resolution merely requested the Commission on Human Rights to study the matter,[218] and that it was a question of extending the Fund's mandate, 'not doing away with it'.[219]

At the following session of the Commission on Human Rights, in 1982, the initiative was taken by Denmark, the only Nordic country represented on the Commission. The draft resolution that Denmark introduced envisaged the extension of the mandate of the UN Trust Fund for Chile to permit the granting of assistance to victims of torture and the redesignation of the Fund into 'a United Nations voluntary fund for victims of torture'.[220] The close vote in the General Assembly appears to have led the sponsors to engage in consultations with other countries. The Danish representative explained the result as follows: 'The general view to be discerned from consultations on the subject seemed to be that the concept of gross and flagrant violation of human rights was too broad to be applied to the designation of a fund.'[221] Accordingly, qualifying cases 'should be of a particularly appalling nature, be well-defined and reveal a special need for assistance. On that basis, it had been decided that the fund should be applied to cases of torture.'[222] The problem noted above, that compensation directed to individual torture victims would constitute allegations of human rights violations, was dealt with by a proposal to channel aid through organizations: 'aid would be extended, for example, through organizations which were in consultative status with the Economic and Social Council and were qualified to channel assistance in

---

[214] UN doc. A/C.3/35/SR.80, para. 9 (India).
[215] UN doc. A/C.3/35/SR.80, para. 84 (UK); A/C.3/35/SR/80, para. 6 (Netherlands); id., para. 20 (Mrs Santander-Downing, Secretary of the Third Committee).
[216] UN doc. A/35/43, para. 9.
[217] Ibid. Other contributors were Cyprus ($1,000) and the Philippines ($250).
[218] UN docs. A/C.3/35/SR.79, para. 84 (UK); A/C.3/35/SR.80, para. 7 (USA).
[219] UN doc. A/C.3/35/SR.79, para. 86 (Australia).
[220] UN doc. E/CN.4/L.1548 (co-sponsored by Finland, Norway, and Sweden).
[221] UN doc. E/CN.4/SR/1637, para. 41.   [222] Ibid.

accordance with normal United Nations' practice'.[223] Also, under the terms of the draft resolution, 'priority would be given to victims in States in which situations had been the subject of resolutions or decisions' in UN bodies.[224]

Continuing to address the objections that had been raised at the General Assembly, the Danish representative argued that 'the fund's new mandate would not imply any lessening of concern over the human rights situation in Chile: cases in that country could still be considered. Moreover, it was not intended that contributions to the fund should be diverted from development assistance.' Certainly Denmark's contributions would not come from development aid resources and 'in any case, it was unlikely that contributions would be so large as to have a noticeable effect on allocations for other purposes'.[225]

The new approach was still not acceptable to all delegations and the USSR proposed a series of draft amendments,[226] the effect of which would have been to forestall an expression of approval for the proposed scheme and promote further discussion in Ecosoc and the General Assembly. The most far-reaching of the proposed amendments was rejected by only three votes (15 for, 12 against, 14 abstentions).[227] Despite this close victory for the integrity of the original resolution, the Commission went on to accept the unamended text by a large margin.[228]

The resolution,[229] whose substance was couched in the form of a draft resolution of the General Assembly, thus reached Ecosoc, its next destination, with some momentum. The USSR proposed a number of amendments to the draft resolution.[230] These 'were designed to maintain the existing title and mandate of the Fund'.[231] After a brief discussion in the Social Committee of Ecosoc,[232] the Soviet amendments were decisively rejected[233] and the original text[234] was easily adopted.[235]

On the recommendation of its Third Committee,[236] the General Assembly in 1981 adopted the draft resolution forwarded by Ecosoc by a strong majority (96 for, 15 against, 33 abstentions). By this resolution (36/151 of 6 December 1981)[237] the General Assembly decided 'to extend the mandate of the United Nations Trust Fund for Chile' to provide aid to victims of torture

---

[223] Id., para. 42. [224] Ibid. [225] Id., para. 43.

[226] Id., paras. 45–52; also UN doc. E/CN.4/SR.1639, paras. 10 and 12.

[227] The proposed amendment would effectively have left the matter for further study. Other draft amendments were defeated 15 for, 11 against, and 13 abstaining: id., para. 13.

[228] 22 for, 7 against, and 14 abstaining: id., para. 15.

[229] Resolution 35 (XXXVII), 11 Mar. 1981, Commission on Human Rights, Report, 37th Session, *ESCOR*, 1981, Supplement No. 5, Chapter XXVIII A.

[230] UN doc. E/1981/46, para. 14. [231] UN doc. E/1981/C.2/SR.18, para. 39.

[232] Id., paras. 36–44. [233] 23 against, 8 for, 16 abstaining: id., para. 45.

[234] Except for a minor technical amendment proposed by Denmark: id., para. 36.

[235] 34 for, 5 against, and 10 abstaining: id., para. 46; Ecosoc res. 1981/39, 8 May 1981.

[236] UN doc. A/36/792, para. 12.

[237] UN doc. A/36/PV.101, 103; GA res. 36/151, 6 Dec. 1981.

without geographical limitation. There had been only perfunctory discussion in the Third Committee,[238] but one new argument of substance had been raised by the Soviet delegation which suggested that 'the establishment of a fund for victims of torture would be an implicit recognition that torture was a normal, everyday occurrence'.[239] One is left with the feeling that this disturbing afterthought deserved further exploration, even if the conclusion were to be a recognition of the reality of the common occurrence of torture and the need at least to alleviate some of its more cruel effects on individual victims.

By the time of the 1982 session of the Commission on Human Rights, the controversy seemed to have abated. In a resolution adopted without a vote[240] the Commission was able to call upon all governments 'to respond favourably to requests for contributions to the Fund'. The General Assembly did the same in 1983 and thereafter.[241] Nevertheless, the continuing reticence of the eastern European countries was evidenced by the fact that the Secretary-General was at first able to appoint only four of the five members of the Board of Trustees set up to supervise the administration of the Fund, and could only later appoint an east European as the fifth member.[242] Meanwhile, using the same language his predecessor had used after the establishment of the Chile Fund,[243] the Secretary-General, in a message to the Board's first meeting, declared:

This fund will provide an excellent opportunity to demonstrate to the peoples of the world that the United Nations, in addition to its role as the conscience of mankind in promoting respect for human rights and fundamental freedoms, is able to respond in a concrete way to the needs arising from violations of human rights.[244]

BENEFICIARIES OF THE FUND

Under General Assembly resolution 36/151 the United Nations Voluntary Fund for Victims of Torture is to provide aid to 'individuals whose human rights have been severely violated as a result of torture and to relatives of such victims' (operative paragraph 11(a)). The wording of the formulation is not

---

[238] UN doc. A/C.3/36/SR.36, paras. 20–30.   [239] Id., para. 20.
[240] Resolution 1982/43, 11 Mar. 1982, Commission on Human Rights, Report, 38th Session, *ESCOR*, 1982, Supplement No. 2, Chapter XXVII A.
[241] GA res. 38/92, 16 Dec. 1983, operative para. 2; see, most recently, GA res. 51/86, 12 Dec. 1996, operative para. 14.
[242] United Nations Voluntary Fund for Victims of Torture Report of the Secretary-General, UN doc. A/39/662 (1984): Mr Hans Danelius (Sweden) Chairman, Ms Elizabeth Odio Benito (Costa Rica), Mr Waleed Sadi (Jordan), and Mr Amos Wako (Kenya) were appointed in 1982; Mr Ivan Tosevski (Yugoslavia) was appointed in 1984. By the time of writing, Mr Jaap Walkate had replaced Mr Danelius as chairman and Mr Ribot Hatano (Japan) had replaced Mr Sadi.
[243] UN doc. A/35/543 (1980), para. 11.
[244] United Nations Information Service, UN Office at Geneva, Press Release (SG/SM/480; HR/1361), 21 Mar. 1983, 2.

ideal: a pedantic reading might suggest that potential claimants may need to show a severe violation of their human rights over and above the torture itself—a violation stemming from the torture. On the other hand, the same approach might suggest that any relative of the primary victim, regardless of the degree of kinship or the social and economic relationship between them, could be a legitimate claimant.

In practice it was to be expected that the Fund would take a pragmatic view of its mandate in this respect. Its primary beneficiaries would be direct victims of torture, whose human rights had been severely violated precisely because they had been tortured. Its secondary beneficiaries would be members of the victims' families who were directly and considerably affected by the fate of the victim.

A number of sensitive questions may well have confronted the Fund in determining who qualifies for consideration as a victim of torture. Should the relatively narrow definition contained in the Declaration against Torture be used, or the possibly wider one contained in the Convention against Torture? How is a conflict between any UN definition and one used by a professional body acting as a channel for funds[245] resolved? Is the Fund, in borderline cases, required to take on a law-determining role? What standards of evidence should it require in assessing the claim of an alleged victim?

Again in practice the Fund is generally in a position to avoid having to grapple with such difficult issues. This is because it does not normally make grants directly to potential beneficiaries, but 'through established channels of assistance'.

INTERMEDIARIES

The term 'established channels of assistance' is also a less than precise formulation, but poses fewer problems. The UN has experience of similar channelling of humanitarian relief through appropriate bodies.[246] Indeed, when challenged in the Commission on Human Rights on the point by the Soviet representative,[247] the Danish representative had observed that 'in the case of Chile, the World Council of Churches and the Red Cross had proved that effective channels could be provided for such assistance'.[248] While there is no formal limitation on possible channels other than that they be 'established', the Fund is in a reasonable position to learn about the work and background of organizations seeking funding for projects aimed at bringing relief to

[245] For example, a medical body applying the World Medical Association's Declaration of Tokyo (see Chapter 12).
[246] For example, the Chile Fund discussed above, and the Southern Africa Trust Fund.
[247] UN doc. E/CN.4/SR.1637, para. 47 (1981).
[248] Id., para. 53. In fact, even a member of the UN family, the High Commissioner for Refugees, has served as an 'implementing channel' for Fund-supported projects (UN doc. A/40/876 (1985), Annex, para. 4).

torture victims. In other words, its function is to establish a relationship of trust with the 'channels' which have already been able to demonstrate the reality of their work for victims of torture.

Thus it is not for the Fund to assess the qualifications of each individual case. This is the function of the 'channels'. The requirements of confidentiality in such sensitive relief ventures preclude such individual assessment. Indeed, the 'channel' would not necessarily itself disburse moneys to particular cases or projects, but might well have to use other channels before the funds reach the intended beneficiaries. This procedure, which is common in relief operations of this type, arises from such factors as difficulty of communications and threats to transmitters and recipients.

COUNTRY PRIORITIES

While there is no geographical limitation on the countries from which there may be beneficiaries, General Assembly resolution 36/151, which established the Fund, provides that priority is to be given 'to aid to victims of violations by States in which the human rights situation has been the subject of resolutions or decisions adopted by either the Assembly, the Economic and Social Council or the Commission on Human Rights' (operative paragraph 1 (a)). The resolution is silent as to whether this would include countries in respect of which the Commission on Human Rights has adopted resolutions or decisions under the confidential procedures of Ecosoc resolution 1503 (XLVIII) referred to at the beginning of this chapter.[249] If such countries were included in the priority category then it will clearly have been necessary for the Board of Trustees of the Fund to have access to the relevant files. This is because although since 1978 the Commission has made public the names of countries that have been the subject of decisions under the resolution 1503 procedure, not all such cases necessarily involve torture and, in any event, the Board would need detailed information.

Opponents of the extension of the Fund's mandate to provide aid to victims of torture without geographical limit feared that this would restrict beneficiaries in Chile, as elsewhere, to victims of torture and their relatives,[250] a fear that was not contested. It does not follow, however, from the language of General Assembly resolution 36/151 of 6 December 1981, that the Fund could

---

[249] There is strong evidence to suggest that such countries are included: of the three countries (Argentina, Guinea, and Uruguay) publicly named as having been the loci of beneficiaries of Fund-supported projects (UN doc. A/40/876 (1985), Annex, para. 5), two have been the subject of UN resolution or decision under the confidential procedure (see Ecosoc decisions 1985/139 (Uruguay) and 1985/156 (Argentina), 30 May 1985, declassifying the files). As of November 1985, the Fund had supported projects in sixteen countries (UN doc. A/40/876 (1985), para. 3); the reference to only three of the sixteen suggests that major changes of government had obviated the need for discretion. The inclusion of Guinea clearly demonstrates that countries not in the priority category can receive Fund support.

[250] UN doc. E/CN.4/SR.1637 (1981), para. 46 (USSR).

not still provide aid to the original broader category of potential beneficiaries in Chile. The intention of the sponsors of the extension may have been to abandon limitation of the Fund to Chile, but geographical extension for a limited purpose (torture) does not automatically require substantive limitation of the broader purpose (general human rights violations) in Chile. In fact, as recently as 1997, the Board reports making a grant to the main Chilean NGO providing assistance specifically to torture victims in that country.[251]

NATURE OF AID

General Assembly resolution 36/151, it may be recalled, authorizes the Fund to distribute its assets as 'humanitarian, legal and financial aid'. Here, too, it is probably unwise to invest this terminology with too much legal precision, since in fact all the Fund's grants will have to be in financial form. If 'financial' has any specific meaning, it probably implies that the ultimate beneficiaries may receive cash as opposed to material support for a particular project designed to assist them. The concept of 'legal aid' is more precise: in the case of torture victims, such aid could be used to secure legal advice and assistance for a range of purposes, such as conducting a defence against criminal charges where incriminatory statements have been obtained by torture, claiming compensation from the authorities responsible for inflicting it, prosecuting or bringing a civil action against alleged torturers and bringing evidence before commissions of inquiry. The concept of 'humanitarian aid' is, in fact, broad enough to cover most, if not all likely applications. If it has any limit, it is probably that such aid could not be used for activities primarily aimed at removal of a government which permits torture, even though such an event could have authentically therapeutic effects.

The kind of aid needed by the torture victim is much influenced by the fact that the suffering of such a victim may not cease with the ill-treatment, and long-term distress of various sorts can remain. Torture takes many forms, physical, psychological, or both, and its effects will be similarly various. The physical and psychological condition of the victim before torture will influence the impact of the torture, as will the aftermath: imprisonment, release into the community (occasioning resocialization or ostracism), exile or flight abroad (entailing adjustment to a new society, possibly in association with or possibly separated from others whose experiences have been similar), and so on. Medical treatment and/or counselling may be needed. In recent years, various bodies have found themselves acquiring a gruesome expertise in the physical and psychological effects of torture on victims. In countries where human rights violations have taken place, ex-prisoners, many of whom have

[251] FASIC (Fundación de Ayuda Social de las Iglesias Cristianas): UN doc. A/52/387 (1997), Annex I.

been tortured, seek assistance from humanitarian institutions or band together in mutual support groups. In countries of refuge, former political prisoners, again many having been tortured, join with other refugees from the countries in which their human rights have been violated. National sections of Amnesty International have been establishing medical groups which have been asked to help refugee torture victims and have a network of information exchange. Indeed, the pioneering work of one such group in the Danish section of Amnesty International led to the establishment of an independent International Rehabilitation and Research Centre for Torture Victims. Amnesty International now identifies centres in some 36 countries.[252]

In November 1993, the Fund reported on the first ten years of its activities. It had recommended grants of over 10 million US dollars raised from 41 governments for 367 programmes.[253] Eighty-three per cent came from Europe, 11 per cent from the Americas and the Caribbean, 6 per cent from Asia and Oceana, and 0.1 per cent from Africa. In addition, organizations had contributed $26,368 and individuals $17,713.[254]

Fifty-six per cent was allocated for medical and psychological assistance and 10 per cent for economic and social rehabilitation.[255] Most of the rest went for the training of health professionals, establishment of treatment centres, and related activities.[256] The report also refers to legal assistance, for which 2 per cent of the funds were designated. The legal needs are described in terms similar to those used above to describe what 'legal aid' for torture victims may consist of, as well as referring to the legal needs of relatives of deceased or missing torture victims.[257] Two years later, the Board was reporting a 'new trend' in its policy of 'encouraging projects designed to defend the right of torture victims to restitution, indemnification and rehabilitation before national courts'.[258] This evolution, involving a genuine contribution to the protection of human rights and clearly mandated by the original terms of the Fund, is nevertheless also justified in humanitarian terms: '[s]uch official acknowledgement of the torture suffered is an essential stage in the psychological rehabilitation of victims'.[259]

In 1994, the United States started making annual donations of 1.5 million dollars, thus, by 1997, putting North America in the position of contributing nearly as much (44.68 per cent) as Western Europe (48.62 per cent). Asia, the Middle East, and Pacific contributed just under 5 per cent, Africa just over 1 per cent and Latin America and the Caribbean just over 0.5 per cent. No contributions came from Central and Eastern Europe.[260] Indeed, a 1990

---

[252] Amnesty International, Medical and Psychological Services for Victims of Human Rights Violations, AI Index: ACT 75/01/98, Feb. 1998.

[253] UN doc. A/48/520 (1993), Annex I, Table 2.   [254] Id., fig. 4.

[255] Id., para. 40; see also para. 42.   [256] Ibid.   [257] Para. 45.

[258] UN doc. A/50/512 (1995), para. 28.   [259] Ibid.

[260] UN doc. A/52/387 (1997), Ch. III, Table 3, Graph 1. The percentage includes Canada's contribution of $18,401, that is, 0.54% of the total available for distribution.

Yugoslav contribution of $5,000 represents the totality of donations to the Fund from governments of that region since the creation of the Fund.[261]

The reports contain an annex listing the organizations receiving funds and their locations, when the recipients have authorized publication of their identity. Several are organizations in Europe and North America 'mainly' providing treatment for 'applicants for asylum and refugee torture victims' coming from other regions of the world.[262] Most of the organizations providing assistance to victims in their own countries come from Latin America, Asia, Africa, and Central and Eastern Europe. Seventy-one organizations are listed in the latest (1997) report. The overwhelming majority are in respect of medical, psychological, or social assistance. Twelve are involved in some combination of that assistance and legal assistance. Two organizations, PCATI (Israel) and Redress (United Kingdom) received funds just for legal assistance projects.[263] No details are given in respect of individual projects.

The Fund's income remained under half-a-million dollars for its first three years, rising gradually to just over one million dollars in 1991. As at 1997, it had some three million dollars available for grant, but requests for assistance of over twice that amount. The Fund is clearly helping to meet a serious need and deserves the resources to enhance its contribution.

SUMMARY

Despite its mandate from the General Assembly in 1975 to take steps to ensure the 'effective observance' of the Declaration against Torture, the Commission on Human Rights proved for several years reluctant to do this. It left the matter to its subordinate body of experts, the Sub-Commission on Prevention of Discrimination and Protection of Minorities, which eventually created a sessional working group. This provided a limited forum for oral NGO denunciations of violations of the rights of prisoners.

However, in 1985 there was a reversal of the Commission's hitherto negative posture on implementation, namely the establishment by the Commission itself of a fact-finding mechanism on torture in the form of a Special Rapporteur. The existence of models created to deal with 'disappearances' and summary executions, together with the resurgence of efforts to raise awareness about the continuing problem of torture, made this possible.

Meanwhile, the General Assembly's request (by means of a questionnaire) for information on states' compliance with the Declaration against Torture yielded a limited number of responses and little concrete information. The discussions in the General Assembly were not sufficient to provoke either

---

[261] UN doc. A/48/520 (1993), Annex, Table III.   [262] UN doc. A/52/387, para. 28.
[263] Id., Annex I.

more replies or more pertinent information from the states that did reply, and the exercise has ceased.

The Convention against Torture was a positive development although it was hardly radical in its provision of optional rights of interstate or individual complaint to the Committee against Torture. Its provision of a power for the Committee to make 'general comments' on each periodic report submitted by states parties, while at the time innovative, cannot of itself ensure effective supervision of compliance with the terms of the Convention. Nor in the near future can hope be placed in the proposed draft optional protocol that would use the preventive technique of arranging routine and *ad hoc* visits to places of detention: not only is the draft protocol explicitly optional (thus likely to attract limited adherence), the protracted negotiations have not yet succeeded in securing agreement on the basic elements that inspired the initiative, and problems of resources, membership, and personnel could, in any event, have a negative impact on the effectiveness of the inspecting body it would set up. Thus, the key to effective implementation is in the Convention's provision that would empower the Committee to inquire of its own initiative into suspected systematic practices of torture. So far the power is used sparingly. At the European level the work of the CPT under the European Convention for the Prevention of Torture, inspired by the UN draft optional protocol, has proven to be an important spur to states to improve their treatment of prisoners.

Finally, as a humanitarian initiative, and bowing to the sad reality of the persisting malignance of torture, the General Assembly established a Voluntary Fund for Victims of Torture. The Fund mainly supports those bodies that are already working to extend relief, especially medical and psychological relief, to those who have suffered at the hands of governments unwilling to comply with the obligation not to torture. It has also started funding projects aimed at providing redress of a legal nature.

6

Extra-legal Executions

When the Universal Declaration of Human Rights proclaimed in its article 3 that 'everyone has the right to life', it raised a number of questions that were left unanswered, including the legitimacy of the death penalty (see Chapter 7) and the permissibility of abortion and euthanasia.[1] However, what was clearly contemplated by the principle was outright murder by government as exemplified by Nazi practices. To the extent that the Declaration may be said to reflect general international law (see Chapter 2), then the prohibition against such murder implicit in the 'right to life' is a norm of general international law.

It is not necessary, however, to rely simply on the juridical status of the Declaration to arrive at this conclusion. The language of the relevant passage of the International Covenant on Civil and Political Rights tends to confirm respect for the right to life as a primary obligation. Article 6, paragraph 1, states, 'Every human being has the inherent right to life. This right shall be protected by law. No one shall be arbitrarily deprived of his life.' No other right contained in the International Bill of Human Rights[2] is described as being 'inherent'. It is possible that this adjective is a redundant invocation of divine or natural law principle, or even of biological fact, but a better view of such terminology in a juridical instrument is that it has juridical meaning. The most likely such meaning would be analogous to that often given to the same word in the Charter of the United Nations: article 51 of the Charter refers to the 'inherent right of . . . self-defence'. In this context 'inherent' is normally understood to suggest that the right is a right attaching to the state, antecedent to the adoption of the Charter. The Covenant seems to be treating the right to life, as it attaches to the individual, similarly.

The Covenant also treats the right to life in the same way as the prohibition against torture and ill-treatment. Thus, no circumstances are indicated as justifying restrictions on the right not to be arbitrarily deprived of life.[3] Nor

[1] Verdoodt, *Naissance et signification de la Déclaration universelle des droits de l'homme* (1964), 95–100.

[2] The International Bill of Human Rights was described in Chapter 2 and consists of the Universal Declaration of Human Rights (1948), the International Covenant on Economic, Social and Cultural Rights, the International Covenant on Civil and Political Rights, and the (first) Optional Protocol to the latter Covenant (all of 1966), as well as its Second Optional Protocol aiming at the abolition of the death penalty (1989—see Chapter 7).

[3] As indicated in Chapter 2, a number of rights contain clauses acknowledging the permissibility of restricting them on grounds such as the need to maintain public order (see articles 18, 19, 21, and 22).

can the right be derogated from, under article 4, even 'in time of public emergency threatening the life of the nation', a protection accorded to only a very limited number of rights. The European and American Conventions on Human Rights treat the right similarly.[4] The African Charter on Human and Peoples' Rights also provides for protection of the right to life, but having no article permitting derogations, it does not need to preserve the specific right to life from such derogations.[5]

With the exception of capital punishment meted out under laws that do not conform to the safeguards contained in Covenant article 6 (see Chapter 7), most incidences of arbitrary deprivations of life by governments would amount to murder under the national laws of the countries where they happen (however immune the perpetrators may be in practice). Accordingly the prohibition against government involvement in or failure to protect from arbitrary deprivations of life is consistent with what the Statute of the International Court of Justice calls 'general principles of law recognized by civilized nations'.

The Human Rights Committee established to monitor compliance with the Covenant has described the right to life as 'the supreme human right'.[6] In the words of the Commission on Human Rights' Special Rapporteur on Summary or Arbitrary Executions (see below), the right to life 'is the most important and basic of human rights. It is the fountain from which all human rights spring. If it is infringed the effects are irreversible . . .'.[7]

Taken together, the foregoing is strongly suggestive of the proposition that, not only is the right to life a treaty rule binding on parties to the relevant treaties, but also, like the prohibition against torture and other ill-treatment (see Chapter 2) and for similar reasons, it is a rule of general international law binding on all states. This view has been challenged with the argument that, since a significant number of governments have practised mass murder, state practice cannot be said to supply a rule prohibiting such murder.[8] This opinion seems incapable of distinguishing between state acts conforming to a rule of law and those that violate it. The argument might seem less preposterous if the governments in question challenged the rule or claimed the murders were a permitted exception to the rule, or admitted that they were committing the

---

[4] European Convention on Human Rights, article 2 (right to life) and article 15 (derogations); American Convention on Human Rights, article 4 (right to life) and article 27 (derogations).
[5] Article 4 of the Charter reads: 'Human beings are inviolable. Every human being shall be entitled to respect for his life and the integrity of his person. No one may be arbitrarily deprived of this right.' This is a clumsy formulation. Presumably the intention was to prohibit arbitrary deprivation of life and personal integrity, rather than of the *right* to life and personal integrity.
[6] General comment 6(16), Report of the Human Rights Committee, *GAOR*. 37th Session, Supplement No. 40 (1982) Annex V.
[7] UN doc. E/CN.4/1983/16, para. 22.
[8] Lane, 'Mass Killing by Governments: Lawful in the World Legal Order?', 12 *New York University Journal of International Law and Politics* 239 (1979).

atrocities in question[9]—such indeed is their approach to capital punishment. But they do no such thing with regard to official murder; they do not contest the rule and they deny the facts, invoking the domestic jurisdiction principle only to avoid effective fact finding. This is hardly the posture of a government asserting the contrary right to kill freely.

The approach by which murder by governments may be considered a violation of general international law tends to be confirmed by resolution 5 ('Extra-legal executions') of the Sixth UN Congress on the Prevention of Crime and the Treatment of Offenders (1980).[10] By this resolution, the Congress 'deplore[d] and condemn[ed] the practice of killing and executing political opponents or suspected offenders carried out by armed forces or by paramilitary or political groups acting with the tacit or other support of such forces or agencies' (operative paragraph 1). Invoking, *inter alia*, article 3 of the Universal Declaration of Human Rights and article 6 of the Covenant (operative paragraphs 2 and 3), the Congress stated the view that 'murder committed or tolerated by Governments is condemned by all national legal systems and, thus, by general principles of law' (operative paragraph 5). Affirming that the acts in question 'constitute a particularly abhorrent crime the eradication of which is a high international priority' (operative paragraph 2), the Congress called upon all governments 'to take effective measures to prevent such acts' (operative paragraph 2) and urged all relevant United Nations organs 'to take all possible action to bring such acts to an end' (operative paragraph 4).

In an especially interesting approach, the resolution expresses the Congress's view that the acts in question 'also violate the Declaration on the Protection of All Persons from Being Subjected to Torture and Other Cruel, Inhuman or Degrading Treatment or Punishment' (see Chapter 1). By this, the Congress is saying that extra-legal executions are not just violations of the right to life: it is apparently propounding the view that the prohibition of such executions has the same status as that prohibiting torture or other ill-treatment (see Chapter 2) and the same consequences as flow from violation of the prohibition of torture or, at least, from violation of the prohibition of 'cruel, inhuman or degrading treatment or punishment' (see Chapter 4).

---

[9] This approach tracks that of the International Court of Justice in *Military and Paramilitary Activities in and against Nicaragua (Nicaragua* v. *United States of America)*, *Merits, Judgment* [1986] ICJ Rep. (1986), 14, at para 186: 'If a State acts in a way prima facie incompatible with a recognized rule, but defends its conduct by appealing to exceptions or justification contained within the rule itself, then whether or not the State's conduct is in fact justifiable on that basis, the significance of that attitude is to confirm rather than weaken the rule.'

[10] *Sixth United Nations Congress on the Prevention of Crime and the Treatment of Offenders— Report*, A/CONF.87/14/Rev. 1 (1981), Chapter 1. Just as the Fifth UN Crime Congress had concentrated on the problem of torture (see Chapter 1), the Sixth Congress devoted much attention to aspects of the right to life, especially the death penalty (see Chapter 7). The governments attending these quinquennial congresses are often represented by officials involved in law enforcement and the administration of justice. Resolutions of the Congress have no binding force *per se*.

While its formal status is merely that of a recommendation from an *ad hoc* meeting, the language of the resolution is more that of a solemn evocation of legal demands. In other words, it seems not so much to be advocating compliance with a desirable standard of moral behaviour as insisting on compliance with a formal rule. The resolution was adopted without dissent, although there were seven abstentions. No reasons are given for these in the Congress report.[11] In any event, by 1982, the Economic and Social Council (Ecosoc) was able to adopt without a vote resolutions that invoked resolution 5 of the Sixth UN Crime Congress. One of these 'strongly deplore[d] the increasing number of summary or arbitrary executions' in terms clearly intended to include extra-legal executions.[12] Later the same year, the General Assembly welcomed the adoption of the Ecosoc resolution, expressing itself to be 'extremely alarmed at the occurrence on a large scale of summary or arbitrary executions including extra-legal executions'.[13]

Two further relevant United Nations instruments deserve to be noted: the Principles on the Effective Prevention and Investigation of Extra-legal, Arbitrary and Summary Executions and the Basic Principles on the Use of Force and Firearms by Law Enforcement Officials. The drafting history of the latter instrument, finalized at the Eighth UN Congress on the Prevention of Crime and the Treatment of Offenders, is summarized in chapter 12. The former also had its origins in preparations for the Eighth Crime Congress, but for unexplained reasons emerged from an inter-regional preparatory meeting for the Congress in the form of a draft resolution of Ecosoc which, after modification by the Committee on Crime Prevention and Control, adopted the instrument in 1989.[14]

While, once again, neither instrument is of itself legally binding, both are relevant in determining the scope of what constitutes unlawful deprivations of life, and will accordingly be referred to below. The question then arises as to what governmentally inflicted or governmentally tolerated killings amount to arbitrary deprivation of life.[15]

---

[11] Resolution 5 was adopted by a roll-call vote of 74 to none, with 7 abstentions (Argentina, Chile, Egypt, Ethiopia, Indonesia, Philippines, and Uruguay): id., para. 214. (It is thought that Argentina sought the roll-call vote because of the linkage in the sixth preambular paragraph with 'disappearances' (recollection of the author, who attended the Congress on behalf of Amnesty International; see Chapter 8.)

[12] Ecosoc res. 1982/35, 7 May 1982. The preceding (seventh) preambular paragraph had described Ecosoc as 'deeply alarmed about the occurrence of summary or arbitrary executions, *including extra-legal executions*, that are widely regarded as being politically motivated' (emphasis added).

[13] GA res. 37/182, 17 Dec. 1982.

[14] Ecosoc res. 1989/65, 24 May 1989, Annex. For more on the drafting history, see Clark, *The United Nations Crime Prevention and Criminal Justice Program* (1994), 115.

[15] See, generally, on the scope of such executions, Amnesty International, *Political Killings by Governments* (1983); also Kaufman and Weiss-Fagan, 'Extrajudicial Executions: an Insight into the Global Dimensions of a Human Rights Violation', *Human Rights Quarterly*, vol. iii, no. 4 (1981), 81.

RACIALLY MOTIVATED KILLING AND GENOCIDE

One particular category of official murder which is singled out for special con-
demnation by international law is that carried out on racial grounds. The
International Convention on the Elimination of All Forms of Racial
Discrimination[16] obliges states parties to it:

to prohibit and eliminate racial discrimination in all its forms and to guarantee the
right of everyone without distinction as to race, colour, or national or ethnic origin, to
equality before the law, notably in the enjoyment of . . . the right to security of person
and protection by the State against violence or bodily harm, whether inflicted by government officials or by any individual, group or institution [article 5].

Similarly, the International Convention on the Suppression and Punishment
of the Crime of *Apartheid*[17] defines apartheid as 'a crime against humanity'
(article I). This covers a number of: 'Inhuman acts committed for the purpose
of establishing and maintaining domination by one racial group of persons
over any other racial group of persons and systematically oppressing them' by
means which include 'denial to a member or members of a racial group or
groups of the right to life and liberty of person . . . by murder of members of
a racial group or groups' (article II).

The legal significance of the *Apartheid* Convention as regards the many
non-parties will be considered below.

A central instrument in the field of racially motivated abuses is the
Convention on the Prevention and Punishment of the Crime of Genocide.[18]
Article II of this Convention defines the offence of genocide to embrace a
number of acts 'committed with intent to destroy, in whole or in part, a
national, ethnical, racial or religious group as such', including 'killing members of the group'. Genocide is prohibited 'in time of peace or in time of war'
(article I). The Convention, is not universally ratified, but the view that it
states a rule of customary international law is beyond serious dispute.[19] It
should be noted, however, that while allegations of genocide are frequently
made by those protesting killings of members of racial or religious groups, it
will rarely be easy to prove 'an intent to destroy' the group 'as such'. The failure of those who framed the Convention to include political groups within its
protection has also been properly criticized,[20] but it will be argued below that
the law has evolved so as to render the omission redundant.

[16] GA res. 2106 A (XX), 21 Dec. 1965.   [17] GA res. 3068 (XXVIII), 30 Nov. 1973.
[18] GA res. 260 A (III), 9 Dec. 1948.
[19] As early as 1951, the International Court of Justice stated that 'the principles underlying the
[Genocide] Convention are principles which are recognized by civilized nations as binding on States,
even without any conventional obligation': *Reservations to the Convention on the Prevention and
Punishment of the Crime of Genocide*, ICJ Rep. (1951), 15, 23. There are 126 States party to the convention, including states representing the overwhelming majority of the world's population.
[20] For example, Kuper, *International Action Against Genocide* (Minority Rights Group,
revised 1984 edn.), part I (Report no. 53); and UN doc. E/CN.4/Sub.2/1985/6, paras. 34-7

EXTRA-LEGAL EXECUTIONS
AS ARBITRARY DEPRIVATIONS OF LIFE

It will be shown in the next chapter that capital punishment inflicted in accordance with certain safeguards is specifically exempted from classification as an arbitrary deprivation of life within the meaning of article 6 of the Covenant. The failure of the Covenant to mention any other exceptions cannot, however, be interpreted as excluding from exemption all other state-inflicted or of state-tolerated killings. There are two categories of such acts that probably cannot be said to be prohibited by the right to life. These are certain killings which may be seen as necessary measures of law enforcement and certain killings committed in armed conflict. Indeed, extra-legal executions may be defined as killings committed outside the judicial process by, or with the consent of, public officials, other than as necessary measures of law enforcement to protect life or as acts of armed conflict carried out in conformity with the rules of international humanitarian law. This definition is offered in the absence of any official definition in any of the treaty or other instruments dealing with the issue.[21]

KILLINGS AS NECESSARY MEASURES OF LAW ENFORCEMENT

Only one international human rights treaty, the European Convention on Human Rights, specifies permitted exceptions to the right not to be deprived of one's life 'intentionally' (article 2). Article 2 excludes from the prohibition against deprivation of life not only judicial death sentences but also such deprivation

when it results from the use of force which is not more than absolutely necessary:

(a) in defence of any person from unlawful violence;
(b) in order to effect a lawful arrest or to prevent the escape of a person lawfully detained;
(c) in action lawfully taken for the purpose of quelling a riot or insurrection.

('Revised and updated report on the question of the prevention and punishment of the crime of genocide prepared by Mr B. Whitaker'). The most recent documented case of genocide, that of Tutsis in Rwanda in 1994, first met controversy in the use of the word, not least because the victims included liberal Hutus: it was only after the recently appointed Special Rapporteur on Rwanda, reporting (some 12 weeks after the massacres began) on his joint mission with the Special Rapporteurs on Extrajudicial, Summary or Arbitrary Executions and on Torture, and building on a statement by the UN Secretary-General describing the massacres as 'genocide', that it became acceptable to use the term in UN bodies, notably the Security Council (UN doc. E/CN.4/1995/7, paras. 41-8).

[21] Note, however, the similar definition in the United States Torture Victims Protection Act, *infra* n. 82.

Proposals for similar formulations in the Covenant were rejected, but it seems to have been understood that the use of the word 'arbitrary' in article 6 of the Covenant was intended to acknowledge such exceptions.[22]

Assuming that the exceptions to the right to life rule contained in the European Convention on Human Rights represent an accurate articulation of the general international law standard of non-arbitrariness, a number of observations may be made. First, the exceptions are realistic, since they represent commonly accepted law enforcement expectations. Second, as frequently occurs in international instruments, they are couched in general language. National law would be expected to give far more precision to defining when it is proper for law enforcement officials to use lethal force. In this connection rules of necessity and proportionality are essential adjuncts in delimiting the scope of exceptions to the right to life rule.[23]

The *necessity* principle is provided for in the formulation quoted above: the use of force is to be 'no more than absolutely necessary' to achieve the stated purposes. To this extent, the European Convention on Human Rights uses terms similar to those of article 3 of the United Nations Code of Conduct for Law Enforcement Officials (see Chapter 12), which states: 'Law enforcement officials may use force only when strictly necessary and to the extent required for the performance of their duty.' More explicitly, principle 4 of the Basic Principles on the Use of Force and Firearms (see Annex 5b) states:

Law enforcement officials, in carrying out their duty, shall, as far as possible, apply non-violent means before resorting to the use of force and firearms. They may use force and firearms only if other means remain ineffective or without any promise of achieving the intended result.

If, as is submitted, these instruments articulate controlling principles, not only must the use of force itself be necessary, so almost must be the level of force used.

The point is illustrated by the *Guerrero* case,[24] which came before the

---

[22] See *GAOR*, 10th Session, Annexes, Agenda item 28 (Part II) (A/2929), chapter VI, paras. 1–3; Dinstein, 'The Right to Life, Physical Integrity and Liberty', in Henkin (ed.), *The International Bill of Rights—The Covenant on Civil and Political Rights* (1981), 114, 114–22; Boyle, 'The Concept of Arbitrary Deprivation of Life', in Ramcharan (ed.), *The Right to Life in International Law* (1985), 221, 222–33; Nowak, *U.N. Covenant on Civil and Political Rights— CCPR Commentary* (1993), 110–11. The word 'intentionally', as found in article 2 of the European Convention, is more appropriate than the word 'arbitrarily' since the Convention specifies the limits on deprivation of life.

[23] Principles of necessity and proportionality are to be found in both traditional areas in which international law deals with the use of force, namely, the law relating to the legitimacy of states' resort to armed force against another state (*jus ad bellum*) (see the World Court judgment in *Military and Paramilitary Activities in and against Nicaragua (Nicaragua v. United States of America)*, Merits, Judgment [1986] ICJ Rep. (1986), 14, para. 194) and the law relating to the use of force in armed conflict (*jus in bello*), in particular as regards the protection of civilian populations (see Rogers, *Law on the Battlefield* (1996), 3 (military necessity) and 14 (rule of proportionality)).

[24] *Guerrero v. Colombia* (45/1979), Report of the Human Rights Committee, *GAOR*, 37th Session, Supplement No. 40 (1982), Annex XI.

Human Rights Committee in 1979. María Fanny Suárez de Guerrero, on whose posthumous behalf a complaint was made under the Optional Protocol to the International Covenant on Civil and Political Rights, was one of seven persons shot dead by the Colombian police.

On 13 April 1978, a police raid took place on a house in Bogotá, the Colombian capital, in the belief that the victim of a kidnap by a guerrilla organization was being held prisoner at the house. The victim was not found and the police patrol decided to hide in the house to await the arrival of the suspected kidnappers. Seven persons who subsequently entered the house, including Mrs Guerrero, were shot by the police and died. A review of the evidence led the Committee to conclude that the police action, involving a deliberate and intentional deprivation of life, 'was apparently taken without warning to the victims and without giving them any opportunity to surrender to the police patrol or to offer any explanation of their presence or intentions' (paragraph 13.2). Referring to criteria that might have justified the police action, the Committee found 'no evidence that the action of the police was necessary in their own defence or that of others, or that it was necessary to effect the arrest or prevent the escape of the persons concerned' (paragraph 13.2). A Colombian forensic report showed that Mrs Guerrero, in particular, 'had been shot several times after she had already died from a heart attack' (paragraph 13.2). In 1982, the Committee concluded that the police action 'was disproportionate to the requirements of law enforcement in the circumstances of the case and that she was arbitrarily deprived of her life contrary to article 6(1)' of the Covenant (paragraph 13.3).

The European Court of Human Rights, in *McCann and Others* v. *United Kingdom*[25] had occasion to stress the notion of absolute necessity. In that case, three Irish Republican Army (IRA) members were shot dead in Gibraltar by members of the British security forces, the Special Air Services (SAS) regiment of the Army. The Court found as a fact that the SAS soldiers did not commence their operation intending to kill, but that they had been briefed on the basis of intelligence assessments to believe, and did believe, that the victims were armed and in possession of a remote-control device capable of detonating a bomb or explosive device said to have been placed in a car (in fact, they were unarmed, had no detonator, and the car contained no bomb), and that they fired intending to kill in order to prevent any detonation of the bomb. The Court neverthless found a violation of Article 2 of the European Convention. It did so after an extensive analysis of the planning and conduct of the whole operation, including a decision to let the IRA members, who were under surveillance, enter Gibraltar from Spain, and concluded:

In sum, having regard to the decision not to prevent the suspects from travelling into Gibraltar, to the failure of the authorities to make sufficient allowances for the possi-

---

[25] Series A, No. 324 (1995), reprinted in 16 *HRLJ* 260 (1995).

bility that their intelligence assessments might, in some respects at least, be erroneous and to the automatic recourse to lethal force when the soldiers opened fire, the Court is not persuaded that the killing of the three terrorists constituted the use of force which was no more than absolutely necessary in defence of persons from unlawful violence within the meaning of Article 2 § 2 (a) of the Convention.[26]

In the closely contested 10–9 decision, the Court's minority argued that, under the circumstances, the operational defects identified by the majority should not have been so characterized. However, there was unanimous agreement on the strictness of the standard.

The concept of necessity applies only to the hierarchy of coercive measures in which lethal or potentially lethal force is reserved as a last resort. It is complemented by the rule of *proportionality*, which applies to the nature of the law enforcement objective. 'Unlawful violence' covers behaviour that may be as dangerous as armed robbery or as trivial as throwing rotten fruit at a public speaker. The authorities may seek to 'effect a lawful arrest' of a suspected pickpocket as well as of a person with a loaded gun, or to 'prevent the escape' of a fine defaulter as well as of a convicted murderer (the abuse which sometimes attends the notion of 'shot while trying to escape' is well known);[27] even riots do not necessarily involve the use of violence, especially against individuals (insurrections probably fall under the rubric of non-international armed conflict which will be dealt with below). It would be subversive indeed of the general rule if it were to be interpreted to permit the use of lethal force, even as a last resort, to achieve the more trivial of the pairs of examples given.

It is, therefore, to be expected that those called upon to give meaning to the right to life and its exceptions will take an approach that recognizes the importance of this aspect of proportionality. Support for such an approach is to be found in the official commentary to article 3 of the UN Code of Conduct for Law Enforcement Officials (see Chapter 12 and Annex 5a). This affirms in general terms that 'in no case should this provision [that is, article 3] be interpreted to authorize the use of force which is disproportionate to the legitimate objective to be achieved'. Indeed, the same commentary goes further and addresses itself specifically to the matter of potentially lethal instruments of coercion: 'In general, firearms should not be used except when a suspected offender offers armed resistance or otherwise jeopardizes the lives of others and less extreme measures are not sufficient to restrain or apprehend the suspected offender.'

The Basic Principles on the Use of Force and Firearms (see Annex 5b) go even further. Having, in principle 5, reaffirmed the general proportionality principle as articulated in the commentary to the Code, its principle 9 proceeds to address directly the use of lethal or potentially lethal force:

[26] Para. 213.
[27] Amnesty International, *The Death Penalty* (1979), 30. The case of *Baboeram et al.* v. *Suriname* mentioned below (see n. 53) affords a vivid illustration of the point.

Law enforcement officials shall not use firearms against persons except in self-defence or defence of others against the imminent threat of death or serious injury, to prevent the perpetration of a particularly serious crime involving grave threat to life, to arrest a person presenting such a danger and resisting their authority, or to prevent his or her escape, and only when less extreme means are insufficient to achieve these objectives. In any event, intentional lethal use of firearms may only be made when strictly unavoidable in order to protect life.

The same principle governs the specific contexts of policing of unlawful assemblies (principle 14) and of persons in custody or detention (principle 16). Thus, firearms, according to the Basic Principles, may only be used to protect life and limb from imminent threat and their intentional *lethal* use may only be effected to protect life.

Clearly neither the Code,[28] together with its commentary, nor the Basic Principles are, of themselves, juridical instruments. Nevertheless, their careful formulation gives them significant interpretative authority. It should not be assumed that the General Assembly would have been so irresponsible as to address to individual law enforcement officials a standard of behaviour that went beyond the requirements that international law imposes on governments.

The case law available, all from Europe, tends to support the requirement of proportionality in this sense. The European Commission of Human Rights has already indicated what its own view would be should an appropriate case come before it. In *Stewart* v. *United Kingdom*,[29] the mother of 13-year-old Brian Stewart, who had been killed in 1976 by a plastic baton round (or 'bullet') fired by the army in Northern Ireland, petitioned the Commission, alleging a violation of article 2 of the European Convention on Human Rights (quoted at the beginning of this section). The Commission accepted the facts as found in the United Kingdom courts: that the boy had been present during a riot of 150 people throwing stones and other missiles at a patrol of eight soldiers; that the soldier who fired the shot was trained and experienced in the use of plastic baton rounds; that the soldier had aimed at the legs of the rioter next to Brian Stewart, but that his 'aim was disturbed at the moment of discharge when he was struck by several missiles'. The Commission also noted that rioting of the kind that occurred in this case 'gives rise to the apprehension . . . that the disturbance will be used as a cover for sniper attack, although no claim has been made in the present case that the patrol actually came under such attack'. Moreover, despite the fact that the plastic baton round 'is a dangerous weapon which can occasion serious injuries and death, particularly if it strikes the head', the Commission felt that 'the weapon is less

[28] GA res. 34/169, 17 Dec. 1979, Annex.
[29] Application no. 10044/82, Decision of the European Commission of Human Rights as to Admissibility (1984).

dangerous than alleged'. It did so in the light of the number of casualties as 'compared with the number of baton rounds discharged'.[30]

Although the Commission declared the application inadmissible, it did not merely rely on the existence of a riot coupled with the use of the minimum necessary force to quell it. It insisted also on a test of proportionality that would relate the means of achieving the ends to the nature of the ends. According to the Commission, for the use of force to be 'no more than absolutely necessary' to achieve the objectives permitted by sub-paragraphs (a), (b), and (c) of article 2(2), it had to be 'strictly proportionate to the achievement of the permitted purpose'. It continued: 'In assessing whether the use of force is strictly proportionate, regard must be had to the nature of the aim pursued, the dangers to life and limb inherent in the situation and the degree of the risk that the force employed might result in loss of life.'[31]

Apparently the Commission concluded that, in the absence of an intentional killing, the issue before it was whether the mere use of plastic baton rounds in the particular case was disproportionate in terms of risk to life and limb; and the further implicit conclusion was that there was no disproportion in the balance of risk. This negative finding on the facts leaves intact the Commission's fundamental approach, which needs to be emphasized here: the use of force that could put life or limb at risk has to be in response to a situation putting life or limb at similar risk.[32]

While not directly relevant to the facts of *McCann*, the European Court in that case reaffirmed the notion of proportionality: 'the force used must be strictly proportionate to the achievement of the aims set out in sub-paragraphs 2 (a), (b) and (c) of Article 2'.[33] It is also worth noting that the Court, while not explicitly applying the provisions, quotes principle 9 of the Basic Principles on the Use of Force or Firearms by Law Enforcement Officials.[34]

---

[30] Id., paras. 20–9.　　　　　　　　　　[31] Id., para. 19.

[32] *Stewart* built on an earlier Commission case which was terminated by a 'friendly settlement': *Farrell* v. *United Kingdom*, Application no. 9013/80, Decision of the European Commission of Human Rights as to Admissibility (1982). The Commission had declared admissible the complaint of a possible violation of article 2 made by the widow of an unarmed man (Farrell) who was one of three men shot dead in 1971 by British soldiers while the three (who were not believed to be armed) were attempting to rob two other men who were leaving money in the night safe of a bank in Northern Ireland. The Commission considered the case raised 'several issues of fact and of the interpretation of Art. 2 of the Convention, mainly as to whether "the use of force was no more than absolutely necessary in order to effect a lawful arrest"'. The details of the 'friendly settlement' between the applicant and the respondent government were not officially made public (see Council of Europe Press Release B (84)50, Dec. 1984). However, according to a press report, the friendly settlement—apparently it consists of the payment, 'on compassionate grounds', to Mrs Farrell of the substantial sum of '£37,000 . . . plus several thousand pounds in legal costs'—was reached after the Commission had in a 'preliminary vote' made a finding on the merits that was 'adverse' to the United Kingdom: Leigh and Lashmar, 'UK Condemned in Strasbourg Rights Ruling', *Observer* (London) 28 Apr. 1985. See also, Boyle, *supra* n. 22, 236–42.

[33] *Supra* n. 25, para. 149.　　　　　　　[34] Para. 139

However, an admissibility decision by the European Commission of Human Rights in *Kelly* v. *United Kingdom*[35] raises some doubts about that body's conception of the role of imminence of threat in its application of the necessity and proportionality rules. Kelly was an unarmed joyrider who was shot while trying to evade an army checkpoint. The Commission considered that this shooting, carried out in the belief that Kelly was a terrorist, was justified 'to effect a lawful arrest' for the purpose of 'prevent[ing] them carrying out terrorist activities'.[36] Clearly, such terrorist activities could, in the Northern Ireland context, include murder. Nevertheless, the Commission's decision that the application was 'manifestly ill-founded' seems to ignore any requirement of imminence of the anticipated threat as part of the necessity or proportionality tests. To sum up, any use of force must be the minimum necessary, with lethal force being only a means of last resort. Also, such force must not be disproportionate to the law enforcement objective, so that lethal or potentially lethal force must be aimed at the preservation of life. Despite *Kelly*, the better view is that the threat to life should not be merely 'hypothetical'; rather, it should be imminent.

KILLINGS IN NON-INTERNATIONAL ARMED CONFLICT

Article 2 of the European Convention on Human Rights refers to 'action taken for the purpose of quelling [an] . . . insurrection' as being outside the prohibition of intentional deprivation of life. Thus international law probably considers non-arbitrary some official killing in non-international armed conflict, but this does not mean that indiscriminate killing may take place in such circumstances. The rules of necessity and proportionality should in principle continue to apply, both in the sense of lethal force being a measure of last resort and, subject to what was said above, necessary to save life in the specific circumstances. Moreover, such an armed conflict also falls under the rules of international humanitarian law.

In its Advisory Opinion on the *Legality of the Threat or Use of Nuclear Weapons*, the World Court addressed the relationship of international human rights law and international humanitarian law, as regards the right to life, in these terms:

The Court observes that the protection of the International Covenant of Civil and Political Rights does not cease in times of war, except by operation of Article 4 of the Covenant whereby certain provisions may be derogated from in a time of national emergency. Respect for the right to life is not, however, such a provision. In principle, the right not arbitrarily to be deprived of one's life applies also in hostilities. The test

[35] Application no. 17579/90, 74 *Decisions and Reports* 139 (1993). See Harris, O'Boyle and Warbrick, *Law of the European Convention on Human Rights* (1995), 50–3, for a penetrating criticism of this case.
[36] Id., 146.

of what is an arbitrary deprivation of life, however, then falls to be determined by the applicable *lex specialis*, namely, the law applicable in armed conflict which is designed to regulate the conduct of hostilities. Thus whether a particular loss of life, through the use of a certain weapon in warfare, is to be considered an arbitrary deprivation of life contrary to Article 6 of the Covenant, can only be decided by reference to the law applicable in armed conflict and not deduced from the terms of the Covenant itself.[37]

Accordingly, we may refer to the body of international humanitarian law in this context. Article 3 common to the four Geneva Conventions of 12 August 1949, which have been ratified by nearly every country in the world,[38] explicitly prohibits in non-international armed conflict 'at any time and in any place whatsoever . . . violence to life and person, in particular murder of all kinds' being inflicted on 'persons taking no active part in the hostilities, including members of armed forces who have laid down their arms and those placed *hors de combat* by sickness, wounds, detention, or any other cause'. In other words, the killings may be inflicted only on persons actively engaged in opposing armed forces.

In addition to restating the above, Additional Protocol II to the Geneva Conventions[39] specifies certain more precise rules. Thus, 'it is prohibited to order that there shall be no survivors' (article 4(1)). Also, civilians not taking a direct part in hostilities are to enjoy 'general protection against the dangers arising from military operations' (article 13(1)). In pursuance of the latter: 'The civilian population as such, as well as individual civilians, shall not be the object of attack. Acts or threats of violence the primary purpose of which is to spread terror among the civilian population are prohibited' (article

[37] ICJ Rep. (1996), 1, para. 25; reprinted in 35 *ILM* 814 (1996).

[38] Indeeed, the World Court has affirmed that common article 3 reflects 'fundamental general principles of humanitarian law' and as such was applicable as against the United States regardless of any treaty obligation: *Military and Paramilitary Activities, supra* n. 22, para. 218. Similarly, the Appeals Chamber of the International Criminal Tribunal for the Former Yugoslavia has gone so far as to determine that 'customary international law imposes criminal liability for serious violations of common article 3': *Tadić* case, Decision on the Defence Motion for Interlocutory Appeal, Case No. IT-94-1-AR72, 2 Oct. 1995, para. 134 (reproduced in 13 *ILM* 35 (1996)). It did this by way of interpretation of the Tribunal's Statute (Security Council res. 827 (1993), Annex) article 3 authorizing its jurisdiction in respect of violations of the laws and customs of war. Article 4 of the Statute of the International Tribunal for Rwanda (Security Council res. 955 (1994), Annex) specifically provides for the Tribunal's jurisdiction over 'serious violations' of common article 3 of the Geneva Conventions. It is clear that the Security Council did not consider itself as creating retrospective criminality, but rather as codifying existing international criminal law. Finally, it should be noted that the International Law Commission's draft Statute for an International Criminal Court (UN doc. A/49355 (1994), 3) provides for the proposed court to have jurisdiction, like the Yugoslav Tribunal, over 'serious violations of the laws and customs applicable in armed conflict' (article 20(c)). See, generally, Meron, 'International Criminalization of Internal Atrocities', 89 *AJIL* 554 (1995); Meindersma, 'Violations of Common Article 3 of the Geneva Conventions as Violations of the Laws and Customs of War under Article 3 of the Statute of the International Criminal Tribunal for the Former Yugoslavia', 42 *Netherlands International Law Review* 375 (1995).

[39] The four Geneva Conventions of 12 August 1949 and the two Protocols of 1977 additional thereto are cited in full in the General Introduction at n. 4.

13(2)). As noted in Chapter 2, this protocol has a limited field of application, namely, situations approaching full-scale civil war, and it has not yet achieved the near-universal ratification that the Geneva Conventions have attracted.[40] Nevertheless, it is submitted that these more precise rules are already implicit in the general rule contained in common article 3 of the Geneva Conventions. Significantly, the second preambular paragraph to Protocol II recalls 'that international instruments relating to human rights offer a basic protection to the human person'. Indeed, the International Criminal Tribunal for the Former Yugoslavia considers that '[m]any of the provisions of this Protocol can now be regarded as declaratory of existing rules or as having crystallized emerging rules of customary international law'.[41] The Statute of the International Tribunal for Rwanda[42] provides explicitly in its article 4 for jurisdiction not only over 'serious violations' of common article 3, but also of Additional Protocol II (to which Rwanda was, however, already a party). It would be extraordinary if any international organ called upon to interpret the scope of the 'insurrection' exception to the right to life were to consider as non-arbitrary killings committed in violation of the Geneva Convention and possibly also the Protocol II rules.

KILLINGS IN INTERNATIONAL ARMED CONFLICTS

As with non-international armed conflict, international law has established rules restricting the permissible use of lethal force even in time of international armed conflict. Indeed, the whole corpus of *jus in bello* is designed to limit violence to what is militarily necessary. In particular, violence against protected persons *hors de combat* and in the hands of a party to the conflict is not considered to be required by military necessity. The prohibition against torture and ill-treatment of such persons has already been described (see Chapter 2). The Geneva Conventions of 12 August 1949 treat killing of such persons similarly.

Thus, wounded and sick members of the armed forces of one party in the hands of another party, as well as those shipwrecked at sea, are to be treated humanely. 'Any attempts upon their lives, or violence to their persons, shall be strictly prohibited; in particular they shall not be murdered or exterminated.'[43] Prisoners of war are also entitled to similarly humane treatment: 'Any unlawful act or omission by the Detaining Power causing death or seriously endangering the health of a prisoner of war in its custody is prohibited and will be regarded as a serious breach of the present Convention.'[44] It is not

---

[40] At the time of writing there are 142 parties to Protocol II and 188 parties to the Geneva Conventions.

[41] Loc. cit. *supra* n. 38, para. 117.   [42] *Supra* n. 38.

[43] Geneva Conventions I and II, common article 12.

[44] Geneva Convention III, article 13. The use of the term 'serious breach' is thought to be intended to reaffirm the fact that infringement of the prohibition is a 'grave breach' (that is, war

clear what might constitute a *lawful* act or omission causing death or endangering health; presumably the infliction of the death penalty in the limited circumstances permitted by the Convention would be an example (see Chapter 7). Possibly death resulting from force necessarily used to prevent escape would also qualify.[45] It will also be recalled that protected civilians in the hands of a party to the conflict may not be subjected to measures that would cause 'physical suffering or extermination'.[46] This is a prohibition that applies 'not only to murder' but to a range of other assaults against the person 'whether applied by civilian or military agents'.[47]

As with torture of persons protected by the Geneva Conventions, 'wilful killing' of such persons is considered to be a grave breach of the Conventions,[48] the significance of which will be discussed below. At this point it needs only to be noted that such killings would be classical examples of 'war crimes'. It may also be noted parenthetically that, in so far as the taking of hostages is also a grave breach of the Conventions,[49] it follows that the killing of hostages would entail the same legal consequences.

There are few examples of international armed conflict wherein persons *hors de combat* would not fall under the protection of at least the Fourth Geneva Convention.[50] Additional Protocol I of 1977 aims at filling any such gap as may exist relating to the scope of application of the Conventions, as well as treating certain matters of substance. The effect of articles 75 and 85 of Protocol I is, *inter alia*, to treat 'violence to life . . . in particular . . . murder' as a grave breach of the Protocol and, as such, a war crime. The almost universal adherence to the Geneva Conventions does not, however, obtain for the Protocol, which means that the gaps intended to be filled by the Protocol will in fact be filled only slowly.[51]

LEGAL CONSEQUENCES OF EXTRA-LEGAL EXECUTIONS

This section follows the approach used in dealing with the legal consequences of torture and other ill-treatment (see Chapter 4), so the doctrinal concepts elaborated in that chapter will be taken as understood.

crime) of the Convention as discussed below (text accompanying n. 48); see Pictet (ed.), *Commentary, III Geneva Convention* (International Committee of the Red Cross, 1960), 140.

[45] Note that prisoners of war who attempt escape and are recaptured may be liable only to (non-capital) disciplinary punishment: Geneva Convention III, articles 91–3.

[46] Geneva Convention IV, article 32.   [47] Ibid.

[48] Geneva Convention I, article 50; Geneva Convention II, article 51; Geneva Convention III, article 130; Geneva Convention IV, article 147.

[49] Ibid.

[50] For example, where there is disputed title to territory, or a population without nationality (as in the occupied territories of the Middle East), questions may arise as to whether certain victims are in fact protected by the Geneva Conventions. Under such circumstances, human rights law would presumably apply.

[51] At the time of writing there are 150 parties to Protocol I.

STATE RESPONSIBILITY

The status under general international law of the prohibition of extra-legal executions has already been examined, with the conclusion that, like torture, extra-legal execution is illegal under international law, regardless of whether or not a state is party to a convention prohibiting the killing. For the same reasons as apply to torture, it may be that, when committed on a systematic basis, extra-legal executions are a species of internationally wrongful act constituting an 'international crime' rather than an 'international delict' (see Chapter 4). The same uncertainty will also apply as to whether this is a valid distinction and, if so, what its implications are. The obligations on a state whose officials have committed such killings are also probably the same as if they had committed torture.

The Principles on Extra-legal Executions (Annex 7) tend to follow the same approach as the Declaration and Convention against Torture. Principle 9 requires 'a thorough, prompt and impartial investigation of all suspected cases of extra-legal, arbitrary and summary executions, including cases where complaints by relatives or other reliable reports suggest unnatural death in the above circumstances'. Indeed, principles 9–17 elaborate a series of procedures aimed at ensuring the effectiveness of any such investigation.[52]

After an investigation has identified persons as having participated in extra-legal executions, governments are required, under principle 18, to bring them to justice. Going further than the instruments on torture, principle 19 explicitly rules out the granting to those involved of blanket immunity from prosecution, a notion manifestly aimed at the practice of some countries, particularly in Latin America, of granting amnesties to state personnel as a means of achieving a transition from military to civilian rule.

Meanwhile, principle 20 entitles families and dependants of victims 'to fair and adequate compensation within a reasonable period of time'.

Finally, following article 3 of the Convention against Torture, principle 5 provides: 'no one shall be involuntarily returned or extradited to a country where there are substantial grounds for believing that he or she may become a victim of extra-legal arbitrary or summary execution in that country'.

Further, the practice of the Human Rights Committee is to treat violations of article 6 (right to life) and 7 (prohibition of torture and other ill-treatment) in the same way. The Committee's approach is illustrated in its findings in respect of a notorious incident in Suriname where '15 prominent persons . . . including journalists, lawyers, professors and businessmen, were arrested in

---

[52] The Principles have since been supplemented by a Model Protocol for a Legal Investigation of Extra-legal, Arbitrary and Summary Executions ('Minnesota Protocol'), a Model Autopsy Protocol and a Model Protocol for Disinterment and Analysis of Skeletal Remains, *Manual on the Effective Prevention and Investigation of Extra-Legal, Arbitrary and Summary Executions* (1991) UN Pub. Sales No. E.91.IV.1 (doc. ST/CSDHA/12), chapters 3, 4, and 5.

their homes' and subsequently 'killed while trying to escape'.[53] Finding an intentional deprivation of life 'as a result of the deliberate action of the military police' against the fifteen, and that Suriname had 'failed to submit any evidence proving that these persons were shot while trying to escape', the Committee found a violation of Covenant article 6(1) protecting the right to life. It went on to urge Suriname 'to take effective steps (i) to investigate the killings of December 1982; (ii) to bring to justice any persons found to be responsible for the death of the victims; (iii) to pay compensation to the surviving families; and (iv) to ensure that the right to life is duly protected in Suriname.'[54]

The European Convention seems to require a similar approach. Thus, in *Kaya* v. *Turkey*, the European Court of Human Rights found a violation of Convention article 2, read together with article 1 (duty to secure Convention rights), resulting from the absence of an effective investigation into a death at the hands of the military in contested circumstances.[55] The Court in *McCann* also stressed the need for an effective investigation, citing the UN Principles, but found that an inquest in Gibraltar, despite certain discrepancies from the requirements of the Principles, had met the Convention standard.[56] No case seems to have arisen directly involving non-prosecution of persons responsible for extra-legal executions. In *Kaya*, there was no possibility of prosecution in the absence of an effective investigation. The issue was elided in *McCann* because the soldiers were found to have acted honestly, albeit mistakenly. While compensation would normally be required and ordered to be awarded as damages by the Court, this did not happen in *McCann* because the victims had in fact 'been intending to plant a bomb in Gibraltar'.[57]

It seems likely that sending somebody to a country where they face a violation of article 2 would be prohibited either as a violation of article 2 itself or of article 3 (torture and ill-treatment). This is the effect of a line of case law, discussed in chapter 4 and culminating in *Soering* v. *United Kingdom* where it was held that to return a person to Virginia to face the death penalty, in the light of the 'death-row phenomenon', the long period before execution (6–8 years), the youth of the applicant at the time the offence was committed (18 years) and certain psychological problems, would be a breach of article 3.[58] The line of cases began precisely with a case potentially involving article 2,

---

[53] *Baboeram et al.* v. *Suriname* (146/1983 and 148–154/1983), Report of the Human Rights Committee, *GAOR*, 40th Session, Supplement No. 40 (1985), Annex X, para. 13.2.

[54] Id., para. 16. To similar effect, see *Dermit* v. *Uruguay* (84/1981), Report of the Human Rights Committee, *GAOR*, 38th Session, Supplement No. 40 (1983), Annex IX. In the *Guerrero* case, *supra* n. 24, the Committee called only for compensation to the victim's husband; but this may be explained by the fact that those responsible were known and had been dismissed from the police force and tried (and acquitted) for the killings.

[55] *Kaya* v. *Turkey* (158/1996/777/978), European Court of Human Rights, Judgment, 19 Feb. 1998, paras. 86–92.

[56] *Supra* n. 25.   [57] Id., para. 219.

[58] Series A, No. 161 (1989), reproduced in 11 *HRLJ* 335 (1990).

namely, *Amekrane* v. *United Kingdom*.[59] Here the second applicant, the widow of a Moroccan air force pilot (the first applicant) who flew to Gibraltar and was returned to Morocco where he was summarily executed after a military court trial, agreed to a friendly settlement in which she received £35,000 compensation. Whether the violation in question, had a formal determination been made by the Commission, was of article 2 itself or of article 3 by virtue of the first applicant's being subjected to a violation of article 2, is of no consequence.

The Inter-American Court of Human Rights has developed a broadly similar pattern. In *Velásquez Rodríguez*, concerning a disappeared prisoner presumed dead, the Court read Convention article 1 (duty to ensure respect for rights) as implying:

The State is obligated to investigate every situation involving a violation of the rights protected by the Convention. If the State apparatus acts in such a way that the violation goes unpunished and the victim's full enjoyment of such rights is not restored as soon as possible, the State has failed to comply with its duty to guarantee the free and full exercise of those rights to the persons within its jurisdiction. The same is true when it allows private persons or groups to act freely and with impunity to the detriment of the rights recognized by the Convention.[60]

It found Honduras had violated article 1 by failing to meet these standards.[61] It also decided that damages were to be paid.[62]

The Special Rapporteur on Extrajudicial, Arbitrary and Summary Executions has affirmed repeatedly, in the words of his annual report to the 1996 session of the UN Commission on Human Rights:

It is the obligation of Governments under international law to carry out exhaustive and impartial investigations into allegations of violations of the right to life, to identify, bring to justice and punish their perpetrators, to grant compensation to the victims or their families, and to take effective measures to avoid future recurrence of such violations. The Principles on the Effective Prevention and Investigation of Extra-legal, Arbitrary and Summary Executions set forth in detail the aforementioned obligations. In addition, regarding deaths as a result of excessive use of force, the Basic Principles on the Use of Force and Firearms by Law Enforcement Officials provide that

---

[59] 16 *Yearbook* 356 (1973).

[60] I/A Court HR, *Velásquez Rodríguez* case, Judgment of 29 July 1988, Series C, No. 4 (Honduras), para. 176; see also paras. 166 and 175.

[61] Id., paras. 180 and 188. Arguably the statement goes too far; not every human rights violation, for instance failure to meet certain standards for a fair trial, involves criminal responsibility. Also it should be noted that in one case where the Court found a violation of article 4, but where there had been unsuccessful attempts to investigate and prosecute the perpetrators, where disciplinary sanctions were imposed on at least one suspected perpetrator, and in which the government accepted responsibility for the killings, the Court decided that only the issue of reparation needed addressing: I/A Court HR, *El Amparo* case, Judgment of 18 Jan. 1995, Series C, No. 19 (Venezuela).

[62] *Supra* n. 59, paras. 189–91; see also follow-up proceedings on damages in Series C, Nos. 7 and 9.

arbitrary or abusive use of force and firearms by law enforcement officials is to be punished as a criminal offence under national law (principle 7).[63]

In the same report, he also opposed expulsion of persons to a country where their lives were in danger.[64]

So, as with torture, international law probably requires that a state responsible for extra-legal execution is required to establish the facts, bring the perpetrators to justice, and compensate the next of kin of the victims. It must also refrain from sending potential victims to a state where there is danger of their becoming victims of extra-legal execution.

INDIVIDUAL RESPONSIBILITY

There is no doubt that extra-legal executions, committed in international armed conflict in violation of the Geneva Conventions of 12 August 1949 open the perpetrators to trial or extradition wherever they may be, since these are grave breaches of the Conventions.[65] The same now appears also true in respect of non-international conflict of serious violations of common article 3 of the Geneva Conventions and of the laws and customs of war under general international law.[66] If so, they would be susceptible of adjudication by a subsequent international penal tribunal and would probably be amenable to universal jurisdiction (see Chapter 4). This is the case under the Convention on *Apartheid* (article V). The same also applies to acts of genocide which, since the adoption of and widespread adherence to the Genocide Convention (see Chapter 4), appears to have become a crime under international law, whether or not committed in connection with an international armed conflict. Further, as was seen in Chapter 4, while the Convention *requires* only jurisdiction by the state in which the genocide was committed, and also envisages a future international penal jurisdiction, it is reasonably certain that international law *permits* the exercise of jurisdiction on a universal basis.

It also seems to have become clear that extra-legal executions committed against *groups* of people, whether or not in connection with any armed conflict, are now to be considered crimes against humanity. This development began in 1954 when the International Law Commission,[67] at the request of the General Assembly, adopted a draft Code of Offences against the Peace and Security of Mankind.[68] The text of the draft code was primarily concerned with elaborating the rules flowing from the Charter and Judgment

---

[63] UN doc. E/CN.4/1996/4, para. 559.   [64] Id., para. 590.

[65] Geneva Convention I, article 49; Geneva Convention II, article 50; Geneva Convention III, article 129; Geneva Convention IV, article 146.

[66] See references, cited *supra* n. 38, concerning the Yugoslav and Rwanda Tribunals and the draft statute of an International Criminal Court.

[67] The General Assembly's expert body on the progressive development and codification of the international law.

[68] *Yearbook of the International Law Commission* (1954), vol. ii (A/2693), para. 54.

of the Nuremberg Tribunal. One provision went clearly beyond these: article 2, paragraph 11, included among offences against the peace and security of mankind:

Inhuman acts such as murder, extermination, enslavement, deportation and persecutions, committed against any civilian population on social, political, racial, religious or cultural grounds by the authorities of a State or by private individuals acting at the instigation or with the toleration of such authorities.

Except for the inclusion of inhuman acts committed on cultural grounds, the text essentially followed the enumeration of crimes against humanity given in the Charter of the Nuremberg Tribunal. It differed radically, however, in one respect: the acts did not have to be committed in connection with crimes against peace or with war crimes. An earlier version of the draft code had, in fact, required the list of 'inhuman acts' to have been 'committed in execution of or in connexion with other offences defined in this article [of the Code]'.[69] The Commission acknowledged that it had 'decided to enlarge the scope of the paragraph so as to make the punishment of the acts enumerated in the paragraph independent of whether or not they are committed in connexion with other offences defined in the draft Code'.[70] It did not give reasons for the change and the disconnection was effected by the closest of votes.[71]

In the event, the General Assembly never took action on the draft, seemingly because it was unable to agree upon a definition of 'aggression', the prototypical crime against peace.[72] The draft code raised its head once more after the General Assembly had finally agreed on a definition of 'aggression'[73] and in 1981 the Assembly returned the matter to the International Law Commission, which was asked to resume its work on the draft.[74]

In 1996, the ILC completed its work on the Draft Code. Article 18 of what is now called the Draft Code of Crimes against the Peace and Security of Mankind, deals with 'crimes against humanity' and reads as follows:

A crime against humanity means any of the following acts, when committed in a systematic manner or on a large scale and instigated or directed by a Government or by any organization or group:

    a. murder;
    b. extermination;
    c. torture;
    d. enslavement;
    e. persecution on political, racial, religious or ethnic grounds;

---

[69] Id., para. 50: Commentary to article 2(1).   [70] Ibid.
[71] 6 for, 5 against, 1 abstaining; id., vol. i, 267th meeting, para. 59 (the preceding debate is found at paras. 40–57).
[72] Ferencz, 'The Draft Code of Offences Against the Peace and Security of Mankind', 75 *AJIL* 674 (1981).
[73] Id., 675.   [74] GA res. 36/106, 10 Dec. 1981.

f. institutionalized discrimination on racial, ethnic or religious grounds involving the violation of fundamental human rights and freedoms and resulting in seriously disadvantaging a part of the population;

g. arbitrary deportation or forcible transfer of population;

h. arbitrary imprisonment; forced disappearance of persons;

i. rape, enforced prostitution and other forms of sexual abuse;

j. other inhumane acts which severely damage physical or mental integrity, health or human dignity, such as mutilation and severe bodily harm.[75]

Extra-legal executions are evidently covered by sub-paragraphs a and b. So such executions, when committed in a systematic manner or on a large scale, will be crimes against humanity, as understood by the ILC. The text of the ILC's commentary confirms the intention not to 'include the requirement that an act was committed in time of war or in connection with crimes against peace or war crimes as in the Nüremberg Charter'.[76]

In fact, the Draft Code has arguably been superseded by (while influencing) more far-reaching initiatives. The first was the adoption by the Security Council of the Statute of the International Tribunal for the Prosecution of Persons Responsible for Serious Violations of International Humanitarian Law Committed in the Territory of the Former Yugoslavia since 1991.[77] Article 5 of the Statute, denominated 'crimes against humanity', includes 'murder' and 'extermination' 'when committed in armed conflict, whether international or internal in character, and directed against any civilian population'. Since such killings are already violations of the Geneva Conventions and of the laws and customs of war, perhaps the only additional element the Statute may offer is to protect a population from its own party to the conflict as opposed to the adverse party. However, the Statute confirms the disconnection of crimes against humanity from international conflict.

The Statute of the International Tribunal for Rwanda[78] removes all formal connection of crimes against humanity with armed conflict. Article 3 lists the same crimes as prosecutable crimes against humanity 'when committed as part of a widespread or systematic attack against any civilian population on national, political, ethnic, racial or religious grounds'. It is true that such an attack implies a situation not comfortably characterized as 'peacetime'. Nevertheless, it is clear that the Geneva Conventions and Protocols criteria for applicability no longer have to be met.

The draft statute of an International Criminal Court includes, without defining, crimes against humanity within the jurisdiction of the proposed court (article 20).[79] The commentary to Article 20 of the International Law

---

[75] Report of the International Law Commission on the Work of its 48th Session, *GAOR*, 51st Session, Supplement No. 10 (1996), ch. II D.

[76] Id., Commentary, para. (6).

[77] Security Council res. 827, 25 May 1993.   [78] Security Council res. 955, 8 Nov. 1994.

[79] Report of the International Law Commission on the Work of its 46th Session, *GAOR*, 49th Session, Supplement No. 10 (1994), 70.

Commission which drafted the text refers to the Draft Code of Offences, as it stood at that time: this had confirmed the disconnection of the notion from armed conflict.[80]

In sum, it may safely be said that crimes against humanity may be understood in the sense contemplated by article 3 of the Rwanda Tribunal Statute. Accordingly, it is plain that, since they include murder and extermination, extra-legal executions meeting those criteria are not only (evidently) triable before an international penal tribunal, but also presumaby susceptible of universal criminal jurisdiction.

The issue becomes less clear when the killings amount neither to war crimes, to acts of genocide, nor to crimes against humanity. In other words, what is the position of an individual perpetrator of an extra-legal execution? To the extent that extra-legal executions violate the Declaration against Torture, then the position of the perpetrator is the same as that of the violator of the Declaration (see Chapter 4).

The Principles on Extra-legal Executions take a clear position. As noted earlier, principle 18 requires that persons identified as responsible for extra-legal executions are to be brought to justice. It goes on to state:

> Governments shall either bring such persons to justice or cooperate to extradite any such persons to other countries wishing to exercise jurisdiction. This principle shall apply irrespective of who and where the perpetrators or the victims are, their nationalities or where the offence was committed.

There would hardly be a simpler formulation of the idea of compulsory universal jurisdiction. The exclusion, in principle 19, of the defence of superior orders also tends to confirm the notion of extra-legal executions as being crimes under international law.

However, there is a dearth of state practice on the point.

The discussion of the *Astiz* case (see Chapter 4) is of interest to the issue of individual responsibility for extra-legal executions as well as to that for torture, since Captain Astiz was accused of both. The judgment in the *Filártiga* case, however, was so heavily couched in the language of the prohibition of torture that, even though the victim allegedly died under torture, it is difficult to analyse the case in terms of extra-legal execution. Nevertheless, many of the suits that have been successfully brought in the United States pursuant to the *Filártiga* litigation have involved claims for murder.[81] Indeed, the Torture Victims Protection Act, which effectively recodifies the Alien Tort Statute in this area, explicitly includes 'extrajudicial killing' as involving liability for damages in a civil action.[82]

---

[80] Id., 76. See, generally, Amnesty International, *The International Criminal Court—Making the Right Choices. Part I* (AI Index: IOR 40/01/97, Jan. 1997), 41–4.

[81] e.g., *Trajano v. Marcos*, 978 F 2d 493 (USCA, 9th Cir., 1992); *Xuncax et al. v. Gramajo*, 886 F Supp. 162 (D Mass., 1995).

[82] Torture Victims Protection Act of 1991, Pub. L No. 102–256; 106 Stat. 73 (1992), s.

This suggests that the perpetrator of an extra-legal execution is as amenable to universal jurisdiction as a torturer. Nevertheless it would be helpful if a specific treaty obligation like that offered by the Convention against Torture applied also in respect of extra-legal execution.

INTERNATIONAL REMEDIES

Until 1982, the UN's concern with official killings was largely focused on arbitrary and summary executions, in the sense of death penalties imposed without the requisite safeguards (see next chapter). Later practice has been to include extra-legal executions as a second category within the concept of summary or arbitrary executions.[83] There is no way of knowing whether the Secretary-General has used his 'best endeavours' called for by a series of General Assembly resolutions in respect of extra-legal executions as well as in respect of procedurally deficient death penalties (see next chapter). By definition, extra-legal executions are not as susceptible of preventive action. The main development in the way of a specific international mechanism on extra-legal executions arose out of the 1982 discussions of the Commission on Human Rights which recommended the establishment of a Special Rapporteur on the problem.

SPECIAL RAPPORTEUR ON EXTRAJUDICIAL, SUMMARY OR ARBITRARY EXECUTIONS

At the thirty-eighth session of the Commission on Human Rights in 1982, the Danish delegation introduced a draft resolution that sought to come to grips with both kinds of arbitrary deprivations of life by expressly including extra-legal executions within its general concern about summary or arbitrary executions.[84] It did so in the context of the introductory statement of the then Director of the Division of Human Rights, Mr Van Boven, which had concentrated on 'deliberate killings perpetrated by organized power' without colour of legality.[85] The draft as adopted by the Commission recommended that Ecosoc should authorize the appointment of a special rapporteur who

2(a)(2). By s. 3(a) '"extrajudicial killing" means a deliberate killing not authorized by a previous judgment pronounced by a regularly constituted court affording all the judicial guarantees which are recognized as indispensable by civilized peoples. Such term however, does not include any such killing that, under international law, is lawfully carried out under the authority of a foreign nation.'

[83] *Supra* text accompanying n. 12.

[84] By 1992, the relevant Commission resolution had been entitled 'Extrajudicial, arbitrary and summary executions': Resolution 1992/72, 5 Mar. 1992, Commission on Human Rights Report, 48th Session, *ESCOR*, Supplement No. 2, Chapter II A.

[85] UN doc. E/CN.4/1982/SR.1.

was to submit to the next session of the Commission 'a comprehensive report
... on the occurrence and extent of the practice of such executions together
with his conclusions and recommendations'.[86] The appointee would be able
to seek and receive information from governments and international governmental and non-governmental organizations. A few weeks later Ecosoc
agreed,[87] whereupon the Chairman of the Commission on Human Rights
appointed to the post S. Amos Wako, Kenyan Secretary-General of the Inter-
African Union of Lawyers and a practising lawyer. He resigned in 1992 and
the Chairman of the 1992 session of the Commission appointed to replace
him Bacre Waly Ndiaye, a Senegalese practising lawyer and former Vice-
Chair of Amnesty International's International Executive Committee.

While the language of the resolution establishing the mandate contained no
words suggesting an action component,[88] this rapidly evolved with the support of the Commission to act in parallel with the earlier established Working
Group on Enforced or Involuntary Disappearances (see chapter 8) and the
later established Special Rapporteur on Torture (see chapter 5).[89]

The Special Rapporteur seems to labour under no explicit limitation on the
sources he can rely on. Although at the beginning of the mandate the only
non-official source from which he could seek and receive information was
non-governmental organizations in consultative status with Ecosoc,[90] by
1986 renewals of his mandate contained no such specification.[91]

When he receives information he feels he can act on,[92] he transmits it to
governments. He seeks to follow up on replies received both by asking sources
of information to comment on those replies and by seeking further information from the governments.[93] He also reminds non-responding governments
of outstanding requests for information. As traditionally expected by the
Commission,[94] he sends urgent appeals in respect of feared extra-legal executions. Thus, in 1997, he sent 65 urgent appeals on behalf of more than 1,888
persons or groups of persons in 19 countries or territories, where there were

---

[86] Resolution 1982/29, 11 Mar. 1982, Commission on Human Rights, Report, 38th Session,
ESCOR, 1982, Supplement No. 2, Chapter XXVI A.

[87] Ecosoc res. 1982/35, 7 May 1982.

[88] Compare the power of the Working Group on Enforced or Involuntary Disappearances to
perform its functions 'in an effective and expeditious manner' and to 'respond effectively to
information that comes before it': Resolution 20 (XXXVI), 29 Feb. 1980, Commission on
Human Rights, Report, 36th Session, *ESCOR*, 1980, Supplement No. 3, Chapter XXVI A.

[89] Thus, in the latest resolution extending his mandate, repeating language used for many
years, the Special Rapporteur is asked to 'respond effectively to information which comes before
him, in particular where an extrajudicial, summary or arbitrary execution is imminent or threatened or when such an execution has occurred'. Resolution 1998/68, 21 Apr. 1998, para. 8(b).

[90] Ecosoc res. 1982/35, 7 May 1982, para. 4.

[91] Ecosoc res. 1986/36, 23 May 1986; note mandate renewals, originally annual, are now tri-
ennial.

[92] He explains his criteria on credibility of sources, including 'non-governmental organizations and individuals' in his 1993 annual report: UN doc. E/CN.4/1994/7, paras. 18–20.

[93] UN doc. E/CN.4/1995/61, para. 24.   [94] See *supra* n. 89.

death threats;[95] he sent communications concerning alleged deaths in custody in 24 countries or territories;[96] communications were sent to 15 countries or territories about alleged deaths involving excessive use of force by law enforcement officials,[97] 8 of which concerned the use of such force against demonstrators in 8 countries;[98] communications were sent to 8 countries concerning deaths due to civil defence or paramilitary groups acting in the service of or in parallel with security forces;[99] urgent appeals went to 2 countries where there was a threat of expulsion of persons to countries where their lives were at risk.[100]

The Special Rapporteur may also undertake on-site visits with the agreement of the government of the country in question. Since the creation of the mandate he has visited eleven countries.[101] As of the end of 1997, he was still seeking invitations to visit three countries.[102] Reports of the visits are usually published as addenda to the annual report or, in the case of joint visits, as separate documents.[103]

The annual reports and mission reports are public documents which provide country-by-country descriptions of the Special Rapporteur's activities. Until the appointment of the present Special Rapporteur, the annual reports tended in practice to follow the model of the Working Group on Enforced or Involuntary Disappearances in not making judgements on the cases or countries reviewed. Since then, it has been increasingly the practice to make observations on the country entries. These tend not so much to be case-specific observations, as observations on the general situation or on legal developments in the countries in question.

The impact of these public activities is enhanced by his resort to press conferences, press releases, and the granting of interviews to organs of the mass media.[104]

---

[95] UN doc. E/CN.4/1998/68, para. 29.   [96] Id., para. 32.   [97] Id., para. 36.
[98] Ibid.   [99] Id., para. 40.   [100] Id., para. 4.
[101] Suriname (twice: UN docs. E/CN.4/1985/17, Annex V; and E/CN.4/1988/22, Annex), Uganda (E/CN.4/1987/20, Annex II), Colombia (twice: E/CN.4/1990/22/Add. 1; E/CN.4/1995/111, the latter jointly with the Special Rapporteur on Torture), Zaïre (E/CN.4/1992/30/Add. 1), Rwanda (E/CN.4/1994/7/Add. 1), Peru (E/CN.4/1994/7/Add. 2), Indonesia and East Timor (E/CN.4/1995/61/Add. 1), Burundi (E/CN.4/1996/4/Add. 1), Papua New Guinea (E/CN.4/1996/4/Add. 2), Sri Lanka (E/CN.4/1998/68/Add. 2), and the United States of America (E/CN.4/1998/68/Add. 3, mainly concerning the death penalty; see Chapter 7). A planned joint mission to Nigeria of the Special Rapporteur on Executions and the Special Rapporteur on the Independence of Judges and Lawyers had failed to materialize by the 1997 session of the Commission, but yielded two reports to the General Assembly (A/51/538 (1996)) and to the Commission (E/CN.4/1997/62). A 1997 joint visit, mandated by the Commission on Human Rights, to the Democratic Republic of the Congo, together with the Special Rapporteur on Zaïre and a member of the Working Group on Enforced or Involuntary Disappearances, proved abortive (UN docs. A/51/1942, Annex; A/52/946, Annex). The Special Rapporteur used also to hold joint hearings, outside South Africa, with the *Ad Hoc* Working Group of Experts on Southern Africa.
[102] UN doc. E/CN.4/1998/68, para. 21: Algeria, India, and Turkey.
[103] See *supra* n. 101.   [104] See UN doc. E/CN.4/1998/68, para. 24.

The Commission's support for the mandate was evident in 1996 when it invited the Special Rapporteur to submit an interim report to the General Assembly.[105] The Assembly, after the first interim report in 1996, invited him to submit a further one in 1998.[106] The first interim report[107] did not have a country-by-country section. Rather it was organized topically, but with country-specific references both statistically (communications and urgent appeals transmitted) and in terms of illustrating particular problems.

SUMMARY

Extra-legal executions are the paradigm violations of the right to life as guaranteed by the Universal Declaration of Human Rights, the International Covenant on Civil and Political Rights, and the regional human rights conventions, as well as being prohibited by the Geneva Conventions of 12 August 1949 and their Additional Protocols, applicable in time of international and non-international armed conflict. The right to life is not one of those rights that can be derogated from, even in time of grave public emergency, under the human rights treaties that permit such derogations. According to the Sixth UN Crime Congress, they may also be violations of the prohibition against torture or other ill-treatment. Like that prohibition (see Chapter 2), it may safely be considered that the right to life is a norm recognized by general international law; this is especially true of the prohibition of racially motivated killings and genocide and other killings aimed at civilian populations (crimes against humanity). Indeed, as also with the prohibition of torture, the right to life has been argued to be a norm of *jus cogens*, that is, a fundamental norm that cannot be varied by consenting states.[108]

Certain killings do not violate the rule, however: killings in connection with law enforcement fall into this category (as long as they are carried out as a measure of last resort and to protect life); similarly, killings of combatants in the actual course of combat do not violate the rule (but once a combatant is *hors de combat* and in the hands of the adverse party, summary execution is forbidden).

Violations of the right to life entail an obligation to investigate the circumstances, bring the perpetrators to justice, and compensate the victims' next of kin. There is also an obligation not to send persons to countries where they risk being victims of extra-legal execution. The responsibility of individual perpetrators of genocide, crimes against humanity, and war crimes is estab-

---

[105] Resolution 1996/74, 23 Apr. 1996, Commission on Human Rights, Report, 52nd session, *ESCOR*, 1996, Supplement No. 3, Chapter II A, para. 19.

[106] GA res. 51/92, 12 Dec. 1996, para. 16.   [107] UN doc. A/51/457 (1996).

[108] Gormley, 'The Right to Life and the Rule of Non-Derogability: Peremptory Norms of *Jus Cogens*', in Ramcharan (ed.), *The Right to Life in International Law* (1985), 120.

lished; perpetrators of the former two are probably liable to trial on the basis of universal jurisdiction, the perpetrators of the latter certainly are. So, under the *Apartheid* Convention, are perpetrators of the crime of apartheid. In peacetime the situation is less clear, but the principles on executions indicate that the perpetrators should be treated no differently from torturers. They may indeed fall into the latter category of persons.

Meanwhile, in the wake of repeated General Assembly condemnation of extrajudicial, arbitrary, and summary executions, the Commission on Human Rights has appointed and maintained a Special Rapporteur on the question. He has brought allegations to the attention of governments, and has reported publicly on summaries of these, together with government replies. He has also intervened with governments (publishing these interventions) in cases where urgent action might prevent further such executions and he has been encouraged to pursue this aspect of his work. He has also undertaken on-site visits to countries, publishing his findings.

7

The Death Penalty

INTRODUCTION: THE OBJECTIVE OF ABOLITION

There is a gradual, but firm movement internationally towards the abolition of the death penalty. As of March 1998, Amnesty International was able to list a majority of states as being abolitionist in law or in practice. While ninety-one states retained the penalty, 104 could be considered as having abolished it. Sixty-three states had abolished it for all crimes and another sixteen for ordinary crimes. In addition, twenty-five states could be considered as abolitionist *de facto*, not having carried out any executions in the previous ten years.[1] While the latter category must be treated with some caution,[2] there seems to be a general trend of about two states becoming abolitionist for ordinary crimes, or all crimes, annually.[3] Indeed, in 1997 or the first three months of 1998, Amnesty International listed Azerbaijan, Estonia, Georgia, and Poland as moving from the ranks of the retentionist to the ranks of totally abolitionist countries; Nepal moved into the same category, having previously been abolitionist for ordinary crimes only; and Bosnia-Herzegovina, having been retentionist, became abolitionist for ordinary crimes.[4]

Nevertheless, the ninety-four countries that retain the death penalty cannot be ignored in assessing the status of the death penalty under general international law. They include three countries (China, Russian Federation, and United States) whose positions in terms of world influence are considerable; they retain the penalty in law and practice.[5] This is so, even though successive UN studies have affirmed, in the words of the first of these, 'that the deterrent effect of the death penalty is, to say the least, not demonstrated'.[6] A later such report put it thus:

With respect to the influence of the abolition of capital punishment upon the incidence of murder, all of the available data suggest that where the murder rate is increasing, abolition does not appear to hasten the increase; where the rate is decreasing, aboli-

---

[1] The Death Penalty—List of Abolitionist and Retentionist Countries (Amnesty International, Apr. 1998) (AI Index: ACT 50/08/98).

[2] For example, Burundi executed six men on 31 July 1997, the first executions there in 16 years: Amnesty International, in *Death Penalty News*, Sept. 1997, 2.

[3] Amnesty International, *supra* n. 1, 1.　　　　　　　　　　　　　　　　　[4] Ibid.

[5] The Russian Federation continued in 1996 to carry out executions, despite a moratorium to which it was committed in the context of its admission to the Council of Europe (Amnesty International, *Death Penalty News*, Mar. 1997, 2); there is, nevertheless, evidence that it has been complying since 1997 and is on the way to formal abolition: see below.

[6] Ancel, *Capital Punishment* (United Nations, 1962).

tion does not appear to interrupt the decrease; where the rate is stable, the presence or absence of capital punishment does not appear to affect it.[7]

Similarly, the latest such study to have examined the deterrence issue considered a number of statistical analyses based on United States experiences and concluded:

Most of those who favour abolition (assuming that they are not opposed to execution under any circumstances) would demand proof that executions have a substantial marginal deterrent effect. Those retentionists who rely on their intuitive belief in deterrence would require substantial proof that there was no additional risk to the lives of citizens before sparing murderers from execution. The balance of evidence, looked at in this way, favours the abolitionist position.[8]

In the light of the number and importance of the retentionist countries, it is hardly surprising that general international law does not expressly require abolition of the death penalty.[9] On the other hand, given the spuriousness of the strongest argument the retentionists can muster—that by taking life the state aims to save other lives or prevent other offences of the type to which the death penalty applies—it is also not surprising that the public stance of the governments of the world, through both treaties and other instruments, has been that the abolition of the death penalty, while not an immediate requirement, is an ultimate goal in the field of human rights. Moreover, as will be seen below, some treaties do commit states parties to abolition.

The Universal Declaration of Human Rights is silent on the issue of the death penalty, although it was discussed in the context of consideration of the right to life. The many proposals that were discussed while the Declaration was being drafted ranged from those that would have provided for the abolition of the death penalty, at least in peacetime, to those that would have maintained it without qualification as an explicit exception to the scope of the right to life.[10] The decision to leave a bare reference to the right to life in the Declaration was partly a reflection of this diversity of view and partly the result of the decision that detailed provisions on the scope of the rights should be left to the planned convention that eventually became the International Covenant on Civil and Political Rights.[11]

Except where it concerns the provisions of the Geneva Conventions relating to armed conflict, the discussion below will deal with norms relating to the

[7] Morris, *Capital Punishment: Developments 1961–1965* (United Nations, 1967).
[8] Hood, *The Death Penalty—A Worldwide Perspective—A Report to the United Nations Committee on Crime Prevention and Control* (1989), 148. The most recent of the UN's quinquennial studies does not address the deterrence question: UN doc. E/1995/78.
[9] See, generally, Schabas, *The Abolition of the Death Penalty in International Law* (2nd edn., 1997) (hereinafter 'Schabas').
[10] Landerer, 'Capital Punishment as a Human Rights Issue before the United Nations', 4 *Revue des droits de l'homme—Human Rights Journal* 511, 513–18 (1971) (hereinafter 'Landerer').
[11] Landerer, 517–18; Schabas, ch. 1.

protection of the right to life, since human rights treaties treat the death penalty as an explicit exception to that right. Had this not been the case, issues relating to the prohibition of torture or other cruel, inhuman, or degrading treatment or punishment could well have arisen. Indeed, the language of this prohibition is occasionally found in contexts concerning the death penalty: the preamble to General Assembly resolution 2393 (XXIII) of 26 November 1968, dealing with safeguards relating to the death penalty (see below), invoked article 5 of the Universal Declaration (prohibiting torture and other ill-treatment), and a Secretariat statement to the Sixth UN Congress on the Prevention of Crime and the Treatment of Offenders described the death penalty as 'cruel, inhuman or degrading punishment'.[12]

The European Court of Human Rights, in *Soering*, which will be discussed below, has confirmed that the circumstances of the imposition and execution of the death penalty may fall foul of the European Convention on Human Rights article 3 prohibition of inhuman or degrading punishment. However, it refused to find that the penalty *per se* violated article 3 in the light of provision for it in article 2, as a limitation on the right to life. Responding to the argument of Amnesty International that the limitation should be considered abrogated in the light of European abolitionist practice, it held that, by the Council of Europe's adopting the 6th Protocol to the Convention on abolition (see below), the states parties had chosen that route to amending article 2, not that of abrogation by state practice.[13]

Nevertheless, it may one day be possible to argue that the death penalty is a violation of the prohibition of torture or cruel, inhuman, or degrading punishment.[14] Meanwhile, it is bizarre that corporal punishment may well fall foul of that prohibition (see Chapter 10), while capital punishment apparently does not.

Consideration of the issue may begin with a review of the various instruments which suggest that abolition of the death penalty is a goal of international human rights law as well as of those that explicitly provide for abolition. The predominant approach in achieving this objective, however, has been the acceptance of certain categories of limitation on the lawfulness of the death penalty. Therefore, after the instruments envisaging abolition have been dealt with, the next three sections will examine these categories: (a) limitations on the nature of the offences that may still attract the death penalty; (b) procedural safeguards that are to be respected in the case of a capitally punishable offence; and (c) exemption of certain categories of

---

[12] *Infra*, n. 22.

[13] *Soering* v. *United Kingdom*, European Court of Human Rights, Judgment, 7 July 1989, reproduced in 11 *HRLJ* 335 (1990), paras. 101–3. The European Parliament has, however, described the death penalty as '*a cruel and inhuman form of punishment* and a violation of the right to life, even where strict legal procedures are applied': Resolution of 17 Jan. 1986 (emphasis added).

[14] Schabas, *The Death Penalty as Cruel Treatment and Torture* (1996).

potential death penalty victims. This is followed by a consideration of remedial measures being undertaken by the UN to promote respect for the standards it has set.

INTERNATIONAL COVENANT ON CIVIL AND POLITICAL RIGHTS

One of the first, if implicit, statements of the goal of abolition is to be found in the International Covenant on Civil and Political Rights, adopted by the General Assembly of the United Nations in 1966.[15] It came into force on 23 March 1976 and 140 countries are now parties to it. Article 6 declares in its first paragraph: 'Every human being has the inherent right to life. This right shall be protected by law. No one shall be arbitrarily deprived of his life.'[16] This general statement cannot be construed as *per se* prohibiting the death penalty, since it is followed by a series of paragraphs stipulating restrictions on the use of the death penalty. The first of these, paragraph 2, which limits the nature of the offences for which the death penalty may be imposed, is introduced by the clause: 'In countries which have not abolished the death penalty . . .'. The specific significance of the phrase will be considered below; here one may note only an implicit suggestion of approval for countries that have abolished the death penalty. The point is strengthened by paragraph 6 of the same article: after the various restrictions on the use of the death penalty have been listed in paragraphs 2 to 5, paragraph 6 states: 'Nothing in this article shall be invoked to delay or to prevent the abolition of capital punishment by any State Party to the present Covenant.'[17] This formulation in article 6 led the Human Rights Committee (the eighteen individual experts elected by the states parties to the Covenant to monitor the Covenant's implementation) to observe: 'The article also refers generally to abolition in terms which strongly suggest (paras. 6(2) and (6)) that abolition is desirable. The Committee concludes that all measures of abolition should be considered as progress in the enjoyment of the right to life . . .'.[18]

[15] GA res. 2200 A (XXI), 16 Dec. 1966. See, generally, Schabas, ch. 2.

[16] For the full text of article 6, see Annex 9b.

[17] This language is an adaptation (*GAOR*, 12th Session, Annexes, Agenda item 33, A/3764 and Add. 1(1957), para. 106) of an Irish proposal aiming to compromise between those that wished at least 'a provision requiring the progressive abolition of the death penalty' and those that did not. *GAOR*, 12th Session, Third Committee, Summary Records, A/C.3/SR.813, para. 41 (1957); see Schabas, 70.

[18] Report of the Human Rights Committee, *GAOR*, 37th Session, Supplement No. 40 (1982), Annex V, general comment 6(16), para. 6. In the same vein, the Inter-American Commission on Human Rights, in a press release issued after its sixty-third regular session (03/84, 5 Oct. 1984), announced that it had 'called upon all the American governments that had not yet done so to abolish the penalty in accordance with the spirit of Article 4 of the American Convention on Human Rights and the universal trend favourable to the abolition of the death penalty'; as quoted in the Commission's *Report on the Situation of Human Rights in Chile*, OAS/Ser. L/V/II.66; doc. 17 (1985). The Commission has also evolved the practice of appealing to

OTHER UN INITIATIVES

Developments in political bodies

Given that it comes from the body whose main function is to assess questions of compliance with the Covenant, the statement of the Human Rights Committee quoted above is persuasive authority. It is also in line with the political direction taken by the United Nations General Assembly and the Commission on Human Rights. After some twelve years of consideration of the topic by the Assembly, Ecosoc, and subordinate bodies of Ecosoc, including the Commission on Human Rights,[19] the Assembly, by resolution 2857 (XXVI) of 20 December 1971, affirmed that 'in order fully to guarantee the right to life, provided for in Article 3 of the Universal Declaration of Human Rights, the main objective to be pursued is that of progressively restricting the number of offences for which capital punishment may be imposed, with a view to the desirability of abolishing this punishment in all countries'.

When, in 1977, on the initiative of Sweden, the General Assembly considered the matter, it reaffirmed the goal it had set in 1971[20] and referred the question to the Sixth United Nations Congress on the Prevention of Crime and the Treatment of Offenders that would take place in 1980 (resolution 32/61 of 8 December 1977). Hope was thus placed in the Congress to produce further normative proscription on the use of the death penalty. Indeed, at the opening of the Congress the Secretary-General of the United Nations, in asking the Congress to give serious consideration to the question of capital punishment, stated that 'the taking of life of human beings violates respect for the dignity of every person and the right to life, as declared in the basic postulates of the United Nations'.[21] In addition, as noted above, the Secretariat working paper on the topic stated that 'the death penalty constitutes "cruel, inhuman or degrading punishment" which even in the light of the behaviour at which it is directed, should not be acceptable'.[22]

In spite of these positive statements, the Congress was unable to agree on a resolution on the death penalty. Austria and Sweden, subsequently joined by Ecuador and the Federal Republic of Germany, introduced a complicated draft resolution that would have declared that 'capital punishment raises serious questions in relation to respect for the dignity of all human beings and

governments not to execute persons sentenced to death and urging abolition, even in cases where no violation of the American Convention on Human Rights can be found: see, for example, Resolution No. 13/84 (Case No. 9054 (Jamaica)), OAS, *Annual Report of the Inter-American Commission on Human Rights 1984–1985* (OEA/Ser.L/V/II.66; doc. 10 rev. 1), 111; see also id., 10 for reference to the above-mentioned general appeal.

[19] See Amnesty International, *The Death Penalty* (1979) (hereinafter '*Death Penalty*'), 24–9.
[20] With the omission of the words 'in all countries'.
[21] *Sixth United Nations Congress on the Prevention of Crime and the Treatment of Offenders—Report*, A/CONF.87/114/Rev. 1 (1981).
[22] UN doc. A/CONF.87/9, para. 98.

for human rights, in particular the right to life, which is the most fundamental of all human rights, and the right not to be subjected to cruel, inhuman or degrading punishment'.[23] It would also have reiterated 'that the ultimate objective is the total abolition of capital punishment throughout the world'. In response to strong opposition, the sponsoring countries then introduced a revised draft in which several paragraphs of the original were weakened.[24] Under the new draft the Congress would merely have declared 'that further restriction in the application of capital punishment and its eventual abolition would be a significant contribution to the strengthening of human rights, in particular the right to life'. While there was some strongly expressed opposition to the very concept of abolition, the doubts of many delegations focused on other aspects of the draft, especially on a proposal for a moratorium on executions (indefinite in the first draft, for five years in the revised one). In the end, 'realizing that there was inadequate time for the completion of work on the question, the sponsors withdrew the revised draft resolution'.[25] This inconclusive result was followed by a further inconclusive, mainly procedural discussion at the thirty-fifth session of the General Assembly (1980). These developments represented a setback for the movement towards enhancing the UN normative proscription of the death penalty. Another attempt, this time initiated by Italy, at the Eighth UN Crime Congress, failed to achieve the necessary two-thirds majority.[26] By the draft resolution, the Congress would have reaffirmed the General Assembly line of the 1970s in favour of the progressive restriction of capitally-punishable offences and asking states to consider imposing a moratorium on executions 'at least on a three-year basis'.[27]

However, Italy returned to the attack at the forty-ninth session of the General Assembly in 1994. It proposed that the Assembly, *inter alia*, invite non-abolitionist states 'to consider the progressive restriction of the number of offences for which the death penalty may be imposed' (arguably a weakening of the language of the pre-1980 resolutions) and that it encourage the same states 'to consider the opportunity of instituting a moratorium on pending executions with a view to ensuring that the principle that no State should dispose of the life of any human being be affirmed in every part of the world by the year 2000'.[28] After a procedurally complicated debate, the resolution failed by 44 votes to 36, with 74 abstentions.[29] This was because a substantial

[23] UN doc. A/CONF.87/C.I/L.1.
[24] UN doc. A/CONF.87/C.I/L.1/Rev. 1; also reproduced in loc. cit. *supra* n. 21, Chapter IV, Report of Committee I, Annex.
[25] *Supra* n. 21, para. 111.
[26] There were 48 votes for, 29 against and 16 abstentions: *Eighth United Nations Congress on the Prevention of Crime and the Treatment of Offenders—Report*, Havana, 27 Aug.–7 Sept. 1990, UN doc. A/CONF.144/28/Rev.1 (1991), para. 358.
[27] Id., para. 352.   [28] UN doc. A/C.3/49/L.32 (1994).
[29] UN doc. A/C.3/49/SR.61 (1994), paras. 55–6.

number of previously sponsoring states joined the ranks of the abstainers after an amendment proposed by Singapore was carried.[30]

Presumably heartened by the fact that a text with an abolitionist thrust could have been successful, Italy brought the matter to the 1997 session of the Commission on Human Rights. The language of the draft[31] was firmer than that proposed to the General Assembly and was adopted unchanged after the defeat of a number of amendments that would have weakened the text, including one modelled on the Singaporean amendment that had been successful at the 1994 General Assembly.[32] By the resulting resolution 1997/12 of 3 April 1997, the Commission 'call[ed] upon' non-abolitionist states 'progressively to restrict the number of offences for which the death penalty may be imposed . . . and to consider suspending executions, with a view to completely abolishing the death penalty'.[33] That this was not a flash in the pan is evidenced by the adoption of a similar resolution in 1998 with the addition of a call for the publication of information on the imposition of the death penalty.[34]

Effectively, then, the issue has moved from the crime prevention organs to the principal human rights organ of the UN. The goal of abolition is reasserted, as is one road to it: progressive restriction of capitally-punishable offences. The addition of requested action of a less long-term nature, in the form of a suspension of, or moratorium on, executions, is a novelty that indicates a new momentum for the abolitionist cause at the universal level. This momentum could be enhanced if the General Assembly could muster the same political will as that found in the Commission. On the other hand, it was the General Assembly itself which, in 1989, was to adopt a path-breaking instrument aimed outright at abolition of the death penalty. To this we now turn.

Optional Protocol to the Covenant on Civil and Political Rights

At the same session of the General Assembly that had in 1980 received the inconclusive results of the Sixth UN Crime Congress debate on the death

[30] UN doc. A/C.3/49/SR.61 (1994), paras. 9–10. The Singapore text would have added a preambular paragraph '[a]ffirming the sovereign right of States to determine the legal measures and penalties which are appropriate in their societies to combat serious crimes effectively' (A/C.3/49/L.73 and Rev.1). It passed even after the Italian draft had already been amended by the 10 sponsors in the direction of the draft Singapore amendment except that the determination had to be 'in accordance with international law, including the Charter of the United Nations' (A/C.3/49/L.32/Rev.1) (1994).

[31] UN doc. E/CN.4/1997/L.20.

[32] Resolution 1997/12, 3 Apr. 1997 (the vote was 27 for, 11 against and 14 abstentions): Commission on Human Rights, Report, 53rd Session, *ESCOR*, 1997, Supplement No. 3, Chapter II A. The draft amendments were contained in UN doc. E/CN.4/1997/L.35.

[33] Operative paras. 4 and 5.

[34] Resolution 1998/8, 3 Apr. 1998, operative para. 4. The resolution was adopted by 26 for, 13 against and 12 abstentions (UN Press Release HR/CN/98/33).

penalty, the governments of Austria, Costa Rica, Italy, the Federal Republic of Germany, Portugal, and Sweden introduced the text of a draft optional protocol to the International Covenant on Civil and Political Rights whereby the parties to such a protocol would commit themselves to abolition.[35] The Assembly decided to consider 'the idea' of such an optional protocol at its next session and sought governments' comments and observations.[36] It did the same at its next (thirty-sixth) session.[37] By the time of the thirty-seventh session in 1982, the Assembly had received replies from only thirty-two governments, revealing no general policy line.[38] At that session it was decided to defer further consideration for two years while the matter (that is, the idea of elaborating an abolitionist optional protocol to the Covenant) was studied by the Commission on Human Rights.[39] Although the issue was then raised at the 1983 session of the Commission,[40] no action was taken and it was not until 1984 that the Commission decided to consult its Sub-Commission on Prevention of Discrimination and Protection of Minorities on how to deal with the proposal.[41]

The Sub-Commission entrusted its Belgian member, Marc Bossuyt, with the task of preparing the analysis.[42] His report was submitted in 1987 and contained a draft optional protocol to the Covenant, somewhat revised from the version originally submitted to the General Assembly in 1980 by the governments that initiated the process.[43] In 1988, the Sub-Commission forwarded the text to the Commission[44] which referred it, through Ecosoc, to the General Assembly. The Assembly adopted the unamended text by resolution 44/128 on 15 December 1989.[45]

It is the first universal abolitionist treaty, entering into force on 11 July 1991 after receiving its tenth instrument of ratification. There are thirty-two states parties as of June 1998. Article 1 contains the basic obligations. The first paragraph provides: 'No one within the jurisdiction of a State Party to the present Protocol shall be executed.' The focus here is on non-execution rather than on legislative abolition. The latter issue is addressed by the

---

[35] Text in *GAOR*, 35th Session, Annexes, Agenda item 65, A/35/742, para. 20. See, generally, Schabas, 168–91.

[36] GA decision 35/437, 15 Dec. 1980.   [37] Resolution 36/59, 25 Nov. 1981.

[38] UN docs. A/36/441 and Adds. 1 and 2 (1981); A/37/407 and Add. 1 (1982).

[39] Resolution 37/192, 18 Dec. 1982.   [40] UN docs. E/CN.4/1983/SR.17–20.

[41] Resolution 1984/19, 6 Mar. 1984, Commission on Human Rights, Report, 40th Session, *ESCOR*, 1984, Supplement No. 4, Chapter II A.

[42] Sub-Commission res. 1984/7, 28 Aug. 1984, UN doc. E/CN.4/1985/3; E/CN.4/Sub.2/1984/43, Chapter XVIII A.

[43] UN doc. E/CN.4/Sub.2/1987/20.

[44] Sub-Commission res. 1988/22, 1 Sept. 1988, UN doc. E/CN.4/1989/3; E/CN.4/Sub.2/1988/45, Chapter II A.; Commission res. 1989/25, 6 Mar. 1989, Commission on Human Rights, Report, 45th Session, *ESCOR*, 1989, Supplement No. 2, Chapter II A.

[45] The Assembly adopted the text by 59 votes to 26, with 48 abstentions. While those voting for were more than double those opposing, they were a minority of those present and voting. Many retentionist states were clearly unhappy with the initiative.

article's second paragraph: 'Each State Party shall take all necessary measures to abolish the death penalty within its jurisdiction.' It would appear from this language which envisages a process—in some states a complicated and protracted one—that the achievement of legislative abolition is not a condition of ratification. Arguably a state that was genuinely taking the prescribed measures could be a party without violating the Protocol, as long as no one was being executed, even if courts had been imposing the death penalty under existing national law. In fact, adherence by a state which is non-abolitionist in law is unlikely.

The only reservations permitted under the Protocol are those that would provide 'for the application of the death penalty in time of war pursuant to a conviction for a most serious crime of a military nature committed during wartime' (article 2(1)). This exception is narrower than that envisaged in the earlier abolitionist 6th Protocol to the European Convention on Human Rights, discussed in the following section. For the reasons there stated, it can be similarly concluded that the war in question must be a formally declared war between states, not a civil war. Such interstate wars have in fact become obsolete; however, many states have left unabrogated laws that entered their statute books when such wars were prevalent. Formal abrogation could be politically sensitive, yet the states in question could still be considered abolitionist and should not be discouraged from adhering to the Protocol. The further restriction, that the offence must be one of a military nature, would seem to suggest that only the 'most serious' crimes committed by military personnel could be the targets of the permitted reservations. The reservation must include the relevant provisions of national legislation (article 2 (2)).

It is also worth noting that, unlike the first Optional Protocol providing for the right to individual petition, there is no provision in the second one for denunciation. If only on the basis of *a contrario* interpretation, this would seem to preclude any going back on the commitment.[46]

Of course, the Protocol is only binding on the states that accept it. Nevertheless, it remains a standard which all states are urged to accept. The fact that this is so, no doubt explains the substantial opposition to its original adoption.[47] As such, it was an important step in the process of reversing the setback that the cause of abolition suffered at the 1980 Sixth UN Crime Congress.

Statutes of international criminal tribunals

In other chapters, especially Chapters 5, 6, and 8, reference is made to the Statutes of the tribunals set up by the UN Security Council to adjudicate

---

[46] The Human Rights Committee has made its view clear that the absence of a denunciation clause in the Covenant itself means that states parties cannot withdraw: see general comment 26(61), 29 Oct. 1997, UN Doc. CCPR/C/21/Rev.1/Add.8/Rev.1 1997.
[47] See n. 45 *supra.*

crimes committed in the former Yugoslavia and in Rwanda, as well as to the proposed statute of a permanent international criminal court. One notable absence from these texts is any provision for the death penalty. Despite the appalling nature of some of the crimes for which they aim to bring the perpetrators to justice—genocide, war crimes, crimes against humanity—the death penalty has been deemed to be incompatible with the values that international justice is meant to represent. This too, then, represents a step towards the abolitionist goal.[48]

EUROPEAN REGIONAL DEVELOPMENTS

The first international treaty prohibiting the use of the death penalty was opened for signature on 8 April 1983. It is Protocol No. 6 to the Convention for the Protection of Human Rights and Fundamental Freedoms [the European Convention on Human Rights] concerning the Abolition of the Death Penalty, which was adopted by the Council of Europe's Committee of Ministers in December 1982.[49] This was the climax of a protracted development towards abolition.

The 'problem of capital punishment in the States of Europe' was on the agenda of the European Committee on Crime Problems as early as 1957 when this body was established.[50] As a result of a 1973 initiative,[51] the Parliamentary Assembly adopted in 1980 a resolution in favour of abolishing the death penalty for crimes committed in peacetime[52] and simultaneously recommended that the Committee of Ministers 'amend article 2 of the European Convention on Human Rights to bring it into line' with the Assembly's peacetime abolition policy.[53] The European Parliament (of the European Community, all of whose member states were Council of Europe members) followed suit in 1981.[54]

[48] The same point is affirmed by the Special Rapporteur on Extrajudicial, Summary or Arbitrary Executions (see below), who himself considers the abolitionist trend as one that states should subscribe to: see, e.g., UN doc. E/CN.4/1997/60, paras. 73–6. Similarly, the Commission on Human Rights has expressed itself as '[w]elcoming the exclusion of capital punishment from the penalties that the [international tribunals] are authorized to impose': resolution 1997/12, *supra* n. 32, preambular para. 5.

[49] Council of Europe doc. H (83)3 containing the text of the protocol and an explanatory memorandum, 5. The Committee of Ministers is the intergovernmental body, composed of representatives of each of the member states of the Council, responsible for taking decisions. See, generally, Leuprecht, 'The First International Treaty for the Abolition of the Death Penalty', 2 *Forum* 2 (1983).

[50] Ibid. It is a body of government experts, advising the Committee of Ministers.

[51] See *Death Penalty*, 29.

[52] Resolution 727, 22 Apr. 1980. The Parliamentary Assembly is composed of nominees of each of the national parliaments of the 40 (then, 21) member states of the Council; it cannot take decisions binding on the states members of the Council.

[53] Recommendation 891, 22 Apr. 1980.

[54] Resolution of 18 June 1981: see also its resolution of 17 Jan. 1986, *supra* n. 13.

Meanwhile steps were under way at the intergovernmental level. At the instigation of the Austrian Minister of Justice, Dr Christian Broda, the issue was commended in 1978 to the attention of the Council of Europe's Committee of Ministers by the eleventh Conference of European Ministers of Justice.[55] This initiative took place six months after the Amnesty International Conference on the Death Penalty, which Dr Broda attended and which recommended that the European Convention on Human Rights should explicitly prohibit 'the introduction or reintroduction of the death penalty'.[56] Subsequent Ministers of Justice conference meetings continued to express interest in the issue and in 1981 the Committee of Ministers asked its Steering Committee for Human Rights[57] 'to prepare a draft additional Protocol to the European Convention on Human Rights abolishing the death penalty in peace time'.[58] The text of the new Protocol was the work of the Steering Committee,[59] and twelve countries signed the Protocol on the day it was opened for signature, at a meeting of Council of Europe Foreign Ministers.[60] Thus an initiative that had started in 1978 with the Ministers of Justice eventually led to a positive response from the Committee of Ministers, prompted by the Parliamentary Assembly.

Article 2 of the European Convention on Human Rights had exempted from the protection of the right to life the intentional deprivation of life 'in the execution of a sentence by a court following . . . conviction of a crime for which this penalty is provided by law'. There was no restriction on the offences for which the death penalty could be provided, nor on the procedural safeguards that were required, nor on categories of prisoner on whom a death sentence may be imposed or inflicted. The effect of the Sixth Protocol is to remove the whole exemption for the death penalty in peacetime. Thus, its article 1 states, with admirable simplicity: 'The death penalty shall be abolished. No one shall be condemned to such penalty or executed.' The first sentence is aimed at defining the obligation on states parties; the second approaches the issue in terms of the right of the individual. According to the official commentary on the text, the first sentence seems to mean that there is an obligation on a state party to 'delete this penalty from its Law'.[61] This view is supported by the wording of the second sentence, which protects people not

[55] Explanatory memorandum, *supra* n. 49, 5. Every two years the Ministers of Justice of the states members of the Council of Europe meet to discuss matters of legal interest.

[56] *Report of the Amnesty International Conference on the Death Penalty, Stockholm, Sweden, 10–11 December 1977*, AI Index: CDP 02/01/78; see Miklau, 'Ein Schritt voran zur Ächtung der Todesstrafe' (A step towards outlawing the death penalty), *Der Staatsbürger* (Salzburg), 37th year, no. 3, 7 Feb. 1984, 9–10.

[57] The Steering Committee on Human Rights is a body of government experts advising the Committee of Ministers.

[58] Explanatory memorandum, *supra* n. 49, 5. [59] Ibid.

[60] Council of Europe Directorate of Press and Information I (83)29, 28 Apr. 1983. At the time of writing, 27 countries have ratified the Protocol, which entered into force on 1 Feb. 1985.

[61] Explanatory memorandum, *supra* n. 49, 6.

only from execution but also from being condemned to death (this probably reflects the practice in some countries of passing death sentences which are then commuted as a matter of course).[62] The reason for couching the second sentence in the language of an individual right is that article 6 envisages the applicability of the rest of the European Convention on Human Rights, including its complaints procedures.

Article 2 contains the permitted exception: 'A State may make provision in its law for the death penalty in respect of acts committed in time of war or imminent threat of war.' Even the exception must operate within the limits of the rule of law. Thus, 'such penalty shall be applied only in the instances laid down in the law and in accordance with its provisions'. This is supplemented by articles 7 and 15 of the Convention itself, which together prohibit retroactive criminality or penalties, even in time of war or other public emergency. Further, a state wishing to avail itself of this exception to the general abolitionist rule in article 1 of the Protocol is obliged by article 2 to 'communicate to the Secretary-General of the Council of Europe the relevant provisions of that law'. It is to be hoped that failure so to communicate would be interpreted as preventing the state in question from invoking the exception.

The ambit of the exception requires comment. The official commentary to the text[63] is silent on the scope of the phrase 'in time of war or imminent threat of war'. It is of note that the formula refers to 'war' rather than 'armed conflict'. 'War' is a legal status, normally declared by at least one of the parties, conferring rights and duties both upon the belligerents and upon third parties in their relations with the belligerents. This is why, for example, the Geneva Conventions of 12 August 1949 are intended by their common article 2 to 'apply to all cases of declared war or other armed conflict which may arise between two or more of the High Contracting Parties, even if the state of war is not recognized by one of them'. If an armed conflict short of formal declared war had been envisaged, other terminology could have been used; it is therefore reasonable to assume that 'war' in the Protocol is intended to exclude other armed conflicts.

The notion of 'imminent threat of war' is somewhat more difficult. The closest international models are to be found in article 39 of the Charter of the United Nations, which permits the Security Council to determine the existence of 'a threat to the peace' with a view to taking enforcement measures that may or may not involve armed action. The Security Council may also 'recommend appropriate procedures or methods of adjustment' (article 36) in the case of a dispute or situation 'likely to endanger the maintenance of

---

[62] It is interesting to note Belgium's signature of the Protocol, despite the fact that it was at the time *de jure* retentionist. *De facto* it was abolitionist for offences unconnected with war, its last execution (for murder) having taken place in 1918; see *Death Penalty*, 108. In 1996, it abolished the penalty for all crimes: Amnesty International, *supra* n. 1.

[63] Explanatory memorandum, *supra* n. 49, 6–7.

international peace and security' (article 33). But these are inherently imprecise concepts, their meanings to be determined by a political body for the purposes of political action. In so far as an 'imminent threat of war' is by definition not a declared war, the exception can apply to a stage of hostile confrontation short of a declared war, as long as it appears that such a war is imminent. The inclusion of such a vaguely worded element in article 2 could lend itself to abusively broad interpretation of 'imminent' by a country wishing to avail itself of the exception. It is to be expected, however, that any case arising out of the passing of a death penalty based on the exception would be most carefully scrutinized by the European Commission and Court of Human Rights.

A final question relating to the exception is whether it applies to international war only. Such would appear to be the case, since although the concept of a civil war is known to international law, a declared civil war, which confers rights and duties on belligerents and third parties, is rare with the notable exception of the Spanish Civil Wár. In practice, the word 'war' is so pervasively used in the sense of 'international armed hostilities' that it would be perverse not to refer specifically to civil war if it had been intended to include this within the article 2 exception. Moreover, the effect of concluding that 'war' includes 'civil war' would be that 'imminent threat of war' includes 'imminent threat of civil war'. This would mean that states could bring within the exception so great a range of circumstances as radically to vitiate the basic abolitionist rule laid down in article 1. It would also give rise to a further anomaly: article 3 of the Protocol precludes the making of derogations from the terms of the Protocol 'in time of war or other public emergency threatening the life of the nation'. This preclusion would be redundant if the basic obligation contained in the Protocol (abolition of the death penalty) could be avoided without formal derogation whenever there was an imminent threat, not only of international war but also of civil war. Such redundancy ought not to be presumed.

This landmark instrument has had more widespread influence than could have been imagined at the time of adoption. First of all, it served as inspiration for the worldwide UN Protocol. It also may well have stimulated the Inter-American version to be discussed below. But by far its major impact has been on the new Europe. The Council of Europe started out as a regional grouping of Western European states, conceived of as those states that were not under Soviet influence. All but Turkey of the original states are now abolitionist, and there have been no executions there since 1984. However, with the collapse of the Soviet Union and the end of the Cold War, most European countries, including the Russian Federation and Ukraine, have now swelled the ranks of the membership to forty. Moreover, a condition of membership is an undertaking to adhere to the European Convention on Human Rights, including the 6th Protocol. Pending ratification of the Protocol, new members are to institute a moratorium on executions. While, in fact, in 1996, executions took place in Latvia, the Russian Federation, and Ukraine, the Council of Europe reacted vigorously, with the Parliamentary Assembly threatening non-ratification of the delegations of the Russian Federation and Ukraine, should executions not be halted.[64] Despite the difficulties faced, especially by the Russian Federation, in securing legislative approval for abolition, there is reason to hope that executions are on the verge of becoming a thing of the past across the continent of Europe.

INTER-AMERICAN DEVELOPMENTS

The legal framework for states parties to the American Convention on Human Rights has, since its adoption in 1969, been more squarely abolitionist than that in respect of other general human rights treaties. While not ruling out the death penalty as such, it effectively imposed a standstill. By article 4(3) abolitionist countries were prohibited from re-establishing it, while retentionist countries could not extend it 'to crimes to which it does not presently apply' (article 4(2)). Thus, when in 1990 the OAS General Assembly adopted the (second) Protocol to the American Convention on Human Rights to Abolish the Death Penalty,[65] it was not in effect adding any new obligation on states that could be expected to adhere to it. Clearly only abolitionist states would do so and they were already bound by article 4 not to reintroduce it. It could perhaps be envisaged that a *de facto* abolitionist state might wish to undertake the obligations of the Protocol's provisions (the obligation in article 1 is not to 'apply the death penalty', which could be interpreted as not requiring *de jure* abolition), but this is hardly likely. Like the Second Optional Protocol to the Covenant, it permits reservations in respect of 'extremely serious' wartime crimes.

Probably the main function of the Protocol is symbolic, indicating a standard to which some states of the region, notably the United States and some English-speaking Caribbean countries, such as Barbados, Jamaica, and Trinidad and Tobago, are still unprepared to subscribe.

---

[64] Council of Europe, Parliamentary Assembly, res. 1111 (1997) (Russian Federation) and 1112 (Ukraine), 29 Jan. 1997. No executions were reported in 1997 in respect of Latvia and, except for Chechnya, the Russian Federation. Executions in Ukraine were reported as continuing up to Mar. 1997 leading to a renewed threat in respect of its parliamentary delegation, despite informal assurances that a *de facto* moratorium was in place: Council of Europe, Parliamentary Assembly, res. 1145 (1998) (Provisional edition), 27 Jan. 1998; also Council of Europe Press Service, 'Assembly gives Ukraine final warning on executions', doc. ref. 50a98, 27 Jan. 1998, and Amnesty International, *Death Penalty News*, Mar. 1998, 3. See, Barry and Williams, 'Russia's Death Penalty Dilemmas', 8 *Criminal Law Forum* 231 (1997).

[65] Approved at Asunción, Paraguay, 8 Jun. 1990, 20th Regular Session of the General Assembly, OAS Treaty Series No. 73. See Schabas, 290–4.

LIMITS TO CAPITALLY PUNISHABLE OFFENCES

In this part, the general starting point for each topic is article 6 of the International Covenant on Civil and Political Rights, as this may indicate, not only the law applicable to the states parties to it, but also the position under general international law. This is because the right to life may, for the reasons given in Chapter 6, be considered as a rule of general international law, if not of *jus cogens*. Accordingly, as the principal universal instrument on the topic, the Covenant may be understood as reflecting the scope of that right. Certainly, as far as the death penalty is concerned, both Special Rapporteurs on Arbitrary or Summary Executions have taken the view that article 6, read with articles 14 and 15, indeed states 'customary international law'.[66] It should also be noted that, by resolution 35/172 of 15 December 1980, the General Assembly urged states 'to respect as a minimum standard the content of the provisions of articles 6, 14 and 15 of the International Covenant on Civil and Political Rights', a call it has frequently reiterated.

However, this position cannot yet be taken as wholly applicable to all parts of article 6, given that the Inter-American Court of Human Rights has interpreted the analogous non-derogable article 4 of the American Convention as permitting reservations in respect of 'certain aspects' of such a non-derogable right, as long as 'the right as a whole' was not deprived of 'its basic purpose'.[67] The Human Rights Committee, it is true, has not been so tolerant, albeit its general comment on reservations has been challenged on various points by France, the United Kingdom, and the USA.[68]

LAWFUL SANCTION

For particular capital offences to be compatible with article 6 of the International Covenant on Civil and Political Rights, the death penalty must be prescribed by national law. This was the clear intention behind the provision that 'no one shall be arbitrarily deprived of his life'.[69] The American Convention on Human Rights (article 4) uses the same language, and that of the African Charter on Human and Peoples' Rights (article 4) is virtually identical. The European Convention on Human Rights expressly permits as an exception to the right to life a deprivation of life that is 'in the execution of a sentence of a court following . . . conviction of a crime for which this penalty

---

[66] UN docs. E/CN.4/1992/30, para. 609; E/CN.4/1993/46, para. 678.

[67] I/A Court HR, *Reservations to the Death Penalty (arts. 4(2) and 6(4) American Convention on Human Rights)*, Advisory Opinion OC-3/83 of 8 Sept. 1983, Series A, No. 3. See also *Roach and Pinkerton* v. *USA* in the Inter-American Commission on Human Rights, *infra* n. 148.

[68] General comment 24 (52), Report of the Human Rights Committee, UN doc. A/50/40 (1995), Annex V; for the comments of the USA and UK, see id., Annex VI; for that of France, see id., UN doc. A/51/40 (1996), Annex VI.

[69] *GAOR*, 10th Session, Annexes, Agenda item 28 (Part II), A/2929, Chapter VI, para. 3.

is provided by law' (article 2). The point need hardly be laboured: unless a punitive killing by the authorities is provided for by national law, it will be an extra-legal execution (see Chapter 6).

ONLY THE 'MOST SERIOUS CRIMES'

According to the International Covenant on Civil and Political Rights, 'sentence of death may be imposed only for the most serious crimes' (article 6(2)). The American Convention on Human Rights (article 4(2)) contains the same limitation. Unfortunately, the term 'the most serious crimes' remains undefined in either instrument. The phrase was adopted in the Covenant despite concerns expressed at the time that it lacked precision, since the concept of 'serious crimes' differed from one country to another;[70] clearly the concept was expected to evolve. It is often thought that the death penalty is reserved for crimes involving loss of life, and it is therefore frequently justified on a principle, however retrograde, of retribution—an eye for an eye, a life for a life. In fact, the 1979 Amnesty International report *Death Penalty*[71] shows that the penalty is often imposed for offences which not only involve no loss of life, but involve no use of violence at all. Violence cannot necessarily therefore be used as the sole measure of the crimes which states consider 'serious' enough to warrant the death penalty. The Human Rights Committee's general comment on the phrase 'the most serious crimes' gives little precision. The Committee says that the expression 'must be read restrictively to mean that the death penalty should be a quite exceptional measure'.[72]

In the 'Safeguards guaranteeing protection of the rights of those facing the death penalty', adopted in 1984, Ecosoc expresses its understanding that the scope of the term 'most serious crimes' 'should not go beyond intentional crimes, with lethal or othĕr extremely grave consequences'.[73] The words 'or other extremely grave' were added after a member of the Committee on Crime Prevention and Control (which drafted the Safeguards) had argued that some acts (for example the provision of secret information to an enemy in wartime) could result in large-scale loss of life, even though the lethal results of the offence could not necessarily be proven.[74]

Neither the Human Rights Committee nor the organs of the American Convention on Human Rights have had occasion to pronounce formally in an individual case whether a particular capitally punishable offence may or

---

[70] Id., para. 6. [71] *Supra* n. 19. [72] *Supra* n. 18, para. 7.
[73] Ecosoc res. 1984/50, 25 May 1984, Annex, para. 1. It is worth noting that the General Assembly endorsed the Ecosoc Safeguards in res. 39/118 of 14 Dec. 1984, and asked the Secretary-General 'to employ his best endeavours in cases where the safeguards . . . are violated' (operative paras. 2 and 5).
[74] Recollection of the author, who attended the eighth session of the Committee on Crime Prevention and Control (1984) on behalf of Amnesty International.

may not be a most serious crime. However, in its review of states' periodic reports, the Committee or, more frequently, its individual members, have been critical of resort to the death penalty for many crimes not resulting in death, notably political crimes, crimes against property, and some drug offences.[75] The Special Rapporteur on Extrajudicial, Arbitrary or Summary Executions similarly considers that the death penalty 'should be eliminated for crimes such as economic crimes and drug-related offences'.[76]

NO OTHER HUMAN RIGHTS VIOLATIONS SHOULD BE INVOLVED

By providing that 'no one shall be arbitrarily deprived of his life', article 6 of the Covenant appears to have intended 'arbitrarily' to mean both 'illegally' and 'unjustly'.[77] The Covenant addresses itself to unjust laws by its proviso that in any event the law providing for capitally punishable crimes must not be 'contrary to the provisions of the present Covenant' (article 6(2)). This stipulation would certainly preclude the use of the death penalty for offences that, in some countries, currently attract it—for example, peaceful dissent or non-violent association and assembly.

It is clear, therefore, that where a particular act of government repression amounts to a violation of human rights as defined in the Covenant then the use of the death penalty in furtherance of the repression is a violation of article 6 of the Covenant. This has more significance than merely that the government in question is violating international law twice. Many of the articles of the Covenant may be suspended 'in time of public emergency which threatens the life of the nation' (article 4), but this is not true of article 6. It may be argued on the basis of the article 6 phrase 'not contrary to the provisions of the present Covenant' that, even when in time of emergency an activity normally protected by a provision of the Covenant (free speech, public assembly, and so on) becomes criminal, the right in question having been suspended, it may still not attract the death penalty.

Article 6(2) also provides that capitally punishable offences must 'not be contrary to the Convention on the Prevention and Punishment of the Crime of Genocide'. Nailing the point down even more firmly, paragraph 3 of the same article provides:

When deprivation of life constitutes the crime of genocide, it is understood that nothing in this article shall authorize any State Party to the present Covenant to derogate in any way from any obligation assumed under the provisions of the Convention on the Prevention and Punishment of the Crime of Genocide.

---

[75] Schabas, 105–8.   [76] UN doc. E/CN.4/1998/68, para. 94.
[77] UN Doc A/2929, *supra* n. 69, para. 3. See Nowak, *U.N. Covenant on Civil and Political Rights—CCPR Commentary* (1993), 110–11.

The intention seems to have been to avoid any interpretation at all by which the Covenant's admission of death sentences 'might be abused to justify' executions punishable under the Genocide Convention.[78]

NON-RETROACTIVITY

A further restriction on crimes that may attract a death sentence is that such sentence may be imposed only 'in accordance with the law in force *at the time of the commission of the crime*' (article 6(2), emphasis added). This seems to be a shorthand way of stating the principle of non-retroactivity contained in article 15 of the Covenant[79] (another article which, like article 6, may not be suspended). That is, that an offence must have been an offence at the time it was committed and that the penalty must have been laid down at that time: *nullum crimen, nulla poena sine lege*. The American Convention on Human Rights (article 4(2)) and the European Convention on Human Rights (article 2(1)) contain a similar restriction. Furthermore, the Covenant (article 15), the European Convention (article 7), and the American Convention (article 9) all provide that, where the law is changed to provide a lighter penalty for the offence in question than that which existed at the time the offence was committed, the convicted person must benefit from the lighter penalty.

In recognition of the standards laid down in the Covenant, the General Assembly, in a resolution on 'Arbitrary or summary executions', urged UN member states to 'respect as a minimum standard the content of the provisions of articles 6, 14 and *15*' (emphasis added) of the Covenant. This resolution (35/172 of 15 December 1980) was adopted without a vote in the context of discussions on the report of the Sixth Congress on the Prevention of Crime and the Treatment of Offenders mentioned above. While such a resolution has the status of a recommendation only, it tends to support the argument that the articles in question, in so far as they touch on the death penalty, may be held to apply to all UN member states, whether or not they are parties to the Covenant. The General Assembly reiterated its position on numerous occasions.[80]

The principle of non-retroactivity is also found in the Geneva Conventions of 12 August 1949 on the protection of victims of war. Thus, article 99 of the Geneva Convention Relative to the Treatment of Prisoners of War (Third Geneva Convention) provides that no prisoner of war 'may be tried or sentenced for an act which is not forbidden by the law of the Detaining Power or by International Law, in force at the time the said act was committed'. It is not clear from this language whether the law has also to prescribe the

---

[78] Landerer, 525.
[79] The provision that was to become article 15 had not been adopted at the time this phrase was inserted; see Landerer, ibid.
[80] See n. 85 *infra*.

penalty before the act is committed. However, in the case of the death penalty the next article (100) meets the point and in some measure goes beyond it:

Prisoners of war and the Protecting Powers shall be informed, as soon as possible, of the offences which are punishable by the death sentence under the laws of the Detaining Power. Other offences shall not thereafter be made punishable by the death penalty without the concurrence of the Power upon which the prisoners of war depend.

Reference will be made later to a similar provision in the Geneva Convention Relative to the Protection of Civilian Persons in Time of War (Fourth Geneva Convention).

POLITICAL OFFENCES

In one region, the Americas, another category of offence may not be made subject to the death penalty. All of the twenty-five parties to the American Convention on Human Rights are bound by paragraph 4 of article 4 which states: 'In no case shall capital punishment be inflicted for political offences or related common crimes.'[81] As has been observed, 'This remarkable provision is consistent with the established tradition among Latin American countries of acknowledging the need for cooperation in maintaining some measure of political tolerance.'[82] The language 'political offences or related common crimes' is borrowed from that used in extradition treaties.[83] Acts falling within the definition are excluded from the obligation to extradite, an exclusion often associated with the concept of political asylum which found fertile soil in the countries of Latin America. The meaning of the formulation in the present context has not received authoritative definition at the international level, and state practice—to be found primarily in the implementation of extradition treaties—is inconsistent.

There is no similar treaty provision at the universal level. However, it is probable that many 'political offences' of the sort covered by the American Convention would be 'contrary to the provisions of the present Covenant' within the meaning of article 6(2) of the Covenant (see above).[84] Further, the UN General Assembly has expressed its concern 'at the occurrence of executions which are widely regarded as being politically motivated',[85] and in 1981

[81] Guatemala alone made a reservation in respect of this paragraph, which it subsequently withdrew.

[82] *Death Penalty*, 20.

[83] See Shearer, *Extradition in International Law* (1971), chapter 7; Gilbert, *Transnational Fugitive Offenders in International Law* (1998), chapter 6; Van den Wijngaert, *The Political Offence Exception to Extradition. The Delicate Problem of Balancing the Right of the Individual and the Public International Order* (1980).

[84] See the generally critical approach of the Human Rights Committee, *supra* n. 75 and accompanying text.

[85] GA res. 35/172, 15 Dec. 1980; and 36/22, 9 Nov. 1981.

the UN Sub-Commission on Prevention of Discrimination and Protection of Minorities called for the abolition of the death penalty for 'political offences'.[86] Once again, the definition of 'political offences' is problematic. In particular, it would be difficult to gain acceptance for the restriction of capital punishment in respect of those politically motivated offences which, without the political motivation, would attract it (the 'related common crimes' of the extradition treaties). Given this difference of definition and the limited likelihood of finding a definition that would meet with general international agreement, an internationally accepted restriction on the use of capital punishment for 'political offences' is unlikely, at least in treaty form.

OFFENCES COMMITTED BY PERSONS UNDER MILITARY OCCUPATION

One other area of limitation on the nature of capitally punishable offences deserves mention here. An occupying power may not arrest, prosecute, or convict civilian persons protected by the Fourth Geneva Convention 'for acts committed or for opinions expressed [*sic*] before the occupation . . . with the exception of breaches of the laws and customs of war' (article 70). As far as offences committed by such a protected person against an occupying power during the occupation are concerned, article 68 of the Fourth Geneva Convention restricts the ability of the legislation of the occupying power to impose the death penalty

to cases where the person is guilty of espionage, of serious acts of sabotage against military installations of the Occupying Power or of intentional offences which have caused the death of one or more persons, provided that such offences were punishable by death under the law of the occupied territory in force before the occupation began.

Thus, there is a double limitation: first, the penalty has to be applicable before the occupation and second, the nature of the capitally punishable offences is limited as far as the powers of the occupying authorities are concerned. However, as has been pointed out, there may be 'cause for concern about the breadth of interpretation given by some jurisdictions to the term "espionage" and "sabotage". It is not unknown for the former to be stretched to cover any unauthorized acquisition of state information, and the latter to cover the unauthorized divulgence of such information.'[87]

NON-REINTRODUCTION

Another approach to limiting the applicability of the death penalty is to prohibit its reintroduction once it has been abolished, or its extension to offences

---

[86] Resolution 1 (XXXIV), 3 Sept. 1981, Report of the Sub-Commission on Prevention of Discrimination and Protection of Minorities, 34th Session (E/CN.4/1512; E/CN.4/Sub.2/495), Chapter XX A.
[87] *Death Penalty*, 22.

for which it is not already laid down. It will be recalled that article 6, paragraph 2, of the Covenant begins: '*In countries which have not abolished the death penalty*, sentence of death may be imposed only for the most serious crimes . . .' (emphasis added). It has been argued above that the emphasized words imply the goal of abolishing the death penalty. The wording also implies that the rules that follow are extended only to countries that have not yet attained that goal. This would contain within it the further implication that abolitionist countries may not avail themselves of the rule—that, therefore, they may not reintroduce the death penalty—and further that the principle on which this would be based (a 'standstill' approach) would require that even in non-abolitionist countries the death penalty not be extended to cover offences for which it does not at present apply.[88] This view is, however, at odds with that taken by a Council of Europe expert committee.[89] The wording quoted above replaced an earlier phraseology ('in countries where capital punishment exists'),[90] leading one commentator to observe that the new language was 'somewhat more emphatic, and possibly more restrictive'.[91] The Human Rights Committee established under the Covenant has not so far, in its general comment on article 6, gone beyond the already quoted formulation that 'all measures of abolition should be considered as progress in the enjoyment of the right to life . . .'.[92] The non-reintroduction/non-extension approach was to be found in the abolitionist draft resolution submitted to, but then withdrawn from, the Sixth UN Crime Congress discussed earlier. Non-reintroduction is also implicit in the Second Optional Protocol to the Covenant.[93] In any event, regardless of what the legal significance of a General Assembly resolution may be, the clear political direction taken by the Assembly—'the main objective to be pursued is that of progressively restricting the number of offences for which capital punishment may be imposed'—seems to require the non-reintroduction/non-extension approach.

There is no comparable doubt in respect of the American Convention on Human Rights. According to its article 4, the application of the death penalty 'shall not be extended to crimes to which it does not presently apply' (paragraph 2), nor may the penalty 'be re-established in states that have abolished it' (paragraph 3). These restrictions apply even where a country may have made a reservation to paragraph 4 that prohibits the death penalty for political offences (see above): such a country may not by virtue of the reservation extend the death penalty to cover political offences for which it did not previously apply.[94]

---

[88] Id., 20.   [89] Id., 32, n. 3.   [90] *Supra* n. 17.
[91] Landerer, 524; see also Schabas, 101–3, who appears to see reintroduction as a retreat from the legally-mandated goal of abolition and, thus, 'incompatible with the Covenant'.
[92] *Supra* n. 18.   [93] *Supra* n. 45 and accompanying text.
[94] I/A Court HR, *Reservations to the Death Penalty (Arts. 4(2) and 4(4) American Convention on Human Rights)*, Advisory Opinion OC-3/83 of 8 Sept. 1983. Series, A, No. 3. For examples of Inter-American Commission on Human Rights reactions against moves to reintroduce the

PROCEDURAL RESTRICTIONS ON
THE IMPOSITION OF THE DEATH PENALTY

In addition to the substantive restrictions on the use of the death penalty described above (it may not be applied except for the most serious crimes, pursuant to law providing the penalty for the offending act, and not contrary to the other provisions of the Covenant), the Covenant also states certain fundamental procedural requirements that must be met in capital cases.

FAIR TRIAL

Article 6 of the Covenant makes no direct reference to a requirement of 'fair trial'. The basic standards for a fair trial, including pre- and post-trial safeguards, are laid down in article 14 of the Covenant,[95] and under normal

death penalty or extend it to new crimes, see, e.g., Annual Report of the Inter-American Commission on Human Rights 1996, OAS Doc. OEA/Ser.L/V/II.95 Doc. 7 rev. (1997), 722 (Guatemala), 739 (Peru), and 834 (El Salvador).

[95] 'Article 14:

1. All persons shall be equal before the courts and tribunals. In the determination of any criminal charge against him, or of his rights and obligations in a suit at law, everyone shall be entitled to a fair and public hearing by a competent, independent and impartial tribunal established by law. The Press and the public may be excluded from all or part of a trial for reasons of morals, public order (*ordre public*) or national security in a democratic society, or when the interest of the private lives of the parties so requires, or to the extent strictly necessary in the opinion of the court in special circumstances where publicity would prejudice the interests of justice; but any judgement rendered in a criminal case or in a suit at law shall be made public except where the interest of juvenile persons otherwise requires or the proceedings concern matrimonial disputes or the guardianship of children.

2. Everyone charged with a criminal offence shall have the right to be presumed innocent until proved guilty according to law.

3. In the determination of any criminal charge against him, everyone shall be entitled to the following minimum guarantees, in full equality:

    (a) To be informed promptly and in detail in a language which he understands of the nature and cause of the charge against him;

    (b) To have adequate time and facilities for the preparation of his defence and to communicate with counsel of his own choosing;

    (c) To be tried without undue delay;

    (d) To be tried in his presence, and to defend himself in person or through legal assistance of his own choosing; to be informed, if he does not have legal assistance, of this right; and to have legal assistance assigned to him, in any case where the interests of justice so require, and without payment by him in any such case if he does not have sufficient means to pay for it;

    (e) To examine, or have examined, the witnesses against him and to obtain the attendance and examination of witnesses on his behalf under the same conditions as witnesses against him;

    (f) To have the free assistance of an interpreter if he cannot understand or speak the language used in court;

    (g) Not to be compelled to testify against himself or to confess guilt.

4. In the case of juvenile persons, the procedure shall be such as will take account of their age and the desirability of promoting their rehabilitation.

5. Everyone convicted of a crime shall have the right to his conviction and sentence being reviewed by a higher tribunal according to law. *over/*

circumstances it would be unnecessary to make reference to them in article 6. However, while, as noted earlier, article 6 is one of those from which no derogation is permitted even in time of public emergency threatening the life of the nation, this is not so for article 14. It may be argued that, despite this gap, an implied obligation not to execute convicted persons who have been denied the benefit of a fair trial must now be read into article 6 by way of ensuring that the deprivation of life not be arbitrary.[96]

In 1968, nine years after it had first initiated a study of the death penalty, the UN General Assembly adopted its first substantive resolution on the topic. By resolution 2393 (XXIII) of 26 November 1968, the Assembly invited member governments, *inter alia*, to 'ensure the most careful legal procedures and the greatest possible safeguards for the accused in capital cases'.[97] By 1980, the Assembly had become more explicit. Its resolution 35/172 of 15 December 1980 urged member states, *inter alia*:

to respect as a minimum standard the content of the provisions of articles 6, 14 and 15 of the International Covenant on Civil and Political Rights and, where necessary, to review their legal rules and practices so as to guarantee the most careful legal procedures and the greatest possible safeguards for the accused in capital cases.

Here the Assembly included reference to article 14 as well as to the non-derogable articles 6 and 15. The Assembly was to reiterate this exhortation in 1981 and on subsequent occasions.[98] Resolution 36/22 of 9 November 1981 asked the Committee on Crime Prevention and Control to examine the problem. That examination culminated in the drafting of the safeguards that Ecosoc was to adopt in 1984.[99] The fifth of these reaffirmed the necessity of fair trials in capital cases, 'including the right to adequate legal assistance at all stages of the proceedings'.

Finally, and especially persuasively, the practice of the Human Rights Committee follows the same approach. In its general comment on article 6 of the Covenant it stated: 'The procedural guarantees . . . prescribed [in article

6. When a person has by a final decision been convicted of a criminal offence and when subsequently his conviction has been reversed or he has been pardoned on the ground that a new or newly discovered fact shows conclusively that there has been a miscarriage of justice, the person who has suffered punishment as a result of such conviction shall be compensated according to law, unless it is proved that the non-disclosure of the unknown fact in time is wholly or partly attributable to him.

7. No one shall be liable to be tried or punished again for an offence for which he has already been finally convicted or acquitted in accordance with the law and penal procedure of each country.'

[96] As Landerer, *supra* n. 10, puts it (footnotes omitted): 'A proposal to tie the trial of capital offences explicitly to the obligations under the Covenant concerning a fair trial was not brought to the vote but it was pointed out that there was no need for such a cross-reference since the Covenant formed an integral "whole".'

[97] This was a formulation first adopted by Ecosoc res. 934 (XXXV), 9 Apr. 1963.

[98] e.g. GA res. 36/22, 9 Nov. 1981; 38/96, 16 Dec. 1983.   [99] *Supra* n. 73.

14] must be observed, including the right to a fair hearing by an independent tribunal, the presumption of innocence, the minimum guarantees for the defence, and the right to review by a higher tribunal.'[100] A year after it formulated this approach, the Committee had occasion to apply it in the *Mbenge* case.[101]

Daniel Monguya Mbenge, a former governor of the province of Shaba in Zaïre was twice sentenced to death *in absentia*. While not precluding the possibility of a judgment *in absentia*, the Committee considered that such a judgment 'requires that, notwithstanding the absence of the accused, all due notification has been made to inform him of the date and place of his trial and to request his attendance'. The Committee seems to have accepted the uncontested claim by Mr Mbenge that he learned of the trials only through press reports after they had taken place, even though the judgment showed that the authorities were aware of his address in Belgium.

The Committee concluded that Zaïre had not respected Mr Mbenge's rights under article 14(3)(a), (b), (d), and (e) of the Covenant.[102] Referring to the requirement in article 6(2) that death sentences must not be contrary to the provisions of the Covenant, the Committee further found that 'the failure of the State party to respect the relevant requirements of article 14(3) leads to the conclusion that the death sentences pronounced against the author of the communication were imposed contrary to the provisions of the Covenant and therefore in violation of article 6(2)' (paragraph 17). Zaïre was, accordingly, under an obligation to provide the victim with effective remedies, including compensation 'for the violations he had suffered' (paragraph 22).

Since then, the Human Rights Committee has had occasion to read article 14 together with article 6 in a series of cases brought by persons on 'death row', mainly in Jamaica.[103] For instance, in one case the victim had been charged with manslaughter and pleaded guilty. The proceedings were then dropped and a murder charge was brought in respect of the same killing, to which he had already pleaded guilty. This was held to violate the article 14(1) guarantee of a fair trial.[104] So, in another case, did the failure to inform the victim of an appeal hearing until after it had taken place.[105]

The Committee has found numerous violations involving deficient or nonexistent legal representation. The refusal of the court to postpone the trial of a person who had been able to consult his court-appointed lawyer only on the

---

[100] *Supra* n. 18, para. 7.

[101] *Monguya Mbenge et al.* v. *Zaïre* (16/1977), Report of the Human Rights Committee, *GAOR*, 38th Session, Supplement No. 40, Annex X.

[102] Paras. 14.1 and 14.2. Article 14 is reproduced in full at n. 95 *supra*.

[103] Jamaica denounced the Optional Protocol on 23 Oct. 1997.

[104] *Richards* v. *Jamaica* (535/1993), UN doc. CCPR/C/59/D/535/1993/Rev. 1(1997), paras. 7.2, 7.5.

[105] *Thomas* v. *Jamaica* (272/1988), Report of the Human Rights Committee, UN doc. A/47/40 (1992), Annex IX G, paras. 11.5, 12 (unaccountably, article 6 is overlooked in the Committee's final views).

day of the trial involved a breach of article 14(3)(b) (adequate time and facilities to prepare defence and communicate with counsel).[106] The same provision was violated in a case where there was only a brief meeting with court-
appointed lawyers before a preliminary hearing, one thirty-minute meeting
one month before the trial, and no consultation by the court-appointed
lawyer before the appeal.[107] In a case from another Caribbean country, the
right to legal assistance of choice (article 14(3)(d)) was violated where an
appeal went ahead with the original counsel at trial, despite the person's wish
to be represented by new counsel.[108] Indeed, the absence of legal aid to file a
constitutional motion to challenge irregularities at trial also involves violation of article 14(3)(d), read with article 6.[109] Also, a failure by a court-
appointed lawyer to call a suggested defence witness without explanation
involved a violation of article 14(3)(e) (right to call defence witnesses under
same conditions as prosecution witnesses).[110] A long delay between a preliminary hearing and the trial, or between conviction and appeal, without adequate explanation, violates article 14(3)(c) (trial without undue delay).[111]

In sum, it may safely be concluded that the Covenant imposes on states
parties to it a requirement in capital cases for a fair trial. Further, the recognition that a violation of article 14 in capital cases entails violation of article
6 suggests the conclusion that, in times of public emergency (when article 14
might be suspended), the force of article 6 (which may not be suspended)
would be to prohibit the imposition of the death penalty in cases where the
provisions of article 14 had not been observed.

To the extent that article 6 may reflect general international law (see
Chapters 4 and 6) and in the light of the repeated statements of the General
Assembly and other UN bodies, it may well be that the right to a fair trial in

[106] *Reid* v. *Jamaica* (No. 250/1987), Report of the Human Rights Committee, *GAOR*, 45th
Session, Supplement No. 40, Vol. II (1990), Annex IX J, paras. 11.3 and 11.5 and 4.
[107] *Little* v. *Jamaica* (No. 283/1988), loc. cit. *supra* n. 105, Annex IX J, paras. 8.4 and 3.2.
[108] *Pinto* v. *Trinidad and Tobago* (no. 232/1987), loc. cit. *supra* n. 106, Annex IX H, paras.
12.5–12.6. (Trinidad and Tobago, like Jamaica (see n. 103), denounced the Optional Protocol on
26 May 1998; on the same day it re-ratified the Protocol, but with a reservation excluding death
sentence related cases.) Similarly, in *Reid*, *supra* n. 106, denial of self-representation and assignment of counsel who refuses to advance arguments on appeal violates the same provision: para.
11.4; see also, on refusal by counsel to advance arguments: *Kelly* v. *Jamaica* (No. 253/1987),
Report of the Human Rights Committee, *GAOR*, 46th Session, Supplement No. 40 (1991),
Annex XI D, paras. 5.10 and 5.14; *Price* v. *Jamaica* (572/1994), UN doc. CCPR/C/58/D/572/1994
(1996), paras. 9.2, 9.3; *Steadman* v. *Jamaica*, *infra* n. 111, paras. 10.3, 11.
[109] *Taylor* v. *Jamaica* (707/1996), UN doc. CCPR/C/60/D/707/1996 (1997), paras. 8.2, 9.
[110] *Supra* n. 107.
[111] *Steadman* v. *Jamaica* (528/1993), UN doc. CCPR/C/59/D/528/1993 (1997), paras. 10.1, 11
(26 months between preliminary hearing and appeal); *Pratt and Morgan* v. *Jamaica* (Nos.
210/1986 and 225/1987), Report of the Human Rights Committee, *GAOR*, 44th Session,
Supplement No. 40 (1989), paras. 13.4, 13.5, 14 (b) (45 months between conviction and appeal).
Johnson v. *Jamaica* (No. 588/1994), UN doc. CCPR/C/56/D/588/1994 (1996), paras. 8.8, 8.9
(51 months between conviction and appeal); *McLawrence* v. *Jamaica* (702/1996), UN doc.
CCPR/C/60/D/702/1996 (1997), paras. 5.11, 5.13 (31 months).

capital cases is one that must be respected by all states. Moreover, in terms which support what has been said above regarding the inapplicability of the death penalty in circumstances where fair trial standards have been suspended, article 3 common to the four Geneva Conventions and relating to armed conflict not of an international character prohibits, with respect to persons in the hands of a party to the conflict, 'at any time and in any place whatsoever . . . the passing of sentences and the carrying out of executions without previous judgment pronounced by a regularly constituted court, affording all the judicial guarantees which are recognised as indispensable by civilized peoples' (emphasis added).

Degree of proof

In 1984, the Ecosoc enunciated a new safeguard that is to be respected in capital cases. Specifically, it envisaged imposition of the death penalty 'only when the guilt of the person charged is based upon clear and convincing evidence leaving no room for an alternative explanation of the facts'.[112] This formulation may well be understood as a gloss on Covenant article 14 that stipulates 'the right to be presumed innocent until proved guilty according to law'. What it does is to establish the burden of proof of guilt, and it is a heavy burden. The effect of the safeguard could be to permit relevant international bodies, such as the Human Rights Committee and the Special Rapporteur on Extrajudicial, Summary or Arbitrary Executions (see below), to look beyond the substantive limitations discussed earlier and the procedural proprieties now under discussion. They can take cognizance of the facts of individual cases so as to ensure that the conviction and resultant death sentence could not have been erroneously arrived at on the basis of inadequate evidence.[113]

APPEALS

Just as article 6 of the Covenant does not expressly require a fair trial, it also does not expressly require a right to appeal. It provides that the death penalty 'can only be carried out pursuant to a final judgment rendered by a competent court', a formulation which is not defined and does not explicitly encompass an appeal. When the General Assembly adopted its resolution 2393 (XXIII) of 26 November 1968 mentioned above, which called for 'the most careful legal procedures and the greatest possible safeguards for the accused in capital cases', it specifically said that these should be arrived at, *inter alia*, 'by providing that . . . a person condemned to death shall not be deprived of the right to appeal to a higher judicial authority or, as the case may be, to petition for pardon or reprieve'. The wording of this formulation is imperfect,

---

[112] *Supra* n. 73, para. 4.
[113] In practice, the Human Rights Committee, wishing to avoid being used as a further appellate court, will look to see that the trial court sought to apply the standard.

since it remains unclear whether a duty not to deprive of a right means that a right has to be afforded, even where such a right would not otherwise exist. Also the language could be taken to suggest that the right of appeal may be an alternative to the right to petition for pardon or reprieve.

The attitude of the General Assembly was again clarified by its 15 December 1980 resolution 35/172 which, it will be recalled, urged member states 'to respect as a minimum standard the content of the provisions of articles 6, 14 and 15' of the Covenant. Since article 14(5) of the Covenant provides for the right to have a conviction and sentence 'reviewed by a higher tribunal according to law', this suggests a General Assembly position in favour of a right to appeal in death penalty cases. The Ecosoc resolution on safeguards in capital cases mentioned above provides: 'Anyone sentenced to death shall have the right to appeal to a court of higher jurisdiction, and steps should be taken to ensure that such appeals shall become mandatory.'[114]

Again, as with the right to a fair trial, the most authoritative statement is that of the Human Rights Committee that the 'procedural guarantees prescribed [by article 6] must be observed, including . . . the right to review by a higher tribunal'.[115] Indeed, in insisting on this right as well as on those relating to a fair hearing mentioned above, the Committee states: 'These rights are applicable in addition to the particular right to seek a pardon or commutation of the sentence.' Thus the same argument applies with the right to appeal as with the right to a fair trial: where the right to appeal has not been afforded, by virtue of suspension of the right in time of public emergency, the death penalty may not, it is submitted, be imposed.

Moreover, the appellate procedure needs to be effective. Thus, failure even by an appellate court to provide a written judgment when that is a condition for a further appeal to a higher tribunal, in this case, the Judicial Committee of the Privy Council, entailed a violation of articles 6 and 14(5). Similarly, a protracted delay in making the judgment available will violate the same provisions.[116]

The possibility of a right of appeal for prisoners of war is envisaged by the Third Geneva Convention, article 106 of which provides:

[114] *Supra* n. 73, para. 6. This is the first instrument to contain an obligation to make the appeal procedure operate independently of the action of the convicted person. States had been urged 'to examine the possibility of making automatic the appeal procedure' by GA res. 35/172, 15 Dec. 1980.

[115] *Supra* n. 18, para. 7.

[116] *Pratt and Morgan* v. *Jamaica* (Nos. 210/1986 and 225/1987), Report of the Human Rights Committee, *GAOR*, 44th Session, Supplement No. 40 (1989), paras. 13.5, 14(b), and 15; *Kelly* v. *Jamaica* (No. 253/1987), Report of the Human Rights Committee, *GAOR*, 4th Session, Supplement No. 40 (1991), Annex XI D, paras. 5.12 and 5.14 (a 5-year wait); *Johnson* v. *Jamaica* (No. 588/1994), UN Doc. CCPR/56/D/588/1994 (1996), paras. 8.8 and 3.3 (over 4 years).

Every prisoner of war shall have, in the same manner as the members of the armed forces of the Detaining Power, the right of appeal or petition from any sentence pronounced upon him, with a view to the quashing or revising of the sentence or the reopening of the trial. He shall be fully informed of his right to appeal or petition and of the time limit within which he may do so.

This language could be taken to mean that the prisoner of war has no better right to appeal than that available to a member of the armed forces of the detaining power, and this may mean none at all. Hopefully the provision is to be interpreted as ensuring the right of appeal or petition and that, where the detaining power already has such a procedure for its own soldiers, prisoners of war will benefit from it to its full extent.

As for civilians protected by the Fourth Geneva Convention, article 73 of the Convention states:

A convicted person shall have the right of appeal provided for by the laws applied by the court. He shall be fully informed of his right to appeal or petition and of the time limit within which he may do so. . . . Where the laws applied by the Court make no provision for appeals, the convicted person shall have the right to petition against the finding and sentence to the competent authority of the Occupying Power.

Thus when the right of appeal or petition is available in the law being applied, it must be accorded to the protected person. If the legal system in question contains no right of appeal, then the Convention imposes the right to petition against the finding and sentence. Such a petition is then one that goes beyond a request merely for pardon or reprieve.

CLEMENCY

Whatever imprecisions there may be regarding the rights to a fair trial and to appeal, there are none regarding the right to petition for clemency (amnesty, pardon, or commutation). Article 6 of the Covenant, from which no derogation is permitted, provides unambiguously in its fourth paragraph: 'Anyone sentenced to death shall have the right to seek pardon or commutation of the sentence. Amnesty, pardon or commutation of the sentence of death may be granted in all cases.' The American Convention on Human Rights (article 4, paragraph 6) is as clear on this point as the Covenant.

A prisoner of war has, according to the terms of article 106 of the Third Geneva Convention quoted above, the same right of petition as a member of the armed forces of the detaining power. In the case of civilians, article 75 of the Fourth Convention states: 'In no case shall persons condemned to death be deprived of the right of petition for pardon or reprieve.' While this does not unambiguously require the provision of the right so to petition, it will be recalled that article 73 at least affords (in the absence of a right to appeal) a right to petition going beyond a petition for clemency.

NON-EXECUTION PENDING APPEAL AND CLEMENCY PROCEDURES

For any right to have meaning there must be opportunity for its enjoyment. Thus, it may well be implicit in the Covenant that the (implicit) right to appeal in article 6 and the express right to seek pardon or commutation of sentence in the same article includes also an obligation on governments not to carry out a death sentence pending appeal or petition. Again the General Assembly addressed this matter in its resolution 2393 (XXIII) of 26 November 1968: 'A death sentence shall not be carried out until the procedures of appeal or, as the case may be, of petition for pardon or reprieve have been terminated.'

The American Convention on Human Rights is explicit as far as applications for amnesty, pardon, or commutation of death sentences are concerned. Article 4, paragraph 6 states: 'Capital punishment shall not be imposed while such a petition is pending decision by the competent authority.'

In so far as it is required that a prisoner of war (Third Geneva Convention, article 106) or a protected civilian (Fourth Geneva Convention, article 73) be informed of the time limit for the exercise of a right to appeal or petition, the existence of such limit within which the death penalty may not be implemented may be presumed. In addition, these Conventions provide for the expiry of a minimum six-month time limit before a death sentence may be carried out (Third Geneva Convention, article 101; Fourth Geneva Convention, article 75). However, in respect of civilians protected by the Fourth Geneva Convention:

The six months period of suspension of the death sentence . . . may be reduced in individual cases in circumstances of grave emergency involving an organized threat to the security of the Occupying Power or its forces, provided always that the Protecting Power is notified of such reduction and is given reasonable time and opportunity to make representations to the competent occupying authorities in respect of such death sentences [article 75].

The existence in the Geneva Conventions of such a time limit presumably inspired the General Assembly's invitation to governments, in its resolution 2393 (XXIII) of 26 November 1968, to

consider whether the careful legal procedures and safeguards [see above] . . . may not be further strengthened by the fixing of a certain time limit or time limits before the expiry of which no death sentence shall be carried out, as has already been recognized in certain international conventions dealing with specific situations.[117]

There has been no further United Nations statement on the subject.

---

[117] See also GA res. 35/172, 15 Dec. 1980, para. 1(c) and Ecosoc res. 1984/50, 25 May 1984, Annex, para. 8.

HUMANE TREATMENT

For many, including the present writer, if international treaties did not permit the death penalty as an exception to the right to life, it would be obvious that it would violate the prohibition of cruel, inhuman, or degrading punishment, such as found in Covenant article 7.[118] Indeed, that view would be irresistable in view of the apparent prohibition by such provisions of corporal punishment. The exception for the death penalty requires us to consider the distasteful notion of whether there can be attendant circumstances which, above and beyond the cruelty and inhumanity inherent in the death penalty, condemns an execution as legally cruel and inhuman. There is now unassailable authority for the proposition.

The leading case is a regional one, *Soering* v. *United Kingdom*.[119] Jens Soering, a German citizen, was sought for extradition from the United Kingdom to the Commonwealth of Virginia in the United States. He argued, *inter alia*, that the 'death row phenomenon' (the harsh conditions on death row) would violate European Convention article 3 prohibiting inhuman or degrading punishment. By six votes to five, the European Commission of Human Rights disagreed, but referred the case to the European Court of Human Rights, as did the United Kingdom and Germany.[120] The Court found in favour of Soering. As noted earlier, it rejected an argument according to which the death penalty *per se* violated article 3. However, it held unanimously that, in the absence of satisfactory assurances that the death penalty would not be carried out, the circumstances of the case indicated that extradition 'would expose him to a real risk of treatment going beyond the threshold set by article 3'.[121] The circumstances were: (1) a predicted period of six to eight years spent on death row, (2) stringent, austere conditions on death row, (3) the young age of the applicant (18 years old) at the time of the offence, (4) his mental state (he was allegedly under the dominating influence of his co-accused girlfriend who was 20 at the time, engaged in the syndrome known as *folie à deux*), and (5) the fact that he could be tried in abolitionist

---

[118] See, generally, Schabas, *supra* n. 14. The Human Rights Committee has also taken the same view: *Ng* v. *Canada* (No. 469/1991), Report of the Human Rights Committee, Vol. II, *GAOR*, 49th Session, Supplement No. 40 (1994), Annex IX CC, para. 16.2; reproduced in 15 *HRLJ* 149, 157 (1994).

[119] European Court of Human Rights, Series A, No. 161; reproduced in 11 *HRLJ* 335 (1990).

[120] This was the only time that a case was referred to the Court by all three entities entitled to make a reference, that is, the Commission, the state against which the application is brought, and the state of nationality of the applicant.

[121] *Supra* n. 119, para. 111. The Court considered that an assurance from the local county attorney that the UK's wish that the death penalty not be carried out would be conveyed to the judge at the time of sentencing was not sufficient to eliminate the risk of the death penalty being imposed: para. 98. The UK had accepted that the US was constitutionally debarred from promising more. After the case, the US Department of State did give a satisfactory assurance, on the basis of which Soering was extradited to Virginia.

Germany.[122] The Court did not single out any one of these circumstances as sufficient in itself. The accent was on their combination. Whether all of them were equally necessary to the finding is also unaddressed.

The principle enshrined in *Soering* applies also at the universal level. The Human Rights Committee has affirmed that the death penalty 'must be carried out in such a way as to cause the least possible physical and mental suffering'.[123] Similarly, the Ecosoc Safeguards require the penalty to be 'carried out so as to inflict the minimum possible suffering' (paragraph 9). Applying the principle in practice the Committee has been cautious. In a series of cases the Committee has refused to consider the time element of itself as a factor bringing the case within article 7.[124] It articulated its position at length in *Johnson* v. *Jamaica*; starting from the premise that the Covenant encourages avoidance of the use of the death penalty, it took the view that to impose a time limit, explicitly or implicitly, would indicate to a state that the penalty should be carried out before the limit expires, thus discouraging initiatives such as moratoria or simply executive reluctance to order executions when abolition (or, presumably, commutation) is not politically feasible, and thereby possibly encouraging use of executions.[125] It is hard not to sympathize with this 'while there's life, there's hope' argument, especially as it makes clear that it is only addressing the relevance of the time factor *per se*, not 'other circumstances connected with detention on death row [that] may . . . turn that detention into cruel, inhuman and degrading treatment or punishment'.[126] In fact, in the actual case, it found a 51–month delay between conviction and appeal to constitute a violation of articles 14(3)(c) and 14(5), together with article 6.[127]

In one case, the Committee found that poor conditions on death row violated article 10(1) (right to be treated with humanity and respect for human dignity), the implication of which is not clear, as it also found a violation of

---

[122] European Court of Human Rights, Series A, No. 161; reproduced in 11 *HRLJ* 335 (1990), paras. 106–11.

[123] General comment 20 (44), Report of the Human Rights Committee, UN Doc. A/47/40 (1992), Annex VI A, para. 6.

[124] e.g., *Cox* v. *Canada* (No. 539/1993), UN Doc. CCPR/C/57/WP.1 (1996), Annex X M and cases listed therein at para. 17.2, footnote 34, reproduced in 15 *HRLJ* 410, 417, footnote 7 (1994).

[125] *Johnson* v. *Jamaica* (No. 558/1994), UN Doc. CCPR/C/56/D/588/1994 (1996), paras. 8.2–8.4. Six members disagreed with the majority view, insisting that the facts of individual cases should be taken into account: Ms Chanet (France), Mr Bhagwati (India), Mr Bruni Celli (Venezuela), Mr Pocar (Italy), Mr Prado Vallejo (Ecuador), Mr Aguilar Urbina (Costa Rica). Also cf. *Pratt and Morgan* in the Judicial Committee of the Privy Council, *infra* n. 129.

[126] Id., para. 8.5.

[127] Id., paras. 8.8–8.9. In two cases the victims spent 16 and 18 years respectively on death row, leading to a common dissent by five Committee members challenging the majority's 'lack of flexibility': *Bickaroo* v. *Trinidad and Tobago* (555/1993), UN doc. CCPR/61/D/555/1993 (1998), Appendix; *La Vende* v. *Trinidad and Tobago* (554/1993), UN doc. CCPR/61/D/554/1993 (1998), Appendix. The dissenters were Mr Pocar (Italy), Mr Bhagwati (India), Ms Chanet (France), Mr Prado Vallejo (Ecuador), and Mr Yalden (Canada).

various other articles, including 14(3)(c) and (d) and (5), with article 6.[128] It also found a particularly gratuitous cruelty involving a delay of close to 20 hours, that is, waiting till 45 minutes before scheduled execution before communicating a reprieve to the accused, violated article 7. This required, in the view of the Committee, commutation of the sentence.[129] However, here too there were violations of articles 14(3)(c) and (5).

The method of execution was decisive in one case. In *Ng* v. *Canada*, it found that Canada, by having extradited Charles Ng to California to face charges 'on 19 criminal counts, including kidnapping and 12 murders', had violated Covenant article 7, because 'execution by gas asphyxiation may cause prolonged suffering and agony and does not result in death as swiftly as possible, as asphyxiation by cyanide gas may take over 10 minutes'.[130] The case can be compared with the Committee's decision in *Kindler* v. *Canada* that no violation was involved in extraditing to Pennsylvania a person already convicted of first-degree murder, who escaped to Canada before sentencing but after the jury recommended the death penalty which is by lethal injection in that state.[131] It is hard to know what other methods of execution would fall foul of article 7. One type was signalled by two members who dissented from the finding in *Ng*: a 'method of execution such as death by stoning, which is intended to and actually inflicts prolonged pain and suffering'.[132] The key point here would seem to lie in the intention.

The observer may be forgiven the suspicion that the Committee might have preferred to avoid treading the path of choosing between different methods of achieving what they themselves agree is already cruel, inhuman, and degrading, but legally permitted by article 6.[133] But they had already decided *Kindler* in favour of Canada. There, they apparently followed *Soering*, but distinguised on the facts.[134] Five dissenters argued cogently that Canada, an abolitionist state (except for certain military offences), could not avail itself of an exception invocable only by non-abolitionist states and indeed it was violating the mandated goal of restriction by exposing the person to the death

---

[128] *Kelly* v. *Jamaica* (No. 253/1987), Report of the Human Rights Committee, *GAOR*, 46th Session, Supplement No. 40 (1991), Annex XI D, paras. 3.8, 5.7, 6.

[129] *Pratt and Morgan* v. *Jamaica* (No. 210/1986 and 225/1987), Report of the Human Rights Committee, *GAOR*, 44th Session, Supplement No. 40 (1989), Annex IX F, paras. 13.7, 15. The case also involved non-production of an appeal judgment preventing appeal to the Judicial Committee of the Privy Council. Eventually such an appeal was made, the panel holding, effectively, that a 5-year period between sentence and execution would probably be inhuman and degrading: *Pratt and another* v. *Attorney General for Jamaica* [1993] 4 All ER 769; reproduced in 14 *HRLJ* 338, 346 (1993).

[130] *Supra* n. 118, paras. 2.1, 16.4.

[131] *Kindler* v. *Canada* (No. 470/1991), Report of the Human Rights Committee, UN Doc. A/48/40 (Part II) (1993), Annex XII J; reproduced in 14 *HRLJ* 307 (1993).

[132] Id., Appendix A: Herndl (Austria); Sadi (Jordan).

[133] *Ng* v. *Canada, supra* n. 118.   [134] *Supra* n. 131, para. 15.3.

sentence.[135] Having been unable to persuade the majority of this view, presumably it was only the issue of method on which a majority could be forged.

PERSONS WHO MAY NOT BE EXECUTED

The foregoing has dealt with restrictions on capitally punishable offences and procedural safeguards that must be respected in such cases. The death penalty is further restricted in that certain categories of individual may not be executed in any circumstances.

PERSONS UNDER 18 YEARS OLD

Under the Covenant, the death sentence may not be imposed 'for crimes committed by persons below eighteen years of age' (article 6, paragraph 5). Also, according to article 37 of the Convention on the Rights of the Child, '[n]either capital punishment nor life imprisonment shall be imposed for offences committed by persons below 18 years of age'.[136] Similarly, the American Convention on Human Rights provides that it may not be imposed 'upon persons who, at the time the crime was committed, were under 18 years of age' (article 4, paragraph 5). This wording is indeed preferable to that of the UN treaties, since it removes any doubt about whether the age of the offender at the time of trial is material. However it is clear that the Covenant's wording means the same:[137] a crime committed by someone who is 18 years or over at the time of coming to trial, but was under 18 at the time of the offence, would be 'a crime committed by [a] person below eighteen years of age'. This is corroborated by the fact that during the process of drafting article 6, a proposal that would have fixed the age of an offender at the time of trial, and thus merely prohibited the passing of a death sentence on one under 18 years old, was rejected.[138]

The use of the specific 18-year-old rule in the Covenant rather than some vaguer concept of 'minors' was borrowed from article 68 of the Fourth Geneva Convention, which deals with civilians;[139] the other Geneva Conventions omit this limitation. The two additional Protocols to the Geneva Conventions (Additional Protocol I relates to international armed conflict; Additional Protocol II relates to non-international armed conflict), adopted in 1977, seek to fill this gap in international humanitarian law: both rule out the death penalty for offenders who were under 18 years of age when the

---

[135] *Ng* v. *Canada, supra* n. 118, Appendix B: Mr Wennergren (Sweden); Appendix C: Mr Lallah (Mauritius); Appendix D: Mr Pocar (Italy); Appendix E: Ms Chanet (France); Appendix F: Mr Aguilar Urbina (Costa Rica).

[136] GA res. 44/25, 20 Nov. 1989.   [137] See Landerer, *supra* n. 10, 526.

[138] Ibid., citing UN doc. A/C.3/SR.820.   [139] Ibid., citing UN doc. A/C.3/SR.819.

crime was committed.[140] The rule is reaffirmed by the Ecosoc Safeguards and reflects overwhelmingly state practice. Nevertheless, a number of states parties have not always adapted their laws to comply with the rule, although there is rarely any evidence of an intention to execute persons under 18.[141]

Of the eight countries that are known to have executed persons below the age of 18 since 1985, four are non-reserving parties to the Covenant.[142] The United States is responsible for nine of the thirty-two juveniles executed.[143] It has entered a controversial reservation to the Covenant effectively preserving the punishment for anyone (except a pregnant woman) 'including such punishment for crimes committed by persons below eighteen years of age'.[144] The Human Rights Committee, in its final comments on the first United States periodic report, considered the reservation to be 'incompatible with the object and purpose of the Covenant',[145] called for its withdrawal,[146] and 'exhort[ed] the authorities to take appropriate steps to ensure that persons are not sentenced to death for crimes committed before they were 18'.[147]

The Inter-American Commission on Human Rights approached the issue in a different way. Since the USA is not a party to the American Convention, the Commission applied the right to life provision of article 1 of the 1948 American Declaration on the Rights and Duties of Man in *Roach and Pinkerton* v. *United States*.[148] This provided an opportunity precisely to consider the matter from the perspective of general international law. It found that there was at least a regional customary international law rule at the level of *jus cogens* against the execution of children.[149] However, it did not find that

---

[140] Additional Protocol I, article 76; Additional Protocol II, article 6.

[141] Schabas, 124–5.

[142] The eight countries are Bangladesh, Iran, Iraq, Nigeria, Pakistan, Saudi Arabia, USA, and Yemen. The four non-reserving states parties are Iran, Iraq, Nigeria, and Yemen. The USA is also a state party, but has made a reservation to article 6, as to which see below: Amnesty International, Juveniles and the Death Penalty—Executions Worldwide since 1985, Jan. 1998, AI Index ACT 50/02/98. The other three (Bangladesh, Pakistan, and Saudi Arabia) are parties to the Convention on the Rights of the Child, article 37a of which prohibits execution of persons under 18; but Pakistan and Saudi Arabia have submitted sweeping reservations subjecting their obligations to the dictates of Islamic law.

[143] See, on the customary international law nature of the rule and its relevance to courts in the United States, Hartman, '"Unusual" Punishment: The Domestic Effects of International Norms Restricting the Application of the Death Penalty', 52 *University of Cincinnati Law Review* 655 (1983).

[144] 31 *ILM* 653 (1992). See Schabas, 83–90; Stewart, 'U.S. Ratification of the Covenant on Civil and Political Rights: The Significance of the Reservations, Understandings and Declarations', 14 *HRLJ* 77 (1993).

[145] Report of the Human Rights Committee, UN Doc. A/50/40 (1995), para. 279. The view is shared by the Special Rapporteur on Extrajudicial, Summary or Arbitrary Executions: UN Doc. E/CN.4/1998/68, Add. 3, para. 140.

[146] Id., para 292.   [147] Id., para 296.

[148] Res. 3/87, case 9647, Annual Report of the Inter-American Commission on Human Rights 1986–1987, OAS Doc. OEA/Ser.L/V/II.71, Doc. 9 rev. 3 (1987), 147; reproduced in 8 *HRLJ* 345 (1987).

[149] Id., para. 56.

the precise 18-year age limit was coextensive with the rule, relying, perversely it may be thought, on US state practice alone.[150] It then found a violation of article 1 on the grounds that the application of the death penalty was arbitrary, because different rules concerning age limits applied in different states of the USA. Article 2 (right to equality before the law) was also violated on this ground.[151] Since many laws in the particular units of a federal system will differ, the same argument could be made in respect of any victim of such differences. The Commission seems not to have realized that its position was simply irreconcilable with the nature of a federal system, in which the criminal law falls within the jurisdiction of the federal units. It is submitted that the basis for a finding of violation is no more convincing than the basis for finding no rule of customary international law. The evidence adduced (US state practice) is at best indicative that such a rule may not be opposable to the United States as a 'persistent objector' to it.[152]

PREGNANT WOMEN AND MOTHERS

The Covenant also prohibits the carrying out of death sentences on pregnant women (article 6(5)). The difference in wording between the language relating to persons under 18 years of age ('shall not be imposed') and that relating to pregnant women ('shall not be carried out') suggests the distasteful conclusion that once the pregnant woman has given birth, she may be executed. The language of the American Convention on Human Rights has the same effect.

The Geneva Conventions do not themselves prohibit the infliction of the death penalty on pregnant women; again the Additional Protocols aim to supply a prohibition on the carrying out of executions on such women.[153] Both Additional Protocols go further than the international human rights instruments in that they also forbid executions of 'mothers having dependent infants' (Additional Protocol I, article 76) or 'mothers of young children' (Additional Protocol II, article 6). Moreover, article 76 of Additional Protocol I requires parties to an international armed conflict, to the 'maximum extent feasible, . . . [to] endeavour to avoid the pronouncement of the death penalty on pregnant women or mothers having dependent infants, for an offence related to the armed conflict'. The Ecosoc Safeguards in capital cases would also forbid the carrying out of executions on 'new mothers'.[154]

[150] Id., paras. 57–60. However, it found the norm to be 'emerging' (para. 60).
[151] Id., paras. 62–5.
[152] See, generally, the powerful analysis in Note by Dinah Shelton, 8 *HRLJ* 355 (1987).
[153] Additional Protocol I, article 76; Additional Protocol II, article 6.
[154] *Supra* n. 73, para. 3.

PERSONS OVER 70 YEARS OLD (AMERICAS REGION)

Only the American Convention on Human Rights places an upper age limit on death sentences. In the Americas, capital punishment is not to be imposed 'upon persons who, at the time the crime was committed were . . . over 70 years of age' (article 4(5)). In a resolution on implementation of the Safeguards, Ecosoc has called for the setting of a maximum age limit.[155]

INSANE PERSONS

Under many, if not most legal systems, insanity is grounds to vitiate criminal responsibility and even to prevent trial in the first place. It is also possible for people to become insane after conviction. In 1984 Ecosoc addressed itself to the issue for the first time and concluded that the death sentence is not to be carried out 'on persons who have become insane'.[156] In its resolution on implementation of the Safeguards, Ecosoc proposes non-execution of 'persons suffering from mental retardation or extremely limited mental competence'.[157] The resolutions are not *per se* legally binding.

INTERNATIONAL REMEDIES

Although the Sixth UN Crime Congress in 1980 and the General Assembly of the same year both failed to strengthen the declared objective of abolition, the Assembly took the first steps towards an attempt to enforce the standards that had already been agreed.

SECRETARY-GENERAL'S 'BEST ENDEAVOURS'

In its resolution 35/172 of 15 December 1980, whose first paragraph, urging member states to 'respect as a minimum standard the content of the provision of articles 6, 14 and 15 of the International Covenant on Civil and Political Rights', has already been frequently cited here, the Assembly also requested the Secretary-General 'to use his best endeavours in cases where the minimum standard of legal safeguards referred to in paragraph 1 above appears not to be respected'. This mandate was reiterated in several General Assembly resolutions. It is understood that the Secretary-General has taken this mandate seriously when apprised of impending executions that may not conform to the safeguards. Accordingly, individuals or organizations having knowledge of such impending executions are known to have invoked these resolutions and

---

[155] Ecosoc res. 1989/64 , 24 May 1989, para. 1c. [156] *Supra* n. 154.
[157] *Supra* n. 155, para. 1(d). As Schabas points out (166–8) this addressed practice in the United States.

presented their information to the Secretary-General, with a view to seeking his intercession.[158]

SPECIAL RAPPORTEUR ON EXTRAJUDICIAL, SUMMARY OR ARBITRARY EXECUTIONS

As indicated in Chapter 6, Ecosoc, at its spring session of 1982, approved a resolution drafted by the Commission on Human Rights at its 1982 (thirty-eighth) session whereby the chairman of the Commission was authorized to appoint a Special Rapporteur on 'summary or arbitrary executions'.[159] The Special Rapporteur was mandated to submit to the Commission at its 1983 session 'a comprehensive report . . . on the occurrence and extent of the practice of such executions together with his conclusions and recommendations'. As was also seen in the same chapter, his mandate has been consistently renewed, most recently in 1998 for a three-year period.[160] The mandate deals with extra-legal executions (see Chapter 6) as well as with death penalties imposed without safeguards described above.

Of especial importance here is the technique developed by the Special Rapporteur of sending 'urgent messages' to governments in the case of imminent or threatened executions falling within his mandate.[161] His most recent report indicates 43 'urgent appeals', as they are now called, on behalf of 78 identified persons to the government or other authorities of 22 countries or territories.[162]

As was noted in Chapter 6, the urgent appeals technique is particularly useful in cases where the death penalty is formally pronounced, however arbitrarily, but may not be so well adapted to cases of extra-legal executions. This was recognized by Ecosoc which at the suggestion of the Commission, when renewing the Special Rapporteur's mandate in 1984, requested him 'to pay special attention to cases in which summary or arbitrary execution is imminent or threatened' and 'to respond effectively to information that comes before him'.[163] Later that year the General Assembly added its authority to a similar request.[164] This language, which borrows from the mandate of the Commission's Working Group on 'disappearances' (see Chapter 8) and which the Working Group has interpreted as authority to engage in 'urgent

---

[158] While the Secretary-General's appeals will normally be confidential, he is free to make his concerns public. For example, the Secretary-General is reported as having appealed, albeit in vain, for the life of James Terry Roach, who was executed in the United States (South Carolina) for murder committed when he was 17. The appeal was because of the 'age issue': *New York Times*, 11 Jan. 1986, p. 7.

[159] Ecosoc res. 1982/35, 7 May 1982.

[160] Commission on Human Rights res. 1998/68, 21 Apr. 1998, (para. 20). The mandate is now described as covering 'extrajudicial, arbitrary or summary executions'.

[161] UN doc. E/CN.4/1984/29, para. 33.

[162] Sixteenth Report, UN doc. E/CN.4/1998/68, para. 27.

[163] Ecosoc res. 1984/35, 24 May 1984.   [164] GA res. 39/110, 14 Dec. 1984.

actions' on behalf of persons allegedly 'disappeared', was an unmistakable endorsement of the Special Rapporteur's technique of urgent messages.

While, as indicated in Chapter 6, the original Commission mandate directed him to seek and receive information from various official sources and non-governmental organizations in consultative status with Ecosoc, this specification has not been reproduced in more recent resolutions renewing the mandate[165] and his Twelfth Report lists main non-official sources as 'non-governmental organizations', without qualification, and indeed 'individuals'.[166] The latter are particularly important given that lawyers and even persons on death row themselves may be valuable sources of information.

Most of his country visits have focused mainly on problems of extra-legal executions (see Chapter 6). His latest one, however, dealt predominantly with the death penalty. This was his 1997 visit to the United States. In the report of that visit, he expressed concern about many facets of the application of the death penalty in that country, the imposition of which is 'marked by arbitrariness. Race, ethnic origin and economic status appear to be key determinants of who will, and who will not, receive a sentence of death.'[167] He makes special note of the execution of juveniles, which 'violates international law', as well as of the reintroduction or extension of the scope of the death penalty, and expresses concern 'about the execution of mentally retarded and insane persons'.[168] His scathing observations on the 'non-existent' knowledge at the state level of the country's international legal obligations will hopefully not represent the measure of the report's impact.[169]

The creation and continuation of the post of Special Rapporteur is evidence that the UN has embarked on a serious, and potentially effective, approach which seeks in specific cases to hold governments to the standards they have proclaimed for themselves and attempts to prevent violations that may be about to occur. Indeed, a sophisticated combined use of both the Secretary-General's 'best endeavours' and the Special Rapporteur's urgent appeals could prove helpful.

SUMMARY

With the last decade, treaty instruments at the European and American, as well as universal, levels have been adopted with the explicit aim of abolishing the death penalty in states parties to them. This development makes unsustainable the contention that the death penalty is not a human rights issue, merely a penal policy matter. General international law does not yet prohibit the death penalty, but it does envisage the goal of abolition. It may be that the

[165] e.g. *supra* n. 160.
[167] UN doc. E/CN.4/1998/68/Add. 3, para. 148.
[169] Id., para. 142.
[166] UN doc. E/CN.4/1994/7, para. 17.
[168] Id., para. 145.

Covenant contains an implicit obligation, analogous to the explicit one contained in the American Convention on Human Rights, not to reintroduce the
death penalty after it has been abolished, nor to extend it to cover crimes for
which it does not at present apply. States are, in any event, expected to restrict
the number of offences for which the death penalty may be applied. Further,
whatever the circumstances, certain offences (non-serious or incompatible
with other human rights standards) may not be made capitally punishable
and certain safeguards (including the right to a fair trial, to appeal, and to
petition for clemency) are to be respected if executions are not automatically
to amount to arbitrary deprivation of life. Moreover, the circumstances of the
death penalty must not be more inhumane than necessarily attendant on an
intrinsically inhumane process. Most of these guarantees are contained in
article 6 of the International Covenant on Civil and Political Rights, which
deals with the right to life and must generally be seen as stating a rule of general international law, binding on all states whether or not they are parties to
the Covenant. In particular, no derogation from the right is permitted, even
in time of grave emergency. Although the right to a fair trial and the right to
appeal are not included expressly in article 6, they should be understood as
being implicitly included. Several categories of people may not be executed in
any circumstances: those 18 years of age or less when they committed a capitally punishable offence, pregnant women, and, in the Americas, persons over
70 years of age at the time the crime was committed. Ecosoc resolutions have
extended this protection to 'new mothers' and 'persons who have become
insane' and the mentally retarded. The relevant rules of international
human rights law and international humanitarian law tend to be mutually
reinforcing.

The UN Commission on Human Rights Special Rapporteur reports on the
incidence of arbitrary and summary executions (which include death penalties carried out without proper safeguards), but can also intercede to seek to
prevent them. This power could well be used effectively in combination with
the 'best endeavours' that the General Assembly has asked the Secretary-
General to deploy.

8

'Disappeared' Prisoners: Unacknowledged Detention

'DISAPPEARANCE'

Most of the chapters of this book refrain from description of the often harrowing practices that are their subject matter, except in so far as such descriptions may be necessary to elucidate the scope of the norms prohibiting them. An exception has to be made for the subject of 'disappearances'. This is because the phenomenon is a special one, with its own characteristics, and no single international standard has been framed to encompass it. In some ways this may be surprising, since its modern genesis was the *Nacht und Nebel* decree of Nazi forces in occupied Europe: according to this decree suspected resistance movement members could be arrested and secretly transferred to Germany 'under cover of night'.[1] This measure would 'have a deterrent effect because (a) the prisoners will vanish without leaving a trace, (b) no information may be given as to their whereabouts or fate'.[2] Given that so much international human rights and humanitarian law was conceived, as has already been noted, in response to Nazi practices in World War II, it may be wondered why the 'disappearance' seems to have been ignored.

In fact, as will be seen, international humanitarian law did address the problem, as understood in 1949, as an 'unlawful deportation or transfer or unlawful confinement' of protected persons, which was characterized as a grave breach of the Fourth Geneva Convention.[3] But the drafters had in mind mainly transfers across frontiers as practised by Nazi forces, rather than secret detention which did not involve trans-frontier abduction, the widespread practice of which seems to have post-dated the Convention. The apparent omission may perhaps best be understood by using the analogy of genocide, the legal framework of which was not set down until after it had happened. The point is that certain actions are so far beyond the pale of accustomed human behaviour that the drafting of legislation to contain them seems morbidly eccentric. Or, more prosaically, it might be argued that to engage in such law-making would risk casting doubt on the current unthinkability of the behaviour.

---

[1] *'Disappearances'—A Workbook* (Amnesty International USA, 1981), 2.
[2] Ibid., citing Gorlitz (ed.), *The Memoirs of Field Marshal Keitel* (1965), 254–6.
[3] Geneva Convention Relative to the Protection of Civilian Persons in Time of War of 12 August 1949, article 147.

The 'disappearance' can best be approached by way of illustration. In the *Bleier* case before the Human Rights Committee, the daughter of Eduardo Bleier stated that:

Her father, Eduardo Bleier, was arrested without a court order in Montevideo, Uruguay, at the end of October 1975. The authorities did not acknowledge his arrest and he was held incommunicado at an unknown place of detention. Her father's detention was, however, indirectly confirmed because his name was on a list of prisoners read out once a week at an army unit in Montevideo where his family delivered clothing for him and received his dirty clothing. His name appeared on that list for several months until the middle of 1976. On 11 August 1976, 'Communiqué No. 1334 of the Armed Forces Press Office' was printed in all the Montevideo newspapers requesting the general public to co-operate in the capture of 14 persons, among whom Eduardo Bleier was listed, 'known to be associated with the banned Communist Party, who had not presented themselves when summoned before the military courts'. The author also alleges that her father was subjected to particularly cruel treatment and torture because of his Jewish origin.

A number of detainees who were held, together with the author's father, and who were later allowed to communicate with their families or were released, gave independent but similar accounts of the cruel torture to which Eduardo Bleier was subjected. They generally agreed that he was singled out for especially cruel treatment because he was a Jew. Thus, on one occasion, the other prisoners were forced to bury him, covering his whole body with earth, and to walk over him. As a result of this treatment inflicted upon him, he was in a very bad state and towards December 1975 had to be interned in the Military Hospital.

At the time of the submission of the communication the author assumed that Eduardo Bleier was either detained incommunicado or had died as a result of torture. The author further states that since her father's arrest, owing to the uncertainty, there has been a complete disruption of family life. She also claims that the honour and reputation of her father were attacked in every possible way by the authorities, in particular by the publication of the above-quoted 'communiqué'.[4]

The Human Rights Committee accepted these facts.[5] This case involves more than incommunicado detention, torture, and possible extra-legal execution, first, because of the official refusal to acknowledge the detention (and the corollary of this refusal: official abandonment of responsibility for the fate of the prisoner). In these circumstances all legal and moral constraint on official behaviour is at once removed. Second, from the point of view of the victim, were he still alive, and even if the physical torture had ceased, there would be the growing despair, as time went by, that the incommunicado detention was to become a permanent denial of his contact with and protection by the outside world. Third, the prisoner's daughter and wife (the latter subsequently became co-author of the 'communication'—i.e., complaint—to the Human

---

[4] *Bleier* v. *Uruguay* (30/1978) Report of the Human Rights Committee, *GAOR*, 37th Session, Supplement No. 40 (1982), Annex X, paras. 2.2–2.4.

[5] Id., paras. 13.4, 14.

Rights Committee) find themselves in a legal and moral limbo: not only is there 'a complete disruption of family life', but there is distress at what the prisoner has suffered and may, were he still alive, be continuing to suffer. There is also the anguish of uncertainty: they must continue to work for his reappearance although aware that he might be dead; they cannot grieve and then try to re-establish themselves, since that would be a betrayal were he still alive. Without official accounting their plight is beyond repair.[6] Thus, the hallmark of the 'disappearance' is mystery: for the family, for the local society, and for the outside world, a nocturnal fog has indeed engulfed the victim.

The terminology used varies: the word 'disappearance' is a non-literal translation of the Spanish *desaparecido* (disappeared person) which has been widely used in Latin America ever since the phenomenon first emerged on a widespread scale in Guatemala in the 1960s. A better term would be 'disappeared prisoner', which conveys more accurately the deliberate and official nature of the practice; the title of this chapter reflects this view. Various other forms are in common use and will occur in this chapter, including 'disappearances', 'enforced or involuntary disappearances', and 'missing persons'. In the interests of brevity, this text will generally follow Amnesty International's practice of using the most common form, 'disappearances', always retaining the quotation marks so that it remains clear that the victims did not vanish accidentally or because they chose to, but that they were caused to disappear.

THE PROBLEM OF DEFINING 'DISAPPEARANCES'

While it is easy to describe a typical 'disappearance', it is difficult to define the nature of the 'disappearance'. It is often called an 'unacknowledged detention' effected or tolerated by public officials. But these words fail to capture the reality. It is not uncommon for detention to be effected without public acknowledgement, perhaps to protect the arrested person from others or to prevent collusion among suspected criminal accomplices, for the purpose of seeking the arrest or preventing the escape of such accomplices or to secure necessary evidence of suspected crimes. The withholding of the information may be lawful at the national level, either under the ordinary law or because normal procedures have been suspended, for example in response to a state of emergency, or it may be unlawful but involve nothing more sinister than a breach of rules for a short period of time. If lawful at the national level, it may be unlawful at the international level (see Chapter 11), but still not amount to

---

[6] See, generally: Shestack, 'The Case of the Disappeared', *Human Rights*, vol. viii, no. 4 (winter 1980) (reprint by the International League for Human Rights); *'Disappearances'—A Workbook*, *supra* n. 1, Chapter IX; Egeland, *Humanitarian Initiative Against Political Disappearances* (Henry Dunant Institute, 1982), Chapters I and II; Berman and Clark, 'State Terrorism: Disappearances', 13 *Rutgers Law Journal* 531 (1982); Reoch, '"Disappearances" and the International Protection of Human Rights', *Yearbook of World Affairs* (1982), 166.

the kind of practice that has aroused international revulsion. The picture gets darker if we refer to a detention which is not only unacknowledged, but explicitly denied. But even here a denial of a detention lasting only a short period of time, while doubtless constituting a case of arbitrary detention, does not raise the case to the level of gravity that is generally associated with the typical case. There is an element of indefiniteness that remains elusive.

Indeed, the time factor provides a central conundrum. In theory, it might be possible to use this element as a pivotal aspect of a definition. That is to say, one could define the practice in terms of a temporal limit on unacknowledged or denied detention, in effect to define, as it were, the point of indefiniteness. The problem here is that there is no limit that could be established that would not have as many disadvantages as advantages. If the limit were too short, say, less than a month, first, governments would probably not accept it (having an eye to particularly acute criminal challenges) and, second, it would trivialize the reality of the phenomenon, blurring the distinction between arbitrary detention and the real enforced disappearance. If the limit were longer, there would be a substantial risk of governments seeing that limit as the authentic test of what behaviour were genuinely out of bounds, thus risking undermining generally the notion of arbitrary detention and specifically the current trend to limit any incommunicado detention ('disappearances' are that too) to 'a matter of days' (see below and Chapter 11). The fact that the only definition so far attempted (to which we return below) refrains from using a temporal test is doubtless attributable to this conundrum.

Is there some other perspective that could help address the problem? It is clear that in the overwhelming majority of situations where the practice has been resorted to, the victims are dead and they died in detention; they are victims of a secret violation of the right to life. Perhaps then we could seek a definition based on the presumption of death. There are two main obstacles to this approach. First, generally the organized voice of the families of the 'disappeared' firmly resists any presumption of death until there has been an official accounting for the fate of their loved ones.[7] That voice is too reasonable to ignore, since the alternative is indirectly to relieve the state of its responsibility to make such an accounting. Second, it would reduce any incentive to the state that has not actually killed the 'disappeared' persons to bring them forth alive, the legal consequences involved for the state being no greater than those which would attend upon an extra-legal execution (see Chapter 6). Third, it is hardly appropriate to such a situation: a presumption can be

---

[7] An attempt by the military government of Argentina in 1979 to dispose of the problem of 'disappearances' by legislating for a presumption of death was met with outrage by the families and the law remained a dead letter: *'Disappearances'—A Workbook*, *supra* n. 1, 11. A vivid example of the resistance is in the very title of a Guatemalan NGO set up by the families of victims of the 'disappeared': Mutual Support Group for the Return of Missing Relatives Alive: UN doc. E/CN.4/1985/15, para. 37.

rebutted and we know of at least one situation where a number of the 'disappeared' reappeared alive after eighteen years.[8] By any standards they were the victims of enforced disappearance within the ordinary understanding of the term.

It was difficulties such as these that led the drafters of the UN Declaration on Enforced Disappearance (see below) to eschew the search for a definition; after all, a Declaration does not *per se* impose binding obligations and, for most purposes, there was no difficulty in identifying the real thing. So it left in a preambular paragraph a 'working description' of the phenomenon, supplied by the Working Group on Enforced or Involuntary Disappearances, a description that boils down to the notion of unacknowledged detention as referred to above,[9] with all its inadequacies as a definition, since a definition as such was not needed.[10]

The Inter-American Convention on Forced Disappearance of Persons includes a definition in its article 2 as follows:

For the purposes of this Convention, forced disappearance is considered to be the act of depriving a person or persons of his or their freedom, in whatever way, perpetrated by agents of the state or by persons or groups of persons acting with the authorization, support, or acquiescence of the state, followed by an absence of information or a refusal to acknowledge that deprivation of freedom or to give information on the whereabouts of that person, thereby impeding his or her recourse to the applicable legal remedies and procedural guarantees.

Surprisingly, this definition, despite variations in wording, involves no substantial change from the UN Declaration's 'working description' and thus precisely suffers from the inadequacies of that approach.

In so far as the text deals with state responsibility for 'disappearances', perhaps the vagueness will not, in practice, be the cause of serious unfairness against states, since they and the intergovernmental bodies they establish may be expected to apply the 'definition' responsibly. Nevertheless, a suspect definition does not enhance respect for the instrument containing it.[11] In any

[8] A number of prisoners were released in 1991 having 'disappeared' in Morocco in 1973, some, such as the Bourequat brothers, having been held at a secret desert fortress (Tazmamert) since 1981: Amnesty International Report 1992, 191.

[9] Preambular paragraph 3 reads in part: '. . . enforced disappearances occur, in the sense that persons are arrested, detained or abducted against their will or otherwise deprived of their liberty by officials of different branches or levels of Government, or by organized groups or private individuals acting on behalf of, or with the support, direct or indirect, consent or acquiescence of the Government, followed by a refusal to disclose the fate or whereabouts of the persons concerned or a refusal to acknowledge the deprivation of their liberty, thereby placing such persons outside the protection of the law'.

[10] However, the absence of a definition may well have contributed to other inadequacies in the text, as governments may well have been reluctant to accept language expressing or implying far-reaching obligations when unsure as to what acts would lead to those obligations (see below).

[11] For example, the vague definition of *apartheid* in article II of the 1973 International Convention on the Suppression and Punishment of the Crime of *Apartheid* (GA res. 3068 (XXVIII), 30 Nov. 1973) was instrumental in the refusal of many states to ratify that treaty.

event, it is not possible to be so sanguine about a definition that purports to establish, at the international level, individual criminal responsibility (see below), which is exactly what the Inter-American Convention does, and the proposed new UN Convention and the Statute of the International Criminal Court (see below) are expected to do.

Another challenge to deriving a definition lies in the fact that it is inherent in the practice (it is no accident) that it will be very difficult to *prove* individual responsibility. Apart from the inherent secrecy necessarily shrouding the whole ghoulish process, it is in fact just that: a process, with various phases. These are the initial capture, the taking to a place of detention, possible removal from place to place of detention, possible interrogation during detention, final removal from the place of detention and eventual disposal of the body, the person having been deprived of life at some point in the process (in Argentina in the 1970s the final removal, deprivation of life, and disposal of the body all took place as part of an operation known as the 'transfer' from the final place of detention).[12] Theoretically all these phases could involve different personnel, with those involved in one phase not necessarily knowing about the other phases or those involved. Yet such knowledge would be an essential element to be proven to support a charge of committing an act of 'disappearance'.

Bearing all this in mind, the closest the present author has been able to come to a definition is one that would essentially track the Declaration's 'working description', culminating with a clause to the effect that the acts have been committed 'with the intention of removing such persons indefinitely from the protection of the law'. This borrows the concluding language from the 'working description', but transforms it into an element of the crime.[13] The *mens rea* would thus contain the missing element, at the same time as accommodating the notion of indefiniteness. It acknowledges the reality that it may be hard to prove the requisite intention in respect of perpetrators acting at different phases of the process, but this is inherent in the nature of the practice. Of course those who organize the process will be easier to identify, as long as the 'disappearance' is part of a systematic practice.

---

[12] See *'Disappearances'—A Workbook*, *supra* n. 1, 10.
[13] For the working description see *supra* n. 9. This approach to the definitional problem emerged from a discussion with Christopher Keith Hall, Amnesty International Legal Adviser, Rome, 23 June 1998, when it began to seem that the existence of a definition was a condition for including enforced disappearance as a 'crime against humanity' within the purview of the Statute of the International Criminal Court being drafted by the United Nations Diplomatic Conference of Plenipotentiaries on the Establishment of an International Criminal Court, Rome, Italy, 15 June–17 July 1998.

THE UN RESPONSE TO 'DISAPPEARANCES'

As with torture, the problem of 'disappearances' first attracted the attention of the United Nations in the context of denunciations by non-governmental organizations (NGOs) and widespread concern with the human rights situation in Chile. The United Kingdom representative to the 1978 General Assembly's Third Committee deplored practices that led to 'the disappearances of individuals'[14] and referred to 'the report of Amnesty International, during the year marking the thirtieth anniversary of the Universal Declaration of Human Rights'[15] and to complaints and appeals 'submitted by groups of people trying to find out what had happened to their friends and relatives'.[16] Rejecting 'the claim that some Governments responsible for such behaviour were acting in defence of democracy, the civilized values of Western civilization, Christianity or law and order', his delegation's view was that 'those actions could only bring shame on their religion, make a mockery of their claim to be civilized, and lead to repudiation of their law and contempt for their order'.[17] The next day the United States representative, having welcomed the report of the Commission on Human Rights *Ad Hoc* Working Group on human rights in Chile,[18] declared that his delegation 'was anxious for an explanation of the problem of missing persons in Chile, since the matter had occasioned too much anguish and torment to those persons' relatives for it to be ignored'.[19] But, he continued, 'the problem of missing persons was not limited to Chile; it also existed in Cyprus and in Argentina, and, in view of its magnitude, he felt that a mechanism should be set up to examine the problem'.[20]

Without further discussion of the issue, Colombia introduced a draft resolution on the problem and this was adopted without a vote in committee[21] and subsequently in plenary as resolution 33/173 of 20 December 1978. The draft resolution will be referred to repeatedly in this chapter; for present purposes, its most important provision, as underlined by the French representative at the time of the draft's adoption in the Third Committee,[22] was that which requested the Commission on Human Rights 'to consider the question of disappeared persons with a view to making appropriate recommendations'. In fact, the Commission at its next (1979) session was unable to take any decision on how to deal with the problem 'because of lack of time' to reach a compromise solution on draft resolutions that would have taken divergent approaches.[23]

---

[14] *GAOR*, 33rd Session, Third Committee, Summary Records, A/C.3/33/SR.69, para. 60.
[15] Ibid.   [16] Id., para. 62.   [17] Id., para. 63.
[18] A/C.3/33/SR.70, para. 5.   [19] Id., para. 6.   [20] Ibid.
[21] A/C.3/33/SR.74, paras. 246–7.   [22] Id., para. 244.
[23] Commission on Human Rights, Report, 35th Session, *ESCOR*, 1979, Supplement No. 6, para. 191; and the draft resolutions are in UN doc. E/CN.4/L.1458/Rev. 1, L. 1460, and L. 1472.

This inconclusive response to the General Assembly's request led the Commission's parent body, the Economic and Social Council (Ecosoc), some two months later, to request the Commission, 'to consider as a matter of priority the question of disappeared persons, with a view to making appropriate recommendations' at its following session (1980). It also requested the Sub-Commission on Prevention of Discrimination and Protection of Minorities 'to consider the subject . . . with a view to making general recommendations to the Commission' at its intervening session later in 1979.[24]

The Sub-Commission came seriously to grips with the problem. It pointed out 'that the danger involved for such [disappeared] persons warrants urgent reaction on the part of all individuals and institutions as well as of the Governments'.[25] Acknowledging the need for 'emergency action called for by this situation', it proposed that a group of experts of the Sub-Commission 'be given all the information available for locating the missing and disappeared persons in different regions of the world and . . . make the necessary contacts with the Governments and families concerned'. The Sub-Commission concluded with the radical suggestion that if the practice of 'disappearances' were to continue, 'its extreme gravity would justify envisaging some form of emergency remedy, based on the notion of *habeas corpus* or any other type of legal protection, designed to induce official organs to devote the necessary means to the search for the missing and disappeared persons in different regions of the world'.

Thus spurred on by Ecosoc from above and the Sub-Commission from below, the Commission, at its 1980 session, eventually responded concretely to the mandate given it by the General Assembly in 1978. The tense debate and complex and sensitive negotiations leading to the adoption of a resolution that created a working group on 'disappearances' has been vividly described elsewhere.[26] The basic terms of the debate were set by two competing draft resolutions. One, introduced by France, would have had the Secretary-General appoint a group of three experts, of international standing in their individual capacities, to investigate 'disappearances'. The appointment would have been without time limit and the group would have reported annually to the Commission. In effect, the experts would have been able both to deal with reports coming to them and to go out and seek information from the governments and families concerned. In responding to urgent situations, their working methods should 'ensure the necessary speed and flexibility of *action*'[27] (emphasis added). This approach was essentially that recommended

[24] Resolution 1979/38, 10 May 1979.
[25] Resolution 5 B (XXXII), 5 Sept. 1979, Report of the Sub-Committee on Prevention of Discrimination and Protection of Minorities (hereinafter 'Sub-Commission Report'). 32nd Session (E/CN.4/1350; E/CN.4/Sub.2/435), Chapter XVI A.
[26] Kramer and Weissbrodt, 'The 1980 UN Commission on Human Rights and the Disappeared', *Human Rights Quarterly*, vol. iii, no. 1 (1981), 18.
[27] UN doc. E/CN.4/L.1502.

by the Sub-Commission but with the advantage that the experts would not be persons elected by governments and the status of the group would be that of a Commission-level body.[28] The second draft was one that Argentina is reported to have circulated informally but which it eventually failed to introduce formally. It opposed creation of any new mechanism as such and proposed that a working group of five Commission members should meet one week before the 1981 session of the Commission. The function of this group would be to evaluate views, to be solicited from governments, as to what procedures might be appropriate to deal with 'disappeared' persons without encroaching on the sovereignty of any nation.[29] If the competing draft resolutions set the terms for conflict of approach, an analogous tone of conflict was set early in the session: the debate was initiated (unusually) by NGOs which referred to situations demonstrating the need for a mechanism on 'disappearances'; Argentina made an unsuccessful attempt to prevent Amnesty International from completing an oral statement referring to thousands of 'disappearances' in Argentina, Afghanistan, Democratic Kampuchea, Ethiopia, Nicaragua, and Uganda.[30]

From the debate emerged resolution 20 (XXXVI) of 29 February 1980, most of the substance of which was contained in written[31] and oral[32] amendments to the French draft, proposed by members of the non-aligned group. By the resolution, which was adopted without a vote, the Commission established a Working Group 'to examine questions relevant to enforced or involuntary disappearances of persons'.[33] The Group was created for only one year and was to consist of five Commission members, to be appointed by the Chairman 'to serve as experts in their individual capacities'. The scheme had some obvious shortcomings: since the Commission is composed of representatives of governments, it might be envisaged that the acts of the Group members might not always have the impartiality and independence that might be achieved by individual experts appointed by the Secretary-General. Second, the geographical distribution implied by having five members, rather than the three suggested in the French draft, is that the Group may thus include a member from each of the UN regions. This might also be seen to imply a certain representative role for the members. Third, the mandate of the Group was vague: 'to examine questions relevant to "disappearances"'. On the other

---

[28] The Commission is an intergovernmental body of 53 representatives (43 at the time); a working group reporting to it would have more authority than a group reporting to its subordinate body, the Sub-Commission, which is composed of 26 individual experts.

[29] Kramer and Weissbrodt, *supra* n. 26.

[30] Commission on Human Rights, Report (Addendum), 36th Session, *ESCOR*, 1980, Supplement No. 3A, Annex IX, 1552nd meeting.

[31] UN doc. E/CN.4/L.1505.   [32] UN doc. E/CN.4/SR.1563.

[33] Resolution 20 (XXXVI), 29 Feb. 1980, Commission on Human Rights, Report, 36th Session, *ESCOR*, 1980, Supplement No. 3, Chapter XXVI A.

hand, the Group was given great latitude in its access to information by making it able both to receive and to seek information from a very broad range of sources, namely, 'governments, intergovernmental organizations, humanitarian organizations and other reliable sources'. It was to perform its functions 'in an effective and expeditious manner' and its working methods should enable it 'to respond effectively to information that comes before it'. It was, however, 'to carry out its work with discretion'.

Upon the adoption of the resolution, there was immediate dispute as to the interpretation of the terms of the mandate. Some countries envisaged a role hardly more far-reaching than that contained in the original Argentinian draft, while others considered that the Group could do anything that the original French draft would have permitted.[34] As will be seen later, when the operation of the Working Group is examined, its mandate was such as to permit it to operate flexibly, subject not so much to formal restrictions flowing from the text as perhaps to such inhibitions as were inherent in its (annually renewed) one-year tenure[35] and its not entirely non-governmental composition.

Later that year the General Assembly welcomed the establishment of the Group[36] and appealed to all governments to co-operate with it. It also requested the Commission 'to continue to study this question as a matter of priority and to take any step it may deem necessary to the pursuit' of its work on the question. It adopted similar resolutions in subsequent years, in the wake of the Commission's renewals of the Group's mandate.[37]

Meanwhile, in 1980 and in 1981 the Sub-Commission's own concern with 'disappearances' led it to urge renewal of the Working Group's mandate.[38] In 1982 it addressed itself to the normative aspects of the problem and suggested that the International Law Commission be invited to consider the issue in the context of its elaboration of the draft code of offences against the peace and security of mankind (see Chapter 6 and below) 'with a view to declaring as a crime against humanity the practice of persons being rendered "missing and disappeared" involuntarily'.[39] Perhaps as a result of the lack of follow-up in the superior bodies, the Sub-Commission decided in 1983 that, at its 1984 session, it would prepare a first draft of a Declaration Against Unacknowledged

---

[34] Commission on Human Rights, Report (Addendum), *supra* n. 30, 1563rd meeting.
[35] Like other thematic mechanisms, such as the Special Rapporteurs on Extrajudicial, Arbitrary and Summary Executions and on Torture, its mandate is presently renewed triennially.
[36] GA res. 35/193, 15 Dec. 1980.
[37] e.g., GA res. 36/163, 16 Dec. 1981; 37/180, 17 Dec. 1982. The latest is GA res. 51/94, 12 Dec. 1996, operative para. 18.
[38] Resolution 18 (XXXIII), 11 Sept. 1980, Sub-Commission Report, 33rd Session (E/CN.4/1413; E/CN.4/Sub.2/459), Chapter XVII A; and resolution 15 (XXXIV), 10 Sept. 1981, Sub-Commission Report, 34th Session (E/CN.4/1512; E/CN.4/495), Chapter XX A.
[39] Resolution 1982/12, 7 Sept. 1982, Sub-Commission Report, 35th Session (E/CN.4/1983/4; E/CN.4/Sub.2/1982/43), Chapter XXI A.

Detention of Persons, Whatever Their Condition.[40] In 1984 a first draft was discussed in the Sub-Commission's Working Group on Detention as a result of which the Sub-Commission asked for a revised draft declaration to be submitted to its 1985 session.[41] By 1985 it was in a position to adopt such a draft,[42] but the Commission on Human Rights to which it was referred was to send it back to the Sub-Commission for reconsideration.[43]

At the 1988 session of the Sub-Commission's Working Group on Detention, French member Louis Joinet presented a draft 'Declaration on the Protection of All Persons from Enforced or Involuntary Disappearances', 'prepared literally overnight by a group of NGOs'.[44] The text was broadly based on the Declaration against Torture (see Annex 1), with some borrowings from the Convention against Torture (see Annex 2a). The Working Group revised the text and forwarded it to the Sub-Commission, which sent it out for comment by governments, NGOs, the Working Group on Enforced or Involuntary Disappearances, and others.[45] A revised draft, prepared by the International Commission of Jurists (ICJ) on the basis of the requested comments and other sources it consulted, was discussed at the 1989 Working Group on Detention and later revised by an expert meeting, convened in March 1990 by the ICJ and chaired by Cuban Sub-Commission member Miguel Alfonso Martínez, who submitted the revised text to the 1990 Working Group on Detention. The Working Group adopted the revised draft 'almost without change' and the Sub-Commission transmitted it to the Commission.[46] The 1991 session of the Commission established an intersessional working group to examine the draft.[47] The Working Group met in November/December 1991 and made certain changes.[48] Having been

[40] Resolution 1983/23, 5 Sept. 1983, Sub-Commission Report, 36th Session (E/CN.4/1984/3; E/CN.4/Sub.2/1983/43), Chapter XXI A.

[41] Resolution 1984/13, 29 Aug. 1984, Sub-Commission Report, 37th Session (ECN.4 1985/3; E/CN.4/Sub.2/1984/43), Chapter XVIII A. The Working Group on Detention is described in Chapter 5.

[42] Resolution 1985/26, 29 Aug. 1985, Sub-Commission Report, 38th Session (E/CN.4/1986/5; E/CN.4/Sub.2/1985/57), Chapter XX A. By the draft the General Assembly would merely declare 'that Governments shall, (a) disclose the identity, location and condition of all persons detained by members of their police, military or security authorities acting with their knowledge, together with the cause of such detention, and (b) seek to locate all other persons who have disappeared. In countries where legislation does not exist to this effect, steps shall be taken to enact such legislation as soon as possible'.

[43] Commission on Human Rights decision 1986/106, 13 Mar. 1986.

[44] Brody and González: 'Nunca Más: An Analysis of International Instruments on "Disappearances"', 19 HRQ 365, 372 (1997); this article identifies the NGOs as Amnesty International, International Commission of Jurists, and Minnesota Lawyers Committee for Human Rights: id., footnote 31.

[45] Sub-Commission res. 1988/17; see Brody and González, supra n. 44.

[46] Brody and González, 372–3. For the text, see Report of the Working Group on Detention, UN doc. E/CN.4/Sub.2/1990/32, Annex, adopted by Sub-Commission res. 1990/33, 31 Aug. 1990.

[47] Commission on Human Rights res. 1991/41, 5 Mar. 1991.

[48] Its report may be found in UN doc. E/CN.4/1992/19/Rev. 1.

adopted by the Commission in 1992[49] and forwarded through Ecosoc to the General Assembly, the Assembly adopted the text the same year.[50] The text of the Declaration on the Protection of All Persons from Enforced Disappearance is reproduced in Annex 8a and will be referred to below.[51]

Meanwhile, the Sub-Commission, following the pattern in respect of torture, has begun working, under the leadership of Louis Joinet, on a draft convention on 'disappearances', basing itself on a draft produced by an expert meeting convened by Amnesty International.[52]

In addition, while it is not proposed to trace its history, it should be noted that in 1994 the Organization of American States adopted the Inter-American Convention on Forced Disappearance of Persons (Annex 8b).[53]

THE INTERNATIONAL LAW PROHIBITION OF 'DISAPPEARANCES'

In international armed conflict, the Fourth Geneva Convention offers a significant range of protection to civilian populations under the control of a party to such a conflict. This is especially so as far as most populations of occupied territories are concerned. There are complex provisions concerning the 'confinement' of protected persons, in terms both of when such confinement is permissible and of the form that such confinement may take (normally, according to article 78, assigned residence or internment). Most 'disappearances' would probably be considered 'unlawful confinement' by these provisions and thus, under article 147, constitute 'grave breaches' of the Convention. In addition, article 49 lays down: 'Individual or mass forcible transfers, as well as deportations of protected persons from occupied territory to the territory of the Occupying Power or to that of any other country, occupied or not, are prohibited, regardless of their motive.' However, the article goes on to allow 'the displacement of protected persons outside the bounds of the occupied territory' under certain specified conditions: (1) either 'the security of the population' or 'imperative military reasons' must so demand, and (2) 'for material reasons it is impossible to avoid such displacement'. At any given moment, it may be a difficult question of fact as to whether these conditions are met. When they are not met, and a transfer or deportation occurs, then it will be unlawful and, according to article 147, a 'grave breach' of the convention.[54]

[49] Commission on Human Rights res. 1992/29, 28 Feb. 1992.
[50] GA res. 47/133, 18 Dec. 1992.
[51] The word 'involuntary' was dropped in the Commission's Working Group, presumably because it was felt to be redundant.
[52] UN doc. E/CN.4/Sub.2/WG.I/CRP.2 (1996), and Brody and González, *supra* n. 44, 405, footnote 216.
[53] Adopted at Belém do Pára, 9 June 1994, 24th regular session of the General Assembly; 5 states parties as of Mar. 1998. For the history, see Brody and González, *supra* n. 44, 374–5.
[54] It would also be a grave breach of article 85(4)(a) of Additional Protocol I.

The harder question is to determine the legal response to 'disappearances' in circumstances other than international armed conflict. Here recourse must again be had to international human rights law.

The Commission on Human Rights Working Group on 'disappearances' has properly pointed out that 'a reading of the Universal Declaration of Human Rights and the International Covenants on Human Rights shows that to a greater or lesser degree practically all basic human rights of . . . a person [who suffers enforced or involuntary disappearance] are infringed'.[55] The practice represents the morally, and thus juridically, unthinkable: the ultimate reduction of the citizen to an object of political expediency. Normal legal constraints are not just snapped, they are erased; it is official rampage. Since, however, not all human rights have the same juridical status, it is necessary to consider more specifically which norms are involved.

Perhaps the best place to start is with what the Working Group identifies as 'the principal human rights' denied to a disappeared prisoner. Three are listed:

(a) The right to liberty and security of person.
(b) The right to humane conditions of detention and freedom from torture, cruel or degrading treatment or punishment.
(c) The right of life.[56]

THE RIGHT TO LIBERTY AND SECURITY OF PERSON

The Working Group considers that 'this is the principal human right denied by the very fact of enforced or involuntary disappearance'.[57] That the right is violated is beyond cavil. Article 1(2) of the Declaration on the Protection of All Persons from Enforced Disappearance identifies the right to liberty and security of the person among the rules of international law violated by an act of enforced or involuntary disappearance. In the *Bleier* case, referred to above, the Human Rights Committee found that among the articles of the International Covenant on Civil and Political Rights violated by Uruguay was article 9,[58] whose paragraph 1 provides: 'Everyone has the right to liberty and security of person. No one shall be subjected to arbitrary arrest or detention. No one shall be deprived of his liberty except on such grounds and in accordance with such procedure as are established by law.' The Committee

---

[55] UN doc. E/CN.4/1983/14, para. 133.

[56] UN doc. E/CN.4/1435, para. 184. The Working Group in addition notes that the right to recognition as a person before the law is also involved. The right is contained in article 16 of the International Covenant on Civil and Political Rights and article 3 of the American Convention on Human Rights; under neither treaty may it be derogated from under any circumstances: see also article 5 of the African Charter on Human and Peoples' Rights. The Declaration against Enforced Disappearance also refers to it as one of the rules of international law violated by an act of enforced disappearance: article 1(2).

[57] Ibid.   [58] *Supra* n. 4, para. 14.

did the same in respect of the *Quinteros* case,[59] which is considered further below. Similarly, in the *Velásquez Rodríguez* case,[60] the Inter-American Court of Human Rights found 'disappearances' to violate the right to personal liberty guaranteed in American Convention on Human Rights article 7, while the European Court of Human Rights in *Kurt* v. *Turkey* found that a 'disappearance' was 'a particularly grave violation' of European Convention on Human Rights article 5, which protects liberty and security of the person.[61]

If the status of the right to liberty and security of person were the same as that of the right to life, or the right not to be tortured, then the matter could be left there. But is it? Certainly, all the human rights instruments contain the right.[62] Indeed, the Universal Declaration of Human Rights has as its first substantive right (article 3): 'Everyone has the right to life, liberty and security of person.' Thus integrated with the right to life, the right to liberty and security of person could hardly be expressed with greater authority. Given that the subsequent universal and regional human rights treaties also contain the right, it may be concluded that the right has as much legal force as may be invested in it by the Declaration. The extent of this is discussed in Chapter 2.

The need for further analysis lies in the fact that, in those treaties that permit, in time of emergency, derogations from some of the rights contained in them, the articles containing the right to liberty and personal security may be made the subject of such derogation. It has been argued in earlier chapters that, where a right is non-derogable (as is the case with the right not to be tortured, for example), this is evidence that it is recognized by general international law as carrying universal obligation, regardless of whether or not a state is party to one of the treaties containing it. The permissibility of derogation need not, however, preclude similar status for other rights, including the right to liberty and personal security. It may just as well mean merely that under emergency conditions it may not always be possible to comply with all elements of the right. For example, paragraph 2 of article 9 of the Covenant requires the provision to an arrested person of reasons for the arrest at the time of the arrest. Compliance with such a rule may well, however regrettably, have to be dispensed with under certain conditions. It cannot follow from this that the right to liberty and security of person as a whole may be rendered nugatory.

[59] *Quinteros* v. *Uruguay* (107/1981), Report of the Human Rights Committee, *GAOR*, 38th Session, Supplement No. 40 (1983), Annex XXII, para. 13. See also *Celis Laureano* v. *Peru* (540/1993), UN doc. CCPR/C/56/D/540/1993 (1996), para. 8.6.

[60] Judgment of 29 July 1988 Series C, No. 4.

[61] *Kurt* v. *Turkey*, European Court of Human Rights, Judgment, 25 May 1998, para. 129; by 6 votes to 3.

[62] International Covenant on Civil and Political Rights, article 9; European Convention on Human Rights, article 5; American Convention on Human Rights, article 7; African Charter on Human and Peoples' Rights, article 6.

Furthermore, one aspect of the right to liberty and personal security as framed in the Covenant strongly suggests that it has an especially important place in the legal hierarchy of human rights norms. Article 9(5) states: 'Anyone who has been a victim of unlawful arrest or detention shall have an enforceable right to compensation.'[63] This is one of the rare occasions wherein compensation is explicitly provided for (and a 'disappeared' person would certainly fit the formula since it is believed that there is no country where a 'disappearance' would not be unlawful detention). Furthermore, the World Court in the *Tehran Hostages* case (see Chapters 2 and 11) used language suggesting that one of the violations of general international law committed in that case was of the right to liberty and security of person.[64]

If the preceding analysis is correct, then the right to liberty and security of person is a rule of general international law, even though it is one which may be suspended in time of public emergency. As will be seen in Chapter 11, however, the possibility of derogation is always limited to 'the extent strictly required by the exigencies of the situation'. It is impossible to accept—nor does it appear to have been maintained—that the secret detention of people for months, years, or even permanently would ever be 'required by the exigencies of the situation'. In the words of the Working Group, 'no special circumstances, armed conflict, states of emergency, situations of internal conflict or tension can justify enforced or involuntary disappearances'.[65] Article 7 of the Declaration against Enforced Disappearance endorses this view. Thus, while some restrictions of the right may be acceptable in emergency situations, 'disappearances' will always be a violation of it.

THE RIGHT TO HUMANE CONDITIONS OF DETENTION AND FREEDOM FROM TORTURE AND ILL-TREATMENT

When invoking the norms on the ill-treatment of prisoners, the Working Group observed: 'Some of the information before the group deals with the conditions of detention, including ill-treatment suffered by the missing or

---

[63] Article 5(5) of the European Convention on Human Rights also provides for an enforceable right to compensation in case of breach of article 5.

[64] According to the *Restatement of the Law: Third Restatement of US Foreign Relations Law*, Vol. 2 (1987), s. 702, 'prolonged arbitrary detention' is a violation of customary international law.

[65] UN doc. E/CN.4/1984/21, para. 172; see, in particular, the discussion in Chapter 11 of *Aksoy* v. *Turkey* (100/1995/606/694), Judgment, 18 Dec. 1996, finding a violation of European Convention article 5(3), despite its purported suspension by a notification of derogation. In *Kurt* v. *Turkey*, the European Commission on Human Rights, referring to an existing derogation in relation to article 5 that had not been invoked by the government, which continued to deny the detention, stated that 'in the case of unacknowledged detention, a derogation which provides for measures relating to detention pursuant to criminal procedures provided for in law can have no application': Application No. 24276/94, Report of the Commission, 5 Dec. 1996, para. 214. The issue of the derogation is not even referred to by the Court in its judgment on the case: *supra* n. 61.

disappeared persons.'[66] This simply states a fact concerning the information presented to the Group, and establishes that 'disappeared' prisoners may also be subjected to prohibited ill-treatment or torture, but in its third report the Group acknowledged the view that a 'disappearance' itself constitutes *ipso facto* torture or other prohibited ill-treatment. It stated: 'The very fact of being detained as a disappeared person, isolated from one's family for a long period is certainly a violation of the right to humane conditions of detention and has been represented to the Group as torture.'[67]

According to article 2(1) of the Declaration against Enforced Disappearance, the rule of international law guaranteeing 'the right not to be subjected to torture and other cruel, inhuman or degrading treatment or punishment' is one of those violated by an act of enforced disappearance. In the version of the draft declaration approved by the Sub-Commission the words 'and other cruel, inhuman or degrading treatment or punishment' did not appear. They were added in the working group of the Commission.[68] The reason for the addition of the full language of the right was not explained. One possible explanation would be that it was out of a concern for completeness. Another might be the absence from the Declaration of a definition of the phenomenon, making governments reluctant to treat a 'disappearance' that may have been of only short duration, perhaps departing in only a small way from legal safeguards against arbitrary arrest and detention, in the same way as the crime of torture.[69]

The early practice of the Human Rights Committee gave uncertain guidance on this point. It found violations of Covenant articles 7 (torture and ill-treatment) and 10(1) (right to be treated with humanity) in the *Bleier* case,[70] but as the Committee pointed out, there were 'the reports of several eyewitnesses that Eduardo Bleier was subjected to severe torture while in detention'.[71] The invocations of articles 7 and 10(1) may therefore be attributable to this aspect of his treatment, and not necessarily reflect the 'disappearance' itself. The same is true for the Committee's similar findings of violations of articles 7 and 10(1) in the *Quinteros* case,[72] when it found that Elena Quinteros had been subjected to torture in a military detention camp in Uruguay.[73] On the other hand, in the latter case, which was brought by Elena Quinteros's mother on her own as well as on her daughter's behalf, the Committee found that the applicant too 'is a victim of the violations of the Covenant, in particular of article 7, suffered by her daughter'.[74] This conclusion flowed from the Committee's understanding of 'the anguish and stress

---

[66] UN doc. E/CN.4/1435, para. 184.   [67] UN doc. E/CN.4/1983/14, para. 131.
[68] *Supra* n. 48, para. 25.
[69] The latter reason was informally put to the author, who was a member of the observer delegation of the ICJ at the meeting, by one of the governments pressing for the inclusion of the new words.
[70] *Supra* n. 4, para. 14.   [71] Id., para. 13.
[72] *Supra* n. 59, para. 13.   [73] Id., para. 12.3.   [74] Id., para. 14.

caused to the mother by the disappearance of her daughter and by the continuing uncertainty concerning her fate and whereabouts. The mother has the right to know what has happened to her daughter.'[75] In so far as 'in these respects' the mother 'is a victim of the violations . . . suffered by her daughter', it appears to follow that the article 7 violation of Elena Quinteros's rights stemmed from her 'disappearance' itself, as well as the torture in the detention centre. In any event, the decision gives formal recognition that the close family of the victim of a 'disappearance' is also subjected to torture or other ill-treatment.

The Committee went a step further in *Mojica v. Dominican Republic.* Finding that the 'circumstances surrounding Rafael Mojica's disappearance . . . give rise to a strong inference that he was tortured or subjected to cruel and inhuman treatment', an inference that had not been rebutted by the government, and being '[a]ware of the nature of enforced or involuntary disappearances of persons in many countries', the Committee concluded 'that the disappearance of persons is inseparably linked to treatment that amounts to a violation of article 7' of the Covenant.[76] The Committee seems here to come close to taking the view that 'disappearances' are themselves a form of torture, but does not do so *expressis verbis.*

By 1996, the Committee could find that 'the abduction and disappearance of' 16-year-old Ana Rosario Celis Laureano and the 'prevention of contact with her family and with the outside world constitute cruel and inhuman treatment in violation of article 7', read together with article 2(1) (obligation to 'respect and ensure' Covenant rights).[77] Here there is no ambiguity that the 'disappearance' in itself violates the prohibition of cruel and inhuman treatment. However, it is not expressly condemned as torture. In this regard, it may be contrasted with an earlier, generally overlooked, case of detention denied for three years by the authorities, in which the Human Rights Committee found a violation of article 7 involving torture. According to his brother, Mohammed Bashir El-Megreisi was detained by Libyan security police in January 1989. The authorities denied the detention and the family learned that he was alive only when his wife was allowed to see him in April 1992. Since that time he had continued to be held, at an unknown place of detention.[78] The Libyan government having provided no information, the Committee found that Mr El-Megreisi, 'by being subjected to prolonged incommunicado detention in an unknown location, is the victim of torture and cruel and inhuman treatment', in violation of articles 7 and 10(1),[79] as

---

[75] Ibid.

[76] (449/1991), Report of the Human Rights Committee, Vol. II, *GAOR*, 49th Session, Supplement No. 40 (1994), Annex IX W, para. 5.7; reproduced in 17 *HRLJ* 18 (1996).

[77] *Celis Laureano* v. *Peru, supra* n. 59, para. 8.5.

[78] *El-Megreisi* v. *Libya*, Report of the Human Rights Committee, Vol. II, *GAOR*, 49th Session, Supplement No. 40 (1994), Annex IX T, paras. 2.1–2.5.

[79] Id., para. 5.4.

well as of 'abritrary arrest and detention, contrary to article 5'.[80] This, then, is the one case where what appears to be a 'disappearance' is described as torture. However, the word 'disappearance' was not used, presumably because by the time the case reached the Committee, the fact of detention had been confirmed, as well as its substantial length. It would be odd if the positive fact of eventual knowledge about the detention permitted a finding of greater gravity than would have been the case had mystery still shrouded the detention.

The Inter-American Court of Human Rights has taken a clear position in two out of three key 'disappearance' cases. In the leading case of *Velásquez Rodríguez*, the Court found a violation by Honduras of American Convention on Human Rights article 5 (humane treatment) because, *inter alia*, 'the mere subjection of an individual to prolonged isolation and deprivation of communication is in itself cruel and inhuman treatment which harms the psychological and moral integrity of the person'.[81] In *Godínez Cruz*, another 'disappearance' case from Honduras, it used identical language.[82] Yet, in the third case, *Caballero Delgado and Santana* v. *Colombia*, it found that there was 'insufficient proof that those detained were tortured or subjected to inhumane treatment' to sustain a violation of article 5.[83] However, the apparent contradiction may well not be real. In this case, the Court was cognizant of 'the short time between capture and presumed death (evidence of execution within hours)'.[84] Thus, the isolation and deprivation of communication was not 'prolonged' in the sense of *Velásquez Rodríguez* and *Godínez Cruz*. There is no reason to believe that the Court would depart from the view expressed in the Honduran case faced with evidence that the detention was prolonged.

The only case law under the European Convention on Human Rights is that of *Kurt* v. *Turkey* where, it will be recalled, the European Court of Human Rights found that Turkey, which denied that the detention had taken place, had violated article 5. In that case, the Court agreed with the Commission that it was not 'appropriate to find a violation' of Article 3.[85] The Court's reasoning was that it had not been presented with any specific evidence of Article 3 ill-treatment, nor of 'an officially tolerated practice of disappearances and associated ill-treatment'.[86] On the other hand, it found that the 'anguish and distress' of the applicant (the victim's mother) and the

---

[80] *El-Megreisi* v. *Libya*, Report of the Human Rights Committee, Vol. II, *GAOR*, 49th Session, Supplement No. 40 (1994), Annex IX T, para. 5.3.

[81] *Supra* n. 60, para. 187.

[82] I/A Court HR, *Godínez Cruz* case, Judgment of 20 Jan. 1989, Series C, No. 5, para. 197.

[83] I/A Court HR, *Caballero Delgado and Santana* case, Judgment of 8 Dec. 1995, Series C, No. 22, para. 65.

[84] Id., para. 64.	[85] *Supra* n. 61, paras. 115–17.

[86] Id., para. 116. The difficulties of proving a systematic practice through the medium of individual applications under the European Convention were noted in Chapter 5.

authorities' 'complacence' in the face of it, led to the result that she had in her own right been the victim of a breach of Article 3 of the Convention.[87]

As far as the Court's analysis in respect of the applicant's disappeared son is concerned, it is submitted that it misses the point. The suffering that the Inter-American Court found as being 'in itself' cruel and inhuman was not based on the existence of a systematic practice.[88] That had nothing to do with the suffering, nor could it. The only possible explanation is that the Court was not prepared to infer anything from the facts other than the existence of a (denied) arbitrary detention: perhaps the son had been detained for a prolonged period, perhaps not. It can be understood that, in so far as the Court is concerned only with state responsibility, there are no necessary legal consequences flowing from the limited finding. Meanwhile, it can only be speculated whether the Court would have followed the Human Rights Committee in the *El-Megreisi* case, if confronted with a belatedly acknowledged case of prolonged secret, denied detention, by finding a violation of the prohibition of torture.

To summarize, there is a trend towards recognizing that to make someone 'disappear' is a form of prohibited torture or ill-treatment, clearly as regards the relatives of the 'disappeared' person and, arguably, in respect of the disappeared person him or herself. The significance of such an analysis, including whether or not it is a question of torture or other ill-treatment, will be addressed below.

THE RIGHT TO LIFE

Because there is evidence that many of the 'disappeared' will never reappear, having lost their lives in captivity, the right to life, as indicated by the Working Group on Enforced or Involuntary Disappearances, is also involved in 'disappearances'. Thus, according to the Declaration against Forced Disappearance, an act of enforced disappearance, in addition to constituting a violation of the rights discussed above, 'also violates or constitutes a grave threat to the right to life' (article 1(2)). Of the 'general comments' adopted by the Human Rights Committee on various articles of the Covenant, only general comment 6(16)[89] dealing with article 6 (the right to life) refers to 'disappearances'. The Committee asserts: 'States parties should also take specific and effective measures to prevent the disappearance of individuals, something which unfortunately has become all too frequent and leads too often to arbitrary deprivation of life' (paragraph 4).

[87] Id., para. 134; by 7 votes to 2: para. 221.
[88] The European Court was evidently, albeit implicitly, at pains to distinguish the present case from *Velásquez Rodríguez*: paras. 101–2, 111, 116. The Commission had done so explicitly: *supra* n. 65, para. 194.
[89] Report of the Human Rights Committee, *GAOR*, 37th Session, Supplement No. 40 (1982), Annex V.

In the *Bleier* case, the Committee, in addition to finding breaches of articles 7, 9, and 10(1), also concluded 'that there are serious reasons to believe that the ultimate violation of article 6 has been perpetrated by the Uruguayan authorities'.[90] This careful wording reveals the main difficulties of categorizing 'disappearances' as violations of the right to life. First, even where there is real fear that the 'disappeared' prisoners have lost their lives, it would be improper for international bodies to presume death: there can be no substitute for the responsibility of the national authorities to account for those their agents have abducted. Second, in some cases there may be grounds for believing that the victim is still alive. This may help to explain the cautious wording used by the Working Group when referring to the right to life as one of the principal human rights being denied: 'Portions of the information received by the Group indicate that during detention the missing or disappeared person may be killed.'[91] Clearly the Group, which, as will be seen below, intervenes rapidly on receipt of information, may wish to refrain from seeming to accuse the authorities of murder, especially at such an early stage. But the fact remains, as noted earlier, that even a long-term 'disappearance' may not necessarily imply that the prisoner is dead.

This is illustrated by the *Quinteros* case considered by the Human Rights Committee.[92] On 18 June 1976 Elena Quinteros was apparently able to evade police officials who had arrested her some days earlier and secure access to the garden of the Venezuelan embassy in Montevideo, where she sought asylum. The Committee found that she was arrested in the embassy grounds by at least one member of the Uruguayan police force. The Uruguayan authorities had, however, refused to acknowledge her detention since that time. The author of the communication to the Human Rights Committee, Elena Quinteros's mother, did not invoke article 6 and the Committee did not refer to it. Had there been evidence of a threat to life, the Committee's silence could be interpreted as sensitive deference to Mrs Quinteros's feelings—and an appropriate reluctance to presume death. In fact, there was evidence of unofficial acknowledgement of the detention (paragraph 1.4), so that the Committee may well have felt that no right to life issue arose.[93]

In another case, where the government did not deny that the alleged victim had disappeared at the hands of 'individuals belonging to the security forces' and where 'the victim's life had previously been threatened by military officers', the Committee found that the right to life of Rafael Mojica had 'not been effectively protected by the Dominican Republic'.[94]

---

[90] *Supra* n. 4, para. 14.   [91] UN doc. E/CN.4/1435, para. 184.
[92] *Supra* n. 59.
[93] However, even since the restoration of constitutional government in Uruguay in 1985, Elena Quinteros is not reported as having reappeared.
[94] *Mojica* v. *Dominican Republic*, *supra* n. 75, para. 5.6. For a similar finding on comparable facts, see *Celis Laureano* v. *Peru*, *supra* n. 59, para. 8.4 (here the victim's grandmother had apparently been told that her granddaughter had been killed).

The European Commission of Human Rights first dealt with 'disappearances' in respect of Greek Cypriots missing in the wake of the military action by Turkey in July 1974. This was one aspect of a case brought by Cyprus against Turkey, alleging numerous violations of the European Convention on Human Rights.[95] The government of Cyprus alleged that at least 3,000 Greek Cypriots, a considerable number of them civilians, had last been seen in the Turkish-occupied area and were still unaccounted for; the government feared they had been killed. Despite evidence that these people had fallen into the hands of the Turkish army, the Turkish authorities denied any knowledge of them.[96] The Commission, accepting that 'a number of persons declared to be missing have been identified as Greek Cypriots taken prisoner by the Turkish army',[97] dealt with the question as an article 2 (right to life) issue, and came to the conclusion:

The Commission considers that there is a presumption of Turkish responsibility for the fate of persons shown to have been in Turkish custody. However, on the basis of the material before it, the Commission has been unable to ascertain whether, and under what circumstances, Greek Cypriot prisoners declared to be missing have been deprived of their life.[98]

One is tempted to sympathize with the statement in the Separate Opinion of Commission member Mr G. Tenekides that 'the impossibility of furnishing . . . tangible proof of a violation of article 2(1), did not absolve the Commission from the duty to draw conclusions from the lack of information, after two years, as to the fate of these people'.[99] Perhaps he might have noted that the problem may have been partly due to the Cyprus government's presentation of the issue solely as an article 2 question.

Similarly, in *Kurt* v. *Turkey*, the European Court of Human Rights was asked, *inter alia*, to find a violation of the right to life, provided for in European Convention on Human Rights article 2, both because of the threat to the right represented by the 'disappearance' and because the absence of an official investigation entailed a failure to provide an effective system of protection of the right to life. Elaborating reasoning similar to that described above in respect of the pertinence of article 3, the Court merely considered that there was insufficient evidence to substantiate that the applicant's son had met his death while in custody, or that there was a practice of violation of the right to life.[100] In the Honduran cases before the Inter-American Court of Human Rights, the Court indeed found violations of the right to life. In these cases, the existence of a systematic practice of 'disappearances' was part of the context for a finding that there was 'reasonable presumption' of the

[95] *Cyprus* v. *Turkey*, 4 EHRR 482 (1976).   [96] Id., para. 316.
[97] Id., para. 349.   [98] Id., para. 351.   [99] Id., 581.
[100] *Supra* n. 61, paras. 108–9.

persons having been killed.[101] In *Caballero Delgado and Santana* there was evidence of actual killing. In *Kurt*, neither factor obtained.

Where there is evidence that the 'disappearances' have ended in murder, then the right to life has clearly been violated. In other cases, the way forward may be in recognizing that the practice of making people 'disappear' is a *threat* to life and, as such, is embraced by a wider understanding of that right. The reluctance of the organs of the European Convention on Human Rights to venture down this path is as difficult to understand as their unwillingness to identify a systematic practice in the first place.

In situations of international armed conflict, it has been seen that most 'disappearances' committed against protected civilians would be considered 'grave breaches' of the Fourth Geneva Convention. In addition to this, the foregoing suggests that 'disappearances' are a flagrant violation of the right to liberty and security of person, a right which, although restrictable in time of public emergency, is recognized by general international law and may not be so restricted as to permit the occurrence of 'disappearances'. There is a trend towards considering 'disappearances' also as a violation of the right to freedom from torture or other cruel, inhuman, or degrading treatment or punishment (see Chapter 2), legitimately susceptible of categorization at the torture end of this scale of prohibited behaviour (see Chapter 3). Further, violation of the families' 'right to know' the fate of their disappeared kin also falls within the prohibition of torture or other ill-treatment. Where death occurs, disappearances are clear violations of the right to life and in all cases may represent a threat to that right.

This analysis is without prejudice to the range of other human rights that are violated by 'disappearances'.[102] It will have failed in its purpose if it merely succeeds in drawing attention to 'disappearances' as a series of individual, technical violations of the international law of human rights. The disdain for the spirit and letter of that law represented by 'disappearances' must be seen cumulatively as the gravest possible transgression and treated as such.

LEGAL CONSEQUENCES OF 'DISAPPEARANCES'

STATE RESPONSIBILITY

To the extent that the practice of 'disappearance' may amount to torture or arbitrary deprivation of life, the consequence of establishing state responsi-

---

[101] *Velásquez Rodríguez, supra* n. 60, para. 188; *Godínez Cruz, supra* n. 82, para. 198.

[102] Loc. cit *supra* n. 55. For example, a 45-hour detention during which the detainees were not allowed to contact their wives has been held to constitute a breach of the right to family life (article 8 of the European Convention on Human Rights): *McVeigh et al.* v. *United Kingdom* (Application Nos. 8022/77, 8025/77, and 8027/77), Report of the European Commission of Human Rights (1981) para. 240. See also *supra* n. 56, on the right to legal personality.

bility for such acts would be the same as if the government has committed acts of torture or has inflicted extra-legal executions (see Chapters 4 and 6).

The UN Declaration on the Protection of All Persons from Enforced Disappearance (Annex 8a) tends to confirm that 'disappearances' are to be treated similarly in their own right. It establishes numerous requirements for the purpose of preventing and taking action in response to 'disappearances'. Of particular note are its provisions for prompt, thorough, and impartial investigation of an alleged 'disappearance' by a 'competent and independent State authority', either on complaint of 'any person having knowledge or a legitimate interest' or without complaint if 'there are reasonable grounds to believe that an enforced disappearance has been committed' (article 13); for prosecution of persons alleged to have perpetrated an act of enforced disappearance (article 14); for compensation to the family (article 19); and for non-expulsion to a country 'where there are substantial grounds to believe' that a person 'would be in danger of forced disappearance' (article 8). In this, it tracks the rules applicable to torture and extra-legal executions.

In both the *Bleier* and *Quinteros* cases the Committee held that Uruguay should take effective steps: (a) to establish what had happened to the victims; (b) to bring to justice those found to be responsible for the death (in the case of *Bleier*), 'disappearance', or ill-treatment; (c) to pay compensation for the wrongs suffered; and (d) to ensure that similar violations do not occur in the future.[103] Apparently mindful of the peculiarly mystifying nature of 'disappearances', the Committee stressed in the *Quinteros* case that 'the author has *the right to know* what happened to her daughter'[104] (emphasis added) and that the Uruguayan government 'has a duty to conduct a full investigation into the matter'.[105]

In *Velásquez Rodríguez* and *Godínez Cruz*, the Inter-American Court of Human Rights affirmed the same position in the clearest terms:

The State has a legal duty to take reasonable steps to prevent human rights violations and to use the means at its disposal to carry out a serious investigation of violations committed within its jurisdiction, to identify those responsible, to impose the appropriate punishment and to ensure the victim adequate compensation.[106]

The absence of a serious investigation of the 'disappearances' leading to the perpetrators' being brought to justice involved not only a violation of the facts of the provisions already referred to, but a further violation of those provisions, read together with American Convention on Human Rights article 1 (state obligation to respect rights).[107] As far as prosecution is concerned, the

---

[103] *Bleier* v. *Uruguay, supra* n. 4, para. 14: *Quinteros* v. *Uruguay, supra* n. 59, para. 16. The first three requirements were also urged in respect of *Mojica* v. *Dominican Republic, supra* n. 76, para. 5.7.

[104] *Supra* n. 59, para. 14. [105] Id., para. 15.

[106] *Supra* nn. 60 and 82, paras. 174 and 184 respectively.

[107] Id., paras. 161–88 and 168–98 respectively.

Court went beyond its usual practice of merely ordering compensation in *Caballero Delgado and Santana*, where it decided 'that the Republic of Colombia is obligated to continue judicial proceedings into the disappearance and presumed death of the persons named and to extend punishment in accordance with internal law'.[108]

In *Cyprus* v. *Turkey*, the European Commission of Human Rights maintained its practice of refraining from specifying the legal consequences of what it found to be the 'presumption of Turkish responsibility for the fate of persons shown to have been in Turkish custody'.[109]

In *Kurt*, the European Court of Human Rights found a violation of European Convention article 13 (right to an effective remedy) which requires 'in addition to the payment of compensation where appropriate, a thorough and effective investigation capable of leading to the identification and punishment of those responsible'.[110]

On the basis of these elements and for the same reasons as stated in Chapter 4, it seems evident that there is an obligation on a state confronted with a 'disappearance' to investigate the matter effectively, to bring the perpetrators to justice, and to compensate the family of the victim, who themselves are victims of at least inhuman and degrading treatment, entitling them to compensation for their own suffering. While there appears to be no international case law on the matter, the Declaration clearly states the prevalent international law on expulsions, as it is inconceivable that sending a person to a country where there is a risk of 'disappearance' should be permitted, when it would be prohibited if the risk were of torture or extra-legal execution.

INDIVIDUAL RESPONSIBILITY

Where 'disappearances' in international armed conflict amount to 'grave breaches' of the Fourth Geneva Convention, then their perpetrators are *ipso facto* liable to trial on the basis of universality of jurisdiction (article 146). Otherwise, the question of the individual responsibility of persons involved in violating the prohibition against torture or the right to life has been explored in Chapters 4 and 6. To the extent that the practice of 'disappearance' falls within the categories of torture or extra-legal execution, the legal implications are the same. That is to say, that general international law probably permits, though may not require, a state to exercise criminal jurisdiction over an alleged perpetrator, regardless of the latter's nationality or the place where the offence was committed. Civil action might also be possible.[111] If 'disappearances' may be considered torture, as defined in the Convention against Torture which requires universality of jurisdiction over alleged torturers, then

---

[108] *Supra* n. 83, para. 72(5).   [109] *Supra* n. 95, para. 351.
[110] *Supra* n. 61, para. 140 (by 5 votes to 2).
[111] See *Filártiga* v. *Peña Irala*, discussed in Chapter 4, and n. 122 *infra* and accompanying text.

at least individuals who are responsible for 'disappearances' and are in the territory of a party to the Convention will be liable to criminal proceedings (see Chapter 4).

The 1990s have seen a rapid evolution of the notion of 'disappearances' constituting a crime against humanity. As indicated in Chapters 4 and 6, the idea of crimes against humanity started with the Charter of the International Military Tribunal at Nuremberg, covering a number of what might now be called human rights offences when committed in connection with international armed conflict.

The connection with international armed conflict has been severed in four recent developments. First, the 1993 Statute of the International Tribunal for the Former Yugoslavia provides for the justiciability of crimes against humanity, 'when committed in armed conflict, whether international or internal in character'.[112] Second, the 1994 Statute of the International Criminal Tribunal for Rwanda effects a complete disconnection of crimes against humanity from armed conflict.[113] Third, the International Law Commission's 1994 draft Statute for an International Criminal Tribunal, while remaining silent on the scope of the offence, is conditioned by the Commission's commentary which refers insistently to the same Commission's Draft Code of Crimes against the Peace and Security of Mankind. As noted in Chapters 4 and 6, the Commission had long ago decided to abandon the link to armed conflict. Fourth, the final text of the Draft Code of Crimes makes no reference in its article on crimes against humanity to the existence of armed conflict. Indeed, the Commentary explicitly confirms the intention to abandon the connection,[114] referring, *inter alia*, to the above-mentioned developments and citing with approval the statement of the Appeals Chamber of the Yugoslav Tribunal: 'It is now a settled rule of customary international law that crimes against humanity do not require a connection to international armed conflict.'[115]

What the four sources clearly have in common is that the acts constituting the crimes have to be committed on an extensive basis against an identifiable group of people: 'directed against any civilian population' (Yugoslav Tribunal); 'committed as part of a widespread or systematic attack against

---

[112] Statute of the International Tribunal for the Prosecution of Persons Responsible for Serious Violations of International Humanitarian Law Committed in the Territory of the Former Yugoslavia since 1991, Report of the Secretary-General, UN doc. S/25704 (1993), Annex, as approved by Security Council res. 827 (1993), 25 May 1993, article 5, reproduced in 32 *ILM* 1192 (1993).

[113] Statute of the International Tribunal for Rwanda, Security Council res. 955 (1994), 8 Nov. 1994, Annex.

[114] Report of the Work of the International Law Commission on the work of its 48th Session (1996), *GAOR*, 51st Session, Supplement No. 10, Chapter II, article 18, and Commentary, para. 6.

[115] *The Prosecutor* v. *Duško Tadić a/k/a/ 'Dule'*, Decision on the Defence Motion for Interlocutory Appeal on Jurisdiction, Case No. IT-94-1-AR72, 20 Oct. 1995.

any civilian population on national, political, ethnic, racial or religious grounds' (Rwanda Tribunal); 'committed in a systematic manner or on a large scale and instigated or directed by a Government or by any organization or group' (Draft Code of Crimes).

Only one of the sources refers explicitly to 'forced disappearance of persons' among the listed forms of crimes against humanity (Draft Code of Crimes), explaining that 'this type of criminal conduct is a relatively recent phenomenon' and proposing its inclusion 'because of its extreme cruelty and gravity'.[116] In any event, to the extent that 'disappearances' were at all part of the events in former Yugoslavia and Rwanda, they would be caught under the rubric common to the Statutes of both tribunals: 'persecutions on political, racial and religious grounds'.

Finally, it may be noted that the preamble to the UN Declaration against Disappearances describes 'the systematic practice of [enforced disappearance] is of the nature of a crime against humanity' and the preamble to the OAS Inter-American Convention on Forced Disappearance of Persons affirms 'that the systematic practice of the forced disappearance of persons constitutes a crime against humanity'.[117]

Again, as indicated in Chapters 4 and 6, the perpetrators of crimes against humanity are amenable to jurisdiction by any international penal tribunal that may be established and by any national tribunal on the basis of universality of jurisdiction. There only remains the question of whether the perpetrators of 'disappearances' committed other than as part of an international armed conflict or of crimes against humanity (that is, on a systematic or widespread scale) may also be triable on the basis of universality of jurisdiction, other than for torture or extra-legal execution. This seems to be the implication of article 14 of the Declaration against Enforced Disappearance:

Any person alleged to have perpetrated an act of enforced disappearance in a particular State shall, when the facts disclosed by an official investigation so warrant, be brought before the competent civil authorities of that State for the purpose of prosecution and trial unless he has been extradited to another State wishing to exercise jurisdiction in accordance with the relevant international agreements in force. All States should take any lawful and appropriate action available to them to bring all persons presumed responsible for an act of enforced disappearance, found to be within their jurisdiction or under their control, to justice.

It was the clear intention of the Sub-Commission draft that universality of jurisdiction be provided for. While the first sentence of its draft was only

---

[116] *Supra* n. 114, article 18, Commentary, para. 15. Moreover, by the time the draft Statute for an International Criminal Court had reached the Diplomatic Conference in Rome (*supra* n. 13), 'enforced disappearance of persons' was listed among the crimes against humanity to be cognizable by the Court: UN doc. A/CONF.183/2/Add. 1 (1998), 25, 26.

[117] UN Declaration, *supra* n. 50; OAS Convention, *supra* n. 53.

slightly amended by the Commission on Human Rights Working Group,[118] the second sentence of the Sub-Commission draft was substantially amended. It had read: 'This provision shall apply regardless of the individual's nationality or the place where the offence was committed.'[119] The effect of this language would have been to affirm compulsory universal jurisdiction (in the sense of an obligation to try or extradite), as provided for in the Convention against Torture (see Chapter 4) and the Basic Principles on the Effective Prevention and Investigation of Extra-Legal, Arbitrary and Summary Executions (see Chapter 6).

The report of the Commission Working Group gives no reasons for the change, nor does it explain the evolution from the Sub-Commission text to the final text. Certainly, there were some states that were nervous about the idea.[120] It appears that the present wording is a compromise providing for 'permissive' rather than compulsory jurisdiction.[121] Indeed, it is language that any state wishing to exercise universal jurisdiction could convincingly invoke to refute a protest from, say, the state of the alleged perpetrator's nationality.

There is no direct case law to permit the analysis to be taken further. The case of Captain Astiz of Argentina was, it will be recalled, resolved inconclusively, because of his prisoner of war status (see Chapter 4). United States cases, building on the precedent of *Filártiga* v. *Peña-Irala* in respect of torture (also, Chapter 4), have found enforced disappearance, like torture, to be a 'tort . . . committed in violation of the law of nations'.[122] Any state wishing to exercise similar jurisdiction for the purposes of *criminal* prosecution, would have little juridical reason to feel inhibited in doing so.

INTERNATIONAL REMEDIES

When the General Assembly adopted resolution 33/173 of 20 December 1978 (see above), among the actions it called for were that the Secretary-General should 'continue his good offices in cases of enforced or involuntary disappearances of persons, drawing, as appropriate, upon the relevant experience

---

[118] Apart from syntactical restructuring, the only substantive amendment to the first sentence was the addition of the word 'civil'. This must be presumed to be aimed at addressing the problem of military and state security officials of many countries being subject to separate, military justice systems that had proven incapable of holding the relevant personnel accountable for atrocities performed in the course of a spurious 'duty'.

[119] UN doc. E/CN.4/Sub.2/1990/32, Annex.

[120] See Brody and González, *supra* n. 44, 391, where the authors cite the unwillingness of some states that a non-binding declaration require states 'to create new bases for personal jurisdiction in [their] domestic law'.

[121] Ibid., cf. Nowak, 'Monitoring Disappearances'; [1996] EHRLR 348, 351, footnote 18, who disagrees without explanation.

[122] e.g., *Xuncax et al.* v. *Gramajo*, 886 F Supp. 162 (D Mass., 1995).

of the International Committee of the Red Cross and of other humanitarian organizations'. Nothing in the debate indicated precisely what 'good offices' the Secretary-General had been exercising on the issue,[123] and it is in the nature of the practice that these 'good offices' remain largely in the confidential sphere. Valuable though the confidential action of the Secretary-General may be, it is fortunate that by 1980 the UN had a more structured and potentially more effective mechanism to begin to come to grips with the problem— this was the Working Group established by the Commission.

WORKING GROUP ON ENFORCED OR INVOLUNTARY DISAPPEARANCES

The background to the establishment of the Working Group has already been described, together with the competing views as to its powers. As will be seen below, these powers have so far been understood by the Working Group to be those of investigation or clarification of cases, rather than of denunciation of specific human rights violations. It is now intended to examine how the Working Group operates.

The scope of the Working Group's concern

The hallmark of the 'disappearance' is that the capture and detention of a prisoner remain unacknowledged by the official authorities whose agents have been directly or indirectly responsible for it. This was recognized by the Working Group from the beginning: it was concerned with cases where the government in question neither accepted responsibility for the arrest, detention, or abduction, nor accounted for these actions.[124]

The Working Group applied this test liberally. Thus, where 'disappeared' prisoners were subsequently found dead, the Group considered 'that cases in which a person's detention between his arrest and his death is not accounted for and his family have not known his whereabouts, do fall within its terms of reference'.[125] Such an incident would, of course, also be an extra-legal execution falling within the mandate of the Special Rapporteur on Summary or Arbitrary Executions (see Chapter 6). When the Working Group was first set up, the office of Special Rapporteur had not yet been established. In any event, until the appearance of a corpse there had been a 'disappearance'. Now the position is that '[i]f a case is clarified but contains information relevant to other thematic mechanisms of the Commission, it is transmitted to the mechanism concerned'.[126]

In one country the law appeared explicitly to permit the authorities to arrest certain categories of person and withhold not only details of the

---

[123] Note, however, that the Assembly had earlier requested the Secretary-General to provide his good offices to support the establishment of an international body to trace and account for missing persons in Cyprus: GA res. 32/128, 16 Dec. 1977.
[124] First Report, UN doc. E/CN.4/1435 (and Add. 1) (1981), para. 3. See generally of the Working Groups work, Nowak, *supra* n. 121.
[125] Id., para. 4.   [126] Sixteenth Report, UN doc. E/CN.4/1996/38, Annex I, para. 17.

person's whereabouts but also the fact of the arrest itself.[127] Although the Working Group was aware of no cases where this had definitely happened,[128] it made clear that it would not be deterred from exercising its functions merely because 'the State has equipped itself with a body of legislation which can ensure that, quite lawfully, a person may disappear without the relatives being able to obtain any information about him'.[129]

The Working Group has not felt it necessary to stipulate a particular lapse of time before someone presumed detained can be considered as 'disappeared'. This is doubtless because 'effective' action by the Group to prevent further abuse or death following the detention requires 'expeditious' action.[130]

General approach

The flexibility in the Working Group's understanding of the scope of its concern meshes well with its general humanitarian approach. The Group has consistently refused to exercise a judgemental role in reporting on its activities on particular countries. Thus, it pointed out that its first report 'does not contain pronouncements or attributions of responsibility'. Rather it had given prominence to a 'humanitarian approach' of seeking to 'help in discovering what has happened to the disappeared'.[131] The Group stressed this approach in its efforts to secure the co-operation of governments,[132] which it presumably sees as the best means of clarifying the facts and which it seems to feel is facilitated by the 'discretion' it is mandated to use.[133] The reports have repeatedly stressed 'the right [of the families] to learn what happened to their relatives'.[134] Furthermore, in 1994, the Working Group began to emulate the (then) novel practice of the Special Rapporteurs on Extrajudicial, Summary and Arbitrary Executions and on Torture in formulating observations on certain countries (see Chapters 5 and 6). These observations had the effect of moving the Group towards a more judgemental posture about the general situation in the country. It still refrains, like the analogous mechanisms, from making case-specific judgements.[135] However, the earlier language of humanitarian and non-accusatory or non-judgemental approach is notably absent from the Group's latest review of its methods of work.[136]

[127] *Supra* n. 124, para. 176 (South Africa).　　[128] Id., para. 175.
[129] Id., para. 183.
[130] The words in quotation marks are from the original Commission resolution establishing the Working Group's mandate, *supra* n. 33.
[131] First Report, para. 9.　　[132] Id., para. 7.
[133] Second Report, UN doc. E/CN.4/1492 (and Add. 1) (1981), para. 180.
[134] e.g., id., paras. 5 and 168.
[135] The observations are now made on countries 'with more than 50 alleged cases of disappearance, or where more than 5 cases were reported during the period under review': Seventeenth Report, UN doc. E/CN.4/1997/34, para. 20.
[136] Sixteenth Report, UN doc. E/CN.4/1996/38, Annex I.

Countries considered

As at the end of 1997, the Working Group had dealt with reports of 'disappearances' from 76 countries or territories, of which only 34 involved less than 10 cases. Of the remaining 42 countries, 22 had reported cases numbering over 100. Of these, there were over 500 cases in three countries: Chile (912), Iran (510), and Philippines (653), while over 1,000 cases were reported in Argentina (3,453), Colombia (1,006), El Salvador (2,661), Guatemala (3,151), Iraq (16,496), Peru (3,004), and Sri Lanka (12,208). Eight of the 22 countries in which over 100 cases were reported reflected a continuing or renewed practice into the 1990s from previous decades (Colombia, India, Indonesia, Iraq, Mexico, Peru, Philippines, and Sri Lanka), while the 1990s saw the introduction of the practice in Algeria, Russia, Sudan, and Turkey.[137] In 1997, the Working Group transmitted allegations in respect of 1,118 cases from 13 countries, not all of which concerned cases occurring in that year.[138]

Sources of information

Information reaches the Working Group from the broad range of sources envisaged by Commission resolution 20 (XXXVI) (see above): 'Governments, intergovernmental organizations, non-governmental organizations in consultative status with the Economic and Social Council, private organizations and relatives of missing persons'.[139] Eyewitnesses of various phases of 'disappearances' also supply information.[140] Clearly, unless the Working Group had been willing to give a generous interpretation to the term 'humanitarian organizations and other reliable sources',[141] it would have been deprived of the richest sources of information, which have been families, national private human rights organizations, and international NGOs.[142]

Despite the absence of anything dictated by the language of the resolution, the Group has developed a notion according to which its 'basic mandate . . . is to assist families in determining the fate and whereabouts of their missing relatives'.[143] In fact, its mandate is to examine and act effectively against enforced disappearance. Of course, an important criterion of success would be in the extent to which the plight of the families has been alleviated and their 'right to know' enhanced. But it is not clear why this is seen as the basic

---

[137] Eighteenth Report, UN doc. E/CN.4/1998/43, Annex II.   [138] Id., Annex I.

[139] First Report, *supra* n. 124, para. 44.   [140] Ibid.

[141] The wording is from the original Commission resolution establishing the Working Group's mandate: *supra* n. 33.

[142] The Tenth Report, UN doc. E/CN.4/1990/13, Annex I, lists 98 such organizations with which the Group has been 'in contact since its inception'; the 12th Report lists another 59 (E/CN.4/1992/18, Annex I); and the 14th Report lists a further 22 (E/CN.4/1994/26, Annex I). Many are national human rights organizations, several specifically dedicated to work for victims of 'disappearances' and their families.

[143] The language comes from the 16th Report containing the latest revised statement of the Group's methods of work: E/CN.4/1996/38, Annex I, para. 3.

element of the mandate. No doubt, it helped the Group sustain the non-judgemental posture referred to on individual cases. However, the Group has taken the further position that '[r]eports on disappearances are considered admissible . . . when they originate from the family or friends of the missing person'. As for other sources, such as non-governmental organizations, they are apparently merely conduits through which information may 'be channelled' and, indeed, they 'must be in a position to follow up with the relatives of the disappeared person concerning his [*sic*] fate'.[144] Again there is nothing in the above quoted language placing the families in such a privileged position or the other sources in such a subordinate position. Nor, in the difficult situations in which 'disappearances' typically occur, is the flow of information, even at the national level, likely to be as simple as the Group's stated position seems to expect. No doubt, in practice, the Group will apply its approach flexibly and experienced NGOs will know how to satisfy the Group, but it is inherently undesirable that an arbitrary mandate restriction be constructed and maintained without any textual support or demonstrated conceptual need.

Screening of information received/admissibility

In so far as the Working Group refrains from passing judgement on specific countries, it obviously does not need to be as scrupulous in its criteria for evaluating information as would be the case were it judgemental. Also, the nature of 'disappearances' is such as to make the gathering of evidence difficult. Further, to the extent that the Group is expected to act sufficiently promptly to prevent the persistence of a 'disappearance' (and the possibly grave consequences attendant on this), it must be prepared to act swiftly and perhaps on less evidence than were it required to come to a formal conclusion.

While the Group naturally seeks 'as many details as possible concerning the identity of the disappeared person and the circumstances of the disappearance', it insists only on the basic 'minimum elements' that would 'enable governments to carry out meaningful investigations'.[145] These are the name of the disappeared person, the date and place of the 'disappearance', an indication of the parties presumed to have held or continuing to detain the person, and information of steps taken to determine the fate or whereabouts of the person.[146] The latter element should not be understood as a formal requirement that domestic remedies be exhausted, but rather as aimed at confirming the fact of refusal to acknowledge the detention.[147]

---

[144] Id., para. 7.   [145] Sixteenth Report, UN doc. E/CN.4/1996/38, Annex I, para. 8.
[146] Ibid.
[147] In its Fifth Report, the Group had 'emphasized the need to exhaust local remedies' (UN doc. E/CN.4/1985/16, para. 78), but it does not continue to use that terminology.

274 'Disappeared' Prisoners

Transmittal of information

Information on cases fulfilling the Group's requirements is transmitted to the governments in question through their Permanent Representatives to the UN in Geneva 'with the request that they carry out investigations and inform the Group about the results'.[148] The Group reminds governments annually of unclarified cases.[149] It also forwards information in government replies to the original sources of information, inviting them to make observations or provide additional details.[150] Failure of the source to respond within six months in the face of governmental information purporting to clarify the case can result in the Group considering the case clarified.[151]

Country visits

One of the most important techniques of the Working Group is the country mission. Such missions take place on the 'invitation' of the government in question. The Group may take 'the initiative of approaching Governments with a view to carrying out visits to countries with a sizeable number of cases of disappearance'.[152]

So far it has visited, by invitation:[153] Mexico (1982),[154] Bolivia (1984),[155] Peru (1985 and 1986),[156] Guatemala (1987),[157] Colombia (1988),[158] Philippines (1990),[159] and Sri Lanka (1991 and 1992).[160] Such visits typically involve two or three members of the Group travelling to the country and having meetings with various branches of government, especially those at the operational level and senior political levels, representatives of the judicial and legislative branches. There will also typically be meetings with local NGOs and indeed witnesses and families. It is in the nature of such missions that the report will need to give an overall assessment of the situation. This makes it difficult credibly to maintain a non-judgemental posture. In its earlier missions, the Group's reports would tend to acknowledge a serious problem, but draw back from direct attribution of responsibility, though this appeared implicitly, not least through recommendations made to constrain the activities of the security forces allegedly implicated in the 'disappearances'. By the time of the Philippines mission the attribution of responsibility was direct, at

---

[148] Sixteenth Report, UN doc. E/CN.4/1996/38, Annex I, para. 10.   [149] Id., para. 13.
[150] Id., para. 14.   [151] Id., para. 15.
[152] Sixteenth Report, UN doc. E/CN.4/1996/38, Annex I, para. 23.
[153] It also undertook a visit (one member) at the request of the Commission's Special Rapporteur on the situation of human rights in the former Yugoslavia: UN doc. E/CN.4/1994/26/Add. 1.
[154] UN doc. E/CN.4/1492/Add. 1 (1982), paras. 2–9.
[155] Fifth Report, UN doc. E/CN.4/1985/15, paras. 51–67.
[156] UN docs. E/CN.4/1986/18/Add. 1 and E/CN.4/1987/15/Add. 1, respectively.
[157] UN doc. E/CN.4/1988/19/Add. 1.   [158] UN doc. E/CN.4/1989/18/Add. 1.
[159] UN doc. E/CN.4/1991/20/Add. 1.
[160] UN docs. E/CN.4/1992/18/Add. 1 and E/CN.4/1993/25/Add. 1, respectively.

least as regards the behaviour of the previous government of President Ferdinand Marcos.[161]

The Sri Lanka report of 1991 represented the final break with the earlier tendency. The Group pointed out that it had recorded a staggering 12,000 cases between 1983 and 1991[162] and that they 'rank as the best documented cases among those from the 40-odd countries appearing in the Group's annual reports'.[163] The report goes on to identify explicitly the army and the police as having been 'involved in disappearances', either directly or through '[d]eath squads, which given the circumstances could only have operated with the acquiescence of government forces'. It also considered implicated 'civil defence units, armed and trained by the army'.[164]

Thus, the country mission has emerged as an important means of exploring in depth and at first hand the reality of the practice of 'disappearance' in a country and the legal and institutional deficiencies that permit them to be practised. It is regrettable that not all countries from which the Group has solicited invitations have responded positively. At the beginning of 1997 the Group reported that it had sought invitations from India, which had 'not reacted positively', Iraq and Turkey, neither of which had responded at all.[165]

Immediate action

Perhaps the most important and, at the time, radical technique agreed upon by the Working Group, at its first session, was the adoption of a procedure for dealing with 'urgent reports . . . requiring immediate action'.[166] Specifically, where such reports were received between sessions of the Group, its chairman was authorized to transmit the reports to the government of the country concerned, inviting the government to respond with 'such information as it might wish'.[167] It based this decision explicitly on its mandate under Commission resolution 20 (XXXVI) to perform its functions 'in an effective and expeditious manner' and 'to respond effectively to information that comes before it'.[168] (The reports are usually faxed direct to the Foreign Minister.[169] The procedure applies to cases reported as being less than three months old and a reminder is sent if there is no clarification after six months.[170]) This was the first time that any UN body had been empowered to take action systematically and routinely in case of a feared violation of

[161] *Supra* n. 159, para. 159.
[162] *Supra* n. 160, para. 184.
[163] Id., para. 187.
[164] Id., para. 193.
[165] Seventeenth Report, UN doc. E/C.4/1997/34, para. 394. By the end of 1997 it reported that Turkey had agreed to a mission that was to take place in 1998; it was also discussing visits with Iran and Yemen, as well as a renewed visit to Colombia: 18th Report, UN doc. E/CN.4/1998/43, paras. 8–11. The Group was also represented (with the Special Rapporteurs on Extrajudicial, Arbitrary and Summary executions and on Zaïre) on a mission to the Eastern Congo that was not eventually permitted to enter the country: id., para. 12.
[166] First Report, *supra* n. 124, para. 30.
[167] Ibid.
[168] Ibid.
[169] Sixteenth Report, UN doc. E/CN.4/1996/38, Annex I, para. 11.
[170] Id., para. 13.

human rights, even where the threat was to life or limb. In its fifth report the Working Group announced that it had, since its creation, acted on 1,121 cases under what it was now calling its 'urgent action procedure'.[171] The Group had earlier drawn attention to statements 'which confirm that prompt international expression of concern can be effective in helping to clarify reports of recent disappearances'.[172] By the time it was reporting the total of 1,121, it noted that it had been possible 'to clarify 216 of those cases—a considerably higher percentage than the clarifications obtained on transmissions under the ordinary procedure'.[173]

The technique continues to be used by the Group. In the period covered by the eighteenth report (23 November 1996–21 November 1997), 141 appeals were made under the urgent action procedure.[174] The Group does not indicate what proportion of the 122 cases it deemed clarified were cases taken up under the urgent action procedure, nor in what year they were first taken up.[175] Accordingly, it is not possible to evaluate the present impact of the procedure.

Annual report

The annual reports of the Working Group, which are the source of the preceding information about the Group's methods of work, are also an integral part of that work. While maintaining its policy on not making judgements in individual cases, it has moved to a position of making judgemental observations on countries where a significant problem exists or has existed or appears to be arising.[176] It publishes informative annual statistical material on cases taken up country-by-country both in the year in question and since its founding.[177] It also publishes graphs on all countries in which there have been more than 100 cases since 1973.[178] The one omission that strikes the reader is the general absence of names of the alleged victims. While this may have been understandable in the Group's early days, when it had to deal with several countries where the problem ran into the thousands, as the Group dealt with cases arising in the 1970s before its creation, it is not clear why the practice should be continued. The use of names could contribute to making the problem seem less abstract and avoid the risk of appearing to perpetuate the very anonymity and depersonalization that is the terrifying hallmark of the enforced disappearance.

---

[171] Fifth Report, UN doc. E/CN.4/1985/15, para. 84.
[172] Third Report, UN doc. E/CN.4/1983/14, para. 13.   [173] *Supra* n. 148.
[174] Eighteenth Report, UN doc. E/CN.4/1998/43, para. 13.
[175] Id., Annex I.   [176] See *supra* n. 135 and accompanying text.
[177] e.g. 18th Report, UN doc. E/CN.4/1998/43, Annexes I and II respectively.
[178] Id., Annex III.

9

Conditions of Imprisonment or Detention

An attempt was made in Chapter 3 to understand the scope of the prohibition against torture or cruel, inhuman, or degrading treatment or punishment of prisoners. Most of the case law discussed in that chapter related to the issue of ill-treatment of prisoners in the period immediately following their arrest, seizure, or capture by the authorities, but preceding formal commitment to a period of pre-trial or post-conviction incarceration, or to institutionalized administrative internment.[1] That is traditionally the period during which prisoners, potentially at the mercy of their captors, tend to be most at risk of abuse; indeed, it is in recognition of this that some of the safeguards discussed below in Chapter 11 were developed. Once people so detained are handed over to a more formal institution of incarceration, the situation will usually change, not least because the personnel responsible for administering the institution will normally be different from those responsible for the initial detention and will not have the same objectives (obtaining information and confessions) as the officials effecting the original detention.

In this chapter it is intended to deal with the question of conditions of imprisonment after the period of initial detention, once the detained person has been formally committed to a place of pre-trial or post-conviction imprisonment (or to formal administrative internment). Nevertheless, it should be understood that torture and other ill-treatment is just as illegal when inflicted on prisoners formally deprived of their liberty as it is when inflicted at the time they are first arrested or captured. Furthermore, while most of the abuses described above tend to occur in the context of the interrogation phase, which is normally coextensive with the period of arrest or capture, this phase may in some cases intrude on the subsequent period of formal detention. Conversely, sometimes pre-trial detainees remain in the hands of the arresting authorities, usually the police, for a prolonged period, but not necessarily for purposes of interrogation.

THE LEGAL RULES

Much of what follows will continue to involve an examination of the scope of the prohibition of torture or other cruel, inhuman, or degrading treatment or punishment, with the accent on 'punishment'. It will be recalled from Chapter

---

[1] As to the lawfulness of which, see Chapter 11.

3 that among the purposes that article 1 of the Declaration against Torture (Annex 1) and article 1 of the UN Convention against Torture (Annex 2a) considered relevant in determining whether or not torture has been inflicted, is the purpose of 'punishing' a person. On the other hand, as was seen in Chapter 1, and will be further considered in Chapter 10, the Declaration against Torture excludes from the definition of torture 'lawful sanctions to the extent consistent with the Standard Minimum Rules for the Treatment of Prisoners'. Clearly then, a punishment which does not violate the Rules (to be considered below) cannot be seen as torture. As appears in Chapters 3 and 10, the UN Convention against Torture excludes altogether 'lawful sanctions' from the definition of torture. If the term 'lawful sanctions' were interpreted to mean lawful under national law (as opposed to lawful under international law—see Chapter 10) then no punishment carried out in accordance with domestic law would, at least for the purposes of the Convention, be capable of amounting to torture. The point is that most of what follows must be seen as elucidating the scope of 'other ill-treatment' rather than 'torture'. The implications of the distinction are discussed in Chapter 4.

In addition to the prohibition against torture or other ill-treatment, the International Covenant on Civil and Political Rights explicitly lays down the principle that prisoners are to be 'treated with humanity and with respect for the inherent dignity of the human person'. The American Convention on Human Rights has the same formula, with the omission of the words 'with humanity and', while the African Charter on Human and Peoples' Rights speaks of the right 'of every individual to the respect of the dignity inherent in a human being'.[2] The juridical status of this principle is more difficult to assess than is the status of the prohibition of torture and other ill-treatment (see Chapter 2). Article 10 of the Covenant, which contains the principle, is not among those from which no derogation is permitted, whereas the comparable rule in the American Convention on Human Rights forms part of article 5, which prohibits torture and other ill-treatment and from which no derogation is possible. The European Convention contains no analogous formulation. The question thus arises as to whether the principle is binding only on states parties to the Covenant, the American Convention, or the African Charter or whether it, like article 7 of the Covenant, reflects a rule of general international law. There are no conclusive indications of the answer, but statements of the Human Rights Committee point in the direction of the latter: in its first 'general comment' on article 10 the Committee points out that the article 'supplements article 7 as regards the treatment of all persons deprived of their liberty' and contains 'a basic standard of universal applica-

---

[2] International Covenant on Civil and Political Rights, article 10(1); American Convention on Human Rights, article 5; and African Charter on Human and Peoples' Rights, article 5; see Annex 9.

tion which cannot depend entirely on material resources'.[3] In parallel, the first general comment on article 7 similarly describes the article 7 prohibition as being 'supplemented by the positive requirement of article 10(1)'.[4] These statements suggest that the better view would be that the principle contained in article 10 of the Covenant (and article 5 of the American Convention) enunciates a rule of general international law.

INSTITUTIONAL ILL-TREATMENT

International law does not reject imprisonment as such,[5] except where incarceration is effected in violation of internationally recognized human rights and fundamental freedoms, for example, by way of infringement of freedom of expression.[6] Nor, in view of the present state of the world's prisons, does it demand a very high standard of treatment for prisoners. A reflection of this is seen in the unambitious title, 'Standard Minimum Rules for the Treatment of Prisoners', given to the main specialized UN instrument for dealing with this topic.

STANDARD MINIMUM RULES FOR THE TREATMENT OF PRISONERS

The first UN Congress on the Prevention of Crime and the Treatment of Offenders adopted the Standard Minimum Rules for the Treatment of Prisoners (SMR) in 1955. The text was endorsed by the Economic and Social Council (Ecosoc) two years later.[7] An additional article 95 was added in 1977 to ensure that persons arrested or imprisoned without charge should benefit from most provisions of the SMR.[8] After stating a basic principle of impartiality and non-discrimination (rule 6), the SMR (reproduced in Annex 3) sets

[3] Report of the Human Rights Committee, *GAOR*, 37th Session, Supplement No. 40 (1982), Annex V, general comment 9(16), paras. 2 and 3 respectively. Similar ideas are stated in the second general comment, with the word 'complements' replacing the word 'supplements': Report of the Human Rights Committee, UN doc. A/47/40 (1992), Annex VI B, general comment 21(44), paras. 3 and 4. Indeed, most of the Human Rights Committee cases referred to below which find violations of article 7 also find violations of article 10(1).

[4] Report of the Human Rights Committee, *GAOR*, 37th Session, Supplement No. 40 (1982), Annex V, general comment 7(16), para. 2. The second general comment on article 7 is similar, the prohibition in the article being '*complemented* by the positive requirements of article 10(1)': Report of the Human Rights Committee, UN doc. A/47/40 (1992), Annex VI A, general comment 20/44, para. 2 (emphasis added).

[5] Nevertheless, a prison sentence grossly disproportionate to the gravity of the offence may fall foul of the prohibition of ill-treatment: see Zellick, 'Human Rights and the Treatment of Offenders', in Andrews (ed.), *Human Rights in Criminal Procedure* (1982), 375, 381.

[6] Thus, the Human Rights Committee will not call for release in case of a violation of the prohibition of torture, but it will for violation of freedom of expression: e.g. *Weinberger* v. *Uruguay* (28/1978), Report of the Human Rights Committee, *GAOR*, 36th Session, Supplement No. 40 (1981), Annex IX.

[7] Ecosoc res. 663 C (XXIV), 31 July 1957.   [8] Ecosoc res. 2076 (LXII), 13 May 1977.

out rules relating to the maintenance of a register of prisoners (7), the separation of categories of prisoner (8), their accommodation (9–14), personal
hygiene (15–16), clothing and bedding (17–19), food (20), exercise and sport
(21), medical services (22–6), discipline and punishment (27–32), instruments
of restraint (33–4), information to and complaints by prisoners (35–6), contact with the outside world (37–9), access to books (40), religion (41–2), reten-
tion of prisoners' property (43), notification of death, illness, transfer, and so
on (44), removal of prisoners (45), institutional personnel (46–54), and
inspection (55). There are also sections dealing with specific categories of prisoner, namely, prisoners under sentence (56–81),[9] insane and mentally abnor-
mal prisoners (82–3), prisoners under arrest or awaiting trial (84–93), and
civil prisoners (94). As noted above, persons arrested or detained without
charge are the subject of additional rule 95.

The SMR is not *per se* a legal instrument, since Ecosoc has no power to legislate. Even when the General Assembly urges the implementation of the
SMR, it does not do so in such a way as to suggest that its pertinent resolutions are anything more than political or moral recommendations.[10] This is
hardly surprising: rule 2, referring to 'the great variety of legal, social, economic and geographical conditions of the world', admits that 'not all of the
rules are capable of application in all places and at all times'. It is no detrac-
tion from the political importance of the SMR to acknowledge their lack of
inherent legal status, since they constitute an important platform for the
activities worldwide of prison reformers.[11]

But the SMR are more than that, since some of their specific rules may also
reflect legal obligations. When rule 31, for example, states that 'corporal punishment, punishment by placing in a dark cell, and all cruel, inhuman or

---

[9] In this section, several articles deal with prison labour (arts. 71–6). Sentenced prisoners are
required to work (art. 71(2)), provided that the labour is not 'of an afflictive nature' (art. 71 (1)),
and subject to certain other conditions. In this respect, the SMR is consistent with the
International Labour Organization's (ILO) Forced Labour Convention, 1930 (No. 29), article 2,
para. 2(c), of which exempts such labour from its provisions prohibiting forced labour. The latter instrument is more stringent than the SMR in so far as the convicted person may not be 'hired
to or placed at the disposal of private individuals, companies or associations'. Compulsory
prison labour of non-convicted prisoners would clearly be incompatible with both instruments.
See also the ILO's Abolition of Forced Labour Convention (1957) No. 105, which commits states
parties to abolish compulsory labour 'as a means of political coercion or education or as a punishment for holding or expressing political views' (art. 1 (a)); normally there should be no need
to apply this to prisoners, as people imprisoned at all in such a connection would be so in violation of their right to freedom of conscience or expression. See generally, ILO, *General Survey of
the Reports relating to the Forced Labour Convention, 1930 (No. 29), and the Abolition of Forced
Labour Convention, 1957 (No. 105)—Report of the Committee of Experts on the Application of
Conventions and Recommendations (Articles 19, 22 and 35 of the Constitution)*—Volume B,
Report III (Part 4B), International Labour Conference, 65th Session, 1979, paras. 35 and
89–109.

[10] See GA res. 2858 (XXVI), 20 Dec. 1971. On other General Assembly resolutions, such as
the Universal Declaration of Human Rights or the Declaration against Torture, see Chapter 2.

[11] See Clifford, 'The Standard Minimum Rules for the Treatment of Prisoners', 66 *AJIL* 232
(1972) (American Society of International Law, Proceedings).

degrading punishments shall be completely prohibited as punishments for disciplinary offences', it does more than just state something desirable: it appears to be restating, in respect of corporal punishment and all cruel, inhuman, or degrading punishments, what has been seen to be a rule of international law (see Chapters 2 and 10); by association, the same might equally be said for the prohibition 'placing in a dark cell'. The same seems to be true for the punitive use of instruments of restraint, such as handcuffs, chains, irons and straitjackets, or any use of chains or irons (rule 33). For example, the use of bar fetters as a disciplinary punishment in prisons in Pakistan was a key concern of the Special Rapporteur on Torture when he visited the country in 1996.[12] He called for termination of their use.[13] Other rules are more easily seen as guidelines only: for example, rule 40, that requires a library 'adequately stocked with both recreational and instructional books'.

Although not every rule may constitute a legal obligation, it is reasonably clear that the SMR can provide guidance in interpreting the general rule against cruel, inhuman, or degrading treatment or punishment. Thus, serious non-compliance with some rules or widespread non-compliance with some others may well result in a level of ill-treatment sufficient to constitute violation of the general rule. The SMR can provide similar guidance in interpreting the general requirement of Covenant article 10(1) of humane treatment and respect for human dignity, as well as the specific requirement in Covenant article 10(3) which states that 'the penitentiary system shall comprise treatment of prisoners the essential aim of which shall be their reformation and social rehabilitation'.[14] The European Commission of Human Rights seemed to be taking a similar position when it decided to use the classifications contained in the SMR for the purposes of dealing with detention conditions in the *Greek* case.[15]

PRISON CONDITIONS IN THE *GREEK* CASE

The findings of the Commission in the *Greek* case provide a useful starting point for an examination of the 'guidance' role of the SMR, since these

---

[12] UN doc. E/CN4/1997/7/Add. 2 (1996), paras. 50–62, 95.

[13] Id., para. 104. The approach of the Human Rights Committee is unclear. In one case, it found that detention conditions involving the person being kept chained violated article 10(1): *Berry* v. *Jamaica* (330/1988), Report of the Human Rights Committee, Vol. II, *GAOR*, 49th Session, Supplement No. 40 (1994), Annex IX D, para. 11.2. In another, it found a violation of articles 7 and 10(1), but it is not evident what practices were relevant to each article: *Bozize* v. *Central African Republic*, id., Annex IX S, paras. 2.3, 5.2.

[14] In its second general comment on article 10, the Committee invited states to indicate in their reports to what extent they were applying *inter alia* the SMR: general comment 21(44), *supra* n. 3, para. 5. In its first general comment the Committee opined that there may also be a flexible threshold for the application of article 10(1), in so far as 'the modalities and conditions of detention may vary with the available resources', provided that they are applied on a non-discriminatory basis: general comment 9(16), *supra* n. 3, para 3.

[15] 12 *Yearbook of the European Convention on Human Rights—The Greek Case* (1969), 468.

findings constituted the first systematic application of the international standard to conditions of detention. Some thirty pages of the Commission's report in this case deal with the findings of its Sub-Commission, which findings it confirmed in respect of the conditions in four places of detention: the security police (*Asphalia*) headquarters in Athens (Bouboulinas Street) and in Piraeus, the Averoff prison in Athens, and the detention camps on the island of Leros. It found that article 3 of the European Convention on Human Rights had been violated by conditions of detention at the Bouboulinas Street premises, at the Averoff prison and at the Leros detention camps, but not at the Piraeus security police headquarters.

The most serious findings related to the basement quarters at Bouboulinas Street.[16] This was the building where the Commission had found that interrogation practices, including *falanga*, amounted to torture (see Chapter 3). When they were not being interrogated, most of the prisoners were kept in the basement area, which consisted of a central courtyard, three further rooms below the central courtyard, and an 'inner isolation block'. The central courtyard had an opaque roof permitting some light to enter, and around it were six cells, each about 1.90 × 1.10 metres, which appear to have been used as isolation cells. In a basement below the courtyard, with virtually no natural light, was the inner isolation block with fourteen cells of similar dimensions. Also below the courtyard were three rooms that apparently had an overall floor space of about 45 square metres. The Sub-Commission had difficulty in determining the numbers of prisoners, political or otherwise, kept in this accommodation. But it accepted the evidence of detainees as to overcrowding during part of 1967. This overcrowding appears to have meant that at least two people were held in very small cells normally used for solitary confinement, that at one time people were even allotted floor space outside the cells, and that at any one time the general basement area may have been inhabited by up to fifty political prisoners, in addition to unnumbered other criminal suspects. On certain occasions, all the prisoners would be pushed back into the underground rooms. Even the central courtyard area itself was described in a report of the International Committee of the Red Cross as 'totally unfit to live in, even for a short period. A veritable pit, it is covered with an almost opaque glass roof and has no ventilation.'[17] According to testimony it received, the Sub-Commission noted at least twenty-eight cases of an alleged detention lasting thirty days or more, including one of almost nine months.[18]

The Sub-Commission cited evidence 'showing that prisoners placed especially under "strict solitary confinement", usually for three days immediately

[16] 12 *Yearbook of the European Convention on Human Rights—The Greek Case* (1969), 468–80.
[17] Id., 469. The report was submitted by the Greek government. There were no prisoners in this area when the Sub-Commission visit took place.
[18] Id., 473.

after their arrest, were deprived of access to elementary sanitary facilities'.[19] They were kept alone for this period, without food. There were no beds or mattresses in the basement area, with only blankets, normally provided by relatives, permitted (often only after the first days of detention).[20] Medical treatment was often not provided on request, given belatedly despite medical instructions recommending urgent treatment, or given inadequately (prisoners were returned to detention within hours—sometimes less than an hour after transfer to a hospital or first aid station in a 'serious state').[21]

The Sub-Commission draws attention to two aspects of the denial to prisoners of contact with the outside world. First, it cites allegations that the security police refused to acknowledge the detention to the prisoners' families in one case for five days, in another for thirty.[22] The Commission was here dealing with a temporary 'disappearance' (see Chapter 8) before the practice had become generally identifiable. The second aspect is the refusal of visits by relatives over 'considerable periods'.[23] The Sub-Commission offers the illustration of one person who was not allowed a visit from his parents until after being held in solitary confinement for fifteen days.[24] Finally, the Sub-Commission notes that the solitary confinement cells in the basement area allowed prisoners hardly any form of recreation; there was no access to the open air; the cells were too small to permit exercise; and the lack of light virtually excluded reading.

The situation described above led both the Sub-Commission and the Commission to conclude that 'the conditions of detention in the basement and the circumstances in which persons have been detained in these cells, are contrary to Article 3 of the Convention'.[25] It did not explain which particular aspects of the conditions involved article 3 violations: while several may well have done, the accumulation of poor conditions was more than sufficient for its finding.

Similarly, no particular conditions were singled out as violations of article 3 with regard to the Averoff prison, in respect of which the Commission found the evidence to reveal 'a combination of conditions of detention of political offenders, which is unjustifiable and amounts to a breach of Article 3',[26] It referred specifically to 'the complete absence of heating in winter, the lack of hot water, the poor lavatory facilities,[27] the unsatisfactory dental treatment,[28] and the close restriction of letters and visits to prisoners'.[29]

---

[19] Id., 474.   [20] Id., 474–5.   [21] Id., 477–8.   [22] Id., 478.
[23] Ibid.   [24] Ibid.   [25] Id., 480.
[26] Id., 489; see Chapter 3 concerning the concept of 'justifiability' in relation to inhuman treatment and torture.
[27] Prisoners were kept locked in cells for 14 hours at a time (from 5.00 p.m.), thus having to use a pot in a cell during the period; id., 484.
[28] The treatment offered seems to have been limited to extraction: id., 485–6.
[29] As few as one visit and one letter per month; oppressive supervision of visits: id., 489.

The Commission also confirmed the findings of its Sub-Commission in respect of detention conditions at the deportation camps on the island of Leros. Here it is possible to obtain a more precise understanding of the Commission's concerns. The Sub-Commission found a violation of article 3 'in the conditions of gross overcrowding and its consequences'.[30] The conditions in question seem to have related mainly to the 'Lakki' camp, about which an International Committee of the Red Cross report, submitted by the government of Greece, is quoted as follows:

The camp . . . comprised two large buildings including one with four storeys.

The detainees are housed in dormitories of a present capacity of 100 to 150 persons. A number of smaller rooms are reserved for elderly detainees. Several beds have even been set up in the corridors. *Owing to the increase in numbers, overcrowding at Leros Lakki, at its present state, constitutes the gravest problems of all the deportation camps.* Because of this situation the ICRC representatives regard living conditions at the Leros-Lakki camp as unacceptable. They consider them likely to endanger, in a very short time, the physical and mental health of the detainee.[31]

The Sub-Commission, not having itself been granted access to the island, gives little detail of the 'overcrowding and its consequences' and was no doubt appropriately influenced by the strong language of the ICRC report which it had the rare opportunity of studying.[32]

It also considered that article 3 was violated 'in the extreme manner of separation of detainees from their families and in particular, the severe limitations, both practical and administrative, on the family visits'.[33] The 'extreme manner of separation' refers to the fact that it could take families in the provinces three to four days to reach the island for visits that were permitted only once every three months.[34] Practical limitations on such visits included the difficulty of travel and, for some families, the prohibitive expense of such travel.[35] The administrative limitations consisted of the restriction of the visit to a two-hour period and the presence of a guard.[36]

Duration of conditions

One factor that appears to be relevant to the Commission's attitude is the duration of the conditions. Thus, in considering the situation on the fourth floor of Bouboulinas Street, where the cells appear to have been 'acceptable as detention quarters' and not overcrowded by the time of the Sub-Commission's visit, it refrained from making a finding of an article 3 violation, despite the fact that 'the situation of the prisoners detained there has been seriously aggravated by overcrowding and the lack of proper washing

---

[30] 12 *Yearbook of the European Convention on Human Rights—The Greek Case* (1969), 497.
[31] Id., 494–5, emphasis in original.
[32] ICRC reports are confidential, unless the government in question makes them public.
[33] *Supra* n. 30, 497.   [34] Id., 493 and 496.   [35] Ibid.   [36] Ibid.

facilities'.[37] Similarly, in considering the Piraeus *Asphalia* it noted that the detention periods there were 'comparatively shorter than those at the *Asphalia* in 1 Bouboulinas Street'.[38] Thus, although isolation cells on the fourth floor of the Piraeus *Asphalia* were 'very small and without any light except such light as comes in through a grille in the door'[39] and although 'the general situation of the detention premises . . . hardly permits any form of recreation' and 'no form of outdoor exercise—even for short periods—is apparently provided for',[40] the Sub-Commission found no violation of article 3, 'subject . . . to the period of detention in [the isolation cells] being comparatively short'.[41]

PRACTICE OF THE EUROPEAN COMMITTEE FOR THE PREVENTION OF TORTURE

It is not intended here to give a detailed analysis of the practice of the European Committee for the Prevention of Torture (CPT).[42] This is because the CPT was not conceived of as having a condemnatory function, but rather to act preventively. It considers, according to its First General Report, that this means that its fact-finding task 'must be geared to *forestalling possible acts or practices* of torture or inhuman or degrading treatment or punishment'.[43] Thus, it seeks to ascertain whether 'there are general or specific conditions or circumstances that are likely to *degenerate into* [such treatment or punishment], or are at any rate conducive to such inadmissible acts or practices'.[44] It looks at general conditions of detention[45] and the historical, social, and economic context of detention,[46] and it considers long-term changes that may be needed.[47] A consequence of these considerations is that it aims 'at a degree of protection that is greater than that upheld by the European Commission and Court of Human Rights when adjudging cases concerning the ill-treatment of persons deprived of their liberty and their conditions of detention'.[48]

In its Second General Report, the CPT spelled out the standards it seeks to implement. They cover the whole range of issues addressed by the SMR and are couched in positive terms.[49] When the CPT finds inhuman or degrading conditions, it will often be as a result of an accumulation of factors. For instance, in three United Kingdom prisons, 'there was a pernicious combination of overcrowding, inadequate regime activities, lack of integral sanitation

---

[37] Id., 480.   [38] Id., 481.   [39] Ibid.   [40] Ibid.   [41] Ibid.

[42] The origins and functioning of the CPT are described in Chapter 5. For preliminary survey of its practice in relation to conditions of detention, see Evans and Morgan, 'The European Convention for the Prevention of Torture: 1992–1997', 46 *ICLQ* 663 (1997), 673–5.

[43] First General Report, Council of Europe doc. CPT(91)3, para. 45 (emphasis in original).

[44] Ibid. (emphasis in original).

[45] Id., para. 48.   [46] Id., para. 49.   [47] Id., para. 50.   [48] Id., para. 51.

[49] Second General Report, Council of Europe doc. CPT/Inf.(92)3, paras. 44–60.

and poor hygiene'.[50] This environment amounted to 'inhuman and degrading treatment'.[51] Its use of such terminology is not, however, systematic. This is appropriate given its non-adjudicatory function. Moreover, it may well wish to avoid the specific categorization if it feels that there is a genuine commitment by the authorities to remove the offending practices.

PRACTICE OF THE HUMAN RIGHTS COMMITTEE

Many of the early cases in which the Human Rights Committee found violations of Covenant article 7 (prohibiting 'torture or cruel, inhuman or degrading treatment or punishment' and, thus, analogous to article 3 of the European Convention on Human Rights) in respect of prison conditions were cases from Uruguay where the conditions were shocking by any standards. For example, in the case of Leopoldo Buffo Carballal,[52] whose testimony was accepted by the Committee, the prisoner was held without charge for over a year; after a period of interrogation, allegedly accompanied by torture,[53] he was held incommunicado, blindfolded, with his hands bound; his only food was a cup of soup in the morning and another at night; relatives were not allowed to bring food or medicine, despite the fact that he suffered from chronic diarrhoea and frequent colds. The Committee found that these conditions violated articles 7 and 10(1) of the Covenant.[54]

The conditions described above were essentially those of the pre-trial period, even though they lasted long after interrogation and even after Mr Buffo's release had been ordered. By contrast, the case of Carmen Améndola Massiotti confronted the Committee with conditions of post-conviction formal detention at two prisons. The Committee based its finding of inhuman treatment within the meaning of article 7 of the Covenant[55] on the following:

Until 1 August 1977 [that is, for nearly two years] she served her sentence at the women's prison 'Ex Escuela Naval Dr. Carlos Nery'. During the rainy period the water was 5 to 10 cm. deep on the floor of the cells. In three of the cells, each measuring 4m by 5m, 35 prisoners were kept. The prison had no open courtyard and the prisoners were kept indoors under artificial light all day. On 1 August 1977 [she] was transferred to Punta Rieles prison. There she was kept in a hut measuring 5m by 10m. The place was overcrowded with 100 prisoners and the sanitary conditions were insuf-

[50] United Kingdom, Council of Europe doc. CPT/Inf.(91) 15, para. 229.
[51] Ibid., also, Bulgaria, Council of Europe doc. CPT/Inf.(97) 1, para. 239; Romania, Council of Europe doc. CPT/Inf.(98) 5, para. 105; and Second General Report, *supra* n. 49, para. 50.
[52] *Buffo v. Uruguay* (33/1978), Report of the Human Rights Committee, *GAOR*, 36th Session, Supplement No. 40 (1981), Annex XI, paras. 2.3, 10, and 13.
[53] Id., para. 2.3; the Committee made no finding on this point as it occurred before the Covenant entered into force (i.e. before 23 Mar. 1976).
[54] Id., para. 13.
[55] *Améndola and Baritussio v. Uruguay* (25/1978), Report of the Human Rights Committee (1982), *supra* n. 3, Annex XVIII, para. 13. The Committee also found a violation of article 10(1) in this case.

ficient.[56] She was subjected to hard labour and the food was poor. The prisoners were constantly subjected to interrogations, harassment and severe punishment.[57]

Similarly, in the case of Elena Beatriz Vasilskis[58] the Committee found a violation of article 7 and of article 10(1) because she 'has not been treated in prison with humanity and with respect for the inherent dignity of the human person'.[59] This finding was made on the basis, *inter alia*, of the allegation that failure to perform her tasks led to punishment by solitary confinement for up to three months and prohibition of visits which were usually half an hour once every fifteen days[60] (see below).

Another Uruguayan case where prison conditions attracted a finding by the Committee of a violation of article 7 was that of Hiber Conteris. This was because he had been subjected to 'harsh and, at times, degrading conditions of detention'.[61] In addition to 'repeated solitary confinements',[62] these prison conditions seem to have involved his being 'held in the coldest part of the prison', despite the fact that he 'was plagued with severe rheumatism in his spine, which often prevented him from leaving his cell for a few minutes exercise when allowed'.[63]

Since the Uruguayan cases, the Committee has dealt with a substantial number of cases from other countries, but especially from prisoners (usually on death row) from Jamaica. In most of these it has found violations of articles 7 and 10(1), relying on uncontested and uninvestigated, but substantiated, claims by or on behalf of the alleged victim. The majority of those in which article 7 was found to have been violated concerned the infliction of beatings by prison warders. The violations are described as involving treatment that is, variously, 'cruel and inhuman',[64] 'cruel, inhuman and degrading',[65] 'degrading',[66] or simply unspecified.[67] There is no discernible pattern

---

[56] One washbasin and four toilets: id., para 1.3 (footnote from original).   [57] Id., para. 11.

[58] *Vasilskis v. Uruguay* (80/1980), Report of the Human Rights Committee, *GAOR*, 38th Session, Supplement No. 40 (1983), Annex XV.

[59] Id., para. 11.   [60] Id., para. 2.6.

[61] *Conteris v. Uruguay* (139/1983), Report of the Human Rights Committee, *GAOR*, 40th Session, Supplement No. 40 (1985), Annex XI, para. 10.

[62] Id., para. 9.2.   [63] Id., para. 1.6.

[64] *Sutcliffe v. Jamaica* (271/1990), Report of the Human Rights Committee, UN doc. A/47/40 (1992), Annex IX F, para. 8.6; *Linton v. Jamaica* (255/1987), Report of the Human Rights Committee, UN doc. A/48/40 (Part II) (1993), Annex XII B, paras. 2.6, 2.7, 8.5; *Hylton v. Jamaica* (407/1990), Report of the Human Rights Committee, Vol. II, *GAOR*, 49th Session, Supplement No. 40 (1994), Annex IX M, para. 9.3.

[65] *Collins v. Jamaica* (240/1987), Report of the Human Rights Committee, UN doc. A/47/40 (1992), Annex IX C, para. 8.7 (no reference to art. 10).

[66] *Francis v. Jamaica* (320/1988), Report of the Human Rights Committee, UN doc. A/48/40 (Part II) (1993), Annex XII K, para. 12.4; *Thomas v. Jamaica* (321/1988), Report of the Human Rights Committee, Vol. II, *GAOR*, 49th Session, Supplement No. 40 (1994), Annex IX A, para. 9.2; *Young v. Jamaica* (615/1995), UN doc. CCPR/C/61/D/615/1995 (1998), para. 5.2 (no reference to art. 10).

[67] *Francis v. Jamaica* (606/1994), UN doc. CCPR/C/57/WP.1 (1996), Annex X N, para. 9.2; *Stephens v. Jamaica* (373/1989), UN doc. CCPR/C/55/D/373/1989 (1995), para. 9.2; *Adams v.*

in the Committee's choice of characterization when finding beatings that violate article 7.

As regards other aspects of conditions of detention that the Committee has found to violate article 7, the overall approach seems to have been set in *Mukong* v. *Cameroon*:[68]

As to the conditions of detention in general, the Committee observes that certain minimum standards regarding the conditions of detention must be observed regardless of a State party's level of development. These include, in accordance with rules 10, 12, 17, 19 and 20 of the Standard Minimum Rules for the Treatment of Prisoners, minimum floor space and cubic content of air for each prisoner, adequate sanitary facilities, clothing which shall be in no manner degrading or humiliating, provision of a separate bed and provision of food of nutritional value adequate for health and strength. It should be noted that these are minimum requirements which the Committee considers should always be observed, even if economic or budgetary considerations may make compliance with these obligations difficult.[69]

This language reinforced the SMR as an aid to interpretation of the Covenant's provisions. How far non-compliance with each of the stipulated rules, as opposed to some combination of them, is central to the violation is left unclarified, as is the identification of the relevant Covenant provision (article 7 or 10). The facts of the case, as reported, do not assist clarification. While the Committee found 'cruel, inhuman and degrading treatment, in violation of article 7 of the Covenant',[70] it pointed out that 'apart from the general conditions of detention', the person had been 'singled out for exceptionally harsh and degrading treatment'.[71] The latter treatment included detention incommunicado for nearly one month, being threatened with torture and death, and being deprived of food and kept locked in a cell for several days without recreation.[72]

The other cases where conditions of detention were found to violate article 7 are too few to permit accurate prediction of further findings. Political opposition leader Primo Mika Miha from Equatorial Guinea was deprived of food and water for a week and, subsequent to severe ill-treatment, was denied medical attention for several weeks. This constituted 'cruel and inhuman treatment within the meaning of article 7' and a violation of article 10(1).[73] Two other cases involved prolonged partial isolation. In one, the person was held

---

Jamaica (607/1994), UN doc. CCPR/C/58/D/607/1994 (1996), para. 3.7; *Reynolds* v. *Jamaica* (587/1994), UN doc. CCPR/C/59/D/587/1994 (1997), para. 10.2. See also *Soogrin* v. *Trinidad and Tobago* (362/1989), Report of the Human Rights Committee, UN doc. A/48/40 (Part II) (1993), Annex XXI Q, para. 14; *Bozize* v. *Central African Republic, supra* n. 13.

[68] (448/1991), Report of the Human Rights Committee, Vol. II, *GAOR*, 49th Session, Supplement No. 40 (1994), Annex IX AA.

[69] Id., para. 9.3.   [70] Id., para. 9.4.   [71] Ibid.   [72] Ibid.

[73] *Mika Miha* v. *Equatorial Guinea* (414/1990), Report of the Human Rights Committee, Vol. II, *GAOR*, 49th Session, Supplement No. 40 (1994), Annex IX O, para. 6.4.

in isolation for 23 hours a day in a small cell, with no more than 10 minutes' sunlight a day.[74] In the other, what would have been an article 10(1) violation (being held alone in a cell measuring less than six square metres and let out for three and a half hours a day, without recreational facilities) was transformed into an article 7 violation 'because of the length of time' (10 years) during which the situation had persisted.[75] In another case, it is not possible to separate out the offending conditions of detention (being shackled, only allowed out of the cell twice a week, and deprived of reading material) from those of earlier maltreatment in identifying which of the two violated articles (7 and 10) applied to what treatment.[76] Moreover, as will be seen below, the Human Rights Committee has in numerous cases found violations of article 10(1) alone, where the facts do not seem to have been substantially dissimilar to those that have given rise to violations of article 7.

Prison conditions which violate human dignity

Article 10(1) of the International Covenant on Civil and Political Rights provides: 'All persons deprived of their liberty shall be treated with humanity and with respect for the inherent dignity of the human person.' This provision has its counterparts in the American and African conventions on human rights.[77] While violations of article 7 of the Covenant usually entail violations of article 10(1), the reverse is not always the case. A number of cases, all concerning prison conditions, have been found by the Human Rights Committee to involve violations of article 10(1) without reference to a possible violation of article 7. The conditions of concern in these cases fall roughly into two categories: incommunicado detention and the penitentiary environment. The former, though itself an important factor in the issue of prison conditions, will be dealt with in Chapter 11. As to the latter, there are four cases which concern general conditions in Uruguay's Libertad Prison.[78]

In the first of these the Committee, finding that David Alberto Cámpora Schweizer was detained 'under inhuman prison conditions',[79] cited Mr Cámpora's description of the treatment to which prisoners were subjected at Libertad Prison[80] where he was held for over two years:

He described the daily life of the prisoners, including their constant harassment and persecution by the guards; the regime of arbitrary prohibitions and unnecessary torments; the combination of solitude and isolation on the one hand and the fact of being constantly watched, listened to and followed by microphones and through peepholes on the other hand; the lack of contact with their families, aggravated by worries about

---

[74] *Polay Campos* v. *Peru* (577/1994), UN doc. CCPR/C/61/D/577/1994 (1998), para. 8.7.
[75] *Edwards* v. *Jamaica* (529/1993), UN doc. CCPR/C/60/D/529/1993 (1997), para. 8.3.
[76] *Bozize* v. *Central African Republic, supra* n. 13.   [77] *Supra* n. 2.
[78] Note the *Larrosa* case, *infra* n. 106, also concerned treatment at Libertad prison.
[79] *Cámpora* v. *Uruguay* (66/1980), Report of the Human Rights Committee, *supra* n. 58, Annex VIII, para. 19.
[80] Id., paras. 11, 17(5).

the difficulties experienced and pressures exerted on their families; the cruel conditions in the punishment wing in which a prisoner might be confined for up to 90 days at a time; the breakdown of physical and mental health through malnutrition, lack of sunshine and exercise, as well as nervous problems created by tension and ill-treatment. In sum, he asserts that the Libertad Prison is 'an institution designed, established and operated with the exclusive objective of totally destroying the individual personality of everyone of the prisoners confined in it.'

This is a summary description of an environment described in detail in the *Estrella* case,[81] in which the Committee made a similar finding.[82] These two findings are cited by the Committee in the two other cases in which it found article 10(1) violations at Libertad Prison.[83]

It is far from obvious how the Committee concluded that such conditions as violate article 10(1) do not also violate article 7. It may have been relevant that the conditions did not, at least explicitly include extreme overcrowding and the infliction of arbitrary and protracted solitary confinement, as had been the case above. Another case raises doubts about this explanation, however. Civil engineer Jorge Manera Lluberas was, according to the Human Rights Committee, a principal founder of the Movimiento de Liberacion Nacional-Tupamaros (whose urban guerrilla activities provoked the gradual military takeover in Uruguay in the early 1970s). The Committee found that:

from January to September 1976 he was held [at a military barracks—'Colonia'] where cells measure 1.6 × 2m, electric lights were kept continuously on, the only piece of furniture was a mattress provided at nights and where detainees had to remain in the cells 24 hours per day in solitary confinement. From September 1976 to August 1977 he was held at Trinidad prison, where the prison conditions were described by two witnesses as being characterized by dirty cells without light, without furniture, very hot in the summer and very cold in the winter. In April 1978, he was transferred to Colonia, where he was kept in complete isolation for six months . . .[84]

This led the Committee to form the view that Covenant article 10(1) had been violated because Manera had 'not been treated with humanity and with respect for the inherent dignity of the human person'.[85]

Later, non-Uruguayan cases have done little to clarify any borderline for the applicability of articles 7 or 10(1) in respect of conditions of detention. In one case, injuries from beatings by warders that the government had not jus-

---

[81] *Estrella* v. *Uruguay* (79/1980), id., Annex XII, paras. 1.10–1.15.   [82] Id., para. 10.

[83] *Estradet* v. *Uruguay* (105/1981), id., Annex XXI, para. 10.2; *Almirati* v. *Uruguay* (92/1981), id., Annex XX, para. 10.4; see also *Berterretche Acosta* v. *Uruguay*, Report of the Human Rights Committee, *GAOR*, 44th Session, Supplement No. 40 (1989), Annex X A. Comparable conditions of the Punta de Rieles political prison for women also elicited a Committee finding of an article 10(1) violation: *Arzuaga Gilboa* v. *Uruguay* (147/1983), Report of the Human Rights Committee, *GAOR*, 41st Session, Supplement No. 40 (1986), Annex VIII B, paras. 4.4, 14.

[84] *Manera* v. *Uruguay* (123/1982), Report of the Human Rights Committee, *GAOR*, 39th Session, Supplement No. 40 (1984), Annex XII, para. 9.2.

[85] Id., para. 10. For further examples of this inconsistent approach, see section on 'solitary confinement' below.

tified as being the result of the use of 'reasonable force' were only sufficient to attract an article 10 violation, despite the fact that many cases of beatings led to the Committee's finding a violation of article 7.[86] In *Griffin* v. *Spain*, the Committee found a violation of article 10(1),[87] 'in the light of the author's detailed account' of the conditions at Metilla prison. According to that account, Gerald Griffin was held in

a 500-year-old prison, virtually unchanged, infested with rats, lice, cockroaches and diseases; 30 persons per cell, among them old men, women, adolescents and an eight-month-old baby; no windows, but only steel bars open to the cold and the wind; high incidence of suicide, self-mutilation, violent fights and beatings; human faeces all over the floor as the toilet, a hole in the ground, was flowing over; sea water for showers and often for drink as well; urine-soaked blankets and mattresses to sleep on in spite of the fact that the supply rooms were full of new bed linen, clothes etc.[88]

According to the author, these conditions, which lasted for over seven months, amounted to cruel, inhuman, and degrading treatment and punishment.[89] It is not evident on what basis the Committee disagreed or could disagree.

In another case, having only a piece of sponge and newspapers to sleep on, with food described by the person as 'not fit for human consumption', and being treated with unspecified brutality by warders when he made complaints, led the Committee to find a violation of article 10(1).[90] The same article was violated where the offending facts consisted of a week in a 'filthy' police cell with seven other prisoners; being held on remand for nearly two years with convicted prisoners 'in a cell without basic sanitary facilities' and being in a death row cell that was 'dirty, smelly and infected [*sic*] with insects', being kept there all day 'except for five minutes to slop out and during visits, once a week for minutes'.[91] In one case, presenting little in the way of detail, the victim of the violation of article 10(1) had spent three months on remand in a small cell with six other occupants and had to sleep on newspapers on the floor.[92] Meanwhile, in a recent case, the denial of food for five days entailed an article 10(1) violation.[93]

It may well be that the Committee should not be understood as precluding the conditions described here from falling also within article 7 of the Covenant. It is virtually impossible to distinguish most of them from conditions where it *has* found a violation of article 7 (see above and some of the solitary confinement cases below). One is hard put to deny them at least the

---

[86] *Chaplin* v. *Jamaica* (596/1994), UN doc. CCPR/C/55/D/596/1994 (1995), para. 8.2.
[87] *Griffin* v. *Spain* (493/1992), UN doc. CCPR/C/57/WP.1 (1996), Annex X G, para. 9.3.
[88] Id., para. 3.1.   [89] Ibid.
[90] *Elahie* v. *Trinidad and Tobago* (533/1993), UN doc. CCPR/C/60/D/533/1993 (1997), para. 8.3.
[91] *Lewis* v. *Jamaica* (708/1996), UN doc. CCPR/C/60/D/708/1996 (1997), para. 8.5.
[92] *Blaine* v. *Jamaica* (696/1996), UN doc. CCPR/C/60/D/696/1996 (1997), para. 8.4.
[93] *Hill* v. *Spain* (526/1993), UN doc. CCPR/C/59/526/1993 (1997), para. 13.

description 'degrading'. The observer is left with the impression that it is sometimes easier for the Committee (which aims to operate by consensus) to agree on what may be considered the lesser violation so as to avoid internal disputes over the greater.[94] Even this assumes an intentional choice. Another explanation could lie in idiosyncrasies of the drafting process. A further possible factor lies within the constraints of the Committee's fact-finding powers. In most of the cases, it is relying on allegations made by the alleged victim. If the government does not effectively contest the allegations, the Committee may be disposed to find for the complainant, yet the information may be skimpy, or inarticulately presented (though this was hardly the case in *Griffin*). In such circumstances the Committee may prefer to find a less serious violation than it would if it were dealing with a well-documented, professionally drafted complaint that had been subjected to and had withstood a rigorous governmental challenge. Certainly, the Committee itself has offered no reasoned argument for its choice of article 10(1) rather than article 7 in these cases.

PRACTICE OF THE SPECIAL RAPPORTEUR ON TORTURE

As described in Chapter 5, the main focus of the work of the Special Rapporteur is the infliction of torture under interrogation. Prison conditions as such do not fall within the remit of the mandate. However, he has encountered on mission practices that he felt obliged to address, presumably because they fall into the 'grey zone' of his mandate, that is, practices that are on the borderline of torture and other ill-treatment (see Chapters 3 and 5).

For instance, in 1994 he received an unsolicited invitation to visit the Russian Federation. In his report of the visit, he described the conditions in 'general cells', measuring some six by twelve metres, holding from 80 to 130 prisoners, or four or five times their capacity,[95] in two remand centres in Moscow. The following extract provides a flavour of what he saw:

Despite having read critical reports and having received first-hand accounts of the conditions of detention in Moscow's Butyrskaya and Matrosskaya Tishina No. 1, the Special Rapporteur was unprepared for the appalling reality he encountered there. When the door to such a general cell is opened, one is hit by a blast of hot, dank, stinking (sweat, urine, faeces) gas that passes for air. These general cells may have one filthy sink and a tap, from which water does not always emerge, near a ground-level toilet around which the inmates may drape some cloth for a minimum of privacy and conceal the squalor of the installation. There is virtually no daylight from covered or

---

[94] One is tempted to speculate whether the identity of the victim in the *Manera* case might not have influenced the attitude of some Committee members. If so, this would be most troubling. The whole point about ill-treatment prohibited by article 7 is that nobody, however atrocious the acts he or she may have committed, may be subjected to such ill-treatment.

[95] UN doc. E/CN.4/1995/34/Add. 1, paras. 42, 53.

barred windows, through which only a small amount of fresh air can penetrate. Artificial lighting is weak and not always functioning.

Due to the overcrowding in the general cells visited at both Butyrskaya and Matrosskaya Tishina No. 1, there is insufficient room for everyone to lie down, sit down or even stand up at the same time. At Matrosskaya Tishina No. 1 the Special Rapporteur saw some detainees lying on the floor underneath the lowest bunk (about 50cm above the floor). All the detainess in these cells suffer from swollen feet and legs due to the fact that they must stand for extensive periods of time. The inmates tend to be half-clothed and are even stripped to their undershorts (at least in the summer, when the Special Rapporteur visited). Their bodies are perspiring and nothing can dry due to the humidity. Despite the existence of some medical and even hospital facilities (often without sufficient medicines), the general cells are the obverse of a hospital regime: they are disease incubators. Festering sores and boils abound; most if not all inmates suffer from skin diseases that cause pervasive itching.

The detainees in all preliminary detention centres are allowed only one hour a day to leave the cell to exercise. Once a week they are able to shower. The food—not always available because of the indebtedness of the institutions—is primitive, of a fat-saturated soupy nature. It is consumed in the cell and is excreted in the cell.[96]

His juridical assessment was that the conditions were 'cruel, inhuman and degrading'.[97] Describing them even as 'torturous', the only thing missing was proof of the purposive element required to justify a characterization of torture (see Chapter 3 above): 'To the extent that suspects are confined there to facilitate the investigation by breaking their wills with a view to eliciting confessions or information, they can be properly be described as being subjected to torture.'[98]

As already indicated, an area of the Special Rapporteur's concern during his 1996 visit to Pakistan was the use of bar fetters, particularly as a disciplinary measure.[99] Another was corporal punishment, used both as a punishment provided by law for criminal offences and as a disciplinary punishment in prisons.[100] He also addressed issues such as denial of medical attention and non-segregation of juveniles from adults.[101]

In another report, on his 1996 visit to Venezuela, he described overcrowding at *La Planta* prison in Caracas that was of an order similar to that described above for Moscow, also at *Sabenata* prison in Maracaibo, where, in addition to a sizeable overcrowding problem, the lack of control exercised by the authorities permitted the place to be described as 'anarchic'.[102] In both instances there had been outbreaks of violence leading to widespread loss of life.[103] There was no separation between convicted and unconvicted

---

[96] Id., paras. 43–5, and UN doc. E/CN.4/1995/34/Add.1/Corr.1, p. 2.   [97] Id., para. 71.
[98] Ibid.   [99] UN doc. E/CN.4/1997/7/Add. 2, paras. 50–62.
[100] Id., paras. 63–72. See Chapter 10 on the legality of corporal punishment.
[101] Id., paras 49 and 73–4.   [102] Id., paras. 58–73, 81.
[103] Id., paras. 68–70.

prisoners. The conditions were 'incompatible with the international prohibition of cruel, inhuman or degrading treatment or punishment'.[104]

To the limited extent that the practice of the Human Rights Committee may distinguish between cruel, inhuman, and degrading treatment, on the one hand, and conditions offensive to human dignity on the other, it would be unwise to compare the Committee's use of the former terminology with that of the Special Rapporteur. Apart from the fact that the latter notion does not fall within the Special Rapporteur's mandate, he has the dubious benefit of confronting the conditions at first hand, which inevitably has an impact that the written word (on which the Committee must rely) fails to convey.

SOLITARY CONFINEMENT

Rule 31 of the SMR prohibits 'punishment by placing *in a dark cell*, and all cruel, inhuman or degrading punishments' (emphasis added), a formula wherein 'placing in a dark cell' is likely to refer to a feature of solitary confinement. Rule 32 acknowledges the possibility of 'close confinement', provided that the medical officer has certified in writing that the prisoner can sustain it,[105] so it would appear that solitary confinement is not absolutely prohibited, but the rule goes on to say that 'in no case may such punishment be contrary to or depart from the principle stated in rule 31'. Thus it is acknowledged that, beyond certain limits, solitary confinement may amount to ill-treatment. Further, it is evident that prolonged solitary confinement may be incompatible with the provisions of the International Covenant on Civil and Political Rights. In another case the Human Rights Committee found a violation of articles 7 and 10(1) in terms similar to those given in the cases described above, at the Libertad prison in Uruguay:

Gustavo Larrosa has been frequently punished at prison and from October 1980 to March 1981 he was allowed to receive only one visit. He has also been held in what is called 'La Isla'—a prison wing of small cells without windows, where the artificial light is left on 24 hours a day and the prisoner was kept in solitary confinement for over a month.[106]

Similarly, the Committee found that articles 7 and 10(1) had been violated, 'because of the inhuman conditions in which Dave Marais, Jr., has been held in prison in Madagascar incommunicado since December 1979'.[107]

---

[104] UN doc. E/CN.4/1997/7/Add. 2, para. 81.

[105] The same applies to 'any other punishment that may be prejudicial to the physical or mental health of a prisoner'. This could raise problems of medical ethics—see Chapter 12. The term 'close confinement' is not defined, and, for the purposes of argument, it is being understood here as not precluding solitary confinement.

[106] *Larrosa* v. *Uruguay* (88/1981), Report of the Human Rights Committee, *supra* n. 58, Annex XVI, para. 10.3.

[107] *Marais* v. *Madagascar* (49/1979), id., Annex XI, para. 19.

Specifically, it concluded that 'in December 1979 Dave Marais was transferred from the Antananarivo Prison to a cell measuring 1m by 2m in the basement of the political police prison at Ambohibao and has been held incommunicado ever since [that is, over three years], except for two brief transfers to Antananarivo for trial proceedings'.[108]

Again, the 'total isolation' of Victor Polay Campos for a year, with restrictions on correspondence with his family was, for the Committee, 'inhuman treatment' under article 7, as well as a violation of article 10(1).[109]

Sometimes the Committee seems satisfied to invoke article 10(1) alone in solitary confinement cases. Thus, the Committee found a breach of article 10(1) because Teresa Gómez de Voituret, a medical doctor, who had been arrested in 1980 in Uruguay, 'was kept in solitary confinement for several months in conditions which failed to respect the inherent dignity of the human person'.[110] The conditions in question seem to refer to the fact that her cell was 'almost without natural light' and that she was not allowed to leave it.[111] Again, there must be doubt as to whether the Committee intended to exclude the possibility of article 7 being applicable here.[112]

The approach of the Committee to solitary confinement is probably summed up in a sentence of its general comment on article 7: 'Even such a measure as solitary confinement may, according to the circumstances, and especially when the person is kept incommunicado, be contrary to this article.'[113] More directly, in its second general comment on article 7, the Committee noted 'that prolonged solitary confinement . . . may amount to acts prohibited by article 7'.[114] Thus, it becomes a question of fact whether the particular form of solitary confinement amounts to a violation of article 7. One factor that may be relevant is whether the enforcement of isolation is more extreme than necessary to achieve reasonable disciplinary objectives or protection of the prisoner from other inmates. Another may be the extent to which, on the one hand, the decision to institute solitary confinement is arrived at by a controlled process of decision making or, on the other, is the

---

[108] Id., para. 17.4. See also *Wight* v. *Madagascar* (115/1982), Report of the Human Rights Committee, *GAOR*, 39th Session, Supplement No. 40 (1985), Annex VIII, which arose out of the same incident that led to the detention of Dave Marais: in Wight's case the ill-treatment, in many respects similar to that of Dave Marais, was aggravated as a result of a prison escape followed by his recapture. This led to a 3½-month period during which he 'was kept in a solitary room . . . chained to a bed spring on the floor, with minimal clothing and severe rationing of food' (para. 15.2). The Committee again found violations of Covenant articles 7 and 10(1).

[109] *Polay Campos* v. *Peru* (577/1994), UN doc. CCPR/C/61/D/577/1994 (1998), para. 8.6.

[110] *Gómez de Voituret* v. *Uruguay* (109/1981), Report of the Human Rights Committee, *supra* n. 57, Annex X, para. 13.

[111] Id., para. 12.2.

[112] It may be relevant that she was able to receive (supervised) visits from her mother every two weeks: id., para. 2.3.

[113] Report of the Human Rights Committee, *supra* n. 3, Annex V, general comment 7(16).

[114] General comment 20 (44), *supra* n. 3, para. 6.

result of arbitrary or even vindictive behaviour by the prison administration. Duration will be a key factor.

Given the diversity of these factors and the variety of combinations of which they are capable, the difficulty of specifying standards could help explain the reluctance of the European Commission of Human Rights to find cases of solitary confinement to be incompatible with article 3 of the European Convention, while nevertheless acknowledging its undesirability.[115] The point is well illustrated by the case of *Kröcher and Möller* v. *Switzerland*.[116] The applicants, who had been arrested 'after an exchange of gun-shots with . . . customs officers' (paragraph 16) and were suspected of 'having taken part in terrorist actions in the past' (paragraph 63), were locked up separately in two non-adjacent cells in the following conditions:

> There was no other prisoner on the same floor. The cells above and below theirs had been evacuated. Both applicants were soon placed under surveillance by closed-circuit television. A 60-watt lamp was continuously kept on in their cells. The cells were in every respect identical with the other cells of the Berne district prison except that the windows had been specially blocked to prevent the applicants from seeing outside. Artificial lighting was thus continuously necessary to make up for lack of daylight. [Paragraph 18.]

The prisoners were placed under the medical supervision of doctors and psychiatrists attached part-time to the prison. After a month the isolation regime was gradually eased (paragraph 69) and after two months, in response to medical advice that it was affecting the prisoners' sleep, the regime of constant artificial lighting was removed. The Commission concluded that there had been no violation of article 3, but a minority argued that the conditions in the first month were sufficient to find a violation of article 3. Clearly the element of time, combined with the element of medical supervision, were strong factors in influencing the Commission's view. The Commission reaffirmed the view stated in previous cases 'that complete sensory isolation coupled with total social isolation, can destroy the personality and constitutes a form of treatment which cannot be justified by the requirements of security or any other reason' (paragraph 62). In this case, however, the sensory isolation was not considered total, apparently because the cells had not been soundproofed (paragraph 66). The task of balancing humane treatment with exceptional security needs is a difficult one, but it seems that, for the Commission, the balance can tilt a long way towards security concerns before article 3 comes into play.

---

[115] See Duffy, 'Article 3 of the European Convention on Human Rights', 32 *ICLQ* 316, 329–35 (1983); Zellick, *supra* n. 5, 382–7; also Sudre, 'La Notion de "peines et traitements inhumains ou degradants" dans la jurisprudence de la Commission et de la Cour européennes des droits de l'homme', 88 *Revue générale de droit international public* 825, 872–8 (1984).
[116] Application No. 8463/78 (1983).

Certainly for the European Committee for the Prevention of Torture (CPT), '[s]olitary confinement can, in certain circumstances, amount to inhuman and degrading treatment; in any event, all forms of solitary confinement should be as short as possible'.[117] Thus, maximum security prisoners held in Spain for 'very long periods' (as much as a year or more) and 'subject to a regime of isolation' in 'austere material conditions of detention with little or nothing by way of activity' were subjected to 'inhuman treatment'.[118]

MEDICAL OR SCIENTIFIC EXPERIMENTATION ON HUMAN BEINGS

As has already been seen, Nazi atrocities of World War II have been the stimulus for much of the development of international humanitarian and human rights law. Nowhere is this clearer than in the international legal response to the medical and scientific experimentation forcibly conducted upon inmates of concentration camps.

Thus, the First and Second Geneva Conventions prohibit the subjection of protected persons to 'biological experiments' (common article 12).[119] Similarly, the Third Geneva Convention provides that no prisoner of war may be subjected 'to physical mutilation or to medical or scientific experiments of any kind which are not justified by the medical, dental or hospital treatment of the prisoner and carried out in his interest' (article 13).[120] The Fourth Geneva Convention gives the same protection to civilians in the hands of a party to the conflict (article 32).[121] All four Conventions specifically include 'biological experiments' within the category of acts of 'torture or inhuman treatment' that constitute 'grave breaches' of the Conventions,[122] that is, war crimes that are subject to universality of jurisdiction (see Chapter 4).

The provisions just mentioned apply in respect of situations of international armed conflict. Article 3 common to the four Geneva Conventions prohibits 'at any time and in any place whatsoever', with respect to persons in the hands of a party to a non-international armed conflict, 'violence to life and person, in particular murder of all kinds, mutilation, cruel treatment and

---

[117] Second General Report, *supra* n. 49, para. 56.

[118] Council of Europe doc. CPT/Inf.(96)9, Part I, para. 113.

[119] Geneva Convention for the Amelioration of the Condition of the Wounded and Sick in Armed Forces in the Field, 12 August 1949 (Geneva Convention I) and Geneva Convention for the Amelioration of the Condition of Wounded, Sick and Shipwrecked Members of Armed Forces at Sea, 12 August 1949 (Geneva Convention II).

[120] Geneva Convention Relative to the Treatment of Prisoners of War, 12 August 1949 (Geneva Convention III).

[121] Geneva Convention Relative to the Protection of Civilian Persons in Time of War, 12 August 1949 (Geneva Convention IV).

[122] Articles 50, 51, 130, and 147 respectively.

torture', as well as 'outrages upon personal dignity, in particular humiliating and degrading treatment'. While this language does not specifically refer to medical, scientific, or biological experimentation, it should be understood to cover these, since the language in the articles quoted above portrays such experimentation as a species of torture or inhuman treatment. Such an interpretation also follows from the meaning of the term 'cruel, inhuman or degrading treatment' as used in the international human rights instruments with which article 3 overlaps. This view is also taken by the official ICRC commentary on the Conventions, which notes that proposals to include reference to biological experiments were rejected in order to avoid the risk of narrowing the scope of the general principle; it was felt that this approach was especially desirable in a brief article designed precisely to lay down general principles.[123]

As noted in Chapter 3, the only specific example of 'cruel, inhuman or degrading treatment' clearly agreed upon by those who framed the Universal Declaration of Human Rights was involuntary human experimentation. Indeed, it was probably because of their concern to equate such practices with torture that they added the second limb to the prohibition against torture. Once the time came to draft a treaty on human rights that would contain provisions of greater specificity than was appropriate for the Declaration, there was an opportunity to include specific reference to human experimentation. Thus, article 7 of the Covenant adds to its prohibition of torture and other ill-treatment: 'In particular, no one shall be subjected without his free consent to medical or scientific experimentation.' The Covenant, then, like the Geneva Conventions, sees such human experimentation as a specific form of torture or other ill-treatment.[124] This means that not only are parties to the relevant treaties prohibited from engaging in the proscribed human experimentation, but that the obligation, like that incurred by torture or other ill-treatment (indeed, human experimentation is seen precisely as a manifestation of such treatment), is one of general international law binding on all governments (see Chapter 2).

Even though the status of the rule may be apparent, its scope is less clear, because the Geneva Conventions and the Covenant approach a single goal from different standpoints: the Geneva Conventions use medical criteria in order to test the lawfulness of any experiment: is it justified or necessitated for the medical welfare of the prisoner? The Covenant asks simply whether the

---

[123] Pictet (ed.), *Commentary—III Geneva Convention* (International Committee of the Red Cross, 1960), 39.

[124] The Human Rights Committee seems to have considered alleged involuntary psychiatric experiments as relevant to a finding of a violation of articles 7 and 10(1). According to the victim's unrefuted allegations, 'he was subjected to psychiatric experiments (giving the name of the doctor) and . . . for three years, against his will, he was injected with tranquilizers every two weeks'. *Viana Acosta* v. *Uruguay* (110/1981), Report of the Human Rights Committee, *supra* n. 84, Annex XI, paras. 2.7 and 15.

subject has agreed to the procedure in question. Thus the Geneva Conventions do not explicitly require the consent of the prisoner, but rely on the concept of medical necessity, while the Covenant requires only consent and does not explicitly consider necessity. No cases at the international level are known to have examined this point. In practice, it is to be hoped that both tests would apply simultaneously: experimental therapy should be used only as a last resort and as a matter of medical necessity, and in no circumstances should it be administered unless the patient, if capable of choosing, accepts it. (For such purposes a prisoner should be treated no differently from any other patient with medical problems.[125]) The matter of consent is especially important where the experimentation in question is aimed at changing the behaviour of convicted offenders so as to avoid repetition of the criminal behaviour or, still less justifiably, to maintain order in the penal institution. Such behaviour modification techniques[126] or enforced rehabilitation are especially open to abuse, even where prisoners do consent. Where they do not, they are illegal under international law.

The next problem is that of determining 'free consent'. This issue arises especially where the experimentation in question is not intended for the benefit of the particular subject, but for the advancement of scientific or medical knowledge in general. The very term 'free consent' suggests that the consent should not be just formal: it should be based on full information about the experiment and should be absolutely voluntary and free from any coercion or improper inducement (such as reduction of sentence, improvement of conditions, and so on). It must then be asked whether a detained or imprisoned person is ever capable of giving free consent so understood. Certainly, an international group of experts convened by the International Association of Penal Law (IAPL) concluded that the objective conditions of detention precluded the possibility,[127] even though in at least one country prisoners are

---

[125] The point seems to have been taken in the two Additional Protocols to the Geneva Conventions of 12 August 1949. Article 11(1) of Protocol I (international armed conflict) prohibits as regards persons in the power of an adverse party or who are deprived of liberty in connection with an international armed conflict 'any medical procedure which is not indicated by the state of health of the person concerned and which is not consistent with generally accepted medical standards which would be applied under similar medical circumstances to persons who are nationals of the Party conducting the procedure and who are in no way deprived of liberty'. Article 11(2) goes on explicitly to prohibit 'medical or scientific experiments' on such persons, 'even with their consent'; this is subject to an exception, i.e. where the acts 'are justified in conformity with the conditions' laid down in article 11(1). In any event, under article 11(5), the persons in question 'have the right to refuse any surgical operation'. Article 5(2)(e) of Additional Protocol II (non-international armed conflict) effectively follows article 11(1) of Additional Protocol I.

[126] These are techniques aimed at disordering and then restructuring the personality to conform to desired behaviour; see Zellick, *supra* n. 5, 384.

[127] Association Internationale de Droit Penal, 'Le Contrlôle de l'expérimentation sur l'homme', 51 *Revue internationale de droit pénal* 35–472 (1980).

invited to, and do, offer themselves for medical and pharmacological experimentation.[128]

The Human Rights Committee did not specifically clarify these points when dealing in its first general comment on article 7 with the second sentence of that article of the Covenant which concerns free consent in this context. Apparently concerned with potentially improper grants of consent on behalf of children or certain mentally handicapped persons,[129] the Committee merely observed that 'special protection in regard to such experiments is necessary in the case of persons not capable of giving their consent'.[130] However, in its second general comment on article 7, it took the view of the IAPL experts. It observed that:

special protection in regard to such experiments is necessary in the case of persons not capable of giving valid consent, and in particular those under any form of detention or imprisonment. Such persons should not be subjected to any medical or scientific experimentation that may be detrimental to their health.[131]

Thus, persons deprived of freedom are indeed not capable of giving valid consent. Accordingly, any potentially detrimental experimentation is ruled out, leaving, implicitly, only the possibility of using unproven techniques with a view to treating health problems when indicated for their medical benefit. Presumably they can, like anyone else, refuse consent.

OTHER AREAS OF POSSIBLE ABUSE OF PRISONERS

This chapter cannot hope to be exhaustive of the cruelties to which persons in the hands of unsympathetic detaining authorities may be subject. It has concentrated for the most part on areas that have been dealt with either by the relevant legal instruments themselves, or by the bodies charged with applying them. Three further areas of concern have received some attention:

PERSONS DETAINED ON MENTAL HEALTH GROUNDS

In the 1970s and 1980s, there was public concern at the manner in which persons could, without their consent, be formally confined in institutions for the mentally ill and, also against their will, be administered certain forms of treatment, such as use of mind-disorientating drugs or electroshock. This concern was aggravated by reports that such forcible confinement or treatment may

---

[128] Association Internationale de Droit Penal, 'Le Controle de l'experimentation sur l'homme', 51 *Revue internationale de droit pénal* 296–322 (USA).

[129] UN doc. CCPR/C/SR.371 (1982).   [130] *Supra* n. 3, general comment 7(16), para. 3.

[131] General comment 20/44, *supra* n. 3, para. 7. Here, the Committee was tracking the language of Principle 22 of the Body of Principles for the Protection of All Persons under Any Form of Detention or Imprisonment (see Annex 4 and Chapter 11).

be administered not because of a genuinely perceived medical problem, but for other motives, such as political repression.[132]

There is an evident distinction to be made between the compulsory detention and treatment in a mental health institution of a person of unsound mind and similar detention and treatment of a person of sound mind. The criteria of distinction include the purpose of the measures and the role of consent, express or implied. In the case of the mentally ill patient, the purpose is the benefit of the patient and consent ought to be sought from the patient, if capable of giving it, otherwise from a person who can reasonably be expected to represent the patient's best interests. In the case of a person of sound mind, however, such detention and treatment on non-medical grounds might well fall within the prohibition of torture or other ill-treatment. International bodies applying the relevant instruments have, for want of jurisdiction over the countries involved, notably the Soviet Union, not had to deal with such cases.[133]

The absence of specific international legal authority on the issue probably explains why the United Nations embarked on what was to be a fourteen-year process of drafting a set of principles concerning the detention and treatment of persons detained on grounds of mental ill health. The UN Commission on Human Rights had requested its Sub-Commission on Prevention of Discrimination and Protection of Minorities to undertake the task in 1977.[134] The Sub-Commission did not complete the task until 1988,[135] despite having the benefit of texts elaborated by the meetings of experts convened by the International Association of Penal Law and the International Commission of Jurists.[136] The Commission did further work on the text from 1989 to 1991, when it forwarded the finalized text, through Ecosoc, to the General Assembly[137] which adopted the 'Principles for the protection of persons with mental illness and the improvement of mental health care' by resolution

---

[132] See, e.g., UN docs. E/CN.4/Sub.2/SR.850, paras. 26–41; E/CN.4/Sub.2/1983/17 and Add. 1; and Amnesty International, *Prisoners of Conscience in the USSR: Their Treatment and Conditions* (2nd edn., 1980).

[133] The organs of the European Convention on Human Rights have dealt with cases where national law has provided inadequate safeguards against erroneous (as opposed to wanton) administrative decisions on the duration of detention, or on the appropriateness of the particular institution. See Duffy, *supra* n. 115, 335–6; also the later *Ashingdane* v. *United Kingdom*, European Court of Human Rights, Judgment of 28 May 1985, Series A, No. 93. The first Special Rapporteur on Torture listed among methods of torture '[a]dministration of drugs, in detention or psychiatric institutions': UN doc. E/CN.4/1986/15, para. 119.

[134] See Commission on Human Rights resolution 10 A (XXXIII), 11 Mar. 1977, Commission on Human Rights, Report, 33rd Session, *ESCOR*, 62nd Session, Supplement No. 6, Chapter XXI A.

[135] UN doc. E/CN.4/Sub.2/1988/23.

[136] International Association of Penal Law, *Protection of Persons Suffering from Mental Disorder* (1981); UN docs. E/CN.4/Sub.2/NGO/81 (1980) and E/CN.4/Sub.2/NGO/85 and 86 (1981).

[137] Res. 1991/46, 5 Mar. 1991, Commission on Human Rights, Report, 47th Session, *ESCOR*, 1991, Supplement No. 2, Chapter II.

46/119 of 17 December 1991. Given that the Soviet Union was the main culprit as regards the abuse of confinement on psychiatric grounds, it was perhaps no accident that the Sub-Commission was only able to complete its task after the period known by the terms *glasnost* (opening up) and *perestroika* (restructuring) had arrived under the presidency of Mikhail Gorbachev and that the Commission was also able to act so rapidly after the demise of the Soviet Union.

The principles indeed establish significant substantive criteria and procedural safeguards on 'involuntary admission'. Principle 16 requires that such admission of a person suffering from mental illness may only be in response to 'a serious likelihood of immediate or imminent harm to that person or to other persons' or to avoid 'a serious deterioration in his or her condition' or failure to give the 'appropriate treatment'. The decision may only be made by at least one qualified medical practitioner. Moreover, it must be only for 'a short period' until it is reviewed by a review body which, according to Principle 17, must be 'a judicial or other independent and impartial body, from which there is to be a further 'right to appeal to a higher court'.

By calling for and adopting principles on both detention and treatment of persons detained on grounds of mental ill health the UN is implicitly recognizing that 'the traditional claim . . . that involuntary admission must necessarily subsume forcible treatment'[138] is not acceptable and that special safeguards on treatment during detention are also necessary. Indeed, Principle 11 provides for a complicated set of such safeguards, starting from the presumption in favour of informed consent by the patient to treatment, even if involuntarily admitted. If the patient lacks the capacity to form such consent, then a personal representative or an independent authority must normally approve treatment. However, the criterion of 'immediate and imminent harm to the patient or to other persons', that is, the key criterion for involuntary admission, will also serve to justify the application of treatment on decision of a 'qualified mental health practitioner', but the treatment must 'not be prolonged beyond the period that is strictly necessary for the purpose' (Principle 11(8)). The possibility of abuse is further restricted by the provision that '[p]sychosurgery and other intrusive and irreversible treatment for mental illness shall never be carried out on . . . an involuntary patient' (Principle 11(14)).

The Principles do not have legal status *per se*, but acts incompatible with them could well be indicative of violations of the prohibition against torture or other ill-treatment or of the principle requiring prisoners to be treated with humanity and with respect for the inherent dignity of the human person.

---

[138] Gostin, 'Consent to Unusually Hazardous, Unestablished or Irreversible Treatments in Psychiatry: A Review of the Draft United Nations Guidelines for the Protection of Persons Suffering from Mental Disorder', in International Association of Penal Law, *supra* n. 136, 73, 74.

FORCIBLE FEEDING

The controversial and emotive issue of the forcible feeding of prisoners who are on hunger-strike is one wherein the infliction of painful treatment has not been clearly established as constituting prohibited ill-treatment, despite the refusal of consent.[139] No authoritative international body has had occasion to pronounce on the substance of the question. While the trend seems to be away from the application of forcible feeding of hunger strikers, some governments assert the right, indeed the obligation, to undertake it. In essence the argument is between two principles: respect for the moral autonomy of the prisoner, against the responsibility of the state for the fate of those it has deprived of liberty.

The ethical posture adopted by the World Medical Association in its Declaration of Tokyo (see Chapter 12), while offering guidance to medical practitioners, may well offer an appropriate general approach to the problem: a doctor should refuse to participate in forcible feeding as long as the prisoner is capable of forming an unimpaired and rational judgement concerning the consequences of refusal of nourishment (article 5). Ascertaining the nature of the prisoner's judgement would be a medical question for at least two doctors. The advantage of this approach is essentially that it reverts to respect for the rule of consent. Once the prisoner's judgement is no longer rational or unimpaired, then he or she is no longer in a position to withhold consent, thus entering a condition wherein a concept of presumed consent as proposed in Chapter 3 can be held to operate. At the least, such an approach is more easily reconciled with 'respect for the inherent dignity of the human person'[140] than is forcibly feeding a conscious and rational prisoner against his or her will.

SEPARATION OF CATEGORIES OF PRISONER

As has been seen, international human rights law has not generally developed specific rules relating to the details of a humane prison regime. The Standard Minimum Rules for the Treatment of Prisoners (SMR), an instrument which is not *per se* legally binding, is the main repository of international aspirations in this field (see above). However, in some respects provisions of the SMR are to be found in international legal instruments. This is especially so in the case of some of the rules relating to the separation of particular categories of prisoner. Article 10 of the Covenant is the key document, and the relevant provisions are also to be found in the American Convention on Human Rights (article 5), though not in the European and African regional human rights conventions.

---

[139] See Zellick, *supra* n. 5, 385.   [140] Covenant article 10(1): see above.

Thus, article 10(2)(a) of the Covenant provides that 'accused persons shall, save in exceptional circumstances, be segregated from convicted persons and shall be subject to separate treatment appropriate to their status as unconvicted persons'.[141] As the Human Rights Committee has pointed out, such segregation is related to the fact that unconvicted prisoners 'are protected by the presumption of innocence stated in article 14, paragraph 2' of the Covenant.[142] In two cases, the Committee has found violations of the provision.[143] So far there is no case law suggesting what 'exceptional circumstances' would justify departure from the rule. In addition, juvenile prisoners, whether accused or convicted, are to be kept separate from their adult counterparts.[144] Subject to certain exceptions, in the interests of the child, this is also the approach of the almost universally ratified UN Convention on the Rights of the Child.[145]

LEGAL CONSEQUENCES OF UNLAWFUL TREATMENT

Where the treatment or conditions referred to in the foregoing amount to violations of the prohibition of torture or other ill-treatment, the legal consequences for such violations have been considered in Chapter 4. In particular it will be recalled that, in respect of unlawful human experimentation, not only may there be state responsibility for the acts in question, the individuals involved in carrying them out may also be liable to trial, possibly without geographical limitation on jurisdiction.

It only remains to consider the legal consequences of those acts that are not considered to amount either to torture or to other cruel, inhuman, or degrading treatment or punishment, but still violate the rule that prisoners are to be treated with humanity and with respect for the inherent dignity of the human person. There is insufficient authority at this stage for a definite conclusion. In one early case where the Human Rights Committee found a violation of article 10(1), it confined itself to expressing the view 'that the state party is under an obligation to take immediate steps to ensure strict observance of the provisions of the Covenant and in particular to extend to [the victim] treat-

---

[141] This corresponds to SMR rules 84(2) and 85(1).

[142] General comment 9(16), *supra* n. 3, para. 8. See also general comment 21 (44), id., para. 9.

[143] *Berry* v. *Jamaica* (330/1988), Report of the Human Rights Committee, Vol. II, *GAOR*, 49th Session, Supplement No. 40 (1994), Annex IX D, para. 11.2; *Griffin* v. *Spain* (493/92), UN doc. CCPR/C/57/WP.1 (1996), Annex X G, para. 9.4

[144] Articles 10(2)(b) and 10(3); corresponding to SMR rules 85(2) and 8(d). See also United Nations Rules for the Protection of Juveniles Deprived of their Liberty, GA res. 45/113, 14 Dec. 1990, especially Rules 28 and 29. The Human Rights Committee has invited states to indicate whether they are applying the Rules: general comment 21(44), *supra* n. 3, para. 13.

[145] GA res. 44/25, 20 Nov. 1989, art. 37c. There are 191 states parties to the Convention, including all UN members except Somalia and the United States.

ment as laid down for detained persons in article 10 of the Covenant'.[146] The Committee is silent on the issue in its general comments to article 10.[147] However, in recent cases it has called for an effective remedy, including compensation.[148] Given the seriousness of the treatment that can violate article 10(1), it is suggested that the approach of requiring compensation for the victim of its violation is the only appropriate response. The Inter-American Commission on Human Rights would have no reason to distinguish between the rules of humane treatment and the prohibition of torture and other ill-treatment, as they are contained in the same article 5; and indeed its practice offers no guidance. Accordingly, any international legal consequences at the universal level for a violation of the Covenant article 10(1) standard would not necessarily involve the attribution of individual responsibility to the relevant personnel, nor would they necessarily require a state to go beyond the provision of compensation to a victim of the violation. They would, of course, require termination of the violation.

INTERNATIONAL REMEDIES

In so far as there are special international procedures relating to the prohibition of torture or other ill-treatment, these have been described in Chapter 5. Of especial note is the existence of the European Committee for the Prevention of Torture and Inhuman or Degrading Treatment or Punishment, the first international body whose central focus is the issue of conditions of detention. Work is at present under way on establishing a similar mechanism at the universal level. Further, in May 1984, on the recommendation of the Committee on Crime Prevention and Control, Ecosoc approved a set of 'procedures for the effective implementation of the Standard Minimum Rules for the Treatment of Prisoners'.[149] Several of the procedures deal with the need to adopt the SMR at the national level and to disseminate them (procedures 1–4). Others would have the Secretary-General disseminate the SMR (procedure 7) and encourage their use in UN programmes of technical co-operation (procedures 9 and 10).

[146] *Estradet* v. *Uruguay, supra* n. 83, para. 11. In other early cases where it is possible to isolate the article 10(1) aspect of its views it has tended to call for the prisoner to be 'treated with humanity': for example, *Martinez* v. *Uruguay* (83/1981), Report of the Human Rights Committee, *supra* n. 84, Annex VII, para. 14; *Gómez de Voituret* v. *Uruguay* (109/1981), id., Annex X, para. 15; *Manera* v. *Uruguay* (123/1982), id., Annex XII, para. 11.

[147] *Supra* n. 3.

[148] e.g., *Griffin* v. *Spain* (493/1992), UN doc. CCPR/C/57/WP.1 (1996), Annex X G, para. 11; *Blaine* v. *Jamaica* (696/1996), UN doc. CCPR/C/60/D/696/1996 (1997), para. 10; *Lewis* v. *Jamaica* (708/1996), UN doc. CCPR/C/60/D/708/1996 (1997), para. 10; *Ellahie* v. *Jamaica* (533/1993), UN doc. CCPR/C/60/D/533/1993 (1997), para. 10.

[149] Ecosoc res. 1984/47, 25 May 1984. See Bassiouni, 'The U.N. Procedures for the Effective Implementation of the Standard Minimum Rules for the Treatment of Prisoners', in Herzberg (ed.), *Festschrift für Dietrich Oehler* (1985), 525.

Of particular interest here is procedure 5, which requires states to report to the Secretary-General every five years on 'the extent of the implementation and the progress made with regard to the application' of the SMR. In preparing his reports, the Secretary-General may enlist the co-operation of certain intergovernmental organizations and non-governmental organizations (NGOs). The request for governments to provide information on a five-yearly basis is not new: indeed it dates from the adoption of the SMR by Ecosoc in 1957.[150] What is new is the explicit role for NGOs, several of which will be in a position to provide relevant information that, it may be assumed, will not appear in the information supplied by governments. By procedure 8, the Secretary-General is to disseminate the reports prepared on the basis of this information. Procedure 11 provides for the Committee on Crime Prevention and Control to 'follow up the present implementing procedures, including periodic reporting under procedure 5'.

The latest report summarized responses from seventy-two countries.[151] In fact, the Commission on Crime Prevention and Criminal Justice, the intergovernmental body successor to the expert Committee on Crime Prevention and Control, devotes only one day of its annual sessions to discussion of responses to a cluster of Secretariat reports on questionnaires on different 'norms and standards'. This does not permit any detailed consideration of particular countries' responses. The Secretariat had recommended the establishment of a 'sub-group' for the purpose, but the Commission did not act on it.[152] Nevertheless, responses were to be placed on the World Wide Web database facility of the United Nations Crime and Justice Information Network.[153]

The report of the Secretary-General could become a useful focus for the analysis of information on the extent of non-compliance with the SMR. As such, it is a notable development in respect of a document whose formal status is no more than that of a recommendation.

SUMMARY

The rule prohibiting torture and ill-treatment was examined in previous chapters largely in the context of the treatment of prisoners when first detained. It can also apply to conditions of detention after formal commitment to pre-trial or post-conviction detention. Another rule found in the Covenant and in two of the three regional human rights conventions (not in the European

---

[150] Ecosoc. res. 663 C (XXIV), 31 July 1957.
[151] UN doc. E/CN.15/1996/16/Add.1, para. 2.
[152] UN doc. E/CN.15/1996/16, para. 103c.
[153] Draft Ecosoc res. VI, Commission on Crime Prevention and Criminal Justice, Sixth Session, Report, UN doc. E/1997/30, p. 93.

Convention on Human Rights) requires prisoners to be treated with 'respect for the inherent dignity of the human person'. In addition, there are the Standard Minimum Rules for the Treatment of Prisoners (SMR) which, though not a legal instrument, can afford guidance interpreting the legal norms.

In the *Greek* case, the European Commission of Human Rights found several violations of article 3 (prohibiting torture or other ill-treatment or punishment) at Bouboulinas Street (a combination of severe overcrowding, incommunicado detention for up to thirty days, no access to open air, limited light, no possibility for exercise, these conditions lasting up to nine months), also at Averoff prison (a combination of no heating in winter, lack of hot water, poor lavatory facilities and dental care, close restriction of letters and visits to prisoners), and at the Leros detention camps (gross overcrowding and extreme separation of detainees from their families). Without indicating precise time limits, the Commission considered the duration of the bad conditions relevant to its findings.

Most findings by international bodies involve a combination of factors, such as overcrowding, prolonged solitary confinement, confinement within cells without any or much activity outside the cell, and poor sanitation facilities. The first two may, by themselves, amount to prohibited ill-treatment under certain circumstances. Of course, brutal treatment by prison personnel will offend the prohibition.

Medical experimentation applied without the consent of the prisoner is a flagrant violation of the norm against torture or ill-treatment, as well as a violation of an explicit term of article 7 of the Covenant. International humanitarian law applicable to international armed conflict expressly requires any such experimentation to be justified by the medical needs of the prisoner. It has been argued that this should also apply to the basic human rights standard, since consent to experimentation for other purposes (for example, advancement of science) cannot genuinely be freely given in a prison context.

Compulsory detention on mental health grounds is recognized as necessary, subject to safeguards that have been developed. In any event, consent should be considered to be required either from the patient or, in case of incapacity, from someone acting in the patient's interests. Such compulsory detention does not automatically entail compulsory treatment. Here again, safeguards have been developed which include the same element of consent.

Unless it is administered so as to cause unnecessary suffering, forcible feeding has not so far been established to be prohibited by international law. Medical ethics require doctors to respect the will of the hunger striker as long as the latter's judgement is rational and unimpaired. Finally, accused persons must normally be kept separate from convicted prisoners, and juvenile prisoners kept separate from adult prisoners.

The legal consequences for violation of the prohibition of torture or ill-treatment are described in Chapter 4. The legal consequences for a violation of the principle of respect for the inherent dignity of the human person have not yet become clear, beyond the obvious requirement that any continuing violation should cease and, probably, be compensated.

Despite the fact that the SMR is not a legal document, Ecosoc has approved a set of procedures to promote its implementation, including a reporting procedure on states' compliance with it. NGOs can contribute to this procedure and it may be hoped that the resultant information which is to appear on the relevant UN website will give a clearer picture than heretofore about observance in practice of the SMR.

10

Corporal Punishment

Corporal punishment differs in a number of ways from the practices discussed in earlier chapters. Unlike torture, extra-legal executions, and 'disappearances', it is a practice which is carried out by way of application of national law, rather than in violation of it. In this respect it is similar to capital punishment, but whereas the latter is a penalty found in the laws of a majority of countries, corporal punishment appears to be comparatively rare. Moreover, it is not a practice that has attracted widespread public attention, or sustained examination by international organizations, governmental or non-governmental. Nor does there appear to be any systematic academic research of a comparative nature that would help to clarify either the number of countries where the law provides for the infliction of physical punishments or the incidence of such infliction in practice.[1]

Nevertheless, international law does deal with the question. Not only is corporal punishment expressly prohibited by the Geneva Conventions in respect of persons in the hands of a party to an international armed conflict, but there is also weighty evidence to suggest that it is illegal under international human rights law. After a brief assessment of the geographical scope of the practice, followed by a report of the rare occasions upon which it has been considered by the General Assembly and other United Nations bodies, the question of its legality under the humanitarian law of armed conflict will be examined. The relevant law, consisting mainly of human rights instruments and the pronouncements of the organs charged with their supervision, will then be analysed with a view to determining the legal status of corporal punishment in circumstances other than those of armed conflict.

THE GEOGRAPHY OF CORPORAL PUNISHMENT

Given the dearth of research material on corporal punishment, the following remarks must be regarded merely as the impressions of an interested observer. The predominant impression is that the use of corporal punishment persists in only a few areas of the world. Few states go as far as those whose consti-

---

[1] Note, however, Amnesty International French Section Medical Group, *Corporal Punishment—a Study on Legislation and Enforcement in 18 Countries* (February 1992); see also (and generally) Bennoune, 'A Practice Which Debases Everyone Involved': Corporal Punishment under International Law', in 20 *Ans consacrés à la réalisation d'une idée* (Association pour la Prévention de la Torture, Geneva, 1997) 203, 204–5 and *passim*.

tutions expressly prohibit 'flogging' (Argentina).[2] Nevertheless corporal punishment is foreign to the modern penal systems of most states.

The main categories of exception appear to be some former British colonies and some states where *shari'a* (Islamic law) is practised. Swaziland is an example of the first category, its legislation permitting caning of minors for certain offences.[3] Saudi Arabia is an example of the latter category: under its interpretation of the *shari'a*, corporal punishment is prescribed in certain circumstances. Thus, amputation of limbs is the normal penalty for theft above a certain value (*Satiqa*) and may be the penalty for brigandage or highwaymanship (*Hiraba*), and flogging is prescribed for adultery (*Zena*), false accusation of adultery or other sexual misbehaviour (*Bhadf*), and drinking alcohol (*Shorh al-Khamr*). Further, where the offender has inflicted physical injury on the victim, the law of retribution (*Quesas*, a version of the *lex talionis*) permits the victim to require the infliction of identical harm on the offender. Resort to punishments which antedate the rise of the modern penitentiary system is undergoing a revival in parts of the Islamic world, as a symptom of the resurgence of Islamic fundamentalism.[4] Until recently, Pakistan, which falls into both of the categories defined above, had sentenced people to be flogged for a wide variety of offences, including peaceful expression of dissent, even though this penalty is not necessarily required even by the sternest interpretation of Islamic law.[5] However, the Abolition of Whipping Act 1996, removes corporal punishment, described as 'violative of human dignity', as a punishment for non-*shari'a*-based offences. This leaves intact their applicability for the offences contemplated by *shari'a*, as well as, apparently, for disciplinary offences in prisons.[6]

In Europe, systematic resort to corporal punishment has been held to be a post-feudal development, occurring as crime came to be seen more as an offence against the state than as a wrong committed against an individual, and as the state came to be more closely identified with a small propertied class needing to defend itself against the unlawful depredations of a large unpropertied class.[7] The development of alternative forms of punishment, especially imprisonment, led to the slow obsolescence and eventual abolition of corporal punishment.[8] It was still practised in an autonomous part of the United Kingdom, however, until the late 1970s (see below), but by that time it had been abandoned in the rest of Western Europe, including the mainland United Kingdom. Few if any Latin American states, juridically the products of the eighteenth-century Enlightenment, know corporal punishment.

[2] Quoted in Ackerman, 'Torture and Other Forms of Cruel and Unusual Punishment in International Law', 11 *Vanderbilt Journal of Transnational Law* 653 (1978), at 691.
[3] See *Corporal Punishment, supra* n. 1.
[4] See, generally, Bassiouni (ed.), *The Islamic Criminal Justice System* (1982).
[5] See, for example, Amnesty International, *Report 1983*, 222–3.
[6] Visit by the Special Rapporteur (on Torture) to Pakistan, UN doc. E/CN.4/1997/7/Add. 2, paras. 63–72.
[7] Weisser, *Crime and Punishment in Early Modern Europe* (1979), 100–1 and 130–2.
[8] Id., 133–42.

UNITED NATIONS ACTIVITIES CONCERNING
CORPORAL PUNISHMENT

In its early years the UN was reluctant to consider human rights issues arising within the jurisdiction of its members, these being considered as matters 'essentially within [their] domestic jurisdiction'.[9] It did, however, find itself dealing with such issues, including that of corporal punishment, in connection with its supervisory powers over the 'international trusteeship system' established under the Charter.[10] One of the 'basic objectives' of this system was 'to encourage respect for human rights and for fundamental freedoms for all'.[11] Thus, the Trusteeship Council, one of the principal organs of the UN,[12] was able to deal with human rights in trust territories. In a number of these territories provision for corporal punishment obtained: the Cameroons (UK), New Guinea (Australia), Ruanda-Urundi (Belgium), Tanganyika (UK), and Togoland (UK); that is, half of the ten territories in the international trusteeship system at the beginning of 1950.[13] In New Guinea corporal punishment was not in fact practised;[14] in the Cameroons and Togoland it was applicable strictly as a judicial punishment; in Ruanda-Urundi and Tanganyika it applied both as a judicial sanction and as a disciplinary measure.[15] In 1948 a Visiting Mission to East Africa had also found in Ruanda-Urundi 'illegal and arbitrary whipping' to compel obedience.[16]

In 1949 the General Assembly, by a resolution invoking only the 'basic objective' of furthering human rights, gave 'full support to the recommendation of the Trusteeship Council that corporal punishment should be abolished immediately in the Cameroons and Togoland under British administration and that corporal punishment should be formally abolished in New Guinea'.[17] The situation in Tanganyika had not been brought before the Council when it drew up its report. Presumably motivated by the Visiting Mission report, the same resolution recommended 'the adoption of strong and effective measures to abolish immediately the corporal punishment of whipping in Ruanda-Urundi'. The Assembly, at its next two sessions, maintained its concern with the issue,[18] albeit with diminishing insistance on

---

[9] UN Charter, article 2(7).

[10] UN Charter, article 75. The trusteeship system was designed to place a number of non-self-governing territories under the administration of another power. Although this acknowledged a quasi-colonial status, the administering power was placed under the supervision of the UN Trusteeship Council.

[11] UN Charter, article 76.   [12] UN Charter, article 7(1).

[13] *Yearbook of the United Nations* (1950), 7.

[14] *GAOR*, Fourth Session, Supplement No. 4 (1949), 66.

[15] *GAOR*, Sixth Session, Supplement No. 4, part II (1951), 47–8,73–4, 120–1, 171–2.

[16] *GAOR*, Fourth Session, Supplement No. 4 (1949), 96.

[17] GA res. 323 (IV), 15 Nov. 1949. Part of the Cameroons and Togoland were under French administration and did not have corporal punishment.

[18] GA res. 440 (V), 2 Dec. 1950; and 562 (VI), 18 Jan. 1952.

immediacy in view of the administering powers' expressed commitment to abolition as soon as possible.

The General Assembly did not specify which human rights issue or issues are raised by the practice of corporal punishment, but statements by the two sponsors of the 1950 resolution left no room for doubt. According to the representative of the Philippines, 'the joint draft resolution postulated . . . the belief, held by all civilized peoples, that corporal punishment was a cruel and inhuman form of State redress for criminal offences'.[19] For the representative of Cuba, it was a question of applying a basic principle of the UN Charter: 'One of those principles, respect for human rights, had been embodied in the Universal Declaration of Human Rights, article 5 of which provided that no one should be subjected to torture or to cruel, inhuman or degrading punishment.'[20]

Another instance of UN concern with corporal punishment was when South Africa began, in the early 1970s, the handing over to 'tribal authorities' of supporters of the South-West Africa Peoples Organization (SWAPO), the Namibian liberation movement recognized by the Organization of African Unity and the UN. These 'tribal authorities', applying what was claimed to be traditional tribal justice, administered public floggings to suspected members and supporters of SWAPO. As a rule the victims were detained without trial by the South African authorities and then handed over to the 'tribal authorities' in Ovamboland which administered the floggings 'with hardly the pretence of a trial'. According to the UN Council for Namibia, 'the floggings generally leave the victims bleeding and unconscious'.[21] An *ad hoc* working group of experts of the Commission on Human Rights gathered extensive evidence of these practices[22] and concluded that the flogging 'is contrary to African tribal custom and tradition and all international standards of human rights and treatment of prisoners'.[23] Calling for the adoption of suitable resolutions by international bodies and for pressure from friendly third-party states, it advocated measures 'aimed at bringing this cruel and barbaric form of punishment to an end'.[24] In response, the Commission on Human Rights deplored 'that public floggings have become a shocking feature of the punishment of opponents of the *apartheid* policy'[25] and requested the UN Commissioner for Namibia to expose the practice. In fact, the latter had already issued a press release denouncing the refusal of a Windhoek court to intervene in such cases.[26] Naturally, this denunciation was in reaction to a

---

[19] *GAOR*, Fifth Session, Fourth Committee, Summary Records, A/C.4/SR.172, para. 11 (1950).
[20] Id., para. 26.
[21] *GAOR*, 29th and 30th Sessions, Supplement No. 24 (1974), paras. 34–9.
[22] UN doc. E/CN.4/1159, paras. 260–71 (1975).
[23] Id., chapter V B 1 (26).   [24] Id., chapter V B 2 (40).
[25] Res. 5 (XXXI), 14 Feb. 1975, Commission on Human Rights, Report, 31st session, *ESCOR*, 58th Session, Supplement No. 4 (1975), Chapter XXIII.
[26] UN Press Release NAM 102, 28 Mar. 1974.

combination of factors: the persecution of dissidents by what the UN considered to be an illegal regime; the absence of a fair trial for the prisoners; and the abuse of the concept of 'traditional customs', as well as to the flogging itself. But it was the last-mentioned that provoked the revulsion.

A later manifestation of UN concern with the issue of corporal punishment arose at the 1984 session of the Sub-Commission on Prevention of Discrimination and Protection of Minorities. The International Commission of Jurists and Amnesty International spoke of the practices of the 'decisive justice courts' in Sudan.[27] According to Amnesty International, '58 sentences of amputation had been imposed and at least 34 had been carried out in the past eight months'.[28] Disabled People's International observed that 'torture, cruel, inhuman or degrading treatment were often closely related to disability—for example, amputation of limbs as a criminal sentence . . .'.[29] The issue was taken up by Zambian Sub-Commission member Mr Mubanga-Chipoya: 'With regard to Sudan, he would simply observe . . . that no rule of law or religious principle, including rules that might draw on the Islamic religion could justify barbarous actions such as amputation.'[30]

Mr Mubanga-Chipoya later evidenced his repugnance at the practice by introducing a draft resolution[31] by which the Sub-Commission would appeal to the government of Sudan 'to cease the infliction of amputations and to remove this cruel penalty from its legislation'.[32] A number of Sub-Commission members questioned the appropriateness of challenging Islamic law, of judging internal penal policies, of relying on the information concerning the Sudan they had so far received, or of singling out the Sudan for special condemnation.[33] Taking account of the last of these points, Mr Mubanga-Chipoya introduced a revised text[34] which, after an essentially procedural debate, the Sub-Commission adopted.[35] By this resolution 1984/22 of 29 August 1984, the Sub-Commission, without mentioning any country by name, noted 'the existence in various countries of legislation or practices providing for the penalty of amputation' and recommended that the Commission on Human Rights 'urge the Governments, which have such legislation or practices to take appropriate measures to provide for other punishment consonant with article 5 [of the Universal Declaration of Human Rights]'.[36] While the Commission did not act on the Sub-Commission's urging at its next

[27] UN doc. E/CN.4/Sub.2/1984/SR.23, paras. 34–9 and paras. 44–8 respectively.
[28] Id., para. 46. [29] UN doc. E/CN.4/Sub.2/1984/SR.24, para. 13.
[30] UN doc. E/CN.4/Sub.2/1984/SR.25, para. 63.
[31] UN doc. E/CN.4/Sub.2/1984/SR.34, para. 86. [32] UN doc. E/CN.4/Sub.2/1984/L.26.
[33] UN doc. E./CN.4/Sub.2/1984/SR.34, paras. 83–104; see also UN docs. E/CN.4/Sub.2/1984/ SR.25, paras. 58–60, and SR.26, paras. 10–13, 28–36.
[34] UN doc. E/CN.4/Sub.2/1984/SR.35, paras. 1–2.
[35] Id., paras. 3–41. The vote was 10 for, 5 against, and 9 abstentions: at para. 41.
[36] Report of the Sub-Commission on Prevention of Discrimination and Protection of Minorities, 37th Session (E/CN.4/1985/3; E/CN.4/Sub.2/1984/43), Chapter XVIII A.

session in 1985, we are left with the formal view of the Sub-Commission that legislation and practices providing for the penalty of amputation are not 'consonant with' article 5 of the Universal Declaration.

Most recently, the matter arose as a general issue at the United Nations Commission on Human Rights. In 1996, the Government of Saudi Arabia challenged the practice of the Special Rapporteur on Torture (see chapter 5) of taking up cases of judicial corporal punishment.[37] The Special Rapporteur accordingly addressed 'the conceptual issues raised by the relationship of the practice' of corporal punishment with his mandate in his annual report to the Commission at its 53rd Session in 1997.[38] The response of the Commission in a resolution adopted without a vote was that it '[r]eminds Governments that corporal punishment can amount to cruel, inhuman or degrading punishment or even to torture'.[39]

This is a decidedly clearer and more vigourous statement even than that of the Sub-Commission. The only question it leaves open is what forms of corporal punishment might not amount to cruel, inhuman, or degrading punishment. While not conclusive of the matter, it is understood that the language that appears to leave intact some forms of corporal punishment is explicable by a desire to leave open the matter of corporal punishment in schools, an issue beyond the purview of this book and not addressed by the present chapter. If that is all the corporal punishment that the Commission considers not prohibited then its line is consistent with the argument made in this chapter.

INTERNATIONAL HUMANITARIAN LAW

The Geneva Conventions of 12 August 1949 are unambiguous in their prohibition of corporal punishment of protected persons in time of *international armed conflict*. The Third Geneva Convention[40] prohibits it in respect of prisoners of war in the following terms: 'collective punishments for individual acts, corporal punishments, imprisonment in premises without daylight and, in general, any form of torture or cruelty, are forbidden' (article 87). The article containing this rule is one of a series of 'general provisions' under the heading 'Penal and Disciplinary Sanctions'. Accordingly it applies both to judicial proceedings and to other proceedings relating to the maintenance of discipline among prisoners of war. The formulation is such that corporal punishment is presented as a specific form of the general category of torture or cruelty.

[37] UN doc. E/CN.4/1997/7/Add. 1, para. 435.   [38] UN doc. E/CN.4/1997/7, paras. 3–11.
[39] Resolution 1997/38, 11 Apr. 1997, Commission on Human Rights, Report, 53rd Session, *ESCOR*, 1997, Supplement No. 3, Chapter II A, para. 9, repeated in resolution 1998/38, para. 3.
[40] Geneva Convention Relative to the Treatment of Prisoners of War of 12 August 1949 (Geneva Convention III).

The language of article 32 of the Fourth Geneva Convention[41] is different. Having prohibited 'any measure of such a character as to cause the physical suffering or extermination of protected persons', the article specifies that the rule applies 'not only to murder, torture, corporal punishments, mutilation and medical or scientific experiments not necessitated by the medical treatment of a protected person, but also to any other measures of brutality whether applied by civilian or military agents'. The specific outrages with which corporal punishments are grouped suggest a categorization similar to that contained in the Third Geneva Convention, despite the differences in formulation. Article 32 applies both to aliens in the territory of a party to the conflict and to civilians in occupied territory, unless the aliens in question are nationals of a state not party to the Convention or of a co-belligerent or neutral state.

The prohibition on corporal punishment is repeated in article 75, paragraph 2 of Additional Protocol I to the Conventions. This more recent and less widely ratified instrument[42] applies to a wider range of armed conflicts.[43] Furthermore, article 75 in particular applies to all persons in the hands of a party to the conflict, 'insofar as they are affected' by an international armed conflict as defined by article 1 of the Protocol.

Thus, the infliction of corporal punishment on prisoners of war or on protected civilians would involve a clear breach of state responsibility by a party to the Geneva Conventions and, given their wide ratification, possibly also by a non-party under general international law as evidenced by the Conventions. So would the same acts committed by a party to the Protocol in respect of persons covered by it, who might not otherwise be covered by the Conventions.

The question arises as to whether the infliction of corporal punishment would entail a 'grave breach' of the Third and Fourth Geneva Conventions within the meaning of articles 130 and 147 respectively. These include 'torture or inhuman treatment, including biological experiments, wilfully causing great suffering or serious injury to body or health . . .'. If, as argued above, the language of article 87 of the Third Convention and article 32 of the Fourth Convention suggests that corporal punishment is a form of torture or inhuman treatment, then its infliction would amount to a grave breach. In any event, where it was inflicted so violently as to cause 'great suffering or serious injury to body or health', then it would *ipso facto* be a grave breach. The implication of this is that anyone involved in committing the practice

---

[41] Geneva Convention Relative to the Protection of Civilian Persons in Time of War of 12 August 1949 (Geneva Convention IV).

[42] The Protocol was adopted in 1977 and there are, at the time of writing, 150 parties to it. There are 188 parties to the Geneva Conventions.

[43] Article 1. See Chapters 4 and 6 for further explanation of the Geneva Conventions and their Additional Protocols.

would be individually liable to trial and punishment by the authorities of any party to the Convention.[44]

As far as *non-international armed conflict* is concerned, article 3 common to the four Geneva Conventions makes no specific reference to corporal punishment. It prohibits 'at any time and in any place whatsoever . . . violence to life and person, in particular murder of all kinds, mutilation, cruel treatment and torture' as well as 'outrages upon personal dignity, in particular, humiliating and degrading treatment'. It would be possible to argue from the language of other parts of the Convention referred to above and from the evolution of international human rights law discussed below that corporal punishment is embraced by this prohibition.

No doubt obtains in respect of Additional Protocol II to the Conventions, which 'develops and supplements' common article 3 (article 1). Its article 4 contains 'fundamental guarantees' of 'humane treatment' and specifies as prohibited acts 'any form of corporal punishment'. This formulation may well suggest that article 3 itself now has to be interpreted to include the prohibition of corporal punishment, regardless of whether or not a state has adhered to the Protocol. The position of the 142 states at present parties to the Protocol could not be clearer.

INTERNATIONAL HUMAN RIGHTS LAW

International human rights instruments mostly do not address themselves explicitly to the question of corporal punishment as a judicial sanction. This is so for the Universal Declaration of Human Rights, the International Covenant on Civil and Political Rights, and the regional human rights conventions.[45] However, as far as corporal punishment for disciplinary offences in prison is concerned, there is strong authority for the proposition that international law rejects this.

The UN Standard Minimum Rules for the Treatment of Prisoners (SMR) provides in its rule 31: 'Corporal punishment, punishment by placing in a dark cell, and all cruel, inhuman or degrading punishments shall be completely prohibited as punishments for disciplinary offences' (see Annex 3). These Rules were first adopted in 1955 by the First UN Congress on the Prevention of Crime and the Treatment of Offenders, endorsed by the

---

[44] Geneva Convention III, article 129 and Geneva Convention IV, article 146 respectively.

[45] An inroad has been made by the UN Standard Minimum Rules for the Administration of Juvenile Justice ('The Beijing Rules'), contained in GA res. 40/33, 29 Nov. 1985, Annex, and adopted on the recommendation of the Seventh United Nations Congress on the Prevention of Crime and the Treatment of Offenders. According to rule 17.3: 'Juveniles shall not be subject to corporal punishment.' The definition of juvenile is left to national practice.

Economic and Social Council (Ecosoc) in 1957,[46] and subsequently commended for implementation by the General Assembly in 1971;[47] they are more fully discussed in Chapter 9. The SMR is not *per se* a legal document. Indeed, it stipulates that 'not all of the rules are capable of application in all places and at all times' (rule 2). This is inevitable in a document that seeks to cover the broad range of factors conducing to a humane prison environment. Nevertheless, the peremptory and absolute language of rule 31 gives it an impact that some of the other rules may not have. Moreover, like the relevant articles of the Geneva Conventions, it appears to place corporal punishment in the general category of 'cruel, inhuman or degrading punishment', a category of practice whose illegality is clearly established (see Chapter 2). Rule 31 of the SMR could therefore be offered as evidence of authoritative interpretation of the scope of such prohibited punishment.[48] The especial concern of General Assembly resolution 562 (within its overall concern about corporal punishment in trust territories) for the complete abolition of corporal punishment 'as a disciplinary punishment in all prisons of the Trust Territories', discussed above, may also be pertinent.[49]

Given the lack of explicit reference in the general human rights instruments to corporal punishment as a judicial sanction, here also it is necessary to turn to the concept of cruel, inhuman, or degrading punishment. The approach of the General Assembly in dealing with the trust territories, of the Sub-Commission in dealing with amputations, of the Commission in respect of corporal punishment generally, and of the Geneva Conventions has already been noted. In 1972 the *Tyrer* case,[50] brought before the European Commission of Human Rights, provided the opportunity to test the compatibility of judicially ordered whipping with article 3 of the European Convention on Human Rights, which prohibits 'torture or inhuman or degrading treatment or punishment'.

A schoolboy, Anthony Tyrer, was convicted by a juvenile court in the Isle of Man, a self-governing territory of the United Kingdom, of unlawful assault, occasioning actual bodily harm, on another schoolboy. He was sentenced to three strokes of the birch, a sentence carried out by a police officer in the presence of a doctor. Tyrer petitioned the European Commission of Human Rights, arguing that his punishment was in violation of article 3.

---

[46] Ecosoc res. 663 C (XXIV), 31 July 1957. Originally intended for persons imprisoned on remand or after conviction, they were in large part extended to cover detention without judicial order—by new rule 95, adopted by Ecosoc res. 2076 (LXII), 13 May 1977.

[47] GA res. 2858 (XXVI), 20 Dec. 1971.

[48] See also, in respect of persons below the age of 18, the analogous rule 67 in the United Nations Rules for the Protection of Juveniles Deprived of their Liberty: GA res. 45/113, 14 Dec. 1990.

[49] GA res. 562 (VI), 18 Jan. 1952.

[50] *Tyrer v. United Kingdom*, Application no. 2856/72, Report of the European Commission of Human Rights, 14 Dec. 1976: European Court of Human Rights, Series B, No. 24, 10.

On the merits of the case, the Commission concluded, with one dissenting opinion (Mr Mangan), that 'judicial corporal punishment constitutes a breach of Article 3 of the Convention and, consequently, its infliction on the applicant was in violation of this provision of the Convention' (paragraph 40). The Commission then referred the case to the European Court of Human Rights, and in 1978 the Court upheld the Commission's view, with one dissenting opinion (Judge Fitzmaurice), deciding that the United Kingdom had violated article 3 of the Convention.[51]

Both the Commission and the Court concluded that the issue at stake was whether the corporal punishment amounted to degrading punishment within the meaning of article 3. The conclusion that it did has been criticized.[52] This criticism is based on the argument that the Court failed to state clearly what element, either as it applied in this case or in general, elevated what may well be undesirable behaviour into prohibited ill-treatment. It appears that both the Court and the Commission wished to take the opportunity to bring all judicial corporal punishment within the ambit of article 3. In consequence, they did not concentrate on particular circumstances of the case that might have been specifically noted as 'degrading' (for example the boy's trousers were removed so that the birching could be administered to the bare posterior). These specific details became merely an aggravating factor.[53] Having decided to address the issue of corporal punishment itself, rather than the details of this particular instance of it, the Court was then obliged to state its test of degrading punishment: that there must be 'humiliation or debasement' such as to 'attain a particular level' other than that involved in judicial punishment generally.[54] The Court then asserted that this test was met by corporal punishment. The Commission had added the element of absence of 'redeeming social value',[55] a point not followed by the Court, which felt that any special deterrent effect (the most relevant redeeming value) would not deprive a punishment of its degrading character,[56] and the Commission had found no deterrent effect. Although the attention of the Commission had been drawn to the relevant provisions of the Geneva Conventions and the SMR,[57] neither it nor the Court relied on these, even though their language tended to include corporal punishment within the category of torture or cruel, inhuman, or degrading punishment. It has rightly been observed[58] that a relevant factor for the Court may well have been its own admission that, in interpreting the Convention as 'a living instrument', it could not 'but be influenced by the developments and commonly accepted standards in the penal policy of

---

[51] *Tyrer* case. European Court of Human Rights, Series A, No. 26.
[52] Judge Sir Gerald Fitzmaurice, ibid.; and by Zellick, 'Corporal Punishment in the Isle of Man', 27 *ICLQ* 665 (1978).
[53] *Supra* n. 51, para. 35.   [54] Id., para. 30.   [55] *Supra* n. 50, para. 39.
[56] *Supra* n. 51, para. 31.   [57] *Supra* n. 50, para. 18.
[58] Zellick, *supra* n. 52, 669.

the member states of the Council of Europe in the field'.[59] Indeed, once it is recognized that, as with the interpretation of constitutional bills of rights, the content and scope of the rights guaranteed will evolve with the changing standards of society, it has to follow that there will be an element of apparent arbitrariness in a judicial finding that what was not prohibited at one stage subsequently has become so.

In any event, criticisms of the Court's reasoning have in no way cast doubt on the legally binding nature of the decision. Even though legislation envisaging corporal punishment remained on the Isle of Man's statute books,[60] judicial corporal punishment has now been formally ruled to be a thing of the past in Western Europe.[61] The implications of the Court's ruling are not confined to Western Europe, however, since the ruling related to a standard which is universal, not just regional. As such this ruling is powerful authority for the scope of standards elsewhere. Nevertheless, its narrow reliance on the terms of the European Convention on Human Rights and on common European practice, without reference to analogous international instruments, makes it desirable to seek further evidence of the wider acceptance of the impermissibility of corporal punishment.

Neither the Human Rights Committee established under the International Covenant on Civil and Political Rights nor the Inter-American Commission and Court of Human Rights have had any cases of corporal punishment to decide. However, at its sixteenth session in 1982, the Human Rights Committee examined the revised, first periodic report of one country, Iran, where severe corporal punishment had been inflicted, and the representative of Iran was challenged on this point.[62] No specific conclusions were reached, since it was not then the practice of the Committee to draw such conclusions on the basis of its examination of country reports. But it had embarked on a process of formulating 'general comments' on the individual articles of the Covenant, on the basis of its experience of examining such reports. The draft comment, before the Committee, on article 7 of the Covenant (prohibiting torture and cruel, inhuman, or degrading treatment or punishment) was prepared by a working group and contained the following statement: 'In the view of the Committee the prohibition must extend to most, if not all, forms of corporal punishment . . .'.[63] By the end of the session, the text was adopted without the words 'most, if not all forms of'. The summary records of the session do not disclose how the change came about. What emerges however, is that

[59] *Supra* n. 51, para. 31.

[60] 21 *Yearbook of the European Convention on Human Rights* 658 (1978).

[61] Zellick, 'Human Rights and the Treatment of Offenders', in Andrews (ėd.), *Human Rights in Criminal Procedure* (1982), 375, 380.

[62] UN doc. CCPR/C/SR.365. The Committee examines reports submitted periodically by states parties to the Covenant (article 40). A revised report had been submitted by the new revolutionary Islamic government to replace a report submitted by the previous government.

[63] UN doc. CCPR/C/SR/371, para. 9.

the view ('the prohibition must extend to corporal punishment') contains no ambiguity.[64]

The Committee's general comments are not binding interpretations of the Covenant, in the sense that decisions of the European Court of Human Rights are binding in respect of the European Convention. However, they represent the consensus views of eighteen persons, nominated by governments, from most juridical, religious, cultural, and political backgrounds, comprising the only organ established by the Covenant itself to monitor compliance with it. As such, its views on the scope of the Covenant's articles represent weighty and persuasive evidence of their meaning.

The prohibition of corporal punishment as a violation of article 7 of the Covenant does not apply to the parties to it alone. As suggested in Chapter 2, the norm contained in article 7 may properly be considered as one of general international law, as evidenced by the adoption in 1975 of the Declaration on the Protection of All Persons from Being Subjected to Torture or Other Cruel, Inhuman or Degrading Treatment or Punishment (Declaration against Torture). While it might be that a country, such as Saudi Arabia, which has always maintained a distinct role for corporal punishment, could claim a historic or regional variation of customary law,[65] the better view would be that in humanitarian matters the uniformity of the rule should prevail, as evidenced by the generally recognized international illegality of the apartheid system.[66]

In a path-breaking decision the Supreme Court of Zimbabwe took this universalist approach in 1987. In *The State* v. *Ncube and Others*,[67] three persons had been found guilty of rape of children, in one case, two children, in another, the man's own daughter, on an unspecified number of occasions over a two-and-a-half-year period. All were sentenced to substantial terms of imprisonment with labour as well as whippings of six strokes. The appeal con-

[64] It may be no accident that the Committee adopted this general comment at the same session as it examined the report of Iran. The position is reaffirmed in the Committee's second general comment on article 7: Report of the Human Rights Committee, *GAOR*, 47th Session, Supplement No. 40 (A/47/40), 1992, Annex VI A, general comment 20(44), para.5.

[65] The existence of regional variations in customary international law has been recognized by the World Court: *Asylum Case* (*Colombia* v. *Peru*), ICJ Rep. 1950, 266.

[66] Note that, according to the International Law Association, 'floggings, the amputation of limbs and other cruel, inhuman or degrading forms of punishment are gross violations of international standards of humane treatment'. International Law Association, Article 6(7) of the Paris Minimum Standards of Human Rights Norms in a State of Emergency, Sixty-First Conference (Paris, 1984). To the extent that the prohibition of torture and other ill-treatment may reflect a rule of *jus cogens* (see Chapter 2), it would be invidious to envisage a regional exception to the rule. See, Rodley, 'Religious Punishments and the Prohibition of Torture and Cruel, Inhuman or Degrading Treatment or Punishment', in *Contemporary International Law Issues: Conflicts and Convergence, 1995 Joint Conference—The American Society of International Law/Nederlandse Vereniging voor International Recht* (1996), 332 and following discussion.

[67] [1987] (2) ZLR246 (SC), 267B–C; [1988] (2) SA 702 (ZSC), 717B–D; also summarized in International Commission of Jurists, *The Review*, No. 41 (Dec. 1988), 61, as reprinted from 14 *Commonwealth Law Bulletin* 593 (1988).

cerned only the whipping. The Court held that the punishment violated the constitutional provision prohibiting inhuman or degrading punishment. It held that it did, despite the fact that the Constitution was framed so as to preserve existing punishments from falling foul of the provision. In so doing it referred to comparative criminal laws and cases from a number of jurisdictions, including the *Tyrer* case. Whipping was incompatible with human dignity.

There remains the question of which branch of the article 7 rule is breached by corporal punishment. Since it is the practice of the European Convention organs to divide up its analogous article 3 rule (torture/inhuman treatment or punishment/degrading treatment or punishment) according to a scale of severity capped by torture, it was understandable that the infliction of three strokes of the birch on a young person should be held to be at the lower end of the scale (degrading). Some of the more injurious manifestations of corporal punishment discussed at the beginning of this chapter would doubtless have risen further up it. The Human Rights Committee is less inclined to draw 'sharp distinctions between the various prohibited forms of treatment and punishment',[68] although it recognizes that the distinctions 'depend on the kind, purpose and severity of the particular treatment'.[69] For juridical purposes, the only significant distinction appears to be between torture on the one hand and the other prohibited forms of ill-treatment on the other. This is because only torture appears automatically to be a crime under international law entailing the individual criminal responsibility of the perpetrator, who may well be triable in the courts of any country, regardless of nationality or of where the offence was committed (see Chapter 4).

Can corporal punishment therefore amount to torture? Logically there is no reason why it should not, though there has been no international decision testing the question. As a practical matter, and as one of fairness, difficulties could arise if people charged with carrying out sanctions laid down by national legislation were to be held liable to universal criminal prosecution. On the other hand, there is important authority from Nuremberg that obedience to national law is not necessarily a defence to a charge of committing a crime under international law.[70] Article 1 of the Declaration against Torture (Annex 1) explicitly excludes from its definition of torture 'pain or suffering arising only from, inherent in or incidental to, lawful sanctions to the extent consistent with the Standard Minimum Rules for the Treatment of Prisoners'. Since the SMR expressly prohibits corporal punishment as a disciplinary measure, this formula does not exclude such corporal punishment from the

[68] Report of the Human Rights Committee, *GAOR*, 37th session, Supplement No. 40 (1982), Annex V, general comment 7(16), para. 2; and *supra* n. 64, general comment 20(44), para 4.
[69] Ibid.
[70] International Military Tribunal (Nuremberg), Judgment and Sentences, 30 September 1946, reproduced in 41 *AJIL* 172 (1947).

definition of torture. Is it as clear that the judicial sanction of corporal punishment should be considered as falling within the definition? All 'lawful sanctions' are excluded from the definition of torture (article 1) in the UN Convention against Torture (Annex 2a). In this it follows the Declaration against Torture, but without the qualifying reference to the Standard Minimum Rules. The original Swedish draft convention had reproduced the qualifying reference to the SMR found in the Declaration but it was later deleted by the working group.[71] Apparently the offending words, by virtue of referring to a document that has no legally binding status (see Chapter 9), were unsuitable for inclusion in what was to become a legally binding treaty.[72] If the exclusion were to be understood as covering any nationally legislated punishment, however gruesome, then it would be difficult to argue that any form of corporal punishment amounts to torture. And yet it is conceptually difficult to withhold this categorization from some manifestations of corporal punishment, such as amputation or other physical punishment leading to serious injury. It may well be, however, that the term 'lawful sanctions' should be understood as referring to sanctions lawful under international law, rather than any sanctions, however cruel, that national law may devise. Here it should be noted that a number of governments have explicitly so interpreted the term, without challenge.[73] Should this interpretation prevail, then corporal punishment will probably not be automatically excluded from the definition of torture since, as argued above, it ought not to be considered as lawful under international law (it being at least prohibited as 'degrading punishment').[74] In that case, some harsh corporal punishment could amount to torture, as affirmed in Commission on Human Rights resolution 1997/38,[75] carrying the same consequences as apply to violations of the prohibition against torture as described in Chapter 4. To the extent that it amounts to ill-treatment falling short of torture, then it may be expected to carry the same consequences (also described in Chapter 4) as are applicable in the case of such ill-treatment.

---

[71] UN doc. E/CN.4/L.1480 (1979), paras. 21 and 29; see also Chapter 1.

[72] Id., para. 21; and UN doc E/CN.4/L.1400, para. 15 (1978).

[73] Italy, Netherlands, United Kingdom, and the United States of America: UN doc. A/39/499 (1984), at 11, 13, 19, and 21 respectively.

[74] See similarly the second paragraph of article 2 of the Inter-American Convention to Prevent and Punish Torture (Annex 2b), which excludes from the definition of torture in that Convention pain or suffering resulting from 'lawful measures, provided that they do not include the performance of the acts or use of the methods referred to in this article'. The proviso seems to deprive the exclusion of all meaning.

[75] *Supra* n. 39 and accompanying text. In the same sense, see the preliminary report of Mr Leandro Despouy, Special Rapporteur on Human Rights and Disability of the Sub-Commission on Prevention of Discrimination and Protection of Minorities, for whom 'penalties deliberately inflicting disability, such as amputation of limbs or mutilation', comprise 'torture or cruel, inhuman or degrading treatment': UN doc. E/CN4/Sub.2/1985/32, para. 18; also para. 27.

SUMMARY

Corporal punishment is provided for in the laws of some countries, though they are probably only a small proportion of the countries in the world. In many of these countries corporal punishment is an inheritance from colonial times, in others it is an aspect of *shari'a* (Islamic law). From the small amount of case law on the subject it may be said that there is strong evidence that the use of corporal punishment by administering powers in trust territories was considered by the General Assembly to be a violation of the prohibition against torture or other ill-treatment, and the Assembly called for its cessation. Similarly, the Commission on Human Rights and the Commissioner for Namibia condemned floggings in Namibia. The Sub-Commission on Prevention of Discrimination and Protection of Minorities has held amputations not to be consonant with the prohibition against torture or other ill-treatment. For the Commission on Human Rights, following the approach of its Special Rapporteur on Torture, 'corporal punishment can amount to cruel, inhuman or degrading punishment or even to torture'.

International humanitarian law applicable in international armed conflicts clearly prohibits the use of corporal punishment on protected persons, either as a penal or as a disciplinary sanction. The only area of doubt is whether or not its infliction would amount to a grave breach of the Geneva Conventions (war crime), and even here there is little doubt that corporal punishment sufficient to cause serious injury to body or health would be such a breach. With regard to non-international armed conflict, there is no specific mention of corporal punishment in common article 3 of the Geneva Conventions, which uses general language closer to that of the international human rights instruments. Parties to Additional Protocol II, however, are explicitly prohibited from using corporal punishment on protected persons and it may be that the prohibition is to be understood as an authoritative interpretation of common article 3.

The Standard Minimum Rules for the Treatment of Prisoners forbid corporal punishment for disciplinary offences in language indicating a rule considered to be legally binding (although in an instrument not *per se* legally binding); other international human rights instruments are silent on the question. The issue, then, is whether corporal punishment is embraced by the international law prohibition of torture or other cruel, inhuman, or degrading punishment. According to the European Court of Human Rights, applying article 3 of the European Convention on Human Rights in the *Tyrer* case, it is. The Human Rights Committee commenting on the analogous article 7 of the Covenant takes the same view. In its least injurious forms corporal punishment clearly does not amount to torture (three strokes of the birch were held to be merely 'degrading' in *Tyrer*). In its more injurious forms it logically could and should do so, an approach that would be compatible with the Declaration against Torture. However, the UN Convention against Torture excluded 'lawful sanctions' from its definition of torture and it may be asked whether this means sanctions lawful under national or international law. If, as may well be the case, the sanctions have to be lawful under international law to be excluded from the definition of torture, then for the purposes of the Convention, and arguably general international law, some of the harsher forms of judicial corporal punishment could be considered torture, as asserted by the UN Commission on Human Rights and its Special Rapporteur on Torture. The legal consequences of the practice of corporal punishment, if it falls into either the torture category or the category of prohibited punishment not amounting to torture, are described in Chapter 4.

Guarantees against Abuses of the Human Person: Arbitrary Arrest and Detention

As early as 1974, the General Assembly of the United Nations had recognized that internationally agreed principles against arbitrary arrest and detention were relevant in the process of combating torture (see Chapter 1). While such principles did not figure prominently in the deliberations leading up to the adoption of the Declaration against Torture (Annex 1), the Assembly immediately thereafter called for the drafting of a body of principles for the protection of all persons under any form of detention or imprisonment, that was to draw upon earlier draft principles on arbitrary arrest, detention, or exile.[1]

This approach reflected an awareness that had already been developed by non-governmental organizations (NGOs) working against torture. In December 1973 the Secretary-General of the International Commission of Jurists (ICJ) argued that effective action could be taken at the national level:

It may prove . . . productive to direct this action . . . to providing legal procedures which will make it unlikely that the event will occur. These could cover such matters as:

   (i) the right to legal assistance, available immediately on arrest and during detention;

  (ii) the right for arrested persons to communicate with their families;

 (iii) strict rules regarding the length of interrogation sessions, with adequate periods for rest and refreshment;

 (iv) medical examination before interrogation and, if requested by the person concerned or his lawyer, after interrogation;

  (v) detailed recording of all relevant facts concerning interrogation, including the length and times of sessions, names of interrogators and guards, particulars and results of medical examinations, etc.;

 (vi) a requirement that arrested persons be brought before a judge within 24 hours and thereafter kept in custody only under order and supervision of the court;

(vii) further interrogations, if any, to be carried out only by the judge;

(viii) adequate remedies for bringing complaints of illegal detention or ill-treatment before the court without any delay (e.g. *habeas corpus, amparo*).[2]

More than a decade later, Amnesty International, in a major report on the problem of torture, felt bound to devote a section to what it called 'the "preconditions" for torture'. It observed:

[1] GA res. 3453 (XXX), 9 Dec. 1975.
[2] 11 *The Review* (International Commission of Jurists, Dec. 1973), 23, 26.

Torture most often occurs during a detainee's first days in custody. These vulnerable hours are usually spent incommunicado, when the security forces maintain total control over the fate of the detainee, denying access to relatives, lawyer or independent doctor. Some detainees are held in secret, their whereabouts known only to their captors. The authorities may deny that certain detainees are held, making it easier to torture or kill them or to make them 'disappear'. Incommunicado detention, secret detention and 'disappearance' increase the latitude of security agents over the lives and well-being of people in custody.

The suspension of *habeas corpus* and other legal remedies, trials of political detainees in military courts, the lack of any independent means to examine and record a prisoner's medical condition—such conditions allow the security forces to conceal evidence of torture from lawyers, civilian magistrates, independent doctors and others who would be capable of taking action against their illegal activities.[3]

Amnesty International was then to include within its '12–Point Program for the Prevention of Torture' (this was to be the focus of a renewed campaign against torture) three points: 'limits on incommunicado detention', 'no secret detention', and 'safeguards during interrogation and custody'.[4]

In 1988, the General Assembly finally adopted the Body of Principles for the Protection of All Persons under Any Form of Detention or Imprisonment.[5] This instrument contains a detailed checklist of safeguards, compliance with which would make threats to, or assaults on, life and limb of prisoners unusual.

After a brief résumé of the drafting process, the main features of the text will be considered in the light of the criteria mentioned in the ICJ text. The Body of Principles does not, of course, *per se* have the force of international law, but will be relevant context to the following section which will involve a treatment of the international law approach to the two most central questions: the extent to which incommunicado detention is prohibited or restricted and whether there is an unrestricted right to challenge the lawfulness of detention. Finally, given that in certain emergency conditions it is possible for states to derogate from these standards to some extent, and that such derogations may create the 'preconditions' for torture, an approach that would limit the extent of 'derogability' will be explored.

UNITED NATIONS BODY OF PRINCIPLES

At its 1976 meeting, the Commission on Human Rights considered the request of the General Assembly to formulate 'a body of principles for the

---

[3] Amnesty International, *Torture in the Eighties* (1984), 110.
[4] Id., 249–50. The organization had first launched its campaign against torture in Dec. 1972: see Chapter 1.
[5] GA res. 43/173, 9 Dec. 1988 (see Annex 4).

protection of all persons under any form of detention or imprisonment on the basis of the Study of the Right of Everyone to be Free from Arbitrary Arrest, Detention and Exile[6] and the draft principles on freedom from arbitrary arrest and detention contained therein'.[7] It decided to ask its Sub-Commission on Prevention of Discrimination and Protection of Minorities to prepare a draft text on the subject.[8] The Sub-Commission met in 1976 and decided that it could best discharge its mandate by appointing one of its members, Mr Nettel, to formulate a first draft.[9] This he did, and the Sub-Commission discussed the result of his work in 1977. This discussion led the Sub-Commission to recommend the establishment of a working group of five members, who would meet in advance of the 1978 session to prepare a revised draft body of principles for consideration at that session.[10] This recommendation was followed, and in 1978 the Sub-Commission adopted a text based on that prepared by the working group, but with some amendments.[11]

After its adoption, the Commission on Human Rights, at its next (1979) session, decided to forward the text to the Economic and Social Council (Ecosoc) for transmission to the General Assembly.[12] It reached the Assembly in the latter part of 1979 and after several years of discussion in a working group of the Assembly's Sixth (Legal) Committee, the text was adopted by the Assembly in resolution 143/173 of 9 December 1988.

The text begins with two paragraphs of a general nature. The first, dealing with the scope of the instrument, reaffirms that the principles 'apply for [*sic*] the protection of all persons under any form of detention or imprisonment.' In other words, any person deprived of freedom by official action would appear to be covered by the text. The second paragraph defines key terms, including the words 'arrest', 'detention', and 'imprisonment' in a way that tends to reinforce the point. It also defines the notion, occurring at several points in the text, of 'judicial or other authority', so as to make clear that where the decision maker is not a judge, the official should possess the main attributes of a judge.[13] Then follow thirty-nine principles, the first thirty-five

---

[6] UN Publications: Sales no. 65.XIV.2 (1965).   [7] GA res. 3453 (XXX), 9 Dec. 1975.

[8] Resolution 10 B (XXXII), 5 Mar. 1976, Commission on Human Rights, Report, 3rd Session, *ESCOR*, 60th Session, Supplement No. 3, chapter XX A.

[9] Decision 2 (XXIX), 20 Aug. 1976, Report of the Sub-Commission on Prevention of Discrimination and Protection of Minorities (hereinafter 'Sub-Commission Report'), 29th Session (ECN4/1218; E/CN.4/Sub.2/378), chapter XVII B.

[10] Resolution 8 (XXX), 31 Aug. 1977, Sub-Commission Report, 30th Session (E/CN.4/1262: E/CN.4/Sub.2/399), Chapter XVII.

[11] The original text is contained in Sub-Commission Report, 31st Session (E/CN.4/1296: E/CN.4/Sub.2/417), para. 109 (1978); it was adopted by resolution 5 C (XXXI), 13 Sept. 1978, id., Chapter XVII A.

[12] Resolution 19 (XXXIV), 7 Mar. 1978, Commission on Human Rights, Report, 34th Session, *ESCOR*, 1978, Supplement No. 4, Chapter XXVI A.

[13] 'For the purposes of the Body of Principles:

(a) "Arrest" means the act of apprehending a person for the alleged commission of an offence or by the action of an authority;   *cont./*

of which are applicable to most detained and imprisoned persons, while the last four are especially applicable to persons suspected of, or charged with, criminal offences.

Analysis of the full text is beyond the scope of this work.[14] This examination will, as indicated, focus on assessment of the extent to which the Body of Principles meets the various points stressed by the ICJ in the passage quoted above.

LEGAL ASSISTANCE

The ICJ advocated the right of detainees to legal assistance immediately upon arrest and during detention. This concern is addressed directly by the Body of Principles. The first paragraph of draft principle 15 as the text had emerged from the Sub-Commission provided: 'A detained person shall be entitled to have legal assistance as soon as possible after the moment of arrest' and the third paragraph would have vouchsafed communication with a lawyer of the detainee's choice 'within the shortest possible period after the arrest'. The final version was substantially weaker after protracted General Assembly consideration of the matter. Principle 17 entitles a detained person 'to have the assistance of a legal counsel' and to be 'informed of his right by the competent authority promptly after arrest'. Principle 18 entitles detained or imprisoned persons to 'communicate and consult' with their legal counsel. The only reference to a time period for contact with legal counsel is principle 18, paragraph 3:

The right of a detained or imprisoned person to be visited by and to consult and communicate, without delay or censorship and in full confidentiality, with his legal counsel may not be suspended or restricted save in exceptional circumstances, to be specified by law or lawful regulations, when it is considered indispensable by a judicial or other authority in order to maintain security and good order.

Although placed within language that would restrict the right to contact with counsel, there does seem to be a recognition of the antecedent notion that the contact be 'without delay'. The meaning of 'without delay' lacks a certain

(b) "Detained person" means any person deprived of personal liberty except as a result of conviction for an offence;
(c) "Imprisoned person" means any person deprived of personal liberty as a result of a conviction for an offence;
(d) "Detention" means the condition of detained persons as defined above;
(e) "Imprisonment" means the condition of imprisoned persons as defined above;
(f) The words "a judicial or other authority" means a judicial or other authority under the law whose status and tenure should afford the strongest possible guarantees of competence, impartiality and independence.'

[14] See Amnesty International, A Guide to the United Nations Body of Principles for the Protection of all Persons under Any Form of Detention or Imprisonment, AI Index IOR/52/04/89, August 1989.

precision, perhaps falling somewhere between the inelastic, objective ICJ preference for 'immediately' and the very elastic, potentially subjective 'within a reasonable time'. It is difficult to conceive of a detention complying with this criterion, especially in view of its purpose, if access were denied for more than twenty-four hours. As far as the 'clawback' language is concerned, it is tightly drawn. The presumption is against suspension or restriction of the right. To rebut the presumption, a decision to suspend or restrict the right must meet several criteria: (1) it must be taken in the light of exceptional circumstances; (2) these circumstances must in turn be specified by law or lawful regulations; (3) there must be a determination of the indispensability of the suspension or restriction; (4) the restriction or suspension must be for the purpose of maintaining security and good order; and (5) it must be taken by a judicial or other authority as defined in the use of terms paragraph (see above). The drafters were clearly aware of the dangers of abuse implicit even in this formulation. Accordingly, to counterbalance the weakening of the Sub-Commission text, a new principle 15 was added:

Notwithstanding the exceptions contained in principle 16, paragraph 4 [notification of arrest and transfer from one place of detention to another], and principle 18, paragraph 3, communication of the detained or imprisoned person with the outside world, and in particular his family or counsel, shall not be denied for more than a matter of days.

The expression 'for a matter of days', while obviously suggesting a period of less than a week, remains imprecise. This was probably inevitable, since a clear specification of a number of days would probably be deemed too high by some states that would calculate the period even in hours rather than days, or too short by others. As will be seen below, international case law is beginning to suggest a period of no more than five and possibly as short as two days. In other respects, principles 17 and 18 contain protections no less than those already provided in rule 93 of the UN Standard Minimum Rules for the Treatment of Prisoners (SMR—see Annex 3) .

COMMUNICATION WITH FAMILIES

The right of detainees to communicate with their families and others is provided for in principle 19:

A detained or imprisoned person shall have the right to be visited by and to correspond with, in particular, members of his family and shall be given adequate opportunity to communicate with the outside world, subject to reasonable conditions and restrictions as specified by law or lawful regulations.

The main part of the text tracks a similar provision in rule 92 of the SMR. However, where the latter envisages restrictions 'in the interests of the administration of justice and of the security and good order of the institution' and the Sub-Commission text (draft principle 17) would have limited restrictions only to those 'to be specified by law for the purposes of detention and for the maintenance of security and good order in the place of detention', the scope of the present clawback is troubling. It is an advance on the SMR in so far as the restrictions must be specified by law or lawful regulations, though the addition of 'lawful regulations' in the General Assembly was clearly intended to provide greater room for legal manoeuvre. More seriously, there is loss of any purposive element to the possible restrictions. They must simply be 'reasonable', a word that tends to allow for almost infinitely flexible interpretation.

LENGTH OF INTERROGATION

The Body of Principles does not establish strict rules regarding the length of interrogation sessions. On the other hand, in principle 23 it does create the framework for determining whether such sessions are coercive or otherwise oppressive by requiring the recording of 'the duration of any interrogation and of the intervals between interrogations, *as well as the identity of the officials who conducted the interrogations and of other persons present*' (emphasis added). Furthermore, detainees and, 'when provided by law', their counsel are to have access to these records. The emphasized words make it possible to establish responsibility in the case of abuse, which in turn is profound discouragement to such abuse. There is no mention of 'adequate periods for rest and refreshment' as the ICJ had suggested.

PRE- AND POST-INTERROGATION MEDICAL EXAMINATIONS

Principle 24 requires that 'a proper medical examination . . . be offered to a detained or imprisoned person as promptly as possible after his admission to the place of detention or imprisonment'. The idea of an offered, rather than automatic medical examination was inserted at the General Assembly, thus opening the way for arguments that in a specific case the offer was refused. The General Assembly also replaced the Sub-Commission's 'promptly' (draft principle 21) by the more elastic 'as promptly as possible' and it dropped the Sub-Commission requirement that examinations be conducted 'thereafter as often as necessary'. However, it does now require that 'thereafter medical care and treatment shall be provided whenever necessary . . . free of charge'. It is thus arguable that a duty attaches to the institution to ensure that medical personnel be in a position to determine, by means of subsequent examinations, when the contemplated care and treatment need to be provided. This does not go as far as requiring medical examinations before and after every interrogation session, and perhaps such a requirement would impose too heavy a burden on professional and financial resources. The problem is hardly addressed in principle 25, which provides for a right to petition a judicial or other authority for a second examination at the request of detainees or their counsel. In the original Sub-Commission version (draft principle 22), there would have been a right, without the need for petition, for an examination by a physician of choice, not merely a second examination or opinion by an (unidentified) person, and a family member would also have been able to initiate exercise of the right. This very limited right may still be 'subject to reasonable conditions to ensure security and good order in the place of detention or imprisonment', traditionally abusable language. Rule 91 of the SMR offers better protection in this respect. On the other hand, principle 26 requires that a record be made of an examination, its results, and the name of the physician, and that access to this record be ensured.

RECORDS OF DETAILS OF INTERROGATIONS, MEDICAL EXAMINATIONS, AND SO ON

These are discussed under the two previous subheadings.

APPEARANCE BEFORE A JUDGE AND JUDICIAL SUPERVISION

The Body of Principles in some ways goes beyond the ICJ suggestion that arrested persons be brought before a judge within twenty-four hours and, thereafter, kept in custody only under order and supervision of a court. Principle 4 provides: 'Any form of detention or imprisonment and all measures affecting the human rights of a person under any form of detention or imprisonment shall be ordered by, or be subject to the effective control of a judicial or other authority.' This effectively brings the judiciary into the process at the pre-arrest stage ('ordered by') or at least immediately upon arrest ('under the effective control of'). The language further suggests that judicial responsibility remains after the original arrest. The term 'or other authority', and so on, makes allowance for those systems, generally found in civil law countries, where a procurator or *fiscal* exercises the powers in question, but the 'use of terms' paragraph referred to above makes clear that the decision has to be taken by an official having the same basic attributes as a judge. In any event, the authority would have to be independent of the agency whose officials effect the arrest.

The formulation has the disadvantage of not requiring, as the ICJ recommendation did, the actual production of the detained person before the judicial or other authority. Yet it also avoids the thorny problem of specifying a time limit for such an appearance: twenty-four hours would be too long in some circumstances and too short in others, and any specified time limit would appear to condone keeping the detainee in custody until the expiry of that limit.

INTERROGATION BY THE JUDICIARY

The Body of Principles does not contain the obligation, suggested by the ICJ, that judges alone would carry out interrogations. It was perhaps too much to expect that countries would be prepared so radically to alter their criminal justice systems as to submit to such a requirement. Nevertheless, principle 4, quoted above, does demand that 'all measures affecting the human rights of a person under any form of detention or imprisonment shall be ... under the effective control of' the judicial or other authority. That such measures may include interrogation is suggested by a number of the principles, for example, principle 21(2): 'no detained person while being interrogated shall be subjected to violence, threats or methods of interrogation which impair his capacity of decision or his judgement'.

CHALLENGING THE LEGALITY OF DETENTION AND TREATMENT

The Body of Principles incorporates the ICJ suggestion concerning challenge to the legality of detention and treatment. Principle 32 permits proceedings before a judicial or other authority (as defined by the 'use of terms' paragraph) to be taken 'at any time ... to challenge the lawfulness of ... detention and to obtain ... release without delay if it is unlawful'. Importantly, the proceedings in question may be brought by the detainee or his or her counsel, but not, as the Sub-Commission text would have provided, 'a member of his family or any citizen having knowledge of the case' (draft principle 28). Nor does the text envisage a challenge to the *necessity* of detention, as opposed to its lawfulness, a possibility the Sub-Commission text provided for. On the other hand, the proceedings must be 'simple and expeditious and at no cost for detained persons without adequate means. The detainee must be produced without delay.' It is not, then, just a question of mere processing of documentation.

In another departure from the Sub-Commission text, the proceedings are not applicable, in the first stage, as regards treatment in detention. Yet principle 33 does allow a 'detained or imprisoned person or his counsel' to 'make a request or complaint regarding his treatment, in particular in case of torture or other cruel, inhuman or degrading treatment'. However, the complaint has to be made, not to a judicial or other authority, but 'to the authorities responsible for the administration of the place of detention, and to higher authorities and, when necessary, to appropriate authorities vested with review or remedial powers'. Such administrative, or, at any rate, non-judicial, recourses could prove to be less than helpful. Tempering the potential dilatoriness of such a procedure is the provision that each request or complaint is to be 'promptly dealt with and replied to without undue delay'. More helpfully, where 'the request or complaint is rejected, or in case of inordinate delay, the complainant shall be entitled to bring it before a judicial or other authority'. Here, then, we seem to have a second stage, where the availability of a habeas corpus type of procedure seems to be required if administrative and similar channels prove ineffective or too protracted. Given the urgency of such situations, the complainant should not be expected to discharge a heavy burden of proof regarding effectiveness and delay of non-judicial channels. A particularly positive aspect of the procedure under principle 33 is that not only may the detainee or his or her counsel be the complainant, but, if they do not have the possibility of instigating the activity, it may be undertaken by a member of the family of the detainee or 'any other person who has knowledge of the case'.

Clearly, the Body of Principles goes far to meeting the ICJ proposals to ensure the existence of an institutional framework at the national level that would prevent the occurrence of conditions that might facilitate the infliction of torture or other ill-treatment. Many of the other principles would reinforce the effect of those described. For example, there is provision in principle 34 for compelling inquiry by 'a judicial or other authority', 'whenever the death or disappearance of a detained or imprisoned person occurs during his detention or imprisonment'.

It should be noted that the Principles contain no references to possible suspension in times of crisis of the guarantees they provide. In this, the document differs from the first draft submitted by Mr Nettel to the working group, which did consider this issue.[15] It is to be assumed that the removal of the relevant text stemmed from the belief that the Principles should obtain under all circumstances. They would otherwise be deprived of their purpose, which was precisely to fill the gap created by the suspension of national legal guarantees in time of emergency.[16]

In approving the Body of Principles, the General Assembly urged 'that every effort be made so that the Body of Principles becomes generally known and respected'.[17] This is strongly supportive language, but certainly not such as to suggest that the Assembly was seeking to promote their recognition as legally binding. Yet the language of many of the principles is peremptory, so clearly they are intended to be persuasive. As is often the case with such 'soft law' instruments, its principal value (from the perspective of international law) will be in assisting governments and relevant international bodies in interpreting and applying broader, but more recognizably legal norms. To these, we now turn.

[15] UN doc. E/CN.4/Sub.2/395 (1978).
[16] This is the recollection of the author (who attended the working group and the subsequent Sub-Commission discussion on behalf of Amnesty International) of the intentions of the working group, although it does not appear in the working group's report (UN doc. E/CN.4/Sub.2/406) nor in the summary records of the Sub-Commission's discussion (UN doc. E/CN.4/Sub.2/SR.807); it is recollected that Mr Nettel also made the point when introducing the working group's text to the Sub-Commission.
[17] GA res. 43/173, 9 Dec. 1988, para. 4.

INCOMMUNICADO DETENTION AND HABEAS CORPUS UNDER
EXISTING LAW AND LEGAL INSTRUMENTS

Given that the Body of Principles is not formally a legal instrument, it is now proposed to discuss existing international law as it addresses itself to the basic guarantees against abuse of detainees. As may be expected, general human rights law, as evidenced by the International Covenant on Civil and Political Rights and the regional human rights conventions, does not deal with treatment of prisoners in the same degree of detail as does the Body of Principles. On the other hand, in these instruments the general scope of the provisions relating to arbitrary arrest and detention is broader than is relevant for present purposes.[18] It is here intended, therefore, to concentrate on just two issues raised by the extract from the Amnesty International report reproduced at the beginning of this chapter: the prohibition of incommunicado detention and the remedy of habeas corpus.

A prisoner who is held incommunicado is simply one who is unable to communicate with the world outside the place of detention. Normally a prisoner, once taken into custody, may be expected to be allowed to have contact with a lawyer, with family members, with a doctor, and possibly with others too. In addition, in so far as persons would not generally be expected to be detained otherwise than pursuant to the preferment of criminal charges, they would have to appear soon after arrest before a judge or magistrate. One who is held incommunicado, then, is one who is denied access to all of these. Such persons are thus at the mercy of their captors, who are subject only to the restraints of their own personal sense of morality and to corporate discipline under the law. As previous chapters have suggested, such restraints may well be inadequate in times of perceived threat to the national social order. This is particularly so given that the captors are part of that social order and the captives in their charge are often felt to embody the threat to it. It must be noted that the anguish of the families of, or others close to, the prisoner held incommunicado may also be formidable. Regardless of reality (if not as a result of it), rumours of abuses will soon begin to spread, increasing their apprehensions.

---

[18] For example, the Human Rights Committee found a violation of Covenant article 9(1) prohibiting arbitrary arrest and detention (see Annex 9b) because the victim was held for eight months 'on account of his political opinions'. This was in addition to a finding that article 19(2) (freedom of expression) had been violated 'because he suffered political persecution on account of his political opinions': *Jaona* v. *Madagascar* (132/1982), Report of the Human Rights Committee, *GAOR*, 40th Session, Supplement No. 40 (1985), para. 14. Thus, article 9(1) covers matters relating to the substantive legitimacy of detention, not just the procedural propriety that is the focus of the present discussion.

INCOMMUNICADO DETENTION UNDER THE COVENANT

For the reasons just given, it is important that persons should not be permitted to be detained incommunicado for any prolonged period of time, but, except in respect of the right to be brought before a judge, the international human rights instruments are not couched in terms that explicitly cover this point. Thus, the Universal Declaration of Human Rights merely asserts that no one shall be subject to 'arbitrary arrest, detention or exile'. The International Covenant on Civil and Political Rights is more specific, in its article 9, which affirms 'the right to liberty and security of person' and prohibits 'arbitrary arrest and detention'. Paragraph 3 of this article requires that a person arrested or detained on a criminal charge be brought 'promptly' before a judge or other officer authorized by law to exercise judicial power. 'Promptly' remains undefined, but guidance may be obtained from the general comment of the Human Rights Committee (on article 9): 'more precise time limits are fixed by law in most States parties and, in the view of the Committee, delays must not exceed a few days'.[19]

Apart from the meaning of 'prompt' which the Committee in non-strict language has nevertheless clearly understood not to permit a prolonged period of time between arrest and appearance before the judicial authority, there are two further problems with the wording of paragraph 9(3). First is the reference to a 'judge *or other officer authorized by law to exercise judicial power*' (emphasis added) which does not contain the definition given in the 'use of terms' paragraph of the Body of Principles discussed above. The problem here is that it is not unknown for officers of a state security agency with powers of arrest and detention also to be vested with judicial power. In other words, the judiciary cannot always be seen as a body to which arresting agents are answerable, since the two may be one and the same.[20] This problem has not been the subject of an individual case before the Human Rights Committee, nor has the Committee addressed it by way of its general comments, so its attitude is not established. It is to be hoped that, confronted with

---

[19] Report of the Human Rights Committee, *GAOR*, 37th Session, Supplement No. 40 (1982), Annex V, general comment 8(16), para. 2; for the shortest period that the Committee has determined to violate article 9(3), see *Terán Jijón* v. *Ecuador* (277/1988), Report of the Human Rights Committee, *GAOR*, 47th Session, Supplement No. 40 (A/47/40), Annex IX I, para. 5.3, where the Committee held that keeping the victim 'incommunicado for five days without being brought before a judge and without having access to counsel . . . entails a violation of article 9, paragraph 3'; cf. *Martínez Portorreal* v. *Dominican Republic* (188/1984) (1988), Selected Decisions of the Human Rights Committee under the Optional Protocol, Vol. 2, UN doc. CCPR/C/OP/2 (1990), where the Committee found that 50 hours of detention did 'not justify a finding as to the alleged violation of article . . . 9, paragraph . . . 3' (para. 10.2), but see below as to articles 7 and 10(1).

[20] See, for example, SAVAK. the security agency of the former government of Iran: *Human Rights in Iran. Testimony on Behalf of Amnesty International Before the Sub-Committee on International Organizations of the Committee on International Relations, House of Representatives, United States Congress*, 28 Feb. 1978 (Amnesty International document AI Index: MDE 13/01/78).

the issue, the Committee would consider such an arrangement to be incompatible with article 9(3). Such an approach would be appropriate both because the general thrust of the provision presupposes that the judicial authority be independent of the detaining authority and because the very concept of 'judicial power' implies a posture of disinterested impartiality.[21]

The second problem is that article 9(3) applies only to persons arrested or detained 'on a criminal charge'. A restrictive reading of this language might be that, as long as formal charges are not preferred, the obligation to produce the detainee before the judicial authority does not apply. Such a reading would, of course, deprive the paragraph of purpose and should therefore be discarded. Such would also seem to be the view of the Human Rights Committee in its finding in, for example, *Netto, Weismann and Lanza* v. *Uruguay*.[22]

Mr and Mrs Lanza were arrested on 2 February 1976 and 17 February 1976 respectively. They were held for investigation under 'prompt security measures' (special legislation effectively suspending habeas corpus) until Mr Lanza was charged with 'subversive association' on 21 September 1976 and Mrs Lanza with aiding such association on 28 September 1976 (that is, more than seven months after that arrest).[23] The Committee found a violation of article 9(3) because, *inter alia*, the Lanzas 'were not *upon their arrest* brought promptly before a judicial officer' (emphasis added).[24]

In non-criminal cases (for example, where a person is held under a system which permits administrative internment) article 9(3) offers no protection. However, the Human Rights Committee has observed in respect of administrative internment that 'if so-called preventive detention is used, for reasons of public security, it must be controlled by these same provisions, i.e. it must not be arbitrary, and must be based on grounds and procedures established by law (paragraph 1) [of article 9]'.[25] It will be rare legislation that permits such preventive detention to be under the sole control of the authority effecting and administering the detention (that is, without some form of external

---

[21] The same is true as regards the Basic Principles on the Independence of the Judiciary, adopted by the Seventh UN Crime Congress: *Seventh United Nations Congress on the Prevention of Crime and the Treatment of Offenders—Report*, A/CONF.121/22/Rev.1, Chapter I D 2; and endorsed by the General Assembly: GA res. 40/32, 29 Nov. 1985, para. 5: also GA res. 40/146, 13 Dec. 1985, para. 2. See also the relevant case law relating to the analogous article 5(3) of the European Convention on Human Rights in the section below on regional conventions.

[22] Report of the Human Rights Committee, *GAOR*, 35th Session, Supplement No. 40 (1980), Annex VI.

[23] Id., para. 8.   [24] Id., para. 16.

[25] General comment 8(16), *supra* n. 19, para. 4. It follows from the terms of the Covenant and the words of the Human Rights Committee that administrative internment is not *per se* prohibited by international law. This is certainly the case in time of public emergency (see below): for example, in *Ireland* v. *United Kingdom*, the UK's internment of suspected IRA terrorists, after the UK had deposited a notice of derogation to article 5 of the European Convention on Human Rights, was held by the European Court of Human Rights not to involve a violation of the Convention: European Court of Human Rights, Series A, No. 25.

and independent supervision). Where this is permitted, however, it might be argued that the process of detention is *per se* arbitrary. As will be seen from the next section, no similar problem arises regarding the right to challenge the legality of detention.

Article 9 is not the only one which acts as a brake on incommunicado detention. Thus, in one case, during a ten-month period, 'while criminal charges against him were being investigated and determined, [the alleged victim] was kept incommunicado without access to legal counsel'. This was sufficient to provoke the Human Rights Committee to find a violation of Covenant article 14(3)(b).[26]

More importantly, in a number of cases the Committee has dealt with incommunicado detention and found it to involve a violation of article 10(1), which states: 'All persons deprived of their liberty shall be treated with humanity and with respect for the inherent dignity of the human person.' Naturally there has to be a lower limit to such detention, below which infringement of the principle contained in article 10(1) does not arise, but the cases dealt with by the Committee do not afford an opportunity to determine what this lower limit may be. The shortest period of detention incommunicado to bring forth a finding of an article 10(1) violation has been fifteen days, but this should not be interpreted as setting the minimum length of time which justifies such a finding—it seems merely to be the shortest period of incommunicado detention to have been considered by the Committee in an individual case in which it considered article 10(1) to be applicable.[27]

Finally, as will be seen below, incommunicado detention may also raise issues relating to article 7 of the Covenant, prohibiting torture or cruel, inhuman, or degrading treatment or punishment.

HABEAS CORPUS UNDER THE COVENANT

The International Covenant on Civil and Political Rights is unambiguous regarding challenges to the legality of detention. Article 9(4) provides:

[26] *Wight* v. *Madagascar* (115/1982), Report of the Human Rights Committee, *GAOR*, 40th Session, Supplement No. 40 (1985), para. 17. Covenant article 14(3) provides: 'In the determination of any criminal charge against him, everyone shall be entitled . . . (b) To have adequate time and facilities for the preparation of his defence and to communicate with counsel of his own choosing'.

[27] *Arzuaga Gilboa* v. *Uruguay* (147/1983), Report of the Human Rights Committee, *GAOR*, 40th Session, Supplement No. 40 (1985), para. 14. The Committee did find a violation of articles 7 and 10(1) in circumstances where a person was held for 50 hours in afflictive prison conditions, but it is not clear to what extent, if any, the length of incommunicado detention was relevant to the finding: *Martínez Portorreal* v. *Ecuador*, loc. cit. n. 19 above. It might also be that *Terán Jijón* v. *Ecuador* (ibid.), where the Committee treated five days' incommunicado detention as violating article 9(3), should be understood as implying that article 10(1) was not violated; however, the ill-treatment of the victim under interrogation led to a finding that articles 7 and 10(1) were violated, making it possible to conclude that the relevance of article 10(1) to the length of incommunicado detention was either overlooked or considered superfluous.

'Anyone who is deprived of his liberty by arrest or detention shall be entitled to take proceedings before a court, in order that such court may decide on the lawfulness of his detention and order his release if the detention is not lawful.' The importance of this provision cannot be overstated. Its benefit extends not only to persons held on suspicion of having committed a criminal offence but to all persons deprived of their liberty by arrest or detention.[28] Moreover, unlike the right of persons arrested or detained on a criminal charge to be brought promptly before 'a judge *or other officer authorized by law* to exercise judicial power' (emphasis added, article 9(3)), here the authority in question is nothing less than a formally constituted court. Further, the court must make its decision 'without delay'. Finally, in the event that the detention is found to be unlawful, the court must order release. The protection afforded by the paragraph is reinforced by article 9(5): 'Anyone who has been the victim of unlawful arrest or detention shall have an enforceable right to compensation.'[29]

Nevertheless, the scope of the right to challenge the legality of detention needs to be understood. It does not appear to prohibit *per se* administrative internment, provided that this internment is for reasons of 'public security', is not arbitrary, and is based on grounds and procedures established by law (see above). Nor does it appear to extend to a challenge to the necessity of detention as an issue separate from its lawfulness; and there is no explicit reference to a challenge to the conditions of detention as opposed to the mere fact of detention. (However, it may be argued that, where such conditions may amount to violations of article 7 or 10(1), then the detention itself will no longer, in its totality, be lawful.) While the right to challenge is vested only in the person deprived of liberty, no interpretation aimed at effectiveness would deny to others the power to initiate the proceedings on behalf of that person. Finally, the language of the article does not explicitly require that the detained person be brought before the court as an integral part of the proceedings. It is to be hoped, however, that an implicit requirement to produce the person before the court (analogous to that contained in article 9(3) in respect of persons arrested or detained on criminal charges) will be held to be contained within the meaning of article 9(4).

---

[28] The same point is stressed by the Human Rights Committee in its general comment 8(16), supra n. 19, para 1. See also *Berry* v. *Jamaica* (330/1988), Report of the Human Rights Committee, Vol. II, *GAOR*, 49th Session, Supplement No. 40 (1994), Annex IX D, para. 9.4, where 2½ months was held to be too long for the purposes of articles 9(3) and 9(4).

[29] The Human Rights Committee interprets the article 9(5) right to compensation, in the case of unlawful arrest and detention, as applying to any arrest or detention violating not only national law but also other provisions of article 9: see *Jaona* v. *Madagascar, supra* n. 18, para. 16.

INCOMMUNICADO DETENTION AND HABEAS CORPUS UNDER THE
REGIONAL CONVENTIONS

The protection against incommunicado detention offered by two of the
regional human rights conventions is largely analogous to that offered by the
Covenant. Thus, article 5 of the European Convention on Human Rights
(Annex 9c) provides that everyone arrested or detained 'on reasonable suspicion of having committed an offence or when it is reasonably considered
necessary to prevent his committing an offence or his fleeing after having
done so' (paragraph 1 (c)) should be 'brought promptly before a judge or
other officer authorized by law to exercise judicial power' (paragraph 3). This
formula is virtually coextensive with the provisions of Covenant article 9(3).
Thus, subject to what will be said below regarding states of emergency, the
European Convention ensures that arrested and detained persons cannot be
held completely at the mercy of the detaining authority: they must be brought
promptly before the judicial authority. Breach of this protection entails an
enforceable right to compensation (article 5 (5)).

In *Brogan et al.* v. *United Kingdom*,[30] the European Court of Human
Rights, in a majority judgment, found that detention of persons suspected of
involvement in terrorism in Northern Ireland for a period of four days and six
hours before being brought before a judge was too long to satisfy the requirement of promptness. This period in itself took account of the context of terrorism in Northern Ireland which the Court decided, dubiously, had the effect
of prolonging the possible period of detention.[31] Accordingly, a period of less
than four days in ordinary criminal cases would run foul of the promptness
requirement of article 5(3).[32] The effect of a notice of derogation in respect of
this provision is considered in the section of states of emergency below. As far
as the meaning of 'or other judicial officer authorized by law to exercise judicial power' is concerned, this has been interpreted to mean that the person
must be independent of the executive and personally hear the detained individual.[33]

The American Convention on Human Rights is particularly far-reaching.
By article 7, paragraph 5, the right to be brought promptly before the judicial
authority applies simply to 'any person detained' (Annex 9d), regardless of

[30] (1988), European Court of Human Rights, Series A, No. 145–B (12 votes to 7).
[31] Id., para. 61.
[32] See, further, Harris, O'Boyle and Warbrick, *Law of the European Convention on Human Rights* (1995), 134–6. Note also that, in one case, it has been held by the European Commission of Human Rights that a 45-hour period of incommunicado detention—in so far as it involved a refusal of permission to contact wives—entailed a violation of article 8 (right to family life) of the European Convention on Human Rights. *McVeigh et al.* v. *United Kingdom*, Applications Nos. 8022/77, 8025/77, and 8027/77 (1981).
[33] *Schiesser* v. *Switzerland* (1979), European Court of Human Rights, Series A, No. 34, para. 31.

the existence or otherwise of a criminal offence. The African Charter on Human and Peoples' Rights does not deal with the point explicitly (see its articles 6 and 7, Annex 9e).

The American Convention on Human Rights virtually repeats Covenant article 10(1), since it provides in article 5 that 'all persons deprived of their liberty shall be treated with respect for the inherent dignity of the human person'; article 5 of the African Charter of Human and Peoples' Rights guarantees the same respect to 'every individual' (see Annex 9e). In this respect, as was noted in Chapter 9, the European Convention on Human Rights has no analogous text. Given that the Human Rights Committee has found prolonged incommunicado detention to contravene this rule as given in the Covenant, the rule stated in the American Convention and the African Charter presumably carries similar weight. It may also be noted that the rule is contained in the same article of the respective instruments as that prohibiting torture and ill-treatment, the significance of which will be addressed below.

The European and American regional conventions have provisions equivalent to article 9(4) of the Covenant, by which the legality of detention may be challenged. In the case of the European Convention, the only notable departure from the Covenant in the wording of its article 5(4) is that the court decision has to be taken 'speedily'. The language of analogous article 7(6) of the American Convention also follows article 9(4) of the Covenant, but makes it explicit that the right may be exercised not only by the 'interested party' but also by 'another person on his behalf'. The language of article 7 of the African Charter does not provide explicitly for the right to challenge legality of detention before a court.

GENERAL INTERNATIONAL LAW

That the Covenant and at least two of the regional human rights conventions have the above elements in common is strong evidence that they express a rule of general international law. These elements may be defined as: (a) the right in criminal cases of a detained person to be brought promptly before a judge and (b) the right of anyone deprived of liberty to challenge the lawfulness of detention and to be released if the detention is found to be unlawful. Only the European Convention fails to express the right to be treated with respect for the inherent dignity of the human person and this is perhaps because it was drafted and adopted earlier than the others.

While, as with the principles considered in other chapters, the rights referred to here are frequently not respected, yet there are few legal systems that do not have provisions reflecting them in their ordinary law.[34] This sug-

[34] See, generally, Andrews (ed.), *Human Rights in Criminal Procedure* (1982); Bassiouni, Hertzberg, and Sammuto, *The Protection of Human Rights in the Criminal Process Under*

gests that, rather than binding only the parties to the relevant instruments, the principles have universal application, reflecting as they appear to do 'general principles of law recognized by civilized nations' (see Chapter 2).

There are also strong indications that the International Court of Justice considers that violation of the right to liberty and security of person and the prohibition of arbitrary arrest and detention is a violation of general international law (see Chapter 2). Here the statement of the World Court in the *Tehran Hostages* case will be recalled:

Wrongfully to deprive human beings of their freedom and to subject them to physical constraint in conditions of hardship is in itself manifestly incompatible with the principles of the Charter of the United Nations, as well as with the fundamental principles enunciated in the Universal Declaration of Human Rights.[35]

This statement appears to have been a specification of the more general finding that, by keeping the hostages effectively imprisoned at the US embassy in Tehran, Iran had committed 'successive and continuing breaches of the obligations laid upon it by the . . . applicable rules of general international law'.[36] The language hardly admits of an interpretation that does not cover the principles concerning arbitrary arrest and detention and liberty and security of person.[37] Since both these principles seem to be the basis for the right to be brought before a judicial authority and the right to challenge the lawfulness of detention and since, indeed, without such rights the principles would be deprived of much of their meaning, it would follow that, in the World Court's view, these rights are enshrined in general international law.

The Universal Declaration does not refer explicitly to the right of prisoners to be treated with humanity and respect for the inherent dignity of the human person.[38] But, as already suggested, the concept may be inherent in the principle of liberty and security of person as well as in the prohibition of torture and other ill-treatment. If this be so, then, in so far as prolonged detention incommunicado is incompatible with respect for the right to be treated with humanity, such detention is also covered by this authoritative judicial statement.

It should also be noted that the UN Special Rapporteur on Torture has persistently argued that the use of (prolonged) incommunicado detention should be considered unlawful, a position that has been upheld by the UN

International Instruments and National Constitutions (1981): and Association Internationale de Droit Pénal, 49 *Revue international de droit pénal*, no. 3 (1978).

[35] ICJ Rep. 1980, 3, at para. 91. [36] Id., para. 90.

[37] Note in the Universal Declaration of Human Rights, the right to liberty and security of person is found linked to the right to life in the first substantive article (article 3), while freedom from arbitrary arrest and detention is found later in article 9. Covenant article 9(1) brings them together.

[38] However, the fifth preambular paragraph of the Universal Declaration describes 'recognition of the inherent dignity of the human family' as 'the foundation of freedom, justice and peace in the world'.

Commission on Human Rights.[39] Also the prohibition in the Body of Principles of such detention for more than a matter of days may be recalled.

STATES OF EMERGENCY

This inquiry cannot conclude with the simple observation that general international law seems to vouchsafe both a rule against incommunicado detention (including the right to be brought promptly before a judicial authority) and a right of habeas corpus. This is because of the specification noted in previous chapters (especially Chapter 2) whereby derogation from certain human rights norms may be permissible in exceptional circumstances.[40]

The circumstances in question are those of public emergencies which threaten the life of the nation, up to and including national or international armed conflict.[41] While certain rights are non-derogable even in such circumstances (for example, freedom from torture and ill-treatment and the right to life), the rights that have been the subject of this chapter are not so immune. Thus, under the International Covenant on Civil and Political Rights, articles 9 (liberty and security of person/arbitrary arrest and detention) and 10

[39] In 1995, the Special Rapporteur issued a compilation of recommendations that had been put forward by the mandate over its first decade, including '[i]ncommunicado detention should be made illegal and persons held incommunicado should be released without delay': E/CN.4/1995/34, paras. 923, 926(d); for the Commission on Human Rights, 'prolonged incommunicado detention may facilitate the perpetration of torture and can in itself constitute a form of cruel, inhuman or degrading treatment': res. 1996/33B, para. 4, 19 Apr. 1996, Commission on Human Rights Report, 52nd Session, *ESCOR*, 1996, Supplement No. 3, Chapter II A. See also *Restatement of the Law: Third Restatement of US Foreign Relations Law*, Vol. 2 (1985), according to s. 702(e) of which, 'prolonged arbitrary detention' violates customary international law.

[40] See, generally, Oraá, *Human Rights in States of Emergency in International Law* (1992); Fitzpatrick, *Human Rights in Crisis—The International System for Protecting Rights During States of Emergency* (1994); Higgins, 'Derogations under the Human Rights Treaties', 48 *BYIL* 281 (1978); Marks, 'Principles and Norms of Human Rights Applicable in Emergency Situations: Underdevelopment, Catastrophes and Armed Conflicts', in Vasak (ed.), *The International Dimensions of Human Rights* (revised English edn. by Alston, 1982), i. 175; International Commission of Jurists, *States of Emergency—Their Impact on Human Rights* (1983); Buergenthal, 'To Respect and to Ensure: State Obligations and Permissible Derogations', in Henkin (ed.), *The International Bill of Human Rights—The Covenant on Civil and Political Rights* (1981), 72; Hartman, 'Derogation from Human Rights Treaties in Public Emergencies—A Critique of Implementation by the European Commission and Court of Human Rights and the Human Rights Committee of the United Nations', 22 *Harvard International Law Journal* 1 (1981); Questiaux, *Study of the Implications for Human Rights of Recent Developments Concerning Situations Known as States of Siege or Emergency*, Sub-Commission on Prevention of Discrimination and Protection of Minorities, UN doc. E/CN.4/Sub.2 1984/15 (hereinafter 'Questiaux').

[41] Covenant, article 4: 'in time of public emergency which threatens the life of the nation'; European Convention on Human Rights, article 15: 'in time of war or other public emergency threatening the life of the nation'; American Convention on Human Rights, article 27: 'in time of war, public danger, or other emergency that threatens the independence or security of a State Party'.

(humane treatment) are derogable. The same is true for the articles analogous to Covenant article 9 in the European Convention on Human Rights (article 5) and the American Convention on Human Rights (article 7). The European Convention has no article analogous to Covenant article 10(1) but the American Convention contains the only instance of a right to humane treatment that applies in all circumstances. This is because the provisions analogous to article 10(1) of the Covenant are to be found in article 5, which also prohibits torture and other ill-treatment and is non-derogable. The temptation to build too much on this regional advance on the other instruments must be resisted, but it would certainly be desirable that 'the list of *rights of absolute inalienability* should be extended by reference to the instrument which specifically confers the most liberal guarantees'.[42] But any such proposal has to be seen as being made *de lege ferenda*.

On the face of it then, international law appears to be permitting the suspension of the very rights that most need to be respected in time of national or international upheaval since, unless they are respected, other rights (freedom from torture, the right to life, and so on—the non-derogable rights or the rights of absolute inalienability) may nevertheless be violated.

In fact, however, such pessimism is not wholly warranted. First of all, the exceptional circumstances must indeed be such as to threaten the life of the nation: they should meet the test of 'the principle of exceptional threat'.[43] This is not the place to rehearse the various elements that might be relevant to such a test;[44] suffice it to say that the emergency in question must be grave, involving at least a violent assault, or the threat thereof, upon the organized social fabric. Moreover, while a certain 'margin of appreciation' may under the European Convention be accorded to the government of the state concerned in determining the existence of such a situation, such determination is not a matter of unilateral discretion for that state.[45] Thus, the European Commission of Human Rights rejected the claim of the Greek government to invoke a state of emergency justifying suspension of certain rights, on the grounds that the emergency did not exist when first proclaimed and was not of sufficient gravity thereafter.[46]

Second, the measures of derogation must be no more than are 'strictly required by the exigencies of the situation' that has provoked them[47] ('the principle of proportionality'[48]). This seems to mean that the measures must be the least stringent available to alleviate or end the emergency situation.[49] Here, too, a 'margin of appreciation' may be afforded the government in

[42] Questiaux, *supra* n. 40, para. 203 B. [43] Id., para. 55. [44] Ibid.
[45] See, for example, *Lawless* v. *Ireland* (Merits) (1961), European Court of Human Rights, Series A, No. 3, 27–67.
[46] 12 *Yearbook of the European Convention on Human Rights—The Greek Case* (1969), 76 and 100.
[47] Language of articles referred to in n. 41 *supra*. [48] Questiaux, para. 60.
[49] Id., para. 63.

question in assessing the facts and requirements, but this does not exclude international scrutiny of the compatibility of the measures taken with the principle of proportionality.[50]

The question that now arises is whether prolonged incommunicado detention and denial of the right to challenge the lawfulness of detention can ever be justified as the minimum strictly required by the exigencies of the situation. Given that such detention and denial of the said right constitute the preconditions for torture and even violations of the right to life—both impermissible under any circumstances—a strong argument can be made for a negative answer to the question. For incommunicado detention and denial of the right to challenge would serve the permitted purpose (of suppressing the state of emergency) only if they were indeed intended to facilitate the prohibited abuses: it may well be that measures are necessary to prevent an arrested or detained person from pursuing violent conspiracies, or colluding with alleged co-offenders, or warning them of the interest of the authorities; it may even be that administrative internment is not yet beyond the bounds of international law and that it may have a certain preventive utility,[51] but none of this requires that the detained person be barred from all contact with the outside world, legal, medical, and family, or that the detention not be effected according to the terms and procedures established by the law authorizing it. If these measures are not 'strictly required by the exigencies of the situation' then they are not permissible.

The European Court of Human Rights cases tend to confirm this approach. The first is the case of *Brannigan and McBride* v. *United Kingdom*.[52] As was considered above, the Court found in *Brogan* that detention for four days and six hours without being brought before a judge or judicial officer was incompatible with the promptness requirement of article 5(3).[53] The reaction of the UK government to this finding was to issue a notice of derogation permitting such detention for up to seven days. This notification and the period of detention it referred to were upheld by the majority in *Brannigan*. But the Court clearly indicated that its conclusion was taken having regard to 'the existence of basic safeguards against abuse'.[54] These safeguards included the availability of habeas corpus to test the legality of the original arrest and detention and the right of the detainees to consult a solicitor after forty-eight hours from the time of arrest.[55]

The importance of this consideration was tested in *Aksoy* v. *Turkey*.[56] Zeki Aksoy, who was killed after lodging his complaint with the European Commission of Human Rights, complained *inter alia* of a violation of article

---

[50] Questiaux, paras. 60–3; see also n. 82 *infra*.   [51] See n. 25 *supra* and accompanying text.
[52] (1993), European Court of Human Rights, Series A, No. 258B (22 votes to 4).
[53] *Supra* n. 30.   [54] *Supra* n. 52, para. 66.   [55] Id., paras. 62–4.
[56] Case of *Aksoy* v. *Turkey* (100/1995/606/694), Judgment of 18 December 1996 (mimeograph).

3 (torture) and article 5(3) (detention without judicial supervision for sixteen days, according to the applicant, or fourteen days, according to the government). Having found a violation of article 3, the Court went on to find a violation of article 5(3), by virtue of the fact that Zeki Aksoy had been detained for at least fourteen days without judicial supervision. The remarkable facet of this aspect of the judgment was that Turkey had deposited a notification of derogation in respect of article 5(3), whose compliance with the formal requirements for such notifications (article 15(3)) was uncontested by the parties. The Court did not, in fact, rule on this issue, precisely because it found that 'the impugned measure was not strictly required by the exigencies of the situation'.[57] In other words, it assumed the validity of the derogation, but found the derogation did not have the effect of completely suspending article 5(3). It looked at the measures taken pursuant to the derogation and 'was not persuaded that the exigencies of the situation necessitated the holding of the applicant on suspicion of involvement in terrorist offences for fourteen days or more in incommunicado detention without access to a judge or other judicial officer'.[58]

In finding the violation, the Court contrasted its present judgment with that in *Brannigan and McBride*. In the latter, it had been 'satisfied that there were effective safeguards in operation in Northern Ireland which provided an important measure of protection against arbitrary behaviour and incommunicado detention', citing the availability of habeas corpus and access to a solicitor after forty-eight hours.[59] In *Aksoy*, on the other hand, the Court considered that

insufficient safeguards were available to the applicant, who was detained over a long period of time. In particular, the denial of access to a lawyer, doctor, relative or friend and the absence of any realistic possibility of being brought before a court to test the legality of detention meant that he was left completely at the mercy of those holding him.[60]

There could be no clearer articulation of the dangers of incommunicado detention.

Under the European Convention, then, the fact that incommunicado detention violates a derogable provision that has in fact been validly derogated from does not prevent a finding that the provision has been violated. In effect, therefore, the Convention has to be read as prohibiting in all circumstances prolonged incommunicado detention, regardless of any state of emergency.

What the limit of such detention is, is unclear. In the UK, *Brannigan and McBride* found seven days' judicially unsupervised detention acceptable after a notification of derogation, when habeas corpus was available from first arrest and there was access to a lawyer after forty-eight hours. In *Aksoy* the excessive period was fourteen days. It could well be that any period of

---

[57] Id., para. 86. [58] Id., para. 84. [59] Id., para. 82. [60] Id., para. 83.

non-judicially supervised incommunicado detention beyond forty-eight hours would fall foul of the Convention. It remains to be tested before the Court.

Can the same conclusion apply in respect of other treaties permitting derogations from their provisions in time of public emergency? As far as the American Convention on Human Rights is concerned, it is almost certainly the case. This is because article 27(2), which lists those articles that may not be subject to derogation, explicitly excludes from derogation 'the judicial guarantees essential for the protection of such rights'. In two advisory opinions the Inter-American Court of Human Rights confirmed that this meant that habeas corpus as provided for in the seemingly derogable article 7(6) (see Annex 9d) could not be suspended. It took the same position in respect of the right contained in article 25(1) to challenge before a court or tribunal a violation of constitutional rights (usually known as *amparo* in Latin America).[61] This means that a simple, prompt judicial remedy has to be available, not only to challenge the lawfulness of detention, but also treatment in detention, as torture and ill-treatment are prohibited in most, if not all, Latin American constitutions, even during a state of emergency. For the purposes of the present discussion, the Court declined an opportunity subsequent to spell out the range of possible non-suspendable judicial guarantees in a further advisory opinion on the grounds that it was

neither possible nor advisable to try to list all the possible 'essential' judicial guarantees that cannot be suspended under Article 27(2). Those will depend in each case upon an analysis of the juridical order and practice of each State Party, which rights are involved, and the facts which give rise to the question.[62]

Although the Court has not specifically ruled, therefore, that article 7(5), the equivalent of article 5(3) of the European Convention, is not suspendable, it is highly improbable that the Court would find non-judicially supervised prolonged incommunicado detention ever to be justified under the American Convention.

It must now be asked whether the International Covenant on Civil and Political Rights affords the same protection.[63] As a general proposition, there

---

[61] I/A Court HR, *Habeas Corpus in Emergency Situations (Arts. 27(2), 25(1) and 7(6) American Convention on Human Rights)*, Advisory Opinion OC-8/87 of January 30, 1987. Series A, No. 8.

[62] I/A Court HR, *Judicial Guarantees in States of Emergency (Arts. 27(2) and 8 American Convention on Human Rights)*, Advisory Opinion OC-9/87 of October 6, 1987. Series A, No. 9, para. 40.

[63] This is precisely the approach taken at a 'high level international conference on the limitation and derogation provisions of the International Covenant on Civil and Political Rights . . . held at Siracusa (Italy) from 30 April to 4 July 1984 . . . sponsored by . . . the International Commission of Jurists, the International Association of Penal Law, the American Association for the International Commission of Jurists, the Urban Morgan Institute of Human Rights and the International Institute of Higher Studies in Criminal Sciences'. (UN doc. E/CN.4/1985/4.) The 'Siracusa Principles' that emerged from the conference elaborated on the approach by specifying: 'No person shall be held in isolation without communication with his family, friend or lawyer for longer than a few days, e.g. three to seven days.' (Id., Annex, para. 70(c).)

would appear to be no reason for the approach to be different from that applicable to the European Convention. Moreover, as far as prolonged incommunicado detention is concerned, there is a further powerful argument that, in one authoritative view, that of the Human Rights Committee, it may already amount to a violation of a rule from which derogation is never permitted: the rule against torture or ill-treatment. This may appear unusual, since, as has been seen, the case law of the Human Rights Committee has tended to invoke article 10(1) rather than article 7 in respect of the individual cases of incommunicado detention that have been before it under the Optional Protocol to the Covenant. On the other hand, the cases in question have not compelled the Committee to arrive at a firm conclusion on the compatibility of such detention with article 7. Despite this, in its general comments,[64] the Committee has gone far towards suggesting that article 7 may also be involved. It has done so in three statements, each of which suggests a distinct approach. First, the Committee states: 'For all persons deprived of their liberty, the prohibition of treatment contrary to article 7 is supplemented by the positive requirement of article 10(1) of the Covenant that they shall be treated with humanity and with respect for the inherent dignity of the human person.'[65] From this an approach may be detected whereby, although article 10 may in certain respects be derogable, the protection of article 10(1) is immune from derogation. That approach would be consistent with the wording of article 10(1): can those who framed the Covenant really have intended to permit, even in times of severe crisis, that people be treated without humanity and respect for the inherent dignity of the human person? The approach would also reconcile the Covenant with the American Convention on Human Rights, which permits no derogation from the principle of humane treatment.

Second, referring to 'cases of torture or similar practices', the Committee states that

it follows from article 7, read together with article 2 of the Covenant, that States must ensure an effective protection through some machinery of control . . . Among the safeguards which may make control effective are provisions against detention incommunicado, granting, without prejudice to the investigation, persons such as doctors, lawyers and family members access to the detainees; provisions requiring that detainees should be held in places that are publicly recognized and that their names and places of detention should be entered in a central register available to persons concerned, such as relatives . . .[66]

---

[64] Report of the Human Rights Committee, *GAOR*, 37th Session, Supplement No. 40 (1982), Annex V, General comment 7(16); Report of the Human Rights Committee, *GAOR*, 47th Session, Supplement No. 40 (1992), Annex VI, general comment 20/44.

[65] General comment 7(16), para 2. See also general comment 20/44, para. 2, to the same effect.

[66] General comment 7(16), *supra* n. 64, para. 1.

By reading article 7 together with article 2 of the Covenant (article 2 requires that states undertake to give effect to the rights recognized by the Covenant) the Committee seems to be incorporating within the scope of article 7 not only the substantive prohibition of torture and ill-treatment, but also the means necessary to make the prohibition a reality. Furthermore, those means appear to include 'provisions against detention incommunicado'. Indeed, the second general comment on article 7 contains in its analagous paragraph the free-standing sentence: 'Provisions should also be made against incommunicado detention.'[67] Such an approach is, of course, absolutely consistent with the argument of this chapter, which has been predicated on the interrelationship between detention incommunicado and practices of torture and illegal deprivations of life. The reference in the statement to the need for detention to be effected in recognized institutions and registered in a form accessible to relatives and others will be immediately perceived as motivated by the practice of 'disappearances'.[68]

Finally, as noted in the previous chapter, the Committee observes in respect of article 7: 'Even such a measure as solitary confinement may, according to the circumstances, and especially when the person is kept incommunicado, be contrary to this article' (paragraph 2). A word on terminology may be in order here. In this text 'solitary confinement' has been used to refer to the practice of isolating individual prisoners from contact with the prison population at large; whereas 'detention incommunicado' has been used to signify detention which deprives the prisoner of contact with the world outside the institution of incarceration. Assuming that the Committee is making similar use of the terms, then it may be saying no more than that the combination of segregation from the communities both within the prison and outside it violates article 7. This is important of itself, but in at least one respect it goes further. For it does not require that the solitary confinement be incommunicado in order to infringe the article, even though such infringement will be 'especially' the case where it does obtain. The reverse must surely also be true: that is that incommunicado detention need not be solitary to infringe the article; the opportunity to mix with the prison population doubtless improves the lot of the prisoner, but if the prisoner is cut off from the outside world—and especially if this is also the case of the other prisoners—then the result may be psychological stress just as severe, if not more so, than solitary confinement which permits communication with the outside world.[69] In particular, the

---

[67] General comment 20/44, *supra* n. 64, para.11.

[68] See Chapter 8. In this it is taking a position congruent with that reflected in OAS, *Annual Report of the Inter-American Commission on Human Rights 1980–1981* (OEA/Ser.L/V/II, 54; doc. 9, rev. I), 113; and in the second report of the UN Working Group on Enforced or Involuntary Disappearances (UN doc. E/CN.4/1492 (1982)), para. 178.

[69] See, generally, OAS Inter-American Commission on Human Rights, *Report on the Situation of Human Rights in Argentina* (OEA/Ser.L/V/II.49; doc. 19, corr. 1), Chapter III (1980). Note, however, that the reference to incommunicado detention in the analogous paragraph of general comment 20/44, *supra* n. 64, para. 6, has disappeared.

knowledge (or even merely the belief) that others so held are being or have been tortured or killed may exacerbate the torment of the person detained incommunicado.

In one particularly extreme individual case, the Human Rights Committee has found 'prolonged incommunicado detention in an unknown location' to be 'torture and cruel and inhuman treatment in violation of articles 7 and 10, paragraph 1 of the Covenant'.[70] In that case, as noted in Chapter 8, Mohammed Bashir El-Megreisi had effectively 'disappeared', having been detained, apparently by Libyan security police, for three years in unacknowledged detention until his wife was allowed to visit him. His subsequent location was unknown and, two years later, the Libyan government had still not responded to the Committee. Untypical and flagrant as the case may be, it still stands clearly for the proposition that prolonged incommunicado detention can violate article 7, even to the extent of constituting torture.

In sum, the underlying logic of the Committee's position would appear to be that the detention of persons in circumstances that give them or others grounds for fearing serious threat to their physical or mental integrity will violate article 7 and as such is not permissible even in time of public emergency.

The Inter-American Court of Human Rights has taken a parallel position. In the *Velásquez Rodríguez* case, involving a disappeared Honduran prisoner, the Court stated that

prolonged isolation and deprivation of communication are in themselves cruel and inhuman treatment, harmful to the psychological and moral integrity of the person and a violation of the right of any detainee to respect for his inherent dignity as a human being. Such treatment, therefore, violates Article 5 of the [American] Convention on Human Rights.[71]

Article 5, it will be recalled, is the article analogous to article 3 of the European Convention and article 7 of the Covenant. The language of the judgment uses the conjunctive (prolonged isolation *and* deprivation of communication) rather than the disjunctive 'or'. However, given that the information before the Court did not suggest that Velásquez was isolated from other prisoners, the wording should not be taken as necessarily implying that both circumstances are required at the same time for article 5 to be violated. If that reading is correct, then, according to the Court, prolonged incommunicado detention violates the article 5 prohibition of cruel and inhuman treatment, a non-suspendable provision.

Finally, the issue of suspendability of the protection of essential safeguards, such as habeas corpus and the prohibition of detention incommunicado,

---

[70] *El-Megreisi* v. *Libya* (440/1990), Report of the Human Rights Committee, Vol. II, *GAOR*, 49th Session, Supplement No. 40, Annex IX T, para. 5.4.
[71] I/A Court HR, *Velásquez Rodríguez* case, Judgment of 29 July 1988, Series C, No. 4, para. 156; see also para. 187.

under general international law must be considered.[72] It has already been argued in this chapter that the relevant rights may well be recognized under general international law. It was also suggested in Chapter 2 that the prohibition of torture and other ill-treatment was a rule of general international law, possibly amounting to a rule of *jus cogens*. Thus, to the extent that general international law would acknowledge the notion of suspendability of rights, for example, under a doctrine of necessity,[73] it would presumably not allow for the suspendability of torture or other ill-treatment. Accordingly, if, as has been suggested, prolonged incommunicado detention is a form of cruel, inhuman, or degrading treatment, then it cannot be resorted to by a state purporting to suspend certain rights in a state of emergency. Even if the detention were too brief to amount to such ill-treatment, but long enough to permit torture or other ill-treatment, the presumption ought to be that general international law follows the same logic as the treaty law, thus prohibiting such detention. Further, it has already been seen that the Body of Principles, which is seemingly intended to apply to *any* form of detention or imprisonment, whatever the circumstances, excludes detention without contact with the outside world for more than a matter of days (principle 15) and provides for a right to challenge the lawfulness of detention before a judicial or similar authority (principle 32), as well as a right to complain in respect of ill-treatment, first to a non-judicial body and then to a judicial or similar authority in the case of rejection of the complaint or inordinate delay (principle 33). The approach of the UN Special Rapporteur on Torture quoted above is set in a context suggesting that even 'exceptional circumstances' would not justify the maintenance of prolonged incommunicado detention.[74] Similarly, the Special Rapporteur on States of Emergency of the UN Sub-Commission on Prevention of Discrimination and Protection of Minorities (referred to in the following section) has taken the position that the remedy of habeas corpus is 'not derogable at any time or under any circumstances'.[75]

---

[72] Oraá, *supra* n. 40, 209–69 and especially 264–5. The International Law Association's Paris Minimum Standards of Human Rights Norms in a State of Emergency, adopted by the ILA's Sixty-First Conference (Paris, 1984) include among 'non-derogable rights and freedoms' the 'right to communicate with, and consult, a lawyer of his own choice, at any time after detention', the right to 'regular visits by the members of the family', and the right to early and periodic medical examinations, together with 'the opportunity at all times to consult a doctor of his own choice', and access to 'the remedy of *habeas corpus* (or *amparo*)' to determine the lawfulness of detention and to ensure treatment 'with humanity' (articles 5(2)(b) and (f), 5(3), and 6(5), as reproduced in 79 *AJIL* 1072, 1077 (1985)).

[73] ORAÁ, 220–6.　　　　　　　　　　　　　　　　　　　[74] *Supra* n. 39 and accompanying text.

[75] UN doc.E/CN.4/Sub.2/1996/19, para.13. A parallel view is taken in a Declaration of Minimum Humanitarian Standards adopted by an expert meeting convened by the Institute for Human Rights, Åbo Akademi University, Turku/Åbo, Finland (30 Nov.–2 Dec. 1990). The text is contained in UN doc. E/CN.4/Sub.2/1991/55, having been submitted to the Sub-Commission on Prevention of Discrimination and Protection of Minorities by two of its members, Mr Van Boven and Mr Eide. It is presently under study with the Commission on Human Rights (resolution 1998/29, 17 Apr. 1998), using the rubric 'fundamental standards of humanity' (see, generally, the UN Secretariat 'analytical report' on the issue (UN doc. E/CN.4/1998/87) for

It is, therefore, probable that any international body called upon to apply juridically the rules of general international law would find prolonged incommunicado detention and, perhaps, denial of the right judicially to challenge at least the lawfulness of detention and even arguably the treatment meted out in detention to be incompatible with that law.

INTERNATIONAL MONITORING OF STATES OF EMERGENCY

The annual review of the human rights of all persons under any form of detention or imprisonment was described in some detail in Chapter 5, but one development, noted in that chapter, deserves particular attention here. At its 1983 session, the Sub-Commission on Prevention of Discrimination and Protection of Minorities decided to request its working group on detention 'to draw up and update a list of countries which proclaim or terminate a state of emergency each year'. It also decided to submit 'an annual special report to the Commission on Human Rights containing reliably attested information on compliance with the rules, internal and international, guaranteeing the legality of the introduction of a state of emergency'.[76] The proposal grew out of the work of the working group on detention which had studied the conclusions and recommendations of its Special Rapporteur Mrs Questiaux.[77] The study had in turn been provoked by the realization 'that there was a connection between situations known as states of siege or emergency and the unfortunate developments noted in the treatment of persons who had been detained or deprived of their liberty'.[78]

The Sub-Commission decided in 1984[79] to appoint a Special Rapporteur to prepare the annual report in question. The first such report was prepared in 1987,[80] the tenth (final) in 1997.[81] This, in turn, could in principle have acted as a restraining influence on the propensity of governments to suspend legal guarantees when they feel threatened. The underlying premise would appear to be that, far from meriting international indulgence when confronted by emergencies and the need to take exceptional measures, the states concerned should be subjected to particular international vigilance.[82] In fact, however,

---

further background. Article 4 of the Turku/Abo declaration deals with the rights to 'communicate with the outside world' (para. 2) and to 'an effective remedy, including *habeas corpus*' (para. 3).

[76] Resolution 1983/30, 6 Sept. 1983, Sub-Commission Report, 36th Session (E/CN.4/1984/3; E/CN.4 Sub.2/1983/43), Chapter XXI A.

[77] Op. cit. *supra* n. 40.   [78] Id., para 11.

[79] Sub-Commission res. 1984/27, 30 Aug. 1984: Sub-Commission Report, 37th Session (E/CN.4/1985/3; E/CN.4/Sub.2/1984/43), Chapter XVIII A.

[80] UN doc. E/CN.4/Sub.2/1987/19/Rev.1 and Adds. 1 and 2.

[81] UN doc. E/CN.4/Sub.2/1997/19 (and Add. 1). The legislative history and background of the mandate may be found in the Ninth Report (UN doc. E/CN.4/Sub.2/1996/19 (paras. 1–9)), as may citations to the first eight reports (para. 6).

[82] The point was central to Mrs Questiaux's approach to the problem: UN doc. E/CN.4/Sub.2/ SR.810 (1978), para. 76. This approach may be contrasted favourably with that of the

the Special Rapporteur, Leandro Despouy (Argentina) was able to do little more than report on the details of which states may have taken measures to introduce, restrict, or abandon states of emergency. The dearth of UN Secretariat resources made available to him prevented him from offering much in the way of serious analysis of the states of emergency and their impact on human rights in specific countries.[83]

While the information contained in the annual reports may have been a helpful starting point from which to examine the effect of states of emergency on human rights in the countries listed, it was no more than that. Expectations of the reports were not realized, nor is there much prospect of effective monitoring of states of emergency as such. For the mandate has effectively been terminated by the Commission on Human Rights which has asked the Secretary-General to submit a biennial list of States under a state of emergency to its Sub-Commission.[84]

SUMMARY

Once the problem of torture had surfaced as a UN concern, it was soon recognized (as had been recognized by the NGOs which drew public attention to the problem) that the practice could be inhibited if there were adequate rules at the national level to ensure that the processes of arrest and detention, especially at the interrogation phase, were effectively controlled and supervised. The General Assembly's call for the drafting of a body of principles on the human rights of imprisoned and detained persons led to the adoption of a draft text by the UN Sub-Commission on Prevention of Discrimination and Protection of Minorities which, with significant amendments, was adopted by the Assembly in 1988.

The Body of Principles contains a number of important safeguards, including the right to legal assistance without delay, the right to communicate with the outside world, obligatory record keeping of details of interrogation, medical examination on admission and continuing medical supervision, judicial supervision of all phases of detention, the right to challenge the lawfulness of detention and the conditions of detention, as well as inquiry, if demanded,

European Court of Human Rights which, in *Brannigan*, reaffirmed its continuing acceptance of a 'wide margin of appreciation' for states that have proclaimed states of emergency and taken measures restricting human rights under them (loc. cit. *supra* n. 52, paras. 41–3). The Human Rights Committee does not seem to have followed the European Court in this regard: see, e.g. General comment 5/13: Report of the Human Rights Committee, *GAOR*, 36th Session, Supplement No. 40 (1981), Annex VII, in which the Committee notes that 'in times of emergency, the protection of human rights becomes all the more important, particularly those rights from which no derogations can be made' (para. 3).

[83] See Fitzpatrick, *supra* n. 40, 168–73. In 1997, Mr Despouy was replaced by Mr Maxim (Romania).

[84] UN Commission on Human Rights dec. 1998/108, 21 April 1998

into a death or 'disappearance' occurring during or shortly after detention. The text does not speak of the possibility of suspending its guarantees in time of emergency. It is not *per se* legally binding.

Of the various safeguards, the prohibition of incommunicado detention and the recourse of habeas corpus are probably the most central, and international law already in large measure requires them to be respected. While not specifically referring to incommunicado detention, the right to be brought before a judicial officer implies a brake on incommunicado detention. This may apply only in criminal cases, but prolonged incommunicado detention in any circumstances may involve violation of principles of respect for the inherent dignity of the human person. The right to challenge the lawfulness of detention (habeas corpus) is clearly established in the human rights instruments. In so far as both guarantees form part of the right to liberty and security of person and of the right not to be subjected to arbitrary arrest and detention, there is authority from the World Court that the rights form part of general international law.

One problem is that these rights may be subject to derogation in times of public emergency. However, it would appear that, as regards prolonged incommunicado detention and denial of the right to challenge the lawfulness of detention, these cannot ever be considered to be 'strictly required by the exigencies of the situation' (a condition for measures to be lawful even under a state of emergency). Furthermore, prolonged incommunicado detention may itself amount to violation of the prohibition of torture or other ill-treatment, a prohibition which, as seen in Chapter 2, may never be derogated from. Hopes for the effective monitoring of states of emergency and their impact on human rights by the Special Rapporteur of the Sub-Commission on Prevention of Discrimination and Protection of Minorities have not been satisfied.

International Codes of Ethics for Professionals

INTRODUCTION

One of the legacies of the Nuremberg and Tokyo war crimes trials was the recognition that, while the organs of the state may be responsible for the most appalling atrocities against those they are supposed to serve and protect, the evil acts themselves are committed not by abstract entities (the police, the judiciary, the military) against other abstract entities (the enemy within or without) but by individual men and women against other men and women. One result of this recognition has been the attribution of individual criminal responsibility to those guilty of some of the more egregious excesses with which this text is concerned (see Chapter 4).

Important as this formal legal response may be, it cannot be the sole solution to the problem. To paraphrase the Constitution of Unesco: since human rights violations begin in the minds of men, it is in the minds of men that the defences of human rights must be constructed.[1] The purpose of a code of ethics is to create a set of desired responses in each individual member of the group or profession to which the code is addressed. Since certain groups may be seen to be more vulnerable to, or more exposed to, demands that they (for example) inflict torture on perceived enemies of society, it is clearly necessary to create within such groups an ethos conducive to the rejection of such demands. The groups most directly concerned with torture and other violations of human rights are the police and other law enforcement officials,[2] including the military, but doctors and other health personnel are also often affected,[3] as too may be members of the legal profession.

As part of its standard-setting work against torture, the United Nations has now adopted ethical texts for law enforcement officials and health personnel. The Council of Europe has adopted its own such text on the police. The background to and content of these codes will be examined, with partic-

---

[1] By the first preambular paragraph of the Constitution of the United Nations Educational, Scientific and Cultural Organization (Unesco), the governments of the states parties declare that 'since wars begin in the minds of men, it is in the minds of men that the defences of peace must be constructed'.

[2] See, generally, Alderson, *The Police and Human Rights* (Council of Europe, 1984); Crawshaw, Devlin and Williamson, *Human Rights and Policing* (1998).

[3] See, generally, *Medicine Betrayed—The Participation of Doctors in Human Rights Abuses* (British Medical Association, 1992); Stover and Nightingale (eds.), *The Breaking of Bodies and Minds—Torture, Psychiatric Abuse, and the Health Professions* (1985).

ular reference to three criteria on which, it has been suggested by Professor Heijder, the merits of the different codes should be judged:

1. Is the code more than a declaration of good intentions? Does it formulate real and detailed norms of conduct?
2. Does the code provide for the mechanisms necessary for its implementation and enforcement?
3. Does the code provide for freedom of information about its norms, reports on deviance, and efforts to enforce its rules?[4]

Ideas for new codes for military personnel and for lawyers will also be discussed, as with the development of ethical principles for lawyers.

UN CODE OF CONDUCT FOR LAW ENFORCEMENT OFFICIALS

BACKGROUND

As early as 1963 a meeting convened under UN auspices proposed consideration of 'the question of a universal police code of ethics'. This was one of the conclusions of a Seminar on the Role of the Police in the Protection of Human Rights, an Asian regional meeting of law enforcement experts, including police officials, held in Canberra, Australia, from 29 April to 13 May 1963.[5] As noted in Chapter 1, the idea had thenceforth been before the Commission on Human Rights without substantive consideration until, at the initiative of the United Kingdom,[6] the Economic and Social Council (Ecosoc) adopted resolution 1794 (LIV) of 18 May 1973. By this resolution Ecosoc invited the Committee on Crime Prevention and Control to consider the matter.

Before the Committee had time to study the issue thoroughly, however,[7] it was referred to the Fifth United Nations Congress on the Prevention of Crime and the Treatment of Offenders: the General Assembly asked the Congress 'to give urgent attention to the question of the development of an international code of ethics for police and related law enforcement agencies'.[8] The Assembly took this action in a resolution dealing with a number of topics under the title 'Torture and other cruel, inhuman or degrading treatment

[4] Heijder, 'Codes of Professional Ethics Against Torture' in *Codes of Professional Ethics* (Amnesty International, 1984), 3.
[5] United Nations, *1963 Seminar on the Role of the Police in the Protection of Human Rights*, ST/TAO/HR/16, para. 209.
[6] UN doc. E/AC.7/SR.722.
[7] Fifth United Nations Congress on the Prevention of Crime and the Treatment of Offenders, *The Emerging Roles of Police and Other Law Enforcement Agencies, With Special Reference to Changing Expectations and Minimum Standards of Performance* (Secretariat working paper), A/CONF.56/5, para. 111 (1975) (hereinafter '*Emerging Roles of the Police*').
[8] GA res. 3218 (XXIX), 6 Nov. 1974.

or punishment in relation to detention or imprisonment', which became known as the 'anti-torture resolution'.[9]

When the Congress met in 1975, it had two main texts before it. One was drafted by 'a meeting of police experts from various regions of the world . . . held at Warrenton, Virginia, United States of America, between 6 and 10 January 1975' (the Warrenton Code).[10] The other was presented by the Netherlands government and consisted of the Declaration of The Hague which had been adopted by a seminar convened by Amnesty International at the Peace Palace in The Hague, Netherlands, in June 1975. The participants 'were members of police forces, police authorities and of national and international police organizations' from eight western European countries.[11] Something of the differing approaches of the two drafts may be conveyed by comparing a paragraph of each. According to article 8 of the Warrenton Code, 'a police officer must obey the orders of the legally constituted authorities and the regulations of the police organization of which the officer is a member, unless he is legally entitled to disregard them'. On the other hand, article 5 of the Declaration of The Hague provided that:

Police officers and all others covered by this code have the right to disobey or disregard any order, instruction or command, even if lawfully made within the context of national legislation, which is in clear and significant contradiction to basic and fundamental human rights, as described in the Universal Declaration of Human Rights. They have a duty to disobey or disregard any order, instruction or command summarily to execute, torture or otherwise to inflict bodily harm upon a person under their custody. They also have the duty, where they have carried out orders, instructions or commands which they believe to be otherwise in clear and significant contradiction to basic and fundamental human rights—such as lengthy detention without effective judicial supervision—to protest against the issuance of such order, instruction or command.

In the event, all the Congress could agree on was that, while there should be an international code of police ethics, 'further expert consideration of the matter' was needed.[12] Thus, the General Assembly had to consider what further attention should be given to this limited development, and at its thirtieth session, also in 1975, it decided to request the Committee on Crime Prevention and Control 'to elaborate, on the basis of, *inter alia*, the proposals submitted to and conclusions arrived at by the Fifth . . . Congress . . ., a draft code of conduct for law enforcement officials . . .'.[13]

The Committee on Crime Prevention and Control, whose fourth session took place in June 1976, had before it a note by the Secretary-General[14] con-

---

[9] *Supra* n. 7.   [10] Id., para. 115 and Annex III: the Warrenton Code.
[11] UN doc. A/CONF.56(V)/Misc.1 (1975).
[12] *Fifth United Nations Congress on the Prevention of Crime and the Treatment of Offenders—Report*, A/CONF.56/10 (1975), paras. 257–8.
[13] GA res. 3453 (XXX), 9 Dec. 1975.   [14] UN doc. E/AC.57/25, Annex (1976).

taining a new text of a 'Draft Code of Conduct for Law Enforcement Officials' and also a statement by Amnesty International drawing attention to the most salient features of the Declaration of The Hague.[15] Representatives of the International Criminal Police Organization (INTERPOL) and the International Police Association attended the session as observers. The text that emerged from the Committee was based on the Secretariat draft.[16] It then went through the Commission for Social Development and Ecosoc to the General Assembly, which began its consideration of the issue in 1977 and adopted the Code of Conduct for Law Enforcement Officials in its final form in 1979.[17]

Before considering the text, a further development needs to be noted. In the context of preparations for the Eighth United Nations Congress on the Prevention of Crime and the Treatment of Offenders, the UN Secretariat brought forward to the preparatory meetings draft basic principles on the use of force and firearms by law enforcement officials. The draft had been formulated by an 'International Expert Meeting on "United Nations and Law Enforcement", held at Baden, near Vienna, in 1987, under the auspices of the United Nations Office at Vienna'.[18] The text was considered in detail by an interregnal Preparatory Meeting of experts and a revised draft was agreed.[19] The text was considered at the 1988[20] and 1990[21] meetings of the Committee on Crime Prevention and Control, the latter approving the text that was submitted to the Congress. The Congress eventually adopted the instrument that is now the Basic Principles on the Use of Force and Firearms by Law Enforcement Officials.[22] This text is essentially a supplement to the Code of Conduct for Law Enforcement Officials and, accordingly, its provisions will be referred to in the following descriptive analysis of the Code.

The texts of the Code and the Basic Principles are reproduced in Annexes 5a and 5b respectively. Space does not permit a close description of the step-by-step evolution of the instruments from the original Secretariat drafts to the final product. Rather it is intended to draw attention to their main features, though reference will be made to the drafting stages where this may assist in construing their terms.

---

[15] UN doc. E/AC.57/NGO/2 (1976).
[16] Committee on Crime Prevention and Control, Report, Fourth Session (E.CN.5/536) (1976), Chapter I A and Annex V.
[17] GA res. 34/169, 17 Dec. 1979.
[18] UN doc. A/CONF.144/PM.1 (1988).   [19] UN doc. A/CONF./144/IPM. 5 (1988).
[20] Report of the Committee on Crime Prevention and Control, 10th Session, *ESCOR* 1988, Supplement No. 10, Chapter I A (draft resolution XIV, para. 11) and Annex IV (topic 5A).
[21] Report of the Committee on Crime Prevention and Control, 11th Session, *ESCOR* 1990, Supplement No. 10, Chapter I B, decision 11/107.
[22] *Eighth United Nations Congress on the Prevention of Crime and the Treatment of Offenders—Report*, Havana, 27 August—7 September 1990, UN doc. A/CONF.144/28/Rev.1 (1991), Chapter I B 2, Annex.

ADDRESSEES OF THE CODE

To the extent that the Code was intended specifically to protect people from being subjected to torture or cruel, inhuman, or degrading treatment, it was clearly necessary that it not be directed only to the behaviour of members of civilian police forces: experience has shown that the worst abuses of human rights are often committed when the armed forces are given the function of maintaining or restoring public order. Sometimes, too, special state security agencies, separate from the regularly constituted armed forces or police, are given such functions, especially where the government seeks to control political opposition.

Accordingly, a commentary to article 1 of the UN Code specifies that 'the term "law enforcement officials" includes all officers of the law, whether appointed or elected, who exercise police powers, especially the powers of arrest or detention', and also 'in countries where police powers are exercised by military authorities, whether uniformed or not, or by state security forces, the definition of law enforcement officials shall be regarded as including officers of such services'. This language is repeated in the Basic Principles.[23] No such specification was to be found in the draft proposed by the UN Secretariat to the Committee on Crime Prevention and Control,[24] but it was contained in the Declaration of The Hague.[25] The formulation was adopted in the draft that emerged from the Committee[26] and was consistent with the movement by the General Assembly from the language of 'an international code of ethics for the police and related law enforcement agencies'[27] to that of 'code of conduct for law enforcement officials'.[28] Nevertheless, the draft is couched in language more applicable to police services than to the military and, as will be seen below, it has been suggested that it may be appropriate to envisage the development of a further code of conduct for military personnel.

THE SCOPE OF THE CODE

Some aspects of the Code seem to fall short of Professor Heijder's first requirement (that it be 'more than a declaration of good intentions'), since much of its language is indeed that of well-meaning generality. Thus, law enforcement officials are expected 'at all times [to] fulfil the duty imposed upon them by law, by serving the community and by protecting all persons against illegal acts, consistent with the high degree of responsibility required by their profession' (article 1). Also, they are to keep confidential 'matters of

---

[23] *Eighth United Nations Congress on the Prevention of Crime and the Treatment of Offenders—Report*, Havana, 27 August—7 September 1990, UN doc. A/CONF.144/28/Rev.1 (1991), Chapter I B 2, Annex, preambular para. 1, footnote.
[24] *Supra* n. 14.   [25] *Supra* n. 15.   [26] *Supra* n. 16.   [27] *Supra* n. 7.
[28] *Supra* n. 13.

a confidential nature in [their] possession . . ., unless the performance of duty or the needs of justice strictly require otherwise' (article 4). Similarly, the Code provides that law enforcement officials 'shall not commit any act of corruption', and goes on to oblige them 'rigorously [to] oppose and combat all such acts' (article 7). Only slightly less blandly, the Code calls on law enforcement officials to 'respect and protect human dignity and maintain and uphold the human rights of all persons' (article 2).

There are, however, other provisions that more nearly fulfil Professor Heijder's requirement of 'real and detailed norms of conduct'. Accordingly, article 3 provides that 'law enforcement officials may use force only when strictly necessary and to the extent required for the performance of their duty'. As the commentary to the article explains:

This provision emphasizes that the use of force by law enforcement officials should be exceptional; while it implies that law enforcement officials may be authorized to use force as is reasonably necessary under the circumstances for the prevention of crime or in effecting or assisting in the lawful arrest of offenders or suspected offenders, no force going beyond that may be used.

The same commentary proceeds to invest this presumption against the use of force, as it might be called, with even greater precision. As noted in Chapter 6, it stipulates that 'in no case should this provision be interpreted to authorize the use of force which is disproportionate to the legitimate objective to be achieved'. Compliance with this rule would certainly reduce the number of occasions on which law enforcement officials resort to force, as well as the level of force used. The commentary achieves yet greater precision in respect of the use of firearms (that is, where the use of force in question would be potentially lethal):

The use of firearms is considered an extreme measure. Every effort should be made to exclude the use of firearms, especially against children. In general firearms should not be used except when a suspected offender offers armed resistance or otherwise jeopardizes the lives of others and less extreme measures are not sufficient to restrain or apprehend the suspected offender. In every instance in which a firearm is discharged, a report should be made promptly to the competent authorities.

The principle of necessity in the use of firearms is thus clearly set out and, in fact, the Basic Principles elaborate the point even further. Having reaffirmed the necessity principle in paragraph 5(a), they go on to impose a principle of proportionality whereby firearms may be used only to avoid death or serious injury and, even more specifically, that 'intentional lethal use of firearms may only be made when strictly unavoidable in order to protect life' (paragraph 9).[29]

Responding to the specific issue that had provoked the General Assembly to mandate the drafting of the Code, article 5 explicitly rules out the infliction,

---

[29] See also to the same effect, para. 14 (dispersing unlawful assemblies) and para. 16 (policing persons in detention).

instigation, or toleration of 'any act of torture or other cruel, inhuman or degrading treatment or punishment'. The commentary reproduces the definition of torture contained in article 1 of the Declaration against Torture (see Chapter 3 and Annex 1). Further, article 6 of the Code specifies a safeguard that could help to reinforce article 5: 'Law enforcement officials shall ensure the full protection of the health of persons in their custody and, in particular, shall take immediate action to secure medical attention whenever required.'

No such provision was included in the original draft proposed to the Committee on Crime Prevention and Control by the UN Secretariat. Its addition may perhaps be attributed to the fact that the Committee was made aware of a principle contained in the Declaration of The Hague, according to which provision should be made for law enforcement officials to 'comply with instructions of medical personnel concerned with the physical and mental health of persons in custody'.[30] While the wording of the final text of article 6 ('full protection', 'whenever required') may be interpreted so as to make the medical needs of the detained person prevail over other considerations, it lacks the vigour of the explicit subordination of the actions of law enforcement officials to the instructions of medical personnel that was present in the wording used in the Declaration of The Hague: 'to comply with the instructions of medical personnel'.

One important principle missing from the Code itself is that of *respondeat superior*, that is, the vicarious responsibility of superior officers for the acts of their subordinates. The action of Lord Caradon, the former British governor of Cyprus, responding to allegations that torture had been committed by British troops, is notable here:

At the detention centre on the Cyprus coast it was well past midnight when a military vehicle stopped abruptly outside. It had driven across the island from Nicosia through the night. Two men went straight inside. One was the colonial Governor, the other his military commander.

'We walked . . . straight into the room where the interrogation was taking place', wrote the governor years afterwards. 'We could see no sign of ill-treatment. Nor could we see any indications of force having been used on the villagers who had been interrogated earlier. But our visit that night was known throughout the island by the next morning. Our night visit did more than all the circulars to prevent the use of torture in the Cyprus emergency.'[31]

The principle of chain-of-command responsibility was contained in the Declaration of The Hague and, in drawing the principle to the attention of the Committee on Crime Prevention and Control, Amnesty International argued that:

it is the view of persons exercising governmental authority, when faced with allegations of ill-treatment committed by subordinates, that the application of this principle

[30] *Supra* n. 15, 3.   [31] Amnesty International, *Torture in the Eighties* (1984), 1.

[that is, of chain-of-command responsibility] has permitted them to take the necessary remedial measures. Similarly, those who have been charged with investigating such allegations and have found them corroborated invariably argue that the principle of responsibility of the superior would, if applied, have prevented the acts in question.[32]

The importance of the principle can hardly be overstated. Anyone familiar with ill-treatment of detainees by their captors knows that written orders to commit excesses are hardly ever to be discovered, and that frequently the ill-treatment is carried out by a process of implicit condonation: those inflicting it are confident that their superiors, if not directly approving the acts, will at least take no action to prevent them. The reasons for the omission of the principle from the Code are not contained in the public record. It is the author's personal recollection that misgivings voiced by members of the Committee centred on two points: first, aversion to the notion that people might be held accountable for acts of which they might have been entirely ignorant. Second, the principle was perceived as being at variance with progressive concepts of community policing whereby the individual police officer would be accountable less to an internal hierarchy than to the local community being served.[33]

On the other hand, while the Code may be silent on the issue of hierarchical responsibility, there is language in the General Assembly resolution adopting it that should not be overlooked. Preambular paragraph 8 of that resolution[34] expresses the Assembly's awareness

that there are additional important principles and prerequisites for the humane performance of law enforcement functions, namely:

... (d) That every law enforcement agency, in fulfilment of the first premise of every profession, should be held to the duty of disciplining itself in complete conformity with the principles and standards herein provided and that the actions of law enforcement officials should be responsive to public scrutiny, whether exercised by a review board, a ministry, a procuracy, the judiciary, an ombudsman, a citizen's committee or any combination thereof, or any other reviewing agency.

From this it could be argued that 'the duty of disciplining itself' imposed on the law enforcement agency at least implies a system of hierarchical responsibility. In any event, the text seems to suggest that there can be no shuffling off of the responsibility by senior governmental authority for the acts of the law enforcement agency as a whole.

[32] *Supra* n. 15, 2. The organization was presumably inspired by precedents such as that found in the case law of the Nuremberg Tribunal: see, e.g., Green, 'Command Responsibility in International Humanitarian Law', 5 *Transnational Law and Contemporary Problems* 319 (1995).
[33] The author represented Amnesty International, which observed the fourth session of the Committee on Crime Prevention and Control. The point was resurrected at a UN seminar attended by 19 government experts from the European region: 'law enforcement agencies should be organized in such a way that the risk of abuse of authority . . . is reduced to a minimum'. (*Symposium on the Role of the Police in the Protection of Human Rights*, UN doc. ST/HR/SER.A/6, para. 117 (2) (viii) (1980).
[34] *Supra* n. 17.

For their part, the Basic Principles leave no room for ambiguity. According to paragraph 24:

Governments and law enforcement agencies shall ensure that superior officers are held responsible if they know, or should have known, that law enforcement officials under their command are resorting, or have resorted, to the unlawful use of force and firearms, and they did not take all measures in their power to prevent, suppress or report such use.

This is a clear statement of the principle of hierarchical responsibility. However, it covers use of force and firearms that is unlawful rather than use incompatible with the Basic Principles. Clearly torture and, arguably, the use of lethal or potentially lethal force contravening the Basic Principles are unlawful under international law (see Chapters 2 and 6 respectively). But paragraph 24 does not specify whether the unlawfulness in question refers to national or international law. In fact, torture will usually, if not always, be unlawful under national law, but not all uses of excessive force, as understood in the Basic Principles, will be unlawful under national systems. Here reference may be made to the discussion in Chapter 10 of the notion of 'lawful sanctions' as an exception to the definition of torture. The argument made there that 'lawful' should be understood as meaning 'lawful under international law' could apply analogously here, that is, that 'unlawful' should mean 'unlawful under national *or* international law'.

EXPECTED RESPONSE TO NON-COMPLIANCE WITH THE CODE

Basing itself on article 5 of the Declaration of The Hague, Amnesty International urged two basic principles upon the Committee on Crime Prevention and Control in respect of orders in contravention of the proposed code. First, the code should provide for 'the DUTY of law enforcement personnel to disregard any order summarily to execute or torture persons under their custody'.[35] Second, it should provide for 'the RIGHT to disregard, or otherwise take action to avoid, orders that would result in a clear and present danger of violating basic human rights and fundamental freedoms'.[36] With regard to the first of these principles it was argued that the principle was 'a prerequisite for the maintenance of law and public order, since the acts in question are illegal in most, if not all, jurisdictions, as are orders to commit them. In addition, international law has recognized the responsibility of the individual for his/her own criminal acts (Nuremberg principles).'[37]

The final text of the UN Code is not as 'strong and audacious'[38] as was the Declaration of The Hague on this question. Instead, law enforcement officials are required 'to the best of their capability' to 'prevent and rigorously oppose any violation' of the law and the Code, which they are also enjoined to

---

[35] *Supra* n. 15, 3.   [36] Ibid.   [37] Ibid.   [38] Heijder, *supra* n. 3, 10.

'respect' (article 8(1)). While this language does not preclude an interpretation that would encompass disobedience to orders to commit such violations, a law enforcement official might well be wary of making such an interpretation. The obligation relates both to the Code and to the law and, in the case where an order creates an apparent conflict between the two, the official would be in an invidious position.

Nevertheless, there may be a presumption that such an order should not be obeyed immediately since the same article states: 'law enforcement officials who have reason to believe that a violation of this Code has occurred or *is about to occur* should report the matter to their superior authorities and, where necessary, to other appropriate authorities or organs vested with reviewing or remedial power' (emphasis added, article 8(2)). A law enforcement official who received an order to commit a violation of the Code (for example, an order to torture or to use excessive force) and who took the action contemplated by this paragraph in respect of a violation 'about to occur' might well achieve the same objective as would be achieved by outright disobedience.[39]

The same paragraph, together with its commentary, also reflects to some extent the concept contained in the Declaration of The Hague which would have imposed 'an obligation to inform the proper national and international bodies of those activities which are in direct contravention of . . . [the] Code . . . and in gross violation of human rights. . . . If necessary as a last resort they should make such information publicly known.'[40] The UN Code seems to differ from the Declaration of The Hague in two respects, however. First, neither article 8(2) nor its commentary refer to international bodies as being among the 'appropriate authorities or organs vested with reviewing or remedial power', to which law enforcement officials should report the violation or threatened violation. Indeed, the Commentary refers to these organs as those 'existing under *national* law' (emphasis added, paragraph (c)). Second, in the UN Code the only reference to publicity, albeit as a last resort, is contained in the commentary to article 8. This provides that law enforcement officials 'may be justified' (though hardly urged, much less required) 'if, as a last resort, . . . they bring violations to the attention of public opinion through the mass media'. But it seems that this justification may be invoked only (a) in those countries where 'the mass media may be regarded as performing complaint review functions'; (b) where such action is 'in accordance with the laws

[39] To the same effect, see Alderson, *supra* n. 2, 27. Nevertheless, the UN symposium referred to at n. 33 *supra* returned to the language of the Declaration of The Hague: 'Law Enforcement Officials have the duty and the right to disobey or disregard any order, instruction or command, even if apparently lawful, which is in clear and significant contradiction of the right not to be subjected to torture or other cruel, inhuman or degrading treatment or punishment.' (Para. 117(2)(vi)(a).)

[40] *Supra* n. 11, article 7 (the text may also be found in Amnesty International document AI Index: CAT 04/01/78).

and customs of their own country'; and (c) where the action also accords 'with the provisions of article 4 of the present Code' (that is, the principle of confidentiality).

Thus, the complaining officers must first report the feared violation to their 'superior authorities' (that is, through the chain of command) and only where this approach proves ineffective may there be resort to another national authority or organ. In certain countries (and one wonders which they are) they may also be justified, as a last resort, in complaining publicly. Thus, the UN Code offers no clear guidance to law enforcement officials concerning the reporting of violations outside the agency in question, even as a last resort, and can hardly be construed as requiring such action.

Again, the Basic Principles are not so shy. Paragraph 26 provides:

Obedience to superior orders shall be no defence if law enforcement officals knew that an order to use force and firearms resulting in the death or serious injury of a person was manifestly unlawful and had a reasonable opportunity to refuse to follow it. In any case, responsibility also rests on the superiors who gave the unlawful orders.

The first sentence implies an obligation not to carry out an order to use the relevant element of force if it is 'manifestly unlawful' and there is a reasonable opportunity to avoid following it. The above discussion of the notion of unlawfulness in connection with paragraph 24 applies *pari passu* to paragraph 26. The notion of 'reasonable opportunity' should be understood as implying, as at the Nuremberg tribunal, that no duress, above and beyond the mere hierarchical relationship, was present so as to exclude moral choice.[41]

The second sentence brings us back to chain-of-command responsibility in respect of those who have given the 'unlawful' order, even if the order was not *manifestly* illegal or the subordinate was under duress to comply with it. In any event, paragraph 25 provides unmistakably, if implicitly, for a right to disobey orders incompatible with the Code or the Basic Principles:

Governments and law enforcement agencies shall ensure that no criminal or disciplinary sanction is imposed on law enforcement officials who, in compliance with the Code of Conduct for Law Enforcement Officials and these basic principles, refuse to carry out an order to use force and firearms, or who report such use by other officials.

It does so by immunizing law enforcement officials from adverse consequences if they choose not to carry out the order. It also reinforces the reporting obligation. So generally does the provision in paragraph (e) of the commentary to the Code, stating that 'law enforcement officials who comply with the provisions of this Code deserve the respect, the full support and the cooperation of the community and of the law enforcement agency in which they serve, as well as of the law enforcement profession'.[42]

[41] See, Eser, 'Defences in War Crimes Trials', in Y. Dinstein and M. Tabory (eds.), *War Crimes in International Law* (1996), 251, at 254–61.
[42] *Supra* n. 11, articles 9 and 11.

IMPLEMENTATION

Aware that compliance with a code of professional ethics can often bring the professional into conflict with persons and bodies (including governments) not only outside the profession but also sometimes within it, the Declaration of The Hague had proposed that the code should provide for 'an impartial complaints mechanism, to which law enforcement officials may have recourse if they feel that the provisions of the Code have been violated or if they have suffered or risk suffering as a result of their own compliance'.[43] In fact, the Code provides for no such thing, and there is thus a certain abandonment of responsibility towards those who are expected to act, possibly at great risk to themselves, in compliance with the Code.

However, the United Nations has subsequently begun to tackle the subject: at the urging of the Sixth UN Congress on the Prevention of Crime and the Treatment of Offenders,[44] the General Assembly in 1980 invited the Committee on Crime Prevention and Control 'to study the application of the Code of Conduct on the basis of . . . information received from Member States . . .'[45] to be elicited by means of a questionnaire. This of itself was no implementation mechanism, but it may be seen as a possible step towards one. The Committee did not deal with the issue at its following (seventh) session in 1982 and, at its eighth session in 1984, it merely sought more replies from governments[46] to the Secretariat questionnaire, so that the Seventh UN Congress on the Prevention of Crime and the Treatment of Offenders could consider the matter. The Congress, in 1985, adopted a resolution by which the Secretary-General was requested to report to the Committee on Crime Prevention and Control, on the basis of information to be supplied by member states 'every five years, beginning in 1987, on the progress achieved in the implementation of the Code'.[47] Indeed Ecosoc went on to adopt a resolution by which it authorized the preparation of such a periodic report, described as 'independent' and which is to draw on 'information received from specialized agencies and relevant intergovernmental and non-governmental organizations in consultative status with the Economic and Social Council'.[48]

[43] *Supra* n. 15, 3.
[44] Resolution 12, *Sixth United Nations Congress on the Prevention of Crime and the Treatment of Offenders—Report*, A/CONF.87/14/Rev. 1 (1980), Chapter I.
[45] GA res. 35/170, 15 Dec. 1980.
[46] There were only 29: UN doc. E/AC.57/1984/4 and Corr. 1.
[47] *Seventh United Nations Congress on the Prevention of Crime and the Treatment of Offenders—Report*, A/CONF.121/22/Rev. 1 (1985), Chapter I E, res. 14, para. 2. The resolution was based on a draft set of Guidelines for the More Effective Implementation of the Code of Conduct for Law Enforcement Officials, proposed by an inter-regional preparatory meeting for the Congress: UN doc. A/Conf.121/IPM/3 (1984).
[48] Ecosoc res. 1986/10 IX, 21 May 1986. The draft was prepared by the Committee on Crime Prevention and Control, at its ninth session, 5–14 Mar. 1986: UN doc. E/AC.57/1986/L.6.

Hopes that the periodic review might be a basis for an international monitoring mechanism of the Code have so far proven unfounded. This may partly be attributable to the attitude of the intergovernmental Commission on Crime Prevention and Criminal Justice which replaced the expert Committee on Crime Prevention and Control in 1992[49] and for which the word 'implementation' proved to be unacceptable, the Commission preferring the use of the term 'promotion of the use and application'.[50] The latest survey which covers both the Code and the Basic Principles is based only on sixty-five government replies,[51] although questionnaires were also sent to non-governmental organizations (NGOs).[52] Much of the reporting is non-country specific.[53] Thus, in the report's section on 'action against torture', two unidentified countries are remarkably said to have reported 'that in order to obtain information or confessions, law enforcement officials were, in special cases, permitted to use interviewing techniques which might cause physical or mental pain or suffering'.[54] Two countries (the same ones?) were noted as reporting that 'such techniques were permitted when there was a threat to national security', and when there was a public 'emergency'.[55] Given the acknowledgement of the apparent illegality of the practices (see Chapter 2), scant encouragement is to be found in the Secretariat observation that the techniques 'were not limited to acceptable international standards in some countries'.[56] In any event, there is nothing here suggesting a mechanism for redress in case of violation of the Code or the Basic Principles.

Meanwhile, in 1989, Ecosoc adopted 'Guidelines for the Effective Implementation of the Code of Conduct for Law Enforcement Officials'.[57] Despite the focus of implementation in the title, the main thrust of the Guidelines is in the field of training and dissemination (see below). Taking

[49] See, generally, Clarke, *The United Nations Crime Prevention and Criminal Justice Program—Formulation of Standards and Efforts at Their Implementation* (1994), especially chapters 2, 3, and 10.

[50] See Report of the Commission on Crime Prevention and Criminal Justice, 2nd Session (E/1993/32; E/CN.15/1993/9), Chapter I, draft res. VII, part III, para. 3. A recent Secretariat document raising the possibility of an inter-sessional working group to review the periodic surveys on the use and application of the norms and standards adopted in the crime and justice area (UN doc. E/CN.15/1997/14) was ignored by the Commission at its 1997 (sixth) session: E/CN.15/1997/L.9/Rev.1.

[51] UN doc. E/CN.15/1996/16/Add. 2, para. 2.   [52] UN doc. E/CN.15/1996/16, para. 6.

[53] Generally, the document is not so loath to mention the name of the responding state when that state is providing information that does not appear to put it in a negative light. In future, it appears that such disguises of reality will be avoidable. At its 1997 (sixth) session the Commission appeared to authorize the Secretariat 'to summarize that information [contained in responses to questionnaires] country by country, and to disseminate it via the World Wide Web database facility of the United Nations Crime and Justice Information Network' (UN doc. E/CN.15/1997/L.9/Rev. 1).

[54] *Supra* n. 51, para. 11.   [55] Ibid.   [56] Id., para. 85.

[57] Ecosoc res. 1989/61, 24 May 1989, Annex, adopted on recommendation of the Committee on Crime Prevention and Control: Report of the Committee on Crime Prevention and Control, 10th Session, *ESCOR*, 1988, Supplement No. 10, Chapter I A, draft resolution VI.

'implementation' to mean adoption and responses to non-compliance, the Guidelines require that '[t]he principles embodied in the Code shall be reflected in national legislation and practice' (paragraph IA1). What is meant by 'principles' is not specified. The only measure contemplating non-compliance is that requiring that 'provisions . . . be made . . . for the receipt and processing of complaints against law enforcement officials by members of the public' (paragraph IB4). However, these provisions are to be 'within . . . mechanisms [that are to] be established to ensure the internal discipline and external control as well as the supervision of law enforcement officials' (paragraphs IB3 and IB4). Since many governments believe that existing systems providing for only judicial recourse (usually dependent on investigations conducted by the very law enforcement agencies whose members' activities may be challenged) are a sufficient external check on the behaviour of such officials, the Guidelines do not appear effectively to address the persistent problem of impunity of the officials. Moreover, the text is silent on recourse by law enforcement officials adversely affected by reason of compliance with the Code. As far as implementation (as described above) at the international level is concerned, the text is silent.

TRAINING AND DISSEMINATION

During its development, it had been recommended that the code should emphasize 'training of law enforcement personnel in the principles of human rights and the terms of the code'.[58] While the UN Code itself does not deal with this issue, the General Assembly resolution adopting it indicates that 'standards as such lack practical value unless their content and meaning, through education and training and through monitoring, become part of the creed of every law enforcement official'.[59] A year later, the Assembly adopted another resolution, by which it called on all states:

(a) To consider favourably the use of the Code of Conduct for Law Enforcement Officials within the framework of national legislation and practice or directives governing law enforcement agencies;
(b) To make the text of the Code of Conduct available to all law enforcement officials in their own language;
(c) To instruct, in basic training programmes and in all subsequent training and refresher courses, law enforcement officials in the provisions of the national legislations [sic] which are connected with the Code of Conduct and other basic texts on human rights.[60]

The Guidelines on implementation of the Code mentioned in the previous section repeat the requirement in points (b) and (c) of the General Assembly

---

[58] *Supra* n. 15.   [59] *Supra* n. 17, eighth preambular paragraph.
[60] *Supra* n. 45.

resolution (paragraphs IIA1 and IA4). They also require governments to disseminate the Code to the public in general (paragraph IIA2). The mere existence of these obligations may be useful to those who have occasion to make recommendations to governments in the context of allegations of abuses by law enforcement officials.

COUNCIL OF EUROPE DECLARATION ON THE POLICE

Some months before the UN Code of Conduct for Law Enforcement Officials was adopted, the Parliamentary Assembly of the Council of Europe adopted the Declaration on the Police.[61] This was the result of an initiative by a number of Assembly members in 1974.[62]

One of the texts before the legal affairs committee of the Parliamentary Assembly which prepared the draft text that the Assembly was to adopt, was one prepared by a group of NGOs in consultative status with the Assembly, including two organizations of police professionals; the International Federation of Senior Police Officers and the European Organization of the International Federation of Employees in the Public Service (Eurofedop).[63] Another text was submitted by the International Union of Police Trade Unions.[64] Both texts reflected many of the principles contained in the Declaration of The Hague; the final text approved by the Assembly in turn reflected similar principles in some respects. The text of Part A of the Declaration on the Police, entitled Ethics, is reproduced as Annex 5c. Here, attention will be drawn to those aspects of the Declaration that more closely follow the Declaration of The Hague than does the UN Code of Conduct, since to some extent it repairs at the European level the omissions of the Code, even as supplemented by the Basic Principles, noted above.

The most obvious respect in which the Declaration on the Police resembles the Declaration of The Hague more than it does the UN Code of Conduct is in the issue of obedience to orders. Having prohibited in all circumstances summary executions, torture, and other forms of cruel, inhuman, or degrading 'treatment or punishment', A(3) of the Declaration states that 'a police officer is under an *obligation to disobey or disregard* any order or instruction involving such measures' (emphasis added). In addition, A(4) requires the officer to 'refrain from carrying out any order he knows, or ought to know, is unlawful'. These vigorous and unambiguous provisions are reinforced by

[61] Resolution 690 (1979) Appendix, 8 May 1979. The Parliamentary Assembly consists of nominees of national parliaments of the now 40 member states of the Council of Europe.
[62] Council of Europe, Consultative Assembly (as it was then called), doc. 3402 revised, 24 Jan. 1974 (proposed by Mr Archer (UK) and 10 others).
[63] Council of Europe doc. H (75) 21, 24 Oct. 1975.
[64] Council of Europe doc. AS/Jur. (28) 8, 1 July 1976.

A(7) which offers special protection: 'No criminal or disciplinary action will be taken against a police officer who has refused to carry out an unlawful order.'

The Declaration also has language which explicitly requires that medical needs should prevail over other considerations. According to A(14), police officers having custody of persons needing medical attention 'shall follow the instructions of doctors and other competent medical workers when they place a detainee under medical care'. The Declaration also adopts the principle of chain-of-command responsibility. A(10) states: 'There shall be a clear chain of command. It should always be possible to determine which superior may be ultimately responsible for acts or omissions of a police officer.'

At the same time as it adopted the Declaration, the Parliamentary Assembly also recommended that the Council of Europe's intergovernmental body, the Committee of the Ministers, should invite the individual governments of the Council's member states 'to give their full support to the declaration . . .'.[65] This recommendation went without response for over three years, and when a reply eventually came the Committee of Ministers expressed 'certain hesitations and objections' that had precluded the granting of 'unqualified support'.[66] Most of these 'hesitations and objections' did not relate to Part A of the Declaration dealing with ethics, but among those that did, the reply noted that 'conflicts might arise by reason of the fact that the principle of obedience is stricter in the armed forces than in the police'.[67] It also found that the word 'unlawful' in A(4) quoted above, was 'too wide and might impair the principles of hierarchy and discipline in the police'.[68] On the other hand there appears to have been no challenge to the obligation not to obey orders involving summary executions, torture, or other ill-treatment. Since such behaviour would also be a grave breach of the Geneva Conventions of 12 August 1949 (see Chapters 4 and 6), the rule is presumably not affected by the fact that the principle of obedience is stricter in the armed forces than in the police.

The Council of Europe has not engaged in implementation of the Declaration. However, it has developed a programme to promote respect for human rights in policing.[69]

---

[65] Recommendation 858 (1979), 8 May 1979.
[66] Council of Europe doc. AS/Jur. (34) 21, 4 Nov. 1982, para. 17.
[67] *Id*, para. 3. A footnote to Part A Ethics clarifies that the text covers 'armed forces . . . performing police duties'.
[68] Id., para. 5.
[69] Council of Europe doc. H(97) 9, 24 Oct., 1997

CODE(S) OF MILITARY ETHICS?

As noted above, the UN Code of Conduct for Law Enforcement Officials and the Council of Europe Declaration on the Police apply not only to the civilian police but to others, including the military, who are engaged in functions which may include the custody of prisoners. It may not therefore be felt necessary to consider the possibility of a separate instrument of professional ethics for military personnel. Certainly the UN has not broached the subject, yet the suggestion has been made and been thought to be worth exploring.[70]

The argument is basically that, while police organizations and representatives were, as has been seen, involved in various stages of developing the codes for law enforcement officials, this was not true as regards the military.[71] Further, it may be said that the principles of humanitarian law, dealing as they do with the conduct of warfare, are familiar to, and understood by, military personnel, whereas principles of human rights aimed at the regulation of civil society may well seem to them to be beyond their mandate. So it is suggested that the military need to be involved in evolving their own codes of conduct.[72] This will clearly require that initiatives be taken at the national level by interested persons and groups, probably with the support of governments, to discuss the ethical problems relating to detention that may confront military personnel. The documentary starting points might well be the UN Code of Conduct for Law Enforcement Officials, as supplemented by the Basic Principles on the Use of Force and Firearms by Law Enforcement Officials, which governments are committed to inculcating into all addressees, and article 3 common to the four Geneva Conventions of 12 August 1949, which represents the distillation of the rules of international humanitarian law applicable in armed conflict (see Chapter 2).

Meanwhile, the Parliamentary Assembly of the Council of Europe has instructed its legal affairs committee 'to consider the possibility of drafting a European code of professional ethics for the armed forces'.[73] The main motivation of the leading sponsor of this initiative appears to be the protection of the human rights of soldiers, so that 'to the greatest possible extent, they should be integrated into our democratic society'.[74] Even if the scope of any such code were to be thus limited it could still well furnish the appropriate

---

[70] See *Report of the International Seminar on Torture and Human Rights*, 1977, *infra* n. 112, Chapter II A, recommendations 13–15, and pp. 12–13; and International Conference on Extrajudicial Executions (Noordwijkerhout, Netherlands, 1982), reported in: Amnesty International, *Political Killings by Governments* (1983), 100–22, at 109–11.

[71] Id., 110.

[72] Ibid. The proposed Declaration of Minimum Humanitarian Standards could provide an opportunity for involving the military: see Chapter 11, n. 75.

[73] Council of Europe, Parliamentary Assembly, Order No. 411(1982), 29 Sept. 1982; and doc. 4719, 12 May 1981 (proposed by Mr Elmquist (Denmark) and 11 others).

[74] Council of Europe, Parliamentary Assembly, doc. AS (34) CR 9, item 11 (1982).

ethos and guidance for soldiers to take seriously their obligations towards the civilian community when called upon to exercise a law enforcement function, and to be protected when they do so. In the event all that emerged from its process was Parliamentary assembly Resolution 903 (1988) of 30 June 1988 calling on states to permit members of armed forces to form, join and participate in professional associations.

UN PRINCIPLES OF MEDICAL ETHICS

BACKGROUND

As was seen in Chapter 1, the idea of developing 'principles of medical ethics which may be relevant to the protection of persons subjected to any form of detention or imprisonment against torture and other cruel, inhuman or degrading treatment or punishment' first surfaced at the intergovernmental level in 1974. In the same resolution by which it had initiated thinking on police ethics, the UN General Assembly invited the World Health Organization (WHO) to draft an outline of such principles.[75] The draft was to be brought before the Fifth UN Congress on the Prevention of Crime and the Treatment of Offenders in 1975.

The World Medical Association (WMA), a non-governmental organization, had already embarked on a similar exercise, apparently in response to a series of events in the United Kingdom: according to Dr A. Wynen, Secretary-General of the WMA, a group of British Parliamentarians had investigated and confirmed allegations of torture in Northern Ireland; the group went on to observe that 'if torture had become inevitable, it was necessary to humanize it and have an attending physician to moderate it, and even stop it if, in his medical opinion, it became physically dangerous!'[76] The British Medical Association apparently reacted to this wisdom by forbidding all British doctors to participate, directly or indirectly, in such practices. It was criticized for taking this position, and so in 1972 turned to the WMA for guidance. The WMA response was its unanimous adoption on 10 October 1975 at the twenty-ninth World Medical Assembly in Tokyo, Japan, of the Declaration of Tokyo—Guidelines for Medical Doctors Concerning Torture and other Cruel, Inhuman or Degrading Treatment or Punishment in relation to Detention or Imprisonment. As will become evident, this was to become an important document for the issue of medical ethics.

Meanwhile, the WHO was able, in the short time available to it, to submit only an inconclusive paper[77] to the Fifth Congress, and the Congress did not

[75] GA res. 3218 (XXIX), 6 Nov. 1974.

[76] Wynen, 'The Physician and Torture', *World Medical Journal*, vol. xxviii, no. 2 (1981), 18.

[77] Fifth United Nations Congress on the Prevention of Crime and the Treatment of Offenders, *Health Aspects of Avoidable Maltreatment of Prisoners and Detainees* (working paper prepared by the World Health Organization), A/CONF.56/9 (1975).

pursue the matter.[78] Accordingly, the General Assembly invited the WHO to 'give further attention to the study and elaboration of [the] principles of medical ethics'.[79] The WHO entrusted the task to the Council for International Organizations of Medical Sciences (CIOMS), a non-governmental organization established with the joint sponsorship of the WHO and Unesco.[80] In October 1978 the CIOMS produced a text of the proposed principles,[81] and these were endorsed in January 1979 by the WHO Executive Board[82] which authorized their transmittal to the UN Secretary-General.[83]

The General Assembly's first act on the matter was to have the text circulated to governments and others, including interested NGOs, for comments and suggestions,[84] and it repeated the exercise the following year.[85] At its 1981 session, the General Assembly authorized the circulation of a revised text for comment[86] by governments only. On 18 December 1982, it adopted the 'Principles of Medical Ethics relevant to the role of health personnel, particularly physicians, in the protection of prisoners and detainees against torture and other cruel, inhuman or degrading treatment or punishment'.[87] In the resolution by which it adopted the Principles, the General Assembly is to be found 'recalling with appreciation the Declaration of Tokyo'.[88] Similarly, the WHO when it forwarded the CIOMS text, made it clear that it, like the CIOMS, saw its text as intending to 'supplement the Declaration of Tokyo ... and the UN Standard Minimum Rules for the Treatment of Prisoners'.[89]

ADDRESSEES OF THE PRINCIPLES

Since the WMA is an organization of national professional associations of medical doctors, its Declaration of Tokyo was naturally aimed at giving ethical guidance to such doctors. Wisely, the UN Principles are not so restricted. The General Assembly resolution that adopted the Principles recognizes, in its sixth preambular paragraph, 'that throughout the world significant medical activities are being performed increasingly by health personnel not licensed or trained as physicians, such as physician-assistants, paramedics, physical therapists and nurse practitioners'.[90] Accordingly, each of the Principles is expressed, like the title, to apply to 'health personnel, particularly physicians'. The Principles may therefore be understood as aimed at the

---

[78] Report, *supra* n. 12.
[79] GA res. 3453 (XXX), 9 Dec. 1975; see also GA res. 31/85, 13 Dec. 1976.
[80] UN doc. A/34/273, Annex, paras. 1.3 and 1.4 (1979).
[81] Reproduced in id., Annex, 4.   [82] Id., para. 2.   [83] Ibid.
[84] GA res. 34/168, 17 Dec. 1979.   [85] GA res. 35/179, 13 Dec. 1980.
[86] GA res. 36/61, 25 Nov. 1981, and Annex.
[87] GA res. 37/194, 15 Dec. 1982, and Annex. Reproduced in Annex 6.   [88] Ibid.
[89] *Supra* n. 80, Annex, para. 2.1 (1979). For the Standard Minimum Rules, see Chapter 9 and Annex 3.
[90] *Supra* n. 87.

broad range of health personnel involved in medical activities, as described in the sixth preambular paragraph of the Assembly resolution. In other words, members of any group of professionals possessing specifically medical expertise are expected to comply with the Principles.

THE SCOPE OF THE PRINCIPLES

The basic thrust of the language in both the Declaration of Tokyo and the UN Principles is similar. Under UN principle 2, it is 'a gross contravention of medical ethics' for health personnel 'to engage, actively or passively, in acts which constitute participation in, complicity in, incitement to or attempts to commit torture or other cruel, inhuman or degrading treatment or punishment'; under the Declaration of Tokyo, doctors are not to 'countenance, condone or participate in' such practices.[91] Both documents therefore prohibit medical personnel from involvement with torture and other ill treatment. The UN Principles go on to define torture, using a definition based, predictably, on that given in the Declaration against Torture, which demands a high threshold of pain or suffering to be passed for the term to apply (see Chapter 3) and excludes certain 'lawful sanctions' (see Chapters 1 and 10). No definition is offered of the second limb of the formula, 'cruel, inhuman or degrading treatment or punishment'. One problem with the UN Principles, therefore, is that they fail to give health personnel any guidance as to what constitutes prohibited ill-treatment other than torture.

As far as the UN Principles are concerned, then, health personnel know that any involvement with outright torture (as considered in Chapter 3 and encompassing also medical or scientific experimentation on human beings without their free consent—Chapter 9) or with the more obvious forms of cruel, inhuman, or degrading treatment not amounting to torture (also described in Chapter 3) is a gross contravention of the Principles. Yet there remain some grey areas where the Principles might usefully offer guidance. These 'grey areas' may be addressed by the following questions:

May a health worker:

(*a*) participate in the infliction of capital punishment?
(*b*) participate in the infliction of corporal punishment?
(*c*) certify a prisoner as fit for capital punishment?
(*d*) certify a prisoner as fit for corporal punishment?
(*e*) evaluate the health of a prisoner to determine fitness for interrogation?
(*f*) treat a prisoner with a view to restoring health prior to interrogation?

Of course, to the extent that corporal punishment may be considered a cruel, inhuman, or degrading punishment or even in some cases torture (as

---

[91] The Declaration of Tokyo is reproduced in *Codes of Professional Ethics, supra* n. 4, Chapter V and in UN doc. A/34/273, Annex 8 (1979).

suggested in Chapter 10), no problem arises with questions (*b*) and (*d*). Any involvement of whatever nature would fall foul of principle 2. The difficulty is that, despite the argument in Chapter 10, a number of countries do resort to judicial corporal punishment, and it might be asking too much of health personnel to be aware of international doctrine and case law suggesting that such punishment is at least cruel, inhuman, or degrading. Similarly, no problem arises where interrogation practices clearly amount to cruel, inhuman, or degrading treatment, as these would again fall foul of principle 2. The difficulty is that treatment potentially injurious to health may not always fall within this category (see Chapters 3 and 9) and it could be difficult for health personnel to be clear on when the threshold is reached.

It is regrettably clear that capital punishment as such cannot yet be categorized as falling with the prohibition against torture or other ill-treatment unless it is inflicted with unnecessary cruelty. Accordingly it is not at present covered by principle 2.

The guidance given by the UN Principles in answering the questions listed above is best approached by considering UN principle 3: 'It is a contravention of medical ethics for health personnel, particularly physicians, to be involved in any professional relationship with prisoners or detainees the purpose of which is not solely to evaluate, protect or improve their physical or mental health.' This principle unambiguously precludes any participation of health personnel in the *infliction* of capital or corporal punishment ((*a*) and (*b*) above), since such participation would be manifestly incompatible with a relationship whose purpose is solely to evaluate, protect, or improve health.[92] However, it may well not cover certification of fitness for such punishment, since such certification may be permitted by the word 'evaluate'. This word did not appear in the CIOMS text, as endorsed by the WHO, and was added by the General Assembly. The word has the same effect regarding evaluation of fitness to endure interrogation (*e*), except, of course, where the methods of interrogation are themselves manifestly cruel, inhuman, or degrading. Finally, the principle does not address the issue of medical treatment for the purpose of rendering the prisoner fit for interrogation (*f*) since its purpose would be the improvement of health. Thus, while principle 3 answers questions (*a*) and (*b*) negatively, (*c*), (*d*), (*e*), and (*f*) remain to be addressed unambiguously.

Principle 4 comes close to offering clear advice, but then shies away from clarity:

It is a contravention of medical ethics for health personnel, particularly physicians:

(*a*) To apply their knowledge and skills in order to assist in the interrogation of prisoners and detainees in a manner that may adversely affect the physical or mental

92 Kemperman, 'Medical Involvement in Capital Punishment', *Lancet* (1983), No. 1, 301 and cited in id., 12 Feb. 1983, 371.

health or condition of such prisoners or detainees *and which is not in accordance with the relevant international instruments*;
(*b*) To certify, or to participate in the certification of, the fitness of prisoners or detainees for any form of treatment or punishment that may adversely affect their physical or mental health *and which is not in accordance with the relevant international instruments*, or to participate in any way in the infliction of any such treatment or punishment *which is not in accordance with the relevant international instruments* [emphasis added].

But for the emphasized words, all the questions set out as (*a*)–(*f*) above would be addressed, including those already treated by principle 3, and would have been answered in the negative. These words, which did not appear in any text before that adopted by the General Assembly and whose inclusion remains unexplained, tend to confuse what had appeared clear. Thus, questions (*c*) and (*d*) at first seem to be answered negatively by principle 4(b) in that certification of fitness for capital or corporal punishment would be certification for punishment 'that may adversely affect their physical or mental health'. But the health personnel seem to be required to assess not only whether the punishment in question may have such an adverse effect but also whether it may nevertheless be in accordance with the relevant international instruments.

Similarly, questions (*e*) and (*f*) would at first sight seem to be answered negatively by principle 4(a) (in fact question (*e*) would also seem to be treated *pari passu* by principle 4(b)) in that both forms of involvement in interrogation practices would constitute an application of knowledge and skills to assist in interrogation in a manner that may adversely affect a detainee's physical or mental health or condition. But here again the health personnel seemingly have to assess not only whether the manner of interrogation is likely to have the adverse effect, but also whether it may nevertheless be in accordance with the relevant international instruments. If questions (*a*) and (*b*) (participation in the infliction of capital or corporal punishment) had not already been answered by principle 3, the effect of principle 4(b) would have raised the same problem for health personnel: they should not 'participate in any way' in the infliction of a punishment adverse to health, *unless*, apparently, the punishment is in accordance with the relevant international instruments.

Thus, the closer reading seems to suggest that the clarity given in the substance of principle 4 is taken away by the reference to the relevant international instruments. Such a reading would imply that principle 4 is redundant, an implication that would leave the reading open to challenge on the principle of interpretation that presumes against redundancy and in favour of words having meaning. Is there then a reading available that would make principle 4 have some meaning, despite the apparent effect of the phrase 'not in accordance with the relevant international instruments'? The

Principles are, after all, not so much a legal document as one intended to offer guidance to health personnel. The above reading notably fails to offer this. An alternative explanation for the inclusion of the phrase would be one that precisely sees the purpose of the Principles as offering such guidance. Approached this way it might be possible to argue that the purpose of the phrase is simply to direct health professionals to the relevant instruments so that they may be further apprised of their contents, as illustrations of, rather than restrictions on, the behaviour they qualify. This approach has the further merit of being more consistent with the General Assembly's stated position when adopting the Principles: it declared itself 'desirous of setting *further* standards in this field' (emphasis added). Since it had just quoted the main relevant international instruments (it had also recalled with appreciation the WMA's Declaration of Tokyo), it should not lightly be presumed that in practice it fails to set such further standards.

It is suggested, therefore, that a reading consistent with offering guidance to health professionals and with the General Assembly's stated intention of setting further standards would read principle 4 to answer questions (*a*) to (*f*) above negatively: health personnel should not do any of the acts suggested by the questions. It must, however, be acknowledged that the more literal (but for many, less acceptable) reading cannot as yet be dismissed. Accordingly, it may be helpful to health professionals, particularly physicians, to be aware of the relevant WMA standards.

The key WMA instrument is the Declaration of Tokyo, whose article 1 is similar to UN principle 2.[93] The difference is that, whereas the latter contains the definition of torture given in the Declaration against Torture, the WMA's definition is 'the deliberate, systematic or wanton infliction of physical or mental suffering by one or more persons acting alone or on the orders of any authority, to force another person to yield information, to make a confession, or for any other reason'. Since the word 'torture' then covers the deliberate infliction or the systematic infliction or the wanton infliction of physical or mental suffering and this may be for the traditional purposes or 'for any other reason',[94] it would appear that any of the practices, in respect of which there may be doubt as to whether they are covered by the UN Principles, would be

[93] Article 1 of the Declaration of Tokyo reads: 'The doctor shall not countenance, condone or participate in the practice of torture or other forms of cruel, inhuman or degrading procedures, whatever the offence of which the victim of such procedures is suspected, accused or guilty, and whatever the victim's beliefs or motives, and in all situations, including armed conflict and civil strife.'

[94] A lawyer interpreting the term 'for any other reason' might apply the *ejusdem generis* rule: this means that when a general word or expression (e.g. 'for any other reason') follows a list of specifics (e.g. reasons such as coercing information or confessions), then the general term must be interpreted to signify a general category exemplified by the preceding list. However, as becomes obvious below, the WMA takes no such approach. For example, the WMA considers that the Declaration applies to punishments, although these would not fall within the category represented by such reasons as coercing confessions or information.

condemned by the Declaration of Tokyo. The practice of the WMA tends to bear this out. Thus, it specifically invoked the Declaration of Tokyo in a vigorous protest which deplored the involvement of surgeons in the amputation of hands of convicted thieves in Mauritania.[95] Similarly, in the wake of a public statement by the WMA Secretary-General expressing concern about possible professional medical involvement in administering the death penalty in Oklahoma, USA,[96] the thirty-fourth World Medical Assembly ratified his action by resolving 'that it is unethical for physicians to participate in capital punishment, although this does not preclude physicians certifying death'.[97]

The only area of medical involvement in such circumstances countenanced by the WMA appears to be certification of death following capital punishment. (Of course, even this may bring to doctors the distasteful task of ensuring that the state had done enough to deprive the condemned person of life.[98] It may nevertheless be understood that the family and associates of an executed person have as much need of official evidence of death as the authorities, and that certification of death may be justified on humanitarian grounds.)

Another topic of controversy in medical ethics is that of forcible feeding, and again the UN Principles are silent upon it. The WMA Declarations of Tokyo and Malta, however, provide a nuanced approach, which has already been dealt with in Chapter 9.

EXPECTED RESPONSE TO NON-COMPLIANCE WITH THE PRINCIPLES

The UN Principles, as has been seen, describe health personnel involvement in torture and other ill-treatment as a 'gross contravention' of medical ethics; acts incompatible with the other principles are considered to be 'contraventions' of medical ethics. The distinction between a contravention and a gross contravention is not explained, and the implications of contravention are not defined.

The concept of disobedience to orders, controversial and difficult for police and military personnel, is less so with regard to doctors. Doctors are not, in principle, members of a hierarchically structured profession: each doctor is theoretically autonomous. Even doctors working in a medical institution are less restricted by the institutional nature of their work than would be police

---

[95] *World Medical Journal*, vol. xxviii, no. 2 (1981), 21; see also n. 107 *infra* and accompanying text.

[96] World Medical Association Press Release, 11 Sept. 1981.

[97] Resolution on Physician Participation in Capital Punishment, adopted by the 34th World Medical Assembly of the World Medical Association, Lisbon, Portugal, 29 Sept. 1981. The text of this resolution and the press release just mentioned are reproduced in *Codes of Professional Ethics*, supra n. 4, Chapter VII, and in *Ethical Codes and Declarations Relevant to the Health Professions* (Amnesty International, 3rd rev. edn., 1994), 11–12.

[98] See, for example, the execution of Charles Books in Huntsville, Texas, USA, described in Amnesty International, *Report 1983*, 173–4.

officers or soldiers. Moreover, there is a venerable tradition of medical adherence to professional ethical principles even in the face of great adversity. Nevertheless, the resolution adopting the Principles contains a preambular paragraph that seems to acknowledge a potential conflict between medical ethics and official authority, in that it described the General Assembly as 'convinced that under no circumstances should a person be punished for carrying out medical activities compatible with medical ethics, regardless of the person benefiting therefrom, or be compelled to perform acts or to carry out work in contravention of medical ethics'.[99] Thus it seems to resolve the conflict in favour of the physician who refuses to compromise medical ethics. It still is not a ringing call for doctors to confront authority by refusal to carry out its wishes.

It is instructive again to compare the UN Principles with the Declaration of Tokyo, since the latter is somewhat more vigorous. In the first place it is generally couched in the peremptory language of what doctors 'shall' or 'shall not' do. Further, as noted above, a doctor's 'fundamental role is to alleviate the distress of his or her fellow man, and no motive—whether personal, collective or political—shall prevail against this higher purpose' (article 4). Indeed, according to the Declaration's preamble, 'the utmost respect for human life is to be maintained even under *threat*' (emphasis added). It seems fairly clear from this that whatever the pressures upon them, doctors are to refuse to act in violation of medical ethics in general and of the Declaration of Tokyo in particular; even here, however, it may not be certain that the individual doctor is being addressed. The language of a similar resolution adopted by the International Council of Nurses[100] is yet more direct: 'the nurse's first responsibility is towards her patients, notwithstanding considerations of national security and interest'. Similarly, the World Psychiatric Association's Declaration of Hawaii[101] prohibits 'maltreatment of individuals or groups' by professional psychiatrists (especially 'compulsory psychiatric treatment in the absence of psychiatric illness') and provides that 'if the patient *or some third party* demands actions contrary to scientific or ethical principles the psychiatrist must refuse to cooperate' (emphasis added).

It will be recalled that law enforcement officials were called upon to 'prevent and rigorously oppose any violations' of the Code's provisions. However, the UN Principles are silent on what should happen if a health worker fails to comply with the Principles. The General Assembly resolution adopting the Principles gives some guidance, however. The paragraph quoted

[99] *Supra* n. 87.

[100] Role of the Nurse in the Care of Detainees and Prisoners (resolution adopted by the Council of National Representatives of the International Council of Nurses, Singapore, Aug. 1975), reproduced in *Codes of Professional Ethics, supra* n. 4, Chapter VIII and *Ethical Codes and Declarations Relevant to the Medical Professions, supra* n. 97, 24.

[101] Declaration of Hawaii of the World Psychiatric Association, Honolulu, Aug. 1977, reproduced in *Ethical Codes and Declarations Relevant to the Medical Professions, supra*, n. 97.

above goes on to express the General Assembly's conviction that 'contravention of medical ethics for which health personnel, particularly physicians, can be held responsible should entail accountability'; it does not, however, indicate what form such accountability would take. The Declaration of Tokyo does not deal with the question at all, and neither instrument gives explicit guidance as to the responsibility of colleagues when confronted by a breach of ethics by fellow health personnel. Indeed, the issue arose at the 1983 session of the WMA World Medical Assembly, where a suggestion that doctors should denounce colleagues who may condone torture or ill-treatment seems to have been given a hostile reception.[102] This may be compared with the approach taken by the International Council of Nurses, whose resolution on the 'Role of the Nurse in the Care of Detainees and Prisoners' is firm that 'nurses having knowledge of physical or mental ill-treatment of detainees [are to] take appropriate action including reporting the matter to appropriate national and/or international bodies'.

IMPLEMENTATION

The need for effective implementation of the UN Principles and other guidelines is reflected in a resolution adopted on 31 August 1983 by the Second World Conference on Prison Health Care, Ottawa, Canada. This called upon the Seventh UN Congress on the Prevention of Crime and the Treatment of Offenders 'to seek to establish a standing commission . . . to visit prisons to monitor compliance with the UN principles of medical ethics'.[103] The Congress did not respond to the call.

As was seen in respect of police codes, there are two aspects to serious implementation of a code of professional ethics. One is that there be a system to support those who find themselves in difficulty as a result of compliance with the code; the other is that there be a system to monitor breaches—in practice usually a mechanism for receiving complaints. The UN Principles offer neither. The resolution by which they are adopted disposes of the matter thus:

noting that in accordance with the Declaration of Tokyo[104] measures should be taken by States and by professional associations and other bodies, as appropriate, against any attempt to subject health personnel or members of their families to threats or

---

[102] *Le Concours médical* (Paris), 12 Nov. 1983, 4.

[103] It is no accident that such a body should take such a line: medical personnel who are part of the prison establishment are at particular risk of their skills being abused; see Buffard, Barral, Do, and Gonin, 'Le Médecin en institution pénitentiaire', *Médecine et Hygiène—Journal suisse d'informations médicales*, vol. xlii, no. 1559, 18 (1984); also Léry, Chambaz, and Labarthe, 'Le Personnel soignaint face à la torture et aux traitements inhumains, cruels et dégradants', id., 20.

[104] Article 6 of the Declaration of Tokyo had also urged this approach, referring to the 'international community' rather than to states.

reprisals resulting from refusal by such personnel to condone the use of torture or other forms of cruel, inhuman or degrading treatment or punishment.[105]

Thus, apart from noting an obligation on states and professional associations, the UN Principles do not offer protection to health personnel complying with them and do not at all address the issue of breaches.

As the UN acknowledged, the Declaration of Tokyo does accept the need to protect doctors who comply with the Declaration. Indeed article 6 specifically pledges WMA support for 'the doctor and his or her family in the face of threats or reprisals resulting from a refusal to condone the use of torture or other forms of cruel, inhuman or degrading treatment or punishment'. This is commendable encouragement to doctors who may be at risk if they take the Declaration seriously.[106] But the WMA has no mechanism by which to receive complaints about doctors who may act in violation of its Declaration of Tokyo. While, as has been seen, it has been prepared nevertheless to act in response to violations, the initiative taken in respect of surgeon involvement in judicial amputations in Mauritania seems to have been addressed to government ministers, not to the surgeons in question. To its great credit, the Mauritanian medical association itself denounced medical involvement in the practices.[107] The World Psychiatric Association has gone further on this issue than any other professional medical body: in August 1977, its Honolulu meeting adopted the Declaration of Hawaii noted above. Having laid down 'ethical guidelines for psychiatrists all over the world' in the Declaration, it went on to establish a mechanism for receiving complaints from member associations alleging breaches of the Code. The activity of this mechanism led to the withdrawal from the WPA of its USSR affiliate.[108] Regrettable as this must have been for the WPA, there could be no stronger evidence that it saw the Declaration as one of more than merely 'good intentions'.

TRAINING AND DISSEMINATION

While the UN Principles are somewhat imperfect, the UN certainly cannot be criticized for failure to advocate their dissemination. In the resolution adopting them, the General Assembly *'call[ed] upon* all Governments to give the Principles of Medical Ethics, together with the present resolution, the widest

---

[105] *Supra* n. 87.

[106] For example, the WMA has been observing trial hearings in respect of a doctor and lawyer working for a torture rehabilitation centre of the Turkish Human Rights Foundation in Adana accused of disobeying an official order to disclose to the authorities the medical records of 167 torture victims: 'The Trial in Turkey' in 6 *Torture—Quarterly Journal on the Rehabilitation and Prevention of Torture* 108 (1996).

[107] Association des médecins, pharmaciens et odontologistes de Mauritanie; see Amnesty International, *Report 1981*, 66; see n. 95 *supra* and accompanying text.

[108] Wynn, 'The Soviet Union and the World Psychiatric Association', *Lancet*, 19 Feb. 1983, 406–8.

possible distribution, in particular among medical and paramedical associations and institutions of detention or imprisonment, in an official language of the State'.[109]

A year later it was to repeat the call and ask the Secretary-General to report 'on the steps taken by the United Nations and the relevant specialized agencies as well as by Governments for the dissemination and implementation' of the Principles.[110] Both resolutions urged international organizations, both governmental ('in particular the World Health Organization') and non-governmental, to bring the principles 'to the attention of the widest possible group of individuals, especially those active in the medical and paramedical field'.

ETHICAL PRINCIPLES FOR LAWYERS?

Law enforcement officials, including military personnel as appropriate, are usually closest to the risk of involvement with torture and ill-treatment of prisoners, with medical personnel coming next. Lawyers too may find themselves faced with problems of professional ethics. There is, for example, the case of the prosecuting lawyer who seeks to introduce into trial proceedings evidence that can reasonably be assumed to have been obtained by torture. Even if no reference to the origins of the evidence is made, the lawyer is confronted with an ethical problem no less than that which faces the forensic pathologist who must decide whether to include evidence of torture in an autopsy report. It would perhaps be negligent of lawyers, who have presumed to assess international codes of ethics for other professions, should they fail to consider the ethical position of their own colleagues.

Indeed, it is not difficult to offer examples of the ways in which lawyers might take ethical action against some of the ill-treatment of prisoners and detainees prohibited by international law. If the prosecuting lawyer posited above were to bring charges against the suspected torturers, instead of introducing the criminally obtained evidence, this would be a powerful deterrent to torture. Examining magistrates might initiate investigations to establish responsibility for extra-legal executions; judges with responsibility for supervising the lawful administration of places of detention might actually exercise their power to visit places of detention where there is credible evidence that ill-treatment is being inflicted; bar associations might come to the aid of lawyers courageous enough to take such initiatives; and law schools might ensure that lawyers are trained to take seriously their responsibilities in this area.

[109] *Supra* n. 87.
[110] GA res. 38/118, 16 Dec. 1983. The Secretary-General's report, containing information supplied by 12 governments, is contained in UN doc. A/39/480 and Adds. 1 and 2 (1984).

Of course, the heaviest burden of protecting people from the practices in question generally falls upon defence lawyers. The conscientious discharge of this burden often leads not only to disbarment but to subjection of the lawyers to the very same atrocities that they have attempted, on behalf of their clients, to combat. A casual reading of the regular bulletins of the Centre for the Independence of Judges and Lawyers established by the International Commission of Jurists reveals the range of persecution to which the diligent judge or lawyer might be subjected. An internationally recognized code of ethics for lawyers might afford some protection from such abuses.

The notion is not new: in 1975 Amnesty International, in consultation with the International Commission of Jurists, presented for public consideration a text of 'Draft Principles for a Code of Ethics for Lawyers, Relevant to Torture and other Cruel, Inhuman or Degrading Treatment or Punishment'.[111] In October 1977 these draft principles were considered by an International Seminar on Torture and Human Rights, which brought together individuals representing thirty-six NGOs interested in human rights, three intergovernmental organizations, and twenty governments.[112] Among the seminar's recommendations were the following:

... that action be taken within the United Nations with a view to the adoption of an appropriate code for lawyers including judges, prosecutors, officials, practitioners and academics, dealing with the protection of prisoners and detainees against torture and other ill-treatment.
    ... that professional lawyers' organizations be urged to consider and comment upon the existing Draft Principles, with a view to the adoption of an appropriate code.[113]

These draft principles were brought to the attention of the United Nations Committee on Crime Prevention and Control at its fifth session in 1978,[114] but it was to be several years before any potentially relevant instruments appeared. In 1985, the Seventh UN Congress on the Prevention of Crime and the Treatment of Offenders adopted the Basic Principles on the Independence of the Judiciary,[115] and, in 1990, the Eighth Congress adopted Basic Principles on the Role of Lawyers[116] and Guidelines on the Role of Prosecutors.[117] Each of these texts is aimed primarily at governmental action to ensure the efficacy of the respective branches of the profession. They are not centrally aimed at the human rights protection dimension of their work, nor, for the most part, are their provisions addressed directly to the individual members of the professions.

---

[111] Reproduced in UN doc. E/AC.57/NGO/2 (1978) and in *Codes of Professional Ethics, supra* n. 4, Chapter X.
[112] *Report of the International Seminar on Torture and Human Rights*, Palais de l'Europe, Strasbourg, 3–5 Oct. 1977 (available from Amnesty International, London), 3–4.
[113] Id., Chapter II A.
[114] UN doc. E/AC.57/NGO/2 (1978).
[115] *Supra* n. 47, Chapter ID2.
[116] *Supra* n. 22, Chapter IB3.
[117] Id., Chapter IC26.

Nevertheless, the *Guidelines on the Role of Prosecutors* do address the issues raised above. It is a largely overlooked text, perhaps because it went through the least sustained drafting process. Although the Seventh Congress in 1985 had called on the Committee on Crime Prevention and Control 'to consider the need for guidelines relating to the selection, professional training and status of prosecutors . . .',[118] the issue did not come before the Committee until its 1990 session. The Committee, acting on the basis of a Secretariat draft,[119] agreed a text and recommended that Ecosoc forward it to the Eighth Congress later that year.[120] So it went through none of the usual preparatory meetings.

One of its provisions is of particular relevance here:

16. When prosecutors come into possession of evidence against suspects that they know or believe on reasonable grounds was obtained through recourse to unlawful methods, which constitute a grave violation of the suspect's human rights, especially involving torture or cruel, inhuman or degrading treatment or punishment, or other abuses of human rights, they shall refuse to use such evidence against anyone other than those who used such methods, or inform the Court accordingly, and shall take all necessary steps to ensure that those responsible for using such methods are brought to justice.

Addressing them directly here, prosecutors are called on either not to avail themselves of evidence by the stated impermissible means or, at least, to inform the court of their provenance. Moreover, they are put under an obligation to act positively, apparently with a view to the initiation of criminal proceedings.

The *Basic Principles on the Independence of the Judiciary* signally fail to require judges to act as suggested above. However, they constitute an important set of guidelines on how the ultimate guarantors of legality and human rights should be enabled to function, constituting an essential point of departure for the work of the Special Rapporteur on the Independence of Judges and Lawyers mandated by the UN Commission on Human Rights.[121]

Work on the *Basic Principles on the Role of Lawyers* started with a resolution of the Seventh UN Crime Congress[122] calling for consideration of the issue by the Committee on Crime Prevention and Control and the Eighth Congress. Like the Basic Principles on the Use of Force and Firearms, the draft lawyers' principles were formulated by the expert meeting in Baden,[123] with a wide range of contributions from governmental and non-governmental sources,[124] and were reviewed by inter-regional and regional preparatory

---

[118] *Supra* n. 47, Chapter IE7, para. 6.
[119] UN doc. E/AC.57/1990/5/Add. 5, draft resolution V.
[120] Committee on Crime Prevention and Control—Report, Eleventh Session (E/1990/31; E/AC.57/1990/8), Chapter I C, decision 11/116, 16 Feb. 1990.
[121] Un doc. E/CN.4/1995/39, para. 36.   [122] *Supra* n. 47, Chapter IE18.
[123] *Supra* n. 22.   [124] UN doc. A/CONF.144/18 (1980), paras. 76–7.

meetings for the Eighth Congress,[125] before preliminary adoption by the Committee which forwarded the text for final consideration and adoption by the Congress.[126]

The Basic Principles do address the concerns mentioned earlier. Thus, paragraph 14 stipulates:

> Lawyers, in protecting the rights of their clients and in promoting the cause of justice, shall seek to uphold human rights and fundamental freedoms recognized by national and international law and shall at all times act freely and diligently in accordance with the law and recognized standards and ethics of the legal profession.

Acknowledging the real risk that such a call may lead lawyers to incur, paragraph 16 requires governments to

> ensure that lawyers (a) are able to perform all of their professional functions without intimidation, hindrance, harassment or improper interference . . . and (c) shall not suffer, or be threatened with, prosecution or administrative, economic or other sanctions for any action taken in accordance with recognized professional duties, standards and ethics.

The text also requires the authorities to safeguard 'the security of lawyers . . . threatened as a result of discharging their functions' (paragraph 17). Moreover, lawyers are not to be 'identified with their clients or their clients' causes' as a result of such discharge (paragraph 18).

As far as UN implementation of these texts is concerned, the questionnaire system applicable to the texts on law enforcement officials (see above) applies also to the principles on prosecutors and on lawyers. At its 1997 (sixth) session, the Commission on Crime Prevention and Criminal Justice called for the surveys of these texts to be undertaken for submission at its following session.[127] In practice, as regards the judges' and lawyers' principles, more serious implementation may be expected of the Special Rapporteur of the UN Commission on Human Rights on the Independence of Judges and Lawyers, for whom these are basic texts for the discharge of his mandate.[128]

---

[125] UN doc. A/CONF.144/18 (1980), paras. 76–7.
[126] *Supra* n. 120, decision 11/109, 16 Feb. 1990.
[127] UN doc. E/CN.15/1997/L.9/Rev. 1, para. 4.   [128] *Supra* n. 121.

General Conclusion—An Agenda

The reader who has worked through the preceding chapters may well be thinking something like: perhaps some points of law need to be clarified, but it is clear that most of the practices described both in the introduction and in some of the substantive chapters are manifest violations of existing law; so what can be done to win greater respect for the law, and to reduce the inhuman treatment inflicted on prisoners and detainees?

In response to this question, this conclusion offers a number of proposals that could be useful steps towards alleviating the ills in question, proposals that are offered with a reminder of something signalled in the introduction: that the rules and machinery of international law are but one element in a global effort to combat the ills. At the international level governments, singly and through constituted bodies, may intercede on behalf of persons who suffer threat to life and limb, and may condemn abuses that have occurred; non-governmental organizations may mobilize public awareness of abuses and expose their perpetrators to shame, or may quietly visit places of detention to give succour to the victims of abuse. Organized special interest groups may work for those who find themselves targets of the abuses. At the national level individuals and groups, politicians, professionals, and concerned persons may undertake decisive and often courageous action to expose abuses, to aid victims, and to forge the changes necessary to prevent further abuses. All may be helped if there is clear legitimation of their efforts by rules and machinery of the organized community of governments.

The proposals are modest. They do not call for an international tribunal to sit in judgement on governments responsible for the abuses. They do not suppose the superiority of one social order or economic system over another. They do not advocate a supranational order whose greater authority would replace that of discredited national orders and so stop the abuses. They aim simply at what seems possible in the short or medium term.

PROPOSALS

GENERAL

1(a). States that have not yet done so should become parties to the International Covenant on Civil and Political Rights, make declarations accepting the right of interstate complaint to the Human Rights Committee, and ratify the (first) Optional Protocol to the Covenant (thus recognizing the right of the Committee to consider complaints from individuals claiming to be victims).

1(b). States members of the Organization of American States that have not yet done so should become parties to the American Convention on Human Rights, and make the declarations necessary for the Inter-American Commission on Human Rights to consider interstate complaints and the Inter-American Court of Human Rights to consider cases that may be referred to it.

1(c). States members of the Organization of African Unity that have not yet done so should take the necessary action to become parties to the African Charter on Human and Peoples' Rights and thus submit themselves to the jurisdiction of the African Commission on Human and Peoples' Rights. The Organization should also establish an African human rights court.

1(d). States that have not yet done so should become parties to the Geneva Conventions of 12 August 1949 on the protection of victims of war, as well as to the two Additional Protocols of 1977.

1(e). States should become parties to the Statute of the International Criminal Court, accepting the full range of its optional powers.

1(f). States should adopt legislation to permit them to exercise universal jurisdiction in respect of violations of human rights amenable to such jurisdiction.

TORTURE AND OTHER ILL-TREATMENT

2(a). States should become parties to the UN Convention against Torture and Other Cruel, Inhuman or Degrading Treatment or Punishment and should make the declarations necessary to permit the Committee against Torture to consider both interstate complaints and complaints from individuals. States members of the Organization of American States should also adhere to the Inter-American Convention to Prevent and Punish Torture.

2(b). The UN Convention against Torture should be supplemented by the adoption of the draft optional protocol that would institute a (properly resourced) system of routine and *ad hoc* visits by delegates of a specially constituted international body to all places of detention. The adherence of all states to such a protocol could do much to prevent torture.

2(c). Meanwhile, states members of the Council of Europe that have not yet done so should adhere to the European Convention for the Prevention of Torture that would institutionalize a similar system of visits to places of detention, as well as to its Protocol 2, whereby non-member states may also be invited to adhere to the Convention.

2(d). The functions of the Special Rapporteur on Torture should be supported with adequate resources.

EXTRA-LEGAL EXECUTIONS AND THE DEATH PENALTY

3(a). States that have not yet done so should become parties to the Convention on the Prevention and Punishment of the Crime of Genocide.

3(b). The functions of the Special Rapporteur on Extrajudicial, Summary or Arbitrary Executions should be supported with adequate resources.

3(c). Efforts should be made to confirm the legislated goal of abolishing the death penalty; for example, appropriate bodies should be brought to acknowledge that, as long as this penalty continues to exist, there can be no complete respect for the right to life, or the right not to be subjected to cruel, inhuman, or degrading punishment.

3(d). States that have not yet done so should adhere to the Second Optional Protocol to the International Covenant on Civil and Political Rights, calling for the abolition of the death penalty.

3(e). Meanwhile, all states members of the Council of Europe should adhere to the sixth Protocol to the European Convention on Human Rights, which calls for the abolition of the death penalty in peacetime, while states parties to the American Convention on Human Rights should adhere to its similar second Protocol.

'DISAPPEARANCES'

4(a). The proposed United Nations convention against enforced disappearance should clarify that 'disappearances' are at least as grave a violation of international law as torture, and indeed constitute a form of torture; also that they should accordingly incur the same international legal consequences as torture.

4(b). The functions of the Working Group on Enforced or Involuntary Disappearances should be supported with adequate resources. Meanwhile, the Working Group should be prepared to identify those on whose behalf it works.

PRISON CONDITIONS

5. Perhaps the most effective mechanism not only to combat torture but also to avoid the worst oppressions found in formal institutions of incarceration, would be the operation of the draft optional protocol to the Convention against Torture mentioned above in 2(b). The preparation of informative reports by the Secretary-General in pursuance of his new mandate on the implementation of the Standard Minimum Rules for the Treatment of Prisoners, as well as publication of state responses to his questionnaires, would be of some value. Even more so would be serious consideration of them by the Commission on Crime Prevention and Criminal Justice.

PROFESSIONAL ETHICS

6(a). The United Nations should establish mechanisms for receiving complaints about law enforcement officials and health workers who do not comply with the codes it has adopted in respect of them. The mechanisms should also be able to take up the cases of those law enforcement officials and health workers who find themselves in jeopardy for having complied with the codes.

6(b). The mandate of the Special Rapporteur on the Independence of Judges and Lawyers should be supported by adequate resources.

HUMAN RIGHTS AWARENESS

7. The United Nations and Unesco should maintain and intensify their work of promoting the widest possible dissemination of the relevant international instruments, as well as information on mechanisms for their implementation. The work of the International Committee of the Red Cross in disseminating international humanitarian law is both a model and deserving of assistance.

Declaration on the Protection of All Persons from Being Subjected to Torture and Other Cruel, Inhuman or Degrading Treatment or Punishment

(adopted by United Nations General Assembly resolution 3452 (XXX) of 9 December 1975)

Article 1

1. For the purpose of this Declaration, torture means any act by which severe pain or suffering, whether physical or mental, is intentionally inflicted by or at the instigation of a public official on a person for such purposes as obtaining from him or a third person information or confession, punishing him for an act he has committed or is suspected of having committed, or intimidating him or other persons. It does not include pain or suffering arising only from, inherent in or incidental to, lawful sanctions to the extent consistent with the Standard Minimum Rules for the Treatment of Prisoners.

2. Torture constitutes an aggravated and deliberate form of cruel, inhuman or degrading treatment or punishment.

Article 2

Any act of torture or other cruel, inhuman or degrading treatment or punishment is an offence to human dignity and shall be condemned as a denial of the purposes of the Charter of the United Nations and as a violation of the human rights and fundamental freedoms proclaimed in the Universal Declaration of Human Rights.

Article 3

No State may permit or tolerate torture or other cruel, inhuman or degrading treatment or punishment. Exceptional circumstances such as a state of war or a threat of war, internal political instability or any other public emergency may not be invoked as a justification of torture or other cruel, inhuman or degrading treatment or punishment.

Article 4

Each State shall, in accordance with the provisions of this Declaration, take effective measures to prevent torture and other cruel, inhuman or degrading treatment or punishment from being practised within its jurisdiction.

Article 5

The training of law enforcement personnel and of other public officials who may be responsible for persons deprived of their liberty shall ensure that full account is taken of the prohibition against torture and other cruel, inhuman or degrading treatment or punishment. This prohibition shall also, where appropriate, be included in such general rules or instructions as are issued in regard to the duties and functions of anyone who may be involved in the custody or treatment of such persons.

Article 6

Each State shall keep under systematic review interrogation methods and practices as well as arrangements for the custody and treatment of persons deprived of their liberty in its territory, with a view to preventing any cases of torture or other cruel, inhuman or degrading treatment or punishment.

Article 7

Each State shall ensure that all acts of torture as defined in article 1 are offences under its criminal law. The same shall apply in regard to acts which constitute participation in, complicity in, incitement to or an attempt to commit torture.

Article 8

Any person who alleges that he has been subjected to torture or other cruel, inhuman or degrading treatment or punishment by or at the instigation of a public official shall have the right to complain to, and to have his case impartially examined by, the competent authorities of the State concerned.

Article 9

Wherever there is reasonable ground to believe that an act of torture as defined in article 1 has been committed, the competent authorities of the State concerned shall promptly proceed to an impartial investigation even if there has been no formal complaint.

Article 10

If an investigation under article 8 or article 9 establishes that an act of torture as defined in article 1 appears to have been committed, criminal proceedings shall be instituted against the alleged offender or offenders in accordance with national law. If an allegation of other forms of cruel, inhuman or degrading treatment or punishment is considered to be well founded, the alleged offender or offenders shall be subject to criminal, disciplinary or other appropriate proceedings.

Article 11

Where it is proved that an act of torture or other cruel, inhuman or degrading treatment or punishment has been committed by or at the instigation of a public official, the victim shall be afforded redress and compensation in accordance with national law.

Article 12

Any statement which is established to have been made as a result of torture or other cruel, inhuman or degrading treatment or punishment may not be invoked as evidence against the person concerned or against any other person in any proceedings.

Convention against Torture and Other Cruel, Inhuman or Degrading Treatment or Punishment

(adopted and opened for signature, ratification and accession by United Nations General Assembly resolution 39/46 of 10 December 1984)

The States Parties to this Convention,

Considering that, in accordance with the principles proclaimed in the Charter of the United Nations, recognition of the equal and inalienable rights of all members of the human family is the foundation of freedom, justice and peace in the world,

Recognizing that those rights derive from the inherent dignity of the human person,

Considering the obligation of States under the Charter, in particular Article 55, to promote universal respect for, and observance of, human rights and fundamental freedoms,

Having regard to article 5 of the Universal Declaration of Human Rights and article 7 of the International Covenant on Civil and Political Rights, both of which provide that no one shall be subjected to torture or to cruel, inhuman or degrading treatment or punishment,

Having regard also to the Declaration on the Protection of All Persons from Being Subjected to Torture and Other Cruel, Inhuman or Degrading Treatment or Punishment, adopted by the General Assembly on 9 December 1975,

Desiring to make more effective the struggle against torture and other cruel, inhuman or degrading treatment or punishment throughout the world,

Have agreed as follows:

PART I

Article 1

1. For the purposes of this Convention, the term "torture" means any act by which severe pain or suffering, whether physical or mental, is intentionally inflicted on a person for such purposes as obtaining from him or a third person information or a confession, punishing him for an act he or a third person has committed or is suspected of having committed, or intimidating or coercing him or a third person, or for any reason based on discrimination of any kind, when such pain or suffering is inflicted by or at the instigation of or with the consent or acquiescence of a public official or other person acting in an official capacity. It does not include pain or suffering arising only from, inherent in or incidental to lawful sanctions.

2. This article is without prejudice to any international instrument or national legislation which does or may contain provisions of wider application.

Article 2

1. Each State Party shall take effective legislative, administrative, judicial or other measures to prevent acts of torture in any territory under its jurisdiction.

2. No exceptional circumstances whatsoever, whether a state of war or a threat of war, internal political instability or any other public emergency, may be invoked as a justification of torture.

3. An order from a superior officer or a public authority may not be invoked as a justification of torture.

Article 3

1. No State Party shall expel, return (*"refouler"*) or extradite a person to another State where there are substantial grounds for believing that he would be in danger of being subjected to torture.

2. For the purpose of determining whether there are such grounds, the competent authorities shall take into account all relevant considerations including, where applicable, the existence in the State concerned of a consistent pattern of gross, flagrant or mass violations of human rights.

Article 4

1. Each State Party shall ensure that all acts of torture are offences under its criminal law. The same shall apply to an attempt to commit torture and to an act by any person which constitutes complicity or participation in torture.

2. Each State Party shall make these offences punishable by appropriate penalties which take into account their grave nature.

Article 5

1. Each State Party shall take such measures as may be necessary to establish its jurisdiction over the offences referred to in article 4 in the following cases:

(*a*) When the offences are committed in any territory under its jurisdiction or on board a ship or aircraft registered in that State;

(*b*) When the alleged offender is a national of that State;

(*c*) When the victim is a national of that State if that State considers it appropriate.

2. Each State Party shall likewise take such measures as may be necessary to establish its jurisdiction over such offences in cases where the alleged offender is present in any territory under its jurisdiction and it does not extradite him pursuant to article 8 to any of the States mentioned in paragraph 1 of this article.

3. This Convention does not exclude any criminal jurisdiction exercised in accordance with internal law.

Article 6

1. Upon being satisfied, after an examination of information available to it, that the circumstances so warrant, any State Party in whose territory a person alleged to have committed any offence referred to in article 4 is present shall take him into custody or take other legal measures to ensure his presence. The custody and other legal measures shall be as provided in the law of that State but may be continued only for such time as is necessary to enable any criminal or extradition proceedings to be instituted.

2. Such State shall immediately make a preliminary inquiry into the facts.

3. Any person in custody pursuant to paragraph 1 of this article shall be assisted in communicating immediately with the nearest appropriate representative of the State of which he is a national, or, if he is a stateless person, with the representative of the State where he usually resides.

4. When a State, pursuant to this article, has taken a person into custody, it shall immediately notify the States referred to in article 5, paragraph 1, of the fact that such person is in custody and of the circumstances which warrant his detention. The State which makes the preliminary inquiry contemplated in paragraph 2 of this article shall promptly report its findings to the said States and shall indicate whether it intends to exercise jurisdiction.

Article 7

1. The State Party in the territory under whose jurisdiction a person alleged to have committed any offence referred to in article 4 is found shall in the cases contemplated in article 5, if it does not extradite him, submit the case to its competent authorities for the purpose of prosecution.

2. These authorities shall take their decision in the same manner as in the case of any ordinary offence of a serious nature under the law of that State. In the cases referred to in article 5, paragraph 2, the standards of evidence required for prosecution and conviction shall in no way be less stringent than those which apply in the cases referred to in article 5, paragraph 1.

3. Any person regarding whom proceedings are brought in connection with any of the offences referred to in article 4 shall be guaranteed fair treatment at all stages of the proceedings.

Article 8

1. The offences referred to in article 4 shall be deemed to be included as extraditable offences in any extradition treaty existing between States Parties. States Parties undertake to include such offences as extraditable offences in every extradition treaty to be concluded between them.

2. If a State Party which makes extradition conditional on the existence of a treaty receives a request for extradition from another. State Party with which it has no extradition treaty, it may consider this Convention as the legal basis for extradition in respect of such offences. Extradition shall be subject to the other conditions provided by the law of the requested State.

3. States Parties which do not make extradition conditional on the existence of a treaty shall recognize such offences as extraditable offences between themselves subject to the conditions provided by the law of the requested State.

4. Such offences shall be treated, for the purpose of extradition between States Parties, as if they had been committed not only in the place in which they occurred but also in the territories of the States required to establish their jurisdiction in accordance with article 5, paragraph 1.

Article 9

1. States Parties shall afford one another the greatest measure of assistance in connection with criminal proceedings brought in respect of any of the offences referred to

in article 4, including the supply of all evidence at their disposal necessary for the proceedings.

2. States Parties shall carry out their obligations under paragraph 1 of this article in conformity with any treaties on mutual judicial assistance that may exist between them.

Article 10

1. Each State Party shall ensure that education and information regarding the prohibition against torture are fully included in the training of law enforcement personnel, civil or military, medical personnel, public officials and other persons who may be involved in the custody, interrogation or treatment of any individual subjected to any form of arrest, detention or imprisonment.

2. Each State Party shall include this prohibition in the rules or instructions issued in regard to the duties and functions of any such person.

Article 11

Each State Party shall keep under systematic review interrogation rules, instructions, methods and practices as well as arrangements for the custody and treatment of persons subjected to any form of arrest, detention or imprisonment in any territory under its jurisdiction, with a view to preventing any cases of torture.

Article 12

Each State Party shall ensure that its competent authorities proceed to a prompt and impartial investigation, wherever there is reasonable ground to believe that an act of torture has been committed in any territory under its jurisdiction.

Article 13

Each State Party shall ensure that any individual who alleges he has been subjected to torture in any territory under its jurisdiction has the right to complain to, and to have his case promptly and impartially examined by, its competent authorities. Steps shall be taken to ensure that the complainant and witnesses are protected against all ill-treatment or intimidation as a consequence of his complaint or any evidence given.

Article 14

1. Each State Party shall ensure in its legal system that the victim of an act of torture obtains redress and has an enforceable right to fair and adequate compensation, including the means for as full rehabilitation as possible. In the event of the death of the victim as a result of an act of torture, his dependants shall be entitled to compensation.

2. Nothing in this article shall affect any right of the victim or other persons to compensation which may exist under national law.

Article 15

Each State Party shall ensure that any statement which is established to have been made as a result of torture shall not be invoked as evidence in any proceedings, except against a person accused of torture as evidence that the statement was made.

Article 16

1. Each State Party shall undertake to prevent in any territory under its jurisdiction other acts of cruel, inhuman or degrading treatment or punishment which do not amount to torture as defined in article 1, when such acts are committed by or at the instigation of or with the consent or acquiescence of a public official or other person acting in an official capacity. In particular, the obligations contained in articles 10, 11, 12 and 13 shall apply with the substitution for references to torture of references to other forms of cruel, inhuman or degrading treatment or punishment.

2. The provisions of this Convention are without prejudice to the provisions of any other international instrument or national law which prohibits cruel, inhuman or degrading treatment or punishment or which relates to extradition or expulsion.

PART II

Article 17

1. There shall be established a Committee against Torture (hereinafter referred to as the Committee) which shall carry out the functions hereinafter provided. The Committee shall consist of ten experts of high moral standing and recognized competence in the field of human rights, who shall serve in their personal capacity. The experts shall be elected by the States Parties consideration being given to equitable geographical distribution and to the usefulness of the participation of some persons having legal experience.

2. The members of the Committee shall be elected by secret ballot from a list of persons nominated by States Parties. Each State Party may nominate one person from among its own nationals. States Parties shall bear in mind the usefulness of nominating persons who are also members of the Human Rights Committee established under the International Covenant on Civil and Political Rights and who are willing to serve on the Committee against Torture.

3. Elections of the members of the Committee shall be held at biennial meetings of States Parties convened by the Secretary-General of the United Nations. At those meetings, for which two thirds of the States Parties shall constitute a quorum, the persons elected to the Committee shall be those who obtain the largest number of votes and an absolute majority of the votes of the representatives of States Parties present and voting.

4. The initial election shall be held no later than six months after the date of the entry into force of this Convention. At least four months before the date of each election, the Secretary-General of the United Nations shall address a letter to the States Parties inviting them to submit their nominations within three months. The Secretary-General shall prepare a list in alphabetical order of all persons thus nominated, indicating the States Parties which have nominated them, and shall submit it to the States Parties.

5. The members of the Committee shall be elected for a term of four years. They shall be eligible for re-election if renominated. However, the term of five of the members elected at the first election shall expire at the end of two years; immediately after the first election the names of these five members shall be chosen by lot by the chairman of the meeting referred to in paragraph 3 of this article.

6. If a member of the Committee dies or resigns or for any other cause can no longer perform his Committee duties, the State Party which nominated him shall appoint

another expert from among its nationals to serve for the remainder of his term, subject to the approval of the majority of the States Parties. The approval shall be considered given unless half or more of the States Parties respond negatively within six weeks after having been informed by the Secretary-General of the United Nations of the proposed appointment.

7. States Parties shall be responsible for the expenses of the members of the Committee while they are in performance of Committee duties.

Article 18

1. The Committee shall elect its officers for a term of two years. They may be re-elected.

2. The Committee shall establish its own rules of procedure, but these rules shall provide, *inter alia*, that:

(*a*) Six members shall constitute a quorum;

(*b*) Decisions of the Committee shall be made by a majority vote of the members present.

3. The Secretary-General of the United Nations shall provide the necessary staff and facilities for the effective performance of the functions of the Committee under this Convention.

4. The Secretary-General of the United Nations shall convene the initial meeting of the Committee. After its initial meeting, the Committee shall meet at such times as shall be provided in its rules of procedure.

5. The States Parties shall be responsible for expenses incurred in connection with the holding of meetings of the States Parties and of the Committee, including reimbursement to the United Nations for any expenses, such as the cost of staff and facilities, incurred by the United Nations pursuant to paragraph 3 of this article.

Article 19

1. The States Parties shall submit to the Committee, through the Secretary-General of the United Nations, reports on the measures they have taken to give effect to their undertakings under this Convention, within one year after the entry into force of the Convention for the State Party concerned. Thereafter the States Parties shall submit supplementary reports every four years on any new measures taken and such other reports as the Committee may request.

2. The Secretary-General of the United Nations shall transmit the reports to all States Parties.

3. Each report shall be considered by the Committee which may make such general comments on the report as it may consider appropriate and shall forward these to the State Party concerned. That State Party may respond with any observations it chooses to the Committee.

4. The Committee may, at its discretion, decide to include any comments made by it in accordance with paragraph 3 of this article, together with the observations thereon received from the State Party concerned, in its annual report made in accordance with article 24. If so requested by the State Party concerned, the Committee may also include a copy of the report submitted under paragraph 1 of this article.

Article 20

1. If the Committee receives reliable information which appears to it to contain well-founded indications that torture is being systematically practised in the territory of a State Party, the Committee shall invite that State Party to co-operate in the examination of the information and to this end to submit observations with regard to the information concerned.

2. Taking into account any observations which may have been submitted by the State Party concerned, as well as any other relevant information available to it, the Committee may, if it decides that this is warranted, designate one or more of its members to make a confidential inquiry and to report to the Committee urgently.

3. If an inquiry is made in accordance with paragraph 2 of this article, the Committee shall seek the co-operation of the State Party concerned. In agreement with that State Party, such an inquiry may include a visit to its territory.

4. After examining the findings of its member or members submitted in accordance with paragraph 2 of this article, the Commission shall transmit these findings to the State Party concerned together with any comments or suggestions which seem appropriate in view of the situation.

5. All the proceedings of the Committee referred to in paragraphs 1 to 4 of this article shall be confidential, and at all stages of the proceedings the co-operation of the State Party shall be sought. After such proceedings have been completed with regard to an inquiry made in accordance with paragraph 2, the Committee may, after consultations with the State Party concerned, decide to include a summary account of the results of the proceedings in its annual report made in accordance with article 24.

Article 21

1. A State Party to this Convention may at any time declare under this article that it recognizes the competence of the Committee to receive and consider communications to the effect that a State Party claims that another State Party is not fulfilling its obligations under this Convention. Such communications may be received and considered according to the procedures laid down in this article only if submitted by a State Party which has made a declaration recognizing in regard to itself the competence of the Committee. No communication shall be dealt with by the Committee under this article if it concerns a State Party which has not made such a declaration. Communications received under this article shall be dealt with in accordance with the following procedure;

(a) If a State Party considers that another State Party is not giving effect to the provisions of this Convention, it may, by written communication, bring the matter to the attention of that State Party. Within three months after the receipt of the communication the receiving State shall afford the State which sent the communication an explanation or any other statement in writing clarifying the matter, which should include, to the extent possible and pertinent, reference to domestic procedures and remedies taken, pending or available in the matter;

(b) If the matter is not adjusted to the satisfaction of both States Parties concerned within six months after the receipt by the receiving State of the initial communication, either State shall have the right to refer the matter to the Committee, by notice given to the Committee and to the other State;

(*c*) The Committee shall deal with a matter referred to it under this article only after it has ascertained that all domestic remedies have been invoked and exhausted in the matter, in conformity with the generally recognized principles of international law. This shall not be the rule where the application of the remedies is unreasonably prolonged or is unlikely to bring effective relief to the person who is the victim of the violation of this Convention;

(*d*) The Committee shall hold closed meetings when examining communications under this article;

(*e*) Subject to the provisions of subparagraph (c), the Committee shall make available its good offices to the States Parties concerned with a view to a friendly solution of the matter on the basis of respect for the obligations provided for in this Convention. For this purpose, the Committee may, when appropriate, set up an ad hoc conciliation commission;

(*f*) In any matter referred to it under this article, the Committee may call upon the States Parties concerned, referred to in subparagraph (b), to supply any relevant information;

(*g*) The States Parties concerned, referred to in subparagraph (b), shall have the right to be represented when the matter is being considered by the Committee and to make submissions orally and/or in writing;

(*h*) The Committee shall, within twelve months after the date of receipt of notice under subparagraph (b), submit a report:

(i) If a solution within the terms of subparagraph (*e*) is reached, the Committee shall confine its report to a brief statement of the facts and of the solution reached;

(ii) If a solution within the terms of subparagraph (*e*) is not reached, the Committee shall confine its report to a brief statement of the facts;
the written submissions and record of the oral submissions made by the States Parties concerned shall be attached to the report. In every matter, the report shall be communicated to the States Parties concerned.

2. The provisions of this article shall come into force when five States Parties to this Convention have made declarations under paragraph 1 of this article. Such declarations shall be deposited by the States Parties with the Secretary-General of the United Nations, who shall transmit copies thereof to the other States Parties. A declaration may be withdrawn at any time by notification to the Secretary-General. Such a withdrawal shall not prejudice the consideration of any matter which is the subject of a communication already transmitted under this article; no further communication by any State Party shall be received under this article after the notification of withdrawal of the declaration has been received by the Secretary-General, unless the State Party concerned has made a new declaration.

Article 22

1. A State Party to this Convention may at any time declare under this article that it recognizes the competence of the Committee to receive and consider communications from or on behalf of individuals subject to its jurisdiction who claim to be victims of a violation by a State Party of the provisions of the Convention. No communication shall be received by the Committee if it concerns a State Party which has not made such a declaration.

2. The Committee shall consider inadmissible any communication under this article

which is anonymous or which it considers to be an abuse of the right of submission of such communications or to be incompatible with the provisions of this Convention.

3. Subject to the provisions of paragraph 2, the Committee shall bring any communications submitted to it under this article to the attention of the State Party to this Convention which has made a declaration under paragraph 1 and is alleged to be violating any provisions of the Convention. Within six months, the receiving State shall submit to the Committee written explanations or statements clarifying the matter and the remedy, if any, that may have been taken by that State.

4. The Committee shall consider communications received under this article in the light of all information made available to it by or on behalf of the individual and by the State Party concerned.

5. The Committee shall not consider any communications from an individual under this article unless it has ascertained that:

(*a*) The same matter has not been, and is not being, examined under another procedure of international investigation or settlement;

(*b*) The individual has exhausted all available domestic remedies; this shall not be the rule where the application of the remedies is unreasonably prolonged or is unlikely to bring effective relief to the person who is the victim of the violation of this Convention.

6. The Committee shall hold closed meetings when examining communications under this article.

7. The Committee shall forward its views to the State Party concerned and to the individual.

8. The provisions of this article shall come into force when five States Parties to this Convention have made declarations under paragraph 1 of this article. Such declarations shall be deposited by the States Parties with the Secretary-General of the United Nations, who shall transmit copies thereof to the other States Parties. A declaration may be withdrawn at any time by notification to the Secretary-General. Such a withdrawal shall not prejudice the consideration of any matter which is the subject of a communication already transmitted under this article; no further communication by or on behalf of an individual shall be received under this article after the notification of withdrawal of the declaration has been received by the Secretary-General, unless the State Party has made a new declaration.

Article 23

The members of the Committee and of the *ad hoc* conciliation commissions which may be appointed under article 21, paragraph 1 (*e*), shall be entitled to the facilities, privileges and immunities of experts on mission for the United Nations as laid down in the relevant sections of the Convention on the Privileges and Immunities of the United Nations.

Article 24

The Committee shall submit an annual report on its activities under this Convention to the States Parties and to the General Assembly of the United Nations.

PART III
Article 25

1. This Convention is open for signature by all States.
2. This Convention is subject to ratification. Instruments of ratification shall be deposited with the Secretary-General of the United Nations.

Article 26

This Convention is open to accession by all States. Accession shall be effected by the deposit of an instrument of accession with the Secretary-General of the United Nations.

Article 27

1. This Convention shall enter into force on the thirtieth day after the date of the deposit with the Secretary-General of the United Nations of the twentieth instrument of ratification or accession.
2. For each State ratifying this Convention or acceding to it after the deposit of the twentieth instrument of ratification or accession, the Convention shall enter into force on the thirtieth day after the date of the deposit of its own instrument of ratification or accession.

Article 28

1. Each State may, at the time of signature or ratification of this Convention or accession thereto, declare that it does not recognize the competence of the Committee provided for in article 20.
2. Any State Party having made a reservation in accordance with paragraph 1 of this article may, at any time, withdraw this reservation by notification to the Secretary-General of the United Nations.

Article 29

1. Any State Party to this Convention may propose an amendment and file it with the Secretary-General of the United Nations. The Secretary-General shall thereupon communicate the proposed amendment to the States Parties with a request that they notify him whether they favour a conference of States Parties for the purpose of considering and voting upon the proposal. In the event that within four months from the date of such communication at least one third of the States Parties favours such a conference, the Secretary-General shall convene the conference under the auspices of the United Nations. Any amendment adopted by a majority of the States Parties present and voting at the conference shall be submitted by the Secretary-General to all the States Parties for acceptance.
2. An amendment adopted in accordance with paragraph 1 of this article shall enter into force when two thirds of the States Parties to this Convention have notified the Secretary-General of the United Nations that they have accepted it in accordance with their respective constitutional processes.
3. When amendments enter into force, they shall be binding on those States Parties which have accepted them, other States Parties still being bound by the provisions of this Convention and any earlier amendments which they have accepted.

Article 30

1. Any dispute between two or more States Parties concerning the interpretation or application of this Convention which cannot be settled through negotiation shall, at the request of one of them, be submitted to arbitration. If within six months from the date of the request for arbitration the Parties are unable to agree on the organization of the arbitration, any one of those Parties may refer the dispute to the International Court of Justice by request in conformity with the Statute of the Court.

2. Each State may, at the time of signature or ratification of this Convention or accession thereto, declare that it does not consider itself bound by paragraph 1 of this article. The other States Parties shall not be bound by paragraph 1 of this article with respect to any State Party having made such a reservation.

3. Any State Party having made a reservation in accordance with paragraph 2 of this article may at any time withdraw this reservation by notification to the Secretary-General of the United Nations.

Article 31

1. A State Party may denounce this Convention by written notification to the Secretary-General of the United Nations. Denunciation becomes effective one year after the date of receipt of the notification by the Secretary-General.

2. Such a denunciation shall not have the effect of releasing the State Party from its obligations under this Convention in regard to any act or omission which occurs prior to the date at which the denunciation becomes effective, nor shall denunciation prejudice in any way the continued consideration of any matter which is already under consideration by the Committee prior to the date at which the denunciation becomes effective.

3. Following the date at which the denunciation of a State Party becomes effective, the Committee shall not commence consideration of any new matter regarding that State.

Article 32

The Secretary-General of the United Nations shall inform all States Members of the United Nations and all States which have signed this Convention or acceded to it of the following:

(a) Signatures, ratifications and accessions under articles 25 and 26;

(b) The date of entry into force of this Convention under article 27 and the date of the entry into force of any amendments under article 29;

(c) Denunciations under article 31.

Article 33

1. This Convention, of which the Arabic, Chinese, English, French, Russian and Spanish texts are equally authentic, shall be deposited with the Secretary-General of the United Nations.

2. The Secretary-General of the United Nations shall transmit certified copies of this Convention to all States.

Inter-American Convention to Prevent and Punish Torture

(signed at Cartagena de Indias, Colombia, on 9 December 1985, at the Fifteenth Regular Session of the OAS General Assembly, OAS Treaty Series No. 67)

The American States signatory to the present Convention,

Aware of the provision of the American Convention on Human Rights that no one shall be subjected to torture or to cruel, inhuman, or degrading punishment or treatment;

Reaffirming that all acts of torture or any other cruel, inhuman, or degrading treatment or punishment constitute an offense against human dignity and a denial of the principles set forth in the Charter of the Organization of American States and in the Charter of the United Nations and are violations of the fundamental human rights and freedoms proclaimed in the American Declaration of the Rights and Duties of Man and the Universal Declaration of Human Rights;

Noting that, in order for the pertinent rules contained in the aforementioned global and regional instruments to take effect, it is necessary to draft an Inter-American Convention that prevents and punishes torture;

Reaffirming their purpose of consolidating in this hemisphere the conditions that make for recognition of and respect for the inherent dignity of man, and ensure the full exercise of his fundamental rights and freedoms,

Have agreed upon the following:

Article 1

The State Parties undertake to prevent and punish torture in accordance with the terms of this Convention.

Article 2

For the purposes of this Convention, torture shall be understood to be any act intentionally performed whereby physical or mental pain or suffering is inflicted on a person for purposes of criminal investigation, as a means of intimidation, as personal punishment, as a preventive measure, as a penalty, or for any other purpose. Torture shall also be understood to be the use of methods upon a person intended to obliterate the personality of the victim or to diminish his physical or mental capacities, even if they do not cause physical pain or mental anguish.

The concept of torture shall not include physical or mental pain or suffering that is inherent in or solely the consequence of lawful measures, provided that they do not include the performance of the acts or use of the methods referred to in this article.

Article 3

The following shall be held guilty of the crime of torture:

(a) A public servant or employee who acting in that capacity orders, instigates or induces the use of torture, or who directly commits it or who, being able to prevent it, fails to do so.

(b) A person who at the instigation of a public servant or employee mentioned in subparagraph (a) orders, instigates or induces the use of torture, directly commits it or is an accomplice thereto.

Article 4

The fact of having acted under orders of a superior shall not provide exemption from the corresponding criminal liability.

Article 5

The existence of circumstances such as a state of war, threat of war, state of siege or of emergency, domestic disturbance or strife, suspension of constitutional guarantees, domestic political instability, or other public emergencies or disasters shall not be invoked or admitted as justification for the crime of torture.

Neither the dangerous character of the detainee or prisoner, nor the lack of security of the prison establishment or penitentiary shall justify torture.

Article 6

In accordance with the terms of Article 1, the States Parties shall take effective measures to prevent and punish torture within their jurisdiction.

The States Parties shall ensure that all acts of torture and attempts to commit torture are offenses under their criminal law and shall make such acts punishable by severe penalties that take into account their serious nature.

The States Parties likewise shall take effective measures to prevent and punish other cruel, inhuman, or degrading treatment or punishment within their jurisdiction.

Article 7

The States Parties shall take measures so that, in the training of police officers and other public officials responsible for the custody of persons temporarily or definitively deprived of their freedom, special emphasis shall be put on the prohibition of the use of torture in interrogation, detention, or arrest.

The States Parties likewise shall take similar measures to prevent other cruel, inhuman, or degrading treatment or punishment.

Article 8

The States Parties shall guarantee that any person making an accusation of having been subjected to torture within their jurisdiction shall have the right to an impartial examination of his case.

Likewise, if there is an accusation or well-grounded reason to believe that an act of torture has been committed within their jurisdiction, the States Parties shall guarantee that their respective authorities will proceed properly and immediately to conduct an investigation into the case and to initiate, whenever appropriate, the corresponding criminal process.

After all the domestic legal procedures of the respective State and the corresponding appeals have been exhausted, the case may be submitted to the international fora whose competence has been recognized by that State.

Article 9

The States Parties undertake to incorporate into their national laws regulations guaranteeing suitable compensation for victims of torture.

None of the provisions of this article shall affect the right to receive compensation that the victim or other persons may have by virtue of existing national legislation.

Article 10

No statement that is verified as having been obtained through torture shall be admissible as evidence in a legal proceeding, except in a legal action taken against a person or persons accused of having elicited it through acts of torture, and only as evidence that the accused obtained such statement by such means.

Article 11

The States Parties shall take the necessary steps to extradite anyone accused of having committed the crime of torture or sentenced for commission of that crime, in accordance with their respective national laws on extradition and their international commitments on this matter.

Article 12

Every State Party shall take the necessary measures to establish its jurisdiction over the crime described in this Convention in the following cases:

(a) When torture has been committed within its jurisdiction;

(b) When the alleged criminal is a national of that State; or

(c) When the victim is a national of that State and it so deems appropriate.

Every State Party shall also take the necessary measures to establish its jurisdiction over the crime described in this Convention when the alleged criminal is within the area under its jurisdiction and it is not appropriate to extradite him in accordance with Article 11.

This Convention does not exclude criminal jurisdiction exercised in accordance with domestic law.

Article 13

The crime referred to in Article 2 shall be deemed to be included among the extraditable crimes in every extradition treaty entered into between States Parties. The States Parties undertake to include the crime of torture as an extraditable offence in every extradition treaty to be concluded between them.

Every State Party that makes extradition conditional on the existence of a treaty may, if it receives a request for extradition from another State Party with which it has no extradition treaty, consider this Convention as the legal basis for extradition in respect of the crime of torture. Extradition shall be subject to the other conditions that may be required by the law of the requested State.

States Parties which do not make extradition conditional on the existence of a treaty shall recognize such crimes as extraditable offenses between themselves, subject to the conditions required by the law of the requested State.

Extradition shall not be granted nor shall the person sought be returned when there are grounds to believe that his life is in danger, that he will be subjected to torture or to cruel, inhuman or degrading treatment, or that he will be tried by special or ad hoc courts in the requesting State.

Article 14

When a State Party does not grant the extradition, the case shall be submitted to its competent authorities as if the crime had been committed within its jurisdiction, for the purposes of investigation, and when appropriate, for criminal action, in accordance with its national law. Any decision adopted by these authorities shall be communicated to the State that has requested the extradition.

Article 15

No provision of this Convention may be interpreted as limiting the right of asylum, when appropriate, nor as altering the obligations of the States Parties in the matter of extradition.

Article 16

This Convention shall not limit the provisions of the American Convention on Human Rights, other conventions on the subject, or the Statutes of the Inter-American Commission on Human Rights, with respect to the crime of torture.

Article 17

The States Parties undertake to inform the Inter-American Commission on Human Rights of any legislative, judicial, administrative, or other measures they adopt in application of this Convention.

In keeping with its duties and responsibilities, the Inter-American Commission on Human Rights will endeavor in its annual report to analyze the existing situation in the member states of the Organization of American States in regard to the prevention and elimination of torture.

Article 18

This Convention is open to signature by the member states of the Organization of American States.

Article 19

This Convention is subject to ratification. The instruments of ratification shall be deposited with the General Secretariat of the Organization of American States.

Article 20

This Convention is open to accession by any other American state. The instruments of accession shall be deposited with the General Secretariat of the Organization of American States.

Article 21

The States Parties may, at the time of approval, signature, ratification, or accession, make reservations to this Convention, provided that such reservations are not incompatible with the object and purpose of the Convention and concern one or more specific provisions.

Article 22

This Convention shall enter into force on the thirtieth day following the date on which the second instrument of ratification is deposited. For each State ratifying or acceding to the Convention after the second instrument of ratification has been deposited, the Convention shall enter into force on the thirtieth day following the date on which that State deposits its instrument of ratification or accession.

Article 23

This Convention shall remain in force indefinitely, but may be denounced by any State Party. The instrument of denunciation shall be deposited with the General Secretariat of the Organization of American States. After one year from the date of deposit of the instrument of denunciation, this Convention shall cease to be in effect for the denouncing State but shall remain in force for the remaining States Parties.

Article 24

The original instrument of this Convention, the English, French, Portuguese, and Spanish texts of which are equally authentic, shall be deposited with the General Secretariat of the Organization of American States, which shall send a certified copy to the Secretariat of the United Nations for registration and publication, in accordance with the provisions of Article 102 of the United Nations Charter. The General Secretariat of the Organization of American States shall notify the member states of the Organization and the States that have acceded to the Convention of signatures and of deposits of instruments of ratification, accession, and denunciation, as well as reservations, if any.

European Convention for the Prevention of Torture and Inhuman or Degrading Treatment or Punishment

(Strasbourg, 26 November 1987, European Treaty Series No. 126)

The member States of the Council of Europe, signatory hereto,

Having regard to the provisions of the Convention for the Protection of Human Rights and Fundamental Freedoms,

Recalling that, under Article 3 of the same Convention, "no one shall be subjected to torture or to inhuman or degrading treatment or punishment";

Noting that the machinery provided for in that Convention operates in relation to persons who allege that they are victims of violations of Article 3;

Convinced that the protection of persons deprived of their liberty against torture and inhuman or degrading treatment or punishment could be strengthened by non-judicial means of a preventive character based on visits,

Have agreed as follows:

CHAPTER I

Article 1

There shall be established a European Committee for the Prevention of Torture and Inhuman or Degrading Treatment or Punishment (hereinafter referred to as "the Committee"). The Committee shall, by means of visits, examine the treatment of persons deprived of their liberty with a view to strengthening, if necessary, the protection of such persons from torture and from inhuman or degrading treatment or punishment.

Article 2

Each Party shall permit visits, in accordance with this Convention, to any place within its jurisdiction where persons are deprived of their liberty by a public authority.

Article 3

In the application of this Convention, the Committee and the competent national authorities of the Party concerned shall co-operate with each other.

CHAPTER II

Article 4

1. The Committee shall consist of a number of members equal to that of the Parties.
2. The members of the Committee shall be chosen from among persons of high

moral character, known for their competence in the field of human rights or having professional experience in the areas covered by this Convention.

3. No two members of the Committee may be nationals of the same State.

4. The members shall serve in their individual capacity, shall be independent and impartial, and shall be available to serve the Committee effectively.

Article 5

1. The members of the Committee shall be elected by the Committee of Ministers of the Council of Europe by an absolute majority of votes, from a list of names drawn up by the Bureau of the Consultative Assembly of the Council of Europe; each national delegation of the Parties in the Consultative Assembly shall put forward three candidates, of whom two at least shall be its nationals.

2. The same procedure shall be followed in filling casual vacancies.

3. The members of the Committee shall be elected for a period of four years. They may only be re-elected once. However, among the members elected at the first election, the terms of three members shall expire at the end of two years. The members whose terms are to expire at the end of the initial period of two years shall be chosen by lot by the Secretary General of the Council of Europe immediately after the first election has been completed.

Article 6

1. The Committee shall meet in camera. A quorum shall be equal to the majority of its members. The decisions of the Committee shall be taken by a majority of the members present, subject to the provisions of Article 10, paragraph 2.

2. The Committee shall draw up its own rules of procedure.

3. The Secretariat of the Committee shall be provided by the Secretary General of the Council of Europe.

CHAPTER III

Article 7

1. The Committee shall organise visits to places referred to in Article 2. Apart from periodic visits, the Committee may organise such other visits as appear to it to be required in the circumstances.

2. As a general rule, the visits shall be carried out by at least two members of the Committee. The Committee may, if it considers it necessary, be assisted by experts and interpreters

Article 8

1. The Committee shall notify the Government of the Party concerned of its intention to carry out a visit. After such notification, it may at any time visit any place referred to in Article 2.

2. A Party shall provide the Committee with the following facilities to carry out its task:

(a) access to its territory and the right to travel without restriction;

(b) full information on the places where persons deprived of their liberty are being held;

(c) unlimited access to any place where persons are deprived of their liberty, including the right to move inside such places without restriction;

(d) other information available to the Party which is necessary for the Committee to carry out its task.

In seeking such information, the Committee shall have regard to applicable rules of national law and professional ethics.

3. The Committee may interview in private persons deprived of their liberty.

4. The Committee may communicate freely with any person whom it believes can supply relevant information.

5. If necessary, the Committee may immediately communicate observations to the competent authorities of the Party concerned.

Article 9

1. In exceptional circumstances, the competent authorities of the Party concerned may make representations to the Committee against a visit at the time or to the particular place proposed by the Committee. Such representations may only be made on grounds of national defence, public safety, serious disorder in places where persons are deprived of their liberty, the medical condition of a person or that an urgent interrogation relating to a serious crime is in progress.

2. Following such representations, the Committee and the Party shall immediately enter into consultations in order to clarify the situation and seek agreement on arrangements to enable the Committee to exercise its functions expeditiously. Such arrangements may include the transfer to another place of any person whom the Committee proposed to visit. Until the visit takes place, the Party shall provide information to the Committee about any person concerned.

Article 10

1. After each visit, the Committee shall draw up a report on the facts found during the visit, taking account of any observations which may have been submitted by the Party concerned. It shall transmit to the latter its report containing any recommendations it considers necessary. The Committee may consult with the Party with a view to suggesting, if necessary, improvements in the protection of persons deprived of their liberty.

2. If the Party fails to co-operate or refuses to improve the situation in the light of the Committee's recommendations, the Committee may decide, after the Party has had an opportunity to make known its views, by a majority of two-thirds of its members to make a public statement on the matter.

Article 11

1. The information gathered by the Committee in relation to a visit, its report and its consultations with the Party concerned shall be confidential.

2. The Committee shall publish its report, together with any comments of the Party concerned, whenever requested to do so by that Party.

3. However, no personal data shall be published without the express consent of the person concerned.

Article 12

Subject to the rules of confidentiality in Article 11, the Committee shall every year submit to the Committee of Ministers a general report on its activities which shall be transmitted to the Consultative Assembly and made public.

Article 13

The members of the Committee, experts and other persons assisting the Committee are required, during and after their terms of office, to maintain the confidentiality of the facts or information of which they have become aware during the discharge of their functions.

Article 14

1. The names of persons assisting the Committee shall be specified in the notification under Article 8, paragraph 1.

2. Experts shall act on the instructions and under the authority of the Committee. They shall have particular knowledge and experience in the areas covered by this Convention and shall be bound by the same duties of independence, impartiality and availability as the members of the Committee.

3. A Party may exceptionally declare that an expert or other person assisting the Committee may not be allowed to take part in a visit to a place within its jurisdiction.

CHAPTER IV

Article 15

Each Party shall inform the Committee of the name and address of the authority competent to receive notifications to its Government, and of any liaison officer it may appoint.

Article 16

The Committee, its members and experts referred to in Article 7, paragraph 2 shall enjoy the privileges and immunities set out in the Annex to this Convention.

Article 17

This Convention shall not prejudice the provisions of domestic law or any international agreement which provide greater protection for persons deprived of their liberty.

Nothing in this Convention shall be construed as limiting or derogating from the competence of the organs of the European Convention on Human Rights or from the obligations assumed by the Parties under that Convention.

The Committee shall not visit places which representatives or delegates of Protecting Powers or the International Committee of the Red Cross effectively visit on a regular basis by virtue of the Geneva Conventions of 12 August 1949 and the Additional Protocols of 8 June 1977 thereto.

CHAPTER V

Article 18

This Convention shall be open for signature by the member States of the Council of Europe. It is subject to ratification, acceptance or approval. Instruments of ratification, acceptance or approval shall be deposited with the Secretary General of the Council of Europe.

Article 19

1. This Convention shall enter into force on the first day of the month following the expiration of a period of three months after the date on which seven member States of the Council of Europe have expressed their consent to be bound by the Convention in accordance with the provisions of Article 18.

2. In respect of any member State which subsequently expresses its consent to be bound by it, the Convention shall enter into force on the first day of the month following the expiration of a period of three months after the date of the deposit of the instrument of ratification, acceptance or approval.

Article 20

1. Any State may at the time of signature or when depositing its instrument of ratification, acceptance or approval, specify the territory or territories to which this Convention shall apply.

2. Any State may at any later date, by a declaration addressed to the Secretary General of the Council of Europe, extend the application of this Convention to any other territory specified in the declaration. In respect of such territory the Convention shall enter into force on the first day of the month following the expiration of a period of three months after the date of receipt of such declaration by the Secretary General.

3. Any declaration made under the two preceding paragraphs may, in respect of any territory specified in such declaration, be withdrawn by a notification addressed to the Secretary General. The withdrawal shall become effective on the first day of the month following the expiration of a period of three months after the date of receipt of such notification by the Secretary General.

Article 21

No reservation may be made in respect of the provisions of this Convention.

Article 22

1. Any Party may, at any time, denounce this Convention by means of a notification addressed to the Secretary General of the Council of Europe.

2. Such denunciation shall become effective on the first day of the month following the expiration of a period of twelve months after the date of receipt of the notification by the Secretary General.

Article 23

The Secretary General of the Council of Europe shall notify the member States of the Council of Europe of:

(a) any signature;

(b) the deposit of any instrument of ratification, acceptance or approval;

(c) any date of entry into force of this Convention in accordance with Articles 19 and 20;

(d) any other act, notification or communication relating to this Convention, except for action taken in pursuance of Articles 8 and 10.

In witness whereof, the undersigned, being duly authorised thereto, have signed this Convention.

Done at Strasbourg, the 26 November 1987, in English and French, both texts being equally authentic, in a single copy which shall be deposited in the archives of the Council of Europe. The Secretary General of the Council of Europe shall transmit certified copies to each member State of the Council of Europe.

Standard Minimum Rules for
the Treatment of Prisoners

*(adopted by the First United Nations Congress on the Prevention of Crime
and the Treatment of Offenders, held at Geneva in 1955, and approved by
United Nations Economic and Social Council resolution 663 C (XXIV) of
31 July 1957; and amended—new rule 95 added—by Economic and Social
Council resolution 2076 (LXII) of 13 May 1977)*

Preliminary Observations

1. The following rules are not intended to describe in detail a model system of penal institutions. They seek only, on the basis of the general consensus of contemporary thought and the essential elements of the most adequate systems of today, to set out what is generally accepted as being good principle and practice in the treatment of prisoners and the management of institutions.

2. In view of the great variety of legal, social, economic and geographical conditions of the world, it is evident that not all of the rules are capable of application in all places and at all times. They should, however, serve to stimulate a constant endeavour to overcome practical difficulties in the way of their application, in the knowledge that they represent, as a whole, the minimum conditions which are accepted as suitable by the United Nations.

3. On the other hand, the rules cover a field in which thought is constantly developing. They are not intended to preclude experiment and practices, provided these are in harmony with the principles and seek to further the purposes which derive from the text of the rules as a whole. It will always be justifiable for the central prison administration to authorize departures from the rules in this spirit.

4. (1) Part I of the rules covers the general management of institutions, and is applicable to all categories of prisoners, criminal or civil, untried or convicted, including prisoners subject to "security measures" or corrective measures ordered by the judge.

(2) Part II contains rules applicable only to the special categories dealt with in each section. Nevertheless, the rules under section A, applicable to prisoners under sentence, shall be equally applicable to categories of prisoners dealt with in sections B, C and D, provided they do not conflict with the rules governing those categories and are for their benefit.

5. (1) The rules do not seek to regulate the management of institutions set aside for young persons such as Borstal institutions or correctional schools, but in general part I would be equally applicable in such institutions.

(2) The category of young prisoners should include at least all young persons who come within the jurisdiction of juvenile courts. As a rule, such young persons should not be sentenced to imprisonment.

PART I
RULES OF GENERAL APPLICATION
Basic principle

6. (1) The following rules shall be applied impartially. There shall be no discrimination on grounds of race, colour, sex, language, religion, political or other opinion, national or social origin, property, birth or other status.

(2) On the other hand, it is necessary to respect the religious beliefs and moral precepts of the group to which a prisoner belongs.

Register

7. (1) In every place where persons are imprisoned there shall be kept a bound registration book with numbered pages in which shall be entered in respect of each prisoner received:

(a) Information concerning his identity;

(b) The reasons for his commitment and the authority therefor;

(c) The day and hour of his admission and release.

(2) No person shall be received in an institution without a valid commitment order of which the details shall have been previously entered in the register.

Separation of categories

8. The different categories of prisoners shall be kept in separate institutions or parts of institutions taking account of their sex, age, criminal record, the legal reason for their detention and the necessities of their treatment. Thus,

(a) Men and women shall so far as possible be detained in separate institutions; in an institution which receives both men and women the whole of the premises allocated to women shall be entirely separate;

(b) Untried prisoners shall be kept separate from convicted prisoners;

(c) Persons imprisoned for debt and other civil prisoners shall be kept separate from persons imprisoned by reason of a criminal offence;

(d) Young prisoners shall be kept separate from adults.

Accommodation

9. (1) Where sleeping accommodation is in individual cells or rooms, each prisoner shall occupy by night a cell or room by himself. If for special reasons, such as temporary overcrowding, it becomes necessary for the central prison administration to make an exception to this rule, it is not desirable to have two prisoners in a cell or room.

(2) Where dormitories are used, they shall be occupied by prisoners carefully selected as being suitable to associate with one another in those conditions. There shall be regular supervision by night, in keeping with the nature of the institution.

10. All accommodation provided for the use of prisoners and in particular all sleeping accommodation shall meet all requirements of health, due regard being paid to climatic conditions and particularly to cubic content of air, minimum floor space, lighting, heating and ventilation.

11. In all places where prisoners are required to live or work,

(a) The windows shall be large enough to enable the prisoners to read or work by natural light, and shall be so constructed that they can allow the entrance of fresh air whether or not there is artificial ventilation;

(*b*) Artificial light shall be provided sufficient for the prisoners to read or work without injury to eyesight.

12. The sanitary installations shall be adequate to enable every prisoner to comply with the needs of nature when necessary and in a clean and decent manner.

13. Adequate bathing and shower installations shall be provided so that every prisoner may be enabled and required to have a bath or shower, at a temperature suitable to the climate, as frequently as necessary for general hygiene according to season and geographical region, but at least once a week in a temperate climate.

14. All pans of an institution regularly used by prisoners shall be properly maintained and kept scrupulously clean at all times.

Personal hygiene

15. Prisoners shall be required to keep their persons clean, and to this end they shall be provided with water and with such toilet articles as are necessary for health and cleanliness.

16. In order that prisoners may maintain a good appearance compatible with their self-respect, facilities shall be provided for the proper care of the hair and beard, and men shall be enabled to shave regularly.

Clothing and bedding

17. (1) Every prisoner who is not allowed to wear his own clothing shall be provided with an outfit of clothing suitable for the climate and adequate to keep him in good health. Such clothing shall in no manner be degrading or humiliating.

(2) All clothing shall be clean and kept in proper condition. Underclothing shall be changed and washed as often as necessary for the maintenance of hygiene.

(3) In exceptional circumstances, whenever a prisoner is removed outside the institution for an authorized purpose, he shall be allowed to wear his own clothing or other inconspicuous clothing.

18. If prisoners are allowed to wear their own clothing, arrangements shall be made on their admission to the institution to ensure that it shall be clean and fit for use.

19. Every prisoner shall, in accordance with local or national standards, be provided with a separate bed, and with separate and sufficient bedding which shall be clean when issued, kept in good order and changed often enough to ensure its cleanliness.

Food

20. (1) Every prisoner shall be provided by the administration at the usual hours with food of nutritional value adequate for health and strength, of wholesome quality and well prepared and served.

(2) Drinking water shall be available to every prisoner whenever he needs it.

Exercise and sport

21. (1) Every prisoner who is not employed in outdoor work shall have at least one hour of suitable exercise in the open air daily if the weather permits.

(2) Young prisoners, and others of suitable age and physique, shall receive physical and recreational training during the period of exercise. To this end space, installations and equipment should be provided.

Medical services

22. (1) At every institution there shall be available the services of at least one qualified medical officer who should have some knowledge of psychiatry. The medical services should be organized in close relationship to the general health administration of the community or nation. They shall include a psychiatric service for the diagnosis and, in proper cases, the treatment of states of mental abnormality.

(2) Sick prisoners who require specialist treatment shall be transferred to specialized institutions or to civil hospitals. Where hospital facilities are provided in an institution, their equipment, furnishings and pharmaceutical supplies shall be proper for the medical care and treatment of sick prisoners, and there shall be a staff of suitably trained officers.

(3) The services of a qualified dental officer shall be available to every prisoner.

23. (1) In women's institutions there shall be special accommodation for all necessary pre-natal and post-natal care and treatment. Arrangements shall be made wherever practicable for children to be born in a hospital outside the institution. If a child is born in prison, this fact shall not be mentioned in the birth certificate.

(2) Where nursing infants are allowed to remain in the institution with their mothers, provision shall be made for a nursery staffed by qualified persons, where the infants shall be placed when they are not in the care of their mothers.

24. The medical officer shall see and examine every prisoner as soon as possible after his admission and thereafter as necessary, with a view particularly to the discovery of physical or mental illness and the taking of all necessary measures; the segregation of prisoners suspected of infectious or contagious conditions; the noting of physical or mental defects which might hamper rehabilitation, and the determination of the physical capacity of every prisoner for work.

25. (1) The medical officer shall have the care of the physical and mental health of the prisoners and should daily see all sick prisoners, all who complain of illness, and any prisoner to whom his attention is specially directed.

(2) The medical officer shall report to the director whenever he considers that a prisoner's physical or mental health has been or will be injuriously affected by continued imprisonment or by any condition of imprisonment.

26. (1) The medical officer shall regularly inspect and advise the director upon:

(*a*) The quantity, quality, preparation and service of food;

(*b*) The hygiene and cleanliness of the institution and the prisoners;

(*c*) The sanitation, heating, lighting and ventilation of the institution;

(*d*) The suitability and cleanliness of the prisoners' clothing and bedding;

(*e*) The observance of the rules concerning physical education and sports, in cases where there is no technical personnel in charge of these activities.

(2) The director shall take into consideration the reports and advice that the medical officer submits according to rules 25(2) and 26 and, in case he concurs with the recommendations made, shall take immediate steps to give effect to those recommendations; if they are not within his competence or if he does not concur with them, he shall immediately submit his own report and the advice of the medical officer to higher authority.

Discipline and punishment

27. Discipline and order shall be maintained with firmness, but with no more restriction than is necessary for safe custody and well-ordered community life.

28. (1) No prisoner shall be employed, in the service of the institution, in any disciplinary capacity.

(2) This rule shall not, however, impede the proper functioning of systems based on self-government, under which specified social, educational or sports activities or responsibilities are entrusted, under supervision, to prisoners who are formed into groups for the purposes of treatment.

29. The following shall always be determined by the law or by the regulation of the competent administrative authority:

(*a*) Conduct constituting a disciplinary offence;

(*b*) The types and duration of punishment which may be inflicted;

(*c*) The authority competent to impose such punishment.

30. (1) No prisoner shall be punished except in accordance with the terms of such law or regulation, and never twice for the same offence.

(2) No prisoner shall be punished unless he has been informed of the offence alleged against him and given a proper opportunity of presenting his defence. The competent authority shall conduct a thorough examination of the case.

(3) Where necessary and practicable the prisoner shall be allowed to make his defence through an interpreter.

31. Corporal punishment, punishment by placing in a dark cell, and all cruel, inhuman or degrading punishments shall be completely prohibited as punishments for disciplinary offences.

32. (1) Punishment by close confinement or reduction of diet shall never be inflicted unless the medical officer has examined the prisoner and certified in writing that he is fit to sustain it.

(2) The same shall apply to any other punishment that may be prejudicial to the physical or mental health of a prisoner. In no case may such punishment be contrary to or depart from the principle stated in rule 31.

(3) The medical officer shall visit daily prisoners undergoing such punishments and shall advise the director if he considers the termination or alteration of the punishment necessary on grounds of physical or mental health.

Instruments of restraint

33. Instruments of restraint, such as handcuffs, chains, irons and strait-jacket, shall never be applied as a punishment. Furthermore, chains or irons shall not be used as restraints. Other instruments of restraint shall not be used except in the following circumstances:

(*a*) As a precaution against escape during a transfer, provided that they shall be removed when the prisoner appears before a judicial or administrative authority;

(*b*) On medical grounds by direction of the medical officer;

(*c*) By order of the director, if other methods of control fail, in order to prevent a prisoner from injuring himself or others or from damaging property; in such instances the director shall at once consult the medical officer and report to the higher administrative authority.

34. The patterns and manner of use of instruments of restraint shall be decided by the central prison administration. Such instruments must not be applied for any longer time than is strictly necessary.

Information to and complaints by prisoners

35. (1) Every prisoner on admission shall be provided with written information about the regulations governing the treatment of prisoners of his category, the disciplinary requirements of the institution, the authorized methods of seeking information and making complaints, and all such other matters as are necessary to enable him to understand both his rights and his obligations and to adapt himself to the life of the institution.

(2) If a prisoner is illiterate, the aforesaid information shall be conveyed to him orally.

36. (1) Every prisoner shall have the opportunity each week day of making requests or complaints to the director of the institution or the officer authorized to represent him.

(2) It shall be possible to make requests or complaints to the inspector of prisons during his inspection. The prisoner shall have the opportunity to talk to the inspector or to any other inspecting officer without the director or other members of the staff being present.

(3) Every prisoner shall be allowed to make a request or complaint, without censorship as to substance but in proper form, to the central prison administration, the judicial authority or other proper authorities through approved channels.

(4) Unless it is evidently frivolous or groundless, every request or complaint shall be promptly dealt with and replied to without undue delay.

Contact with the outside world

37. Prisoners shall be allowed under necessary supervision to communicate with their family and reputable friends at regular intervals, both by correspondence and by receiving visits.

38. (1) Prisoners who are foreign nationals shall be allowed reasonable facilities to communicate with the diplomatic and consular representatives of the State to which they belong.

(2) Prisoners who are nationals of States without diplomatic or consular representation in the country and refugees or stateless persons shall be allowed similar facilities to communicate with the diplomatic representative of the State which takes charge of their interests or any national or international authority whose task it is to protect such persons.

39. Prisoners shall be kept informed regularly of the more important items of news by the reading of newspapers, periodicals or special institutional publications, by hearing wireless transmissions, by lectures or by any similar means as authorized or controlled by the administration.

Books

40. Every institution shall have a library for the use of all categories of prisoners, adequately stocked with both recreational and instructional books, and prisoners shall be encouraged to make full use of it.

Religion

41. (1) If the institution contains a sufficient number of prisoners of the same religion, a qualified representative of that religion shall be appointed or approved. If the number of prisoners justifies it and conditions permit, the arrangement should be on a full-time basis.

(2) A qualified representative appointed or approved under paragraph (1) shall be allowed to hold regular services and to pay pastoral visits in private to prisoners of his religion at proper times.

(3) Access to a qualified representative of any religion shall not be refused to any prisoner. On the other hand, if any prisoner should object to a visit of any religious representative, his attitude shall be fully respected.

42. So far as practicable, every prisoner shall be allowed to satisfy the needs of his religious life by attending the services provided in the institution and having in his possession the books of religious observance and instruction of his denomination.

Retention of prisoners' property

43. (1) All money, valuables, clothing and other effects belonging to a prisoner which under the regulations of the institution he is not allowed to retain shall on his admission to the institution be placed in safe custody. An inventory thereof shall be signed by the prisoner. Steps shall be taken to keep them in good condition.

(2) On the release of the prisoner all such articles and money shall be returned to him except in so far as he has been authorized to spend money or send any such property out of the institution, or it has been found necessary on hygienic grounds to destroy any article of clothing. The prisoner shall sign a receipt for the articles and money returned to him.

(3) Any money or effects received for a prisoner from outside shall be treated in the same way.

(4) If a prisoner brings in any drugs or medicine, the medical officer shall decide what use shall be made of them.

Notification of death, illness, transfer, etc.

44. (1) Upon the death or serious illness of, or serious injury to a prisoner, or his removal to an institution for the treatment of mental affections, the director shall at once inform the spouse, if the prisoner is married, or the nearest relative and shall in any event inform any other person previously designated by the prisoner.

(2) A prisoner shall be informed at once of the death or serious illness of any near relative. In case of the critical illness of a near relative, the prisoner should be authorized, whenever circumstances allow, to go to his bedside either under escort or alone.

(3) Every prisoner shall have the right to inform at once his family of his imprisonment or his transfer to another institution.

Removal of prisoners

45. (1) When the prisoners are being removed to or from an institution, they shall be exposed to public view as little as possible, and proper safeguards shall be adopted to protect them from insult, curiosity and publicity in any form.

(2) The transport of prisoners in conveyances with inadequate ventilation or light, or in any way which would subject them to unnecessary physical hardship, shall be prohibited.

(3) The transport of prisoners shall be carried out at the expense of the administration and equal conditions shall obtain for all of them.

Institutional personnel

46. (1) The prison administration, shall provide for the careful selection of every grade of the personnel, since it is on their integrity, humanity, professional capacity and personal suitability for the work that the proper administration of the institutions depends.

(2) The prison administration shall constantly seek to awaken and maintain in the minds both of the personnel and of the public the conviction that this work is a social service of great importance, and to this end all appropriate means of informing the public should be used.

(3) To secure the foregoing ends, personnel shall be appointed on a full-time basis as professional prison officers and have civil service status with security of tenure subject only to good conduct, efficiency and physical fitness. Salaries shall be adequate to attract and retain suitable men and women; employment benefits and conditions of service shall be favourable in view of the exacting nature of the work.

47. (1) The personnel shall possess an adequate standard of education and intelligence.

(2) Before entering on duty, the personnel shall be given a course of training in their general and specific duties and be required to pass theoretical and practical tests.

(3) After entering on duty and during their career, the personnel shall maintain and improve their knowledge and professional capacity by attending courses of in-service training to be organized at suitable intervals.

48. All members of the personnel shall at all times so conduct themselves and perform their duties as to influence the prisoners for good by their example and to command their respect.

49. (1) So far as possible, the personnel shall include a sufficient number of specialists such as psychiatrists, psychologists, social workers, teachers and trade instructors.

(2) The services of social workers, teachers and trade instructors shall be secured on a permanent basis, without thereby excluding part-time or voluntary workers.

50. (1) The director of an institution should be adequately qualified for his task by character, administrative ability, suitable training and experience.

(2) He shall devote his entire time to his official duties and shall not be appointed on a part-time basis.

(3) He shall reside on the premises of the institution or in its immediate vicinity.

(4) When two or more institutions are under the authority of one director, he shall visit each of them at frequent intervals. A responsible resident official shall be in charge of each of these institutions.

51. (1) The director, his deputy, and the majority of the other personnel of the institution shall be able to speak the language of the greatest number of prisoners, or a language understood by the greatest number of them.

(2) Whenever necessary, the services of an interpreter shall be used.

52. (1) In institutions which are large enough to require the services of one or more full-time medical officers, at least one of them shall reside on the premises of the institution or in its immediate vicinity.

(2) In other institutions the medical officer shall visit daily and shall reside near enough to be able to attend without delay in cases of urgency.

53. (1) In an institution for both men and women, the part of the institution set aside for women shall be under the authority of a responsible woman officer who shall have the custody of the keys of all that part of the institution.

(2) No male member of the staff shall enter the part of the institution set aside for women unless accompanied by a woman officer.

(3) Women prisoners shall be attended and supervised only by women officers. This does not, however, preclude male members of the staff, particularly doctors and teachers, from carrying out their professional duties in institutions or parts of institutions set aside for women.

54. (1) Officers of the institutions shall not, in their relations with the prisoners, use force except in self-defence or in cases of attempted escape, or active or passive physical resistance to an order based on law or regulations. Officers who have recourse to force must use no more than is strictly necessary and must report the incident immediately to the director of the institution.

(2) Prison officers shall be given special physical training to enable them to restrain aggressive prisoners.

(3) Except in special circumstances, staff performing duties which bring them into direct contact with prisoners should not be armed. Furthermore, staff should in no circumstances be provided with arms unless they have been trained in their use.

Inspection

55. There shall be a regular inspection of penal institutions and services by qualified and experienced inspectors appointed by a competent authority. Their task shall be in particular to ensure that these institutions are administered in accordance with existing laws and regulations and with a view to bringing about the objectives of penal and correctional services.

PART II
RULES APPLICABLE TO SPECIAL CATEGORIES
A. PRISONERS UNDER SENTENCE
Guiding principles

56. The guiding principles hereafter are intended to show the spirit in which penal institutions should be administered and the purposes at which they should aim, in accordance with the declaration made under Preliminary Observation 1 of the present text.

57. Imprisonment and other measures which result in cutting off an offender from the outside world are afflictive by the very fact of taking from the person the right of self-determination by depriving him of his liberty. Therefore the prison system shall not, except as incidental to justifiable segregation or the maintenance of discipline, aggravate the suffering inherent in such a situation.

58. The purpose and justification of a sentence of imprisonment or a similar measure deprivative of liberty is ultimately to protect society against crime. This end can only be achieved if the period of imprisonment is used to ensure, so far as possible, that upon his return to society the offender is not only willing but able to lead a law-abiding and self-supporting life.

59. To this end, the institution should utilize all the remedial, educational, moral, spiritual and other forces and forms of assistance which are appropriate and available, and should seek to apply them according to the individual treatment needs of the prisoners.

60. (1) The regime of the institution should seek to minimize any differences between prison life and life at liberty which tend to lessen the responsibility of the prisoners or the respect due to their dignity as human beings.

(2) Before the completion of the sentence, it is desirable that the necessary steps be taken to ensure for the prisoner a gradual return to life in society. This aim may be achieved, depending on the case, by a pre-release regime organized in the same institution or in another appropriate institution, or by release on trial under some kind of supervision which must not be entrusted to the police but should be combined with effective social aid.

61. The treatment of prisoners should emphasize not their exclusion from the community, but their continuing part in it. Community agencies should, therefore, be enlisted wherever possible to assist the staff of the institution in the task of social rehabilitation of the prisoners. There should be in connection with every institution social workers charged with the duty of maintaining and improving all desirable relations of a prisoner with his family and with valuable social agencies. Steps should be taken to safeguard, to the maximum extent compatible with the law and the sentence, the rights relating to civil interests, social security rights and other social benefits of prisoners.

62. The medical services of the institution shall seek to detect and shall treat any physical or mental illnesses or defects which may hamper a prisoner's rehabilitation. All necessary medical, surgical and psychiatric services shall be provided to that end.

63. (1) The fulfilment of these principles requires individualization of treatment and for this purpose a flexible system of classifying prisoners in groups; it is therefore desirable that such groups should be distributed in separate institutions suitable for the treatment of each group.

(2) These institutions need not provide the same degree of security for every group. It is desirable to provide varying degrees of security according to the needs of different groups. Open institutions, by the very fact that they provide no physical security against escape but rely on the self-discipline of the inmates, provide the conditions most favourable to rehabilitation for carefully selected prisoners.

(3) It is desirable that the number of prisoners in closed institutions should not be so large that the individualization of treatment is hindered. In some countries it is considered that the population of such institutions should not exceed five hundred. In open institutions the population should be as small as possible.

(4) On the other hand, it is undesirable to maintain prisons which are so small that proper facilities cannot be provided.

64. The duty of society does not end with a prisoner's release. There should, therefore, be governmental or private agencies capable of lending the released prisoner effi-

cient after-care directed towards the lessening of prejudice against him and towards his social rehabilitation.

Treatment

65. The treatment of persons sentenced to imprisonment or a similar measure shall have as its purpose, so far as the length of the sentence permits, to establish in them the will to lead law-abiding and self-supporting lives after their release and to fit them to do so. The treatment shall be such as will encourage their self-respect and develop their sense of responsibility.

66. (1) To these ends, all appropriate means shall be used, including religious care in the countries where this is possible, education, vocational guidance and training, social casework, employment counselling, physical development and strengthening of moral character, in accordance with the individual needs of each prisoner, taking account of his social and criminal history, his physical and mental capacities and aptitudes, his personal temperament, the length of his sentence and his prospects after release.

(2) For every prisoner with a sentence of suitable length, the director shall receive, as soon as possible after his admission, full reports on all the matters referred to in the foregoing paragraph. Such reports shall always include a report by a medical officer, wherever possible qualified in psychiatry, on the physical and mental condition of the prisoner.

(3) The reports and other relevant documents shall be placed in an individual file. This file shall be kept up to date and classified in such a way that it can be consulted by the responsible personnel whenever the need arises.

Classification and individualization

67. The purposes of classification shall be:

(a) To separate from others those prisoners who, by reason of their criminal records or bad characters, are likely to exercise a bad influence;

(b) To divide the prisoners into classes in order to facilitate their treatment with a view to their social rehabilitation.

68. So far as possible separate institutions or separate sections of an institution shall be used for the treatment of the different classes of prisoners.

69. As soon as possible after admission and after a study of the personality of each prisoner with a sentence of suitable length, a programme of treatment shall be prepared for him in the light of the knowledge obtained about his individual needs, his capacities and dispositions.

Privileges

70. Systems of privileges appropriate for the different classes of prisoners and the different methods of treatment shall be established at every institution, in order to encourage good conduct, develop a sense of responsibility and secure the interest and co-operation of the prisoners in their treatment.

Work

71. (1) Prison labour must not be of an afflictive nature.

(2) All prisoners under sentence shall be required to work, subject to their physical and mental fitness as determined by the medical officer.

(3) Sufficient work of a useful nature shall be provided to keep prisoners actively employed for a normal working day.

(4) So far as possible the work provided shall be such as will maintain or increase the prisoners ability to earn an honest living after release.

(5) Vocational training in useful trades shall be provided for prisoners able to profit thereby and especially for young prisoners.

(6) Within the limits compatible with proper vocational selection and with the requirements of institutional administration and discipline, the prisoners shall be able to choose the type of work they wish to perform.

72. (1) The organization and methods of work in the institutions shall resemble as closely as possible those of similar work outside institutions, so as to prepare prisoners for the conditions of normal occupational life.

(2) The interests of the prisoners and of their vocational training, however, must not be subordinated to the purpose of making a financial profit from an industry in the institution.

73. (1) Preferably institutional industries and farms should be operated directly by the administration and not by private contractors.

(2) Where prisoners are employed in work not controlled by the administration, they shall always be under the supervision of the institution's personnel. Unless the work is for other departments of the government the full normal wages for such work shall be paid to the administration by the persons to whom the labour is supplied, account being taken of the output of the prisoners.

74. (1) The precautions laid down to protect the safety and health of free workmen shall be equally observed in institutions.

(2) Provision shall be made to indemnify prisoners against industrial injury, including occupational disease, on terms not less favourable than those extended by law to free workmen.

75. (1) The maximum daily and weekly working hours of the prisoners shall be fixed by law or by administrative regulation, taking into account local rules or custom in regard to the employment of free workmen.

(2) The hours so fixed shall leave one rest day a week and sufficient time for education and other activities required as part of the treatment and rehabilitation of the prisoners.

76. (1) There shall be a system of equitable remuneration of the work of prisoners.

(2) Under the system prisoners shall be allowed to spend at least a part of their earnings on approved articles for their own use and to send a part of their earnings to their family.

(3) The system should also provide that a part of the earnings should be set aside by the administration so as to constitute a savings fund to be handed over to the prisoner on his release.

Education and recreation

77. (1) Provision shall be made for the further education of all prisoners capable of profiting thereby, including religious instruction in the countries where this is possible. The education of illiterates and young prisoners shall be compulsory and special attention shall be paid to it by the administration.

(2) So far as practicable, the education of prisoners shall be integrated with the educational system of the country so that after their release they may continue their education without difficulty.

78. Recreational and cultural activities shall be provided in all institutions for the benefit of the mental and physical health of prisoners.

Social relations and after-care

79. Special attention shall be paid to the maintenance and improvement of such relations between a prisoner and his family as are desirable in the best interests of both.

80. From the beginning of a prisoner's sentence consideration shall be given to his future after release and he shall be encouraged and assisted to maintain or establish such relations with persons or agencies outside the institution as may promote the best interests of his family and his own social rehabilitation.

81. (1) Services and agencies, governmental or otherwise, which assist released prisoners to re-establish themselves in society shall ensure, so far as is possible and necessary, that released prisoners be provided with appropriate documents and identification papers, have suitable homes and work to go to, are suitably and adequately clothed having regard to the climate and season, and have sufficient means to reach their destination and maintain themselves in the period immediately following their release.

(2) The approved representatives of such agencies shall have all necessary access to the institution and to prisoners and shall be taken into consultation as to the future of a prisoner from the beginning of his sentence.

(3) It is desirable that the activities of such agencies shall be centralized or co-ordinated as far as possible in order to secure the best use of their efforts.

B. INSANE AND MENTALLY ABNORMAL PRISONERS

82. (1) Persons who are found to be insane shall not be detained in prisons and arrangements shall be made to remove them to mental institutions as soon as possible.

(2) Prisoners who suffer from other mental diseases or abnormalities shall be observed and treated in specialized institutions under medical management.

(3) During their stay in a prison, such prisoners shall be placed under the special supervision of a medical officer.

(4) The medical or psychiatric service of the penal institutions shall provide for the psychiatric treatment of all other prisoners who are in need of such treatment.

83. It is desirable that steps should be taken, by arrangement with the appropriate agencies, to ensure if necessary the continuation of psychiatric treatment after release and the provision of social-psychiatric after-care.

C. PRISONERS UNDER ARREST OR AWAITING TRIAL

84. (1) Persons arrested or imprisoned by reason of a criminal charge against them, who are detained either in police custody or in prison custody (jail) but have not yet been tried and sentenced, will be referred to as "untried prisoners," hereinafter in these rules.

(2) Unconvicted prisoners are presumed to be innocent and shall be treated as such.

(3) Without prejudice to legal rules for the protection of individual liberty or prescribing the procedure to be observed in respect of untried prisoners, these prisoners shall benefit by a special regime which is described in the following rules in its essential requirements only.

85. (1) Untried prisoners shall be kept separate from convicted prisoners.

(2) Young untried prisoners shall be kept separate from adults and shall in principle be detained in separate institutions.

86. Untried prisoners shall sleep singly in separate rooms, with the reservation of different local custom in respect of the climate.

87. Within the limits compatible with the good order of the institution, untried prisoners may, if they so desire, have their food procured at their own expense from the outside, either through the administration or through their family or friends. Otherwise, the administration shall provide their food.

88. (1) An untried prisoner shall be allowed to wear his own clothing if it is clean and suitable.

(2) If he wears prison dress, it shall be different from that supplied to convicted prisoners.

89. An untried prisoner shall always be offered opportunity to work, but shall not be required to work. If he chooses to work, he shall be paid for it.

90. An untried prisoner shall be allowed to procure at his own expense or at the expense of a third party such books, newspapers, writing materials and other means of occupation as are compatible with the interests of the administration of justice and the security and good order of the institution.

91. An untried prisoner shall be allowed to be visited and treated by his own doctor or dentist if there is reasonable ground for his application and he is able to pay any expenses incurred.

92. An untried prisoner shall be allowed to inform immediately his family of his detention and shall be given all reasonable facilities for communicating with his family and friends, and for receiving visits from them, subject only to such restrictions and supervision as are necessary in the interests of the administration of justice and of the security and good order of the institution.

93. For the purposes of his defence, an untried prisoner shall be allowed to apply for free legal aid where such aid is available, and to receive visits from his legal adviser with a view to his defence and to prepare and hand to him confidential instructions. For these purposes, he shall if he so desires be supplied with writing material. Interviews between the prisoner and his legal adviser may be within sight but not within the hearing of a police or institution official.

D. CIVIL PRISONERS

94. In countries where the law permits imprisonment for debt, or by order of a court under any other non-criminal process, persons so imprisoned shall not be subjected to any greater restriction or severity than is necessary to ensure safe custody and good order. Their treatment shall be not less favourable than that of untried prisoners, with the reservation, however, that they may possibly be required to work.

E. PERSONS ARRESTED OR DETAINED WITHOUT CHARGE

95. Without prejudice to the provisions of article 9 of the International Covenant on Civil and Political Rights, persons arrested or imprisoned without charge shall be accorded the same protection as that accorded under part I and part II, section C. Relevant provisions of part II, section A, shall likewise be applicable where their application may be conducive to the benefit of this special group of persons in custody, provided that no measures shall be taken implying that re-education or rehabilitation is in any way appropriate to persons not convicted of any criminal offence.

Body of Principles for the Protection of All Persons under Any Form of Detention or Imprisonment

(approved by United Nations General Assembly resolution 43/173 of 9 December 1988)

Scope of the Body of Principles

These principles apply for the protection of all persons under any form of detention or imprisonment.

Use of Terms

For the purposes of the Body of Principles:

(*a*) "Arrest" means the act of apprehending a person for the alleged commission of an offence or by the action of an authority;

(*b*) "Detained person" means any person deprived of personal liberty except as a result of conviction for an offence;

(*c*) "Imprisoned person" means any person deprived of personal liberty as a result of conviction for an offence;

(*d*) "Detention" means the condition of detained persons as defined above;

(*e*) "Imprisonment" means the condition of imprisoned persons as defined above;

(*f*) The words "a judicial or other authority" means a judicial or other authority under the law whose status and tenure should afford the strongest possible guarantees of competence, impartiality and independence.

Principle 1

All persons under any form of detention or imprisonment shall be treated in a humane manner and with respect for the inherent dignity of the human person.

Principle 2

Arrest, detention or imprisonment shall only be carried out strictly in accordance with the provisions of the law and by competent officials or persons authorized for that purpose.

Principle 3

There shall be no restriction upon or derogation from any of the human rights of persons under any form of detention or imprisonment recognized or existing in any State pursuant to law, conventions, regulations or custom on the pretext that this Body of Principles does not recognize such rights or that it recognizes them to a lesser extent.

Principle 4

Any form of detention or imprisonment and all measures affecting the human rights of a person under any form of detention or imprisonment shall be ordered by, or be subject to the effective control of, a judicial or other authority.

Principle 5

1. These principles shall be applied to all persons within the territory of any given State, without distinction of any kind, such as race, colour, sex, language, religion or religious belief, political or other opinion, national, ethnic or social origin, property, birth or other status.

2. Measures applied under the law and designed solely to protect the rights and special status of women, especially pregnant women and nursing mothers, children and juveniles, aged, sick or handicapped persons shall not be deemed to be discriminatory. The need for, and the application of, such measures shall always be subject to review by a judicial or other authority.

Principle 6

No person under any form of detention or imprisonment shall be subjected to torture or to cruel, inhuman or degrading treatment or punishment.* No circumstance whatever may be invoked as a justification for torture or other cruel, inhuman or degrading treatment or punishment.

Principle 7

1. States should prohibit by law any act contrary to the rights and duties contained in these principles, make any such act subject to appropriate sanctions and conduct impartial investigations upon complaints.

2. Officials who have reason to believe that a violation of this Body of Principles has occurred or is about to occur shall report the matter to their superior authorities and, where necessary, to other appropriate authorities or organs vested with reviewing or remedial powers.

3. Any other person who has ground to believe that a violation of this Body of Principles has occurred or is about to occur shall have the right to report the matter to the superiors of the officials involved as well as to other appropriate authorities or organs vested with reviewing or remedial powers.

Principle 8

Persons in detention shall be subject to treatment appropriate to their unconvicted status. Accordingly, they shall, whenever possible, be kept separate from imprisoned persons.

---

* The term "cruel, inhuman or degrading treatment or punishment" should be interpreted so as to extend the widest possible protection against abuses, whether physical or mental, including the holding of a detained or imprisoned person in conditions which deprive him, temporarily or permanently, of the use of any of his natural senses, such as sight or hearing, or of his awareness of place and the passing of time.

Principle 9

The authorities which arrest a person, keep him under detention or investigate the case shall exercise only the powers granted to them under the law and the exercise of these powers shall be subject to recourse to a judicial or other authority.

Principle 10

Anyone who is arrested shall be informed at the time of his arrest of the reason for his arrest and shall be promptly informed of any charges against him.

Principle 11

1. A person shall not be kept in detention without being given an effective opportunity to be heard promptly by a judicial or other authority. A detained person shall have the right to defend himself or to be assisted by counsel as prescribed by law.

2. A detained person and his counsel, if any, shall receive prompt and full communication of any order of detention, together with the reasons therefor.

3. A judicial or other authority shall be empowered to review as appropriate the continuance of detention.

Principle 12

1. There shall be duly recorded:
(*a*) The reasons for the arrest;
(*b*) The time of the arrest and the taking of the arrested person to a place of custody as well as that of his first appearance before a judicial or other authority;
(*c*) The identity of the law enforcement officials concerned;
(*d*) Precise information concerning the place of custody.

2. Such records shall be communicated to the detained person, or his counsel, if any, in the form prescribed by law.

Principle 13

Any person shall, at the moment of arrest and at the commencement of detention or imprisonment, or promptly thereafter, be provided by the authority responsible for his arrest, detention or imprisonment, respectively with information on and an explanation of his rights and how to avail himself of such rights.

Principle 14

A person who does not adequately understand or speak the language used by the authorities responsible for his arrest, detention or imprisonment is entitled to receive promptly in a language which he understands the information referred to in principle 10, principle 11, paragraph 2, principle 12, paragraph 1, and principle 13 and to have the assistance, free of charge, if necessary, of an interpreter in connection with legal proceedings subsequent to his arrest.

Principle 15

Notwithstanding the exceptions contained in principle 16, paragraph 4, and principle 18, paragraph 3, communication of the detained or imprisoned person with the outside world, and in particular his family or counsel, shall not be denied for more than a matter of days.

Principle 16

1. Promptly after arrest and after each transfer from one place of detention or imprisonment to another, a detained or imprisoned person shall be entitled to notify or to require the competent authority to notify members of his family or other appropriate persons of his choice of his arrest, detention or imprisonment or of the transfer and of the place where he is kept in custody.

2. If a detained or imprisoned person is a foreigner, he shall also be promptly informed of his right to communicate by appropriate means with a consular post or the diplomatic mission of the State of which he is a national or which is otherwise entitled to receive such communication in accordance with international law or with the representative of the competent international organization, if he is a refugee or is otherwise under the protection of an intergovernmental organization.

3. If a detained or imprisoned person is a juvenile or is incapable of understanding his entitlement, the competent authority shall on its own initiative undertake the notification referred to in the present principle. Special attention shall be given to notifying parents or guardians.

4. Any notification referred to in the present principle shall be made or permitted to be made without delay. The competent authority may however delay a notification for a reasonable period where exceptional needs of the investigation so require.

Principle 17

1. A detained person shall be entitled to have the assistance of a legal counsel. He shall be informed of his right by the competent authority promptly after arrest and shall be provided with reasonable facilities for exercising it.

2. If a detained person does not have a legal counsel of his own choice, he shall be entitled to have a legal counsel assigned to him by a judicial or other authority in all cases where the interests of justice so require and without payment by him if he does not have sufficient means to pay.

Principle 18

1. A detained or imprisoned person shall be entitled to communicate and consult with his legal counsel.

2. A detained or imprisoned person shall be allowed adequate time and facilities for consultation with his legal counsel.

3. The right of a detained or imprisoned person to be visited by and to consult and communicate, without delay or censorship and in full confidentiality, with his legal counsel may not be suspended or restricted save in exceptional circumstances, to be specified by law or lawful regulations, when it is considered indispensable by a judicial or other authority in order to maintain security and good order.

4. Interviews between a detained or imprisoned person and his legal counsel may be within sight, but not within the hearing, of a law-enforcement official.

5. Communications between a detained or imprisoned person and his legal counsel mentioned in the present principle shall be inadmissible as evidence against the

detained or imprisoned person unless they are connected with a continuing or contemplated crime.

Principle 19

A detained or imprisoned person shall have the right to be visited by and to correspond with, in particular, members of his family and shall be given adequate opportunity to communicate with the outside world, subject to reasonable conditions and restrictions as specified by law or lawful regulations.

Principle 20

If a detained or imprisoned person so requests, he shall if possible be kept in a place of detention or imprisonment reasonably near his usual place of residence.

Principle 21

1. It shall be prohibited to take undue advantage of the situation of a detained or imprisoned person for the purpose of compelling him to confess, to incriminate himself otherwise or to testify against any other person.

2. No detained person while being interrogated shall be subject to violence, threats or methods of interrogation which impair his capacity of decision or his judgement.

Principle 22

No detained or imprisoned person shall, even with his consent, be subjected to any medical or scientific experimentation which may be detrimental to his health.

Principle 23

1. The duration of any interrogation of a detained or imprisoned person and of the intervals between interrogations as well as the identity of the officials who conducted the interrogations and other persons present shall be recorded and certified in such form as may be prescribed by law.

2. A detained or imprisoned person, or his counsel when provided by law, shall have access to the information described in paragraph 1 of the present principle.

Principle 24

A proper medical examination shall be offered to a detained or imprisoned person as promptly as possible after his admission to the place of detention or imprisonment, and thereafter medical care and treatment shall be provided whenever necessary. This care and treatment shall be provided free of charge.

Principle 25

A detained or imprisoned person or his counsel shall, subject only to reasonable conditions to ensure security and good order in the place of detention or imprisonment, have the right to request or petition a judicial or other authority for a second medical examination or opinion.

Principle 26

The fact that a detained or imprisoned person underwent a medical examination, the name of the physician and the results of such an examination shall be duly recorded. Access to such records shall be ensured. Modalities therefore shall be in accordance with relevant rules of domestic law.

Principle 27

Non-compliance with these principles in obtaining evidence shall be taken into account in determining the admissibility of such evidence against a detained or imprisoned person.

Principle 28

A detained or imprisoned person shall have the right to obtain within the limits of available resources, if from public sources, reasonable quantities of educational, cultural and informational material, subject to reasonable conditions to ensure security and good order in the place of detention or imprisonment.

Principle 29

1. In order to supervise the strict observance of relevant laws and regulations, places of detention shall be visited regularly by qualified and experienced persons appointed by, and responsible to, a competent authority distinct from the authority directly in charge of the administration of the place of detention or imprisonment.

2. A detained or imprisoned person shall have the right to communicate freely and in full confidentiality with the persons who visit the places of detention or imprisonment in accordance with paragraph 1 of the present principle, subject to reasonable conditions to ensure security and good order in such places.

Principle 30

1. The types of conduct of the detained or imprisoned person that constitute disciplinary offences during detention or imprisonment, the description and duration of disciplinary punishment that may be inflicted and the authorities competent to impose such punishment shall be specified by law or lawful regulations and duly published.

2. A detained or imprisoned person shall have the right to be heard before disciplinary action is taken. He shall have the right to bring such action to higher authorities for review.

Principle 31

The appropriate authorities shall endeavour to ensure, according to domestic law, assistance when needed to dependent and, in particular, minor members of the families of detained or imprisoned persons and shall devote a particular measure of care to the appropriate custody of children left with out supervision.

Principle 32

1. A detained person or his counsel shall be entitled at any time to take proceedings according to domestic law before a judicial or other authority to challenge the lawfulness of his detention in order to obtain his release without delay, if it is unlawful.

2. The proceedings referred to in paragraph 1 of the present principle shall be simple and expeditious and at no cost for detained persons without adequate means. The detaining authority shall produce without unreasonable delay the detained person before the reviewing authority.

Principle 33

1. A detained or imprisoned person or his counsel shall have the right to make a request or complaint regarding his treatment, in particular in case of torture or other cruel, inhuman or degrading treatment, to the authorities responsible for the administration of the place of detention and to higher authorities and, when necessary, to appropriate authorities vested with reviewing or remedial powers.

2. In those cases where neither the detained or imprisoned person nor his counsel has the possibility to exercise his rights under paragraph 1 of the present principle, a member of the family of the detained or imprisoned person or any other person who has knowledge of the case may exercise such rights.

3. Confidentiality concerning the request or complaint shall be maintained if so requested by the complainant.

4. Every request or complaint shall be promptly dealt with and replied to without undue delay. If the request or complaint is rejected or, in case of inordinate delay, the complainant shall be entitled to bring it before a judicial or other authority. Neither the detained or imprisoned person nor any complainant under paragraph 1 of the present principle shall suffer prejudice for making a request or complaint.

Principle 34

Whenever the death or disappearance of a detained or imprisoned person occurs during his detention or imprisonment, an inquiry into the cause of death or disappearance shall be held by a judicial or other authority, either on its own motion or at the instance of a member of the family of such a person or any person who has knowledge of the case. When circumstances so warrant, such an inquiry shall be held on the same procedural basis whenever the death or disappearance occurs shortly after the termination of the detention or imprisonment. The findings of such inquiry or a report thereon shall be made available upon request, unless doing so would jeopardize an ongoing criminal investigation.

Principle 35

1. Damage incurred because of acts or omissions by a public official contrary to the rights contained in these principles shall be compensated according to the applicable rules or liability provided by domestic law.

2. Information required to be recorded under these principles shall be available in accordance with procedures provided by domestic law for use in claiming compensation under the present principle.

Principle 36

1. A detained person suspected of or charged with a criminal offence shall be presumed innocent and shall be treated as such until proved guilty according to law in a public trial at which he has had all the guarantees necessary for his defence.

2. The arrest or detention of such a person pending investigation and trial shall be carried out only for the purposes of the administration of justice on grounds and under conditions and procedures specified by law. The imposition of restrictions upon such a person which are not strictly required for the purpose of the detention or to prevent hindrance to the process of investigation or the administration of justice, or for

the maintenance of security and good order in the place of detention shall be forbidden.

Principle 37

A person detained on a criminal charge shall be brought before a judicial or other authority provided by law promptly after his arrest. Such authority shall decide without delay upon the lawfulness and necessity of detention. No person may be kept under detention pending investigation or trial except upon the written order of such an authority. A detained person shall, when brought before such an authority, have the right to make a statement on the treatment received by him while in custody.

Principle 38

A person detained on a criminal charge shall be entitled to trial within a reasonable time or to release pending trial.

Principle 39

Except in special cases provided for by law, a person detained on a criminal charge shall be entitled, unless a judicial or other authority decides otherwise in the interest of the administration of justice, to release pending trial subject to the conditions that may be imposed in accordance with the law. Such authority shall keep the necessity of detention under review.

General clause

Nothing in this Body of Principles shall be construed as restricting or derogating from any right defined in the International Covenant on Civil and Political Rights.

Code of Conduct for Law Enforcement Officials

(adopted by United Nations General Assembly resolution 34/169 of 17 December 1979)

Article 1

Law enforcement officials shall at all times fulfil the duty imposed upon them by law, by serving the community and by protecting all persons against illegal acts, consistent with the high degree of responsibility required by their profession.

Commentary:

(*a*) The term "law enforcement officials", includes all officers of the law, whether appointed or elected, who exercise police powers, especially the powers of arrest or detention.

(*b*) In countries where police powers are exercised by military authorities, whether uniformed or not, or by State security forces, the definition of law enforcement officials shall be regarded as including officers of such services.

(*c*) Service to the community is intended to include particularly the rendition of services of assistance to those members of the community who by reason of personal, economic, social or other emergencies are in need of immediate aid.

(*d*) This provision is intended to cover not only all violent, predatory and harmful acts, but extends to the full range of prohibitions under penal statutes. It extends to conduct by persons not capable of incurring criminal liability.

Article 2

In the performance of their duty, law enforcement officials shall respect and protect human dignity and maintain and uphold the human rights of all persons.

Commentary:

(*a*) The human rights in question are identified and protected by national and international law. Among the relevant international instruments are the Universal Declaration of Human Rights, the International Covenant on Civil and Political Rights, the Declaration on the Protection of All Persons from Being Subjected to Torture and Other Cruel, Inhuman or Degrading Treatment or Punishment, the United Nations Declaration on the Elimination of All Forms of Racial Discrimination, the International Convention on the Elimination of All Forms of Racial Discrimination, the International Convention on the Suppression and Punishment of the Crime of Apartheid, the Convention on the Prevention and Punishment of the Crime of Genocide, the Standard Minimum Rules for the Treatment of Prisoners and the Vienna Convention on Consular Relations.

(*b*) National commentaries to this provision should indicate regional or national provisions identifying and protecting these rights.

Article 3

Law enforcement officials may use force only when strictly necessary and to the extent required for the performance of their duty.

Commentary:

(*a*) This provision emphasizes that the use of force by law enforcement officials should be exceptional; while it implies that law enforcement officials may be authorized to use force as is reasonably necessary under the circumstances for the prevention of crime or in effecting or assisting in the lawful arrest of offenders or suspected offenders, no force going beyond that may be used.

(*b*) National law ordinarily restricts the use of force by law enforcement officials in accordance with a principle of proportionality. It is to be understood that such national principles of proportionality are to be respected in the interpretation of this provision. In no case should this provision be interpreted to authorize the use of force which is disproportionate to the legitimate objective to be achieved.

(*c*) The use of firearms is considered an extreme measure. Every effort should be made to exclude the use of firearms, especially against children. In general, firearms should not be used except when a suspected offender offers armed resistance or otherwise jeopardizes the lives of others and less extreme measures are not sufficient to restrain or apprehend the suspected offender. In every instance in which a firearm is discharged, a report should be made promptly to the competent authorities.

Article 4

Matters of a confidential nature in the possession of law enforcement officials shall be kept confidential, unless the performance of duty or the needs of justice strictly require otherwise.

Commentary:

By the nature of their duties, law enforcement officials obtain information which may relate to private lives or be potentially harmful to the interests, and especially the reputation, of others. Great care should be exercised in safeguarding and using such information, which should be disclosed only in the performance of duty or to serve the needs of justice. Any disclosure of such information for other purposes is wholly improper.

Article 5

No law enforcement official may inflict, instigate or tolerate any act of torture or other cruel, inhuman or degrading treatment or punishment, nor may any law enforcement official invoke superior orders or exceptional circumstances such as a state of war or a threat of war, a threat to national security, internal political instability or any other public emergency as a justification of torture or other cruel, inhuman or degrading treatment or punishment.

Commentary:

(*a*) This prohibition derives from the Declaration on the Protection of All Persons from Being Subjected to Torture and Other Cruel, Inhuman or Degrading Treatment or Punishment, adopted by the General Assembly, according to which: "[Such an act is] an offence to human dignity and shall be condemned as a denial of the purposes of the Charter of the United Nations and as a violation of the human rights and fundamental freedoms proclaimed in the Universal Declaration of Human Rights [and other international human rights instruments]."

(*b*) The Declaration defines torture as follows: ". . . torture means any act by which severe pain or suffering, whether physical or mental, is intentionally inflicted by or at the instigation of a public official on a person for such purposes as obtaining from him or a third person information or confession, punishing him for an act he has committed or is suspected of having committed, or intimidating him or other persons. It does not include pain or suffering arising only from, inherent in or incidental to, lawful sanctions to the extent consistent with the Standard Minimum Rules for the Treatment of Prisoners."

(*c*) The term "cruel, inhuman or degrading treatment or punishment" has not been defined by the General Assembly but should be interpreted so as to extend the widest possible protection against abuses, whether physical or mental.

Article 6

Law enforcement officials shall ensure the full protection of the health of persons in their custody and, in particular, shall take immediate action to secure medical attention whenever required.

Commentary:

(*a*) "Medical attention", which refers to services rendered by any medical personnel, including certified medical practitioners and paramedics, shall be secured when needed or requested.

(*b*) While the medical personnel are likely to be attached to the law enforcement operation, law enforcement officials must take into account the judgement of such personnel when they recommend providing the person in custody with appropriate treatment through, or in consultation with, medical personnel from outside the law enforcement operation.

(*c*) It is understood that law enforcement officials shall also secure medical attention for victims of violations of law or of accidents occurring in the course of violations of law.

Article 7

Law enforcement officials shall not commit any act of corruption. They shall also rigorously oppose and combat all such acts.

Commentary:

(*a*) Any act of corruption, in the same way as any other abuse of authority, is incompatible with the profession of law enforcement officials. The law must be enforced fully with respect to any law enforcement official who commits an act of corruption, as Governments cannot expect to enforce the law among their citizens if they cannot, or will not, enforce the law against their own agents and within their agencies.

(b) While the definition of corruption must be subject to national law, it should be understood to encompass the commission or omission of an act in the performance of or in connection with one's duties, in response to gifts, promises or incentives demanded or accepted, or the wrongful receipt of these once the act has been committed or omitted.

(c) The expression "act of corruption" referred to above should be understood to encompass attempted corruption.

Article 8

Law enforcement officials shall respect the law and the present Code. They shall also, to the best of their capability, prevent and rigorously oppose any violations of them.

Law enforcement officials who have reason to believe that a violation of the present Code has occurred or is about to occur shall report the matter to their superior authorities and, where necessary, to other appropriate authorities or organs vested with reviewing or remedial power.

Commentary:

(*a*) This Code shall be observed whenever it has been incorporated into national legislation or practice. If legislation or practice contains stricter provisions than those of the present Code, those stricter provisions shall be observed.

(*b*) The article seeks to preserve the balance between the need for internal discipline of the agency on which public safety is largely dependent, on the one hand, and the need for dealing with violations of basic human rights, on the other. Law enforcement officials shall report violations within the chain of command and take other lawful action outside the chain of command only when no other remedies are available or effective. It is understood that law enforcement officials shall not suffer administrative or other penalties because they have reported that a violation of this Code has occurred or is about to occur.

(*c*) The term "appropriate authorities or organs vested with reviewing or remedial power" refers to any authority or organ existing under national law, whether internal to the law enforcement agency or independent thereof, with statutory, customary or other power to review grievances and complaints arising out of violations within the purview of this Code.

(*d*) In some countries, the mass media may be regarded as performing complaint review functions similar to those described in subparagraph (c) above. Law enforcement officials may, therefore, be justified if, as a last resort and in accordance with the laws and customs of their own countries and with the provisions of article 4 of the present Code, they bring violations to the attention of public opinion through the mass media.

(*e*) Law enforcement officials who comply with the provisions of this Code deserve the respect, the full support and the co-operation of the community and of the law enforcement agency in which they serve, as well as the law enforcement profession.

Basic Principles on the Use of Force and Firearms by Law Enforcement Officials

(adopted by the Eighth United Nations Congress on the Prevention of Crime and the Treatment of Offenders, Havana, Cuba, 27 August to 7 September 1990)

Whereas the work of law enforcement officials* is a social service of great importance and there is, therefore, a need to maintain and, whenever necessary, to improve the working conditions and status of these officials,

Whereas a threat to the life and safety of law enforcement officials must be seen as a threat to the stability of society as a whole,

Whereas law enforcement officials have a vital role in the protection of the right to life, liberty and security of the person, as guaranteed in the Universal Declaration of Human Rights and reaffirmed in the International Covenant on Civil and Political Rights,

Whereas the Standard Minimum Rules for the Treatment of Prisoners provide for the circumstances in which prison officials may use force in the course of their duties,

Whereas article 3 of the Code of Conduct for Law Enforcement Officials provides that law enforcement officials may use force only when strictly necessary and to the extent required for the performance of their duty,

Whereas the preparatory meeting for the Seventh United Nations Congress on the Prevention of Crime and the Treatment of Offenders, held at Varenna, Italy, agreed on elements to be considered in the course of further work on restraints on the use of force and firearms by law enforcement officials,

Whereas the Seventh Congress, in its resolution 14, *inter alia*, emphasizes that the use of force and firearms by law enforcement officials should be commensurate with due respect for human rights,

Whereas the Economic and Social Council, in its resolution 1986/10, section IX, of 21 May 1986, invited Member States to pay particular attention in the implementation of the Code to the use of force and firearms by law enforcement officials, and the General Assembly, in its resolution 41/149 of 4 December 1986, *inter alia*, welcomed this recommendation made by the Council,

Whereas it is appropriate that, with due regard to their personal safety, considera-

---

* In accordance with the commentary to article 1 of the Code of Conduct for Law Enforcement Officials, the term "law enforcement officials" includes all officers of the law, whether appointed or elected, who exercise police powers, especially the powers of arrest or detention. In countries where police powers are exercised by military authorities, whether uniformed or not, or by State security forces, the definition of law enforcement officials shall be regarded as including officers of such services.

tion be given to the role of law enforcement officials in relation to the administration of justice, to the protection of the right to life, liberty and security of the person, to their responsibility to maintain public safety and social peace and to the importance of their qualifications, training and conduct,

The basic principles set forth below, which have been formulated to assist Member States in their task of ensuring and promoting the proper role of law enforcement officials, should be taken into account and respected by Governments within the framework of their national legislation and practice, and be brought to the attention of law enforcement officials as well as other persons, such as judges, prosecutors, lawyers, members of the executive branch and the legislature, and the public.

General provisions

1. Governments and law enforcement agencies shall adopt and implement rules and regulations on the use of force and firearms against persons by law enforcement officials. In developing such rules and regulations, Governments and law enforcement agencies shall keep the ethical issues associated with the use of force and firearms constantly under review.

2. Governments and law enforcement agencies should develop a range of means as broad as possible and equip law enforcement officials with various types of weapons and ammunition that would allow for a differentiated use of force and firearms. These should include the development of non-lethal incapacitating weapons for use in appropriate situations, with a view to increasingly restraining the application of means capable of causing death or injury to persons. For the same purpose, it should also be possible for law enforcement officials to be equipped with self-defensive equipment such as shields, helmets, bullet-proof vests and bullet-proof means of transportation, in order to decrease the need to use weapons of any kind.

3. The development and deployment of non-lethal incapacitating weapons should be carefully evaluated in order to minimize the risk of endangering uninvolved persons, and the use of such weapons should be carefully controlled.

4. Law enforcement officials, in carrying out their duty, shall, as far as possible, apply non-violent means before resorting to the use of force and firearms. They may use force and firearms only if other means remain ineffective or without any promise of achieving the intended result.

5. Whenever the lawful use of force and firearms is unavoidable, law enforcement officials shall:

(*a*) Exercise restraint in such use and act in proportion to the seriousness of the offence and the legitimate objective to be achieved;

(*b*) Minimize damage and injury, and respect and preserve human life;

(*c*) Ensure that assistance and medical aid are rendered to any injured or affected persons at the earliest possible moment;

(*d*) Ensure that relatives or close friends of the injured or affected person are notified at the earliest possible moment.

6. Where injury or death is caused by the use of force and firearms by law enforcement officials, they shall report the incident promptly to their superiors, in accordance with principle 22.

7. Governments shall ensure that arbitrary or abusive use of force and firearms by law enforcement officials is punished as a criminal offence under their law.

8. Exceptional circumstances such as internal political instability or any other public emergency may not be invoked to justify any departure from these basic principles.

Special provisions

9. Law enforcement officials shall not use firearms against persons except in self-defence or defence of others against the imminent threat of death or serious injury, to prevent the perpetration of a particularly serious crime involving grave threat to life, to arrest a person presenting such a danger and resisting their authority, or to prevent his or her escape, and only when less extreme means are insufficient to achieve these objectives. In any event, intentional lethal use of firearms may only be made when strictly unavoidable in order to protect life.

10. In the circumstances provided for under principle 9, law enforcement officials shall identify themselves as such and give a clear warning of their intent to use firearms, with sufficient time for the warning to be observed, unless to do so would unduly place the law enforcement officials at risk or would create a risk of death or serious harm to other persons, or would be clearly inappropriate or pointless in the circumstances of the incident.

11. Rules and regulations on the use of firearms by law enforcement officials should include guidelines that:

(*a*) Specify the circumstances under which law enforcement officials are authorized to carry firearms and prescribe the types of firearms and ammunition permitted;

(*b*) Ensure that firearms are used only in appropriate circumstances and in a manner likely to decrease the risk of unnecessary harm;

(*c*) Prohibit the use of those firearms and ammunition that cause unwarranted injury or present an unwarranted risk;

(*d*) Regulate the control, storage and issuing of firearms, including procedures for ensuring that law enforcement officials are accountable for the firearms and ammunition issued to them;

(*e*) Provide for warnings to be given, if appropriate, when firearms are to be discharged;

(*f*) Provide for a system of reporting whenever law enforcement officials use firearms in the performance of their duty.

Policing unlawful assemblies

12. As everyone is allowed to participate in lawful and peaceful assemblies, in accordance with the principles embodied in the Universal Declaration of Human Rights and the International Covenant on Civil and Political Rights, Governments and law enforcement agencies and officials shall recognize that force and firearms may be used only in accordance with principles 13 and 14.

13. In the dispersal of assemblies that are unlawful but non-violent, law enforcement officials shall avoid the use of force or, where that is not practicable, shall restrict such force to the minimum extent necessary.

14. In the dispersal of violent assemblies, law enforcement officials may use firearms only when less dangerous means are not practicable and only to the minimum extent necessary. Law enforcement officials shall not use firearms in such cases, except under the conditions stipulated in principle 9.

Policing persons in custody or detention

15. Law enforcement officials, in their relations with persons in custody or detention, shall not use force, except when strictly necessary for the maintenance of security and order within the institution, or when personal safety is threatened.

16. Law enforcement officials, in their relations with persons in custody or detention, shall not use firearms, except in self-defence or in the defence of others against the immediate threat of death or serious injury, or when strictly necessary to prevent the escape of a person in custody or detention presenting the danger referred to in principle 9.

17. The preceding principles are without prejudice to the rights, duties and responsibilities of prison officials, as set out in the Standard Minimum Rules for the Treatment of Prisoners, particularly rules 33, 34 and 54.

Qualifications, training and counselling

18. Governments and law enforcement agencies shall ensure that all law enforcement officials are selected by proper screening procedures, have appropriate moral, psychological and physical qualities for the effective exercise of their functions and receive continuous and thorough professional training. Their continued fitness to perform these functions should be subject to periodic review.

19. Governments and law enforcement agencies shall ensure that all law enforcement officials are provided with training and are tested in accordance with appropriate proficiency standards in the use of force. Those law enforcement officials who are required to carry firearms should be authorized to do so only upon completion of special training in their use.

20. In the training of law enforcement officials, Governments and law enforcement agencies shall give special attention to issues of police ethics and human rights, especially in the investigative process, to alternatives to the use of force and firearms, including the peaceful settlement of conflicts, the understanding of crowd behaviour, and the methods of persuasion, negotiation and mediation, as well as to technical means, with a view to limiting the use of force and firearms. Law enforcement agencies should review their training programmes and operational procedures in the light of particular incidents.

21. Governments and law enforcement agencies shall make stress counselling available to law enforcement officials who are involved in situations where force and firearms are used.

Reporting and review procedures

22. Governments and law enforcement agencies shall establish effective reporting and review procedures for all incidents referred to in principles 6 and 11(f). For incidents reported pursuant to these principles, Governments and law enforcement agencies shall ensure that an effective review process is available and that independent administrative or prosecutorial authorities are in a position to exercise jurisdiction in appropriate circumstances. In cases of death and serious injury or other grave consequences, a detailed report shall be sent promptly to the competent authorities responsible for administrative review and judicial control.

23. Persons affected by the use of force and firearms or their legal representatives

shall have access to an independent process, including a judicial process. In the event of the death of such persons, this provision shall apply to their dependants accordingly.

24. Governments and law enforcement agencies shall ensure that superior officers are held responsible if they know, or should have known, that law enforcement officials under their command are resorting, or have resorted, to the unlawful use of force and firearms, and they did not take all measures in their power to prevent, suppress or report such use.

25. Governments and law enforcement agencies shall ensure that no criminal or disciplinary sanction is imposed on law enforcement officials who, in compliance with the Code of Conduct for Law Enforcement Officials and these basic principles, refuse to carry out an order to use force and firearms, or who report such use by other officials.

26. Obedience to superior orders shall be no defence if law enforcement officials knew that an order to use force and firearms resulting in the death or serious injury of a person was manifestly unlawful and had a reasonable opportunity to refuse to follow it. In any case, responsibility also rests on the superiors who gave the unlawful orders.

Declaration on the Police—Part A

(adopted by resolution 690 (1979) of the Parliamentary Assembly of the Council of Europe)

A. Ethics[1]

1. A police officer shall fulfil the duties the law imposes upon him by protecting his fellow citizens and the community against violent, predatory and other harmful acts, as defined by law.

2. A police officer shall act with integrity, impartiality and dignity. In particular he shall refrain from and vigorously oppose all acts of corruption.

3. Summary executions, torture and other forms of inhuman or degrading treatment or punishment remain prohibited in all circumstances. A police officer is under an obligation to disobey or disregard any order or instruction involving such measures.

4. A police officer shall carry out orders properly issued by his hierarchical superior, but he shall refrain from carrying out any order he knows, or ought to know, is unlawful.

5. A police officer must oppose violations of the law. If immediate or irreparable and serious harm should result from permitting the violation to take place he shall take immediate action, to the best of his ability.

6. If no immediate or irreparable and serious harm is threatened, he must endeavour to avert the consequences of this violation, or its repetition, by reporting the matter to his superiors. If no results are obtained in that way he may report to higher authority.

7. No criminal or disciplinary action shall be taken against a police officer who has refused to carry out an unlawful order.

8. A police officer shall not co-operate in the tracing, arresting, guarding or conveying of persons who, while not being suspected of having committed an illegal act, are searched for, detained or prosecuted because of their race, religion or political belief.

9. A police officer shall be personally liable for his own acts and for acts of commission or omission he has ordered and which are unlawful.

10. There shall be a clear chain of command. It should always be possible to determine which superior may be ultimately responsible for acts or omissions of a police officer.

11. Legislation must provide for a system of legal guarantees and remedies against any damage resulting from police activities.

---

[1] Parts A and B of the declaration cover all individuals and organisations, including such bodies as secret services, military police forces, armed forces or militias performing police duties, that are responsible for enforcing the law, investigating offences, and maintaining public order and state security.

12. In performing his duties, a police officer shall use all necessary determination to achieve an aim which is legally required or allowed, but he may never use more force than is reasonable.

13. Police officers shall receive clear and precise instructions as to the manner and circumstances in which they should make use of arms.

14. A police officer having the custody of a person needing medical attention shall secure such attention by medical personnel and, if necessary, take measures for the preservation of the life and health of this person. He shall follow the instructions of doctors and other competent medical workers when they place a detainee under medical care.

15. A police officer shall keep secret all matters of a confidential nature coming to his attention, unless the performance of duty or legal provisions require otherwise.

16. A police officer who complies with the provisions of this declaration is entitled to the active moral and physical support of the community he is serving.

Principles of Medical Ethics relevant to the Role of Health Personnel, particularly Physicians, in the Protection of Prisoners and Detainees against Torture and Other Cruel, Inhuman or Degrading Treatment or Punishment

(adopted by United Nations General Assembly resolution 37/194 of 18 December 1982)

Principle 1

Health personnel, particularly physicians, charged with the medical care of prisoners and detainees have a duty to provide them with protection of their physical and mental health and treatment of disease of the same quality and standard as is afforded to those who are not imprisoned or detained.

Principle 2

It is a gross contravention of medical ethics, as well as an offence under applicable international instruments, for health personnel, particularly physicians, to engage, actively or passively, in acts which constitute participation in, complicity in, incitement to or attempts to commit torture or other cruel, inhuman or degrading treatment or punishment.[1]

Principle 3

It is a contravention of medical ethics for health personnel, particularly physicians, to be involved in any professional relationship with prisoners or detainees the purpose of which is not solely to evaluate, protect or improve their physical and mental health.

Principle 4

It is a contravention of medical ethics for health personnel, particularly physicians:

(*a*) To apply their knowledge and skills in order to assist in the interrogation of prisoners and detainees in a manner that may adversely affect the physical or mental health or condition of such prisoners or detainees and which is not in accordance with the relevant international instruments;[2]

---

[1] See the Declaration on the Protection of All Persons from Being Subjected to Torture and Other Cruel. Inhuman or Degrading Treatment or Punishment (resolution 3452 (XXX), annex).

[2] Particularly the Universal Declaration of Human Rights (resolution 217 A (3)), the International Covenants on Human Rights (resolution 2200 A (XXI). annex), the Declaration on the Protection of All Persons from Being Subjected to Torture and Other Cruel, Inhuman or

(*b*) To certify, or to participate in the certification of, the fitness of prisoners or detainees for any form of treatment or punishment that may adversely affect their physical or mental health and which is not in accordance with the relevant international instruments, or to participate in any way in the infliction of any such treatment or punishment which is not in accordance with the relevant international instruments.

Principle 5

It is a contravention of medical ethics for health personnel, particularly physicians, to participate in any procedure for restraining a prisoner or detainee unless such a procedure is determined in accordance with purely medical criteria as being necessary for the protection of the physical or mental health or the safety of the prisoner or detainee himself, of his fellow prisoners or detainees, or of his guardians, and presents no hazard to his physical or mental health.

Principle 6

There may be no derogation from the foregoing principles on any ground whatsoever, including public emergency.

Degrading Treatment or Punishment (resolution 3452 (XXX), annex) and the Standard Minimum Rules for the Treatment of Prisoners (First United Nations Congress on the Prevention of Crime and the Treatment of Offenders: report by the Secretariat (United Nations publication, Sales No. E.1956.IV.4, annex I.A).

Principles on the Effective Prevention and Investigation of Extra-legal, Arbitrary and Summary Executions

(recommended by United Nations Economic and Social Council resolution 1989/65 of 24 May 1989)*

Prevention

1. Governments shall prohibit by law all extra-legal, arbitrary and summary executions and shall ensure that any such executions are recognized as offences under their criminal laws, and are punishable by appropriate penalties which take into account the seriousness of such offences. Exceptional circumstances including a state of war or threat of war, internal political instability or any other public emergency may not be invoked as a justification of such executions. Such executions shall not be carried out under any circumstances including, but not limited to, situations of internal armed conflict, excessive or illegal use of force by a public official or other person acting in an official capacity or by a person acting at the instigation, or with the consent or acquiescence of such person, and situations in which deaths occur in custody. This prohibition shall prevail over decrees issued by governmental authority.

2. In order to prevent extra-legal, arbitrary and summary executions, Governments shall ensure strict control, including a clear chain of command over all officials responsible for apprehension, arrest, detention, custody and imprisonment, as well as those officials authorized by law to use force and firearms.

3. Governments shall prohibit orders from superior officers or public authorities authorizing or inciting other persons to carry out any such extra-legal, arbitrary or summary executions. All persons shall have the right and the duty to defy such orders. Training of law enforcement officials shall emphasize the above provisions.

4. Effective protection through judicial or other means shall be guaranteed to individuals and groups who are in danger of extra-legal, arbitrary or summary executions, including those who receive death threats.

5. No one shall be involuntarily returned or extradited to a country where there are substantial grounds for believing that he or she may become a victim of extra-legal, arbitrary or summary execution in that country.

---

* In resolution 1989/65, paragraph 1, the Economic and Social Council recommended that the Principles on the Effective Prevention and Investigation of Extra-legal, Arbitrary and Summary Executions should be taken into account and respected by Governments within the framework of their national legislation and practices.

6. Governments shall ensure that persons deprived of their liberty are held in officially recognized places of custody, and that accurate information on their custody and whereabouts, including transfers, is made promptly available to their relatives and lawyer or other persons of confidence.

7. Qualified inspectors, including medical personnel, or an equivalent independent authority, shall conduct inspections in places of custody on a regular basis, and be empowered to undertake unannounced inspections on their own initiative, with full guarantees of independence in the exercise of this function. The inspectors shall have unrestricted access to all persons in such places of custody, as well as to all their records.

8. Governments shall make every effort to prevent extra-legal, arbitrary and summary executions through measures such as diplomatic intercession, improved access of complainants to intergovernmental and judicial bodies, and public denunciation. Intergovernmental mechanisms shall be used to investigate reports of any such executions and to take effective action against such practices.

Governments, including those of countries where extra-legal, arbitrary and summary executions are reasonably suspected to occur, shall cooperate fully in international investigations on the subject.

Investigation

9. There shall be thorough, prompt and impartial investigation of all suspected cases of extra-legal, arbitrary and summary executions, including cases where complaints by relatives or other reliable reports suggest unnatural death in the above circumstances. Governments shall maintain investigative offices and procedures to undertake such inquiries. The purpose of the investigation shall be to determine the cause, manner and time of death, the person responsible, and any pattern or practice which may have brought about that death. It shall include an adequate autopsy, collection and analysis of all physical and documentary evidence and statements from witnesses. The investigation shall distinguish between natural death, accidental death, suicide and homicide.

10. The investigative authority shall have the power to obtain all the information necessary to the inquiry. Those persons conducting the investigation shall have at their disposal all the necessary budgetary and technical resources for effective investigation. They shall also have the authority to oblige officials allegedly involved in any such executions to appear and testify. The same shall apply to any witness. To this end, they shall be entitled to issue summonses to witnesses, including the officials allegedly involved and to demand the production of evidence.

11. In cases in which the established investigative procedures are inadequate because of lack of expertise or impartiality, because of the importance of the matter or because of the apparent existence of a pattern of abuse, and in cases where there are complaints from the family of the victim about these inadequacies or other substantial reasons, Governments shall pursue investigations through an independent commission of inquiry or similar procedure. Members of such a commission shall be chosen for their recognized impartiality, competence and independence as individuals. In particular, they shall be independent of any institution, agency or person that may be the subject of the inquiry. The commission shall have the authority to obtain all information necessary to the inquiry and shall conduct the inquiry as provided for under these Principles.

12. The body of the deceased person shall not be disposed of until an adequate autopsy is conducted by a physician, who shall, if possible, be an expert in forensic pathology. Those conducting the autopsy shall have the right of access to all investigative data, to the place where the body was discovered, and to the place where the death is thought to have occurred. If the body has been buried and it later appears that an investigation is required, the body shall be promptly and competently exhumed for an autopsy. If skeletal remains are discovered, they should be carefully exhumed and studied according to systematic anthropological techniques.

13. The body of the deceased shall be available to those conducting the autopsy for a sufficient amount of time to enable a thorough investigation to be carried out. The autopsy shall, at a minimum, attempt to establish the identity of the deceased and the cause and manner of death. The time and place of death shall also be determined to the extent possible. Detailed colour photographs of the deceased shall be included in the autopsy report in order to document and support the findings of the investigation. The autopsy report must describe any and all injuries to the deceased including any evidence of torture.

14. In order to ensure objective results, those conducting the autopsy must be able to function impartially and independently of any potentially implicated persons or organizations or entities.

15. Complainants, witnesses, those conducting the investigation and their families shall be protected from violence, threats of violence or any other form of intimidation. Those potentially implicated in extra-legal, arbitrary or summary executions shall be removed from any position of control or power, whether direct or indirect. over complainants, witnesses and their families, as well as over those conducting investigations.

16. Families of the deceased and their legal representatives shall be informed of, and have access to, any hearing as well as to all information relevant to the investigation, and shall be entitled to present other evidence. The family of the deceased shall have the right to insist that a medical or other qualified representative be present at the autopsy. When the identity of a deceased person has been determined, a notification of death shall be posted, and the family or relatives of the deceased shall be informed immediately. The body of the deceased shall be returned to them upon completion of the investigation.

17. A written report shall be made within a reasonable period of time on the methods and findings of such investigations. The report shall be made public immediately and shall include the scope of the inquiry, procedures and methods used to evaluate evidence as well as conclusions and recommendations based on findings of fact and on applicable law. The report shall also describe in detail specific events that were found to have occurred and the evidence upon which such findings were based, and list the names of witnesses who testified, with the exception of those whose identities have been withheld for their own protection. The Government shall, within a reasonable period of time, either reply to the report of the investigation, or indicate the steps to be taken in response to it.

Legal proceedings

18. Governments shall ensure that persons identified by the investigation as having participated in extra-legal, arbitrary or summary executions in any territory under their jurisdiction are brought to justice. Governments shall either bring such persons

to justice or cooperate to extradite any such persons to other countries wishing to exercise jurisdiction. This principle shall apply irrespective of who and where the perpetrators or the victims are, their nationalities or where the offence was committed.

19. Without prejudice to principle 3 above, an order from a superior officer or a public authority may not be invoked as a justification for extra-legal, arbitrary or summary executions. Superiors, officers or other public officials may be held responsible for acts committed by officials under their authority if they had a reasonable opportunity to prevent such acts. In no circumstances, including a state of war, siege or other public emergency, shall blanket immunity from prosecution be granted to any person allegedly involved in extra-legal, arbitrary or summary executions.

20. The families and dependents of victims of extra-legal, arbitrary or summary executions shall be entitled to fair and adequate compensation within a reasonable period of time.

Declaration on the Protection of All Persons from Enforced Disappearance

(proclaimed by United Nations General Assembly resolution 47/133 of 18 December 1992)

The General Assembly,

Considering that, in accordance with the principles proclaimed in the Charter of the United Nations and other international instruments, recognition of the inherent dignity and of the equal and inalienable rights of all members of the human family is the foundation of freedom, justice and peace in the world,

Bearing in mind the obligation of States under the Charter, in particular Article 55, to promote universal respect for, and observance of, human rights and fundamental freedoms,

Deeply concerned that in many countries, often in a persistent manner, enforced disappearances occur, in the sense that persons are arrested, detained or abducted against their will or otherwise deprived of their liberty by officials of different branches or levels of Government, followed by a refusal to disclose the fate or whereabouts of the persons concerned or a refusal to acknowledge the deprivation of their liberty, which places such persons outside the protection of the law,

Considering that enforced disappearance undermines the deepest values of any society committed to respect for the rule of law, human rights and fundamental freedoms, and that the systematic practice of such acts is of the nature of a crime against humanity,

Recalling its resolution 33/173 of 22 December 1978, in which it expressed concern about the reports from various parts of the world relating to enforced or involuntary disappearances, as well as about the anguish and sorrows caused by those disappearances, and called upon Governments to hold law enforcement and security forces legally responsible for excesses which might lead to enforced or involuntary disappearances of persons,

Recalling also the protection afforded to victims of armed conflicts by the Geneva Conventions of 12 August 1949 and the Additional Protocols thereto, of 1977,

Having regard in particular to the relevant articles of the Universal Declaration of Human Rights and the International Covenant on Civil and Political Rights, which protect the right to life, the right to liberty and security of the person, the right not to be subjected to torture and the right to recognition as a person before the law,

Having regard also to the Convention against Torture and Other Cruel, Inhuman or Degrading Treatment or Punishment, which provides that States parties shall take effective measures to prevent and punish acts of torture,

Bearing in mind the Code of Conduct for Law Enforcement Officials, the Basic Principles on the Use of Force and Firearms by Law Enforcement Officials, the

Declaration of Basic Principles of Justice for Victims of Crime and Abuse of Power and the Standard Minimum Rules for the Treatment of Prisoners,

Affirming that, in order to prevent enforced disappearances, it is necessary to ensure strict compliance with the Body of Principles for the Protection of All Persons under Any Form of Detention or Imprisonment contained in the annex to its resolution 43/173 of 9 December 1988, and with the Principles on the Effective Prevention and Investigation of Extra-legal, Arbitrary and Summary Executions, set forth in the annex to Economic and Social Council resolution 1989/65 of 24 May 1989 and endorsed by the General Assembly in its resolution 44/162 of 15 December 1989,

Bearing in mind that, while the acts which comprise enforced disappearance constitute a violation of the prohibitions found in the aforementioned international instruments, it is none the less important to devise an instrument which characterizes all acts of enforced disappearance of persons as very serious offences and sets forth standards designed to punish and prevent their commission,

1. *Proclaims* the present Declaration on the Protection of All Persons from Enforced Disappearance, as a body of principles for all States;

2. *Urges* that all efforts be made so that the Declaration becomes generally known and respected.

Article 1

1. Any act of enforced disappearance is an offence to human dignity. It is condemned as a denial of the purposes of the Charter of the United Nations and as a grave and flagrant violation of the human rights and fundamental freedoms proclaimed in the Universal Declaration of Human Rights and reaffirmed and developed in international instruments in this field.

2. Any act of enforced disappearance places the persons subjected thereto outside the protection of the law and inflicts severe suffering on them and their families. It constitutes a violation of the rules of international law guaranteeing, *inter alia*, the right to recognition as a person before the law, the right to liberty and security of the person and the right not to be subjected to torture and other cruel, inhuman or degrading treatment or punishment. It also violates or constitutes a grave threat to the right to life.

Article 2

1. No State shall practise, permit or tolerate enforced disappearances.

2. States shall act at the national and regional levels and in cooperation with the United Nations to contribute by all means to the prevention and eradication of enforced disappearance.

Article 3

Each State shall take effective legislative, administrative, judicial or other measures to prevent and terminate acts of enforced disappearance in any territory under its jurisdiction.

Article 4

1. All acts of enforced disappearance shall be offences under criminal law punishable by appropriate penalties which shall take into account their extreme seriousness.

2. Mitigating circumstances may be established in national legislation for persons who, having participated in enforced disappearances, are instrumental in bringing the victims forward alive or in providing voluntarily information which would contribute to clarifying cases of enforced disappearance.

Article 5

In addition to such criminal penalties as are applicable, enforced disappearances render their perpetrators and the State or State authorities which organize, acquiesce in or tolerate such disappearances liable under civil law, without prejudice to the international responsibility of the State concerned in accordance with the principles of international law.

Article 6

1. No order or instruction of any public authority, civilian, military or other, may be invoked to justify an enforced disappearance. Any person receiving such an order or instruction shall have the right and duty not to obey it.

2. Each State shall ensure that orders or instructions directing, authorizing or encouraging any enforced disappearance are prohibited.

3. Training of law enforcement officials shall emphasize the provisions in paragraphs 1 and 2 of the present article.

Article 7

No circumstances whatsoever, whether a threat of war, a state of war, internal political instability or any other public emergency, may be invoked to justify enforced disappearances.

Article 8

1. No State shall expel, return (*refouler*) or extradite a person to another State where there are substantial grounds to believe that he would be in danger of enforced disappearance.

2. For the purpose of determining whether there are such grounds, the competent authorities shall take into account all relevant considerations including, where applicable, the existence in the State concerned of a consistent pattern of gross, flagrant or mass violations of human rights.

Article 9

1. The right to a prompt and effective judicial remedy as a means of determining the whereabouts or state of health of persons deprived of their liberty and/or identifying the authority ordering or carry out the deprivation of liberty is required to prevent enforced disappearances under all circumstances, including those referred to in article 7 above.

2. In such proceedings, competent national authorities shall have access to all places where persons deprived of their liberty are being held and to each part of those places, as well as to any place in which there are grounds to believe that such persons may be found.

3. Any other competent authority entitled under the law of the State or by any international legal instrument to which the State is a party may also have access to such places.

Article 10

1. Any person deprived of liberty shall be held in an officially recognized place of detention and, in conformity with national law, be brought before a judicial authority promptly after detention.

2. Accurate information on the detention of such persons and their place or places of detention, including transfers, shall be made promptly available to their family members, their counsel or to any other persons having a legitimate interest in the information unless a wish to the contrary has been manifested by the persons concerned.

3. An official up-to-date register of all persons deprived of their liberty shall be maintained in every place of detention. Additionally, each State shall take steps to maintain similar centralized registers. The information contained in these registers shall be made available to the persons mentioned in the preceding paragraph, to any judicial or other competent and independent national authority and to any other competent authority entitled under the law of the State concerned or any international legal instrument to which a State concerned is a party, seeking to trace the whereabouts of a detained person.

Article 11

All persons deprived of liberty must be released in a manner permitting reliable verification that they have actually been released and, further, have been released in conditions in which their physical integrity and ability fully to exercise their rights are assured.

Article 12

1. Each State shall establish rules under its national law indicating those officials authorized to order deprivation of liberty, establishing the conditions under which such orders may be given, and stipulating penalties for officials who, without legal justification, refuse to provide information on any detention.

2. Each State shall likewise ensure strict supervision, including a clear chain of command, of all law enforcement officials responsible for apprehensions, arrests, detentions, custody, transfers and imprisonment, and of other officials authorized by law to use force and firearms.

Article 13

1. Each State shall ensure that any person having knowledge or a legitimate interest who alleges that a person has been subjected to enforced disappearance has the right to complain to a competent and independent State authority and to have that complaint promptly, thoroughly and impartially investigated by that authority. Whenever there are reasonable grounds to believe that an enforced disappearance has been committed, the State shall promptly refer the matter to that authority for such an investigation, even if there has been no formal complaint. No measure shall be taken to curtail or impede the investigation.

2. Each State shall ensure that the competent authority shall have the necessary powers and resources to conduct the investigation effectively, including powers to compel attendance of witnesses and production of relevant documents and to make immediate on-site visits.

3. Steps shall be taken to ensure that all involved in the investigation, including the complainant, counsel, witnesses and those conducting the investigation, are protected against ill-treatment, intimidation or reprisal.

4. The findings of such an investigation shall be made available upon request to all persons concerned, unless doing so would jeopardize an ongoing criminal investigation.

5. Steps shall be taken to ensure that any ill-treatment, intimidation or reprisal or any other form of interference on the occasion of the lodging of a complaint or during the investigation procedure is appropriately punished.

6. An investigation, in accordance with the procedures described above, should be able to be conducted for as long as the fate of the victim of enforced disappearance remains unclarified.

Article 14

Any person alleged to have perpetrated an act of enforced disappearance in a particular State shall, when the facts disclosed by an official investigation so warrant, be brought before the competent civil authorities of that State for the purpose of prosecution and trial unless he has been extradited to another State wishing to exercise jurisdiction in accordance with the relevant international agreements in force. All States should take any lawful and appropriate action available to them to bring to justice all persons presumed responsible for an act of enforced disappearance, who are found to be within their jurisdiction or under their control.

Article 15

The fact that there are grounds to believe that a person has participated in acts of an extremely serious nature such as those referred to in article 4, paragraph 1, above, regardless of the motives, shall be taken into account when the competent authorities of the State decide whether or not to grant asylum.

Article 16

1. Persons alleged to have committed any of the acts referred to in article 4, paragraph 1, above, shall be suspended from any official duties during the investigation referred to in article 13 above.

2. They shall be tried only by the competent ordinary courts in each State, and not by any other special tribunal, in particular military courts.

3. No privileges, immunities or special exemptions shall be admitted in such trials, without prejudice to the provisions contained in the Vienna Convention on Diplomatic Relations.

4. The persons presumed responsible for such acts shall be guaranteed fair treatment in accordance with the relevant provisions of the Universal Declaration of Human Rights and other relevant international agreements in force at all stages of the investigation and eventual prosecution and trial.

Article 17

1. Acts constituting enforced disappearance shall be considered a continuing offence as long as the perpetrators continue to conceal the fate and the whereabouts of persons who have disappeared and these facts remain unclarified.

2. When the remedies provided for in article 2 of the International Covenant on Civil and Political Rights are no longer effective, the statute of limitations relating to acts of enforced disappearance shall be suspended until these remedies are re-established.

3. Statutes of limitations, where they exist, relating to acts of enforced disappearance shall be substantial and commensurate with the extreme seriousness of the offence.

Article 18

1. Persons who have or are alleged to have committed offences referred to in article 4, paragraph 1, above, shall not benefit from any special amnesty law or similar measures that might have the effect of exempting them from any criminal proceedings or sanction.

In the exercise of the right of pardon, the extreme seriousness of acts of enforced disappearance shall be taken into account.

Article 19

The victims of acts of enforced disappearance and their family shall obtain redress and shall have the right to adequate compensation, including the means for as complete a rehabilitation as possible. In the event of the death of the victim as a result of an act of enforced disappearance, their dependents shall also be entitled to compensation.

Article 20

1. States shall prevent and suppress the abduction of children of parents subjected to enforced disappearance and of children born during their mother's enforced disappearance, and shall devote their efforts to the search for and identification of such children and to the restitution of the children to their families of origin.

2. Considering the need to protect the best interests of children referred to in the preceding paragraph, there shall be an opportunity, in States which recognize a system of adoption, for a review of the adoption of such children and, in particular, for annulment of any adoption which originated in enforced disappearance. Such adoption should, however, continue to be in force if consent is given, at the time of the review, by the child's closest relatives.

3. The abduction of children of parents subjected to enforced disappearance or of children born during their mother's enforced disappearance, and the act of altering or suppressing documents attesting to their true identity, shall constitute an extremely serious offence, which shall be punished as such.

4. For these purpose, States shall, where appropriate, conclude bilateral and multilateral agreements.

Article 21

The provisions of the present Declaration are without prejudice to the provisions enunciated in the Universal Declaration of Human Rights or in any other international instrument, and shall not be construed as restricting or derogating from any of those provisions.

Inter-American Convention on the Forced Disappearance of Persons

(adopted at Belém do Pará, Brazil, on 9 June 1994, at the Twenty-fourth Regular Session of the OAS General Assembly)

The Member States of the Organization of American States,

DISTURBED by the persistence of the forced disappearance of persons;

REAFFIRMING that the true meaning of American solidarity and good neighborliness can be none other than that of consolidating in this Hemisphere, in the framework of democratic institutions, a system of individual freedom and social justice based on respect for essential human rights;

CONSIDERING that the forced disappearance of persons is an affront to the conscience of the Hemisphere and a grave and abominable offense against the inherent dignity of the human being, and one that contradicts the principles and purposes enshrined in the Charter of the Organization of American States;

CONSIDERING that the forced disappearance of persons violates numerous non-derogable and essential human rights enshrined in the American Convention on Human Rights, in the American Declaration of the Rights and Duties of Man, and in the Universal Declaration of Human Rights;

RECALLING that the international protection of human rights is in the form of a convention reinforcing or complementing the protection provided by domestic law and is based upon the attributes of the human personality;

REAFFIRMING that the systematic practice of the forced disappearance of persons constitutes a crime against humanity;

HOPING that this Convention may help to prevent, punish, and eliminate the forced disappearance of persons in the Hemisphere and make a decisive contribution to the protection of human rights and the rule of law,

RESOLVE to adopt the following Inter-American Convention on the Forced Disappearance of Persons:

Article I

The States Parties to this Convention undertake:

(a) Not to practice, permit, or tolerate the forced disappearance of persons, even in states of emergency or suspension of individual guarantees;

(b) To punish within their jurisdictions those persons who commit or attempt to commit the crime of forced disappearance of persons and their accomplices and accessories;

(c) To cooperate with one another in helping to prevent, punish and eliminate the forced disappearance of persons;

(d) To take legislative, administrative, judicial, and any other measures necessary to comply with the commitments undertaken in this Convention.

Article II

For the purposes of this Convention, forced disappearance is considered to be the act of depriving a person or persons of his or their freedom, in whatever way, perpetrated by agents of the state or by persons or groups of persons acting with the authorization, support, or acquiescence of the state, followed by an absence of information or a refusal to acknowledge that deprivation of freedom or to give information on the whereabouts of that person, thereby impeding his or her recourse to the applicable legal remedies and procedural guarantees.

Article III

The States Parties undertake to adopt, in accordance with their constitutional procedures, the legislative measures that may be needed to define the forced disappearance of persons as an offense and to impose an appropriate punishment commensurate with its extreme gravity. This offense shall be deemed continuous or permanent as long as the fate or whereabouts of the victim has not been determined.

The States Parties may establish mitigating circumstances for persons who have participated in acts constituting forced disappearance when they help to cause the victim to reappear alive or provide information that sheds light on the forced disappearance of a person.

Article IV

The acts constituting the forced disappearance of persons shall be considered offenses in every State Party. Consequently, each State Party shall take measures to establish its jurisdiction over such cases in the following instances:

(a) When the forced disappearance of persons or any act constituting such offense was committed within its jurisdiction;

(b) When the accused is a national of that state;

(c) When the victim is a national of that state and that state sees fit to do so.

Every State Party shall, moreover, take the necessary measures to establish its jurisdiction over the crime described in this Convention when the alleged criminal is within its territory and it does not proceed to extradite him.

This Convention does not authorize any State Party to undertake, in the territory of another State Party, the exercise of jurisdiction or the performance of functions that are placed within the exclusive purview of the authorities of that other Party by its domestic law.

Article V

The forced disappearance of persons shall not be considered a political offense for purposes of extradition.

The forced disappearance of persons shall be deemed to be included among the extraditable offenses in every extradition treaty entered into between State Parties.

The States Parties undertake to include the offense of forced disappearance as one which is extraditable in every extradition treaty to be concluded between them in the future.

Every State Party that makes extradition conditional on the existence of a treaty and receives a request for extradition from another State Party with which it has no extradition treaty may consider this Convention as the necessary legal basis for extradition with respect to the offense of forced disappearance.

State Parties which do not make extradition conditional on the existence of a treaty shall recognize such offense as extraditable, subject to the conditions imposed by the law of the requested state.

Extradition shall be subject to the provisions set forth in the constitution and other laws of the requested state.

Article VI

When a State Party does not grant the extradition, the case shall be submitted to its competent authorities as if the offense had been committed within its jurisdiction, for the purposes of investigation and when appropriate, for criminal action, in accordance with its national law. Any decision adopted by these authorities shall be communicated to the state that has requested the extradition.

Article VII

Criminal prosecution for the forced disappearance of persons and the penalty judicially imposed on its perpetrator shall not be subject to statutes of limitations.

However, if there should be a norm of a fundamental character preventing application of the stipulation contained in the previous paragraph, the period of limitation shall be equal to that which applies to the gravest crime in the domestic laws of the corresponding State Party.

Article VIII

The defense of due obedience to superior orders or instructions that stipulate, authorize, or encourage forced disappearance shall not be admitted. All persons who receive such orders have the right and duty not to obey them.

The States Parties shall ensure that the training of public law-enforcement personnel or officials includes the necessary education on the offense of forced disappearance of persons.

Article IX

Persons alleged to be responsible for the acts constituting the offense of forced disappearance of persons may be tried only in the competent jurisdictions of ordinary law in each state, to the exclusion of all other special jurisdictions, particularly military jurisdictions.

The acts constituting forced disappearance shall not be deemed to have been committed in the course of military duties.

Privileges, immunities, or special dispensations shall not be admitted in such trials, without prejudice to the provisions set forth in the Vienna Convention on Diplomatic Relations.

Article X

In no case may exceptional circumstances such as a state of war, the threat of war, internal political instability, or any other public emergency be invoked to justify the forced disappearance of persons. In such cases, the right to expeditious and effective judicial procedures and recourse shall be retained as a means of determining the whereabouts or state of health of a person who has been deprived of freedom, or of identifying the official who ordered or carried out such deprivation of freedom.

In pursuing such procedures or recourse, and in keeping with applicable domestic law, the competent judicial authorities shall have free and immediate access to all detention centers and to each of their units, and to all places where there is reason to believe the disappeared person might be found, including places that are subject to military jurisdiction.

Article XI

Every person deprived of liberty shall be held in an officially recognized place of detention and be brought before a competent judicial authority without delay, in accordance with applicable domestic law.

The States Parties shall establish and maintain official up-to-date registries of their detainees and, in accordance with their domestic law, shall make them available to relatives, judges, attorneys, any other person having a legitimate interest, and other authorities.

Article XII

The States Parties shall give each other mutual assistance in the search for, identification, location, and return of minors who have been removed to another state or detained therein as a consequence of the forced disappearance of their parents or guardians.

Article XIII

For the purposes of this Convention, the processing of petitions or communications presented to the Inter-American Commission on Human Rights alleging the forced disappearance of persons shall be subject to the procedures established in the American Convention on Human Rights and to the Statute and Regulations of the Inter-American Commission on Human Rights and to the Statute and Rules of Procedure of the Inter-American Court of Human Rights, including the provisions on precautionary measures.

Article XIV

Without prejudice to the provisions of the preceding article, when the Inter-American Commission on Human Rights receives a petition or communication regarding an alleged forced disappearance, its Executive Secretariat shall urgently and confidentially address the respective government and shall request that government to provide as soon as possible information as to the whereabouts of the allegedly disappeared person together with any other information it considers pertinent, and such request shall be without prejudice as to the admissibility of the petition.

Article XV

None of the provisions of this Convention shall be interpreted as limiting other bilateral or multilateral treaties or other agreements signed by the Parties.

This Convention shall not apply to the international armed conflicts governed by the 1949 Geneva Conventions and their Protocols, concerning protection of wounded, sick, and shipwrecked members of the armed forces; and prisoners of war and civilians in time of war.

Article XVI

This Convention is open for signature by the member states of the Organization of American States.

Article XVII

This Convention is subject to ratification. The instruments of ratification shall be deposited with the General Secretariat of the Organization of American States.

Article XVIII

This Convention shall be open to accession by any other state. The instruments of accession shall be deposited with the General Secretariat of the Organization of American States.

Article XIX

The states may express reservations with respect to this Convention when adopting, signing, ratifying or acceding to it, unless such reservations are incompatible with the object and purpose of the Convention and as long as they refer to one or more specific provisions.

Article XX

This Convention shall enter into force for the ratifying states on the thirtieth day from the date of deposit of the second instrument of ratification.

For each state ratifying or acceding to the Convention after the second instrument of ratification has been deposited, the Convention shall enter into force on the thirtieth day from the date on which that state deposited its instrument of ratification or accession.

Article XXI

This Convention shall remain in force indefinitely, but may be denounced by any State Party. The instrument of denunciation shall be deposited with the General Secretariat of the Organization of American States. The Convention shall cease to be in effect for the denouncing state and shall remain in force for the other State Parties one year from the date of deposit of the instrument of denunciation.

Article XXII

The original instrument of this Convention, the Spanish, English, Portuguese and French texts of which are equally authentic, shall be deposited with the General Secretariat of the Organization of American States, which shall forward certified copies thereof to the United Nations Secretariat, for registration and publication, in accordance with Article 102 of the Charter of the United Nations. The General Secretariat of the Organization of American States shall notify member states of the

Organization and states acceding to the Convention of the signatures and deposit of instruments of ratification, accession or denunciation, as well as of any reservations that may be expressed.

Geneva Conventions of 12 August 1949

Common Article 3

In the case of armed conflict not of an international character occurring in the territory of one of the High Contracting Parties, each Party to the conflict shall be bound to apply, as a minimum, the following provisions:

1. Persons taking no active part in the hostilities, including members of armed forces who have laid down their arms and those placed *hors de combat* by sickness, wounds, detention, or any other cause, shall in all circumstances be treated humanely, without any adverse distinction founded on race, colour, religion or faith, sex, birth or wealth, or any other similar criteria.

To this end, the following acts are and shall remain prohibited at any time and in any place whatsoever with respect to the above-mentioned persons:

(a) violence to life and person, in particular murder of all kinds, mutilation, cruel treatment and torture;

(b) taking of hostages;

(c) outrages upon personal dignity, in particular humiliating and degrading treatment;

(d) the passing of sentences and the carrying out of executions without previous judgment pronounced by a regularly constituted court, affording all the judicial guarantees which are recognized as indispensable by civilized peoples.

2. The wounded and sick shall be collected and cared for.

An impartial humanitarian body, such as the International Committee of the Red Cross, may offer its services to the Parties to the conflict.

The Parties to the conflict should further endeavour to bring into force, by means of special agreements, all or part of the other provisions of the present Convention.

The application of the preceding provisions shall not affect the legal status of the Parties to the conflict.

International Covenant on Civil and Political Rights

Article 6

1. Every human being has the inherent right to life. This right shall be protected by law. No one shall be arbitrarily deprived of his life.

2. In countries which have not abolished the death penalty, sentence of death may be imposed only for the most serious crimes in accordance with the law in force at the time of the commission of the crime and not contrary to the provisions of the present Covenant and to the Convention on the Prevention and Punishment of the Crime of Genocide. This penalty can only be carried out pursuant to a final judgement rendered by a competent court.

3. When deprivation of life constitutes the crime of genocide, it is understood that nothing in this article shall authorize any State Party to the present Covenant to derogate in any way from any obligation assumed under the provisions of the Convention on the Prevention and Punishment of the Crime of Genocide.

4. Anyone sentenced to death shall have the right to seek pardon or commutation of the sentence. Amnesty, pardon or commutation of the sentence of death may be granted in all cases.

5. Sentence of death shall not be imposed for crimes committed by persons below eighteen years of age and shall not be carried out on pregnant women.

6. Nothing in this article shall be invoked to delay or to prevent the abolition of capital punishment by any State Party to the present Covenant.

Article 7

No one shall be subject to torture or to cruel, inhuman or degrading treatment or punishment. In particular, no one shall be subjected without his free consent to medical or scientific experimentation.

Article 9

1. Everyone has the right to liberty and security of person. No one shall be subjected to arbitrary arrest or detention. No one shall be deprived of his liberty except on such grounds and in accordance with such procedure as are established by law.

2. Anyone who is arrested shall be informed, at the time of arrest, of the reasons for his arrest and shall be promptly informed of any charges against him.

3. Anyone arrested or detained on a criminal charge shall be brought promptly before a judge or other officer authorized by law to exercise judicial power and shall be entitled to trial within a reasonable time or to release. It shall not be the general rule that persons awaiting trial shall be detained in custody, but release may be subject to guarantees to appear for trial, at any other stage of the judicial proceedings, and should occasion arise, for execution of the judgement.

4. Anyone who is deprived of his liberty by arrest or detention shall be entitled to take proceedings before a court, in order that that court may decide without delay on the lawfulness of his detention and order his release if the detention is not lawful.

5. Anyone who has been the victim of unlawful arrest or detention shall have an enforceable right to compensation.

Article 10

1. All persons deprived of their liberty shall be treated with humanity and with respect for the inherent dignity of the human person.

2. (*a*) Accused persons shall, save in exceptional circumstances, be segregated from convicted persons and shall be subject to separate treatment appropriate to their status as unconvicted persons;

(*b*) Accused juvenile persons shall be separated from adults and brought as speedily as possible for adjudication.

3. The penitentiary system shall comprise treatment of prisoners the essential aim of which shall be their reformation and social rehabilitation. Juvenile offenders shall be segregated from adults and be accorded treatment appropriate to their age and legal status.

European Convention on Human Rights

Article 2

1. Everyone's right to life shall be protected by law. No one shall be deprived of his life intentionally save in the execution of a sentence of a court following his conviction of a crime for which this penalty is provided by law.

2. Deprivation of life shall not be regarded as inflicted in contravention of this Article when it results from the use of force which is no more than absolutely necessary:

(*a*) in defence of any person from unlawful violence;

(*b*) in order to effect a lawful arrest or to prevent the escape of a person lawfully detained;

(*c*) in action lawfully taken for the purpose of quelling a riot or insurrection.

Article 3

No one shall be subjected to torture or to inhuman or degrading treatment or punishment.

Article 5

1. Everyone has the right to liberty and security of person.

No one shall be deprived of his liberty save in the following cases and in accordance with a procedure prescribed by law:

(*a*) the lawful detention of a person after conviction by a competent court;

(*b*) the lawful arrest or detention of a person for non-compliance with the lawful order of a court or in order to secure the fulfilment of any obligation prescribed by law;

(*c*) the lawful arrest or detention of a person effected for the purpose of bringing him before the competent legal authority on reasonable suspicion of having committed an offence or when it is reasonably considered necessary to prevent his committing an offence or fleeing after having done so;

(*d*) the detention of a minor by lawful order for the purpose of educational supervision or his lawful detention for the purpose of bringing him before the competent legal authority;

(*e*) the lawful detention of persons for the prevention of the spreading of infectious diseases, of persons of unsound mind, alcoholics or drug addicts or vagrants;

(*f*) the lawful arrest or detention of a person to prevent his effecting an unauthorised entry into the country or of a person against whom action is being taken with a view to deportation or extradition.

2. Everyone who is arrested shall be informed promptly, in a language which he understands, of the reasons for his arrest and of any charge against him.

3. Everyone arrested or detained in accordance with the provisions of paragraph

1(*c*) of this Article shall be brought promptly before a judge or other officer authorised by law to exercise judicial power and shall be entitled to trial within a reasonable time or to release pending trial. Release may be conditioned by guarantees to appear for trial.

4. Everyone who is deprived of his liberty by arrest or detention shall be entitled to take proceedings by which the lawfulness of his detention shall be decided speedily by a court and his release ordered if the detention is not lawful.

5. Everyone who has been the victim of arrest or detention in contravention of the provisions of this Article shall have an enforceable right to compensation.

American Convention on Human Rights

Article 4. Right to Life

1. Every person has the right to have his life respected. This right shall be protected by law and, in general, from the moment of conception. No one shall be arbitrarily deprived of his life.

2. In countries that have not abolished the death penalty, it may be imposed only for the most serious crimes and pursuant to a final judgment rendered by a competent court and in accordance with a law establishing such punishment, enacted prior to the commission of the crime. The application of such punishment shall not be extended to crimes to which it does not presently apply.

3. The death penalty shall not be reestablished in states that have abolished it.

4. In no case shall capital punishment be inflicted for political offenses or related common crimes.

5. Capital punishment shall not be imposed upon persons who, at the time the crime was committed, were under 18 years of age or over 70 years of age; nor shall it be applied to pregnant women.

6. Every person condemned to death shall have the right to apply for amnesty, pardon, or commutation of sentence, which may be granted in all cases. Capital punishment shall not be imposed while such a petition is pending decision by the competent authority.

Article 5. Right to Humane Treatment

1. Every person has the right to have his physical, mental, and moral integrity respected.

2. No one shall be subjected to torture or to cruel, inhuman, or degrading punishment or treatment. All persons deprived of their liberty shall be treated with respect for the inherent dignity of the human person.

3. Punishment shall not be extended to any person other than the criminal.

4. Accused persons shall, save in exceptional circumstances, be segregated from convicted persons, and shall be subject to separate treatment appropriate to their status as unconvicted persons.

5. Minors while subject to criminal proceedings shall be separated from adults and brought before specialized tribunals, as speedily as possible, so that they may be treated in accordance with their status as minors.

6. Punishments consisting of deprivation of liberty shall have as an essential aim the reform and social readaptation of the prisoners.

Article 7. Right to Personal Liberty

1. Every person has the right to personal liberty and security.

2. No one shall be deprived of his physical liberty except for the reasons and under the conditions established beforehand by the constitution of the State Party concerned or by a law established pursuant thereto.

3. No one shall be subject to arbitrary arrest or imprisonment.

4. Anyone who is detained shall be informed of the reasons for his detention and shall be promptly notified of the charge or charges against him.

5. Any person detained shall be brought promptly before a judge or other officer authorized by law to exercise judicial power and shall be entitled to trial within a reasonable time or to be released without prejudice to the continuation of the proceedings. His release may be subject to guarantees to assure his appearance for trial.

6. Anyone who is deprived of his liberty shall be entitled to recourse to a competent court, in order that the court may decide without delay on the lawfulness of his arrest or detention and order his release if the arrest or detention is unlawful. In States Parties whose laws provide that anyone who believes himself to be threatened with deprivation of his liberty is entitled to recourse to a competent court in order that it may decide on the lawfulness of such threat, this remedy may not be restricted or abolished. The interested party or another person in his behalf is entitled to seek these remedies.

7. No one shall be detained for debt. This principle shall not limit the orders of a competent judicial authority issued for nonfulfillment of duties of support.

African Charter on Human and Peoples' Rights

Article 4

Human beings are inviolable. Every human being shall be entitled to respect for his life and the integrity of his person. No one may be arbitrarily deprived of this right.

Article 5

Every individual shall have the right to the respect of the dignity inherent in a human being and to the recognition of his legal status. All forms of exploitation and degradation of man particularly slavery, slave trade, torture, cruel, inhuman or degrading punishment and treatment shall be prohibited.

Article 6

Every individual shall have the right to liberty and to the security of his person. No one may be deprived of his freedom except for reasons and conditions previously laid down by law. In particular, no one may be arbitrarily arrested or detained.

Article 7

1. Every individual shall have the right to have his cause heard. This comprises:
   (*a*) The right to an appeal to competent national organs against acts of violating his fundamental rights as recognized and guaranteed by conventions, laws, regulations and customs in force;
   (*b*) the right to be presumed innocent until proved guilty by a competent court or tribunal;
   (*c*) the right to defence, including the right to be defended by counsel of his choice;
   (*d*) the right to be tried within a reasonable time by an impartial court or tribunal.
2. No one may be condemned for an act or omission which did not constitute a legally punishable offence at the time it was committed. No penalty may be inflicted for an offence for which no provision was made at the time it was committed. Punishment is personal and can be imposed only on the offender.

Index

Index